Protection of Sexual Minorities since Stonewall

I0083890

Progress and Stalemate in Developed and Developing Countries

Edited by Phil C.W. Chan
Foreword by Archbishop Desmond Tutu

Routledge
Taylor & Francis Group
LONDON AND NEW YORK

First published 2010 by Routledge
2 Park Square, Milton Park, Abingdon, Oxon, OX14 4RN

Simultaneously published in the USA and Canada
by Routledge
711 Third Avenue, New York, NY 10017

Routledge is an imprint of the Taylor & Francis Group, an informa business

First issued in paperback 2011

This book is a reproduction of *The International Journal of Human Rights*, volume 13, issue 2/3. The Publisher requests to those authors who may be citing this book to state, also, the bibliographical details of the special double issue on which the book was based.

Typeset in Times New Roman by Value Chain, India

British Library Cataloguing in Publication Data
A catalogue record for this book is available from the British Library.

ISBN13: 978-0-415-41850-8 (hbk)
ISBN13: 978-0-415-50888-9 (pbk)

For Paul, my mother,
and my grandmother in memory of whom I endure

Protection of Sexual Minorities since Stonewall

The Stonewall Riots in New York in 1969 marked the birth of the sexual minority rights movement worldwide. In the subsequent four decades, equality and related rights on grounds of sexual orientation and gender identity have been enshrined in many African, Asian, Australasian, European and North American countries, thanks to better informed discourses of the natures of sexual orientation, gender identity, equality and rights that systematic scientific and socio-legal research has generated.

Discrimination, harassment and persecution on grounds of a person's sexual orientation or gender identity, however, continue to pervade the laws and social norms in all developed and developing countries. In tribute to the courage of those who participated in the Stonewall Riots, this book examines the progress and stalemate in various countries on five continents, as well as in the development of international law, concerning the rights of persons belonging to sexual minorities. This book covers issues including homophobic bullying and gay–straight alliances in schools; the merits and problems that legislation prohibiting hate speech on grounds of sexual orientation presents; criminal justice systems in relation to male rape victims and to criminalisation of HIV exposure and transmission; the development of sexual minority rights, from historical and socio-legal perspectives, in Hong Kong, Japan, Singapore, and Zimbabwe; the lives of transgender persons in Asian countries; the evolution, operation and impact of international and domestic refugee laws on sexual orientation and gender identity as grounds for refugee status and asylum; and the conflicts between law, religion and sexual minority equality rights that inhere in the same-sex marriage debate in Ireland.

This book was previously published as a special double issue of *The International Journal of Human Rights*.

Phil C.W. Chan is currently Visiting Research Fellow at the University of Otago Faculty of Law, while completing his doctoral thesis on China and international law for examination at the National University of Singapore Faculty of Law. He has held visiting research positions at universities including Cambridge, Keele, St Andrews, ANU, Ottawa, Toronto, Freiburg and Vanderbilt.

CONTENTS

Notes on contributors

Phil C.W. Chan is Editor of this book. Since graduating from the University of Hong Kong with his law degree and the Rowdget W. Young Medal in Law in 2002 at the age of 19 and from the University of Durham with his LL.M. in 2004, he has published over 50 articles in international refereed journals including *The International Journal of Human Rights*, *Chinese Journal of International Law*, *Criminal Law Forum*, *European Business Law Review*, *International Journal of Punishment and Sentencing*, *Journal of Intellectual Property Law and Practice*, *King's College Law Journal*, *Nottingham Law Journal*, *Sexuality & Culture* and *Singapore Journal of Legal Studies* and book chapters, and is a contributor to *Encyclopedia of Modern China*. He was Editor of *Equality in Asia-Pacific: Reality or a Contradiction in Terms?* (Routledge, 2007), published also as a special double issue of *The International Journal of Human Rights*. He is Editorial Board Member of the *Journal of Homosexuality* and *Sexuality & Culture*, and of *The International Journal of Human Rights* between 2004 and 2009. He has delivered over 40 specially invited guest lectures and seminars on his research at universities worldwide, including ANU, Melbourne, Auckland, Otago, Cambridge, St Andrews, Copenhagen, Frankfurt, Lund, Ottawa, Toronto, Berkeley, Harvard, Vanderbilt and Virginia. Having held visiting research positions at universities including Cambridge, Keele, St Andrews, ANU, Ottawa, Toronto, Freiburg and Vanderbilt, he is currently Visiting Research Fellow at the University of Otago Faculty of Law, while completing his doctoral thesis, *China's Exercise of Sovereignty and the International Legal Order: Appraisal of a Symbiotic Relationship*, for examination at the National University of Singapore Faculty of Law. His contribution 'Shared values of Singapore: sexual minority rights as Singaporean value' in this book received the inaugural Rascals Prize (2009).

Kay Goodall is Senior Lecturer in Law and Director of Research at the School of Law, University of Stirling, and an Editorial Board Member of *The International Journal of Human Rights*. She specialises in statutory interpretation, anti-discrimination, and hate crime laws. With Ian McLeod, she is Co-Editor of forthcoming editions of *Bennion's Statutory Interpretation*. She has carried out empirical research in several areas, in particular the policing of crimes involving violence or racism.

Eric Heinze is Professor of Law and Humanities at Queen Mary, University of London, and an Editorial Board Member of *The International Journal of Human Rights*. He received his JD from Harvard Law School and his PhD from the University of Leiden, in addition to undergraduate and post-graduate study in the Universities of Paris (Licence, Maîtrise) and Berlin. His books include *The Logic of Constitutional Rights* (2005); *The Logic of Liberal Rights* (2003); *The Logic of Equality* (2003) and *Sexual Orientation: A Human Right* (Kluwer 1995) (Russian translation 2004), as well as an edited collection entitled *Of Innocence and Autonomy: Children, Sex and Human Rights* (Ashgate 2000). He has contributed chapters to such anthologies as *Extreme Speech and Democracy* (Weinstein & Hare, OUP, 2009), *Religious Pluralism and Human Rights* (Loenen & Goldschmidt, Intersentia, 2007) and *Minority and Group Rights Toward the New Millennium* (Bowring & Fottrell, Kluwer, 1999), and articles in *Oxford Journal of Legal Studies*, *Harvard Human Rights Journal*, *Modern Law*

Review, Legal Studies, Ratio Juris, Law & Critique, Social & Legal Studies, Law & Literature, Canadian Journal of Law & Jurisprudence, National Black Law Journal, Michigan Journal of International Law, Indiana International & Comparative Law Review, Nordic Journal of International Law, Howard Law Journal, Netherlands Quarterly of Human Rights, and other scholarly journals.

Alana Klein is Assistant Professor at the Faculty of Law, McGill University, where she teaches in the areas of criminal law, constitutional law, administrative law, and human rights, and an Editorial Board Member of *The International Journal of Human Rights*. She has previously served as Senior Policy Analyst at the Canadian HIV/AIDS Legal Network, a Commissioner of the Ontario Human Rights Commission, and a law clerk to (former) Justice Louise Arbour of the Supreme Court of Canada, in addition to teaching at Columbia Law School and Columbia University. Her publications include 'Judging as Nudging: New Governance Approaches for the Enforcement of Constitutional Social and Economic Rights', *Columbia Human Rights Law Review* (2008); *Sticking Points: Barriers to Access to Needle and Syringe Programs in Canada* (2007); and *HIV/AIDS and Immigration: Final Report* (2001).

Nicole LaViolette is Associate Professor and Vice Dean at the Faculty of Law, University of Ottawa. Her research and publications are devoted mainly to international human rights, international humanitarian law, and the rights of refugees. She is also interested in lesbian and gay legal issues, feminist theory and transnational family law. Professor LaViolette has published several articles on sexual minorities and the refugee determination system. In 1999, she was awarded the *Lambda Foundation Award for Excellence in Gay and Lesbian Studies* for her work on the Canadian Immigration and Refugee Board's *Gender Guidelines* and their impact on sexual orientation and sexual identity claims. Prior to joining the law faculty, Professor LaViolette worked as a legislative assistant in the House of Commons of Canada and collaborated with both governmental and non-governmental organisations specialising in human rights.

Mark McLelland is Associate Professor and Convenor of the Sociology Program at the University of Wollongong and was Toyota Visiting Professor of Japanese at the University of Michigan, Ann Arbor, in 2007–8. He is author or co-editor of numerous books on sexuality in post-war Japanese society, including *Male Homosexuality in Modern Japan* (2000), *Genders, Transgenders and Sexualities in Japan* (2005), and *Queer Japan from the Pacific War* (2005).

Matthew T. Mercier is a 2008 JD graduate of the University of Virginia School of Law and holds a BA from New York University.

Jenni Millbank is Professor of Law at the Faculty of Law, University of Technology, Sydney. Her research forms part of a larger comparative project on refugee claims made on the basis of sexual orientation and gender across Australia, the United Kingdom, Canada and New Zealand from 1994 to 2007. Earlier publications include: '"The Ring of Truth": A Case Study of Credibility Assessment in Particular Social Group Refugee Determinations', *International Journal of Refugee Law* (2009); 'A Preoccupation with Perversion: The British Response to Refugee Claims on the Basis of Sexual Orientation 1989–2003', *Social & Legal Studies* (2005); 'The Role of Rights in Asylum Claims on the Basis of

Sexual Orientation', *Human Rights Law Review* (2004); 'Gender, Sex and Visibility in Refugee Decisions on Sexual Orientation', *Georgetown Immigration Law Journal* (2003); 'Imagining Otherness: Refugee Claims on the Basis of Sexuality in Canada and Australia', *Melbourne University Law Review* (2002); and, with Catherine Dauvergne, 'Forced Marriage and the Exoticisation of Gendered Harms in US Asylum Law', *Columbia Journal of Gender and Law* (2010); 'Forced Marriage as a Harm in Domestic and International Law', 73 *Modern Law Review* (2010); and 'Before the High Court: *Applicants S396/2002 and S395/2002*, A Gay Refugee Couple from Bangladesh', *Sydney Law Review* (2003).

Aisling O'Sullivan is currently pursuing doctoral research at the Irish Centre for Human Rights, National University of Ireland, Galway, investigating the principle of *aut dedere aut judicare* and the concept of universal jurisdiction. Previously, she was a Doctoral Fellow at the Centre for three years, where she served as principal researcher on a government-/Irish Research Council for the Humanities and Social Sciences-funded research project on 'Ireland's Participation in International Human Rights Law and Institutions' involving archival and interview-based research. She graduated with an LLB from the University of Limerick and an LLM with Distinction from the University of Durham.

Oliver Phillips is Reader in Law and Research Director at the School of Law, University of Westminster, and an Editorial Board Member of *The International Journal of Human Rights*. He holds criminology and law degrees from the University of Cape Town and an MPhil and a PhD in criminology from the University of Cambridge. He has worked at Columbia University, Keele University, Universiteit van Amsterdam, the University of London, and the University of Zimbabwe as well as with a number of advocacy organisations in Southern Africa. He has published articles on sexuality, HIV/AIDS, and human rights and the law in Southern Africa and his monograph *Sexuality and the Politics of Rights in Post-Colonial Southern Africa: The Legacy of Venus Monstrosa* will appear in 2010.

Sean Rehaag is Assistant Professor at the Osgoode Hall Law School, York University. He has been a visiting scholar at the Center for Gender and Refugee Studies at the University of California, Hastings, and visiting researcher at the International Gay and Lesbian Human Rights Commission's Asylum Documentation Program. During his doctoral studies at the University of Toronto Faculty of Law, he provided pro bono legal services at the FCJ Refugee Centre with his work focusing on incorporating international legal norms in gender and sexual orientation-based refugee and immigration applications. His previous scholarly publications include an analysis of the experience of bisexuals in Canada's refugee determination system in *McGill Law Journal* and an empirical study of variations in refugee claim success rates across Canadian Immigration and Refugee Board members in *Ottawa Law Review.*

Philip N.S. Rumney is Reader in Law at the Department of Law, University of the West of England, where he teaches criminal justice courses. He has a particular interest in the treatment of rape cases within the criminal justice system and has had articles published in a number of leading journals including *Cambridge Law Journal, Modern Law Review,* and *Oxford Journal of Legal Studies.* His research examines male sexual victimisation, issues of sentencing, law reform, false rape allegations, and attitudes to rape. With Natalia Hanley, he is currently conducting research involving the use of focus groups to examine student attitudes towards male rape and the impact, if any, of educational evidence on those attitudes. He is also working on two articles that consider the use of torture as a tool of interrogation in the 'war on terror'.

Katsuhiko Suganuma is Assistant Professor at the Center for International Education and Research, Oita University. His research focuses on contemporary Japanese sexuality politics, queer globalisation, and post-colonial feminism. He has published critical essays on gay and lesbian sexualities in contemporary Japan in *Inter-Asia Cultural Studies* and *Intersections*. He is co-editor (with Mark McLelland and James Welker) of *Queer Voices from Japan* (2007) and Editorial Board Member of the *Journal of Queer Studies Japan*.

Sam Winter is Associate Professor and Associate Dean (Research) at the Faculty of Education, University of Hong Kong. He has academic and professional qualifications in psychology and has worked as a psychologist for 31 years, initially as an educational psychologist in the UK, and then as a member of teaching and research faculty of the University of Hong Kong for 24 years. He is author or co-author of around 100 journal articles and book chapters. For the last ten years he has researched and taught sexual and gender diversity in Asia. He has also been involved in a community group working for transpeople's rights in Hong Kong, and is Director of the TransgenderASIA Centre, which aims to encourage research, education and social activism for transpeople in Asia. He runs a course, 'Sexual and Gender Diversity', for 500 undergraduates each year. Some of his recent publications include: 'Measuring Hong Kong students' attitudes towards transpeople' (with Beverley Webster and Eleanor Cheung) in *Sex Roles* (Vol.59 Nos.9-10 (2008)); 'Transwomen in the Philippines: a close focus' (with Sass Rogando-Sasot and Mark King) in *International Journal of Transgenderism* (Vol.10 No.2 (2007)); 'Transpeople, hormones and health risks in Southeast Asia: a Lao study' (with Serge Doussantousse) in *International Journal of Sexual Health* (Vol.21 No.1 (2009)); and 'Transpeople, transprejudice and pathologisation: a seven-country factor analytic study (with Pornthip Chalungsooth, Yik Koon Teh and others) in *International Journal of Sexual Health* (Vol. 21 No.2 (2009)). He is currently focusing on a research project on 'Trans Lives: Asian Voices', a compilation of autobiographies (oral and written, in various languages) by transpeople across Asia.

Foreword

Human rights are elusive. Once they are secured, they are taken for granted. It seldom occurs to us that human rights were brought into being and continue to be defended at a very high human price. We tend to forget that any of the human rights that we take for granted may be eroded by the state or by our fellow citizens at a stroke or in a gradual yet devious process. It took centuries of suffering, struggles, and sacrifices for international human rights law to finally take hold and develop. Equally, persons belonging to sexual minorities – lesbians, gay men, bisexuals, and transgender persons – have been persecuted and oppressed for centuries, and their right to live free and full lives continues to be undermined. The beginning of the global sexual minority rights movement dates back to 1969 when a group of individuals decided to stand up for themselves in Greenwich Village, New York.

I am therefore very heartened to commend and congratulate *The International Journal of Human Rights* for its dedication and Phil C.W. Chan for his editorship of an admirable special double issue that attests to, and no doubt will invigorate, the conviction and courage of persons belonging to sexual minorities in their struggles for full realisation of their human rights irrespective of sexual orientation or gender identity and for true equality within society generally. This special double issue, in which dedicated scholars explore and address many neglected issues affecting persons belonging to sexual minorities in various developed and developing countries on five continents, provides in-depth and authoritative insights into the state of sexual minority protection or oppression, and contributes to an invaluable understanding of persons belonging to sexual minorities as nothing more, and nothing less, than full, complete and equal human beings.

Desmond M. Tutu
Archbishop Emeritus of Cape Town
Chairman, The Elders

Preface

The International Journal of Human Rights is very pleased to publish this special double issue that explores the lives of persons belonging to sexual minorities and examines the protection they enjoy, or persecution and oppression they endure, from society and the state, in both developed and developing countries. Through transnational and multidisciplinary lenses our authors address many neglected issues including homophobic bullying and gay–straight alliances in schools; the compatibility between sexual minority protection and freedom of expression; the responses of the criminal justice system to gay male rape victims and to HIV exposure and transmission; the meaning of being a person belonging to sexual minorities in Singapore, Hong Kong, Japan and Zimbabwe as well as the lives, struggles and sufferings of transgender persons in Asia; the obstacles persons belonging to sexual minorities must overcome in order to find a refuge away from home; and the viability of same-sex marriage in Ireland, a country permeated socially and constitutionally with Catholic teachings.

This special double issue would not have been possible without the tireless and superb efforts that Phil C.W. Chan, as Guest Editor, has dedicated to it. His inspirational commitment to the cause of the rights of sexual minorities in particular and human rights in general must be commended.

I am confident this special double issue will be an authoritative contribution to the academic literature and a valuable resource for advocates and practitioners who, together with scholars, work towards the achievement of real protection of all human beings and their human rights everywhere.

Frank Barnaby
Editor

Protection of sexual minorities since Stonewall: their lives, struggles, sufferings, love, and hope

Phil C.W. Chan

Faculty of Law, National University of Singapore, Singapore

THEY CAME FIRST for the Communists,
  and I didn't speak up because I wasn't a Communist.
THEN THEY CAME for the Jews,
  and I didn't speak up because I wasn't a Jew.
THEN THEY CAME for the trade unionists,
  and I didn't speak up because I wasn't a trade unionist.
THEN THEY CAME for the Catholics,
  and I didn't speak up because I was a Protestant.
THEN THEY CAME for me,
  and by that time no one was left to speak up.[1]

– Martin Niemöller

Solidarity is not discovered by reflection but created. It is created by increasing our sensitivity to the particular details of the pain and humiliation of other, unfamiliar sorts of people. Such increased sensitivity makes it more difficult to marginalise people different from ourselves by thinking 'They do not feel as *we* would', or 'There must always be suffering, so why not let *them* suffer?'. This process of coming to see other human beings as 'one of us' rather than as 'them' is a matter of detailed description of what unfamiliar people are like and of redescription of what we ourselves are like.[2]

– Richard Rorty

The horrors of World War II profoundly changed the mindset of governments and citizens around the world regarding the nature, causes, and consequences of discrimination, oppression and persecution of persons belonging to minority groups due to particular personal characteristics or fundamental personal convictions, and led to the advent and progressive development of international human rights law. In 1948, the United Nations General Assembly proclaimed the Universal Declaration of Human Rights[3] which has since been regarded as reflecting norms of customary international law binding on all States.[4] In the Declaration, States agreed by consensus that '[a]ll human beings are born free and equal in dignity and right. They are endowed with reason and conscience and should act towards one another in a spirit of brotherhood.'[5] However, amid the jubilation accompanying international human rights law, the struggles, sufferings, tortures, and executions of persons belonging to sexual minorities – gay men, lesbians, bisexuals, and transgender persons – in countries around the world have continued unabated.[6]

It was the patrons of Stonewall, a gay bar, who amid a climate of hostility and intolerance decided to stand up for themselves with courage through what are now known as the

Stonewall Riots, thereby setting off the global sexual minority rights movement. Sexual minorities began to assert their collective and individual right to live their lives in safety, in peace, in dignity, and in full. A series of legal and social reforms ensued, such as the decriminalisation of consensual male/male sexual activity in England and Wales in 1967 and in Canada in 1969, the de-pathologisation of homosexuality as a mental disorder by the American Psychiatric Association in 1973,[7] the legal reform efforts initiated by Harvey Milk and George Moscone protecting persons belonging to sexual minorities in San Francisco against discrimination and the increased awareness of the plight and rights of sexual minorities within the general American public during their office and after their assassinations,[8] and the 1981 landmark decision of the European Court of Human Rights in *Dudgeon* v. *United Kingdom*[9] that recognised the right of persons belonging to sexual minorities to privacy in their family and sexual life, a decision that continues to influence sexual minority rights development around the world, including in Hong Kong[10] and the United States.[11]

As with all rights movements, the sexual minority rights movement has endured its highs and lows. Sexual minorities found themselves as scapegoats with the onset of the HIV epidemic in the 1980s when medical understanding of the epidemic was still insufficient and uncertain. Through the United States Supreme Court decision in *Bowers* v. *Hardwick*[12] and the purported Colorado state constitutional amendment that, if it had been allowed to stand, would have had Colorado *prohibit protection* of sexual minorities and their minority status,[13] a message was renewed time and again during the 1980s and early 1990s that sexual minorities were not part of society and must not be allowed the room to assert or to *have* their human rights. Under the Thatcher government Parliament in the United Kingdom passed legislation that until its repeal in 2000 in Scotland and in 2003 in England and Wales forbade the teaching in schools of homosexuality as a 'pretended family relationship'.[14] As Ann Hartman has stated, '[t]here is no better way to subjugate human beings than to silence them. There is nothing more oppressive than denying another's reality.'[15]

Nevertheless, since the early 1990s the sexual minority rights movement resurfaced with resilience and vigour. In 1994, the United Nations Human Rights Committee in *Toonen* v. *Australia*[16] came to the view that criminalisation of consensual same-sex sexual activity violated a person's right to privacy and that 'sex' in the equality and non-discrimination guarantees of the International Covenant on Civil and Political Rights must be taken as encompassing sexual orientation.[17] A series of national court decisions around the world and opinions of international human rights bodies recognising a person's right of equality and other human rights regardless of sexual orientation or gender identity ensued.[18] Legal reforms celebrating the fundamental rights and freedoms of persons belonging to sexual minorities have by no means been confined to countries in Australasia, Europe, and North America. After decades-long apartheid, South Africa promulgated the first national constitution in the world in 1996 that expressly protects against sexual orientation discrimination, in such terms that '[t]he state may not unfairly discriminate directly or indirectly against anyone on one or more grounds, including race, gender, sex, pregnancy, marital status, ethnic or social origin, colour, sexual orientation, age, disability, religion, conscience, belief, culture, language and birth.'[19] The Constitution also requires that private individuals respect and uphold the principle of equality of all and mandates enactment of national anti-discrimination legislation.[20] In addition, the Constitution affirms unequivocally that '[e]veryone has inherent dignity and the right to have their dignity respected and protected.'[21] As part and parcel of the general right of equality and inherent dignity of a person regardless of sexual orientation, a number of countries have embraced the right of a person to marry another person of the same sex.[22]

However, amid these successes the vast majority of persons belonging to sexual minorities continue to remain invisible and to live in fear and under conditions of discrimination, harassment, oppression and persecution as hetero-normative society and governments around the world continue to refuse to accept them as equal human beings entitled to equal rights and dignity. It is therefore important that when one conducts research or policy reviews on protection or otherwise of sexual minorities, persons belonging to sexual minorities are seen, heard and understood as human beings and not as some abstract notion of academic discourse. As A. Belden Fields and Wolf-Dieter Narr have pointed out, '[i]f people are not aware of the historical and contextual nature of human rights and not aware that human rights become realized only by the struggles of real people experiencing real instances of domination, then human rights are all too easily used as symbolic legitimizers for instruments of that very domination.'[23] It is only through deep and genuine understanding that true discernment of the lives, struggles and sufferings of persons belonging to sexual minorities can be had and true progress of sexual minority protection and general human rights and equality achieved.

At the same time, there remains a fundamental and invidious invisibility of minorities within sexual minorities. In the midst of battles for general recognition of sexual minority rights as equal human rights, and behind the frontlines of more publicly visible issues such as same-sex marriage, an array of issues that affect the lives of particular groups of persons belonging to sexual minorities in peculiar ways remain fundamentally neglected, not only by society and the state, but also by many scholars and advocates of human rights and sexual minority rights. Practices and discourses of human rights and sexual minority rights continue to suffer stratification on the basis of the perceived importance of issues. Invariably, these minorities within minorities consist of the most disadvantaged and disempowered groups in society, including children and adolescents, sexual abuse victims, people living with HIV, and refugees.

I am therefore very honoured and pleased to edit and introduce this special double issue on behalf of *The International Journal of Human Rights* at the 40th anniversary of the Stonewall Riots, which explores and examines, from multifaceted lenses and perspectives, the current state and continuing implications of protection or otherwise of persons belonging to sexual minorities in various developed and developing countries on five continents, and which highlights many of the neglected issues in the current practices and discourses of sexual minority protection and oppression. This special double issue includes the insightful contributions of many fine and dedicated scholars in their respective fields without whose efforts it could not have materialised.

We begin with a discussion of the most fundamental sexual orientation-related issue affecting children and adolescents, that is, homophobic bullying in schools. As Phil C.W. Chan points out in 'Psychosocial implications of homophobic bullying in schools: a review and directions for legal research and the legal process', homophobic school bullying, with which school bullying not attributable to sexual orientation is *always* intertwined, is a universal problem affecting children and adolescents of all ages around the world. Through a systematic review of the extant research literature in medical sciences, educational studies and social sciences, Chan examines the nature, likelihood, causes, onset, course, consequences, resolution and prevention of school bullying and addresses the added implications of homophobia with the role of family taken into account. Despite the tremendous harm school bullying generally and homophobic school bullying in particular causes, school authorities, parents, and society typically deny its occurrence and impact. Their denial of the struggles and sufferings of innumerable children and adolescents and their right 'to form relationships of trust, meaning, and affection with people in their daily lives and their broader communities'[24] is continually reinforced, perpetuated and exacerbated by the responses, or the lack thereof, of the legal system as reflected by the paucity of legal research on the problem. A thorough understanding of relevant empirical research, and of the real lives of all children and adolescents, is essential in exploring how the law, including international law, and those professing the law may redress, deter and prevent school bullying, including homophobic school bullying, and some directions as to how these roles should be explored through legal research and the legal process are suggested by the author.

In undermining the rights of persons belonging to sexual minorities, very often silence speaks louder than action, and heterosexuals need not necessarily be the enemy. In 'Fighting to fit in: gay–straight alliances in schools under United States jurisprudence', Matthew T. Mercier explores how school students across the United States have sought to create and promote safer school environments for all students including those belonging to sexual minorities through gay–straight alliances, and the obstacles they encounter when attempting to do so. Mercier examines how the Equal Access Act, which prohibits restriction of limited open forum on prohibited grounds of discrimination,[25] and the First Amendment to the United States Constitution, which protects free speech,[26] may be invoked in establishing a constitutional and statutory basis for heterosexual and sexual minority students to join together to foster safer school environments through informed dialogues over matters that affect all of them and society as a whole, and how courts in the United States have supported the creation of gay–straight alliances in schools through a series of seminal decisions.

Staying on free speech yet moving to wider society, we present an instructive debate on whether hate speech attributable to sexual orientation should be criminalised. In 'Cumulative jurisprudence and human rights: the example of sexual minorities and hate speech', Eric Heinze argues that norms of non-discrimination enshrined in many international human rights treaties and resolutions since World War II have been correctly and successfully invoked to embrace and protect the right of all persons, including persons belonging to sexual minorities, to equality through which a 'cumulative jurisprudence' for the recognition of other sexual minority rights has developed. However, Heinze maintains that, however tempting, these norms should not be hastily resorted to in banning hate speech attributable to sexual orientation through the operation of the criminal law, and argues that hate speech bans in longstanding and stable democracies embody such deep flaws that reliance upon them in endeavours to protect the rights of sexual minorities entails real dangers of betraying, and thereby disintegrating, fundamental principles of human rights law without which protection of sexual minorities cannot be achieved.

Kay Goodall in 'Challenging hate speech: incitement to hatred on grounds of sexual orientation in England, Wales and Northern Ireland' disagrees. Through a detailed discussion of the relevant pieces of legislation in England, Wales and Northern Ireland that criminalise incitement to hatred on the basis of sexual orientation, Goodall argues that those pieces of legislation can be and have been sufficiently narrowed such that freedom of expression is not jeopardised. The author also addresses criticisms, particularly those by Heinze, of such legislation on the bases of equal protection and of cause and effect. However, Goodall laments that such legislation will not achieve significant social change unless all other sources of discriminatory discourse are tackled in a comprehensive and sustained manner.

The potential overreach or neglect of the criminal justice system over issues of sexual orientation and gender identity is not confined to speech alone. The failure of the criminal justice system to respond to male rape victims, including male rape victims who are gay precisely due to the 'taint of homosexuality',[27] and the incoherent rationales and approaches of the criminal justice system to the HIV epidemic are two examples. In 'Gay male rape victims: law enforcement, social attitudes and barriers to recognition', Philip N.S. Rumney explores empirical studies of experiences of gay male rape victims with the criminal justice system and of police attitudes. Rumney also examines the impact of social attitudes to homosexuality and gay men which reinforce, and are in turn reinforced by, the responses of the criminal justice system to male rape. It is to be understood that the treatment by the criminal justice system, and society at large, of male rape, homosexuality, and gay men has serious repercussions not only for male victims of sexual assault who are gay but for all male victims of sexual assault, as the fact of their having been assaulted and penetrated calls into question their previously assumed heterosexuality and attendant male impenetrability and ascribed attributes of innocence and normalcy. Rumney identifies three barriers to genuine recognition by the criminal justice system and wider society of male rape, and proposes two strategies for improving the treatment of male sexual victimisation in England and Wales through human rights legislation and education.

Similarly, the issue of criminalisation of HIV exposure and transmission does not affect, or even primarily affect, gay men or persons belonging to other sexual minority groups, even though the popular myth of HIV as a gay plague continues to be perpetuated in many quarters of society around the world. As Alana Klein shows in 'Criminal law, public health, and governance of HIV exposure and transmission', the prosecutions brought to date in the United Kingdom, the United States, and Canada for HIV exposure and transmission have principally concerned sexual intercourse between a man and a woman in which either party failed or was presumed to have failed to inform his/her sex partner of his/her HIV-seropositivity. Klein draws lessons from the public health and human rights movement to explain the theoretical bases that underlie why the criminal justice system, on its own through prosecution of people living with HIV, is an ineffective and inappropriate mechanism for efforts to halt the HIV epidemic. Instead, the author argues that the criminal justice system should co-ordinate with the public health system in structured approaches which she assesses through new governance and restorative justice perspectives, so that a more focused operation of the criminal law that takes into account the sensitivities and sexual behaviours of people living with HIV may be developed.

We then move to explore the *polity* with which persons belonging to sexual minorities must come to terms, and which constitutes the primary obstacle to full realisation of human rights including sexual minority rights and the primary venue where battles must be fought and lives lived. The vast majority of governments around the world continue to rely on constructed notions of sovereignty and culture in stonewalling sexual minority rights development. Such reliance is by no means confined to developing or non-Western countries, as the fervent and continuing battles for full recognition of all sexual minority rights in the United States have shown. However, in putting forward a 'culture' in order to override fundamental rights and freedoms, the state must first define what that culture is, in order to discern whether such a culture in fact exists. Sally Engle Merry has explained that culture must not be seen as static, rigid, and isolated within a polity: 'Its boundaries are fluid, meanings are contested, and meaning is produced by institutional arrangements and political economy. Culture is marked by hybridity and creolization rather than uniformity or consistency.'[28] Furthermore, as Abdullahi Ahmed An-Na'im reminds us, in the construction of culture, 'powerful individuals and groups tend to monopolize the interpretation of cultural norms and manipulate them to their own advantage'.[29] One must, in addition, explore whether and why that culture should have such controlling normative force capable of overriding fundamental rights and freedoms.

In 'Shared values of Singapore: sexual minority rights as Singaporean value', Phil C.W. Chan points out that in the process of self-exploration as to the compatibility or otherwise between sexual minority rights and a particular culture, it must be kept in mind at all times that no matter one's position on sexual minority rights with, and within, that culture as well as generally, in order for one's position to be valid, one must not simply dismiss *a priori* and must understand and critically assess any alleged incompatibility. For the same reason, one must also explore and explain whether and how sexual minority rights may in fact and in law be developed as a national value and a constitutional and legal right. By examining the position of the Singapore government on human rights through deconstructing Singapore 'culture' and by deconstructing the relevant laws affecting persons belonging to sexual minorities in Singapore, Chan argues that the legal situation affecting persons belonging to sexual minorities in Singapore in fact provides useful insight into the development of human rights and governance in the country in general. While Singapore constitutional jurisprudence has prescribed that Singapore courts should look within the 'four walls' of the Singapore Constitution and resulting Singapore case law when interpreting the Singapore Constitution and statutes and developing Singapore common law, the author explores whether and how Singapore may develop its own jurisprudence on sexual minority rights under the framework of legitimate constitutional comparativism.

What is legitimate constitutional comparativism? In his keynote address to the annual meeting of the American Society of International Law in 2003, United States Supreme Court Justice Stephen Breyer referred to his colleague Justice Ruth Ginsburg as she stated extra-judicially that 'comparative analysis emphatically is relevant to the task of interpreting constitutions and enforcing human rights'.[30] However, as Roger Alford has explained, comparative law concerns the central development of a constitutional theory in a particular jurisdiction with comparativism as an interpretive paradigm.[31] 'The legitimacy of constitutional comparativism', Alford argues, 'should be determined by constitutional theory. Comparativism is not a constitutional theory; it is a methodology that is employed depending on a judge's particular theory.'[32] In 'Keeping up with (which) Joneses: a critique of constitutional comparativism in Hong Kong and its implications for rights development', Phil C.W. Chan delves into the merits, advantages, and dangers presented by constitutional comparativism in Hong Kong in the development of human rights, including sexual minority rights. By examining Hong Kong courts' recourse to foreign and international legal materials in the interpretation of the two most important rights instruments governing Hong Kong both generally and in two specific cases concerning freedom of expression and the age of consent for male/male sexual activity, Chan explains that constitutional comparativism may be capable of both undermining and augmenting the protection of fundamental rights and freedoms, including sexual minority rights. The author calls for a consistent and principled approach for constitutional comparativism to be legitimate and for the protection of human rights, including sexual minority rights, and for the rule of law to progress and be safeguarded in Hong Kong. A proper understanding of constitutional comparativism at work will furthermore enable other jurisdictions, such as Singapore, that resist participating in 'transnational judicial conversations'[33] to observe the intrinsic values and advantages of such conversations as a juridical enterprise and engine for thoughtful judicial and legislative decisions with carefully discerned insights and experiences from other jurisdictions.

As Clare Hemmings has argued, '[f]or national spokesmen for a range of African and Asian nation-states, among others, homosexuality is ... framed as a betrayal in two ways:

as a failure of appropriate gendered and sexual citizenship, and as a marker of Western influence. By suturing nation to heterosexuality through positing "gayness ... as a polluting foreign influence", state representatives can deny any history of same-sex practice in the national context at stake, and dismiss global sexual rights movements as straightforwardly imperialistic.'[34] The notion that homosexuality had been non-existent in Asian and African societies – China continues to claim that sexual minorities do not exist within its territory[35] – until corrupt Westerners invaded or colonised their countries and spread their immorality must thus be investigated. As An-Na`im discerns, 'the possibilities of cultural reinterpretation and reconstruction through internal cultural discourse and cross-cultural dialogue, as a means to enhancing the universal legitimacy of human rights', ought to be explored.[36] There are many approaches through which to deconstruct a culture both from within and from without in relation to homosexuality/heterosexuality/bisexuality/transgender identity and sexual minority rights development. One such approach is by placing homosexuality/heterosexuality/bisexuality/transgender identity in the historical context of the polity to determine whether sexual minority rights are an essential or implied value of – or precisely to protect against – that culture and how they have been enacted in reality. Another approach is to look at and through actual instances of struggles, sufferings, and/or successes in living in fear and in safety, by talking and listening to real people and placing their individual experiences in the context of their societies, in the light of their societies' historical and contemporary circumstances.

In 'Sexual minorities and human rights in Japan: an historical perspective', Mark McLelland and Katsuhiko Suganuma point out that Japan has always enjoyed longstanding and well-documented traditions of same-sex eroticism. As has been noted, culture is not static, rigid, and isolated within a polity, and this has been true in the case of Japan and the contexts and identities of sexual minorities through which same-sex eroticism has been expressed, as McLelland and Suganuma explain. The authors note that changes in notions of Japanese sexual identity and sexual citizenship have been particularly profound after World War II as discourses of rights implanted by the United States began to develop, even though true linkage between sexual minorities and human rights began to be built only since the 1980s, through which gay men, lesbians, bisexuals, and transgender persons must face their current and future challenges respectively and collectively.

Shifting to Africa, by analysing an actual scenario involving participants with whom he has conducted extensive interviews, Oliver Phillips in 'Blackmail in Zimbabwe: troubling narratives of sexuality and human rights' highlights the significance of discourse and rhetoric in the operation of the law, in particular the criminal law on blackmail and consensual same-sex sexual activity, in Zimbabwe. Phillips argues that the historical and contemporary sexual politics in Zimbabwe – a former British colony where, as in Singapore and Hong Kong, criminalisation of consensual same-sex sexual activity was implanted as part of British colonial rule – and the racial and sexual identities of persons belonging to sexual minorities in the country ascribe sexual minorities the attribute of unvarying and perpetual guilt, and those who engage in blackmail and extortion of sexual minorities the attribute of innocence in defence of the heterosexuality of the state. The author explains that such attributes of guilt and innocence prevent human agency and rights development. It is to be recalled that attributes of guilt and innocence also have primary and serious repercussions for all male rape victims, including gay male rape victims, of sexual assault, as Rumney has explained.

Meanwhile, attention must be paid to transgender persons, whose voices, experiences, struggles, sufferings, and desires are often dismissed by gay men and lesbians (who themselves suffer a degree of relegation by gay men due to their gender) – a similar fate has befallen bisexuals, as Sean Rehaag illustrates later in this special double issue. In 'Lost in transition: transpeople, transprejudice and pathology in Asia', Sam Winter explores the lives of transgender persons – persons who are gender variant or gender identity variant – in Asia. In particular, Winter examines the hurdles and desires transgender persons encounter if and when making a transition to a gender that does not match the one assigned to them at birth but which corresponds to their inner identities and feelings; their prevalence and visibility across the continent; issues of healthcare, documentation, and stealth; and prejudice and discrimination on the basis of gender identity. The author also argues that by classifying gender identity variance as a mental disorder in the same manner *vis-à-vis* homosexuality until the American Psychiatric Association reversed course in 1973, psychiatry exacerbates prejudice and discrimination against transgender persons through pathologisation.

As the horrors of World War II illuminated, intolerance of persons belonging to minorities may rise to the level of persecution and these minorities who find themselves in such conditions and circumstances must find refuge away from their homes instead of continuing to hope that they will ever be able to live a life in full without fear. Jurisprudence on refugee protection has been developed in a progressive and authoritative manner and *non-refoulement* as embodied in the 1951 Convention Relating to the Status of Refugees,[37] under which '[n]o Contracting State shall expel or return (*"refouler"*) a refugee in any manner whatsoever to the frontiers of territories where his life or freedom would be threatened on account of his race, religion, nationality, membership of a particular social group or political opinion',[38] has been described as a principle of customary international law if not one of the rarefied pre-emptory norms of international law binding upon all States[39] whether or not they have ratified the Convention (whether or not together with the subsequent 1967 Protocol Relating to the Status of Refugees[40]). Jurisprudence in major host states such as Australia, Canada, New Zealand, the United Kingdom, and the United States now regards persecution on grounds of sexual orientation or gender identity as a basis upon which refugee status and asylum may be claimed.

However, persons belonging to sexual minorities have found that claims for refugee status and asylum on the basis of sexual orientation or gender identity continue to be difficult to succeed in practice, as courts and refugee determination tribunals criticise, question, and disbelieve the validity of their sexual orientation or gender identity. In 'From discretion to disbelief: recent trends in refugee determinations on the basis of sexual orientation in Australia and the United Kingdom', Jenni Millbank explores the impact of *Appellants S395/2002 and S396/2002* v. *Minister for Immigration and Multicultural Affairs*[41] – the first decision in the world by an ultimate national court to consider a claim for refugee status based on sexual orientation – on the refugee jurisprudence of Australia and the United Kingdom five years since it was decided in 2003. In its majority decision the High Court of Australia rejected the notion propounded in previous decisions that refugee claimants ought to protect themselves through 'discretion', that is, concealment of one's sexual orientation through what Kenji Yoshino has termed 'covering'.[42] Millbank describes how courts and refugee determination tribunals in the two countries have still been slow to acknowledge that concealment of sexual orientation is not predicated upon choice but upon discrimination, oppression and persecution in society and by the state. Furthermore, the author points to a clear shift in Australian refugee jurisprudence from the premise of discretion towards outright disbelief of refugee claimants' sexual orientation on the basis of stereotypical notions of what it means to be a sexual minority person that also ignore how the lives of sexual minority refugee claimants in their countries of origin, in Asia, Africa, Latin America, and the Middle East, are and must be lived.

As noted above, practices and discourses of human rights and sexual minority rights continue to suffer stratification on the basis of perceived importance of issues. Indeed, they also question the validity of certain issues in a manner alarmingly akin to the prejudicial approaches in Australian refugee jurisprudence that Millbank has illustrated. One issue that continues to be sidelined consists of the unique struggles and sufferings bisexuals must endure in order to realise their right of equality and their right to safety. Through an empirical assessment of the success rates of refugee claims on grounds of bisexuality in Canada, the United States, and Australia, Sean Rehaag in 'Bisexuals need not apply: a comparative appraisal of refugee law and policy in Canada, the United States, and Australia' examines the reasons why the struggles and sufferings of bisexuals have been regarded as of lesser severity than the struggles and sufferings of gay men and lesbians, which have rendered bisexuals largely invisible in the sexual minority rights movement. Rehaag points out that bisexuals are significantly less successful than gay men or lesbians in obtaining refugee status in the three countries, and explains that persecution of a person on grounds of his or her bisexuality should be recognised as an equal basis under refugee law upon which refugee status and asylum may be claimed.

The journey from discretion to disbelief that Millbank has explored is for a significant part fuelled by the lack or inadequacy of independent country information on the lives and persecution of sexual minority refugee claimants and the general state of human rights in their countries of origin. In 'Independent human rights documentation and sexual minorities: an ongoing challenge for the Canadian refugee determination process', Nicole LaViolette notes that a sexual minority refugee claimant, be he or she a gay man, lesbian, bisexual or transgender person, must meet the same evidentiary burden imposed upon all other refugee claimants. However, refugee claimants belonging to sexual minorities must first have made their sexual orientation or gender identity explicit in their countries of origin and thereby subjected themselves to persecution on the basis of a personal characteristic 'unchangeable or changeable only at unacceptable personal costs'[43] (hence discretion). LaViolette explains that that is why independent country information assembled by international and local human rights organisations, including those dedicated to sexual minority issues, plays an instrumental role in sexual minority refugee claimants' ability to meet their evidentiary burden. However, many of these organisations continue to be unwilling or unable to assemble the kinds of information necessary for sexual minority refugee claimants to prove their claims amid shifting legal questions, and courts and refugee determination tribunals, such as in Canada on which LaViolette focuses her study, have relied on the paucity of such independent country information to reject claims based on sexual orientation or gender identity as unfounded, have failed to understand the issues raised in the independent country information that is available, and have further discriminated between international and local human rights organisations and between general human rights and sexual minority rights organisations on the basis of perceived repute and objectivity (hence disbelief).

Amid the struggles and sufferings that our papers have illustrated, we wish to underscore and convey a message of love. While arguments based on religion have continued to fuel prejudice, discrimination, oppression and persecution of persons belonging to sexual minorities, persons holding particular religious beliefs and persons belonging to sexual minorities *can* embrace each other in the spirit of love. As Rhoda Howard-Hassmann has pointed out, '[t]he truly rights-protective society is one that is "inclusive". These three key words – celebration, diversity, and inclusivity – typify a very recent social attitude that mere tolerance is a type of racism or prejudice, reflecting an unwillingness of the dominant, "tolerant" group to acknowledge that the diverse Other is as morally respectable as the conforming Us.'[44] The recent reform in predominantly Catholic Spain that has recognised the right to marry another person of the same sex is a good example. In Ireland, which is equally permeated by Catholic teachings in its social and constitutional structures, discourses and legal reforms have been progressively developed to embrace and protect persons belonging to sexual minorities as equal human beings. In 'Same-sex marriage and the Irish Constitution', Aisling O'Sullivan examines the recent Irish High Court case of *Zappone and Gilligan* v. *Revenue Commissioners and Others*,[45] a challenge to the constitutionality of the state's interpretation of taxation legislation that excludes a same-sex couple from certain benefits available to a different-sex couple. As the right to marry and the nature of marriage are undefined in the Irish Constitution, O'Sullivan argues that a progressive interpretation of the Irish Constitution and laws may take into account contemporary scientific and normative understandings of sexuality, sexual orientation, and, above all, norms of equality and non-discrimination, so as to embrace and protect a person's right to marry another person of the same sex in Ireland in the spirit of prudence, justice and charity as the Constitution prescribes.[46]

While there remains a lack of formal legal instruments at the international level that would guarantee and protect the rights of persons belonging to sexual minorities in similar manners as the rights of women and racial, ethnic, religious, and linguistic minorities are guaranteed and protected, sexual minorities need not, indeed must not, perpetuate silence through their own silence and inaction, and battles for true and full realisation of sexual minority rights as equal human rights that were asserted forcefully through the Stonewall Riots four decades ago must continue – through loud and vigorous persuasion. Under the auspices of the International Commission of Jurists and the International Service for Human Rights on behalf of a coalition of human rights organisations around the world, a distinguished group of experts on human rights met in Yogyakarta, Indonesia, in 2006 and assembled an admirably comprehensive set of fundamental rights and freedoms to which persons belonging to sexual minorities are entitled on the basis of existing international human rights law for the simple reason that they are full and equal human beings, in the form of the Yogyakarta Principles on the Application of International Human Rights Law in relation to Sexual Orientation and Gender Identity. While we are not able to include the Yogyakarta Principles in this special double issue, readers are urged to consult the Yogyakarta Principles, available in all six official languages of the United Nations, in tandem.[47] The Yogyakarta Principles affirm the primary obligation of each and every State to implement all human rights, including sexual minority rights, and assist their implementation with carefully discerned recommendations. At the same time, as the drafters of the Yogyakarta Principles remind us, all actors, including international organisations, state apparatuses especially national courts, human rights commissions and ombudsmen, educational institutions, the media, and, ultimately, all individuals, have responsibilities to promote and protect all human rights – discrimination or stratification between human rights will only render *all* human rights vulnerable to attack and demise. This special double issue, thus, ends with United States President Barack Obama's words, 'the audacity of hope'.

Acknowledgements

While preparations for this special double issue began in early 2005, they could not have been proceeded but for the facilities and assistance I received during my visiting fellowships and extended academic visits at Gender, Sexuality and Law Research Group, School of Law, Keele University; Lauterpacht Research Centre for International Law, University of Cambridge; Asia-Pacific College of Diplomacy, Australian National University; Faculty of Law, University of Ottawa; Asian Institute, Munk Centre for International Studies, University of Toronto; Institut für Öffentliches Recht, Albert-Ludwigs-Universität Freiburg; Department of Political Science, Vanderbilt University; and School of International Relations, University of St Andrews, between April 2006 and June 2008. Special thanks must also extend to Simon Chesterman, Juliette Gregory Duara, Andrew Harding, John and Lynette Lim, and Andrew Simester for their tremendous support and forbearance as I conducted the final and most critical stage of preparations for this special double issue while contending with my doctoral research at the Faculty of Law, National University of Singapore. Last but not least, I wish to thank Paul Serfaty, Frank Barnaby, and Taylor & Francis, especially Stacey Davies and Jessica Vivian, for their support and assistance to this project, as well as each and every anonymous reviewer for so kindly volunteering their valuable time to enable this special double issue to be an authoritative source of scholarly analyses of issues affecting persons belonging to sexual minorities, and ultimately all persons and societies, around the world.

Notes

1. As inscribed on a stone in New England Holocaust Memorial, Boston, United States.
2. R. Rorty, *Irony, Contingency and Solidarity* (Cambridge: Cambridge University Press, 1989), xvi.
3. Adopted and proclaimed by UN GA Res. 217A(III) of 10 December 1948.
4. For discussions of the legal status and ethical significance of the Universal Declaration of Human Rights, see, e.g., C. Brown, 'Universal Human Rights: A Critique', *International Journal of Human Rights* 1 (1997): 41; T. Pogge, 'The International Significance of Human Rights', *Journal of Ethics* 4 (2000): 45; B. Simma and P. Alston, 'The Sources of Human Rights Law: Custom, Jus Cogens, and General Principles', *Australian Year Book of International Law* 12 (1992): 82; L.B. Sohn, 'The New International Law: Protection of the Rights of Individuals rather than States', *American University Law Review* 32 (1982): 1.
5. Universal Declaration of Human Rights, Art. 1.
6. See Amnesty International, *Breaking the Silence: Human Rights Violations Based on Sexual Orientation* (London: Amnesty International, 1997); N. LaViolette and S. Whitworth, 'No Safe Haven: Sexuality as a Universal Human Right and Gay and Lesbian Activism in International Politics', *Millennium: Journal of International Studies* 23 (1994): 563.
7. See American Psychiatric Association, 'Position Statement on Homosexuality and Civil Rights', *American Journal of Psychiatry* 131 (1973): 497. In 1998, the American Psychiatric Association unanimously adopted a Position Statement on Psychiatric Treatment and Sexual Orientation, *American Journal of Psychiatry* 156 (1999): 1131, that condemned the use of 'reparative therapy' for homosexuality, stating that '[t]he potential risks of reparative therapy are great, including depression, anxiety and self-destructive behavior, since therapist alignment with societal prejudices against homosexuality may reinforce self-hatred already experienced by the patient. Many patients who have undergone reparative therapy relate that they were inaccurately told that homosexuals are lonely, unhappy individuals who never achieve acceptance or satisfaction. The possibility that the person might achieve happiness and satisfying interpersonal relationships as a gay man or lesbian is not presented, nor are alternative approaches to dealing with the effects of societal stigmatization discussed. ... Therefore, the American Psychiatric Association opposes any psychiatric treatment, such as reparative or conversion therapy which is based upon the assumption that homosexuality per se is a mental disorder or based upon the *a priori* assumption that the patient should change his/her sexual homosexual orientation.' In 2000, the American Psychiatric Association adopted a further Position Statement on Therapies Focused on Attempts to Change Sexual Orientation (Reparative or Conversion Therapies), *American Journal of Psychiatry* 157 (2000): 1719, which expanded and elaborated the 1998 position statement.
8. See E.A. Armstrong, *Forging Gay Identities: Organizing Sexuality in San Francisco, 1950–1994* (Chicago and London: University of Chicago Press, 2002).
9. (1981) 4 EHRR 149.
10. *Leung T.C. William Roy* v. *Secretary for Justice* [2005] 3 HKLRD 657 (Hong Kong Court of First Instance); *Secretary for Justice* v. *Leung T.C. William Roy* [2006] 4 HKLRD 211 (Hong Kong Court of Appeal).
11. 539 US 558 (2003) (Supreme Court of the United States).

12. 478 US 186 (1986).
13. *Romer* v. *Evans*, 517 US 620 (1996) (Supreme Court of the United States).
14. Local Government Act 1986 (c. 10), s. 2A(1), as inserted by Local Government Act 1988 (c. 9), s. 28(1). The legislation was not applicable in Northern Ireland: Local Government Act 1988, s. 42(2). The legislation was repealed by the devolved Scottish Parliament for Scotland in 2000: Ethical Standards in Public Life etc. (Scotland) Act 2000 (2000 asp 7), s. 36(1) and Sch. 4, para. 1; and by Parliament in Westminster for England and Wales in 2003: Local Government Act 2003 (c. 26), s. 127(2) and Sch. 8(1), para. 1.
15. A. Hartman, 'Out of the Closet: Revolution and Backlash', *Social Work* 38 (1993): 245, 245.
16. 1(3) IHRR 97 (1994).
17. Article 2(1) of the International Covenant on Civil and Political Rights, adopted and opened for signature, ratification and accession by UN GA Res. 2200A(XXI) of 16 December 1966 and entered into force on 23 March 1976, states that '[e]ach State Party to the present Covenant undertakes to respect and to ensure to all individuals within its territory and subject to its jurisdiction the rights recognised in the present Covenant, without distinction of any kind, such as race, colour, sex, language, religion, political or other opinion, national or social origin, property, birth or other status.' Article 26, ibid., states that '[a]ll persons are equal before the law and are entitled without any discrimination to the equal protection of the law. In this respect, the law shall prohibit any discrimination and guarantee to all persons equal and effective protection against discrimination on any ground such as race, colour, sex, language, religion, political or other opinion, national or social origin, property, birth or other status.'
18. See, e.g., *R.* v. *M. (C.)* (1995) 98 CCC (3d) 481 (Ontario Court of Appeal); *R.* v. *Roy* (1998) 101 DLR (4th) 148 (Québec Court of Appeal); *Vriend* v. *Alberta* (1998) 156 DLR (4th) 385 (Supreme Court of Canada); *Reference re Same-Sex Marriage* [2004] 3 SCR 698 (Supreme Court of Canada); *Leung T.C. William Roy* v. *Secretary for Justice* [2005] 3 HKLRD 657 (Hong Kong Court of First Instance); *Secretary for Justice* v. *Leung T.C. William Roy* [2006] 4 HKLRD 211 (Hong Kong Court of Appeal); *National Coalition for Gay and Lesbian Equality* v. *Minister of Justice*, 1999 (1) SA 6 (Constitutional Court of South Africa); *National Coalition for Gay and Lesbian Equality* v. *Minister of Home Affairs*, 39(4) ILM 798 (2000) (Constitutional Court of South Africa); *Fourie* v. *Minister of Home Affairs*, Case CCT 232/03, 30 November 2004 (Supreme Court of Appeal of South Africa); *Minister of Home Affairs* v. *Fourie*, Case CCT 60/04, 1 December 2005 (Constitutional Court of South Africa); *Lawrence* v. *Texas*, 539 US 558 (2003) (Supreme Court of the United States); *Goodridge* v. *Department of Public Health*, 440 Mass 309 (2003) (Massachusetts Supreme Judicial Court); *In re Opinions of the Justices to the Senate*, 440 Mass 1201 (2004) (Massachusetts Supreme Judicial Court); *Sutherland* v. *United Kingdom* (1997) 24 EHRR CD22 (European Commission of Human Rights); *Salgueiro da Silva Mouta* v. *Portugal* (2001) 31 EHRR 1055 (European Court of Human Rights); *Smith and Grady* v. *United Kingdom* (2000) 29 EHRR 493 (European Court of Human Rights); *Young* v. *Australia*, United Nations Human Rights Committee, Communication No. 941/2000, CCPR/C/78/D/941/2000, 6 August 2003 (cf., however, *Joslin* v. *New Zealand*, United Nations Human Rights Committee, Communication No. 902/1999, CCPR/C/75/D/902/1999, 17 July 2002).
19. Final Constitution of the Republic of South Africa of 1996, Art. 9(3). Article 9(5), ibid., states that discrimination on any of the grounds specified in Article 9(3) is deemed to be unfair 'unless it is established that the discrimination is fair'.
20. Article 9(4), ibid., states that '[n]o person may unfairly discriminate directly or indirectly against anyone on one or more grounds in terms of subsection (3). National legislation must be enacted to prevent or prohibit unfair discrimination.'
21. Ibid., Art. 10.
22. For a comprehensive, cross-national discussion of the debate on the right of a person to marry another person of the same sex, see P.C.W. Chan, 'Same-Sex Marriage/Constitutionalism and their Centrality to Equality Rights in Hong Kong: A Comparative–Socio-Legal Appraisal', *International Journal of Human Rights* 11 (2007): 33.
23. A. Belden Fields and Wolf-Dieter Narr, 'Human Rights as a Holistic Concept', *Human Rights Quarterly* 14 (1992): 1, 5.
24. M. Minow, 'Rights for the Next Generation: A Feminist Approach to Children's Rights', *Harvard Women's Law Journal* 9 (1986): 1, 24.
25. Equal Access Act of 1984, Title 20 USCA, ss. 4071–4.

26. The First Amendment to the United States Constitution states that 'Congress shall make no law respecting an establishment of religion, or prohibiting the free exercise thereof; or abridging the freedom of speech, or of the press; or the right of the people peaceably to assemble, and to petition the Government for a redress of grievances.'

27. S. Sivakumaran, 'Male/Male Rape and the "Taint" of Homosexuality', *Human Rights Quarterly* 27 (2005): 1274.

28. S.E. Merry, 'Human Rights Law and the Demonization of Culture (and Anthropology along the Way)', *Political and Legal Anthropology Review* 26 (2003): 55, 67. See also A.-B.S. Preis, 'Human Rights as Cultural Practice: An Anthropological Critique', *Human Rights Quarterly* 18 (1996): 286.

29. A.A. An-Na'im, 'Toward a Cross-Cultural Approach to Defining International Standards of Human Rights', in *Human Rights in Cross-Cultural Perspectives: A Quest for Consensus*, ed. A.A. An-Na'im (Philadelphia, PA: University of Pennsylvania Press, 1992), 19, 27–8.

30. S. Breyer, 'Keynote Address', *American Society of International Law Proceedings* 97 (2003): 265, 265, quoting R.B. Ginsburg and D.J. Merritt, 'Affirmative Action: An International Human Rights Dialogue', *Cardozo Law Review* 21 (1999): 253, 282.

31. R.P. Alford, 'In Search of a Theory for Constitutional Comparativism', *UCLA Law Review* 52 (2005): 639, 644.

32. Ibid., 641.

33. See, e.g., V.C. Jackson, 'Comparative Constitutional Federalism and Transnational Judicial Discourse', *International Journal of Constitutional Law* 2 (2004): 91; C. McCrudden, 'A Common Law of Human Rights?: Transnational Judicial Conversations on Constitutional Rights', *Oxford Journal of Legal Studies* 20 (2000): 499; A.-M. Slaughter, 'Judicial Globalization', *Virginia Journal of International Law* 40 (1999–2000): 1103; L.-A. Thio, 'Beyond the "Four Walls" in an Age of Transnational Judicial Conversations: Civil Liberties, Rights Theories, and Constitutional Adjudication in Malaysia and Singapore', *Columbia Journal of Asian Law* 19 (2005–6): 428.

34. C. Hemmings, 'What's in a Name? Bisexuality, Transnational Sexuality Studies and Western Colonial Legacies', *International Journal of Human Rights* 11 (2007): 13, 16, quoting P.A. Jackson, 'Pre-Gay, Post-Queer: Thai Perspectives on Proliferating Gender/Sex Diversity in Asia', *Journal of Homosexuality* 40 nos 3–4 (2001): 1, 8.

35. See F.-F. Ruan, 'China', in *Sociolegal Control of Homosexuality: A Multi-Nation Comparison*, ed. D.J. West and R. Green (New York: Plenum Press, 1997), 57.

36. A.A. An-Na'im, 'Introduction', in *Human Rights in Cross-Cultural Perspectives: A Quest for Consensus*, ed. A.A. An-Na'im (Philadelphia, PA: University of Pennsylvania Press, 1992), 1, 3.

37. Adopted by United Nations Conference of Plenipotentiaries on the Status of Refugees and Stateless Persons convened under UN GA Res. 429(V) of 14 December 1950 on 28 July 1951 and entered into force on 22 April 1954.

38. Ibid., Art. 33(1).

39. P.C.W. Chan, 'The Protection of Refugees and Internally Displaced Persons: *Non-Refoulement* under Customary International Law?', *International Journal of Human Rights* 10 (2006): 231.

40. Entered into force on 4 October 1967.

41. (2003) 216 CLR 473.

42. K. Yoshino, 'Covering', *Yale Law Journal* 111 (2002): 769; K. Yoshino, *Covering: The Hidden Assault on Our Civil Rights* (New York: Random House, 2006).

43. *Egan* v. *Canada* (1995) 124 DLR (4th) 609, 619 (per La Forest J., Supreme Court of Canada).

44. R.E. Howard-Hassmann, 'Gay Rights and the Right to a Family: Conflicts between Liberal and Illiberal Belief Systems', *Human Rights Quarterly* 23 (2001): 73, 79.

45. [2006] IEHC 404.

46. Bunreacht na hÉireann (Constitution of Ireland) 1937, Preamble.

47. See http://yogyakartaprinciples.org.

Psychosocial implications of homophobic bullying in schools: a review and directions for legal research and the legal process

Phil C.W. Chan

Faculty of Law, National University of Singapore, Singapore

This review paper explores the medical, educational and sociological research literature on the nature, likelihood, causes, onset, course, consequences, resolution and prevention of school bullying and addresses the added implications of homophobia, with the role of family taken into account. A thorough understanding of relevant empirical research is essential to exploring the contributory, remedial, retributive and deterrent roles of the law, including international law. Some directions as to how these roles may be explored through legal research and the legal process are suggested.

Introduction

Homophobic school bullying, with which school bullying not attributable to sexual orientation is *always* intertwined, is a universal and the most fundamental sexual orientation-related problem affecting all children and adolescents of all ages around the world. Yet despite the tremendous harms school bullying in general and homophobic school bullying in particular causes, school authorities, parents, and society typically deny its occurrence and impact. Their denial is continually reinforced, perpetuated and exacerbated by the responses, or the lack thereof, of the legal system as reflected by the paucity of legal research on the problem. Such denial is rooted in society's general and pervasive unease with matters of sexuality and individual differences, and in its constructed image of childhood that, except for poverty, a child *cannot* struggle or suffer. Many children struggle and suffer a great deal, only to find their struggles and sufferings unseen, unheard, ignored and disbelieved. For a child, school bullying is to him/her the biggest terror of all; for some, death means life. Contrary to O'Neill's claim that the child's 'main remedy is to grow up',[1] as a bullied child reaches adulthood his or her traumatic past will not, as society likes to think, simply disappear. As Herman in her groundbreaking *Trauma and Recovery*[2] states, '[r]epeated trauma in adult life erodes the structure of the personality already formed, but repeated trauma in childhood forms and deforms the personality.'[3]

Through a review of the medical, educational and sociological research literature on the nature, likelihood, causes, onset, course, consequences, resolution and prevention of school bullying, in which the added implications of homophobia are addressed and the role of family taken into account, this paper demonstrates that school bullying in general and homophobic school bullying in particular entails traumatic consequences for the bullied child and his or her later life. A thorough understanding of relevant empirical research is essential to exploring the contributory, remedial, retributive and deterrent roles of the law, including international law. Some directions as to how these roles may be explored through legal research and the legal process are then suggested.

Psychosocial implications of (homophobic) school bullying: a review of research literature

The nature and prevalence of (homophobic) school bullying

The late developmental psychoanalyst Erikson pointed out that the formation of identity 'has its normative crisis in adolescence, and is in many ways determined by what went before and determines much that follows'.[4] It involves the adolescent's attempts at synchronisation of his or her inner being, through 'a process of simultaneous reflection and observation, a process taking place on all levels of mental functioning',[5] with his or her external environs and attendant values.[6] This process, which culminates in '[i]dentity consolidation, social integration, and intimacy [that] are after all the hallmarks of the transition to adulthood',[7] is, maintained Erikson, 'luckily, and necessarily, for the most part unconscious except where inner conditions and outer circumstances combine to aggravate a painful, or elated, "identity-consciousness".'[8] Needless to say, growing up realising that one belongs to a sexual minority (inner conditions) in a hetero-normative and oftentimes aggressively homophobic society (outer circumstances) is one instance where such identity-consciousness is generated but nevertheless is 'a primary developmental task for homosexual adolescents'.[9] As Schneider discerns, '[b]eing lesbian or gay influences much more than the expression of one's sexuality. It affects relationships with family and friends and is an integral part of one's identity as a male or female.'[10] I have argued elsewhere that children and adolescents have the right to sexual minority identity[11] as well as the rights to non-discrimination, to education and to health under the United Nations Convention on the Rights of the Child,[12] a point to which I will return as I explore the contributory, remedial, retributive and deterrent roles of the law, including international law, in school bullying in general and homophobic school bullying in particular.

Confused as to whether any sexual activity may or may not be an appropriate matter in life, many adolescents and indeed many adults perceive sexuality as outright threatening. Gonsiorek observes that '[a]dolescents are frequently intolerant of differentness in others and may castigate or ostracize peers, particularly if the perceived differentness is in the arena of sexuality or sex roles.'[13] Gonsiorek also notes that '[d]uring adolescence, individuals are more polarized in their sex roles than at any other time in their lives. Males experience intense peer pressure to be "tough" and "macho", and females to be passive and compliant. Although social sex roles are not intrinsically related to sexual orientation, the distinction is poorly understood by most adolescents, as well as by most adults.'[14] Society's negative treatment of homosexuality – through 'a *diverse set of social practices* – from the linguistic to the physical, in the public sphere and the private sphere, covert and overt – *in an array of social arenas* (e.g. work, home, school, media, church, courts, streets, etc.), *in which the homo/hetero binary distinction is at work whereby heterosexuality is privileged*'[15] – reinforces adolescents' (and adults') belief that only heterosexuality is acceptable. The constant flow of negative information and indoctrination adolescents receive over the badness of differences and the goodness of conformity from their parents and those in positions of authority, such as teachers and religious pastors who preach divine eternal punishment for non-conformity, further reinforces their fear. (Gill, however, cautions that a positive use of a discourse that 'explains and embraces' individual differences may have as its disguised purpose 'justifying injustice' and 'serves further to play down any notion of structural inequality or institutional practices'.[16]) As psychoanalytic observations have affirmed, '[t]he more subtle methods by which children are induced to accept historical or actual people as prototypes of good and evil consist of minute displays of emotions such as affection, pride, anger, guilt, anxiety, and sexual tension. They themselves, rather than merely the words used, the meanings intended, or the philosophy implied, transmit to the human child the outlines of what really counts in his world'.[17] Matters are worse for those with a sexual orientation other than heterosexuality. Savin-Williams observes that '[f]or the youth struggling with a stigmatizing sexual identity, adolescence can be a time of conflict and distress. With pressures from family and peers to be heterosexual, gay male, lesbian and bisexual youths face unique hurdles in their efforts to forge a healthy sense of self.'[18] In an attempt to dislodge their identity confusions and fears, many adolescents – including those in fear of being or being perceived as non-heterosexual and those in denial or rejection of their minority sexual orientations – resort to bullying behaviours towards their peers which serve a dual performative purpose for both self and others. As Nayak and Kehily observed through their school-based research at two secondary schools in the West Midlands, England:

> In the constant struggle for coherence subjects engage in various forms of splitting, projection and displacement which are 'articulated' in the homophobic performance. The performance is enacted to expel fears, desires and the vulnerability of ambivalence. These processes of self-production appear to go largely unacknowledged by the individuals concerned, as they struggle to achieve the illusion of internal consistency. In order to fabricate a coherent heterosexual masculinity, ambivalences must be managed in external social arenas through public perfor-mace, and at internal levels within the subject. Homophobic performances are part of the self-convincing rituals of masculinity young men engage in. The performance is as much for self as others, where heterosexual masculinities are constituted through action. The acts are not simply a momentary social performance for an external audience, but form a technique for styling a particular masculine self-identity.[19]

In other words, from a psychoanalytic viewpoint, the bully believes that so long as he/she distances him/herself from a particular attribute – such as but by no means limited to a non-heterosexual sexual orientation – that his or her victim possesses or is perceived to possess, he or she simply cannot possess that attribute.[20] No one was born to be a bully – bullying is *always* a learned behaviour; the same goes for the victim.

McFarland notes that 'the struggle for identity and control is endemic to every class-room'.[21] Propensity to bullying behaviours has been found to increase and peak during early adolescence and decrease subsequently.[22] Equally, resistance to bullying prevention and intervention programmes peaks during adolescence.[23] According to Olweus, who pio-neered research on bullying with his large-scale study in Norway in the 1970s,[24] '[a] student is being bullied or victimized when he or she is exposed, repeatedly and over time, to nega-tive actions on the part of one or more other students.'[25] Negative actions in bullying may manifest in various forms, including name-calling, rumours, shunning, exclusion from a group, yelling, having belongings damaged or taken, and threats and acts of physical aggression and violence. Systematic abuse of an imbalance of power underlies school bullying; one cannot bully another person who is of equal or superior physical and mental strength.[26]

School bullying is 'an important public health issue'[27] and a universal problem affecting all children and adolescents of all ages around the world. Prevalence of victimisation has been found to range from 11.3% in a sample of 5813 primary school children in Finland[28] to 49.8% in a sample of 7290 primary school children in Ireland.[29] Prevalence of victimisation in secondary schools has been found to vary between 4.2% in a British sample[30] and 25% in an Australian sample.[31] In a study of 11,535 pupils in England and Wales aged between 13 and 15, fear of bullying was reported by a quarter of the respondents.[32] In another study involving 703 secondary school pupils in England, 32% of the respondents reported having recurring memories of bullying incidents.[33] In the United States, it has been found that 15–20% of school children are victimised on a regular basis.[34] In terms of frequency, Whitney and Smith in a survey of 6758 pupils in Sheffield, England, found 27% of junior/middle school and 10% of secondary school pupils to have been bullied at least 'sometimes' while 10% of the former and 4% of the latter group had been bullied at least 'once a week'.[35] The researchers observed comparable results in Ireland, Spain, Sweden, and the Netherlands.[36] Smith and Shu found that in England 65% of victims reported having been bullied for one week to one month, 13% the entire term, 9% one year, and 13% several years.[37] In the United States, as Nansel and her colleagues found, 10.6% of school children bullied others 'sometimes' and 8.8% once a week or more often, leading to a national estimate of 2,027,254 youth who were involved in moderately frequent bullying and 1,681,030 youth in frequent bullying, while 8.5% were bullied 'sometimes' and 8.4% once a week or more often, leading to a national estimate of 1,634,095 pupils who were bullied with moderate frequency and 1,611,809 pupils bullied frequently.[38] There is also high stability among participants in school bullying: according to a British study by Boulton and Smith, both the bully and victim statuses based on peer nominations were highly stable for three separate assessment periods during a school year and at the start of the next year within a group of eight- to nine-year-olds.[39] The commonality, frequency and stability of school bullying, Rodkin and Hodges discern, is one reason why teachers and parents typically regard school bullying as having an insignificant impact on the psychosocial development of children.[40]

Participants in a school bullying situation

In a bullying situation, instead of a bully–victim binary, there are six participant roles. From a sample of 573 Finnish sixth-graders, Salmivalli found that 8.2% were bullies; 11.7% were victims; 6.8% were assistants, who although not instigators would join in bullying; 19.5% were reinforcers, who would encourage bullying by providing an audience; 23.7% were outsiders, who would avoid involvement in bullying by staying away or not taking sides and would yet play a role in bullying through their silence; and, finally, 17.3% were defenders of victims, who would assist victims and try to stop bullying through positive action.[41] It has been noted that while most pupils are either opposed or neutral to bullying,[42] when bullying occurs many pupils will reinforce the bullying as assistants, reinforcers or outsiders, and the presence of bystander peers has been found to contribute to the persistence of particular bullying situations and relationships.[43] A 1993 survey found that two main reasons why adolescents carried weapons in schools were to impress or gain acceptance from friends (66%) and to feel important (56%).[44] Twenlow and his colleagues distinguish two types of bystanders: those who feel they are not able to stop the bullying and those who draw pleasure in watching the distress of their peers[45] (there are, of course, also bystanders who are simply indifferent). Nansel and her colleagues observed that victims were avoided by their peers, who feared getting bullied or losing social status themselves.[46] In a study of Toronto elementary schools, it was observed that peers were present 88% of the time when bullying occurred, while they intervened 19% of the time and their intervention was effective in stopping the bullying 57% of the time.[47] Research has also found that children with similar tendency to aggression and anti-social behaviours tend to associate with each other,[48] and Salmivalli, Lappalainen, and Lagerspetz observe that a powerful predictor of how a particular child will behave in bullying situations is how his friends behave in such situations.[49] In the words of Rodkin and Hodges, '[n]othing can be as powerful an obstacle or as effective a tool in preventing bullying as the forces create by socialising one another.'[50] Salmivalli suggests that in a climate where group conformity is overwhelming, peers' attitudes towards bullying and their actual actions, or inactions, do not necessarily converge. The researcher also warns that the participant roles tend to be rigid and self-fulfilling, with the result that bullies who are unchecked will end up believing and behaving as if entirely incapable of behaviours other than those expected of bullies. The same is true of other participant roles, especially victims who may find that even in a new class with no former classmates, bullying will start afresh.[51]

The roles of bully and victim are also not mutually exclusive. Most bullies suffer bullying at times; these are known as aggressive victims or bully/victims.[52] In particular, Smith and his colleagues reported that victims who endured bullying on a continuing basis were the most likely to bully others[53] (which should not be at all surprising, as bullying is, as has been noted, always a learned behaviour – who else is better positioned than continuing victims to learn the power dynamics and vulnerabilities of bullying?). Bully/victims are also at greater risk than victims of lack of peer acceptance,[54] and they are the most aggressive among bullies.[55]

Meanwhile, research has found that boys are more likely than girls to engage in bullying behaviours involving physical acts of aggression and violence[56] while boys and girls are equally likely to engage in non-physical bullying.[57] Boys generally are bullied by other boys and not by girls while girls suffer bullying by boys and girls equally.[58] In their study of 452 boys in fourth to sixth grades from schools in Chicago and North Carolina, Rodkin, Farmer, Pearl, and van Acker found a strong correlation, particularly among older adolescent boys, between aggression and popularity[59] (significantly, being popular is not the same as being well-liked; Parkhurst and Hopmeyer found that popular pupils were generally not well-liked by their peers and well-liked pupils were generally not popular[60]). Although non-physical bullying is perceived by school children to be more common than physical bullying,[61] Hazler and his colleagues found that non-physical bullying was less likely to be identified by teachers as warranting positive action,[62] and Boulton found that fewer than half of teachers in England regarded social exclusion as a bullying behaviour.[63] Salmivalli and her colleagues found that boys were more likely than girls to be assistants or reinforcers while girls were more likely than boys to be outsiders or defenders.[64] In her study of 196 Finnish secondary school pupils aged between 13 and 15, Salmivalli found that anti-bullying campaigns that were implemented by peers had positive effects among girls but not among boys. Indeed, among boys there was a significant increase in pro-bullying attitudes. The majority of boys also did not see such campaigns to have a beneficial impact. The researcher explained that such gender-specific results were likely due to the fact that all of those who implemented such campaigns were girls.[65] Naylor and Cowie similarly found that male pupils in England, particularly those in early adolescence, regarded rendering or seeking support in a bullying situation to be a threat to their masculinity.[66] In her study of two primary and seven secondary schools in England where peer support systems had been established for at least one year as part of a school anti-bullying policy, Cowie found involvement in peer support to lead to teasing or taunts from pupils outside the peer support groups, especially among boys. Male peer supporters in particular found offering support to be a daunting experience due to its perceived incompatibility with masculinity.[67]

What motivates bullying behaviours in schools?

Longitudinal research has indicated that bullies tend to target children who are physically weak, lack social skills and have low self-esteem, each of which contributes to increased victimisation over time.[68] Egan and Perry observe that '[p]oor self-concept may play a central role in a vicious cycle that perpetuates and solidifies a child's status as a victim of peer abuse.'[69] As with all victims of abuse,[70] there is a strong tendency, especially among aggressive youth,[71] to blame their victims in order to validate or justify their bullying behaviours,[72] and the tendency becomes more widespread and entrenched as children become older.[73] In a study in the United States involving 212 school children, respondents tended to blame victims for bullying and to regard bullying as meant 'for fun' while also 'helping' victims become tougher.[74] A larger study involving 1312 elementary school pupils in Greece found that 60% would not keep company with bullies while 26% did not think about how they would feel about them, and 6% reported liking bullies 'because they are cool'. After engaging in bullying behaviours, 33.7% reported that they felt 'pity' for the victim, 29.7% felt the victim 'deserved it', 26.7% felt 'bad', 24.7% were 'worried about being told off by teachers or parents', and 20.8% felt that 'it was fun'.[75] In a nationwide survey involving 6282 pupils between fifth and tenth grades in 29 state primary and 21 state secondary schools in Malta, 49.8% of bullies reported feeling 'sorry', 40.6% feeling 'indifferent', and 20.9% feeling 'satisfied'.[76] Boulton and Underwood interviewed 25 children and found that 44% of bullies responded that the victim provoked the bully, and 20% of bullies responded that they did not know why they bullied others. Thirty-six per cent of bullies responded that the victim was smaller and weaker and did not fight back. When asked if they bullied others because bullying others allowed them to feel good about themselves, 75% of bullies responded in the negative (from which, however, came the corollary that 25% of bullies, a substantial proportion, did *not* respond in the negative).[77] Björkqvist, Ekman, and Lagerspetz reported that bullies derived satisfaction by causing their victims to demonstrate behavioural correlates of emotional problems during acts of bullying, especially fear, submissiveness, submission to extortion and displays of suffering, which enabled the bullies to believe that they were indeed powerful and superior.[78] Roland suggests that emotional issues on the part of victims can be both a cause and a consequence of their victimisation by peers.[79] Salmivalli and her colleagues have found that both submissiveness and counter-aggression are only provocative and are ineffective in stopping bullying.[80] It has been observed that children generally accept the hierarchical structure of peer ecology and attendant social power, even if they personally dislike it.[81] As membership in a peer group becomes extremely important during late childhood and early adolescence,[82] the transition to adolescence requires a re-negotiation of social relationships and many adolescents resort to bullying behaviours in order to attain dominance.[83]

The roles of social environment, peers and teachers in (homophobic) school bullying

Thus, the social environment surrounding bullies and victims is instrumental to the likelihood and severity of victimisation by peers. Research has found that bullies have a significantly poorer perception of the social climate of their schools than do victims or bully/victims,[84] and that the presence of a reciprocated best friend significantly lowers the likelihood and severity of victimisation by peers.[85] However, victims tend to befriend those who are victims themselves[86] or those who are physically weak or exhibit emotional issues.[87] Partly due to their low social status, victims tend to be marginalised also by their non-bully peers, as evidenced by research across diverse ages, races and countries.[88] In their Australian study, Rigby and Slee found that the majority of pupils opposed bullying and felt sympathetic towards victims. However, one in five pupils responded that they 'would not be friends with kids who allowed themselves to be pushed around', and one in seven responded that 'soft kids make me sick'. A significant minority of the respondents felt disdain for victims for being weak and admiration of bullies for their aggressiveness, and sympathy and inclination to intervene for victims decreased with age.[89] Sutton, Smith, and Swettenham suggest that bullies, especially ringleader bullies, tend to be adept at social manipulation.[90] In fear of retaliation and shame, many victims do not seek help from their peers.[91] Whitney and Smith found that half of victims did not tell anyone about the bullying they endured,[92] while in their research on escaped victims, continuing victims and new victims of school bullying, Smith and his colleagues found that two-thirds of escaped victims reported talking to someone about an actual incident of bullying whereas fewer than half of new or continuing victims did.[93]

Research has confirmed that teachers have a unique role in the development of positive social dynamics among children[94] and that teachers' attitudes towards their pupils and their pupils' behaviours are mutually reinforcing.[95] Olweus argues that teachers' attitudes are of 'major significance for the extent of bully/victim problems'.[96] Roland and Galloway found a strong correlation between teachers' management and the social structure of a class,[97] and Norwegian and British studies on school-based interventions found that such interventions led to reductions in bullying by 30–50%.[98] In relation to homophobic bullying in schools, the Department for Education and Skills and the Department of Health in the United Kingdom jointly maintain that '[a]ll schools, particularly early years settings and primary schools, are ideally placed to challenge homophobia because they make a significant contribution to the development of values and attitudes in young children that are likely to be highly resistant to change in later life.'[99]

However, the beliefs and prejudices that many teachers, school administrators and counsellors as well as parents hold about the rightfulness of certain behaviours and inner characteristics, particularly regarding sexuality and sexual orientation, preclude their willingness to acknowledge and forestall the presence or extent of bullying behaviours among their pupils and children. These adults may instead condone or encourage or even perpetuate or assist in their pupils' or children's behaviours.[100] In the nationwide survey involving 6282 pupils in Malta noted above, 24.7% of victims reported feeling indifferent and 24% feeling helpless, which Borg attributed to teachers' and school administators' scepticism, unwillingness or inability to support and protect victims.[101] In a study conducted by Stonewall, the largest human rights organisation in the United Kingdom dedicated to tackling issues affecting persons belonging to sexual minorities, it was found that 65% of sexual minority pupils experienced homophobic bullying and 97% heard derogatory terms used with prejudicial sexual orientation-related overtones. Fifty-eight per cent of victims never reported their victimisation to their teachers, half of whom failed to respond to situations of homophobic bullying and only 7% of whom always took action when derogatory terms were used. Only a quarter of schools explicitly objected to homophobic bullying; in those schools sexual minority pupils were 60% less likely to be bullied.[102] Twemlow and his colleagues note that a major factor contributing to aggression in children consists of the negative behaviours their parents and teachers display[103] and the adults' attempts to dominate and humiliate others.[104] In another study of 116 teachers from seven elementary schools in the United States, Twemlow and his colleagues found that teachers who had endured bullying when they were pupils were more likely as teachers to bully their pupils and to be bullied by their pupils both within and outside the school setting.[105] Adolescents, ill-equipped to understand individual differences particularly regarding sexuality and sexual orientation, emulate adults in positions of authority so that their beliefs – inculcated by adults – as to how their peers should be and behave will not be jeopardised. Overt or tacit condonation or encouragement on the part of teachers and parents further amplifies the frequency and severity of peer victimisation that a great number of sexual minority adolescents endure on a daily basis. It is to be lamented that many school counsellors, who are expected to be understanding of individual differences, similarly hold adverse attitudes towards sexual minority adolescents,[106] and their purported solidarity with and outward appearance of concern for pupils enables them to instil in adolescents belonging to sexual minorities an equally entrenched and equally devastating prejudice that what they *might* be feeling is merely a passing phase, which the adolescents are likely to interpret as evidence that their feeling must be wrong. As McCann points out, '[h]eterosexism does not disappear simply because the therapist decides to ignore it'.[107] It has been observed that hetero-normativity is prevalent in schools due to 'its taken-for-grantedness, the fact that it goes unexplained, unchallenged and is assumed',[108] and it leads to 'stigmatization of gay and lesbian identities [that] is a routine feature of student/pupil life'.[109] Power dynamics, I argue, are a central motivation for the condoning or encouraging behaviours of many teachers, school administrators and counsellors as they attempt to foster social conformity. As Gilmore and Somerville have noted, '[p]ower relationships are central to stigmatization. Stigmatization is an exercise of power over people and a manifestation of disrespect for them.'[110] One of the main reasons why hetero-sexism pervades society and schools is not sexual minorities' 'deviant' sexualities but in order to preserve the status quo. To declare systematically and in concert another person's inner feelings as unreal and to deny altogether the existence of others holding similar inner feelings is the best way to achieve enforced conformity, as '[t]here is no better way to subjugate human beings than to silence them. There is nothing more oppressive than denying another's reality.'[111] One result of having their bullying behaviours condoned or encouraged, let alone perpetuated or assisted, by adults in positions of authority is that adolescents 'build partitions of aggression or seeming indifference between themselves and the rest of the world so that no-one sees their vulnerabilities. These partitions are dangerous because they prevent both the world gaining a clear view of the person behind them and that person having a clear view of the world.'[112] Nayak and Kehily are adamant that the likelihood that 'these negative reactions may continue into adulthood and other work situations is worrying'.[113]

In addition to condonation or encouragement of pupils' and children's bullying behaviours, Astor, Pitner, and Duncan suggest that avoidance of feelings of guilt or personal responsibility for allowing bullying behaviours to have taken place or for failing to intervene when they do may underlie the unwillingness of many teachers and parents to acknowledge problems of school bullying and to intervene.[114] Farrington argues that solidarity and collective acknowledgment of issues of school bullying among teachers and school administrators is essential to tackling their pupils' bullying behaviours,[115] and Olweus calls on teachers to closely supervise interactions among their pupils during recess and to intervene upon the slightest hint of bullying taking place.[116] Any bullying prevention and intervention programmes must involve all participants in bullying situations including all pupils, teachers, school administrators and counsellors as well as parents,[117] and, as Twemlow and his colleagues point out, '[s]ocial aggression in schools is not likely to ameliorate until the aggressiveness of adults, both teachers and parents, is also admitted and dealt with.'[118]

Lastly, many teachers simply are incapable of recognising or tackling the presence or severity of a bullying situation when it occurs. A British study reported that 98.6% of teachers felt they had a responsibility to prevent school bullying but did not feel confident in their ability to do so, and 87% wanted more training.[119] While many teachers recognise that bullying behaviours take varying forms, they nonetheless tend to regard verbal or indirect bullying to be of lesser consequence than physical bullying.[120] A Canadian study found that although 85% of teachers reported that they intervened often or nearly always to stop their pupils' bullying behaviours, only 35% of pupils from the same schools reported intervention by their teachers.[121] Even so, pupils were still more confident in teachers' ability to intervene than in their peers'.[122]

The role of family in (homophobic) school bullying

Meanwhile, family – of both bully and victim – plays a significant role in the nature, likelihood, causes, onset, course, consequences, resolution and prevention of (homophobic) school bullying, as many children and adolescents who are bullied by their peers do not receive support from their families and may in fact be victimised by their own families.[123] Research has found that victims tend to come from harsh home environments[124] and have intrusive, demanding, less responsive and less supportive parents and a parent–child relationship that is marked by insecure or inconsistent attachment styles.[125] Bullies generally lack adult role models[126] and are more likely than children not directly involved in bullying situations to have authoritarian,[127] less responsive and less supportive parents[128] with inconsistent discipline and to come from harsh home environments[129] with hostility within the family and poor parent–child communication.[130] Fagot and Kavanagh found that anxious attachment to parents in four-year-olds was predictive of more aggressive or difficult peer relationships,[131] while Karr-Morse and Wiley noted that insecure attachment to parents during infancy increased the likelihood of later aggression and delinquency.[132] By contrast, Troy and Sroufe reported that children with secure attachment to parents were later able to distance themselves from bullying situations either as victims or as bullies.[133] Renken and his colleagues suggest that bullies are likely to have avoidant–insecure attachment to parents and to develop distrust and expectations of hostile situations, while victims are likely to have ambivalent–insecure attachment to parents due to unpredictable care and to develop lack of self-esteem and of self-confidence.[134] Greater likelihood of later victimisation by peers ensues for a child whose parents engage in rearing practices that impede the development of autonomy in the child or fundamentally threaten the parent–child relationship.[135] Olweus reported that four particular factors significantly correlated with bullying behaviours on the part of boys: the boy's temperament, his mother's general negative outlook, her permissiveness towards aggression, and parental assertion of power.[136] Maternal hostility strongly predicts later victimisation by peers, with intrusive demands, coercion and threats of rejection significantly linked to later peer victimisation, especially if the child is a girl. However, over-protectiveness by a mother equally correlates with her child's later victimisation by peers, especially if the child is a boy.[137] C. Patterson and her colleagues found that socially rejected aggressive children reported receiving least affection, companionship and satisfaction from their fathers,[138] while paternal involvement in a child's life has been found to contribute to a small but significant decrease in the likelihood of victimisation by peers.[139] Bully/victims reported more troubled relationships with parents and lowest parental warmth as well as highest parental over-protection and neglect simultaneously.[140] Loeber and Dishion found inconsistent or highly aversive discipline coupled with corporal punishment to increase the likelihood of later aggression in the child.[141] Meanwhile, G. Patterson has noted the role of siblings in the development of anti-social behavioural problems,[142] and in their study of 193 children aged between 8 and 11 attending three middle schools in a relatively deprived area of Sheffield, Bowers, Smith, and Binney found in bullies a high ambivalent involvement with siblings and others whom they regarded as powerful as well as lack of cohesion and preoccupation with power within their families.[143] High levels of conflict within the family together with familial preoccupation with power or parental drug use or incarceration significantly increase aggression in the child.[144] Child abuse is a major precipitating factor of either victimisation or bullying behaviours.[145] Shields and Ciccihetti reported that victims and bullies were each 2.2 times more likely than children not directly involved in bullying situations to have experienced child abuse, and explained that child abuse directly and substantially elevated emotional dysregulation among those who had been abused by their immediate or extended families.[146] In a study involving 558 middle school pupils in the United States, anger was found to be the strongest predictor of propensity to bullying behaviours.[147] Indicative of a degree of generational continuity, fathers who were bullies when they were at school are likely to have sons who are bullies at school,[148] and bully/victims tend to come from especially troubled or abusive families.[149] In fact, some parents teach their children to physically fight others when they perceive that they have been wronged.[150] By contrast, caring and loving relationships with parents have been shown to sustain empathy and pro-social behaviours in children,[151] and responsive and supportive parenting has been associated with decreased levels of bullying[152] and victimisation.[153] Children of lower socio-economic status are more likely to become victims or bullies.[154]

Consequences of school bullying generally

School bullying carries grave consequences. Contrary to the popular beliefs that school bullying is an inevitable phase during childhood and adolescence – the claim of 'inevitability' is meant to disguise the negativity of bullying, unlike the 'passing phase' of non-heterosexual sexual attraction the transient nature of which is meant to be a blessing – and that any emotional problems that may be had as a result of school bullying are suffered by victims only, research has established that a wide range of psychiatric, psychological and emotional problems are suffered by victims, bullies and bully/victims alike in living under fear or in perpetration of school bullying.

In respect of victims of school bullying, victimisation may be the sole direct cause of as much as 20% of their emotional problems.[155] In particular, research has consistently found that victims suffer from negative reactions towards themselves, feelings of loneliness, low self-esteem, generalised anxiety, and depression;[156] helplessness;[157] diminution of 'a youngster's healthy sense of narcissism and sense of identity';[158] higher rates of school refusal, school absenteeism, and dropping out;[159] physical health problems;[160] psychiatric problems including eating disorders;[161] and suicidal ideation, attempted suicides, and complete suicides.[162] A British study of 8–13-year-old children found a significant negative correlation between self-reported levels of bullying and levels of academic achievement, among both victims and bullies (although victims were more affected),[163] and it has been found that there is a significant positive correlation between bullying and school avoidance and 'victimized children tend to become more … school avoidant after they are victimized by peers. Further, no support was found for the counter argument that school adjustment difficulties precede exposure to victimization.'[164] Former victims have been reported to suffer higher levels of depression and lower self-esteem than non-victims at the age of 23,[165] and new and continuing victims have reported higher rates of loneliness and lower self-worth than former victims and non-victims, which Juvonen, Nishina, and Graham suggest points to good prospects of recovery upon cessation of victimisation.[166] However, Smith and his colleagues noted that one-third of continuing victims reported that fear of bullying led them to be truant from school, and that continuing victims both rated themselves and were rated by their teachers as especially high on emotional problems and problems with peers, conduct disorders and hyperactivity. As noted above, continuing victims were also more likely to engage in bullying behaviours themselves.[167] Bully/victims have been found to be poorest when compared with victims and bullies in psychosocial functioning;[168] while victims are four times[169] and bullies 2.8 to 4.3 times more likely[170] to suffer from depression when compared with children not directly involved in bullying situations, bully/victims are 6.3 to 8.8 times more likely[171] to be depressed. Bully/victims also tend to be the most aggressive[172] and to have a higher rate of severe suicidal ideation (2.5 times) than victims (2.1 times).[173]

Significantly, victims have been found to suffer from revenge fantasies;[174] research has implicated revenge for school bullying to be a prime contributor to school shootings,[175] and a study of school shootings between 1974 and 2000 in the United States indicated that two-thirds involved attackers who 'felt persecuted, bullied, threatened, attacked, or injured by others prior to the incident',[176] and 'a number of the attackers had experienced bullying and harassment that was longstanding and severe. In those cases, the experience of bullying appeared to play a major role in motivating the attack at school.'[177] Seventy-eight per cent of attackers suffered from suicidal ideation or had attempted suicide, and 61% suffered from severe depression.[178]

Meanwhile, research has found that bullies suffer from an equally wide array of psychiatric, psychological and emotional problems and attendant consequences, including depression;[179] psychiatric problems including eating disorders;[180] substance abuse;[181] criminal delinquency;[182] psychosexual problems including premature dating and physical aggression towards their dating partners;[183] lower academic achievement;[184] and suicidal ideation.[185] In his Norwegian study, Olweus observed an aggressive personality pattern in bullies, whose aggression was directed not only towards their victims but also towards their teachers, parents and siblings, and who had a more positive attitude towards violence. Olweus suggested that stable aggression of bullies predicted later adjustment problems and noted that bullies were four times more likely to be found to engage in criminal delinquency at the age of 24, 60% with at least one conviction and 35–40% at least three convictions.[186] A British study also reported similar results.[187] In addition, positive correlations between aggression and suicidal ideation, attempted suicides and complete suicides have been reported.[188] In fact, bullies are four times more likely than children not directly involved in bullying situations to report severe suicidal ideation, as opposed to 2.1 times in the case of victims and 2.5 times in the case of bully/victims.[189]

Additional consequences of school bullying attributable to sexual orientation

Meanwhile, with homophobia entrenched in society, schools and families and confusions over sexuality and sexual orientation permeating adolescence, school bullying that is attributable to one's actual or perceived sexual orientation leads to consequences of a different nature *in addition to* and more severe than those that result from school bullying not attributable to sexual orientation.[190] The United States Center for Population Options has found that sexual minority adolescents

> face tremendous challenges to growing up physically and mentally healthy in a culture that is almost uniformly anti-homosexual. Often, these youth face an increased risk of medical and psychosocial problems, caused not by their sexual orientation, but by society's extremely negative reaction to it. Gay, lesbian and bisexual youth face rejection, isolation, verbal harassment and physical violence at home, in school and in religious institutions. Responding to these pressures, many lesbian, gay and bisexual young people engage in an array of risky behaviors.[191]

As Erikson observed, '[t]herapeutic as well as reformist efforts verify the sad truth that in any system based on suppression, exclusion, and exploitation, the suppressed, excluded, and exploited unconsciously accept the evil image they are made to represent by those who are dominant.'[192] Sexual minority adolescents' problems with alcohol and substance abuse[193] and with running away or expulsion from home and subsequent homelessness[194] – which exposes them to sexual exploitation and abuse including unsafe sex and prostitution[195] rendering them susceptible to sexually transmitted diseases including HIV/AIDS[196] – are well documented. Finding themselves entirely alone, a significant number of sexual minority adolescents will find the 'school environment [that] is a focal point of adolescent growth and development'[197] too intimidating and resort to truancy and dropping out which are then 'taken as evidence that sexual minority youth are a particularly problematic population. Yet this behavior should more properly be seen as a coping strategy, born of desperation when authorities fail to provide a safe learning environment.'[198] Many confused and tormented adolescents may eventually 'consider suicide as an escape, not from issues related to their sexual orientation, but as a result of challenges they encounter in the broader social context'.[199] The suicide rates for sexual minority adolescents have been found to be significantly higher than those for heterosexual adolescents; a study conducted on behalf of the United States Department of Health and Human Services found that sexual minority adolescents were more than three times more likely to attempt suicide than their heterosexual peers.[200] However, due to pressures from conservative lobby groups, the findings were repudiated by the United States Congress as contrary to the 'calling' of the Department of Health and Human Services.[201] Proctor and Groze argue that '[s]uch a refusal to acknowledge the difficulties of gay, lesbian, and bisexual youths leaves very few sanctioned avenues for investigation of suicide risk factors.'[202] Notably, it has been found that 'bisexual and questioning youth may be at higher risk for suicidal behavior than self-identified homosexual youth',[203] which attests to the importance of acknowledging an adolescent's sexual orientation, whatever it be, fully, respectfully and supportively. Thus, Sullivan stresses:

> If this population is to be appropriately served, both in the interests of the youths themselves and in the interests of a society that must bear the cost of their marginalization in epidemiological vulnerability and lost potential, society must begin by recognizing their existence as a population with distinct developmental needs. The tacit denial of both the existence of gay youths and the need to develop programs to protect them was a luxury and a folly even before the advent of AIDS.[204]

Where are the lawyers?

The extensive and substantial research in medical sciences, educational studies and social sciences on school bullying in general and homophobic school bullying in particular is admirable and imperative for a greater understanding of issues that precipitate and perpetuate the problem. At the same time, however, those professing the law, including legal researchers, lawyers, lawmakers and judges, have thoroughly failed to examine or address the problem. Indeed, notwithstanding the progressive development of international human rights law since the end of World War II during which countless persons belonging to sexual minorities had been persecuted,[205] sexual minorities today continue to be harassed, tortured or executed by the state. The adoptions of the Universal Declaration of Human Rights,[206] the International Covenant on Civil and Political Rights,[207] the International Covenant on Economic, Social and Cultural Rights[208] and other major international human rights treaties have not ameliorated the position of sexual minorities in international law, as those instruments invariably do not explicitly prohibit sexual orientation discrimination which they directly perpetuate through deafening silence.[209] The same can be said of most municipal constitutions or legislation that purport to guarantee and protect human rights.

Focus should thus be laid on the one treaty that directly, substantively and substantially concerns and impacts the rights of children, namely, the United Nations Convention on the Rights of the Child, which, adopted in 1989, currently enjoys the ratification and participation of 193 states parties excluding only the United States[210] and Somalia.[211] In furtherance of the right of a child (generally defined as a person below the age of 18[212]) to education as enshrined in Article 28 of the Convention,[213] Article 29(1) of the Convention states that:

States Parties agree that the education of the child shall be directed to:
  (a) The development of the child's personality, talents and mental and physical abilities to their fullest potential;
  (b) The development of respect for human rights and fundamental freedoms, and for the principles enshrined in the Charter of the United Nations;
  (c) The development of respect for the child's parents, his or her own cultural identity, language and values, for the national values of the country in which the child is living, the country from which he or she may originate, and for civilisations different from his or her own;
  (d) The preparation of the child for responsible life in a free society, in the spirit of understanding, peace, tolerance, equality of sexes, and friendship among all peoples, ethnic, national and religious groups and persons of indigenous origin;
  (e) The development of respect for the natural environment.[214]

In its *General Comment No. 1 on the Aims of Education*,[215] the United Nations Committee on the Rights of the Child[216] reaffirmed that the key goal of education as agreed by all states parties is 'the development of the individual child's personality, talents and abilities, in recognition of the fact that every child has unique characteristics, interests, abilities, and learning'[217] and 'to empower the child by developing his or her skills, learning and other capacities, human dignity, self-esteem and self-confidence. "Education" in this context goes far beyond formal schooling to embrace the broad range of life experiences and learning processes which enable children, individually and collectively, to develop their personalities, talents and abilities and to live a full and satisfying life within society.'[218] The Committee reiterated that the aims of education enshrined in Article 29(1) are interconnected with the rights and freedoms embodied in other provisions of the Convention, including Article 2 which protects a child's right of non-discrimination; Article 3 which ensures the best interests of the child; Article 6 which guarantees the right to life, survival and development; Article 12 which enshrines a child's right to express views and to have them taken into account in decision-making that impacts his or her welfare; Article 13 which protects a child's freedom of expression and Article 14 his or her freedom of thought; Article 17 which enshrines a child's right to information; and Article 24 which ensures a child's right to proper education in relation to matters of health.[219] The Committee stated that discrimination on any of the grounds prohibited in Article 2(1), 'whether it is overt or hidden, offends the human dignity of the child and is capable of undermining or even destroying the capacity of the child to benefit from educational opportunities.'[220] The Committee also pointed out that 'the school environment itself must thus reflect the freedom and the spirit of understanding, peace, tolerance, equality of sexes, and friendship among all peoples ... called for in article 29(1)(b) and (d). A school which allows bullying or other violent and exclusionary practices to occur is not one which meets the requirements of article 29(1).'[221]

While the Convention does not mention sexual orientation in its entire text, its provisions can be and have been interpreted to address issues affecting adolescents belonging to sexual minorities. For example, the Committee in its *General Comment No. 4 on Adolescent Health and Development*[222] interpreted the non-discrimination provision in Article 2(1), that 'States Parties shall respect and ensure the rights set forth in the present Convention to each child within their jurisdiction without discrimination of any kind, irrespective of the child's or his or her parent's or legal guardian's race, colour, sex, language, religion, political or other opinion, national, ethnic or social origin, property, disability, birth or other status',[223] as prohibiting sexual orientation discrimination.[224] As I have argued elsewhere, Article 8 of the Convention, which states that 'States Parties undertake to respect the right of the child to preserve his or her identity, including nationality, name and family relations as recognised by law without unlawful interference',[225] can and should be interpreted as encompassing the right of a child to his or her sexual minority identity and to have his or her sexual orientation, whatever it be, acknowledged fully, respectfully and supportively.[226]

It might be hoped accordingly that the Committee would address issues of school bullying and homophobic school bullying as well as matters related to sexual orientation discrimination rigorously and vigorously in its concluding observations of states parties' implementation of the Convention. However, in its concluding observations between 2004 and 2008 of 101 states parties' implementation of the Convention,[227] the Committee took note of issues of school bullying or school violence in only 22 instances[228] and issues related to sexual orientation generally (namely, criminalisation of consensual same-sex sexual activity or lack of sexual orientation anti-discrimination legislation in conflict with Article 2 of the Convention) in only five instances.[229] Only in the case of the United Kingdom did the Committee express specific concern over lesbian, gay, bisexual, and transgender children who alongside children belonging to other minority groups 'continue to experience discrimination and social stigmatization'.[230] The scant attention the Committee has paid to the problem of school bullying in general and homophobic school bullying in particular only serves to illuminate and perpetuate the indifference of those professing the law, including legal researchers, lawyers, lawmakers and judges, and society as a whole to the struggles and sufferings of innumerable children and adolescents – including a substantial number of sexual minority children and adolescents[231] burdened with 'the experience of being gay or bisexual [or lesbian or transgender] in our society [which] overwhelms any potential differences in social categories involving age, ethnicity, race, social class or geographical region'[232] – and their right 'to form relationships of trust, meaning, and affection with people in their daily lives and their broader communities'.[233]

Directions for legal research and the legal process

Herman identifies three stages of recovery to be central for victims of prolonged and repeated traumas, namely, establishment of safety, remembrance and mourning, and reconnection with ordinary life.[234] As an essential part of reconnection, a victim must be able to embrace and to redress – by telling, and through the legal process, if *he or she* wishes – his or her struggles and sufferings. As Herman states, '[i]t is at this point that survivors are ready to reveal their secrets, to challenge the indifference and censure of bystanders, and to accuse those who have abused them.'[235] Silence, including of self that is involuntary, such as precisely the kind that enables all forms of abuse and injustice to begin, grow and continue, is not an option. Thus, this paper suggests some directions as to how the contributory, remedial, retributive and deterrent roles of the law, including international law, may be explored through legal research and the legal process.

First of all, within common law jurisdictions,[236] the civil process should be explored to see whether the law of torts has already addressed the problem of school bullying in general and homophobic school bullying in particular and, if not, how the law may be so engaged, in particular by examining how (homophobic) school bullying may be covered by such causes of action as negligence, assault, battery, breach of statutory duty, occupiers' liability, harassment, intentional infliction of emotional distress, and/or interference with proper educational opportunities, and reference may be had to and lessons learned from the judicial decisions and legal literature concerning child sexual abuse.[237] As the appropriate causes of action are identified, the issues of duty of care – including the direct and/or vicarious, and individual and/or joint and several, liability of school authorities, including the direct liability of teachers and school administrators, parents of bullies and, of course, bullies – and of remedies (compensatory and exemplary) should be examined. The possibility that a fiduciary relationship exists between a pupil and his or her teachers and school, given the asymmetry and heightened levels of trust, confidence and dependence, ought also to be explored. Given that most if not all victims will not be able to initiate legal proceedings against their tormentors until at least when they reach adulthood and are financially and emotionally capable, the impact of limitation legislation must be scrutinised to address the peculiar problems facing victims of (homophobic) school bullying in initiating legal proceedings against those who have violated their physical, psychological and emotional integrity. It is suggested that reference may again be had to and lessons learned from the judicial decisions and legal literature concerning child sexual abuse.[238]

The contributory role of the criminal justice system in homophobic school bullying through criminalisation of consensual same-sex sexual activity has already been noted. Nevertheless, the criminal justice system also may serve remedial, retributive and deterrent roles in (homophobic) school bullying, as school bullying may already, or may otherwise be held to, constitute criminal harassment, criminal battery, and/or criminal assault including assault occasioning actual or grievous bodily harm,[239] and, in the case of homophobic school bullying, hate speech or hate crime.[240] The question of whether a legislature should explicitly classify (homophobic) school bullying as a criminal offence *per se* given its prevalence and consequences should be explored. Meanwhile, teachers and parents who condone, encourage, perpetuate or assist in their pupils' or children's bullying behaviours at school may be held criminally liable for aiding and abetting, as accessories or as part of a joint venture. The close correlation between (homophobic) school bullying and school truancy also requires research on how the law may be appropriate and useful in tackling school truancy with underlying causes and consequences taken into account, and on where legal liability, both civil and criminal, for a child's school truancy should lie.

Then comes the liability of the state. Research should be conducted to examine how the state, through its educational policies or perpetuation of a particular educational culture or through continual state discrimination against certain minority groups, facilitates (homophobic) school bullying to take place and to continue. A particularly apt example of such policies is that which was mandated by section 2A of the Local Government Act 1986 (colloquially known as 'Section 28', as in the 1988 amending legislation), applicable in England, Wales and Scotland but not Northern Ireland[241] before its repeal in Scotland in 2000[242] and in England and Wales in 2003,[243] that '[a] local authority shall not (a) intentionally promote homosexuality or publish material with the intention of promoting homosexuality; (b) promote the teaching in any maintained school of the acceptability of homosexuality as a pretended family relationship.'[244] The provision has been cited as a major factor that continues even after its repeal to contribute to homophobic school bullying *and* school bullying generally in schools in the United Kingdom.[245] At the same time, we should explore how the state may encourage a culture of mutual respect among school children and between pupils and their teachers and parents through comprehensive and sustained legal reform on equality, human rights, and the welfare of children. As Evan states, '[l]aw emerges not only to *codify* existing customs, morals, or mores, but also to *modify* the behavior and the values presently existing in a particular society.'[246]

Finally, the United Nations Convention on the Rights of the Child protects the right of a child to education the aims of which must be understood and implemented in tandem with and in the context of other provisions of the Convention as a whole. In the spirit of the Convention and its *General Comments Nos 1 and 4*, the United Nations Committee on the Rights of the Child must rigorously and vigorously scrutinise (homophobic) school bullying and general phenomena that give rise to and perpetuate the problem within states parties, including discrimination on the basis of sexual orientation or other personal characteristics 'unchangeable or changeable only at unacceptable personal costs',[247] and request that states parties implement without delay measures that will reduce if not eliminate a problem that affects all children and adolescents of all ages around the world and one that is not only a public health issue, an educational issue, a social issue, but also a human rights issue.

Acknowledgements

This paper could not have been proceeded with but for the facilities and assistance I received during my extended academic visits at Faculty of Law, University of Ottawa; Institut für Öffentliches Recht, Albert-Ludwigs-Universität Freiburg; Department of Political Science, Vanderbilt University; and School of International Relations, University of St Andrews, between February 2007 and June 2008. I am also particularly indebted to Kay Goodall, Philip Rumney, Paul Serfaty, and Andrew Simester for their valuable comments on earlier versions of this paper given to them at very short notice, and Sasan Ansari and Mark King for their assistance in locating certain materials. Any error or omission in this paper is mine alone.

This paper could not have begun, and I could not have become who I have become, but for the tremendous support and understanding of so many individuals in the past ten years, who, as mentors, friends or colleagues and through their mentorship or friendship and personal and professional advice, have showed me the kindness and hope that had so fundamentally been denied me. I am greatly indebted to Jon Austin for changing my life course so entirely, Sylvia Acevedo, Andrew Byrnes, Johannes Chan, Robin Corcos, John Harris, and Robert Morgan for making allowances for my depression and helping me survive law school, Jill Cottrell for her stimulating tort classes that inspired me to pursue a project on homophobic school bullying and the law, and Donald Lewis for fortifying my interest in legal research and for his kindness during a difficult time in October 2005. I am very fortunate meanwhile to have made many wonderful friends and colleagues with many wonderful memories during these ten years, particularly Anita and Terry in

Toronto, Detlev Pusch and Marianne in Berlin, Klint Alexander, Michelle Chong, Linda Christie, Juliette Gregory Duara, Linn Edvartsen, Pierre François-Laval, Richard Gardiner, Sarah Gardiner, Robin Hansen, Mariko Iijima, Juyon Kim, Alana Klein, Felizmina Lutucuta, Tamara McKen, Annalisa Meloni, Maria Frederica Moscati, Mark Nolan, Aisling O'Sullivan, Oliver Phillips, Nicky Priaulx, Lucy Richmond, Philip Ridgway, Alisoun Roberts, Dominika Švarc, Sarah Wennberg, Julie Wong, and Vivien Yip, whose friendships, company and personal and professional advice I will always cherish. Above all, I am grateful to my mother and my late grandmother, in whose memory this paper was completed, for supporting as best they can the opportunities presented to me and the life choices that I have made, and to Paul Serfaty for so unwaveringly supporting my academic endeavours over the past seven years and helping me heal with his enduring kindness and understanding.

Notes

1. O. O'Neill, 'Children's Rights and Children's Lives', in *Children, Rights, and the Law*, ed. P. Alston, S. Parker, and J. Seymour (Oxford: Clarendon, 1992), 24, 39.
2. J. Herman, *Trauma and Recovery: The Aftermath of Violence – from Domestic Abuse to Political Terror* (New York: Basic Books, 1992).
3. Ibid., 96. Herman, ibid., 121, argues that the psychiatric diagnosis of post-traumatic stress disorder is not sufficiently accurate to describe prolonged and repeated traumas endured in captivity or captivity-like situations, including child abuse, and attendant profound deformations of a victim's personality including, most significantly, a coherent sense of self. The clinician calls for diagnostic recognition of complex post-traumatic stress disorder (C-PTSD) and recommends that complex post-traumatic stress disorder be diagnosed on the basis of seven criteria including: '1. A history of subjection to totalitarian control over a prolonged period (months to years). Examples include hostages, prisoners of war, concentration-camp survivors, and survivors of some religious cults. Examples also include those subjected to totalitarian systems in sexual and domestic life, including survivors of domestic battering, childhood physical or sexual abuse, and organized sexual exploitation. 2. Alterations in affect regulation, including persistent dysphoria; chronic suicidal preoccupation; self-injury; explosive or extremely inhibited anger (may alternate); compulsive or extremely inhibited sexuality (may alternate). 3. Alterations in consciousness, including amnesia or hypermnesia for traumatic events; transient dissociative episodes; depersonalization/derealization; reliving experiences, either in the form of intrusive post-traumatic stress disorder symptoms or in the form of ruminative preoccupation. 4. Alterations in self-perception, including sense of helplessness or paralysis of initiative; shame, guilt, and self-blame; sense of defilement or stigma; sense of complete difference from others (may include sense of specialness, utter aloneness, belief no other person can understand, or nonhuman identity). 5. Alterations in perception of perpetrator, including preoccupation with relationship with perpetrator (includes preoccupation with revenge); unrealistic attribution of total power to perpetrator (caution: victim's assessment of power realities may be more realistic than clinician's); idealization or paradoxical gratitude; sense of special or supernatural relationship; acceptance of belief system or rationalizations of perpetrator. 6. Alterations in relations with others, including isolation and withdrawal; disruption in intimate relationships; repeated search for rescuer (may alternate with isolation and withdrawal); persistent distrust; repeated failures of self-protection. 7. Alterations in systems of meaning, including loss of sustaining faith; sense of hopelessness and despair.' Complex post-traumatic stress disorder has since been included in the World Health Organisation's *International Statistical Classification of Diseases and Related Health Problems*, 10th Revision, Version for 2007, as 'enduring personality change after catastrophic experience' (F62.0).
4. E.H. Erikson, *Identity: Youth and Crisis* (London: Faber & Faber, 1968), 23.
5. Ibid., 22.
6. Ibid., 23.
7. T.R. Sullivan, 'Obstacles to Effective Child Welfare Service with Gay and Lesbian Youths', *Child Welfare* 73 (1994): 291, 294.
8. Erikson, *Identity*, 23.
9. D.F. Morrow, 'Social Work with Gay and Lesbian Adolescents', *Social Work* 38 (1993): 655, 657, citing E.S. Hetrick and A.D. Martin, 'Developmental Issues and their Resolution for Gay and Lesbian Adolescents', *Journal of Homosexuality* 14, nos 1–2 (1987): 25.

10. M. Schneider, 'Developing Services for Lesbian and Gay Adolescents', *Canadian Journal of Mental Health* 10 (1991): 133, 136.

11. P.C.W. Chan, 'No, it is not just a Phase: An Adolescent's Right to Sexual Minority Identity under the United Nations Convention on the Rights of the Child', *International Journal of Human Rights* 10 (2006): 161.

12. Adopted and opened for signature, ratification and accession by UN GA Res. 44/25 of 20 November 1989 and entered into force on 2 September 1990.

13. J.C. Gonsiorek, 'Mental Health Issues of Gay and Lesbian Adolescents', *Journal of Adolescent Health Care* 9 (1988): 114, 116.

14. Ibid.

15. K. Plummer, 'Speaking its Name: Inventing a Lesbian and Gay Studies', in *Modern Homosexualities: Fragments of Lesbian and Gay Experience*, ed. K. Plummer (London: Routledge, 1992), 3, 19 (emphasis in original).

16. R. Gill, 'Justifying Injustice: Broadcasters' Accounts of Inequality in Radio', in *Discourse Analytic Research: Repertoires and Readings of Texts in Action*, ed. E. Burman and I. Parker (London: Routlege, 1993), 75, 79.

17. Erikson, *Identity*, 55.

18. R.C. Savin-Williams, 'Lesbian, Gay Male, and Bisexual Adolescents', in *Lesbian, Gay, and Bisexual Identities over the Lifespan: Psychological Perspectives*, ed. A.R. D'Augelli and C.J. Patterson (New York: Oxford University Press, 1995), 165, 174.

19. A. Nayak and M.J. Kehily, 'Playing it Straight: Masculinities, Homophobias and Schooling', *Journal of Gender Studies* 5 (1996): 211, 225. On the performative nature of school bullying generally, see S.A. Everett and J.H. Price, 'Students' Perceptions of Violence in the Public Schools: The MetLife Survey', *Journal of Adolescent Health* 17 (1995): 345; A.H. Gorman, J. Kim, and A. Schimmelbusch, 'The Attributes Adolescents Associate with Peer Popularity and Teacher Preference', *Journal of School Psychology* 40 (2002): 143; D.L. Hawkins, D.J. Pepler, and W.M. Craig, 'Naturalistic Observations of Peer Interventions in Bullying', *Social Development* 10 (2001): 512; K.M. LaFontana and A.H.N. Cillessen, 'The Nature of Children's Stereotypes of Popularity', *Social Development* 7 (2002): 301; P. O'Connell, D. Pepler, and W. Craig, 'Peer Involvement in Bullying: Insights and Challenges for Intervention', *Journal of Adolescence* 22 (1999): 437; M.J. Prinstein and A.H.N. Cillessen, 'Forms and Functions of Adolescent Peer Aggression Associated with High Levels of Peer Status', *Merrill-Palmer Quarterly* 44 (2003): 310; P.C. Rodkin, T.W. Farmer, R. Pearl, and R. van Acker, 'Heterogeneity of Popular Boys: Antisocial and Prosocial Configurations', *Developmental Psychology* 36 (2000): 14; P.C. Rodkin and E.V.E. Hodges, 'Bullies and Victims in the Peer Ecology: Four Questions for Psychologists and School Professionals', *School Psychology Review* 32 (2003): 384; E. Roland, 'Bullying, Depressive Symptoms and Suicidal Thoughts', *Educational Research* 44 (2002): 55; C. Salmivalli, A. Huttunen, and K.M.J. Lagerspetz, 'Peer Networks and Bullying in Schools', *Scandinavian Journal of Psychology* 38 (1997): 305; C. Salmivalli, K. Lagerspetz, K. Björkqvist, K. Österman, and A. Kaukiainen, 'Bullying as a Group Process: Participant Roles and their Relations to Social Status within the Group', *Aggressive Behavior* 22 (1996): 1; S. Twemlow, F. Sacco, and P. Williams, 'A Clinical and Interactional Perspective on the Bully–Victim–Bystander Relationship', *Bulletin of the Menninger Clinic* 60 (1996): 297.

20. See A. Freud, *The Ego and the Mechanisms of Defence*, trans. C. Baines (New York: International Universities Press, 1946).

21. D.A. McFarland, 'Student Resistance: How the Formal and Informal Organization of Classrooms Facilitate Everyday Forms of Student Defiance', *American Journal of Sociology* 107 (2001): 612, 665.

22. T.R. Nansel, M. Overpeck, R.S. Pilla, W.J. Ruan, B. Simons-Morton, and P. Scheidt, 'Bullying Behaviors among US Youth: Prevalence and Association with Psychosocial Adjustment', *Journal of the American Medical Association* 285 (2001): 2094; A.D. Pellegrini and M. Bartini, 'Dominance in Early Adolescent Boys: Affiliative and Aggressive Dimensions and Possible Functions', *Merrill-Palmer Quarterly* 47 (2001): 142; P.K. Smith, K.C. Madsen, and J.C. Moody, 'What Causes the Age Decline in Reports of Being Bullied at School? Toward a Developmental Analysis of Risks of Being Bullied', *Educational Research* 41 (1999): 267.

23. P.A. Adler and P. Adler, *Peer Power: Preadolescent Culture and Identity* (New Brunswick, NJ: Rutgers University Press, 1998); A.A. Ferguson, *Bad Boys: Public Schools in the Making of Black Masculinity* (Ann Arbor: University of Michigan Press, 2000).

24. D. Olweus, *Aggression in the Schools: Bullies and Whipping Boys* (Washington, DC: Hemisphere, 1978).

25. D. Olweus, 'Bullying at School: Basic Facts and Effects of a School-Based Intervention Program', *Journal of Child Psychology and Psychiatry* 35 (1994): 1171, 1173.

26. J.A. Dake, J.H. Price, and S.K. Telljohann, 'The Nature and Extent of Bullying at School', *Journal of School Health* 73 (2003): 173; P. Naylor and H. Cowie, 'The Effectiveness of Peer Support Systems in Challenging School Bullying: The Perspectives and Experiences of Teachers and Pupils', *Journal of Adolescence* 22 (1999): 467; D. Olweus, 'Bullying/ Victim Problems in School: Knowledge Base and an Effective Intervention Project', *Irish Journal of Psychology* 18 (1997): 170; K. Rigby, 'Attitudes and Beliefs about Bullying among Australian School Children', *Irish Journal of Psychology* 18 (1997): 202; E. Roland, 'Bullying: A Developing Tradition of Research and Management', in *Understanding and Managing Bullying*, ed. D.P. Tattum (Oxford: Heinemann, 1993); E. Roland and E. Munthe, 'The 1996 Norwegian Program for Preventing and Managing Bullying in Schools', *Irish Journal of Psychology* 18 (1997): 233; P.K. Smith, Y. Morita, J. Junger-Tas, D. Olweus, R. Catalano, and P. Slee, eds, *The Nature of School Bullying: A Cross-National Perspective* (London: Routledge, 1999).

27. E.L. Lipman, 'Don't Let Anyone Bully You into Thinking Bullying Is Not Important!', *Canadian Journal of Psychiatry* 48 (2003): 575, 575.

28. K. Kumpulainen, E. Räsänen, and K. Puura, 'Psychiatric Disorders and the Use of Mental Health Services among Children Involved in Bullying', *Aggressive Behavior* 27 (2001): 102.

29. M. O'Moore and C. Kirkham, 'Self-Esteem and its Relationship to Bullying Behavior', *Aggressive Behavior* 27 (2001): 269.

30. I. Whitney and P.K. Smith, 'A Survey of the Nature and Extent of Bullying in Junior/Middle and Secondary Schools', *Educational Research* 35 (1993): 3.

31. L. Peterson and K. Rigby, 'Countering Bullying at an Australian Secondary School with Students as Helpers', *Journal of Adolescence* 22 (1999): 481.

32. L.J. Francis and S.H. Jones, 'The Relationship between Eysenck's Personality Factors and Fear of Bullying among 13–15 Year Olds in England and Wales', *Evaluation and Research in Education* 8 (1994): 111.

33. S. Sharp, 'How Much Does Bullying Hurt? The Effects of Bullying on the Personal Well-Being and Educational Progress of Secondary Aged Students', *Educational and Child Psychology* 12 (1995): 81.

34. G.M. Batsche and H.M. Knoff, 'Bullies and their Victims: Understanding a Pervasive Problem in the Schools', *School Psychology Review* 23 (1994): 165.

35. Whitney and Smith, 'A Survey of the Nature and Extent of Bullying in Junior/Middle and Secondary Schools'.

36. Ibid.

37. P.K. Smith and S. Shu, 'What Good Schools Can Do about Bullying: Findings from a Survey in English Schools after a Decade of Research and Action', *Childhood* 7 (2000): 193.

38. Nansel et al., 'Bullying Behaviors among US Youth'.

39. M. Boulton and P.K. Smith, 'Bully/Victim Problems in Middle-School Children: Stability, Self-Perceived Competence, Peer Perceptions and Peer Acceptance', *British Journal of Developmental Psychology* 12 (1994): 315.

40. Rodkin and Hodges, 'Bullies and Victims in the Peer Ecology'.

41. C. Salmivalli, 'Participant Role Approach to School Bullying: Implications for Interventions', *Journal of Adolescence* 22 (1999): 453.

42. E. Menesini, M. Eslea, P. Smith, M.L. Genta, E. Giannetti, A. Fonzi, and A. Constabile, 'Cross-National Comparison of Children's Attitudes towards Bully/Victim Problems in School', *Aggressive Behavior* 23 (1997): 245; Whitney and Smith, 'A Survey of the Nature and Extent of Bullying in Junior/Middle and Secondary Schools'.

43. O'Connell et al., 'Peer Involvement in Bullying'; Salmivalli et al., 'Bullying as a Group Process'.

44. Everett and Price, 'Students' Perceptions of Violence in the Public Schools'.

45. Twemlow et al., 'A Clinical and Interactional Perspective on the Bully–Victim–Bystander Relationship'.
46. Nansel et al., 'Bullying Behaviors among US Youth'.
47. Hawkins et al., 'Naturalistic Observations of Peer Interventions in Bullying'.
48. D.L. Espelage, M.K. Holt, and R.R. Henkel, 'Examination of Peer-Group Contextual Effects on Aggression during Early Adolescence', *Child Development* 74 (2003): 205; G.J.T. Haselager, W.W. Hartup, C.F.M. van Lieshout, and J.M. Riksen-Walraven, 'Similarities between Friends and Nonfriends in Middle Childhood', *Child Development* 69 (1998): 1198; M. McPherson, L. Smith-Lovin, and J.M. Cook, 'Birds of a Feather: Homophily in Social Networks', *Annual Review of Sociology* 27 (2001): 415; A.D. Pellegrini, M. Bartini, and F. Brooks, 'School Bullies, Victims, and Aggressive Victims: Factors Relating to Group Affiliation and Victimization in Early Adolescence', *Journal of Educational Psychology* 91 (1999): 216.
49. C. Salmivalli, M. Lappalainen, and K.M.J. Lagerspetz, 'Stability and Change of Behavior in Connection with Bullying in Schools: A Two-Year Follow-up', *Aggressive Behavior* 24 (1998): 205.
50. Rodkin and Hodges, 'Bullies and Victims in the Peer Ecology', 396.
51. Salmivalli, 'Participant Role Approach to School Bullying'. See also D. Rabiner and J. Coie, 'Effects of Expectancy Inductions on Rejected Children's Acceptance by Unfamiliar Peers', *Developmental Psychology* 25 (1989): 450; Salmivalli et al., 'Stability and Change of Behavior in Connection with Bullying in Schools'.
52. Pellegrini et al., 'School Bullies, Victims, and Aggressive Victims'; D. Schwartz, K.A. Dodge, G.S. Pettit, and J.E. Bates, 'The Early Socialisation of Aggressive Victims of Bullying', *Child Development* 68 (1997): 665; M.M. Vermande, E. van den Oord, P.P. Goudena, and J. Rispens, 'Structural Characteristics of Aggressor–Victim Relationships in Dutch School Classes of 4- to 5-Years Olds', *Aggressive Behavior* 26 (2000): 11.
53. P.K. Smith, L. Talamelli, H. Cowie, P. Naylor, and P. Chauhan, 'Profiles of Non-Victims, Escaped Victims, Continuing Victims and New Victims of School Bullying', *British Journal of Educational Psychology* 74 (2004): 565.
54. H. Mynard and S. Joseph, 'Bully/Victim Problems and their Association with Eysenck's Personality Dimensions in 8 to 13 Year Olds', *British Journal of Educational Psychology* 67 (1997): 51.
55. R.N. Olafsen and V. Viemero, 'Bully/Victim Problems and Coping with Stress in School among 10- to 12-Year-Old Pupils in Åland, Finland', *Aggressive Behavior* 26 (2000): 57.
56. A.C. Baldry and D.P. Farrington, 'Types of Bullying among Italian School Children', *Journal of Adolescence* 22 (1999): 423; Nansel et al., 'Bullying Behaviors among US Youth'; G.K. Natvig, G. Albrektsen, and U. Qvarnstrom, 'School-Related Stress Experience as a Risk Factor for Bullying Behavior', *Journal of Youth and Adolescence* 30 (2001): 561; Olweus, 'Bullying at School: Basic Facts and Effects of a School-Based Intervention Program'; Peterson and Rigby, 'Countering Bullying at an Australian Secondary School with Students as Helpers'; G. Salmon, A. James, and D.M. Smith, 'Bullying in Schools: Self Reported Anxiety, Depression and Self Esteem in Secondary School Children', *British Medical Journal* 317 (1998): 924; A. Sourander, L. Helstelä, H. Helenius, and J. Piha, 'Persistence of Bullying from Childhood to Adolescence – A Longitudinal 8-Year Follow-up Study', *Child Abuse and Neglect* 24 (2000): 873; Whitney and Smith, 'A Survey of the Nature and Extent of Bullying in Junior/Middle and Secondary Schools'.
57. Baldry and Farrington, 'Types of Bullying among Italian School Children'; Nansel et al., 'Bullying Behaviors among US Youth'; Olweus, Aggression in the Schools; Peterson and Rigby, 'Countering Bullying at an Australian Secondary School'; G. Siann, M. Callahan, P. Glissov, R. Lockhart, and L. Rawson, 'Who Gets Bullied? The Effect of School, Gender, and Ethnic Group', *Educational Research* 36 (1994): 123; Whitney and Smith, 'Survey of the Nature and Extent of Bullying'.
58. M.J. Boulton and K. Underwood, 'Bully/Victim Problems among Middle School Children', *British Journal of Educational Psychology* 62 (1992): 73; Whitney and Smith, 'Survey of the Nature and Extent of Bullying'.
59. Rodkin et al., 'Heterogeneity of Popular Boys'. See also Gorman et al., 'The Attributes Adolescents Associate with Peer Popularity and Teacher Preference'; LaFontana and Cillessen, 'The Nature of Children's Stereotypes of Popularity'; Prinstein and Cillessen, 'Forms and Functions of Adolescent Peer Aggression Associated with High Levels of Peer Status'.

60. J.T. Parkhurst and A. Hopmeyer, 'Sociometric Popularity and Peer-Perceived Popularity: Two Distinct Dimensions of Peer Status', *Journal of Early Adolescence* 18 (1998): 125.

61. W.A. Corsaro and D. Eder, 'Children's Peer Cultures', *Annual Review of Sociology* 16 (1993): 197; R.J. Hazler, *Breaking the Cycle of Violence: Interventions for Bullying and Victimization* (Washington, DC: Accelerated Development, 1996); K. Rigby, *Bullying in Schools and What to Do about It* (Bristol, PA: Jessica Kingsley, 1996); Smith et al., 'What Causes the Age Decline in Reports of Being Bullied at School?'.

62. R.J. Hazler, D.L. Miller, J.V. Carney, and S. Green, 'Adult Recognition of School Bullying Situations', *Educational Research* 43 (2001): 133.

63. M.J. Boulton, 'Teachers' Views on Bullying Definitions, Attitudes and Ability to Cope', *British Journal of Educational Psychology* 67 (1997): 223.

64. Salmivalli et al., 'Bullying as a Group Process'; Salmivalli et al., 'Stability and Change of Behavior in Connection with Bullying in Schools'.

65. C. Salmivalli, 'Peer-Led Intervention Campaign against School Bullying: Who Considered it Useful, Who Benefited?', *Educational Research* 43 (2001): 263.

66. Naylor and Cowie, 'The Effectiveness of Peer Support Systems in Challenging School Bullying'.

67. H. Cowie, 'Perspectives of Teachers and Pupils on the Experience of Peer Support against Bullying', *Educational Research and Evaluation* 4 (1998): 108.

68. S.K. Egan and D.G. Perry, 'Does Low Self-Regard Invite Victimization?', *Developmental Psychology* 34 (1998): 299; E.V.E. Hodges, M. Boivin, F. Vitaro, and W.M. Bukowski, 'The Power of Friendship: Protection against an Escalating Cycle of Peer Victimization', *Developmental Psychology* 35 (1999): 94; E.V.E. Hodges and D.G. Perry, 'Personal and Interpersonal Consequences of Victimization by Peers', *Journal of Personality and Social Psychology* 76 (1999): 677; A.D. Pellegrini, 'A Longitudinal Study of Boys' Rough-and-Tumble Play and Dominance during Early Adolescence', *Journal of Applied Developmental Psychology* 16 (1995): 77; E.M. Vernberg, 'Psychological Adjustment and Experiences with Peers during Early Adolescence: Reciprocal, Incidental, or Unidirectional Relationships?', *Journal of Abnormal Child Psychology* 18 (1990): 187.

69. Egan and Perry, 'Does Low Self-Regard Invite Victimization?', 299.

70. L. Montada and M. Lerner, *Responses to Victimizations and Belief in a Just World: Critical Issues in Social Justice* (New York: Plenum, 1998).

71. E.M. Vernberg, A.K. Jacobs, and S.L. Hershberger, 'Peer Victimization and Attitudes about Violence during Early Adolescence', *Journal of Clinical Child Psychology* 28 (1999): 386.

72. D.M. Ross, *Childhood Bullying and Teasing* (Alexandria, VA: American Counseling Association, 1996).

73. E.M. Vernberg, A.K. Jacobs, S.W. Twemlow, F. Sacco, and P. Fonagy, 'Developmental Patterns in Aggression, Victimization, and Violence-Related Cognitions', paper presented at American Psychological Association symposium: 'Violence against Peers: Developmental Inevitability or Unacceptable Risk?', Washington, DC, United States, August 2000, as cited in E.M. Vernberg and B.K. Gamm, 'Resistance to Violence Prevention Interventions in Schools: Barriers and Solutions', *Journal of Applied Psychoanalytic Studies* 5 (2003): 125, 128–9.

74. R. Oliver, J.H. Hoover, and R. Hazler, 'The Perceived Roles of Bullying in Small-Town Midwestern Schools', *Journal of Counseling Development* 72 (1994): 416.

75. A. Houndoumadi and L. Pateraki, 'Bullying and Bullies in Greek Elementary Schools: Pupils' Attitudes and Teachers'/Parents' Awareness', *Educational Research* 53 (2001): 19.

76. M.G. Borg, 'The Emotional Reactions of School Bullies and their Victims', *Educational Psychology* 18 (1998): 433.

77. Boulton and Underwood, 'Bully/Victim Problems among Middle School Children'.

78. K. Björkqvist, K. Ekman, and K. Lagerspetz, 'Bullies and Victims: Their Ego Picture, Ideal Ego Picture, and Normative Ego Picture', *Scandinavian Journal of Psychology* 23 (1982): 307. See also D.G. Perry, J.C. Williard, and L.C. Perry, 'Peers' Perceptions of the Consequences that Victimized Children Provide Aggressors', *Child Development* 61 (1990): 1310; D. Schwartz, K.A. Dodge, and J.D. Coie, 'The Emergence of Chronic Peer Victimization in Boys' Play Groups', *Child Development* 64 (1993): 1755.

79. Roland, 'Bullying, Depressive Symptoms and Suicidal Thoughts'.

80. C. Salmivalli, J. Karhunen, and K.M.J. Lagerspetz, 'How Do the Victims Respond to Bullying?', *Aggressive Behavior* 22 (1996): 99.

81. R. Lippitt, N. Polansky, F. Redl, and S. Rosen, 'The Dynamics of Power: A Field Study of Social Influence in Groups of Children', in *Readings in Social Psychology*, ed. G.E. Swanson, T.M. Newcomb, and E.L. Hartley, rev. edn (New York: Holt, 1952), 623; Rodkin and Hodges, 'Bullies and Victims in the Peer Ecology'.

82. J.S. Eccles, A. Wigfield, and U. Schiefele, 'Motivation to Succeed', in *Handbook of Child Psychology: Social, Emotional, and Personality Development*, vol. 3, ed. N. Eisenberg, 5th edn (New York: Wiley, 1998), 1017; K.H. Rubin, W. Bukowski, and J.G. Parker, 'Peer Interactions, Relationships, and Groups', in Eisenberg, *Handbook of Child Psychology*, 619.

83. A.D. Pellegrini, 'Bullying and Victimization in Middle School: A Dominance Relations Perspective', *Educational Psychologist* 37 (2002): 151.

84. Nansel et al., 'Bullying Behaviors among US Youth'.

85. M.J. Boulton, M. Trueman, C. Chau, C. Whitehand, and K. Amatya, 'Concurrent and Longitudinal Links between Friendships and Peer Victimization: Implications for Befriending Interventions', *Journal of Adolescence* 22 (1999): 461; Hodges et al., 'The Power of Friendship'.

86. Hodges et al., 'The Power of Friendship'.

87. Haselager et al., 'Similarities between Friends and Nonfriends in Middle Childhood'; E.V.E. Hodges, M.J. Malone, and D.G. Perry, 'Individual Risk and Social Risk as Interacting Determinants of Victimization in the Peer Group', *Developmental Psychology* 33 (1997): 1032; Pellegrini et al., 'School Bullies, Victims, and Aggressive Victims'; Salmivalli et al., 'Peer Networks and Bullying in Schools'.

88. M. Boivin, S. Hymel, and W.M. Bukowski, 'The Roles of Social Withdrawal, Peer Rejection, and Victimization by Peers in Predicting Loneliness and Depressed Mood in Childhood', *Development and Psychopathology* 7 (1995): 765; Boulton and Smith, 'Bully/Victim Problems in Middle-School Children'; E.S. Buhs and G.W. Ladd, 'Peer Rejection as an Antecedent of Young Children's School Adjustment: An Examination of Mediating Processes', *Developmental Psychology* 37 (2001): 550; N.R. Crick, J.F. Casas, and H.C. Ku, 'Relational and Physical Forms of Peer Victimization in Preschool', *Developmental Psychology* 35 (1999): 376; R. Forero, L. McLellan, C. Rissel, and A. Bauman, 'Bullying Behaviour and Psychosocial Health among School Students in New South Wales, Australia: Cross Sectional Survey', *British Medical Journal* 319 (1999): 344; L.D. Hanish and N.G. Guerra, 'Predictors of Peer Victimization among Urban Youth', *Social Development* 9 (2000): 521; Hodges et al., 'The Power of Friendship'; K.M.J. Lagerspetz, K. Björkqvist, M. Berts, and E. King, 'Group Aggression among School Children in Three Schools', *Scandinavian Journal of Psychology* 23 (1982): 45; D. Olweus, *Bullying at School: What We Know and What We Can Do* (Oxford: Blackwell, 1993); Pellegrini et al., 'School Bullies, Victims, and Aggressive Victims'; D.G. Perry, S.J. Kusel, and L.C. Perry, 'Victims of Peer Aggression', *Developmental Psychology* 24 (1988): 807.

89. K. Rigby and P. Slee, 'Bullying among Australian School Children: Reported Behaviour and Attitudes to Victims', *Journal of Social Psychology* 131 (1991): 615.

90. J. Sutton, P.K. Smith, and J. Swettenham, 'Social Cognition and Bullying: Social Inadequacy or Skilled Manipulation?', *British Journal of Developmental Psychology* 17 (1999): 435.

91. P. Bijttebier and H. Vertommen, 'Coping with Peer Arguments in School-Age Children with Bully/Victim Problems', *British Journal of Educational Psychology* 68 (1998): 387; Naylor and Cowie, 'The Effectiveness of Peer Support Systems in Challenging School Bullying'; P. Naylor, H. Cowie, and R. del Rey, 'Coping Strategies of Secondary School Children in Response to Being Bullied', *Child Psychology and Psychiatry Review* 6 (2001): 114.

92. Whitney and Smith, 'A Survey of the Nature and Extent of Bullying in Junior/Middle and Secondary Schools'.

93. Smith et al., 'Profiles of Non-Victims, Escaped Victims, Continuing Victims and New Victims of School Bullying'.

94. L. Chang, 'Variable Effects of Children's Aggression, Social Withdrawal, and Prosocial Leadership as Functions of Teacher Beliefs and Behaviors', *Child Development* 74 (2003): 535; T.W. Farmer, 'Misconceptions of Peer Rejection and Problem Behavior: Understanding Aggression in Students with Mild Disabilities', *Remedial and Special Education* 21 (2000): 194.

95. M.G. Borg, 'Secondary School Teachers' Perception of Pupils' Undesirable Behaviours', *British Journal of Educational Psychology* 68 (1998): 67; C.M. Clark and P.L. Peterson, 'Teachers' Thought Processes', in *Handbook of Research on Teaching*, ed. M.C. Wittrock, 3rd edn (New York: Macmillan, 1986), 255; G.B. Helton and T.D. Oakland, 'Teachers'

Attitudinal Responses to Differing Characteristics of Elementary School Students', *Journal of Educational Psychology* 69 (1977): 261; D.M. Kagan, 'Implications of Research on Teacher Belief', *Educational Psychologist* 27 (1992): 65; M.L. Silberman, Behavioral Expression of Teachers' Attitudes toward Elementary School Students', *Journal of Educational Psychology* 60 (1969): 402.

96. Olweus, *Bullying at School*, 26.
97. E. Roland and D. Galloway, 'Classroom Influences on Bullying', *Educational Research* 44 (2002): 299.
98. D. Olweus, 'Bully/Victim Problems among School Children: Basic Facts and Effects of a School Based Intervention Program', in *The Development and Treatment of Childhood Aggression*, ed. D. Pepler and K.H. Rubin (Hillsdale, NJ: Lawrence Erlbaum, 1991), 411; D. Olweus, 'Bullying at School: Long-Term Outcomes for the Victims and an Effective School-Based Intervention Program', in *Aggressive Behavior: Current Perspectives*, ed. L.R. Huesmann (New York: Plenum, 1994); S. Sharp and P.K. Smith, 'Bullying in UK Schools: The DES Sheffield Bullying Project', *Early Child Development Care* 77 (1991): 47; P.K. Smith, 'Bullying in Schools: The UK Experience and the Sheffield Anti-Bullying Project', *Irish Journal of Psychology* 18 (1997): 191.
99. Department for Education and Skills and Department of Health, *Stand up for Us: Challenging Homophobia in Schools* (London: Department for Education and Skills and Department of Health, 2004), 4.
100. See M. Bochenek and A.W. Brown, *Hatred in the Hallways: Violence and Discrimination against Lesbian, Gay, Bisexual, and Transgender Students in U.S. Schools* (New York: Human Rights Watch, 2001), 79–87.
101. Borg, 'The Emotional Reactions of School Bullies and their Victims'.
102. R. Hunt and J. Jensen, *Education for All: The Experiences of Young Gay People in Britain's Schools* (London: Stonewall, 2007), 3.
103. S.W. Twemlow, P. Fonagy, and F.C. Sacco, 'Modifying Social Aggression in Schools', *Journal of Applied Psychoanalytic Studies* 5 (2003): 211.
104. S.W. Twemlow, 'The Roots of Violence: Converging Psychoanalytic Explanatory Models for Power Struggles and Violence in Schools', *Psychoanalytic Quarterly* 69 (2000): 741.
105. S.W. Twemlow, P. Fonagy, F.C. Sacco, and J.R. Brethour, Jr, 'Teachers Who Bully Students: A Hidden Trauma', *International Journal of Social Psychiatry* 52 (2006): 187.
106. J.T. Sears, 'Educators, Homosexuality, and Homosexual Students: Are Personal Feelings Related to Professional Beliefs?', *Journal of Homosexuality* 22, nos 3–4 (1992): 29 (finding that two-thirds of school counsellors held adverse attitudes towards sexual minority students).
107. D. McCann, 'Lesbians, Gay Men, their Families and Counselling: Implications for Training and Practice', *Educational and Child Psychology* 10 (2001): 78, 78.
108. Nayak and Kehily, 'Playing it Straight', 224.
109. D. Epstein and R. Johnson, 'On the Straight and Narrow: The Heterosexual Presumption, Homophobias and Schools', in *Challenging Lesbian and Gay Inequalities in Education*, ed. D. Epstein (Buckingham: Open University Press, 1994), 197, 223.
110. N. Gilmore and M.A. Somerville, 'Stigmatization, Scapegoating and Discrimination in Sexually Transmitted Diseases: Overcoming "Them" and "Us"', *Social Science and Medicine* 39 (1994): 1339, 1342.
111. A. Hartman, 'Out of the Closet: Revolution and Backlash', *Social Work* 38 (1993): 245, 245.
112. C. Lee, *The Ostrich Position: Sex, Schooling, Mystification* (London: Unwin, 1986), 34.
113. Nayak and Kehily, 'Playing it Straight', 220.
114. R.A. Astor, R.O. Pitner, and B.B. Duncan, 'Ecological Approaches to Mental Health Consultation with Teachers on Issues Related to Youth and School Violence', *Journal of Negro Education* 65 (1998): 336.
115. D.P. Farrington, 'Understanding and Preventing Bullying', in *Crime and Justice: A Review of Research*, vol. 17, ed. M. Tonry (Chicago: University of Chicago Press, 1993), 381.
116. Olweus, *Bullying at School*.
117. A.M. Horne, C.L. Bartolomucci, and D. Newman-Carlson, *Bully Busters: A Teacher's Manual for Helping Bullies, Victims, and Bystanders* (Champaign, IL: Research Press, 2003); J. Larson, D.C. Smith, and M.J. Furlong, 'Best Practices in School Violence Prevention', in *Best Practices in School Psychology*, vol. IV, ed. A. Thomas and J. Grimes (Bethesda, MD: National Association of School Psychologists, 2002), 1081; D. Olweus, S. Limber, and

S. Mihalic, *Blueprints for Violence Prevention: Bullying Prevention Program* (Boulder, CO: Institute of Behavioral Science, University of Colorado, 1999).

118. Twemlow et al., 'Modifying Social Aggression in Schools', 215.
119. Boulton, 'Teachers' Views on Bullying Definitions, Attitudes and Ability to Cope'.
120. Ibid.; Hazler et al., 'Adult Recognition of School Bullying Situations'.
121. D.J. Pepler, W.M. Craig, S. Ziegler, and A. Charach, 'An Evaluation of an Anti-Bullying Intervention in Toronto Schools', *Canadian Journal of Community Mental Health* 13 (1994): 95.
122. Menesini, Eslea, Smith, Genta, Giannetti, Fonzi, and Constabile, 'Cross-National Comparison of Children's Attitudes towards Bully/Victim Problems in School'.
123. See, e.g., L. Berdondini and P.K. Smith, 'Cohesion and Power in the Families of Children Involved in Bully/Victim Problems at School: An Italian Replication', *Journal of Family Therapy* 18 (1996): 99; Bochenek and Brown, *Hatred in the Hallways*; L. Bowers, P.K. Smith, and V. Binney, 'Perceived Family Relationships of Bullies, Victims and Bully/Victims in Middle Childhood', *Journal of Social and Personal Relationships* 11 (1994): 215; Dake et al., 'The Nature and Extent of Bullying at School'; D.L. Espelage and S.M. Swearer, 'Research on School Bullying and Victimization: What Have We Learned and Where Do We Go from Here?', *School Psychology Review* 32 (2003): 365; R.C. Savin-Williams, 'Verbal and Physical Abuse as Stressors in the Lives of Lesbian, Gay Male, and Bisexual Youths: Associations with School Problems, Running Away, Substance Abuse, Prostitution, and Suicide', *Journal of Consulting and Clinical Psychology* 62 (1994): 261; P.K. Smith and S. Sharp, *School Bullying: Insights and Perspectives* (London: Routledge, 1994); P.R. Smokowski and K.H. Kopasz, 'Bullying in School: An Overview of Types, Effects, Family Characteristics, and Intervention Strategies', *Children and Schools* 27 (2005): 101; V. Stevens, I. de Bourdeaudhuij, and P. van Oost, 'Relationship of the Family Environment to Children's Involvement in Bully/Victim Problems at School', *Journal of Youth and Adolescence* 31 (2002): 419.
124. R.D. Duncan, 'Maltreatment by Parents and Peers: The Relationship between Child Abuse, Bully Victimization, and Psychological Distress', *Child Maltreatment* 4 (1999): 45; D. Schwartz, K.A. Dodge, G.S. Pettit, J.E. Bates, and Conduct Problems Prevention Research Group, 'Friendship as a Moderating Factor in the Pathway between Early Harsh Home Environment and Later Victimization in the Peer Group', *Developmental Psychology* 36 (2000): 646; A. Shields and D. Cicchetti, 'Parental Maltreatment and Emotion Dysregulation as Risk Factors for Bullying and Victimization in Middle Childhood', *Journal of Clinical Child Psychology* 30 (2001): 349.
125. G.W. Ladd and B.K. Ladd, 'Parenting Behaviors and Parent–Child Relationships: Correlates of Peer Victimization in Kindergarten?', *Developmental Psychology* 34 (1998): 1450. For discussions of attachment theory generally, see M.D.S. Ainsworth, *Infancy in Uganda: Infant Care and the Growth of Love* (Baltimore: Johns Hopkins University Press, 1967); M.D.S. Ainsworth, *Patterns of Attachment* (Hillsdale, NJ: Lawrence Erlbaum, 1978); J. Bowlby, *Attachment and Loss*, vol. 1: Attachment (London: Hogarth, 1969); J. Bowlby, *Attachment and Loss*, vol. 2: Separation: Anxiety and Anger (London: Hogarth, 1972); J. Bowlby, *Attachment and Loss*, vol. 3: Loss: Sadness and Depression (London: Hogarth, 1980); J. Bowlby, *A Secure Base: Parent–Child Attachment and Healthy Human Development* (New York: Basic Books, 1988); M. Rutter, *Maternal Deprivation Reassessed*, 2nd edn (London and New York: Penguin Books, 1981).
126. D.L. Espelage, K. Bosworth, and T.R. Simon, 'Short-Term Stability and Prospective Correlates of Bullying in Middle School Students: An Examination of Potential Demographic, Psychosocial, and Environmental Influences', *Violence and Victims* 16 (2001): 411.
127. A.C. Baldry and D.P. Farrington, 'Bullies and Delinquents: Personal Characteristics and Parental Styles', *Journal of Community and Applied Social Psychology* 10 (2000): 17.
128. Ibid.; Espelage et al., 'Short-Term Stability and Prospective Correlates of Bullying in Middle School Students'; K. Rigby and I.K. Cox, 'The Contributions of Bullying and Low Self-Esteem to Acts of Delinquency among Australian Teenagers', *Personality and Individual Differences* 21 (1996): 609.
129. Duncan, 'Maltreatment by Parents and Peers'; D.P. Farrington, 'Childhood Aggression and Adult Violence: Early Precursors and Later-Life Outcomes', in *The Development and Treatment of Childhood Aggression*, ed. D. Pepler and K.H. Rubin (Hillsdale, NJ: Lawrence Erlbaum, 1991), 8; D. Gorman-Smith, P.H. Tolan, A. Zelli, and L.R. Huesmann, 'The Relation

of Family Functioning to Violence among Inner-City Minority Youths', *Journal of Family Psychology* 10 (1996): 115; R. Loeber and T. Dishion, 'Early Predictors of Male Delinquency: A Review', *Psychological Bulletin* 94 (1983): 68; A.N. Schore, *Affect Regulation and the Origin of the Self: The Neurobiology of Emotional Development* (Hillsdale, NJ: Lawrence Erlbaum, 1994); Schwartz et al., 'Friendship as a Moderating Factor in the Pathway between Early Harsh Home Environment and Later Victimization in the Peer Group'; Shields and Cicchetti, 'Parental Maltreatment and Emotion Dysregulation as Risk Factors for Bullying and Victimization in Middle Childhood'; P.H. Tolan, R.E. Cromwell, and M. Braswell, 'The Application of Family Therapy to Juvenile Delinquency: A Critical Review of the Literature', *Family Process* 15 (1986): 619.

130. K.A. Berthold and J.H. Hoover, 'Correlates of Bullying and Victimization among Intermediate Students in the Midwestern USA', *School Psychology International* 21 (2000): 65; E.V.E. Hodges and D.G. Perry, 'Victims of Peer Abuse: An Overview', *Journal of Emotional and Behavioral Problems* 5 (1996): 23.

131. B. Fagot and K. Kavanagh, 'The Prediction of Antisocial Behavior from Avoidant Attachment Classifications', *Child Development* 61 (1990): 864; P. Turner, 'Relations between Attachment, Gender, and Behavior with Peers in Preschool', *Child Development* 62 (1991): 1475.

132. R. Karr-Morse and D.B. Wiley, *Ghosts from the Nursery* (New York: Atlantic Monthly Press, 1997).

133. M. Troy and L.A. Sroufe, 'Victimization among Preschoolers: Role of Attachment Relationship Theory', *Journal of the American Academy of Child and Adolescent Psychiatry* 26 (1987): 166.

134. B. Renken, B. Egeland, D. Marvinney, S. Mangelsdorf, and L.A. Sroufe, 'Early Childhood Antecedents of Aggression and Passive-Withdrawal in Early Elementary School', *Journal of Personality* 57 (1989): 257.

135. R.A. Finnegan, E.V.E. Hodges, and D.G. Perry, 'Victimization by Peers: Associations with Children's Reports of Mother–Child Interaction', *Journal of Personality and Social Psychology* 75 (1998): 1076; Ladd and Ladd, 'Parenting Behaviors and Parent–Child Relationships'.

136. D. Olweus, 'Familial and Temperamental Determinants of Aggressive Behavior in Adolescent Boys: A Causal Analysis', *Child Development* 16 (1980): 644.

137. Berdondini and Smith, 'Cohesion and Power in the Families of Children Involved in Bully/ Victim Problems at School'; Bowers et al., 'Perceived Family Relationships of Bullies, Victims and Bully/Victims in Middle Childhood'; Schwartz et al., 'Friendship as a Moderating Factor in the Pathway between Early Harsh Home Environment and Later Victimization in the Peer Group'; P.K. Smith and R. Myron-Wilson, 'Parenting and School Bullying', *Clinical Child Psychology and Psychiatry* 3 (1998): 405.

138. C.J. Patterson, J.B. Kupersmidt, and P.C. Griesler, 'Children's Perceptions of Self and of Relationships with Others as a Function of Sociometric Status', *Child Development* 61 (1990): 1335.

139. E. Flouri and A. Buchanan, 'Life Satisfaction in Teenage Boys: The Moderating Role of Father Involvement and Bullying', *Aggressive Behavior* 28 (2002): 126.

140. Bowers et al., 'Perceived Family Relationships of Bullies, Victims and Bully/Victims in Middle Childhood'.

141. R. Loeber and T.J. Dishion, 'Boys Who Fight at Home and School: Family Conditions Influencing Cross-Setting Consistency', *Journal of Consulting and Clinical Psychology* 52 (1984): 759.

142. G.R. Patterson, 'The Contribution of Siblings to Training for Fighting: A Microsocial Analysis', in *Development of Antisocial and Prosocial Behavior: Research Theories and Issues*, ed. D. Olweus, J. Block, and M. Radke-Yarrow (New York: Academic Press, 1986), 235.

143. Bowers et al., 'Perceived Family Relationships of Bullies, Victims and Bully/Victims in Middle Childhood'.

144. Ibid.; S.W. Henggeler, S.K. Schoenwald, C.M. Borduin, M.D. Rowland, and P.B. Cunningham, *Multisystemic Treatment of Antisocial Behavior in Children and Adolescents* (New York: Guilford Press, 1998); P.K. Smith and K. Ananiadou, 'The Nature of School Bullying and the Effectiveness of School-Based Interventions', *Journal of Psychoanalytic Studies* 5 (2003): 189.

145. Duncan, 'Maltreatment by Parents and Peers'; Shields and Cicchetti, 'Parental Maltreatment and Emotion Dysregulation as Risk Factors for Bullying and Victimization in Middle Childhood'.

146. Shields and Cicchetti, 'Parental Maltreatment and Emotion Dysregulation'.

147. K. Bosworth, D.L. Espelage, and T. Simon, 'Factors Associated with Bullying Behavior in Middle School Students', *Journal of Early Adolescence* 19 (1999): 341.
148. Farrington, 'Understanding and Preventing Bullying'.
149. Schwartz et al., 'The Early Socialisation of Aggressive Victims of Bullying'.
150. M.H. Futrell, 'Violence in the Classroom: A Teacher's Perspective', in *Schools, Violence, and Society*, ed. A.M. Hoffman (Westport, CT: Praeger, 1996), 3.
151. M.A. Barnett, J.A. Howard, L.M. King, and G.A. Dino, 'Antecedents of Empathy: Retrospective Accounts of Early Socialization', *Personality and Social Psychology Bulletin* 6 (1980): 361; N. Eisenberg, *Altruistic Emotion, Cognition, and Behavior* (Hillsdale, NJ: Lawrence Erlbaum, 1986).
152. Baldry and Farrington, 'Bullies and Delinquents'.
153. Ladd and Ladd, 'Parenting Behaviors and Parent–Child Relationships'.
154. D. Wolke, S. Woods, K. Stanford, and H. Schultz, 'Bullying and Victimization of Primary School Children in England and Germany: Prevalence and School Factors', *British Journal of Psychology* 92 (2001): 673.
155. D.S. Hawker and M.J. Boulton, 'Twenty Years' Research on Peer Victimization and Psychosocial Maladjustment: A Meta-Analytic Review of Cross-Sectional Studies', *Journal of Clinical Psychology and Psychiatry* 41 (2000): 441.
156. Boivin et al., 'The Roles of Social Withdrawal, Peer Rejection, and Victimization by Peers in Predicting Loneliness and Depressed Mood in Childhood'; L. Bond, J.B. Carlin, L. Thomas, K. Rubin, and G. Patton, 'Does Bullying Cause Emotional Problems? A Prospective Study of Young Teenagers', *British Medical Journal* 323 (2001): 480; Boulton and Underwood, 'Bully/Victim Problems among Middle School Children'; J.V. Carney, 'Bullied to Death: Perceptions of Peer Abuse and Suicidal Behavior during Adolescence', *School Psychology International* 21 (2000): 44; N.R. Crick and J.K. Grotpeter, 'Children's Treatment by Peers: Victims of Relational and Overt Aggression', *Development and Psychopathology* 8 (1996): 367; Egan and Perry, 'Does Low Self-Regard Invite Victimization?'; Forero et al., 'Bullying Behaviour and Psychosocial Health among School Students in New South Wales, Australia'; Hazler, *Breaking the Cycle of Violence*; Hodges and Perry, 'Personal and Interpersonal Consequences of Victimization by Peers'; J. Juvonen, A. Nishina, and S. Graham, 'Peer Harassment, Psychological Adjustment, and Social Functioning in Early Adolescence', *Journal of Educational Psychology* 92 (2000): 349; R. Kaltiala-Heino, M. Rimpelä, M. Marttunen, A. Rimpelä, and P. Rantenan, 'Bullying, Depression, and Suicidal Ideation in Finnish Adolescents: School Survey', *British Medical Journal* 319 (1999): 348; R. Kaltiala-Heino, M. Rimpelä, P. Rantenan, and A. Rimpelä, 'Bullying at School – An Indicator of Adolescents at Risk for Mental Disorders', *Journal of Adolescence* 23 (2000): 661; B.J. Kochenderfer and G.W. Ladd, 'Peer Victimization: Cause or Consequence of School Maladjustment?', *Child Development* 67 (1996): 1305; Kumpulainen et al., 'Psychiatric Disorders and the Use of Mental Health Services among Children Involved in Bullying'; Nansel et al., 'Bullying Behaviors among US Youth'; Olweus, 'Bullying at School: Long-Term Outcomes for the Victims and an Effective School-Based Intervention Program'; O'Moore and Kirkham, 'Self-Esteem and its Relationship to Bullying Behavior'; Salmon et al., 'Bullying in Schools'; Vernberg, 'Psychological Adjustment and Experiences with Peers during Early Adolescence'; K. Williams, M. Chambers, S. Logan, and D. Robinson, 'Association of Common Health Symptoms with Bullying in Primary School Children', *British Medical Journal* 313 (1996): 17.
157. Borg, 'The Emotional Reactions of School Bullies and their Victims'.
158. C.R. Pfeffer, 'Manifestation of Risk Factors', in *Suicide in Children and Adolescents*, ed. G. MacLean (Toronto: Hogrefe & Huber, 1990), 65, 81.
159. Boivin et al., 'The Roles of Social Withdrawal, Peer Rejection, and Victimization by Peers in Predicting Loneliness and Depressed Mood in Childhood'; Egan and Perry, 'Does Low Self-Regard Invite Victimization?'; Hodges and Perry, 'Personal and Interpersonal Consequences of Victimization by Peers'; Juvonen et al., 'Peer Harassment, Psychological Adjustment, and Social Functioning in Early Adolescence'; Kochenderfer and Ladd, 'Peer Victimization'; J.G. Parker and S.R. Asher, 'Peer Relations and Later Personal Adjustment: Are Low-Accepted Children at Risk?', *Psychological Bulletin* 102 (1987): 357; G. Salmon, A. James, E.L. Cassidy, and M.A. Javaloyes, 'Bullying a Review: Presentations to an Adolescent Psychiatric Service and within a School for Emotionally and Behaviourally Disturbed Children',

Clinical Child Psychology and Psychiatry 5 (2000): 563; Schwartz et al., 'The Emergence of Chronic Peer Victimization in Boys' Play Groups'; P.T. Slee, 'Situational and Interpersonal Correlates of Anxiety Associated with Peer Victimization', *Child Psychiatry and Human Development* 25 (1994): 97; Vernberg, 'Psychological Adjustment and Experiences with Peers during Early Adolescence'.

160.   Kaltiala-Heino et al., 'Bullying, Depression, and Suicidal Ideation in Finnish Adolescents'; K. Rigby, *Bullying in Schools: And What to Do about It* (Camberwell, Victoria: Australian Council for Educational Research, 1996); K. Rigby, 'Peer Victimisation at School and the Health of Secondary School Students', *British Journal of Educational Psychology* 68 (1999): 95; Williams et al., 'Association of Common Health Symptoms with Bullying in Primary School Children'.

161.   Kaltiala-Heino et al., 'Bullying, Depression, and Suicidal Ideation'; Kumpulainen et al., 'Psychiatric Disorders and the Use of Mental Health Services among Children Involved in Bullying'.

162.   Kaltiala-Heino et al., 'Bullying, Depression, and Suicidal Ideation'; Olweus, *Bullying at School*; K. Rigby, 'Effects of Peer Victimization in Schools and Perceived Social Support on Adolescent Well-Being', *Journal of Adolescence* 23 (2000): 57; Slee, 'Situational and Interpersonal Correlates of Anxiety Associated with Peer Victimization'; J.M. Stillion, 'Sucide: Understanding those Considering Premature Exits', in *Dying, Death, and Bereavement: Theoretical Perspectives and Other Ways of Knowing*, ed. I.B. Corless, B.B. Germino, and M. Pittman (Boston: Jones & Bartlett, 1994), 273.

163.   Mynard and Joseph, 'Bully/Victim Problems and their Association with Eysenck's Personality Dimensions in 8 to 13 Year Olds'.

164.   Kochenderfer and Ladd, 'Peer Victimization', 1314.

165.   Olweus, 'Bullying at School: Long-Term Outcomes for the Victims and an Effective School-Based Intervention Program'.

166.   Juvonen et al., 'Peer Harassment, Psychological Adjustment, and Social Functioning in Early Adolescence'.

167.   Smith et al., 'Profiles of Non-Victims, Escaped Victims, Continuing Victims and New Victims of School Bullying'.

168.   S. Austin and S. Joseph, 'Assessment of Bully/Victim Problems in 8 to 11 Year-Olds', *British Journal of Educational Psychology* 66 (1996): 447; Forero et al., 'Bullying Behaviour and Psychosocial Health among School Students in New South Wales, Australia'.

169.   Bond et al., 'Does Bullying Cause Emotional Problems?'; Kaltiala-Heino et al., 'Bullying, Depression, and Suicidal Ideation in Finnish Adolescents'; Kaltiala-Heino et al., 'Bullying at School'.

170.   Kaltiala-Heino et al., 'Bullying, Depression, and Suicidal Ideation in Finnish Adolescents'; Kaltiala-Heino et al., 'Bullying at School'; Salmon et al., 'Bullying in Schools'.

171.   Kaltiala-Heino et al., 'Bullying, Depression, and Suicidal Ideation in Finnish Adolescents'; Kaltiala-Heino et al., 'Bullying at School'.

172.   Olafsen and Viemero, 'Bully/Victim Problems and Coping with Stress in School among 10- to 12-Year-Old Pupils in Åland, Finland'.

173.   Kaltiala-Heino et al., 'Bullying, Depression, and Suicidal Ideation in Finnish Adolescents'.

174.   D.S. Elliot, B.A. Hamburg, and K.R. Williams, 'Violence in American Schools: An Overview', in *Violence in American Schools*, ed. D.S. Elliot, B.A. Hamburg, and K.R. Williams (Cambridge: Cambridge University Press, 1998), 3.

175.   Vernberg and Gamm, 'Resistance to Violence Prevention Interventions in Schools'; B. Vossekuil, R.A. Fein, M. Reddy, R. Borum, and W. Modzeleski, *Safe School Initiative: An Interim Report on the Prevention of Targeted Violence in Schools* (Washington, DC: United States Secret Service and United States Department of Education, 2000).

176.   Vossekuil et al., *Safe School Initiative*, 7.

177.   Ibid.

178.   B. Vossekuil, R.A. Fein, M. Reddy, R. Borum, and W. Modzeleski, *The Final Report and Findings of the Safe School Initiative: Implications for the Prevention of School Attacks in the United States* (Washington, DC: United States Secret Service and United States Department of Education, 2002).

179.   Austin and Joseph, 'Assessment of Bully/Victim Problems in 8 to 11 Year-Olds'; S. Callagan and S. Joseph, 'Self-Concept and Peer Victimization among Schoolchildren', *Personality and*

Individual Differences 18 (1995): 161; Kaltiala-Heino et al., 'Bullying, Depression, and Suicidal Ideation in Finnish Adolescents'; Kaltiala-Heino et al., 'Bullying at School'; A. Neary and S. Joseph, 'Peer Victimization and its Relationship to Self-Concept and Depression among Schoolgirls', *Personality and Individual Differences* 16 (1994): 183; Salmon et al., 'Bullying in Schools'; P.T. Slee, 'Peer Victimization and its Relationship to Depression among Australian Primary School Students', *Personality and Individual Differences* 18 (1995): 57.

180. Kaltiala-Heino et al., 'Bullying at School'; Kumpulainen et al., 'Psychiatric Disorders and the Use of Mental Health Services among Children Involved in Bullying'.

181. Baldry and Farrington, 'Bullies and Delinquents'; Berthold and Hoover, 'Correlates of Bullying and Victimization among Intermediate Students in the Midwestern USA'; Forero et al., 'Bullying Behaviour and Psychosocial Health among School Students in New South Wales, Australia'; Nansel et al., 'Bullying Behaviors among US Youth'.

182. Baldry and Farrington, 'Bullies and Delinquents'; Berthold and Hoover, 'Correlates of Bullying and Victimization'; A.D. Pellegrini and M. Bartini, 'A Longitudinal Study of Bullying, Victimization, and Peer Affiliation during the Transition from Primary School to Middle School', *American Educational Research Journal* 37 (2000): 699; Rigby and Cox, 'The Contributions of Bullying and Low Self-Esteem to Acts of Delinquency among Australian Teenagers'.

183. J.A. Connolly, D. Pepler, W. Craig, and A. Taradash, 'Dating Experiences of Bullies in Early Adolescence', *Child Maltreatment* 5 (2000): 297.

184. Nansel et al., 'Bullying Behaviors among US Youth'; Juvonen et al., 'Peer Harassment, Psychological Adjustment, and Social Functioning in Early Adolescence'; Mynard and Joseph, 'Bully/Victim Problems and their Association with Eysenck's Personality Dimensions in 8 to 13 Year Olds'

185. Kaltiala-Heino et al., 'Bullying, Depression, and Suicidal Ideation in Finnish Adolescents'.

186. D. Olweus, 'Bullying among Schoolchildren: Intervention and Prevention', in *Aggression and Violence throughout the Life Span*, ed. R.D. Peters, R.J. McMahon, and V.L. Quinsey (London: Sage, 1992), 100.

187. Farrington, 'Understanding and Preventing Bullying'.

188. Olweus, *Aggression in the Schools*; Roland, 'Bullying, Depressive Symptoms and Suicidal Thoughts'; E. Roland and T. Idsoe, 'Aggression and Bullying', *Aggressive Behavior* 27 (2001): 446; D. Shaffer and J. Piacentini, 'Suicide and Attempted Suicide', in *Child and Adolescent Psychiatry*, ed. M. Rutter, E. Taylor, and L. Hersov (Oxford: Blackwell Science, 1994), 407.

189. Kaltiala-Heino et al., 'Bullying, Depression, and Suicidal Ideation in Finnish Adolescents'.

190. N. Adams, T. Cox, and L. Dunstan, '"I am the Hate that Dare Not Speak its Name": Dealing with Homophobia in Secondary Schools', *Educational Psychology in Practice* 20 (2004): 259; N. Douglas, I. Warwick, S. Kemp, and G. Whitty, *Playing it Safe: Responses of Secondary School Teachers to Lesbian, Gay and Bisexual Pupils, Bullying, HIV and AIDS Education and Section 28* (London: Terrence Higgins Trust, 1997); L. Robertson and J.J. Monsen, 'Issues in the Development of a Homosexual Identity: Practice Implications for Educational Psychologists', *Educational and Child Psychology* 18 (2001): 13.

191. Center for Population Options, *Lesbian, Gay and Bisexual Youth: At Risk and Underserved* (Washington, DC: Center for Population Options, 1992), 1.

192. Erikson, *Identity*, 59.

193. D.B. Kandel, 'Drug and Drinking Behavior among Youth', *Annual Review of Sociology* 6 (1980): 235; D.J. McKirnan and P.L. Peterson, 'Alcohol and Drug Use among Homosexual Men and Women: Epidemiology and Population Characteristics', *Addictive Behaviors* 14 (1989): 545; D.J. McKirnan and P.L. Peterson, 'Psychosocial and Cultural Factors in Alcohol and Drug Abuse: An Analysis of a Homosexual Community', *Addictive Behaviors* 14 (1989): 555; J.P. Paul, R. Stall, and K.A. Bloomfield, 'Gays and Alcoholism: Epidemiologic and Clinical Issues', *Alcohol Health and Research World* 15 (1991): 151; G.J. Remafedi, 'Adolescent Homosexuality: Issues for Pediatricians', *Pediatrics* 79 (1987): 331.

194. A.M. Boxer, J.A. Cook, and G. Herdt, 'Double Jeopardy: Identity Transitions and Parent–Child Relations among Gay and Lesbian Youth', in *Parent–Child Relations throughout Life*, ed. K. Pillemer and K. McCartney (Hillsdale, NJ: Lawrence Erlbaum, 1991), 59; J.A. Farrow, R.W. Deisher, R. Brown, J.W. Kulig, and M.D. Kipke, 'Health and Health Needs of Homeless and Runaway Youth: A Position Paper of the Society for Adolescent Medicine', *Journal of*

Adolescent Health 13 (1992): 717; G. Kruks, 'Gay and Lesbian Homeless/Street Youth: Special Issues and Concerns', *Journal of Adolescent Health* 12 (1991): 515.

195. D. Boyer, 'Male Prostitution and Homosexual Identity', *Journal of Homosexuality* 17, nos 1–2 (1989): 151; E. Coleman, 'The Development of Male Prostitution Activity among Gay and Bisexual Adolescents', *Journal of Homosexuality* 17, nos 1–2 (1989), 131; C.M. Earls and H. David, 'A Psychosocial Study of Male Prostitution', *Archives of Sexual Behavior* 18 (1989): 401; R.S. Gold and M.J. Skinner, 'Situational Factors and Thought Processes Associated with Unprotected Intercourse in Young Gay Men', *AIDS* 6 (1992): 1021; R.S. Gold and M.J. Skinner, 'Desire for Unprotected Intercourse Preceding its Occurrence: The Case of Young Gay Men with Anonymous Partners', *International Journal of STD and AIDS* 4 (1993): 326; V. Minichiello, R. Mariño, J. Browne, M. Jamieson, K. Peterson, B. Reuter, and K. Robinson, 'Commercial Sex between Men: A Prospective Diary-Based Study', *Journal of Sex Research* 37 (2000): 151; J. Wade, 'Children on the Edge – Patterns of Running Away in the UK', *Child and Family Law Quarterly* 15 (2003): 343.

196. D. Barrett and M. Melrose, 'Courting Controversy – Children Sexually Abused through Prostitution – Are They Everybody's Distant Relatives but Nobody's Children?', *Child and Family Law Quarterly* 15 (2003): 371; T. Calhoun and B. Pickerill, 'Young Male Prostitutes: Their Knowledge of Selected Sexually Transmitted Diseases', *Journal of Human Behavior* 25, no. 3 (1988): 1; R.B. Hays, S.M. Kegeles, and T.J. Coates, 'High HIV Risk Taking among Young Gay Men', *AIDS* 4 (1992): 901; A.R. Markos, A.A.H. Wade, and M. Walzman, 'The Adolescent Male Prostitute and Sexually Transmitted Diseases, HIV and AIDS', *Journal of Adolescence* 17 (1994): 123; M.J. Rotheram-Borus, H. Reid, and M. Rosario, 'Factors Mediating Changes in Sexual HIV Risk Behaviors among Gay and Bisexual Male Adolescents', *American Journal of Public Health* 84 (1994): 1938; P.M. Simon, E.V. Morse, P.M. Balson, H.J. Osofsky, and H.R. Gaumer, 'Barriers to Human Immunodeficiency Virus Related Risk Reduction among Male Street Prostitutes', *Health Education Quarterly* 20 (1993): 261; P.M. Simon, E.V. Morse, H.J. Osofsky, and P.M. Balson, 'HIV and Young Male Street Prostitutes: A Brief Report', *Journal of Adolescence* 17 (1994): 193.

197. Morrow, 'Social Work with Gay and Lesbian Adolescents', 658.

198. K. Whitlock, *Bridges of Respect: Creating Support for Lesbian and Gay Youth* (Philadelphia: American Friends Service Committee, 1988), 16.

199. P.A. Rutter and E. Soucar, 'Youth Suicide Risk and Sexual Orientation', *Adolescence* 37 (2002): 289, 291.

200. P. Gibson, 'Gay Male and Lesbian Youth Suicide', in *Prevention and Intervention in Youth Suicide, Report to the Secretary's Task Force on Youth Suicide*, vol. 3, ed. M.R. Feinlieb (Washington, DC: Department of Health and Human Services, 1989), 110.

201. C.D. Proctor and V.K. Groze, 'Risk Factors for Suicide among Gay, Lesbian, and Bisexual Youths', *Social Work* 39 (1994): 504, 504.

202. Ibid.

203. Rutter and Soucar, 'Youth Suicide Risk and Sexual Orientation', 290, citing A.R. D'Augelli and S.L. Hershberger, 'Lesbian, Gay and Bisexual Youth in Community Settings: Personal Challenges and Mental Health Problems', *American Journal of Community Psychology* 21 (1993): 421; S.L. Hershberger, N.W. Pilkington, and A.R. D'Augelli, 'Predictors of Suicide Attempts among Gay, Lesbian, and Bisexual Youth', *Journal of Adolescent Research* 12 (1997): 477; M.J. Rotheram-Borus, J. Piacentini, S. Miller, F. Graae, and D. Castro-Blanco, 'Brief Cognitive Behavioral Treatment for Suicide Attempters and their Families', *Journal of the American Academy for Child and Adolescent Psychiatry* 3 (1994): 508.

204. T.R. Sullivan, 'The Challenge of HIV Prevention among High-Risk Adolescents', *Health and Social Work* 21 (1996): 58, 64.

205. For an account of the Nazi persecution of sexual minorities, see R. Plant, *The Pink Triangle: The Nazi War against Homosexuals* (New York: H. Holt, 1986).

206. Adopted and proclaimed by UN GA Res. 217A(III) of 10 December 1948.

207. Adopted and opened for signature, ratification and accession by UN GA Res. 2200A(XXI) of 16 December 1966 and entered into force on 23 March 1976.

208. Adopted and opened for signature, ratification and accession by UN GA Res. 2200A(XXI) of 16 December 1966 and entered into force on 3 January 1976.

209. See E. Heinze, 'Sexual Orientation and International Law: A Study in the Manufacture of Cross-Cultural "Sensitivity"', *Michigan Journal of International Law* 22 (2001): 283. Cf. E. Heinze, *Sexual Orientation: A Human Right* (Dordrecht: Martinus Nijhoff, 1995).
210. The United States signed the United Nations Convention on the Rights of the Child on 16 February 1995. For a discussion of the reasons for the United States' failure to ratify the Convention, see S. Kilbourne, 'The Wayward Americans – Why the USA Has Not Ratified the UN Convention on the Rights of the Child', *Child and Family Law Quarterly* 10 (1998): 243.
211. Somalia signed the United Nations Convention on the Rights of the Child on 9 May 2002. Somalia's failure to ratify the Convention is likely due to its lack of a functioning central government.
212. United Nations Convention on the Rights of the Child, Art. 1.
213. Article 28(1), ibid., states that 'States Parties recognise the right of the child to education, and with a view to achieving this right progressively and on the basis of equal opportunity, they shall, in particular: (a) Make primary education compulsory and available free to all; (b) Encourage the development of different forms of secondary education, including general and vocational education, make them available and accessible to every child, and take appropriate measures such as the introduction of free education and offering financial assistance in case of need; (c) Make higher education accessible to all on the basis of capacity by every appropriate means; (d) Make educational and vocational information and guidance available and accessible to all children; (e) Take measures to encourage regular attendance at schools and the reduction of drop-out rates.' Article 28(2), ibid., states that 'States Parties shall take all appropriate measures to ensure that school discipline is administered in a manner consistent with the child's human dignity and in conformity with the present Convention.' Article 28(3), ibid., states that 'States Parties shall promote and encourage international cooperation in matters relating to education, in particular with a view to contributing to the elimination of ignorance and illiteracy throughout the world and facilitating access to scientific and technical knowledge and modern teaching methods. In this regard, particular account shall be taken of the needs of developing countries.'
214. Ibid., Art. 29(1).
215. United Nations Committee on the Rights of the Child, *General Comment No. 1: The Aims of Education*, CRC/GC/2001/1, 17 April 2001.
216. On the powers and functions of the United Nations Committee on the Rights of the Child, see United Nations Convention on the Rights of the Child, Arts 43–5.
217. United Nations Committee on the Rights of the Child, *General Comment No. 1*, para. 9.
218. Ibid., para. 2.
219. Ibid., para. 6.
220. Ibid., para. 10.
221. Ibid., para. 19.
222. United Nations Committee on the Rights of the Child, *General Comment No. 4: Adolescent Health and Development in the Context of the Convention on the Rights of the Child*, CRC/GC/2003/4, 1 July 2003.
223. United Nations Convention on the Rights of the Child, Art. 2(1)
224. United Nations Committee on the Rights of the Child, *General Comment No. 4*, para. 6.
225. United Nations Convention on the Rights of the Child, Art. 8(1).
226. Chan, 'No, It is not just a phase'.
227. United Nations Committee on the Rights of the Child, 35th Session, *Concluding Observations: Indonesia*, CRC/C/15/Add.223, 26 February 2004; *Concluding Observations: Guyana*, CRC/C/15/Add.224, 26 February 2004; *Concluding Observations: Armenia*, CRC/C/15/Add.225, 26 February 2004; *Concluding Observations: Germany*, CRC/C/15/Add.226, 26 February 2004; *Concluding Observations: Kingdom of the Netherlands (Netherlands and Aruba)*, CRC/C/15/Add.227, 26 February 2004; *Concluding Observations: India*, CRC/C/15/Add.228, 26 February 2004; *Concluding Observations: Papua New Guinea*, CRC/C/15/Add.229, 26 February 2004; *Concluding Observations: Slovenia*, CRC/C/15/Add.230, 26 February 2004; *Concluding Observations: Japan*, CRC/C/15/Add.231, 26 February 2004; 36th Session, *Concluding Observations: El Salvador*, CRC/C/15/Add.232, 30 June 2004; *Concluding Observations: Panama*, CRC/C/15/Add.233, 30 June 2004; *Concluding Observations: Rwanda*, CRC/C/15/Add.234, 1 July 2004; *Concluding Observations: São Tomé and Príncipe*, CRC/C/15/Add.235, 1 July 2004; *Concluding Observations: Liberia*,

CRC/C/15/Add.236, 1 July 2004; *Concluding Observations: Myanmar*, CRC/C/15/Add.237, 30 June 2004; *Concluding Observations: Dominica*, CRC/C/15/Add.238, 30 June 2004; *Concluding Observations: Democratic People's Republic of Korea*, CRC/C/15/Add.239, 1 July 2004; *Concluding Observations: France*, CRC/C/15/Add.240, 30 June 2004; 37th Session, *Concluding Observations: Brazil*, CRC/C/15/Add.241, 3 November 2004; *Concluding Observations: Botswana*, CRC/C/15/Add.242, 3 November 2004; *Concluding Observations: Croatia*, CRC/C/15/Add.243, 1 October 2004; *Concluding Observations: Kyrgyzstan*, CRC/C/15/Add.244, 3 November 2004; *Concluding Observations: Equatorial Guinea*, CRC/C/15/Add.245, 3 November 2004; *Concluding Observations: Angola*, CRC/C/15/Add.246, 3 November 2004; *Concluding Observations: Antigua and Barbuda*, CRC/C/15/Add.247, 3 November 2004; 38th Session, *Concluding Observations: Sweden*, CRC/C/15/Add.248, 30 March 2005; *Concluding Observations: Albania*, CRC/C/15/Add.249, 31 March 2005; *Concluding Observations: Luxembourg*, CRC/C/15/Add.250, 31 March 2005; *Concluding Observations: Austria*, CRC/C/15/Add.251, 31 March 2005; *Concluding Observations: Belize*, CRC/C/15/Add.252, 31 March 2005; *Concluding Observations: The Bahamas*, CRC/C/15/Add.253, 31 March 2005; *Concluding Observations: Islamic Republic of Iran*, CRC/C/15/Add.254, 31 March 2005; *Concluding Observations: Togo*, CRC/C/15/Add.255, 31 March 2005; *Concluding Observations: Bolivia*, CRC/C/15/Add.256, 11 February 2005; *Concluding Observations: Nigeria*, CRC/C/15/Add.257, 13 April 2005; 39th Session, *Concluding Observations: Saint Lucia*, CRC/C/15/Add.258, 21 September 2005; *Concluding Observations: The Philippines*, CRC/C/15/Add.259, 21 September 2005; *Concluding Observations: Bosnia and Herzegovina*, CRC/C/15/Add.260, 21 September 2005; *Concluding Observations: Nepal*, CRC/C/15/Add.261, 21 September 2005; *Concluding Observations: Ecuador*, CRC/C/15/Add.262, 21 September 2005; *Concluding Observations: Norway*, CRC/C/15/Add.263, 21 September 2005; *Concluding Observations: Mongolia*, CRC/C/15/Add.264, 21 September 2005; *Concluding Observations: Nicaragua*, CRC/C/15/Add.265, 21 September 2005; *Concluding Observations: Costa Rica*, CRC/C/15/Add.266, 21 September 2005; *Concluding Observations: Yemen*, CRC/C/15/Add.267, 21 September 2005; 40th Session, *Concluding Observations: Australia*, CRC/C/15/Add.268, 20 October 2005; *Concluding Observations: Algeria*, CRC/C/15/Add.269, 12 October 2005; *Concluding Observations: Finland*, CRC/C/15/Add.272, 20 October 2005; *Concluding Observations: China (including Hong Kong and Macau Special Administrative Regions)*, CRC/C/CHN/CO/2, 24 November 2005; *Concluding Observations: Denmark*, CRC/C/DNK/CO/3, 23 November 2005; *Concluding Observations: Russian Federation*, CRC/C/RUS/CO/3, 23 November 2005; *Concluding Observations: Uganda*, CRC/C/UGA/CO/2, 23 November 2005; 41st Session, *Concluding Observations: Azerbaijan*, CRC/C/AZE/CO/2, 17 March 2006; *Concluding Observations: Ghana*, CRC/C/GHA/CO/2, 17 March 2006; *Concluding Observations: Hungary*, CRC/C/HUN/CO/2, 17 March 2006; *Concluding Observations: Liechtenstein*, CRC/C/LIE/CO/2, 16 March 2006; *Concluding Observations: Lithuania*, CRC/C/LTU/CO/2, 17 March 2006; *Concluding Observations: Mauritius*, CRC/C/MUS/CO/2, 17 March 2006; *Concluding Observations: Peru*, CRC/C/PER/CO/3, 14 March 2006; *Concluding Observations: Saudi Arabia*, CRC/C/SAU/CO/2, 17 March 2006; *Concluding Observations: Thailand*, CRC/C/THA/CO/2, 17 March 2006; *Concluding Observations: Trinidad and Tobago*, CRC/C/TTO/CO/2, 17 March 2006; 42nd Session, *Concluding Observations: Colombia*, CRC/C/COL/CO/3, 8 June 2006; *Concluding Observations: Latvia*, CRC/C/LVA/CO/2, 28 June 2006; *Concluding Observations: Lebanon*, CRC/C/LBN/CO/3, 8 June 2006; *Concluding Observations: Mexico*, CRC/C/MEX/CO/3, 2 June 2006; *Concluding Observations: Turkmenistan*, CRC/C/TKM/CO/1, 2 June 2006; *Concluding Observations: United Republic of Tanzania*, CRC/C/TZA/CO/2, 21 June 2006; *Concluding Observations: Uzbekistan*, CRC/C/UZB/CO/2, 2 June 2006; 43rd Session, *Concluding Observations: Benin*, CRC/C/BEN/CO/2, 20 October 2006; *Concluding Observations: Ethiopia*, CRC/C/ETH/CO/3, 1 November 2006; *Concluding Observations: Ireland*, CRC/C/IRL/CO/2, 29 September 2006; *Concluding Observations: Jordan*, CRC/C/JOR/CO/3, 29 September 2006; *Concluding Observations: Kiribati*, CRC/C/KIR/CO/1, 29 September 2006; *Concluding Observations: Oman*, CRC/C/OMN/CO/2, 29 September 2006; *Concluding Observations: Republic of the Congo*, CRC/C/COG/CO/1, 20 October 2006; *Concluding Observations: Samoa*, CRC/C/WSM/CO/1, 16 October 2006; *Concluding Observations: Senegal*, CRC/C/SEN/CO/2, 20 October 2006; *Concluding Observations: Swaziland*, CRC/C/SWZ/CO/1, 16

October 2006; 44th Session, *Concluding Observations: Chile*, CRC/C/CHL/CO/3, 23 April 2007; *Concluding Observations: Honduras*, CRC/C/HND/CO/3, 3 May 2007; *Concluding Observations: Kenya*, CRC/C/KEN/CO/2, 19 June 2007; *Concluding Observations: Malaysia*, CRC/C/MYS/CO/1, 2 February 2007; *Concluding Observations: Mali*, CRC/C/MLI/CO/2, 3 May 2007; *Concluding Observations: Marshall Islands*, CRC/C/MHL/CO/2, 19 November 2007; *Concluding Observations: Suriname*, CRC/C/SUR/CO/2, 18 June 2007; 45th Session, *Concluding Observations: Kazakhstan*, CRC/C/KAZ/CO/3, 19 June 2007; *Concluding Observations: The Maldives*, CRC/C/MDV/CO/3, 13 July 2007; *Concluding Observations: Slovakia*, CRC/C/SVK/CO/2, 10 July 2007; *Concluding Observations: Uruguay*, CRC/C/URY/CO/2, 5 July 2007; 46th Session, *Concluding Observations: Venezuela*, CRC/C/VEN/CO/2, 5 October 2007; 47th Session, *Concluding Observations: Dominican Republic*, CRC/C/DOM/CO/2, 11 February 2008; *Concluding Observations: Timor-Leste*, CRC/C/TLS/CO/1, 14 February 2008; 48th Session, *Concluding Observations: Bulgaria*, CRC/C/BGR/CO/2, 23 June 2008; *Concluding Observations: Eritrea*, CRC/C/ERI/CO/3, 23 June 2008; *Concluding Observations: Georgia*, CRC/C/GEO/CO/3, 23 June 2008; *Concluding Observations: Republic of Serbia*, CRC/C/SRB/CO/1, 20 June 2008; *Concluding Observations: Sierra Leone*, CRC/C/SLE/CO/2, 20 June 2008; 49th Session, *Concluding Observations: Bhutan*, CRC/C/BTN/CO/2, 8 October 2008; *Concluding Observations: Djibouti*, CRC/C/DJI/CO/2, 7 October 2008; *Concluding Observations: United Kingdom of Great Britain and Northern Ireland*, CRC/C/GBR/CO/4, 20 October 2008.

228. United Nations Committee on the Rights of the Child, *Indonesia*, paras 61(e) and 63(h); *Germany*, paras 40 and 41(a); *Slovenia*, paras 38–9; *Japan*, paras 6 and 50(b); *Croatia*, paras 37 and 58(h); *Sweden*, paras 4 and 35–6; *Bosnia and Herzegovina*, paras 58(b) and 59(f); *Norway*, paras 39–40; *Australia*, paras 60 and 61(b); *Finland*, paras 46–7; *China (including Hong Kong and Macau)*, paras 76 and 78 (on Hong Kong), and paras 76 and 79 (on Macau); *Denmark*, paras 50–1; *Liechtenstein*, paras 20–1; *Lithuania*, paras 56–7; *Trinidad and Tobago*, para. 59(a); *Latvia*, paras 50 and 51(c); *Ireland*, para. 59(c); *Kazakhstan*, paras 34 and 35(d); *Bulgaria*, para. 29(d); *Georgia*, para. 3(c); *Serbia*, paras 60(h) and 62(c); *United Kingdom*, paras 66(c) and 67(f).

229. United Nations Committee on the Rights of the Child, *China (including Hong Kong and Macau)*, paras 31 and 33 (on Hong Kong); *Samoa*, paras 28–9; *Chile*, paras 29–30; *Malaysia*, para. 31; *Slovakia*, paras 27–8.

230. United Nations Committee on the Rights of the Child, *United Kingdom*, paras 24 and 25(b).

231. It has been estimated that sexual minority adolescents constitute 5–6% of the general adolescent population: Bochenek and Brown, *Hatred in the Hallways*, 24.

232. M. Rosario, J. Hunter, and M.J. Rotheram-Borus, 'HIV Risk Acts of Lesbian Adolescents' (unpublished manuscript, Columbia University), 19, quoted in Savin-Williams, 'Verbal and Physical Abuse as Stressors in the Lives of Lesbian, Gay Male, and Bisexual Youths', 267.

233. M. Minow, 'Rights for the Next Generation: A Feminist Approach to Children's Rights', *Harvard Women's Law Journal* 9 (1986): 1, 24.

234. See Herman, *Trauma and Recovery*, 133–236.

235. Ibid., 200.

236. Needless to say, legal researchers, lawyers, lawmakers and judges in civil law jurisdictions are equally urged to explore how their laws and legal systems may be used to redress and to deter school bullying in general and homophobic school bullying in particular.

237. See, e.g., B. Feldthusen, 'The Civil Action for Sexual Battery: Therapeutic Jurisprudence?', *Ottawa Law Review* 25 (1993): 203; B. Feldthusen, 'Discriminatory Damage Quantification in Civil Actions for Sexual Battery', *University of Toronto Law Journal* 44 (1994): 133; B. Feldthusen, O. Hankivsky, and L. Greaves, 'Therapeutic Consequences of Civil Actions for Damages and Compensation Claims by Victims of Sexual Abuse', *Canadian Journal of Women and the Law* 12 (2000): 66.

238. See, e.g., *A. v. Hoare, C. (F.C.) v. Middlesbrough Council, X. (F.C.) and another (F.C.) v. London Borough of Wandsworth, H. (F.C.) v. Suffolk County Council, Young v. Catholic Care (Diocese of Leeds) and others* [2008] UKHL 6, 30 January 2008 (House of Lords); C. Brennan, '"An Instrument of Injustice"? Child Abuse and the Reform of Limitation Law', *Child and Family Law Quarterly* 18 (2006): 67; M. Fordham, 'Sexual Abuse and the Limitation of Actions in Tort – A Case for Greater Flexibility?', *Singapore Journal of Legal Studies* (2008): 292; J. Mosher, 'Challenging Limitation Periods: Civil

Claims by Adult Survivors of Incest', *University of Toronto Law Journal* 44 (1994): 169; A.C.L. Mullis, 'Compounding the Abuse? The House of Lords, Childhood Sexual Abuse and Limitation Periods', *Medical Law Review* 5 (1997): 22.

239. See in particular *R.* v. *Savage, R.* v. *Parmenter* [1992] 1 AC 699 (House of Lords).

240. For an instructive debate over whether sexual orientation-related hate speech should be held accountable as a criminal offence, see E. Heinze, 'Cumulative Jurisprudence and Human Rights: The Example of Sexual Minorities and Hate Speech', *International Journal of Human Rights* 13 (2009): 193; K. Goodall, 'Challenging Hate Speech: Incitement to Hatred on Grounds of Sexual Orientation in England, Wales and Northern Ireland', *International Journal of Human Rights* 13 (2009), 211.

241. Local Government Act 1988 (c. 9), s. 42(2).

242. Ethical Standards in Public Life etc. (Scotland) Act 2000 (2000 asp 7), s. 36(1) and Sch. 4, para. 1.

243. Local Government Act 2003 (c. 26), s. 127(2) and Sch. 8(1), para. 1.

244. Local Government Act 1986 (c. 10), s. 2A(1), as inserted by Local Government Act 1988 (c. 9), s. 28(1).

245. Adams et al., '"I am the Hate that Dare Not Speak its Name"'; Douglas et al., *Playing it Safe*; I. Warwick, E. Chase, and P. Aggleton, with S. Sanders, *Homophobia, Sexual Orientation and Schools: A Review and Implications for Action* (London: Thomas Coram Research Unit, University of London, 2004).

246. W.M. Evan, 'Law as an Instrument of Social Change', in *Applied Sociology: Opportunities and Problems*, ed. A.W. Gouldner and S.M. Miller (New York: Free Press, 1965), 285, 286 (emphasis in original).

247. *Egan* v. *Canada* (1995) 124 DLR (4th) 609, 619 (per La Forest J., Supreme Court of Canada).

Fighting to fit in: gay–straight alliances in schools under United States jurisprudence

Matthew T. Mercier

JD, University of Virginia School of Law, Charlottesville, USA

Schools in the United States have long sought to limit what students can and cannot say in the school setting. As students across the country have sought to foster safer environments for gay and lesbian students through the creation of gay–straight alliances, many have encountered resistance from their schools' administrations or local school boards. They, however, have not been helpless. American courts have been overwhelmingly supportive of gay and lesbian students and their allies as they have invoked the Equal Access Act and the First Amendment in their fight for equality and inclusion in schools. In examining the status of students' rights to form gay–straight alliances in United States schools under the Equal Access Act and the First Amendment, I explore seminal American cases regarding the formation of gay–straight alliances in schools as the vehicle for exploring the legality, methods, and motivations of school boards' and school districts' attempts to prevent their formation.

Introduction

From *Tinker* to *Morse*, schools in the United States have sought to constrain what students can and cannot say within their walls.[1] Whether it was John Tinker's black armband worn to school to symbolise his objection to American involvement in Vietnam or Joseph Frederick's unfurling of a large banner reading 'BONG HiTS 4 JESUS' across from his high school during a school event, school officials have not been shy in taking administrative actions against students who discuss issues or express viewpoints that they deem inappropriate or undesirable.[2] Students, however, have been equally assertive in invoking their First Amendment rights, often turning to the courts for relief. Controversies over student speech and expression in schools are far from recent.

It is not difficult to comprehend that as students have sought to form school groups that deal with issues specific to gay and lesbian youth in schools across the United States, tensions with school officials have been a familiar occurrence. Indeed, a school group that even tangentially deals with issues of student sexuality is likely to be subjected to increased scrutiny from school officials. As gay–straight alliances (GSAs) have gone from being a rarity in the late 1980s to rather commonplace today, the formation of them in schools has already spawned a number of court battles. From *Bowers* to *Lawrence*, as the pursuit of equal rights for gays and lesbians has shifted its focus from rights in the private realm to rights of equal participation and expression in the public realm, the inclusion of GSAs in schools has become a particularly salient issue.[3] The convergence of considerations of free speech rights, youth, sexuality, and, for some, religion creates ideal conditions for conflict. While the legal outcome of the struggle by gay and gay-friendly youth to create a safe forum in America's schools to discuss their concerns is not completely certain, their cause has thus far proved to be compelling and largely successful. The legal framework supporting the formation of GSAs is still not fully settled, courts thus far reaching varying conclusions about the legality and constitutionality of school districts' efforts to ban the formation of GSAs, and employing wholly different reasoning in doing so.[4]

This paper will explore the status of United States students' rights to form GSAs in schools under the Equal Access Act (EAA) and the First Amendment. It will examine the legality, methods, and motivations of school boards' and school districts' attempts to prevent the meeting of GSAs on school premises. This will be accomplished through thorough analysis, comparison, and contrast of free speech claims brought by students attempting to form GSAs in their schools. Though case law is not yet well developed, a federal district court judge noting in a 2000 lawsuit that it was apparently only the fourth in the nation regarding GSAs,[5] clear and consistent patterns of legal theories, defences, and outcomes have emerged. Finally, this paper will carry out this legal analysis within the unique framework of the gay rights movement and discuss the extent to which decisions of schools and judges are motivated by the message of GSAs and a desire to suppress it.

Gay–straight alliances: the contours of a concept

While GSAs have been in existence in America's schools since 1988,[6] widespread litigation of students' rights to form GSAs and gain access to school resources for meeting and organisational purposes through the EAA and the First Amendment began to appear in the mid-1990s. An examination of the geographical locations where these disputes have arisen suggests that this increase in litigation is partially the result of increased student assertiveness to form GSAs in locales where their message is most controversial. Accordingly, we see recent litigation in Utah, Texas, central Florida, and Minnesota, and an absence of such litigation in more liberal parts of the country. Finally, the invalidation of sodomy laws (in the 13 remaining states with such laws on the statute books) by *Lawrence v. Texas*[7] now precludes states from arguing that allowing GSAs to meet on school premises and using school resources would be tantamount to implicit approval of criminal behaviour.

At issue in much of the litigation between GSA proponents and opposing local school boards is the purpose and activities of GSAs. An argument that is repeatedly proffered by hostile school boards is that a GSA's primary function is to articulate pro-sex and anti-abstinence views, and accordingly that those groups are inappropriate for a school audience.[8] A closer examination reveals, however, that in reality the functions of GSAs are much more nuanced and rarely place emphasis on sex. Gay–straight alliances primarily focus on 'anti-[gay, lesbian, bisexual, and transgender] name calling, bullying, and harassment' of sexual minority students, as well as fostering a general atmosphere of respect and tolerance for all students.[9] Additionally, GSAs engage in organising awareness and con-sciousness-raising events, such as the National Day of Silence.[10] As will be demonstrated in this paper, the objection of local school boards to the formation of GSAs and their attempts to prevent recognition of GSAs represent not an equal and neutral application of existing legal principles, but rather an ad hoc, ex post attempt to justify what is purely content and viewpoint discrimination.

In the instances in which school boards have attempted to prevent the formation of GSAs, one sees a familiar pattern of school board actions. The extreme measures that school boards are willing to take to prevent GSAs from organising and meeting on school premises reveal that the deep animus of local communities and school board officials towards gay and lesbian individuals is in fact the driving force behind their actions. Indeed, it is certainly not uncommon for school officials to ignore or even participate in harassment of gay and lesbian students.[11] The factual background of *White County High School Peers Rising in Diverse Education* v. *White County School District* is chiefly characteristic of the type of situation that gives rise to GSA litigation. [12]

In *White*, a group of high school students in a rural Georgia community sought to form a GSA at their school. While the administration initially denied the request, it later agreed to allow formation of the group conditional upon a list of stringent requirements. Among those conditions was submission of a list to the principal of all students who would be a member of the organisation, a condition imposed solely on the GSA and not on other student organ-isations.[13] Upon renaming the organisation and expanding its mission to include anti-bullying measures inclusive of all students (not just bullying based on actual or perceived sexual orientation), the school allowed the student group to meet for the remainder of the academic year.[14] The following year, however, in what can only be seen as an attempt to disallow the GSA from meeting on school premises, the school board adopted a measure whereby *all* non-curricular school groups were prevented from meeting on school premises.[15] Despite the implementation of this ban, several non-curricular groups, including Cheerleaders, Dance Team, and Student Council, were permitted to meet on school premises during non-instructional time, while the GSA was not.[16] The students thus sued alleging, *inter alia*, violation of EAA rights and First Amendment freedom of speech rights. Charac-teristic of much GSA litigation is the attempt by school boards to prevent GSAs from meeting by the extreme measure of banning *all* 'non-curricular' groups from meeting on school premises. Schools wishing to only actually ban GSAs, however, attempt to articulate a definition of 'curricular' that would include groups such as cheerleaders, Future Home-makers of America, and other traditional school groups, and exclude only the GSA.

Having a fundamental knowledge of the context in which students attempt to form GSAs, schools' attempts to ban them, and the types of claims which students may bring, I now proceed to a legal analysis of seminal GSA cases, and their implications.

Caudillo: a legal framework for excluding GSAs

While proponents of GSAs have been largely successful in establishing the right to form GSAs and use school resources based on the EAA and the First Amendment, *Caudillo* v. *Lubbock Independent School District*,[17] a 2004 case before the Federal District Court for the Northern District of Texas, provides us with an example of the legal framework articulated for upholding a school district's ban on the formation of a GSA. Though the court validated the Lubbock Independent School District's denial of students' rights to form a GSA, it is unclear, based on subsequent legal developments, whether the result could be reached today.

The plaintiff students in *Caudillo* sought to form a GSA and the right to distribute fliers on school premises, gain access to the school's public address system, and be recognised as an extracurricular organisation.[18] As the defendants stipulated that the school had created a limited open forum, thus triggering the EAA, it was incumbent on the school board officials to demonstrate that they had not engaged in content-based discrimination. This stood in stark contrast to the legal strategy used by other schools where the school denied the fact that it had created a limited open forum, thus shifting the legal burden to plaintiff students to establish the relatedness of their group to the school curriculum.[19]

The Equal Access Act, Title 20 USCA §§ 4071–4, enacted by Congress in 1984, and upheld by the Supreme Court in 1990 in the context of a school denying extracurricular group status to a Christian student organisation,[20] provides in pertinent part:

§ 4071. Denial of equal access prohibited

(a) Restriction of limited open forum on basis of religious, political, philosophical, or other speech content prohibited

It shall be unlawful for any public secondary school which receives Federal financial assistance and which has a limited open forum to deny equal access or a fair opportunity to, or discriminate against, any students who wish to conduct a meeting within that limited open forum on the basis of the religious, political, philosophical, or other content of the speech at such meetings.

(b) 'Limited open forum' defined

A public secondary school has a limited open forum whenever such school grants an offering to or opportunity for one or more noncurriculum related student groups to meet on school premises during noninstructional time.

Thus the fact that the school stipulated that a limited open forum existed triggered the EAA, meaning that no student group could be denied equal treatment or be discriminated against on the basis of the content of the student group's speech.[21] A school may wish to readily admit the existence of a limited open forum in order to allow it to continue to permit traditional but non-curricular groups (such as cheerleaders) to meet on school premises without running foul of content neutrality requirements. Though upon cursory examination it appeared that GSA proponents would be successful with their claim based on the EAA's promise of content-neutral school policies, the defendant school district sought refuge in the numerous exceptions found in the EAA.

While the EAA generally requires decisions regarding the formation of school groups to be content neutral, a school need not provide equal access where doing so would 'sanction meetings that are otherwise unlawful', prevent the school from 'maintain[ing] order and discipline on school premises', or prevent the school from 'protect[ing] the well-being of students'.[22] Of great importance, and perhaps essential to the court's ultimate holding in *Caudillo*, is that when the students brought their claim, though not at the time Judge Cummings ultimately issued the court decision, Texas still maintained a sodomy statue that forbade sexual acts between persons of the same sex.[23] Additionally, Texas criminalised all sex between minors of the same sex and sex between minors of different sexes more than three years apart in age.[24] Finally, the Lubbock Independent School District itself had a strict policy of abstinence-only sex education.

Among the original material GSA proponents sought approval to distribute included a link to <http://www.gay.com>, which contained frank discussion of same-sex sexual activity, contraception, and other material that the court concluded as a matter of law to be lewd, indecent, and obscene.[25] This finding had the effect of precluding the students' First Amendment claim, as the court concluded that such material was not protected by the First Amendment, particularly in the context of a secondary school. As the determinations of the court were necessarily subjective and dependant upon the 'average person, applying community standards',[26] the First Amendment rights of students wishing to distribute material dealing with sex and sexuality will vary geographically. As discussed above, this conditioning of rights on community standards necessarily means that litigation dealing with GSAs will be more likely to occur in more conservative locales where the average person in the community would find the material a GSA seeks to distribute to be indecent and lewd.[27]

Even assuming the material in question not to be lewd, indecent, and obscene, the court was willing to find the Lubbock Independent School District's limitation to be permissible under First Amendment jurisprudence. The court began with the premise, as articulated in *Perry*,[28] that in the context of a limited public forum the First Amendment requires only that it be neutral with respect to viewpoints. The significance of this is that a school may suppress the expression of certain content by suppressing discussion of the entire subject matter, rather than individual viewpoints on that subject. Accordingly, because the entire subject of sexual activity was banned, the court found the school's actions to be constitutionally appropriate in denying GSA members to espouse any particular viewpoint of sexuality. This conclusion, however, only follows if one construes the teaching of abstinence not to be a viewpoint regarding sexuality. It is doubtful that if a Christian group at the school had attempted to organise an abstinence pledge, the school would have sought to disband the group for its discussion of sexual activity.

The determination of lewdness or indecency, as well as illegality of the conduct advocated, had serious implications for the *Caudillo* EAA analysis as well. First, because of the criminal nature of sodomy in Texas at the time, a GSA that distributed information with links to material that discussed criminal conduct was susceptible to characterisation by the school board as undeserving of EAA protection. Yet it is not readily clear that the distribution alone (absent actual likelihood that illegal conduct will take place) even constitutes the sanctioning 'of a meeting that is otherwise illegal'. Paragraph (c)(4) of Section 4071 of the EAA, however, provides in addition that a school need not provide equal access to meetings that would 'materially' or 'substantially' interfere with the orderly conduct of education activities within the school'. Because the school had made an educational decision to maintain an abstinence-only policy with respect to sex, the distribution of materials that espoused a contrary view was deemed to interfere with the school's education goals.

Regarding the EAA's student well-being exception, the court found that exposing students, some as young as 12 years old, to material about sexual activity and sexually transmitted diseases would endanger student welfare by increasing the likelihood that students would be exposed to sexually transmitted infections. Furthermore, the defendants asserted, and the court agreed, that exposing young students to material about sexual activity was in itself detrimental to well-being.[29] Lastly, in what seems to be the most shocking rationale, the court accepted the defendants' paternalistic and circular view that it was necessary to prevent the formation of the GSA because allowing the students to form the group would subject its members to harassment, potentially subjecting the school to liability for failing to prevent harassment of students based on their sexual orientation. Such a view equates to a heckler's veto, with disapproval of a particular viewpoint by some as grounds for completely barring a controversial school group. It seems completely implausible that in another context (religion, say,) a court would permit a school to deny equal access to, say, a fundamentalist Christian group because they might be subjected to harassment as a result of their membership. Whatever Congress meant in enacting school anti-discrimination legislation in Title IX, 20 USC § 1681(a), on which the court relied, it seems wholly improbable that it meant to allow schools to ban student groups on the basis that group participation would subject members to harassment. If anything, the court completely stood Congressional intent on its head in this instance.

If the real fault with the GSA was in fact their distribution of material dealing with frank discussion of sex, it is unclear why the remedy should not simply have been forbidding the GSA from discussing or distributing sexual material, rather than allowing the school to completely bar the group from meeting on school premises. Such a remedy could only be logically imposed if a judge believed that *any* activity that a GSA engaged in would necessarily be sex based. Yet other courts have validated GSAs as performing functions wholly unrelated to sex, such as anti-bullying activities, creation of a safe space for gay and lesbian youth,[30] and organising a day of silence.[31]

It is equally puzzling that Judge Cummings placed so much reliance on Texas's criminalisation of sodomy when his decision was issued almost a full year after *Lawrence*. In Judge Cummings's opinion, the briefest of treatment was given to the fact that at the time of the decision the state's sodomy law was already invalidated and much of the decision's rationale undermined by this fact. Considering the great extent to which the decision relied on the criminalisation of same-sex sexual acts, it is simply not clear to what extent *Caudillo* remains good law in the Northern District of Texas, and as a precedent in the United States. Finally, the court made an obvious error in finding that the issue presented was one entirely novel to any court; it wrongly noted that other cases finding for plaintiffs did not present circumstances where the school had an abstinence-only policy. Yet in *Colin*, which the court specifically cited, the school did in fact have an abstinence-only policy, teaching 'the benefits of abstinence, including it being the only totally effective prevention method'.[32] Though *Caudillo* seemed to give broad latitude to school districts in barring GSAs as extracurricular groups, and a number of rationales by which to do so, an examination of case law indicates that *Caudillo* is very much in the minority and represents a significantly lesser threat to the First Amendment rights of gay and lesbian students than is immediately apparent.

By conceding to the existence of a 'limited open forum' in its school, the Lubbock Independent School District necessarily subjected itself to the requirements of the EAA, namely the requirement that the school not 'deny equal access or a fair opportunity, or discriminate against' students on the basis of 'religious, political, philosophical' or other content to students seeking access to that limited open forum.[33] In *East High School PRISM Club* v. *Seidel*, however, the school board explicitly denied that it had created a 'limited open forum' as defined by the EAA, in an effort to limit the scope of permissible school clubs to those that were 'directly related to the curriculum'.[34] Doing so would prevent students from bringing an EAA challenge, and leave only the possibility of a First Amendment viewpoint discrimination claim. Though not explicitly stated in the opinion, the fact that this curriculum-related-only policy regarding school clubs was adopted in 1996, a time when the first wave of GSA litigation was just beginning, suggests that this policy was adopted with the goal of prohibiting the formation of a GSA at East High School.[35] Having asserted that a limited open forum had not been created (for the purpose of excluding GSAs), the challenge for the school board became to articulate a standard of curriculum-relatedness that would exclude a GSA but allow other extracurricular groups, such as the Vegetarian Club, the Polynesian Club, and the CHARABANC Club (a Salt Lake City culture club). Merely setting the standard for forming a school club at curriculum-relatedness is not enough, however, and the United States Supreme Court has held that schools must proffer substantive standards for allowing and excluding specific clubs.[36] The very purpose of this requirement is to ensure that schools do not engage the very 'post hoc rationalization' and 'shifting or illegitimate criteria' that they have been so willing to do in order to exclude GSAs from their schools.[37]

The standards for determining whether a prospective student group was in fact curriculum related, as articulated by the school board in *Seidel*, required that:

1. The subject matter of the groups is actually taught or soon will be taught in a regular course; or

2. The subject matter of the group concerns the body of courses as a whole; or
3. Participation in the group is required for a particular course, or results in academic credit.[38]

With these standards in place, a potential student group submits a form to a school district official, listing goals, objectives, and activities of the club as well as the basis for its curriculum-relatedness (e.g. if the club relates to subject matter actually taught, the form must include to what courses, and specifically to what course objectives, the student club will be related). In its application for club status, PRISM (People Recognizing Important Social Movements)[39] argued that its subject matter was 'actually taught'.[40] The club was intentioned to expand on the body of information taught in 'American History, government, law, and sociology', serving as 'a prism through which historical and current events, institutions, and culture can be viewed in terms of the impact, experience, and contributions of gays and lesbians'.[41] The school's ultimate denial of PRISM's application for club status was based on what school officials asserted was implicit in the curriculum-relatedness standard itself, 'that the *subject matter* of the club not be too narrow'.[42] Yet this is exactly the kind of post hoc rationalisation of a student group access denial decision that the requirement that written standards be promulgated seeks to prevent.

The court's analysis of the plaintiff's claim therefore focused on whether the no-narrowing requirement in fact was implicit in the school district's standards, as well as whether all school groups (and not just PRISM) were equally subject to the alleged no-narrowing requirement. In looking to the text of the written policies of the Salt Lake City School District, taken in conjunction with the cross-examination of the Salt Lake City School District Superintendent at trial, where the Superintendent stated that the standards required nothing above the fact that 'the subject matter of the club be directly related',[43] the court was forced to the reasonable conclusion that no such no-narrowing principle in fact existed, implicitly or explicitly, within the school district's standards. The more interesting inquiry, however, was the extent to which the no-narrowing principle the school asserted had been equally applied. While the court took note of denial of group status of SADD (Students Against Drunk Driving) and the Women's Studies Club (WSC), it summarily determined that these dismissals did not demonstrate the existence of a no narrowing of the subject matter rule.[44]

However, the court did find instructive on the subject of equal application the fact that group status was granted to the Polynesian Club and CHARABANC. The Polynesian Club based its meeting the curriculum-relatedness test on the teaching of the Tongan language.[45] Yet the fit between Polynesia and the Tongan language is far from perfect. The subject of Polynesia is much broader than Tonga and the Tongan language. Similarly, focusing on the Tongan language only to the extent that it is spoken in Polynesia, 'to the exclusion of other Tongan-speakers world-wide',[46] should implicate the no-narrowing rule.

An even-handed application of the no narrowing of subject matter rule should have in fact excluded the Polynesian Club from being recognised by the school. Similarly, CHARABANC Humanities Club, with the ostensible goal of appreciating the humanities taught in school through outings solely in Salt Lake City, should seemingly have been barred by equal application of the alleged no-narrowing rule as well. The court also firmly rejected a viewpoint-neutral/non-neutral distinction between PRISM and the Polynesian Club and CHARBANC Club, for if PRISM was viewpoint selective because it primarily concerned itself with gay and lesbian issues, then the Polynesian Club and CHARABANC Club were viewpoint exclusive in focusing on solely Polynesian Tongan and Salt Lake City humanities, respectively.[47] Therefore, even assuming the existence of a no-narrowing rule, the school had arguably run afoul of that standard and selectively applied it to single out and exclude gay-positive viewpoints. Ultimately, the post hoc articulation of the no-narrowing rule was found to be no more than a selectively employed method of creating a legal framework for viewpoint discrimination, which thus ought to fail.

The court's comparison of the application of the no-narrowing rule to the Polynesian Club and the CHARBANC Club with the application to PRISM, though interesting, side-stepped that actual rationale for a finding for the plaintiffs. As the requested relief in *Seidel* was an injunction requiring recognition of PRISM and allowing it equal access to school resources, the court only concluded that an injunction was proper because of PRISM's sub-stantial likelihood of success on the merits.[48] It is not clear, however, on what grounds the court believed that PRISM would have ultimately succeeded. The requested relief in most GSA cases is injunctive in nature, and after an injunction is initially granted based on like-lihood of success on the merits, many schools simply choose to discontinue their legal opposition to GSAs.[49] The end result, however, is that the specific legal rationales requiring that GSAs are allowed to meet are not fully developed, since the actual merits analysis is ultimately not carried out. Thus, in *Seidel*, it is not clear the rationale forbidding exclusion of PRISM was whether, (1) though not intending to, the school created a limited open forum by allowing non-curricular groups to meet (Polynesian Club and CHARBANC), and thus was subject to EAA requirements forbidding them from limiting access based on political or philosophical content; or, (2) though no limited open forum was created, the no-narrowing standard articulated post hoc by school officials as a reason for denying PRISM club status was not implicit in the actual promulgated standards and was applied in a manner that impermissibly constituted viewpoint discrimination barred by the First Amendment. As the court engaged in very little discussion of the EAA or the creation of a limited open forum, a reasonable conclusion is that the rationale behind its grant of relief was the latter, even as the former would seem to have been equally appropriate and sound. The relief requested, the procedural posture, and the unwillingness of many school districts to further litigate the matter create a lack of clear and concise case law on the matter, and may explain the case-by-case manner in which GSA issues are litigated.

In reading *Caudillo* and *Seidel* together, however, the distinction between a limited open forum and a closed forum seems more theoretical, as it has little bearing on the ulti-mate outcome of the cases. In fact, paradoxically, in *Seidel*, where the court found there to be no open limited open forum, the plaintiffs fared better than in *Caudillo*, where, although defendants admitted the existence of a limited open forum, they lost. On a larger scale, however, the courts' general intolerance and disdain for blatant viewpoint discrimination has consistently translated into rulings in favour of GSAs. The importance of the distinction between a limited open forum and a closed forum is simply outweighed by considerations of viewpoint neutrality, making the EAA less important in GSA cases than would first seem apparent.

Colin: a clear application of limited open forum analysis

While the exact legal theory upon which the success of the plaintiffs in *Seidel* was predi-cated was not clearly articulated, the *Colin* court, in contrast, put forth a straightforward limited open forum analysis. The plaintiffs in *Colin* submitted the routine paperwork for the purpose of establishing the Gay–Straight Alliance Club of El Modena High School. The way in which school officials treated the group, however, was far from customary. Plaintiff Colin and a friend desired to form a GSA in the wake of the attack on Matthew Shepherd on the basis of his sexual orientation. The ostensible purpose of their organisation was to promote tolerance and fight homophobia.[50] Gay–Straight Alliance Club proponents experienced great delays in their application for approval and received notice from the school principal that the proposed name was inappropriate, with suggestions of alternatives such as 'The Alliance' and 'Tolerance Club'.[51] No other proposed school group was subjected to similar scrutiny, delays, or required name change.[52] The school board ultimately denied the plaintiffs' request to form a GSA, allegedly for the inappropriate sexually charged nature of the club, though statements of school board members gave clearer suggestions about the motivating factors behind the board's denial.[53] The plaintiffs then filed a lawsuit asserting violations of their rights under the EAA and the First Amendment.[54]

The EAA was clearly applicable in this instance, as the El Modena School Board had an explicit policy of allowing curriculum- *and* non-curriculum-related groups to meet using school resources.[55] Indeed, the existence of a limited open forum was clear, with groups such as 'Asian Club', 'Black Student Union', 'Christian Club', and 'Gentleman's Club' meeting at the school.[56] The presence of a limited open forum in the school triggered EAA protection. In an initial effort to legally justify the denial of Colin's group, the school board proffered a tortured statutory construction of the EAA. It asserted that the curriculum-relatedness or -non-relatedness distinction was important in determining not only whether a limited open forum had been created in the first place, but also whether a given group was protected by the EAA where a limited open forum had been created. According to the school, where a limited open forum had been created, only non-curriculum-related groups were protected under the EAA, and the GSA in question was a curriculum-related group. Yet the language of the EAA, Title 20 USC § 4071(a), offers protection to 'any students who wish[es] to conduct a meeting within the limited open forum' and makes no distinction between curriculum- and non-curriculum-related groups once EAA protection is triggered. Though the court easily disposed of this illogical construction of the EAA,[57] the school's argument was yet another example of attempted post hoc rationalisation of illegal content discrimination.

The defendants found their final rationalisation of the exclusion of the GSA in the EAA itself as well. Because the EEA does not provide protection to student groups that 'non-school persons ... direct, conduct [or] control', the school argued that the similarity between the student group name 'Gay–Straight Alliance Club' and the name 'GLSEN' (Gay, Lesbian, and Straight Education Network; a national organisation seeking to counter homophobia in schools) was indicative of control or direction from an outside organisation.[58] This argument too was easily disposed of. Even assuming that a school club is not protected by the EAA merely because it shares the name of an outside organisation (the court articulated that something more substantial than a similar name must be proffered to infer outside control or direct), the school had unevenly applied the requirement, overlooking other school groups that shared names or were affiliated with a national organisation, such as Red Cross/Key Club and Movimiento Estudiantil Chicano de Aztlán.[59] Presented with an ample array of evidence, the court found not just 'content-based denial of student recognition, but a pattern of delay and discrimination against the Plaintiffs on the basis of sexual orientation or perceived sexual orientation'.[60]

The clearest articulation at the US Court of Appeals level of treating groups unequally within a limited open forum came from the Eight Circuit in *SAGE* (Students and Gays for Equality) v. *Osseo*.[61] At the district level, the court granted a preliminary injunction allowing SAGE to meet based on an EAA theory. The underlying claim was a violation of the EAA and the First Amendment in treating other non-curricular groups more favourably than SAGE, namely by allowing those non-curricular groups use of the school public address system, the school yearbook, the 'scrolling screen', and other school resources.[62]

The district court, pointing to the more favourable access granted to the non-curricular synchronised swimming and cheerleading groups to school resources, found substantial likelihood that the plaintiffs would prevail on the merits of their EAA claim. The defendants appealed, arguing that, given the physical education curriculum of the school, synchronised swimming and cheerleading were in fact curriculum related and could validly be granted more access to school resources than non-curriculum-related groups.[63] Though the Eighth Circuit court defined the contours of curriculum-relatedness in substantially the same manner as the policy in *Seidel*, its application of the standard was more rigid than that by the *Seidel* court. Ironically, the Eighth Circuit read into those policies a standard similar to the no-narrowing standard that the *Seidel* defendants alleged unsuccessfully was implicit in the curriculum-relatedness standards, but it still found for the plaintiffs.

The most interesting and unique portion of the Eighth Circuit court's opinion, however, was its offering of suggested alternatives to the legal situation in which the court's ruling left the school. First, the court noted that the school was 'free to wipe out all of its noncurriculum related student groups and totally close its forum'.[64] If the school ultimately wishes to exclude the GSA, however, simply abolishing the limited open forum and allowing only curriculum-related groups may not be a viable alternative. The Eighth Circuit did not address the possibility of the GSA in question being considered curriculum related, but *Seidel* articulated a conceptual theory for finding the GSA to be in fact curriculum related and illustrated the plausibility of a court doing so. Accordingly, the court's first alternative may in practice simply be inadequate. Its application of a curriculum-relatedness standard less stringent than the *Seidel* defendants' proposed no-narrowing rule but more rigorous than the standard the *Seidel* court actually adopted may mean that, should the issue arise in the future, courts within the Eighth Circuit would find GSAs not to be curriculum related. Ultimately, however, the scant legal analysis the court leaves us with is inconclusive on the matter.

Second, the court stated that its holding 'does not prevent [the school] from legitimately categorizing cheerleading, synchronized swimming, and any other athletic groups as "curriculum related" by granting physical education academic credit to students who participate in such groups'.[65] This solution too may be an inadequate means by which the school may legitimately prevent the formation of a GSA. Enacting school policy changes so that swimming and cheerleading clubs relate to curriculum simply means that the school has closed its forum. This is simply a more roundabout way of getting to the court's first alternative. As in the first instance, this would still not preclude characterisation of a GSA as curriculum related, requiring the school to permit the group to meet. Additionally, even if a school modifies its policies to make all previously non-curriculum-related groups curriculum related, with the exception of the GSA, plaintiffs still may succeed on a pure First Amendment theory of pretextual actions to effect viewpoint discrimination.[66] Though the Eighth Circuit offered school officials what it believed to be viable alternatives to permitting the GSA access to school resources, the body of pertinent case law in other jurisdictions suggests that those alternatives may be merely theoretical in nature and unavailable in practice.

Modern trends and the limiting of *Caudillo*

Though litigation regarding GSAs in schools is indeed a recent phenomenon, a clear and consistent pro-free-expression trend has developed, with only the *Caudillo* court finding against the plaintiff GSA. The case-by-case nature of these disputes, a result of the procedural posture of the litigation and the reluctance of school boards to continue litigation after unfavourable grants of preliminary injunctions, means the presence of GSAs in the United States' schools will continue to be litigated. The issuance of a preliminary injunction by a federal district court in Florida in April 2007 illustrated the current nature of this issue.[67] *Gay–Straight Alliance of Okeechobee High School* (*GSA of OHS*) exemplified the extent to which subsequent courts have severely limited and undermined the rationale of *Caudillo*.

In *GSA of OHS*, Okeechobee High School initially delayed and subsequently denied the GSA access to the school's admitted limited open forum.[68] The defendant school board, after initial significant delay, predicated its denial of GSA access to its limited open forum on the rationale of the *Caudillo* court, specifically that the school could legally deny access to its limited open forum by a 'sex-based' club based on the school's interest in maintaining order, discipline, and protecting the well-being of its students.[69] The *GSA of OHS* court found the *Caudillo* rationale distinguishable, however, in that the GSA in question was not 'sex-based', but rather that it specifically denoted in its charter that it did not seek to advocate or discuss sex.[70] Although the court noted that this was a distinction from rather than a rejection of *Caudillo*, its logic has had an equally expansive effect in practice. If students wish to form a GSA, they simply may state in their charter that the group will not discuss or advocate sex, but instead will seek to accomplish some other purpose, such as promoting tolerance, addressing homophobia, or creating a safe space in which vulnerable students may meet. The ease with which GSAs may circumvent the rationale underlying the *Caudillo* decision may in part explain why there have been few if any decisions against GSAs since *Caudillo*. In July 2008, in a major victory for GSAs, an order was issued in *GSA of OHS* requiring that the School Board of Okeechobee County offer the GSA of OHS 'all attendant benefits uniformly afforded to each of [the school's] noncurricular student groups'.[71]

Conclusion

The requirement that schools articulate written standards regarding their student club policies serves the purpose of preventing schools from engaging in post hoc rationalisation of discrimination based on the content or viewpoint of the prospective club. The legal battles that have ensued between students seeking to form GSAs and the schools seeking to prevent their formation must be understood in the context of the larger sexual minority rights movement, as students are seeking to establish a group that discusses content and articulates a viewpoint (acceptance and tolerance of sexual minority individuals) of which many individuals and communities disapprove. The courts have more often than not been willing to side with GSA proponents, within certain limits, using a variety of rationales. First, where schools maintain a limited open forum, courts (with the exception of *Caudillo*) have found it impermissible to deny GSAs access to school resources while allowing other non-curriculum-related groups access. Second, even where schools have not created a limited open forum, thus not triggering the EAA, courts have been willing to read 'curriculum related' in a manner that includes GSAs. Finally, where the totality of the circumstances suggested that facially neutral school policies were implemented solely to prevent the formation of GSAs, the courts have hinted that sufficient evidence of such a situation could support a finding of a First Amendment violation. It appears that the courts simply find pure content and viewpoint discrimination intolerable, whatever the form.

While it seems that jurisprudence regarding issues of the rights of gays and lesbians may have departed from the jurisprudence that would apply to other groups in the school context, the courts' intolerance of discrimination against GSAs indicates that the 'gay exception' may be disappearing. In fact, the *Colin* court declared that 'if [the court] were to allow the School Board to deny recognition to the Gay–Straight Alliance, it would be guilty of the current evil of "judicial activism', carving out an exception from the bench to the statute enacted by the politically accountable Congress ... it would be complicit in the discrimination against students who want to raise awareness about homophobia and discuss how to deal with harassment directed towards gay youth'.[72] As the GSA question continues to play out in America's communities, one can only hope that the courts will rise to the challenge and eradicate impermissible content and viewpoint discrimination wherever found.

Acknowledgements

The author would like to acknowledge the support of University of Virginia School of Law Professor Robert M. O'Neil in the preparation of this paper.

Notes

1. *Tinker* v. *Des Moines Independent Community School District*, 393 US 503 (1969); *Morse* v. *Frederick*, 127 S. Ct. 2618 (2007).
2. *Tinker*, ibid.; *Morse*, ibid.
3. Sonia K. Katyal, 'Sexuality and Sovereignty: The Global Limits and Possibilities of *Lawrence*', *William and Mary Bill of Rights Law Journal* 14 (2006): 1429.
4. See *East High Gay/Straight Alliance* v. *Board of Education*, 81 F.Supp. 2d 1166 (1999), finding that an East High School's GSA's rights under the EAA were violated. Cf. *Caudillo* v. *Lubbock Independent High School District*, 311 F.Supp.2d 550 (2004), holding that the school district's denial of permission to form a GSA was not impermissible viewpoint discrimination under the EAA or the First Amendment.
5. *Colin* v. *Orange Unified School District*, 83 F.Supp.2d 1135 (2000), 1139.
6. GLSEN, 'FAQs about Student Organizing', http://www.glsen.org/cgi-bin/iowa/all/news/record/1876.html (accessed 24 December 2008).
7. See *Lawrence* v. *Texas*, 539 US 558 (2003), invalidating sodomy statues remaining in force in Texas, Kansas, Oklahoma, Missouri, Alabama, Florida, Idaho, Louisiana, Mississippi, North Carolina, South Carolina, Utah, and Virginia. It is no coincidence that many of the states in which modern GSA litigation has arisen are states that had sodomy laws in effect until 2003. These states expressed a legislative policy of hostility towards sexual minority individuals, presumably a reflection of the general social attitudes of the states' populations, thus making it more likely that school boards and communities in those states could and would display hostility towards groups that treat sexual diversity in a positive manner.
8. The anti-abstinence until marriage view – a view that school boards assert GSA will contradict – is itself problematic and is another example of the way in which sexual minority youth are simply excluded from the life-goal paradigm that routinely exists in high schools. While schools teach abstinence until marriage as the primary form of sex education, with the exception of Massachusetts, California, and possibly New York, such a system assumes away the existence of sexual minority youth who find themselves in a jurisdiction where marriage with the person of their choice is simply not an option.
9. GLSEN, 'FAQs about Student Organizing'.
10. The National Day of Silence entails sexual minority students and their allies wearing a tee-shirt expressing acceptance and tolerance of sexual minority individuals. Additionally, students may remain silent for the duration of the school day to raise awareness to the oppression that sexual minority students endure on a daily basis. This practice has spawned organised as well as ad hoc opposition, primarily from religious students, whereby those students themselves wear tee-shirts condemning homosexuality and sexual minority students. Some schools, in turn, have sought to prevent students from wearing clothing that depicts other students in a threatening, derogatory, or demeaning manner. For a sampling of the legal treatment of this practice, see *Zamecnik ex rel. Zamecnik* v. *Indian Prairie School District*, Slip Copy, 2007 WL 1141597 (N.D.Ill.), denying a request for an injunction by students wishing to wear clothing that expressed opposition to homosexuality, on the grounds that students had a right not to be verbally, or graphically,

attacked on the basis of core identifying characteristics such as sexual orientation, race, gender, etc. Cf. *Nixon* v. *Northern Local School District Board of Education*, 383 F. Supp.2d. 965 (2005), granting an injunction requiring a school to allow a student to wear a tee-shirt with the message 'Homosexuality is a sin ... some issues are just black and white'.

11. Phil C. W. Chan, 'No, it is not just a Phase: An Adolescent's Right to Sexual Minority Identity under the United Nations Convention on the Rights of the Child', *International Journal of Human Rights* 10 (2006): 165.

12. *White County High School Peers Rising in Diverse Education* v. *White County School District*, Order, Civil Action No. 2:06-CV-29-WCO, 2006.

13. Ibid., 3.

14. Ibid., 4.

15. Ibid., 5.

16. Ibid.

17. *Caudillo* v. *Lubbock Independent High School District*.

18. Ibid., 556.

19. For an example of a case in which a school board asserted that they had not created a limited open forum, thus shifting the legal paradigm in which the case was analysed, see *East High School PRISM Club* v. *Seidel*, 94 F.Supp.2d 1239 (2000).

20. *Board of Education* v. *Mergens*, 496 US 226 (1990).

21. Examination of the situation where a school explicitly denies the creation of a limited open forum despite the appearance of one is reserved for discussion in a later section of this paper.

22. Title 20 USCA § 4071(d)(5) and (f).

23. Texas Penal Code Ann. § 21.06 (Vernon 2003).

24. Ibid., § 21.11(a).

25. *Caudillo* v. *Lubbock Independent High School District*, 561.

26. Ibid.

27. Yet not all GSAs necessarily deal with sexual material. See *Gay–Straight Alliance of Okeechobee High School* v. *School Board of Okeechobee County*, 483 F.Supp.2d 1224 (S.D.Fla. 2007), and a discussion of it below, specifically finding that the GSA in question was not 'sex-based'.

28. *Perry Education Association* v. *Perry Local Educators' Association*, 460 US 37 (1983).

29. This argument which was accepted by the court, however, assumed that somehow the abstinence-only education did not address sexual activity and was wholly implausible. Furthermore, the fact that sexual minority students subject to abstinence-only education that simply does not account for their existence (e.g. abstinence until marriage simply is inapplicable to individuals who date members of the same sex but do not have the legal option to marry) could plausibly dictate that it is necessary for the well-being of sexual minority individuals to receive information that the school otherwise does not provide.

30. It is again difficult to see how creating a safe space where sexual minority students can gather without fear is not in furtherance of or even required for the well-being of students. Consider examples of hostility that sexual minority students routinely face, as discussed in *Boyd County Gay Straight Alliance* v. *Board of Education of Kentucky*, Civil Action No. 03-17-DLB (2003): one plaintiff was subjected to a statement by a fellow student in class that 'they needed to take all the fucking faggots out in the back woods and kill them'. Ibid., 3, n. 1.

31. See *Gay–Straight Alliance of Okeechobee High School* v. *School Board of Okeechobee County*.

32. *Colin* v. *Orange Unified School District*, 1144.

33. Title 20 USCA § 4071(a).

34. *East High School PRISM Club* v. *Seidel*, 1240.

35. The issue of whether the adoption of the 1996 policy of the Board of Education of Salt Lake City School District was in fact merely a pretextual measure aimed solely at denying students the ability to form a GSA was discussed in a case that was the precursor to the *Seidel* litigation. In *East High Gay/Straight Alliance* v. *Board of Education*, the plaintiff GSA challenged the validity of the 1996 policy as 'pretextual and ... substantially motivated by an intent to silence "gay-positive" views', despite the fact that the policy remained viewpoint neutral on its face. Neither plaintiffs nor defendants were granted summary judgment on the issue, and, due to the procedural posture of the case, the nature of subsequent and satellite litigation, and the ultimate decision of the school district to cease litigating the matter, the issue of whether the adoption of the 1996 policy itself was anti-gay viewpoint discrimination impermissible under the First and Fourteenth Amendments was not decided.

36. *City of Lakewood* v. *Plain Dealer Publishing Co.*, 486 US 750 (1988).

37. *East High School PRISM Club* v. *Seidel*, 1244. The absence of clear written standards would render it almost impossible for a court to determine when a school has made decisions regarding the formation of school clubs for impermissible reasons.

38. Ibid., 1241.

39. Although the name PRISM did not ostensibly suggest that it was in fact a GSA, at this point in the litigation the name had been changed, presumably for legal strategic purpose ('PRISM' sounded less provocative than 'Gay/Straight Alliance'), from 'East High Gay/Straight Alliance'.

40. In its application for group status, PRISM explicitly stated that the group was not about '"advocating homosexuality", promoting a partisan platform, or discussing sexual behavior', thereby eliminating the *Caudillo* rationale for preventing the formation of a GSA. *East High School PRISM Club* v. *Seidel*, 1242 (emphasis added).

41. Ibid., 1243.

42. Ibid., 1247 (emphasis added). Taking the school official's no-narrowing argument to its logical extreme, a student group would have to discuss all subjects matter included in classes to which it purports to be related from all viewpoints to satisfy the 'subject matter is actually taught' requirement. This proposition seems absurd as well as impossible given the amount of time that would be required to accomplish such a goal.

43. Ibid., 1241.

44. The court's treatment and analysis of the no-narrowing rule was inarticulate at best. While the defendants alleged the policy to be one solely of no narrowing of subject matter, the court bifurcated the analysis, without explanation, into a no narrowing of subject matter and a no narrowing of viewpoint rule. It seems from the *Siedel* opinion that if a club narrows its scope to one viewpoint (e.g. a gay-positive viewpoint) the club would be deemed inherently political and non-curriculum related, as curriculum generally seeks to address both sides of a contentious social issue where applicable. The court seemed to partially rest its conclusion that the school must allow PRISM to meet on the fact that it only narrowed the subject matter, and not the viewpoint, that is, it will primarily focus on the history, contributions, and civil rights movement of sexual minority individuals as subject matter, but viewpoints of members and meeting attendees were in no way limited to a sexual-minority-positive viewpoint. Statements such as 'The "no narrowing of subject matter" rule appears to have been applied in these two cases [referring to SADD and WSC exclusion from club status]' and 'The court finds no reason to think that a "no narrowing of the club's viewpoint" rule was applied in either case', however, illustrated the clumsy and inadequate treatment by the court on this issue.

45. *East High School PRISM Club* v. *Seidel*, 1249.

46. Ibid., 1250.

47. Ibid.

48. Ibid., 1251.

49. School districts are generally hesitant to continue litigation after a court has already determined that the plaintiff GSAs are likely to ultimately succeed on the merits. The spectre of large sums of money spent on litigating an issue before a court that has already determined that the school district is likely to ultimately lose encourages many defendant school boards to discontinue legal opposition to the formation of GSAs.

50. *Colin* v. *Orange Unified School District*, 1138. Protesters expressed opposition to the group Colin sought to form by displaying 'Grades Not AIDS' signs at a school board meeting discussing the group's formation. This indeed suggests a great need for a student organisation that combats stereotypes and promotes tolerance of gay sexual minority individuals. Ibid., 1139.

51. Ibid., 1139–40.

52. Ibid., 1139.

53. See ibid., where one board member said of the GSA proponent's request for official recognition, 'The Bible says we're all sinners, but this, in my opinion, is asking us to legitimize sin', and another, 'We know the law is on their side, but our community members don't want it.' These represented the opinions of two of the seven board members who voted against allowing the formation of the GSA. The vote was 7–0 against the plaintiffs.

54. As the court ruled in favour of the plaintiffs on EAA grounds, the court did not assess their First Amendment claim. Accordingly, only the EAA analysis will be discussed for the purposes of this case.

55. Ibid., 1143.
56. Ibid., 1138.
57. Ibid., 1145–6.
58. Ibid., 1146.
59. Ibid., 1146–7.
60. Ibid., 1149. Other instances of viewpoint discrimination on which the judge relied to determine systematic discrimination included the school's repeated insistence that the group change its name to one that would be 'less divisive'; suggestions that the group adopt tenets limiting topics to be discussed within the group; an assistant superintendent's warning to the school principal to 'be on the lookout' for a GSA; the board's opposition to state legislation that would prohibit discrimination based on sexual orientation in schools as expressed in a board resolution; and school board member statements expressing moral disapproval of sexual minority individuals. This pattern of behaviour was illustrative that at the core of schools' denials of equal access to GSAs lies disapproval of sexual-minority-positive viewpoints that GSA members wish to espouse.
61. *SAGE* v. *Osseo*, 471 F.3d 908 (2006). Incidentally, a detailed search reveals that *SAGE* is the only Circuit Court decision addressing First Amendment issues regarding GSAs in schools. Apparently Osseo Area Schools–District 279 has thus far been the only school district willing to continue litigation after a lower court had already issued a preliminary injunction predicated on a finding of likelihood of success on the merits.
62. Ibid., 910.
63. The school strategically did not make the argument that a no narrowing of subject matter rule would keep the GSA from forming as in *Seidel*, as application of that rule would almost certainly lead to the conclusion that swimming and cheerleading were non-curricular. Here, the school ultimately sought to create a curriculum-relatedness framework that would only exclude SAGE.
64. *SAGE* v. *Osseo*, 913.
65. Ibid.
66. See *East High Gay/Straight Alliance* v. *Board of Education*, 1188–9, suggesting that although plaintiffs had not yet met their burden to obtain summary judgment (on the issue of whether the school's actions were pretextual and, though neutral on their face were impermissible viewpoint discrimination) 'the existence of a blanket unwritten viewpoint exclusion is a question that may be further addressed' at a later state in the litigation.
67. *Gay–Straight Alliance of Okeechobee High School* v. *School Board of Okeechobee County.*
68. Ibid.
69. Ibid.
70. Ibid.
71. *Yaminez* v. *School Board of Okeechobee County*, 571 F.Supp. 2d 1257 (S.D.Fla. 2008).
72. *Colin* v. *Orange Unified School District*, 1149.

Cumulative jurisprudence and human rights: the example of sexual minorities and hate speech

Eric Heinze

School of Law, Queen Mary, University of London, UK

Leading non-discrimination norms in post-1945 human rights instruments have generally enumerated specified categories for protection, such as race, ethnicity, sex, and religion. They have often omitted express reference to sexual minorities. However, through 'such as' or 'other status' clauses, or otherwise open-ended phrasing or interpretation, such instruments have generated a 'cumulative jurisprudence', whereby sexual minorities subsequently become incorporated through analogical reasoning. That cumulative jurisprudence has yielded protections for sexual minorities through norms governing, e.g., privacy, employment, age of consent, and freedoms of speech and association. Hate speech bans, too, have often been formulated with reference only to more traditionally recognised categories, particularly race and religion, rarely making express reference to sexual minorities. It might therefore be expected that the same cumulative jurisprudence should be applied, such that their scope might be extended to encompass sexual minorities. In this paper, however, that approach is challenged. It is argued that hate speech bans suffer in themselves from deep flaws. Either they promote discrimination by limiting the number of protected categories, or, by including all meritorious categories, they would dramatically limit free speech. While sexual minorities within longstanding, stable and prosperous democracies should generally enjoy all human rights, it is argued that they should not seek the protection of hate speech bans, which run real risks of betraying fundamental principles of human rights law.

Introduction

On the evening of 13 September 2002, three boys, aged 16–20, entered a city park in Reims, France. Their plan was to 'smash an Arab' (*casser de l'Arabe*). Instead they found François Chenu. Chenu was 29 years old, an openly gay man. So they decided to 'smash a faggot' (*cassé du pédé*). They taunted him, beat him, then threw him in a pond, where he was later discovered drowned.[1]

Queer-bashing is never just about physical assaults. A society casual about words like 'queer' or 'poof' is one in which sexual minorities[2] are maimed and murdered. Queer-bashing without words is like a dirge without music. Queer-bashing is that torrent of blows and words, every kick and punch chanted with 'queer', 'poof', 'faggot', 'cock-sucker', or 'lesbo'; like a racist, anti-Semitic, or Islamophobic attack, the same kinds of words spewed with the same kinds of blows.

In recent years, violence of words has provided powerful justifications for hate speech bans.[3] It is understandable that sexual minorities would seek protection under them as part of a broader effort to combat prejudice. In so doing, they would be pursuing an otherwise legitimate and often successful strategy, which I shall call 'cumulative jurisprudence'. Gains for sexual minorities have frequently resulted from activists, lawyers, and scholars citing protections, such as privacy, free expression, free association, or non-discrimination, which may not originally have been adopted with sexual minorities in mind, but then showing how those protections can and should be interpreted to include sexual minorities. In the following discussion, I shall argue that cumulative jurisprudence is appropriate for sexual minorities as a general matter, but should not be assumed to apply mechanically to all norms that may emerge within the human rights corpus, without any deeper enquiry into the legitimacy of the underlying norms themselves. Norms against hate speech provide an example.

I shall begin by examining the concept of cumulative jurisprudence as a systematic application of general human rights norms to categories of persons not expressly named or intended in leading human rights instruments. A cumulative jurisprudence has allowed sexual minorities to gain increasing recognition within human rights systems, and might seem prima facie to justify the extension of hate speech bans to include sexual minorities. I shall then argue, however, that hate speech bans pose a dilemma intolerable for human rights law: either they promote discrimination by unfairly limiting the protected categories and individuals; or, if they do include all similarly situated categories and individuals, they represent more than just minimal limits on free speech. I conclude that sexual minorities should generally enjoy all guarantees available within human rights law, but should not seek refuge in bans that may serve more to betray fundamental principles of human rights law than to promote them.

Sexual minorities and cumulative jurisprudence

Michel Foucault's publication of *Histoire de la sexualité*[4] in 1976 sparked a revolution in our understandings of dominant and subordinated social groups. Foucault described the post-Enlightenment appropriation of sexuality within the sphere of scientific enquiry. Purportedly neutral, objectivist – professionalised and therefore exclusive – scientific discourses of sexuality, presupposing unacknowledged standards of normativity and deviance,[5] came to pervade language and consciousness to the extent that what we now know as 'heterosexuality', 'homosexuality', 'transsexualism', and a long train of similar terms came to construct, and thereby to control, our everyday sense of sexual experience and sexual identity. The objectivist, scientific discourses have persisted, of course, providing ample fodder for debates between 'essentialist' and 'social constructionist' approaches. Foucault nevertheless shed real light on how dominant social discourses regiment everyday experiences and attitudes.

Social constructionism reminds us that when gay-bashers cry 'queer', 'poof', 'faggot', and 'cocksucker' they are not merely describing some 'outside world' that 'contains' such individuals. Rather, they are 'constructing' that world, to control those individuals. Compare a story told by Randall Kennedy:

> Although they typically travelled on public buses, my mother had failed to notice that her mother, Big Mama, always took her to the back of the bus where Negroes were segregated. One day, Big Mama asked my mother to run an errand that required her to catch a bus on which they had often ridden together. This errand marked the first time that my mother rode

the bus on her own. She stood at the correct stop, got on the right bus, and deposited the appropriate fare. Being a bit scared, however, she sat down immediately behind the bus driver. After about a block, the driver pulled the bus over to the curb, cut the engine, and suddenly wheeled around and began to scream at my mother who was all of about eight or nine years old – 'Nigger, you know better than to sit there! Get to the back where you belong.'[6]

Randall Kennedy's mother was not born a 'nigger'. She was made one, as Chenu was made a *pédé*, within a world whose fundamental relationship to such individuals was one of social dominance and subordination.

The phrase 'hate speech' is recent, having arisen in the 1980s in the United States. More recently, the phrase has been adopted in Europe and elsewhere.[7] But the problem itself is ancient. Blasphemy laws, for example, may not in every sense be identical to current hate speech laws, as they have often protected beliefs themselves, regardless of whether any group's individuals might be personally offended by speech against those beliefs, which, moreover, have generally been the ideas of the dominant group, and not of a minority.[8] Functionally, however, they have served to protect sensibilities and to avoid offence. In recent jurisprudence, blasphemy laws have often been maintained precisely insofar as they serve the same aims as hate speech laws – prohibiting speech likely to be found offensive or unduly disruptive.[9]

Article 20(2) of the International Covenant on Civil and Political Rights (ICCPR),[10] currently binding on 160 states,[11] provides that 'any advocacy of national, racial or religious hatred that constitutes incitement to discrimination, hostility or violence shall be prohibited by law'. Drafted in the 1960s, the ICCPR does not use the phrase 'hate speech'. However, it captures the overall aims that have emerged in post-1945 regulations of speech deemed to be highly offensive.

From the perspective of sexual minorities, it might well be argued that the enumeration of three specific kinds of target groups in article 20(2) – national, racial, and religious – should be deemed only 'illustrative', and not final or exhaustive.[12] On that approach, it could be argued that article 20(2) represents only an early attempt to deal with intolerance through human rights instruments, which can grow to encompass additional target groups as each group's history and circumstances come to light. In support of that approach, it could be noted that, like similar provisions in other international, regional, or national instruments, article 19(3), which limits freedom of expression on grounds of 'public order', 'morals', or even 'rights or reputation of others', remains amenable to hate speech bans protective of sexual minorities.[13] Some national legal systems have already extended hate speech bans to protect sexual minorities, either by specific legislative amendment or through subsequent judicial interpretation.[14]

The International Convention on the Elimination of All Forms of Racial Discrimination[15] (CERD), also drafted in the 1960s, includes a detailed prohibition on hate speech, which, albeit expressly limited to race, exemplifies the broad reach of hate speech bans that have been promoted within international law and institutions.[16] Article 4 requires that states parties shall

(a) declare an offence punishable by law all dissemination of ideas based on racial superiority or hatred, incitement to racial discrimination, as well as all acts of violence or incitement to such acts against any race or group of persons of another colour of ethnic origin . . .

(b) declare illegal and prohibit organizations, and also organized and all other propaganda activities, which promote and incite racial discrimination, and shall recognize participation in such organizations or activities as an offence punishable by law.

CERD is of particular interest, insofar as post-1945 movements for the rights of sexual minorities have often followed in the footsteps of anti-racism movements, as illustrated, for example, in the United States, where the African-American civil rights movements of the 1950s and 1960s, joined by the feminist movements of the 1960s and 1970s, became decisive in inspiring America's gay rights movements.[17] In the post-1945 period, gay rights movements have frequently pursued a strategy of cumulative (or 'analogical') jurisprudence, whereby rights first recognised for racial, ethnic, religious, or national minorities, or women, would be seen to set the stage for rights of sexual minorities.[18]

The question I am asking is whether the considerable success of a cumulative jurisprudence in achieving rights for sexual minorities should be applied so as to extend hate speech bans to embrace sexual minorities. In the mid-1990s, when sexual minorities were first beginning[19] to gain attention within the United Nations, I argued that their rights must not primarily be seen as 'innovations'. They must be seen as necessary applications of existing international norms, without which the interpretation of those norms would be inherently contradictory. I recommended some jurisprudential principles for the recognition of rights of sexual minorities within existing international human rights law.[20] One of them, which I called the 'Principle of Extant Rights', was formulated as follows: 'Rights of sexual orientation are required by extant human rights law to the degree, and only to the degree, that they derive from extant rights.'[21]

By including the restriction 'only to the degree', I conceded the minor, arguably tautological, point that fundamental rights of sexual minorities could not be said to exist *already* within the existing international human rights corpus except insofar as those rights existed within the corpus for human beings generally. That slight limitation having been acknowledged, the more important point was that protections already existing for human beings generally had to be extended ipso facto to sexual minorities. Cumulative jurisprudence has provided an important vehicle for realising the Principle of Extant Rights.

The aim of the Principle of Extant Rights was to play both prescriptive and descriptive roles. As a prescriptive matter, it suggests that fundamental international human rights must be construed to apply to sexual minorities if they are to avoid falling into internal contradiction. As a descriptive matter, it provides a sense of how, in general, advocacy for rights of sexual minorities has in fact tended to proceed: once the post-1945 frameworks for human rights were firmly in place – originally drafted with little regard to rights of sexual minorities – sexual orientation and identity have subsequently been incorporated at international, regional, and national levels, be it through national legislation and adjudication, or through the judgments or opinions of international or regional human rights bodies.[22]

In its prescriptive role, the Principle of Extant Rights takes as axiomatic – that is, it merely assumes, insofar as international human rights count as norms within positive international, regional, or national law – that existing rights within the international corpus are normatively legitimate, in particular such fundamental norms as privacy, expression, association, and non-discrimination. In proposing it, I conceded from the outset that human rights may not be historically or cross-culturally universal. They may be artefacts of specific historical, political, and economic circumstances. Or, even if we take as given a general corpus of human rights, certain rights within that corpus may be challenged in their formulation or interpretation.[23] Many a human rights norm – such as privacy, expression, association, non-discrimination – could be independently contested on its own terms, before any more specific inquiry into its applicability to sexual minorities would even arise. Is the norm genuinely universal? Does it, in all cases, stand as a legitimate trump over worthy, competing interests?

The prescriptive approach, then, simply assumes the validity of the general corpus of fundamental human rights, without undertaking any inquiry into the overall validity either of any specific right or of the human rights corpus, as such. Its role is merely to state that, insofar as the existing corpus *is* accepted and applied, it must be applied equally to sexual minorities. For nuts-and-bolts human rights practice, that assumption poses few problems. Everyday advocacy can assume, as a general matter, that sexual minorities as such merit, say, privacy,[24] freedoms of expression or association,[25] and non-discrimination[26] insofar as all human beings merit them.

The cumulative jurisprudence of non-discrimination for sexual minorities has not been mechanical or straightforward. Consider the example of the United States. Having adopted the most demanding standard of judicial review – 'strict scrutiny' – for racial classifications,[27] the road to gender equality was rockier, starting from a highly deferential 'rational basis' standard,[28] then swinging towards a strict scrutiny standard,[29] until finally settling upon a standard of intermediary review ('heightened', but not always 'strict'), which – often in the interest of respecting gender differences that would accrue to women's advantage – had to take into account complexities of difference that tend to be specific to gender.[30]

The road for sexual minorities was at least as rocky. After a major defeat in the 1986 case of *Bowers* v. *Hardwick*,[31] the United States Supreme Court began to recognise rights for sexual minorities only in the 1996 case of *Romer* v. *Evans*[32] and then the 2003 case of *Lawrence* v. *Texas*.[33] Even in those cases, the Court created the oddity of applying a remarkably rigorous standard of review in practice, while remaining ambivalent about declaring the adoption of a stricter level of scrutiny as a formal or final matter.[34] Despite that erratic approach, it seems that, overall, a jurisprudence originating in anti-racist movements has expanded to encompass other targets of discrimination,[35] with sexual minorities gradually included through a cumulative jurisprudence.[36]

In Europe, the evolution of article 14 of the European Convention on Human Rights[37] (ECHR) also provides an example of cumulative jurisprudence. Article 14 sets forth a standard non-discrimination provision:

> The enjoyment of the rights and freedoms set forth in this Convention shall be secured without discrimination on any ground *such as* sex, race, colour, language, religion, political or other opinion, national or social origin, association with a national minority, property, birth *or other status*. (Emphasis added)

While specifically referring to sex (originally construed as applying to men and women), race, colour, and other categories, 'such as' and 'other status' have long been interpreted to mean that the expressly enumerated categories are not exhaustive. In *Marckx* v. *Belgium*, the European Court of Human Rights held discriminatory treatment of unwed mothers to be in violation of article 14.[38] In *Inze* v. *Austia* the Court interpreted 'other status' to encompass children born out of wedlock.[39] In *Darby* v. *Sweden* the Court extended the clause further to include persons not registered as resident.[40] Recognition of homosexuality came as early as 1981, with *Dudgeon* v. *United Kingdom*[41] (although subsequent developments, notably for transsexuals, have not been uniformly positive[42]). The United Nations Human Rights Committee, too, has increasingly recognised sexual orientation[43] along with other classifications under the 'other status' clause of ICCPR.[44]

Cumulative or contradictory?

Is there a limit to the Principle of Extant Rights, in particular, to the axiomatic assumption of the overall validity either of the corpus in general or of any given background norm? How shall we proceed when it is by no means obvious that a particular norm *should* carry the kind of authority that can be accorded to norms such as privacy, expression, association, or professional or educational non-discrimination? Should sexual minorities accept the overall background norm of prohibitions on hate speech wholesale, insisting on equal protection under them, without any independent analysis of the merits of those norms themselves?

Article 4 of CERD may refer only to race, and article 20(2) of ICCPR may include only the two other categories of nationality and religion. Sexual minorities might nevertheless reason as follows: once we have shown that homophobic speech is similarly harmful, easily associated with precisely the kinds of danger or violence that those provisions sought to avert, extending hate speech bans to encompass sexuality should proceed as a matter of course. Some states have already begun to protect sexual minorities under hate speech bans.[45] In 1997, a resolution of the Committee of Ministers of the Council of Europe (COM-COE) urged a more extensive regime of hate speech bans. Unlike article 4 of CERD or article 20(2) of ICCPR, it is worded more like a standard non-discrimination norm, employing an open-ended 'other forms' clause, suggesting a potentially unlimited range of individuals or groups for protection under hate speech bans. Sexual minorities would count as obvious candidates. The resolution calls upon member states to combat

> statements ... which may reasonably be understood as hate speech, or as speech likely to produce the effect of legitimising, spreading or promoting racial hatred, xenophobia, anti-Semitism *or other forms* of discrimination or hatred based on intolerance.[46]

Although the resolution is non-binding, such a statement represents an authoritative synthesis of views, either on the current status or on a plausible further evolution of their respective states' approaches. To date, the European Court of Human Rights has accepted a principle of wide latitude towards states' decisions to censor speech found to be offensive,[47] and United Nations human rights bodies have advised European states to strengthen further their censorship activity.[48] The more specialised European Commission against Racism and Intolerance has also continued to push for stronger censorship.[49]

Standard non-discrimination norms aim to secure benefits and burdens spread throughout society, to prevent any individuals or groups being unfairly treated[50] on grounds of irrelevant characteristics. The modern non-discrimination norm is amenable to a cumulative jurisprudence because it is cumulative in its conception.[51] To exclude one group holding a claim that is equal in merit to that of an included group is itself to discriminate. Any such disparity impeaches the non-discrimination norm altogether. To expand the norm's scope – as long as that expansion retains the aim of eliminating such recourse to irrelevant characteristics in the distribution of burdens and benefits – is to perfect it, and thus to perfect the whole of the human rights corpus. The same is true of any legitimate extensions of norms of privacy, expression, association, and the like.

That same observation cannot be made about hate speech bans. Consider an analogy to persons who are mentally or physically disabled.[52] The analogy reveals flaws in hate speech bans, and distinguishes such bans from rights of privacy, employment, speech, association, and other human rights. Bringing disabled persons within the scope of a standard non-discrimination norm may occasionally pose practical problems (e.g. questions about expenditure for 'reasonable accommodation'[53]); however, under today's non-discrimination norms, it can no longer be denied that a given disabled individual who, for all relevant purposes, is equally situated to others in terms of qualifications for such matters as housing, education, or employment must be accorded equal access.

Similarly, unless their specific health or welfare dictates otherwise, arguments can scarcely be made against their equal rights of expression, association, and belief, right to life, and other fundamental rights. Nor can it be claimed that their enjoyment of such rights in any serious way diminishes the rights of others. In a word, taking into account any such pragmatic considerations, the application of 'other status' clauses to encompass physically or mentally disabled persons within non-discrimination norms would widely be seen today not merely as feasible, but as a moral imperative.

What would it mean, however, to include disabled persons within hate speech bans? Consonant with concepts of social constructionism, advocates of hate speech bans argue that, insofar as derogatory terms remain standard within ordinary speech, their underlying prejudices – blacks are inferior, Jews are greedy, sexual minorities are dangerous deviants or predatory perverts – are expressly or tacitly disseminated and reinforced as social norms.[54] Similarly, words like 'idiot', 'moron', 'spas', 'spack', 'lame', 'pscyho', 'loony', and 'schizo' construct physical, mental, or psychological disability as inferior, inept, bumbling, misbegotten, or ridiculous.[55] They are so engrained within our language and usage as to seem innocuous, not unlike the casual racism or homophobia of earlier times, when words like 'nigger' or 'queer' passed easily in polite society. According to guidelines adopted by the American Psychological Association, '[t]he use of certain words or phrases can express gender, ethnic, or racial bias, either intentionally or unintentionally. *The same is true of language referring to persons with disabilities*, which in many instances can express negative and disparaging attitudes.'[56]

Nor has disability been the only category generally excluded from protection under hate speech bans. Age is another. Epithets like 'old bag' or 'senile' stigmatise both real and mythical infirmities.[57] Consider also physical fitness or appearance: 'fatso' or 'fat slob' degrades those who are overweight (leaving aside questions of when obesity would count as a disability), even through medical conditions beyond their control, such as congenital diabetes.[58] Eddie Murphy's 2006 film *Norbit* was rebuked for courting laughter at the expense of obesity.[59] Had his portrayals featured similarly conceived caricatures of groups, such as racial, ethnic, or religious groups, protected under hate speech bans in European states, serious questions of censorship could have been raised about the film's European distribution.[60] In the words of the COM-COE resolution, such a film can 'reasonably be understood' to be 'spreading or promoting' discriminatory attitudes.

In 1999, English Football Association manager Glenn Hoddle publicly stated that individual disabilities were justly deserved, through 'bad karma' accumulated in former lives. Hoddle lost his job thereafter,[61] but only as a matter of public relations, due to his high profile, and not through the application of any hate speech ban. Even in the rare cases where physical, mental, or psychological disability has been contemplated for inclusion under hate speech bans,[62] no serious attempt has been made to explain how such inclusion could occur without either massive, or wholly random, censorship of speech. Either whole categories such as physical, mental, or psychological disability, age, or obesity, must be excluded, or, if they are included, essentially random, and therefore individually discriminatory, choices must be made about which members of those groups will and will not be protected from terms so ubiquitously used.

A cardinal aim of hate speech bans is to protect groups or individuals with scant political influence. While ethnic or religious minorities in several Western countries have organised visible political movements, disabled persons are often isolated; limited in their ability even to associate effectively, let alone to mobilise strategic lobbying efforts. They are often restricted in their ability to earn, let alone to pool resources, and can generally direct few of their resources towards activities like anti-hate-speech campaigns, given the ongoing and more pressing expenses of primary care.[63] It would come as no surprise nowadays for leading celebrities or commentators to shun terms like 'nigger', 'dirty Jew', or 'queer' while directing terms like 'idiot' or 'moron' at leading political figures, indeed in the belief that they are speaking in a socially critical vein. Obvious examples have included former United States President George W. Bush and Vice President Dan Quayle, not to mention countless uses of such terms, sometimes passionately, sometimes nonchalantly, in everyday speech.[64] The problem arises not from the prospect of offence caused to a Bush or a Quayle. Rather, the problem is that such terms offend all persons whose conditions are thereby degraded.[65]

This shift in focus – from the disparagement of a classification targeted against someone belonging to that classification, to its use against someone not belonging to it – requires some explanation, as it may appear to change considerably the nature of the hate speech concerned. As James Weinstein, for example, has commented on a previous statement of my views:

> It is very rare nowadays that anyone, at least in the US or UK, would use a term to knowingly disparage the mentally retarded or physically handicapped. Nor is there a massive amount of hate speech readily available on the Internet against the mentally retarded or the physically disabled, as there is with respect to blacks, Jews and gays. There is not nearly the same reason to try to use the force of law to eradicate 'hate speech' against these groups. People nowadays simply do not hate the mentally retarded or physically disabled in the way that too many people hate blacks, Jews, or gays. I think the same is true of the elderly. There may be more hostility towards this group, but nothing like that directed towards people on the basis of race, ethnicity or religion. Moreover and more significantly, though there may be cases of people using 'fighting words' against the elderly, the disabled, or the obese in the street when they get annoyed, there is to my knowledge no hate literature against these groups at all, and even if there is some, it is nothing like the virulent tracts directed against Jews, blacks and sexual minorities.[66]

Weinstein's objection is empirical. There is no evidence of widespread hostility towards mentally or physically disabled persons, or elderly or obese persons, comparable to that against certain racial, ethnic, religious, and sexual categories. Therefore, by definition, there can be no substantial causal link between derogatory language against those groups and any such hostility.

If Weinstein's objection were correct, however, governments, courts and human rights bodies would endorse hate speech bans only if some threshold level of hostility against a protected group could be demonstrated. In *Otto-Preminger-Institut* v. *Austria*,[67] the European Court of Human Rights rejected any such condition placed on a state's prerogative to combat intolerance through censorship. The Court did not require any showing of systemic hostility or discrimination towards Roman Catholics in Austria, who have long constituted the overwhelming numerical and socio-cultural majority of the country's population.[68] The prosecution was originally brought under traditional blasphemy principles, and not a hate speech ban in the modern sense; however, the Court upheld the conviction on general grounds of overall tolerance,[69] and not on grounds of any sui generis exceptions to free speech principles carved out for blasphemy laws.

In essence, the Court treated anti-Catholic expression as an evil in itself, evil simply on grounds of its expression of intolerance, and not merely as evil on the condition that some independent history, or future possibility, of material detriment be adduced. Nor, despite some criticism of *Otto-Preminger-Institut*, was the decision an aberration. The Court reiterated its view in *Wingrove* v. *United Kingdom*, in which it once again upheld censorship on the grounds that the material in question was offensive to Christians or Christian beliefs.

No international human rights body has recommended any principles that would contradict or limit such an approach. (The censored materials in *Otto-Preminger-Institut* and *Wingrove* were not 'hate' materials in any straightforward sense. They were merely art-house films that, respectively, lampooned and sexualised Christian symbols.)

Nor could these human rights bodies easily do otherwise, once they had started down the road of endorsing hate speech bans. To require threshold showings of some sufficient number of acts of hostility would entail a 'more-victim-than-thou' jurisprudence that, far from combating discrimination, would only entrench it. Intolerant attitudes may disadvantage the designated groups or individuals in ways subtler than concerted campaigns of hate. For example, if someone who is mentally or physically disabled is denied housing or employment despite possessing the competence to fulfil all requirements – precisely as if a person belonging to a racial, ethnic, religious, or sexual minority were denied – it may be impossible in any given case to determine whether or to what degree overall social attitudes are a contributing factor.

Unsurprisingly, advocates of hate speech bans have not insisted upon rigorous empirical evidence to demonstrate links between broader attitudes and discrete detriments suffered in particular instances. The crucial premise of hate speech bans has never been that hate speech *demonstrably* causes detriment to the disparaged groups, as no such evidence has been adduced vis-à-vis longstanding, stable, and prosperous democracies,[70] no more than it has been shown that violent films promote social violence, or that pornography augments incidents of rape. Rather, advocates of hate speech bans proceed on the broader assumption that hate speech *might plausibly* cause such detriment, indeed in ways that are often subtle and pernicious, and therefore not amenable to precise empirical observation.

Nor can it be argued that blacks, Jews, or sexual minorities have more burdened histories. Nazism showed how physically or mentally disabled persons, along with all the propaganda – hate speech – concerning their threats to Aryan purity and perfection, led to extermination on the grounds of their putative sub-humanity.[71] Might Chenu's attackers not just as eagerly have assaulted someone mentally or physically disabled, or someone elderly or obese? Can anyone argue that such an attack would not have been motivated by a cultural arsenal stockpiled with age-old barbs of 'idiot', 'spas', 'old bag', and 'fat slob'? It would require a leap of sociological imagination to argue that such an assault would be ignited by a consciousness promoted by hate speech when racially motivated but not when motivated by stereotypes of mental or physical conditions.

At first blush, one might wonder whether such disparities between classifications included within, and excluded from, hate speech bans are insurmountable. One might argue, in the spirit of the COM-COE resolution, that *any* actual or potential victims of discrimination should be protected by hate speech bans. But what would it mean to extend the bans so widely? We can safely assume that the films, newspaper or magazine articles, radio and television shows, and websites in which terms like 'idiot' and 'moron' appear – the same media that would no longer use 'nigger' or 'queer' in non-ironic or non-critical contexts – are innumerable. Remarkably broad censorship of both the media and everyday speech, backed up by legal penalties, would be required. Hate speech bans can only succeed either through enormous measures of censorship or through discriminatory selection of target categories or individuals.

To date, of course, the latter course has been chosen. Few have seriously proposed massive censorship. Rather, leading proponents of hate speech bans, often justifying bans as a necessary means of listening to society's unheard, excluded voices, have generally excluded physical, mental, and psychological disability, and age and obesity from the categories for which they seek protection.[72] Indeed, so common is the use of terms degrading to members of these latter groups that proponents of bans on racial and ethnic hate speech unwittingly use those terms. For instance, Richard Delgado, a leading critical race theorist and passionate advocate of penalties for racist speech, has used the word 'schizophrenic' derisively to mean 'inept'.[73] As Delgado and Jean Stefancic state, 'we *are* our current stock of narratives, and they us'.[74]

It might be argued that the increasing numbers of vocal elderly and overweight persons show that they are now able to defend themselves in the public arena. However, the relative political stature of an otherwise numerical minority has not generally been deemed by advocates of hate speech bans to constitute grounds for excluding the affected members from protection. Again, in *Otto-Preminger-Institut*, the fact that Roman Catholicism has long been Austria's overwhelmingly dominant faith, far from preventing censorship, was cited by Austrian authorities, unchallenged by the European Court of Human Rights, to suggest that there was ipso facto 'a pressing need for the preservation of religious peace'.[75]

Hate speech bans collide, then, with either of the following two principles of human rights law: (1) If they are narrowly drawn so as to limit their application, they violate the principle of non-discrimination by censoring or punishing some offences, while permitting similar offences against equally vulnerable persons. (2) If they are broadly drawn to include all target groups or individuals, they potentially capture large quantities of expression. In applying the Principle of Extant Rights, my concerns about the inclusion of sexual minorities within hate speech bans stem not from any specific characteristics of sexual minorities, but from the inadequacies of hate speech bans themselves. The fact that some or all persons of sexual minorities *might* be amenable to inclusion under hate speech bans provides no moral compensation for the exclusion of other equally vulnerable groups or individuals. Sexual minorities, or any groups – racial, ethnic, religious – cannot legitimately accept the protections of such norms within a framework of *fundamental, universal rights* when equally vulnerable groups or individuals are excluded.

Some objections and replies

Hate speech bans may be required as temporary measures within weak or newly emerging democracies, or under legitimately declared states of emergency. Such circumstances cannot, however, overcome the bans' discriminatory character. Within longstanding, stable, and prosperous democracies, it becomes questionable whether sexual minorities, or any other groups, should be seeking protection from norms that are fundamentally exclusive of some of society's most vulnerable.

I cannot examine all possible objections to my criticism of hate speech bans, as any such discussion would require a full-blown analysis of the overall problem of hate speech bans, which has been the subject of countless scholarly studies. It is worthwhile, however, to note some concerns arising specifically from an understanding of cumulative jurisprudence as a central instrument of rights for sexual minorities.

An anonymous reviewer of this piece objected that I noted 'no ground peculiar to sexual minorities' use of hate speech which ... makes them particularly vulnerable to its misapplication'.[76] The objection effectively makes the following assumption: if some groups or individuals, such as sexual minorities, are satisfied with the protections they can receive from hate speech bans, the bans are therefore legitimate *for those groups*. Yet this is precisely the assumption I am rejecting. The view of human rights I am assuming is the opposite: even if a hate speech ban could be both drafted and applied so as to protect some groups, or some individuals, in ways generally seen as beneficial, we would still be contradicting the founding assumptions of the leading human rights norms – certainly, of all those that have been central to rights of sexual minorities – if we were to maintain that a norm is legitimate even if it cannot be enjoyed equally by all similarly situated persons.[77]

The premise of international human rights since the Universal Declaration of Human Rights[78] has been that norms of the human rights corpus can claim universal legitimacy only insofar as they can, in principle, be framed and applied so as to encompass all human beings.[79] For sexual minorities, or any other actual or potential beneficiary group, to claim protection of norms that cannot be extended to other equally vulnerable groups should prompt the gravest ethical concerns about whether such norms properly belong within the international human rights corpus (except, again, as temporary measures in unstable states), despite the fact that hate speech bans have been endorsed within international human rights law.[80]

The same reviewer objected that '[n]one of the international laws . . . or indeed national hate speech laws that exist internationally, defines every insult or offence as hate speech. To do so would be ridiculous. Yet [Heinze] argues . . . that every insult against an overweight or disabled or elderly [person] should be considered hate speech as the only alternative is to discriminate selectively, which is anathema to human rights principles.'[81] I have not had to argue, however, that *every* such insult would have to count as hate speech. No such broad claim is required to demonstrate the discriminatory nature of hate speech bans. It suffices to ask whether there is *any* body of insults that can be covered under leading international and regional norms without either discriminatory application, whereby *equally dangerous or hurtful* terms go unregulated, or highly rigorous censorship.

Even avid proponents of, for example, race-based hate speech bans do not generally insist that 'every' racist insult be banned, for the simple reason that insults are context bound, and not amenable to exhaustive enumeration. 'Queer bastard' might be benign if used, for example, in an ironic, comical, or in-group situation. Meanwhile, 'funny gay man' might be offensive in an overtly anti-gay context. In view of the grey areas that render many contexts ambiguous, neither I nor anyone else could provide any conceptually exhaustive account of what counts as 'every' insult against any given category of persons. The view that '[t]o do so would be ridiculous' is, then, precisely the problem. Any serious step towards non-discriminatory application of hate speech bans, even in cases of overall parity in the level of offence to the targeted group or individual ('easy cases'), would indeed be a step towards a 'ridiculously' censorious regime, whereby much freedom of speech would be exercised not as a right, but as a contingent government concession. Yet any step away from that order of censorship becomes a step towards discriminating between protected and unprotected victims of speech acts that are otherwise equally offensive.

One might also raise a more pragmatic objection. Consider the following argument: 'Perhaps terms like "idiot" or "old bag" are indeed difficult to eradicate. However, the fact that we cannot protect all individuals does not mean we should protect none. We don't live in an ideal world. We must achieve what we can, even if we can't achieve everything.' That objection might carry some weight in many other areas of law (it may be legitimate to renovate Hyde Park even if there is not enough money to clean up St James's Park, or to catch more speeding motorists on the M1 than on the M4), but raises grave concerns for human rights. By analogy, there is no doctrine of human rights law which states that torture of some is justified as long as torture of most can be prevented; or that privacy or freedom of conscience is justified for some, even if it cannot be extended to all (such results may often occur in practice, for reasons of material constraint or political will, but are never justified by any principle of human rights law). Everyday legislation on ordinary issues must certainly deal in horse-trading and compromises, which presumably underlies much routine legislative activity: 'We'll agree to reduce taxes on the wealthy if you agree to reduce them on the poor;' 'We'll agree to raise the speed limit if you agree to build safety ramps.' That reasoning cannot transpose *simpliciter* to human rights law.[82] Even under a validly declared state of emergency, we could hardly adopt approaches such as 'We don't have enough money to protect the Catholics, so we'll just protect the Protestants' or 'If you agree not to torture the children, we'll allow you to torture the adults.' One reason for the credibility of such fundamental rights to life, privacy, expression, and non-discrimination is that, despite breaches in practice, there is absolutely no conceptual difficulty in postulating their universal application in principle. Insofar as hate speech bans are not, and cannot be, extended to protect all vulnerable groups or individuals, they violate the principle of universality.

Where does this all leave François Chenu? In calling for coherence in human rights, does one risk overlooking some of the concrete problems that hate speech bans might help to solve? Not at all. Another error among advocates of hate speech bans is their frequent failure to distinguish between, on one hand, a broader arena of public discourse – the arena of radio, television, film, the press, or the speaker in the public common – and, on the other hand, invective specifically and immediately directed by certain individuals against other, more or less specifically targeted individuals in face-to-face situations.[83] Opponents of hate speech bans rarely deny that offensive speech of the second type may legitimately be proscribed. In the United States, the doctrine of 'fighting words' allows the punishment of personally targeted insults in live, hostile encounters.[84] In principle, the protections afforded by that traditional doctrine are far broader than those by modern hate speech bans; they allow punishment of *any* kind of strongly offensive remark, which may include, yet need not be limited to, insults on grounds of race, ethnicity, religion, or other such identity. Certainly, traditional bans on 'fighting words' require periodic review of their content or application, in view of changing social conditions. However, in itself, an approach like the United States Supreme Court's upholding of bans on fighting words contains all that is required to protect *all* individuals from direct and unduly hostile verbal assaults. Moreover, as to actual crimes, involving non-speech acts such as killing, battery, theft, rape, or vandalism, the Supreme Court has found that no violation of free speech arises when hate speech is used as evidence of a hate-based criminal motive, or when crimes motivated by racial or other group-based animus are punished more harshly than others.[85]

Again, my focus in this paper has been on stable, longstanding, and prosperous democracies. What makes a democracy sufficiently stable, longstanding, and prosperous to be able to abolish hate speech bans? There will always be room for debate in borderline cases. But, as a general matter, Western European states certainly fit the bill. At the very least, a sufficiently stable, longstanding, and prosperous democracy is presupposed by any binding civil rights instrument, as suggested (1) by the inclusion, in modern instruments, of derogations clauses, authorising suspension of certain rights during legitimately declared states of emergency,[86] as well as (2) the judicial application of derogation principles to older instruments.[87] Derogation principles effectively require that a state guarantee rights unless it is rendered materially unable to do so.[88] Certainly, many states, in Europe and elsewhere, albeit not fully stable, longstanding, and prosperous democracies, are parties to the ICCPR or the ECHR, without regularly invoking the derogations clauses. However, as to weaker or emerging democracies, the totality of their political, social, and economic standards would warrant them to invoke those clauses against political or social unrest with far greater latitude (both under the ICCPR's 'proportionality' principle and under the 'margin of appreciation' doctrine deduced by the European Court of Human Rights from the ECHR) than would be expected for the wealthier and more stable Western European countries.[89]

It is stable, longstanding, and prosperous democracies that I have had in mind in noting that no correlation has been shown between levels of hate speech and incidence of hate crime. However, it is by no means certain that such correlation is absent today in weaker or emerging democracies. In some emerging democracies, for example, it has been suggested that a newly liberalised press can harshly impact on vulnerable groups without democratic institutions or traditions, or the sheer resources, required to redress the effects.[90] Meanwhile, in such societies, attitudes towards sexual minorities have often remained harsh and have even worsened.[91] Accordingly, I have refrained from taking a position on hate speech in such societies. Bans may indeed be required where some likely causation from hate speech to hate crime can be shown. Overall, however, the growing strength of democratic institutions and practices, along with the resources to protect vulnerable groups, should be displayed in a society's gradual ability to reduce its reliance on hate speech bans.

Today, compared with just a few decades ago, the increasing disdain for persons who casually drop epithets like 'nigger', 'dirty Jew', or 'queer' gives testimony not so much to the efficacy of prosecutions, which have scarcely had any systematic character in Europe, but to the fact that, in essentially open, liberal democracies, maintaining faith in the free and robust exchange of ideas,[92] informal, social pressures have always had the potential to effectuate needed change without the need for coercive laws that at best accomplish nothing and, at worst, operate in unjustifiably discriminatory ways. In general, sexual minorities have been right to follow a cumulative jurisprudence – to insist that norms of even-handedness intrinsic to the very idea of human rights be rigorously implemented and respected in practice. However, cumulative jurisprudence is only as worthy as the norms to which it is applied. Hate speech bans, despite their wide acceptance within international law and in most national jurisdictions, raise grave concerns about both their conceptual and their practical compatibilities with the norms and principles of human rights law.

Conclusion

A cumulative jurisprudence of human rights has been and remains an important means of advancing the interests of sexual minorities within the dominant contemporary framework of international, regional, and national human rights regimes. Even non-discrimination norms not originally conceived to apply to sexual minorities have been interpreted to extend to them with little conceptual or practical difficulty. That does not mean, however, that a cumulative jurisprudence should be applied willy-nilly to any norm that may emerge within human rights regimes. Hate speech bans are by definition conceived as limitations on fundamental rights of free speech and expression. They cannot be applied in a non-discriminatory way without raising serious questions about the fundamental status of free speech. Again, any step away from discriminatory application becomes a step towards massive censorship; and any step away from massive censorship becomes a step towards discriminatory application. Either hate speech bans must arbitrarily exclude persons who are just as vulnerable as those who enjoy protection, or the bans must extend so far as to undermine the rights of free speech and expression. Hate speech bans have no place within longstanding, stable, and prosperous democracies, which have ample means at their disposal to protect sexual minorities and other vulnerable groups from hate crime and discrimination without having to impose inevitably arbitrary limits on free speech.

Acknowledgements

The ideas presented in this piece benefited from a staff seminar held at Durham University in April 2007, chaired by Erika Rackley and facilitated by Helen Fenwick and Gavin Phillipson, and from a subsequent one-day conference at Durham entitled 'Sexuality, Hatred and Law', 6 May 2008, organised by Neil Cobb and Gavin Phillipson. Thanks also to James Weinstein and two anonymous reviewers for their detailed comments, and to Phil Chan for his kind assistance.

Notes

1. See *Au-delà de la Haine*, documentary film directed by Olivier Meyrou (2005). Cf. Caroline Constant, 'Leçon d'humanité', *L'Humanité*, 14 March 2007, http://www.humanite.presse.fr/journal/2007-03-14/2007-03-14-847695 (accessed 19 September 2008).

2. Like concepts of 'race', 'ethnicity', and 'religion', concepts of 'sexual orientation' and 'sexual minorities' may be fluid and are not amenable to conclusive definitions. For the limited purposes of human rights law, the term 'sexual minorities' may be used generally 'to denote people whose preferences, intimate associations, lifestyles, or other forms of personal identity or expression actually or imputedly derogate from a dominant normative-heterosexual paradigm'; see Eric Heinze, *Sexual Orientation: A Human Right* (Dordrecht, The Netherlands: Martinus Nijhoff, 1995), 61.

3. For a landmark text, see, e.g., Mari Matsuda, Charles Lawrence III, Richard Delgado, and Kimberle Williams Crenshaw, eds, *Words that Wound: Critical Race Theory, Assaultive Speech, and the First Amendment* (Boulder, CO: Westview, 1993). For other works, see, e.g., authors cited in Richard Delgado, 'About Your Masthead: A Preliminary Inquiry into the Compatibility of Civil Rights and Civil Liberties', *Harvard Civil Rights–Civil Liberties Law Review* 39 (2004): 1.

4. Michel Foucault, *Histoire de la sexualité I: La volonté de savoir* (Paris: Gallimard, 1976).

5. See also Michel Foucault, *Histoire de la folie à l'âge classique* (Paris: Gallimard, 1972).

6. Randall Kennedy, *Nigger: The Strange History of a Troublesome Word* (New York: Vintage, 2003), xii.

7. See, e.g., Kevin Boyle, 'Hate Speech: The United States *versus* the Rest of the World?', *Maine Law Review* 53 (2001): 487, 489.

8. See, e.g., *Otto-Preminger-Institut* v. *Austria*, Eur. Ct. H. R., Ser. A, No.295-A [1994] (upholding a blasphemy law protective of the Roman Catholic majority). See also *Wingrove* v. *United Kingdom* [1996] Eur. Ct. H. R. 1937.

9. Cf. Eric Heinze, 'Viewpoint Absolutism and Hate Speech', *Modern Law Review* 69 (2006): 543, 558–9. Cf. also Eric Heinze, 'Towards the Abolition of Hate Speech Bans: A "Viewpoint Absolutist" Perspective', in *Religious Pluralism and Human Rights in Europe*, ed. Titia Loenen and Jenny Goldschmidt (Antwerp: Intersentia, 2007), 295.

10. 993 UNTS 3, entered into force on 3 January 1976.

11. For periodically updated data on ratifications, accessions, successions, reservations, and declarations, see, e.g., Office of the United Nations High Commissioner for Human Rights (UNHCR), 'Ratifications and Reservations', http://www.ohchr.org/english/countries/ratification/index.htm (accessed 19 September 2008).

12. Cf., e.g., Heinze, *Sexual Orientation*, section 12.3; Eric Heinze, 'Equality: Between Hegemony and Subsidiarity', *Review of the International Commission of Jurists* 52 (1994): 56. Cf. also, e.g., Marc Bossuyt, *L'interdiction de la discrimination dans le droit international des droits de l'homme* (Brussels: Bruylant, 1976).

13. See Heinze, 'Viewpoint Absolutism and Hate Speech', 556–9.

14. See, e.g., ibid., 544 (discussing the French case of Dominique Vanneste). See also, e.g., Jan-Peter Loof, 'Freedom of Expression and Religiously-Based Ideas on Homosexuality: European and Dutch Standards', in *Religious Pluralism and Human Rights in Europe*, ed. Titia Loenen and Jenny Goldschmidt (Antwerp: Intersentia, 2007), 267.

15. 660 UNTS 195, entered into force on 4 January 1969.

16. Cf. UNHCR, note 11 above.

17. For some standard accounts, see, e.g., John D'Emilio, *Sexual Politics, Sexual Communities: The Making of a Homosexual Minority in the United States, 1940–1970* (Chicago: University of Chicago Press, 1983); Toby Johnson and Toby Marotta, *The Politics of Homosexuality* (Boston: Houghton Mifflin, 1981). Similarly, Marxist and left-wing approaches in Europe tended to aggregate the interests of outsider groups. See, e.g., Mario Mieli, *Elementi di critica omosessuale* (Turin: Giuliu Einaudi, 1977).

18. Cf. text accompanying notes 32–44 below.

19. Cf., e.g., *Sexual Orientation*, 12, n. 55 (noting limited attention to sexual orientation within the United Nations through the 1980s).
20. Ibid., ch. 8.
21. Ibid., 136.
22. Cf. text accompanying notes 32–44 below.
23. Heinze, *Sexual Orientation*, ch. 3.
24. Ibid., ch.10.
25. Ibid., sections 14.3–14.5.
26. Ibid., chs 12–13.
27. See *Korematsu* v. *United States*, 323 US 214 (1944); *Brown* v. *Board of Education*, 347 US 483 (1954); *Loving* v. *Virginia*, 388 US 1 (1967).
28. See *Reed* v. *Reed*, 404 US 71 (1971). Since the Supreme Court in *Reed* did strike down the gender discrepancy in dispute, however, it could be argued that the Court was already anticipating a more stringent approach.
29. See *Frontiero* v. *Richardson*, 411 US 677 (1973). The application of strict scrutiny by a plurality of only four justices, however, suggested a continuing unease about the appropriate judicial standard.
30. See *Craig* v. *Boren*, 429 US 190 (1976); *United States* v. *Virginia*, 518 US 515 (1996).
31. *Bowers* v. *Hardwick*, 478 US 186 (1986).
32. *Romer* v. *Evans*, 517 US 620 (1996)
33. *Lawrence* v. *Texas*, 539 US 558 (2003).
34. See the various views taken on the Supreme Court's standards of review in, e.g., Randy E. Barnett, 'Justice Kennedy's Libertarian Revolution: *Lawrence* v. *Texas*', *Cato Supreme Court Review* (2002–03): 21; Laurence H. Tribe, '*Lawrence* v. *Texas*: The "Fundamental Right" that Dare Not Speak Its Name', *Harvard Law Review* 117 (2004): 1893.
35. Although *Lawrence* was not decided primarily on grounds of equal protection (non-discrimination), the Court noted the consistency of its holding with equal protection principles. *Lawrence* v. *Texas*, 574–5 (describing as 'tenable' a disposition of the case on equal protection grounds). See also ibid., 579 (O'Connor J., concurring) (arguing that the sodomy statute should be struck down on equal protection grounds).
36. See, e.g., John E. Nowak and Ronald D. Rotunda, *Constitutional Law*, 6th edn (St Paul, MN: West, 2000), §§ 14.11–14.30.
37. Convention for the Protection of Human Rights and Fundamental Freedoms, 213 UNTS 222 (entered into force on 3 September 1953), as amended by Protocols Nos 3, 5, 8, and 11 (entered into force on 21 September 1970, 20 December 1971, 1 January 1990, and 1 November 1998, respectively).
38. See *Marckx* v. *Belgium*, Judgment of 13 June 1979, Eur. Ct. H. R., Ser. A, No. 31.
39. See *Inze* v. *Austria*, Judgment of 28 October 1987, Eur. Ct. H. R., Ser. A, No. 126.
40. See *Darby* v. *Sweden*, Judgment of 23 October 1990, Eur. Ct. H. R., Ser. A, No. 187.
41. *Dudgeon* v. *United Kingdom*, Judgment of 22 October 1981, Eur. Ct. H. R., Ser. A, No. 45.
42. See generally, e.g., Eric Heinze, 'Sexual Orientation and International Law: A Study in the Manufacture of Cross-Cultural "Sensitivity"', *Michigan Journal of International Law* 22 (2001): 283.
43. See, e.g., United Nations Human Rights Committee, *Toonen* v. *Australia*, Communication No. 488/1992, UN GAOR, UN Doc. CCPR/C/50/D/488/1992 (1994); *Concluding Observations of the Human Rights Committee: Colombia*, UN Doc. CCPR/C/79/Add.76 (1997), para.16; *Concluding Observations of the Human Rights Committee: Sudan*, UN Doc. CCPR/C/79/Add.85 (1997), para.8; *Young* v. *Australia*, Communication No. 941/2000, UN Doc. CCPR/C/78/D/941/2000 (2003). But see, e.g., *Joslin* v. *New Zealand*, Communication No. 902/1999, UN Doc. A/57/40 (2002), 214. Cf., e.g., Heinze, 'Sexual Orientation and International Law', 292.
44. See Scott Davidson, 'Equality and Non-Discrimination', in *Defining Civil and Political Rights: The Jurisprudence of the United Nations Human Rights Committee*, ed. Alex Conte, Scott Davidson, and Richard Burchill (Aldershot: Ashgate, 2004), 161, 172–4.
45. See text accompanying note 14 above.
46. Recommendation No. R (97) 20E (1997), Principle 1 (emphasis added). Cf., e.g., Boyle, 'Hate Speech', 489 (advocating incorporation of sexual orientation within hate speech bans).
47. See, e.g., *Otto-Preminger-Institut* v. *Austria*; *Wingrove* v. *United Kingdom* [1996] Eur. Ct. H. R. 1937. In *Jersild* v. *Denmark*, Eur. Ct. H. R., Ser. A, No.298 [1995], the Court struck down a

penalty imposed for the broadcast of racist views solely because they were broadcast within the context of expository journalism, not presented as the views of the journalist or broadcaster. There was no suggestion that the original speakers merited any freedom of speech.

48. See, e.g., *Conclusions and Recommendations of the Committee on the Elimination of Racial Discrimination: Denmark*, UN Doc. CERD/C/304/Add.2 (1996), para. A.3 (suggesting that, notwithstanding the European Court of Human Rights' judgment, Denmark retained an obligation under CERD to punish the offensive speech in *Jersild*). See generally, e.g., Committee on the Elimination of Racial Discrimination, *General Recommendation No.7: Measures to Eradicate Incitement to or Acts of Discrimination* (32nd Session, 1985), UN Doc. A/40/18 (1985), para. 120, reprinted in *Compilation of General Comments and General Recommendations Adopted by Human Rights Treaty Bodies*, UN Doc. HRI/GEN/1/Rev.6 (2003), 199.

49. See, e.g., ECRI General Policy Recommendation No. 1: Combating Racism, Xenophobia, Anti-Semitism and Intolerance, adopted on 4 October 1996; ECRI General Policy Recommendation No. 7 on National Legislation to Combat Racism and Racial Discrimination, adopted on 13 December 2002; European Commission against Racism and Intolerance (ECRI), General Policy Recommendation No. 8, adopted on 17 March 2004; ECRI General Policy Recommendation No. 9 on the Fight against Anti-Semitism, adopted on 25 June 2004.

50. On the concept of 'treatment' under non-discrimination norms, cf. Eric Heinze, *The Logic of Equality* (Aldershot: Ashgate, 2003), part 1.

51. Cf. generally Bossuyt, *L'interdiction de la discrimination*.

52. Cf. generally, e.g., 'What Is Disability', Disability Knowledge and Research, http://www.disabilitykar.net/learningpublication/whatisdisability.html (accessed 19 September 2008) (noting controversy about the concept of 'disability').

53. Cf., e.g., Heinze, *The Logic of Equality*, ch. 16.

54. See, e.g., Matsuda et al., *Words that Wound*.

55. See, e.g., Joseph Shapiro, 'Label Falls Short for Those with Mental Retardation', report of 22 January 2007, National Public Radio, http://www.npr.org/templates/story/story.php?storyId=6943699 (accessed 19 September 2008).

56. American Psychological Association, 'Guidelines for Non-handicapping Language in APA Journals', http://apastyle.apa.org/disabilities.html (accessed 19 September 2008) (emphasis added).

57. On age discrimination generally, see, e.g., American Association of Retired People, 'Age Discrimination at Work', http://www.aarp.org/money/careers/jobloss/a2004-04-28-agediscrimination.html (accessed 19 September 2008).

58. See, e.g., Obesity Society, http://www.obesity.org (accessed 19 September 2008).

59. See, e.g., *Guidelive.com*, review by Robert W. Butler of 9 February 2007, http://www.guidelive.com/portal/page?_pageid=33,97283&_dad=portal&_schema=PORTAL&item_id=52579 (accessed 19 September 2008) (reprinted from *Dallas Morning Post*).

60. See text accompanying notes 46–7 above.

61. See, e.g., 'Sport: Football Hoddle Sacked', *BBC Online Network*, 3 February 1999, http://news.bbc.co.uk/1/hi/sport/football/270194.stm (accessed 19 September 2008).

62. See, e.g., Tania Branigan and Alan Travis, 'Straw Moves to Ban Incitement against Gays', *The Guardian*, 9 October 2007, http://www.guardian.co.uk/gayrights/story/0,,2186690,00.html (accessed 19 September 2008).

63. At a global level, most disabled persons lack the basic services they require: see, e.g., Committee on Economic, Social and Cultural Rights, *General Comment No. 5: Persons with Disabilities* (11th Session, 1994), UN Doc. E/1995/22 (1995), 19, reprinted in *Compilation of General Comments and General Recommendations Adopted by Human Rights Treaty Bodies*, UN Doc. HRI/GEN/1/Rev.6 (2003), 24.

64. Recall the popular jibe long directed at Bush, 'Somewhere in Texas a Village Is Missing an Idiot!'; see, e.g., Michael Honigsbaum, 'Divided We Stand', *The Guardian*, 17 October 2004, http://observer.guardian.co.uk/review/story/0,6903,1329057,00.html (accessed 19 September 2008).

65. To draw an analogy, it is not merely Falstaff but Jews who are smeared when Mistress Page disparages Falstaff's deceit by calling him 'A Herod of Jewry'. William Shakespeare, *The Merry Wives of Windsor*, II.i.20.

66. Private communication of 24 December 2007, on file with author.

67. *Otto-Preminger-Institut* v. *Austria*.

68. According to *Encyclopaedia Britannica*: 'In the early 1990s the [Austrian] population was 84 percent Roman Catholic and 6 percent Protestant (mainly of the Augsburg Confession). Some 4 percent followed other religions – including the Old Catholic and Orthodox churches, Judaism, and Islam – while some 6 percent had no religious affiliation.' *Britannica Online*, http://www.britannica.com/eb/article-33395 (accessed 19 September 2008).

69. See *Otto-Preminger-Institut* v. *Austria*, para. 47 (interpreting article 9 of ECHR as protecting 'the religious feelings of believers' from 'provocative portrayals of objects of religious veneration').

70. Despite their advocacy of hate speech bans, Jean Stefancic and Richard Delgado have inadvertently noted that racist and other discriminatory incidents had *increased* in Europe after hate speech bans were introduced; 'A Shifting Balance: Freedom of Expression and Hate Speech Regulation', *Iowa Law Review* 78 (1992–3): 737, 745. Cf., critically, Heinze, Viewpoint Absolutism and Hate Speech', 577–8.

71. See, e.g., Disability Rights Commission, 'The Holocaust – Perfection Is the Issue, Says Disability Rights Commission', 26 January 2006, http://www.drc.org.uk/newsroom/news_releases/2001/the_holocaust_perfection_is.aspx (accessed 19 September 2008).

72. See, e.g., Matsuda et al., *Words that Wound*; Delgado, 'About Your Masthead'.

73. Delgado, ibid., 15.

74. Richard Delgado and Jean Stefancic, 'Images of the Outsider in American Law and Culture', in *Critical Race Theory: The Cutting Edge*, ed. Richard Delgado and Jean Stefancic, 2nd edn (Philadelphia: Temple University Press, 2000), 131, 225, 229 (reprinted from *Cornell Law Review* 77 (1992): 1258) (emphasis in original).

75. *Otto-Preminger-Institut* v. *Austria*, para. 52. Cf. R.A. Lawson and H.G. Schermers, *Leading Cases of the European Court of Human Rights*, 2nd edn (Leiden: Ars Aequi Libri, 1999), 573.

76. Report of anonymous reviewer for publication in *International Journal of Human Rights*, delivered to me via electronic communication on 2 August 2007.

77. See Eric Heinze, 'Even-handedness and the Politics of Human Rights', *Harvard Human Rights Journal* 21 (2008): 7.

78. UN GA Res. 217A (III), UN Doc. A/810 (1948), para. 71.

79. Universal Declaration of Human Rights, arts 1, 2, 7, and 28.

80. See notes 46–9 above.

81. Report of anonymous reviewer, note 76 above.

82. Cf. generally, e.g., Ronald Dworkin, *Taking Rights Seriously* (Cambridge, MA: Harvard University Press, 1977) (distinguishing between concepts of 'policy' and 'principle').

83. See, e.g., Matsuda et al., *Words that Wound*.

84. See *Chaplinsky* v. *New Hampshire*, 315 US 568, 571–3 (1942). Cf., e.g., Heinze, 'Viewpoint Absolutism and Hate Speech', 575–7.

85. See *Wisconsin* v. *Mitchell*, 508 US 476 (1993).

86. ECHR, art. 15; ICCPR, art. 4.

87. See, e.g., *Korematsu* v. *United States*, 323 US 214 (1944) (finding that national security may constitute a compelling government interest in abridging a constitutionally protected right).

88. Cf. ECHR, art. 1; ICCPR, art. 2(2).

89. Thus, for example, the United Nations Human Rights Committee's reference to 'exigency' inevitably presupposes levels of available resources to prevent violence or harm: *General Comment No. 29: States of Emergency (article 4)*, UN Doc. CCPR/C/21/Rev.1/Add.11 (2001), reprinted in *Compilation of General Comments and General Recommendations Adopted by Human Rights Treaty Bodies*, UN Doc. HRI/GEN/1/Rev.6 (2003), 186.

90. See, e.g., *Conclusions and Recommendations of the Committee on the Elimination of Racial Discrimination: Bulgaria*, UN Doc. CERD/C/304/Add.29 (1997), paras 8–9 (expressing concern about hate speech and hate crimes in Bulgaria).

91. See European Parliament Resolution of 26 April 2007 on homophobia in Europe, P6_TA-PROV(2007)0167, http://www.europarl.europa.eu/sides/getDoc.do?Type=TA&Reference=P6-TA-2007-0167&language=EN (provisional edition) (with special reference to Poland) (accessed 19 September 2008).

92. For a classic judicial statement, see, e.g., *Whitney* v. *California*, 274 US 357 (1927) (Brandeis J., concurring).

Challenging hate speech: incitement to hatred on grounds of sexual orientation in England, Wales and Northern Ireland

Kay Goodall

School of Law, University of Stirling, UK

In England and Wales (in 2008) and Northern Ireland (in 2004) legislation has been enacted to render it a criminal offence to incite hatred based on sexual orientation. This paper examines the relevant pieces of legislation and considers whether they can be kept sufficiently narrow in operation to protect one's freedom of expression. The paper also addresses criticism of such legislation, notably by Eric Heinze, based on arguments on equal protection and cause and effect. It concludes that in the UK, narrowly drafted legislation may have a useful, if marginal, impact and will not necessarily lead to the immense restrictions on freedom of expression that Heinze fears. Nor, however, will the legislation be likely to achieve radical social change while other powerful sources of discriminatory discourse remain uncontrolled.

Introduction

Less than half a century ago, consensual sex in private between adult males was a crime in the United Kingdom. If we read now the parliamentary records from that time, it is striking how supporters of reform sounded like today's persecutors. In the first of several debates on the famous *Wolfenden Report*,[1] the mover, Kenneth Robinson, Member of Parliament, remarked:

> I have no wish to suggest that I regard homosexuality as a desirable way of life. It is in my view undesirable for reasons which I will tell the House. It is undesirable because it leads so often to unhappiness, to loneliness and to frustration, because it entails in many cases heavy burdens of guilt and shame on those affected by it and because it seldom provides a basis for a stable emotional relationship. It may also possibly be undesirable on moral grounds because it is a sin, but these are matters on which I am not competent to pass judgment. Surely all this suggests that these unfortunate people deserve our compassion rather than our contempt.[2]

Another supporter, Antony Greenwood, Member of Parliament, noted:

> Tonight, we have had various estimates of the number of homosexuals in the country. Obviously, it is difficult for any of us to be positive about it. The lowest estimate which I have been able to find is 500,000, approximately the population of the City of Leeds. The highest estimate I have found is that they are nearly as numerous as the population of Wales.[3]

In 1960 – even with the growing support of broadsheet editors and moderate clergymen – it was a brave decision to speak in favour of the motion. Today, it is opponents of equality who regard themselves as the brave ones to speak out. The arguments they use, from accusations of paedophilic tendencies[4] to the description of same-sex sexual orientation as a sin and an abomination,[5] were however used almost fifty years ago. The difference now is that a bundle of sexual minority rights has been achieved. Society in the United Kingdom has changed so spectacularly that, in 2008, Stonewall and other campaigners successfully persuaded Parliament to render it a crime in England and Wales to incite hatred against any person based on his or her actual or perceived sexual orientation.

In this paper I examine this new law and its Northern Irish counterpart enacted in 2004 and ask whether this is the right direction for us to take. In particular, I consider the cogent arguments of Eric Heinze against sexual orientation-based hate speech bans. I conclude, with some reservations, that the legislation was the correct course to take.

Prior developments

There has been a whirlwind of decriminalisation and equality legislation in the UK in the last decade pertaining to sexual minorities. The ages of consent for different-sex and male/male sexual conduct are now finally equal;[6] criminal laws governing sexual behaviour in England and Wales no longer distinguish between different-sex and male/male participants;[7] civil partnership, albeit not marriage,[8] has been enabled;[9] adoption by same-sex couples has been made possible;[10] and a person may seek redress if he or she suffers sexual orientation-based discrimination in some areas of employment and provision of goods and services.[11] Once, consensual male/male sexual activity was a criminal matter; now the battle against homophobic crime is an official priority for the UK police forces.[12] Offences found to have a homophobic element are more severely punished.[13] These are only some of the more important developments. Policy too is changing, gradually taking account of the rights even of sexual minority children:

> if nothing else, surely realising that he ought to have been using the word *we* instead of always just that same cross, worn-out I in his angry mutterings would have helped ... He cannot account for himself; he cannot describe what he sees.[14]

In Neil Bartlett's poignant tale set in London in 1967, the protagonist toils to identify what he is feeling in a society in which he has never heard of homosexuality. Now, guidance to most schools issued by the Department for Children, Schools and Families requires that they provide sex education 'relevant' and 'sensitive' to the needs of all children, and that they are able to deal with homophobic bullying.[15] As we will see, the modern UK is still far from being a society in which it is entirely safe to express alternative sexual orientations. Nevertheless, it has come far. It is in this context that we should take a closer look at the new law.

UK laws concerning incitement to hatred on grounds of sexual orientation

Incitement to hatred on grounds of sexual orientation will constitute a criminal offence[16] in England and Wales[17] – not Scotland – when the relevant legislative provisions amending Part 3A of the Public Order Act 1986 are brought into force.[18] It has been an offence in Northern Ireland since 2004 under Part 3 of the Public Order (Northern Ireland) Order 1987;[19] indeed the Northern Irish legislation is considerably wider than that applicable in England and Wales, although no prosecutions appear to have been brought so far.[20] I will not discuss Scots law in this paper because there is as yet no corresponding legislation in the Scottish legal system. There is, however, potential for an interesting debate about the extent to which the flexibility of Scots common law could allow for a conviction for similar activities.

The provisions for England and Wales in Part 3A cover 'threatening' activities intended to stir up hatred against a group of persons because of their sexual orientation. This could be in the form of spoken words or behaviour or written material or a recording. Displaying material or publishing or distributing written material is an offence, as is distributing, showing or playing a recording. The offence can also (with some exclusions) include performing a play in public, broadcasting a programme or including it in a programme service, or possessing such material with the intention of broadcasting it. The offence can be committed in public or in private, but can only take place within a dwelling if the offending words or behaviour were heard or seen outside the dwelling and were intended to be heard or seen. It is essentially, then, a *public order* offence.

Sometimes commentators have described the offence as 'homophobic incitement', but Part 3A in fact covers persons of any sexual orientation, including heterosexual (although it does not make specific provision for those who are transgender[21]). Section 29AB refers to 'hatred against a group of persons defined by reference to sexual orientation (whether towards persons of the same sex, the opposite sex or both)'. There is no definition of sexual orientation in the Northern Irish Part 3. (One interesting question is whether the English Part 3A excludes asexuality – absence of sexual attraction.[22])

What is important is that the offence focuses on hatred directed against a *group*, rather than hatred targeting individuals. Another key element is the audience, which does not necessarily include the victim, but is rather a separate audience who can be stirred up (hate speech delivered directly at the victim can be usually covered within the ordinary criminal law[23]). What is important too is that there need not be an aim to incite a crime. Advocating violence or other criminal action is already covered by the law.[24] Rather, the offence consists of an incitement to *hatred*, which is not otherwise criminal behaviour. It was modelled very closely on the existing English provisions on incitement to hatred on grounds of religion, and, as we will see, both are worded extremely narrowly.[25]

There are now three areas covered by incitement to hatred legislation in England and Wales: race, religion, and sexual orientation. The oldest is that which covers incitement to racial hatred. The classic example of an incitement to hatred offence in the UK has been a leaflet through the ordinary public's doors, or a speaker at a meeting of a racist group, deliberately stirring up the intended audience with provocative, hate-filled statements about an ethnic minority. Any prosecution of all incitement to hatred offences must first be approved by the Attorney General.[26] The early convictions under the first specific offence (incitement to racial hatred, created by section 6 of the Race Relations Act 1965) involved extreme language and the ringleaders and active members of openly racist organisations.[27] This was how Parliament had intended the legislation to be used – for the most brazen activities.[28] Indeed, as the first version of the offence required proof of specific intent, it was often difficult to secure a conviction.

Part 3 of the 1987 Northern Irish Order was drafted much like the English Part 3A. It covers the same basic offences in similar wording, but it also goes much further. First, it does not necessarily require specific intent: it extends to acts that are *likely to* stir up hatred; 'likely', in this area of law, is to be objectively assessed in the light of all the circumstances.[29] Second, it also covers acts that 'arouse fear'. Third, it extends not just to threatening words or behaviour, but also to those which are abusive or insulting.

The aim of these sorts of legislation is to fill a perceived gap in the law. In most circumstances, those who stir up hatred are likely to commit an offence, such as when they abuse an identifiable individual, or when they incite others to commit a criminal act. Inciting others to hatred alone, however (rather than inciting them to commit an offence), is usually not unlawful except where it has been specifically provided for by statute. When the Bill that contained the amended Part 3A was introduced to Parliament, Ben Summerskill of Stonewall, a non-governmental organisation for sexual minority causes in the UK, produced evidence to the House of Commons Bill Committee that cited popular reggae lyrics that exhorted listeners to kill gay men and lesbians (these could, however, depending on context, amount to incitement to violence or to murder, which *would* be an offence). He also produced evidence of British National Party leaflets that explicitly linked paedophilic murders with homosexuality. When asked whether there was anything to suggest that such material had led to an increase in violence, he drew attention to the possibility of a link by citing Crown Office statistics showing a 167% rise over the two preceding years in convictions for crimes aggravated on grounds of sexual orientation.[30] Such links do not prove causation but they appear to have been sufficient for the Bill to succeed.

Neither statute provides a detailed explanation of what 'hatred' or 'incitement' is to mean (other than a list of the groups to which they are to apply), nor does the Northern Irish Part 3 define 'arousing fear', 'abuse', or 'insult'. It is likely that such words will be seen as 'ordinary' words and therefore a matter for the court of first instance.[31] Prior case law may be relevant, although in the case of the English Part 3A, the fact that it is a separate Part to the Public Order Act, rather than a simple amendment to the existing law on racial hatred, renders previous decisions less persuasive than they would otherwise have been.

The English Part 3A does, however, contain a saving[32] on freedom of expression (section 29JA), which states:

> In this Part, for the avoidance of doubt, the discussion or criticism of sexual conduct or practices or the urging of persons to refrain from or modify such conduct or practices shall not be taken of itself to be threatening or intended to stir up hatred.

This section was neither originally included in the provisions proposed by the government nor thought necessary by the Parliamentary Joint Committee on Human Rights.[33] It was inserted by the House of Lords at the eleventh hour. They had done the same thing two years before when they forced through an amendment to religious hatred provisions to include a similar provision.[34]

The sexual orientation hatred provision is less emphatic than its religious hatred counterpart, which provides that '[n]othing in this Part shall be read or given effect in a way which prohibits or restricts discussion, criticism or expressions of antipathy, dislike, ridicule, insult or abuse of particular religions [etc.]'.[35] The concern among Members of Parliament and the media about the religious hatred provisions was that they would discourage robust criticism and comic mockery of religious practices. The comedian Rowan Atkinson was given a great deal of media attention for his campaign over several years about the chilling potential of such legislation.[36] Less media time was given to concerns about the sexual orientation hatred provisions – and the main thrust of these was simply that the provisions would discourage criticism by those with religious beliefs. Presumably, those moving the amendment creating the second saving did not therefore regard it necessary to emphasise the continuing right of comedians to mock gay men and lesbians.

However, the express protection was not strictly necessary. This is because freedom of expression is already implicit as an aid to interpreting all UK legislation. Any UK statute must insofar as is possible to do so be construed in a manner compatible with the

Human Rights Act 1998.[37] Courts must take account of the relevant jurisprudence under the European Convention on Human Rights (hereinafter referred to as ECHR or 'the Convention').[38] The Human Rights Act requires that particular regard be had to the importance of freedom of expression embodied in Article 10 of the Convention.[39] Section 13 of the Human Rights Act similarly lays emphasis on upholding freedoms of thought, conscience, and religion, in accordance with Article 9 of the Convention. There are other kinds of protection under the Human Rights Act. Under section 19, ministers introducing a government Bill to Parliament must make a statement that in their view the Bill is compatible with the Convention rights listed in the Act.[40] All public authorities must also, under section 6, act compatibly with those Convention rights unless primary legislation expressly requires otherwise. This places a duty on the police and prosecution services to take human rights into account when investigating cases and deciding whether to initiate a prosecution.

It was therefore – as a matter of UK statutory interpretation principles – unnecessary to add the saving. Also, superfluous words risk making it harder for judges to interpret the law.[41] There is, however, a reasonable argument that, since one saving already exists for the religious hatred provisions, inserting another clarifies the legal position for those who are not familiar with the principles of statutory interpretation. Both may deter overzealous policing. They may also help protect against the effects of malicious or misinformed exaggeration of the extent of the law.[42]

Consistency and analogical extensions of human rights norms

Campaigners relied on what Heinze calls 'cumulative jurisprudence' to achieve the revision of the English Part 3A. They argued that it was logical to extend the established categories of the incitement laws (racial and religious) to include hatred on grounds of sexual orientation. Heinze defines cumulative jurisprudence as 'a systematic application of general human rights norms to categories of persons not expressly named or intended in leading human rights instruments'.[43] Here, the argument was that the experience of hate crime and incitement to hatred suffered by sexual minorities was similar to that experienced by ethnic and religious minorities on ethnic and religious grounds. With demonstrated evidence of this hatred towards individuals, and towards sexual minorities as a group, it would be equitable to extend the law on racial and religious hatred to cover sexual minorities.

Stonewall has successfully used this strategy before: indeed it has been their focused approach to campaigning for one incremental advance at a time which has been one of the organisation's most significant tactics in the twenty-first century, and which has attracted it considerable respect. The tactic has helped bring about some radical changes in law for sexual minorities in the UK, and it is an approach that, in general, Heinze supports. He has maintained that developments in sexual minorities law have been justified on a 'Principle of Extant Rights': they are necessary extensions of existing norms, because the differences between the existing norms and the proposed new one cannot be distinguished in any ethically relevant way (in the context of the surrounding norms of that particular society or international social order) in the light of the task the rights instrument is being asked to perform.

Obviously, this argument from indistinguishability is contextual and relative. There are legal orders in which societal norms (such as a constitution based on a moral principle of the inseparability of law and a governing state religion) could cast sexual orientation as a legally relevant ground justifying extensive discrimination. The human rights instruments Heinze considers here, however, have developed in a historical context in which religion – the only powerful current ethical framework in Western states which holds sexual orientation to be a relevant factor by which to make fundamental judgments about the worth of individuals – has been increasingly irrelevant as a ground on which to interpret the key norms of those instruments. (Individual states may, however, uphold religious norms within the discretion permitted within their margins of appreciation.[44]) To maintain a legal distinction that includes some victim groups but not others whose plight is ethically similar would therefore render the existing law capricious.

Heinze argues, however, that sexual orientation-based hate speech bans should be regarded differently. In his view, it is not appropriate to extend the law by deriving legitimacy in this way. The reason behind this is the consequences of providing fully equal protection.

Heinze takes the radical view that hate speech bans are inconsistent because they are seriously incomplete. His argument here is not that extending the law to sexual minorities would logically be a step too far. Rather, it is that it would not be *enough*. Whenever a group is systematically disadvantaged by discrimination it is entitled to the assistance of the law. Why draw the line at sexual minorities when there is such widespread verbal abuse directed at elderly and disabled persons? Better, he argues, that there be no hate speech bans, which are a threat to freedom of expression than that the legitimacy of human rights law be undermined by fragmentary developments.

During the parliamentary debate on amending the English Part 3A, Heinze's views were echoed by Gareth Crossman, the policy director of Liberty (the most prominent human rights campaigning body in the UK). Crossman argued that there was 'no logical reason' for creating an incitement law protecting on some grounds but not on the grounds of sex or disability. He suggested that new offences in this area seemed to develop in response to 'those who lobby most effectively to introduce that offence', adding that:

> If we are determining that some areas are suitable for that to be an offence, then unless you can show a logical reason why you should not extend it to any other area where somebody could be discriminated against, then it has to be piecemeal and slapdash. Let me make this absolutely clear. I am not saying – please let me make this absolutely clear – and nor is Liberty saying, 'Do away with all incitement to hate law. Do away with all speech offences.' What we are saying is that the way that the law is developing at the moment is undesirable.[45]

Equally, however, Crossman expressed concern about the proportionality of creating a generic offence of incitement to hatred.

Certainly, it is a fundamental value of human rights law that everyone is entitled to equal protection under the law. Indeed, this is the heart of Protocol 12 to the ECHR, which requires that all rights 'set forth by law' be secured without discrimination. They must be made available to everyone without discriminating between persons unless there is reasonable and objective justification for doing so. The official Explanatory Report for the Protocol observes that Article 1 (the general prohibition of discrimination principle)

> is not intended to impose a general positive obligation on the Parties to take measures to prevent or remedy all instances of discrimination in relations between private persons ... On the other hand, it cannot be totally excluded that the duty to 'secure' under the first paragraph of Article 1 might entail positive obligations. For example, this question could arise if there is a clear lacuna in domestic law protection from discrimination ... Nonetheless, the extent of any positive obligations flowing from Article 1 is likely to be limited.[46]

Thus, if there is differential treatment in the enjoyment of a right already set forth in national law, such as under the protection offered by incitement offences, this might amount to a breach of Protocol 12. The Protocol builds on and extends the limited anti-discrimination principle in Article 14. The UK has not yet ratified it,[47] but its adoption by the Council of Europe buttresses the argument for equality which Heinze makes.

There is an argument against Heinze here, though, which is that it would be justifiable to draw a line where the characteristics of the excluded groups make it in some way too difficult and unwieldy in practice for a revised law to operate successfully (i.e. where there is objective and reasonable justification to differentiate). It has in practice been more difficult to define disability for legal purposes than 'race' or religion or sexual orientation – and much harder to work out what would be reasonable accommodation to what can be a genuine and relevant difference.[48] But disability is no more a relevant reason for stirring up hatred than 'race', religion, or sexual orientation is. And in any case the ingenuity of modern human rights developments such as fourth-generation human rights that create anticipatory duties[49] should allow us to put this objection aside for now and consider Heinze's argument more fully. It forces our attention to the very heart of a niggling uncertainty that I suspect has stirred in the thoughts of any fair-minded jurist who follows the developments in anti-discrimination law.

An ad hoc answer, which would enable imperfect but necessary new laws to be enacted, is that the law has focused on those groups which can be shown to have suffered the deepest systematic discrimination over a long period of time in that state or social order. There is certainly good support for this argument. However, it is clearly not the whole or only explanation. Anti-discrimination law of all kinds has been enacted not only on the grounds of just desserts, but also where elite political opinion has been swung in favour of a group, often because of a calamitous event. In the UK we only need think of the legal changes brought about by the Race Relations (Amendment) Act 2000 after the immense publicity given to a critical report that (eventually) followed the murder of the young black student Stephen Lawrence.[50] Another precipitating factor is the successful mobilising of lobbying activity by effective campaign groups. Therefore, although it may in fact have been the most deserving social groups who have benefited from these events and activities, it is not necessarily so. Indeed, the persistence of disadvantage on the grounds of social class in the UK, most convincingly demonstrated by researchers such as Goldthorpe,[51] makes it clear that there remain large groups of deserving individuals who are silently excluded from the full benefits of current anti-discrimination law.

Furthermore, the law need not protect only the most needy. It could protect all who suffer significant disadvantage to the extent that this could legitimately be described as systematic or, if not systematic, at least significant in the likely life course of an individual. It might well be that there is a line that should be drawn where the benefit to society is overall reduced by the enactment of new law, because of the further complexity added to the legal regime when weighed against a sufficiently slight benefit to a group. But the position of that line needs to be identified by rigorous research, not implicitly assumed as at present. Heinze's argument is open to criticism, but we have yet to muster sufficient evidence to decide whether it is wrong, so debate should be had on whether UK laws deal with the appropriate range of concerns.

Implications for freedom of expression

Heinze develops this point to strengthen his case against hate speech bans. He maintains that, although this legal development by analogical extension is ethically justified in other areas of law, it is inappropriate in the case of hate speech bans.

Having argued that protection should extend further, he then invites us to consider the effect on other rights if broader hate speech bans were enacted. If we were fairly to acknowledge the harm caused by hate speech, Heinze insists, we would admit that the damage caused by words such as 'moron' used against those with learning difficulties or 'old bag' used against an elderly woman could cause the same level of harm as does the word 'nigger' used against someone of African or Caribbean origin or 'queer' used against a gay man. In his view, the amount of censorship that would be required for such broad bans is immense, so immense that he does not need to lay out for us what the deleterious effects would be; they are obvious.

Although Heinze's arguments at first glance might seem risible, there is no good reason for that gut reaction. Why should the fierce, contemptuous, or mocking use of a derogatory label against a member of a highly vulnerable group not amount to a potentially serious harm? Can we really say with confidence that a political figure, say, publicly describing a person with minor learning difficulties as a moron *cannot* cause distress, hurt, or fear among those with similar disabilities? Can we argue with any certainty that this cannot shore up a form of discourse which constructs such individuals as objects of contempt or antipathy?

That Heinze fully recognises this harm is one of the strongest reasons to think very seriously before disagreeing with his decision to oppose hate speech bans. An important question that Heinze does not fully address, however, is whether there is a difference, if not in character, in degree. Equal protection does not require identical treatment if the circumstances are relevantly different. The current UK incitement laws have been enacted where there is some evidence of a history or culture of stirring up hatred against those particular groups. Is there evidence of a comparable culture of *stirring up hatred* against those with learning difficulties, elderly individuals or those with learning difficulties in the UK?

Referring to a particularly brutal attack on an openly gay man, Heinze observes:

> [It cannot] be argued that blacks, Jews, or sexual minorities have more burdened histories. Nazism showed how physically or mentally disabled persons, along with all the propaganda—hate speech—concerning their threats to Aryan purity and perfection, led to extermination on the grounds of their putative sub-humanity. Might Chenu's attackers not just as eagerly have assaulted someone mentally or physically disabled, or someone elderly or obese? Can anyone argue that such an attack would not have been motivated by a cultural arsenal stockpiled with age-old barbs of 'idiot', 'spas', 'old bag', and 'fat slob'? It would require a leap of sociological imagination to argue that such an assault would be ignited by a consciousness promoted by hate speech when racially motivated but not when motivated by stereotypes of mental or physical conditions.[52]

It is a powerful point and this problem should be raised as a human rights argument much more often than it has been. Nevertheless, it needs qualification. Stereotyping language takes on a particular virulence in certain contexts. Words such as 'nigger' and 'dirty Jew' have become especially derogatory in Western states because of the particular history associated with, for instance, slavery and the Holocaust (and its predecessors such as the Russian pogroms), and because of the *continuing* evidence of hatred against those groups. Words such as 'Paki', for instance, clearly fall into the same category of disparaging labelling, but are not – yet – always regarded as equally toxic.[53] It may well be that the rising level of vilification directed at Muslims may lead to that changing.

When the Bill containing the amended Part 3A for England and Wales was introduced to Parliament, the government justified it by reference to vile examples of bigotry and violence, as noted above. Likewise, the official Explanatory Notes on the amending legislation for Part 3 for Northern Ireland specifically stated that there had been 'increases in recorded incidents involving victims defined by their sexual orientation'.[54]

Homophobic aggression remains a serious problem. According to recent research carried out for Stonewall, one in five gay men and lesbians in Britain stated that they had experienced a homophobic hate crime or incident in the preceding three years.[55] This is despite the fact that of those polled

> A third of lesbian and gay people alter their behaviour so they are not perceived as being gay specifically to prevent being a victim of crime. This includes not showing affection for their partners in public, dressing differently and avoiding areas where they could be identified as lesbian or gay.[56]

Stonewall rather naughtily called this study the 'Gay British Crime Survey', though it is nothing of the sort. The costly British Crime Survey was close to a miniature census of around 51,000 people,[57] carefully targeting a representative sample of the population in their homes, whereas Stonewall paid for a YouGov survey of 1721 people in which self-selected participants answered questions online. However, the British Crime Survey cost millions, and, given that it posed no questions covering this sort of hate crime, Stonewall's only option was to pay what it could afford (with some Home Office support) to get some-what nearer the precious statistics needed to convince government policy-makers. There is, however, strong supporting evidence in Northern Ireland, where state-funded research found a high and rising level of homophobic crime in some parts of Northern Ireland. It concluded that '[s]tudies conducted in Northern Ireland have consistently recorded high levels of homophobic attacks, both verbal and physical'.[58]

While Heinze rightly cites the history of Nazi persecution of persons with mental disabilities, he has not shown why words such as 'idiot' and 'moron' carry a connotation quite as sinister as 'nigger' and 'Jew' do when used in societies that participated in the slave trade and have been profoundly affected by the mass murder and expulsion of Jews across the world. Nor has he provided evidence of current persecution equal to that suffered by sexual minorities in the UK. Likewise, although there has long been evidence, for example, of severe domestic abuse carried out against elderly individuals,[59] there is less evidence of persecution of them as a group. Here, the difference is a question not of character, but of degree. We *can* relevantly distinguish.

Certainly, it was concluded that the problem of hatred on grounds of disability was sufficiently serious to justify creating a corresponding hate speech ban in Northern Ireland. This seems to have been based, however, on research on persons with learning difficulties carried out in England in 1999 by Mencap, a mental health charity. As a result of this research, and because disability has now been included as a specific statutory ground for sentencing enhancement in English law,[60] Parliament's Northern Ireland Committee report on hate crime had recommended extending the incitement law to include disability.[61] There appears to have been no other published evidence; another report by the same committee the following year noted that '[h]ate incidents and crimes against the disabled in Northern Ireland are the least well documented by the police and no statistics are available'.[62]

This is not to say, of course, that disability-based hate crimes are not a real problem, either in Northern Ireland or in England and Wales. Convictions for offences found to be aggravated on grounds of disability are now monitored, and in 2008 the magazine *Disability Now* featured a list of horrific examples.[63] However, evidence of widespread hate crimes against persons with disabilities is not the same as evidence of widespread *incitement to hatred* against persons with disabilities. The case remains to be made for a change in the English Part 3A to encompass disability. Nevertheless, it may well be that such a case can and soon will be made, and thus Heinze's argument must be taken seriously.

Cause and effect

Heinze has put forward another compelling argument against hate speech bans. He argues that although there are correlations between hate speech and hate crime, there is no evidence that the speech causes the crime. Without this evidence, hate speech that is less direct than 'fighting words'[64] should not be made subject to the criminal law. The distinction he makes is not based on any facile assumption that hate speech is harmless; he is astutely aware of the ways in which social understandings help construct and reproduce social roles. He is also quick to acknowledge that the speaking of words is an act with consequences, so that (to cite one of his examples) a person is not born a 'nigger' but is made one.

We should not forget that provocative words can have quite tangible results. Every nation has its history of incendiary demagogues who have not specifically advocated violence, but who have roused their audiences to a level of prejudice that has later spilled over into violence. One of the most frustrating and upsetting aspects of researching legal writing on hate speech is having to endure the mealy-mouthed or ignorant, or both, views of commentators who minimise the sting of hate speech while claiming that protection should not be available because victim groups are over-sensitive and too easily offended. It has been seriously unhelpful for legal debate that there are two common connotations of offensiveness in this context. One is displeasure – insulted sensibilities – and the other is aggressive hostility, likely to cause hurt or fear among vulnerable persons. It may be difficult in legal practice to distinguish the two, but that does not justify ignoring the distinction when discussing why legislation may be needed in the first place. Heinze does not make this mistake; rather he argues only that without sufficient evidence of cause and effect such speech should not be faced with the full force of the criminal law.

Given, however, that Heinze accepts that discourse helps reproduce social roles (it is the labelling that identifies the 'nigger'), it is odd that he steps back from accepting that hate speech can cause hate crime. Perhaps here we could distinguish between a sociological concept of cause in social research and a forensic concept of cause in criminal law. The law in the UK requires evidence of the stirring up to hate, not of the crime that may result, and so causation is not the concern here, which is what worries Heinze. It is extremely difficult to see how one could demonstrate direct causation between, say, the intemperate speeches of a far-right racist politician and an increase in assaults on ethnic minority individuals in their constituency, unless perhaps one of the assailants confessed that they had been motivated to act by the politician's bile. Such examples of course exist, but we are a long way from being able to extrapolate from particular examples to carry out the extraordinarily difficult task of predicting, in all the circumstances, which incidents of hate speech will lead to hate crime. Social sciences can achieve such a thing only in science fiction.

Nevertheless, research on racist discourse clearly shows general patterns. It shows that the impact of repeated discriminatory speech operates in an insidious way, not simply as individual acts of speech affecting relatively immediate audiences. It can take many forms, of which hate discourse is one, and we know that it can succeed. What we do not know to a high standard of reliability is how to predict when and where particular instances of hate speech will result in hate crime. But we do know that when it is successful, hate discourse acts as strategic persuasion, reinforcing and regenerating prejudiced beliefs and unequal treatment, and promoting – or, more accurately, undermining – social solidarity by distinguishing outsiders.[65] Where is the cut-off point that would prevent this leading to hate crime? The question then is not whether hate speech can lead, directly or indirectly, to hate crime. History shows that it can. It is whether, given our inability to tell *what* hate speech will achieve this and when in a particular context it *will*, we should ban any of it.

The difficulty, then, is that this process of causation is indirect and contingent. It is near impossible to show that one particular act or individual has caused or even is likely to cause this nebulous damage except in the unusual situation where there is compelling evidence such as perpetrator testimony. At best we can look at the wider discourse and context, then try and disentangle causes from correlations more broadly.[66] The distinction in ECHR jurisprudence between 'concrete expression'[67] and expression that spreads hatred more indirectly has been underdeveloped, legal debate about this problem being thus unhelpfully vague.

The important question, meanwhile, becomes where it is right in criminal law to draw a line. If the only concern was to prevent the reproduction of hate, we could prohibit even the most subtle forms of discriminatory speech, trampling gaily over freedom of expression. At the other end, if we require that a person can only be regarded as criminally responsible if we can prove to the criminal law's standard of proof, that is, beyond reasonable doubt, that their particular speech will cause their particular audience to commit a particular crime, then it is arguable that even fighting words should be excluded from the criminal law. What proof is there that *this* angry man whipping up *this* particular angry crowd will beyond reasonable doubt turn them into a mob? His behaviour may be deeply irresponsible, but we do not know enough about his audience to prove that he needs to be silenced. In reality, almost all of us accept that there should be some limitation of personal liberty in the interests of a public order that we can never be sure will result. This is the terrible problem we face, and Heinze's response, though clarifying the terms of the debate, does not solve it.

Legal threshold and protection of freedom of expression

This does not dispose of the discussion in the UK, however. What also needs to be considered is the history of prosecutions under incitement to hatred laws, and what threshold needs to be crossed for this offence. How much threat has it posed to freedom of expression thus far? What risks lie ahead? Heinze observes:

> We can safely assume that the films, newspaper or magazine articles, radio and television shows, and websites in which terms like 'idiot' and 'moron' appear—the same media that would no longer use 'nigger' or 'queer' in non-ironic or non-critical contexts—are innumerable. Remarkably broad censorship of both the media and everyday speech, backed up by legal penalties, would be required. Hate speech bans can only succeed either through enormous measures of censorship or through discriminatory selection of target categories or individuals.[68]

It may well be that the non-ironic or non-critical[69] use of 'nigger', which is regarded as an extraordinarily inflammatory label, would raise the possibility of prosecution for incitement to racial hatred, but there would need to be evidence that the speaker intended to stir up hatred or that in the particular context the word was likely to stir up hatred. The word alone would not constitute grounds for a civil action or a criminal prosecution in the UK, though if uttered by a public figure, it would likely lead to calls for his or her resignation or dismissal,[70] and not much more than the use of the word might suffice to provide grounds for a civil action or a criminal prosecution.

The threshold for sexual orientation hatred is higher and it is likely that any future extension of the law to new groups will be similarly restricted. The new English Part 3A applies only to *threatening* words and behaviour *intended* to stir up hatred on grounds of sexual orientation. Abuse and insult do not constitute incitement to hatred; it is clear from both the wording of the statute and from parliamentary materials – which are admissible evidence in court – that they are not encompassed in the offence.[71] Even if the English Part 3A were to be extended to include the grounds of disability, it still would not matter that a person expressed hatred in the form of words such as 'idiot' or 'moron' unless there were something more – an intended threat.

I have argued elsewhere that because the near-identical offence of incitement to religious hatred requires proof of both threat and specific intent (to be construed in the light of the freedom of expression provision) it will be almost unenforceable unless the accused confesses.[72] Equally, how easy will it be to prove, in the face of a not-guilty plea, that words were not just insulting or abusive, but were actually intended to be threatening and furthermore were intended to stir up others to hatred of gay men and lesbians as a group?

The history of racial hatred provisions in the UK – even when they have *not* required proof of intent – has been that prosecutions have been few and convictions consequently rare.[73] Similarly worded legislation in the Republic of Ireland under the Incitement to Hatred Act 1989 (which extends to sexual orientation) appears to have resulted in no convictions on grounds of sexual orientation[74] – and indeed by 2001 there had only been one conviction on *any* ground.[75] There have also been no prosecutions in Northern Ireland for incitement to hatred on grounds of either sexual orientation or disability – despite the wide wording that includes acts intended *or likely to* stir up hatred *or arouse fear*. On the other hand, there is no information to indicate whether this is because of a lack of will to prosecute; because the legislation is hard to enforce; because complaints to the police are not forthcoming; or because prosecutors suspect that juries would tend to acquit.[76] One government report did, however, suggest that the lack of convictions was due to 'problems of definition'.[77] If so, whatever the criminal justice context, it is a poor day for civil liberties and the fundamental value of legal equality if, instead of legislative clarity, we have prosecutorial restraint. As Lord Bingham observed in the House of Lords decision in *R. v. K.*:

> The rule of law is not well served if a crime is defined in terms wide enough to cover conduct which is not regarded as criminal and it is then left to the prosecuting authorities to exercise a blanket discretion not to prosecute to avoid injustice.[78]

Prosecutions in practice

The law in the UK needs to be understood, then, both in the light of its narrow wording and in the context of prosecutorial practice. Both should worry us. Bailey, Harris, and Jones have argued that one reason for the lack of case law on incitement to racial hatred was that racist literature had been less 'intemperate' than before.[79] Rumney has mounted a particularly spirited and well-researched defence of the legislation in practice.[80] But it is notable that for many years the practice was to prosecute only relatively severe cases of incitement to hatred – and not always some of those. Powerful interests can deter prosecutions. Geoffrey Bindman, one of the most respected human rights barristers and jurists in the UK, wrote recently of a decision to prosecute *The Sun* newspaper in 1986 for incitement to racial hatred. The decision was revoked after the paper's fearsome lawyer put pressure on the Attorney General behind the scenes.[81]

The most relentless assaults on some groups in the UK come from the print media. Research in 2008 on news stories about Muslims demonstrated a pattern of misrepresentation in which two-thirds of the 'news hooks' involved terrorism, religious difference, or extremism.[82] The worst offences by the press include publishing inflammatory stories that are nothing more than invention.[83] The United Nations Committee on the Elimination of Racial Discrimination commented in 2003 that the UK Press Complaints Commission needed to be made 'more effective' in dealing with racial discrimination,[84] a view the UK Parliamentary Joint Committee on Human Rights supported.[85] An academic study in 2008 found that the Commission had not upheld a single complaint about discrimination on grounds of race or ethnicity.[86]

It is unlikely, then, that the media targets Heinze identifies would be those who would face prosecution in the UK under a law criminalising incitement to hatred against persons with disability. This becomes clear if we look at the more recent prosecutions for incitement to racial hatred for analogous examples (ignoring for the moment the greater breadth of the racial hatred provisions than would be likely in the new legislation). The prosecutions encompassed such activities as preaching sermons that vilify Jews;[87] making speeches to supporters stating that Islam sanctions rape;[88] distributing leaflets alleging that 'Muslims' (which was held to be a codeword for Pakistanis) were 'running amok' and carrying out attacks in parts of Glasgow;[89] and chanting hate-filled language during a demonstration.[90] It is outsiders, albeit not ineffective outsiders, who are being prosecuted for perpetrating the offence.

In bleak contrast, there has been no suggestion of prosecuting the *Daily Mail* for claiming in 2003 that asylum-seekers infected with HIV were placing public health at risk when the parliamentary report from which this story originated had specifically stated that they were not the source of HIV infection from overseas. Worse still, the original report had expressed the view that it was prejudicial media reports that were in fact creating a situation where politicians felt obliged to isolate asylum-seekers, so that an asylum-seeker who did become infected would be less likely to get necessary medical care.[91]

Nor would even a mild reprimand from the Press Complaints Commission seem likely to be forthcoming for the likes of the *Daily Mail*. Chris Frost notes that in 2000 the Commission failed to find *The Sun*'s bileful language – singled out in examples such as 'scrounging Romanian gypsies' and 'our land is being swamped by a flood of fiddlers' – to be either racist or discriminatory. It appears that the Commission defended its decision on the grounds that the 'opinions' were not directed at individuals.[92]

Heinze posits two options: either hate speech bans exclude some groups discriminatorily or include all and so unacceptably limit free speech. There is a third option, however, which is that they include as many groups as need protection, but serve a primarily symbolic or expressive function, because they are so difficult to make use of. This is the approach the UK seems to be taking. It is open to criticism – particularly if the religious and sexual orientation provisions turn out to be almost unusable – but it does not suggest a high risk of an immense increase in censorship. It needs to be remembered that states parties to the ECHR are required not only to uphold Articles 9 and 10, but also to meet their Article 17 duty not to permit the deprivation of other Convention rights and freedoms.[93]

Are the UK laws really 'hate speech bans'?

It is worth asking whether the English Part 3A and the Northern Irish Part 3 genuinely amount to 'hate speech bans'. On the face of them, both would, particularly the Northern Irish Part 3. In his discussion of hate speech bans, Heinze focuses on two examples in international human rights instruments. Article 20(2) of the International Covenant on Civil and Political Rights requires the prohibition of 'advocacy' of specified grounds of 'hatred' that constitute 'incitement to discrimination, hostility or violence'. Article 4 of the International Convention on the Elimination of All Forms of Racial Discrimination requires states parties to prohibit among other things the 'dissemination of ideas based on racial superiority or hatred' and 'incitement to discrimination'. Article 4 is potentially very broad, but Article 20(2) is quite specific. The resemblance between these provisions and the language of the UK legislation is obvious.

There would be two difficulties with referring to the English Part 3A as a hate speech ban, however. First, it is not a ban on hate-filled speech as such – rather it is a ban on speech that seeks to incite others to hate. This is a significantly narrower category. It requires proof of specific intent to stir up others, which places a substantial burden on the prosecution. It also requires evidence of threat, not merely abuse or insult. The threat must be intentional, so it is not enough that abusive behaviour might in effect be threatening – the perpetrator must have intended that it be. Taking all these together, we see for instance that merely referring angrily to 'queers' would be far from enough to constitute an offence.

Second, it tends to focus judicial thought on acts affecting a relatively circumscribed audience, whether that be those in the immediate vicinity or those likely to view a recording or broadcast. Its primary task is to maintain public order, not to tackle aggressive bigotry in whatever form it occurs. While it may be that the Northern Irish provisions have been little used as a matter of political caution, the English legislation is very restrictively drafted.

The English Part 3A, then, does not ban all immoderate expressions of hate, but it does extend further than the classic prohibition of 'fighting words'. It deals not with inciting violence (which is a separate crime), or with inciting hatred against specific individuals (which is again subject to the ordinary criminal law), but with inciting hate against a group (where actual individuals need not be specified). What restricts it are the principles and rules I have discussed above.

This does not justify any complacency. I have argued that the English Part 3A (the religion and sexual orientation hatred provisions) is so narrow as to be almost unusable. The English racial hatred provisions are significantly broader and have for many years been a better example of legislation that is workable and that has not opened floodgates to prosecutions. It should also now be restrained by the freedom of expression provisions of the Human Rights Act 1998. However, decisions have been reached recently both in incitement to hatred law and in other areas of the criminal law which should cause concern. In *Hammond* v. *DPP*,[94] an evangelical Christian preacher was in the habit of setting up in a city centre square a large double-sided sign bearing the words 'Stop Immorality', 'Stop Homosexuality', and 'Stop Lesbianism'. This had previously attracted protest. On the occasion in question, members of the public found it distressing and insulting. A group of protesters assaulted Mr Hammond. Police officers asked him to take down the sign and leave but he refused. They then formed the view that he was provoking violence and arrested him for breach of the peace. He was convicted of an offence under section 5 of the Public Order Act 1986, aggravated on grounds of sexual orientation, for displaying an insulting sign within the hearing or sight of a person likely to be caused harassment, alarm or distress thereby. The appellate court held that it was proportionate to restrict his freedoms of expression and of thought, conscience, and religion because it had been open to the lower court to conclude that Hammond had knowingly gone 'beyond legitimate protest' and was provoking violence and disorder, which interfered with the rights of others, and that he had failed to demonstrate a defence that his behaviour was reasonable. There was therefore a legitimate aim of preventing disorder and thus a pressing social need for the restriction. Further appeal to the European Court of Human Rights was refused.

The court observed that a 'heckler's veto' was not justifiable, but it is hard to see how someone in Hammond's position could otherwise peacefully express his or her views in the face of persistent unrest. Ironically, in the light of the discussion here, it has been claimed that Hammond suffered from Asperger's syndrome.[95] If so, an impaired ability to make fine judgments about social situations would have made it harder for Hammond to identify when his actions had gone beyond legitimate protest.

Another question that remains is who the targets of the English Part 3A are. The offence of incitement to racial hatred, as we have seen, has a wider compass than the other incitement offences. There is no freedom of expression saving in the legislation to confine judicial attention, and it can be applied not just where there is intent to stir up hatred, but where this is merely a *likely* outcome. It covers not just threats, but also abusive and insulting words. I have mentioned above that it has long been used only for dealing with ringleaders and activists of organisations whose core activities promote racial division, but a recent decision has called this into question.

In *R. v. Saleem*,[96] one of the defendants, Saleem, was convicted of incitement to racial hatred after taking part in a demonstration about the Danish cartoons depicting Mohammed.[97] Saleem had led chants of, *inter alia*, 'democracy hypocrisy', 'UK you will pay', 'with your blood', and '7/7 on its way'. Similar chants were led against Denmark, Norway, and 'Europe'. For this, he was sentenced to four years' imprisonment (reduced to 30 months on appeal). What is disturbing about this conviction is, first, the presumption that the hatred likely to be stirred up was racial and, second, the context of the offence. Lord Phillips of Worth Matravers, Lord Chief Justice of England and Wales, delivering the judgment of the Court of Appeal of England and Wales, stated:

> The offences with which we are concerned involved a one-off demonstration, mounted at short notice without sophisticated planning. It has been urged on behalf of the appellants that re-publication of the cartoons caused worldwide outrage on the part of Muslims. Peaceful and lawful demonstrations in these circumstances would not have been objectionable. But, as Miss Ezekiel for the Crown pointed out, this demonstration was not lawful and was objectionable. It attracted ultimately a band of some 300 demonstrators, most of whom were young men. We have viewed each of the individual videos prepared for the purpose of the separate trials. Most taking part in the demonstration appeared to be joining readily in chanting the slogans that were led over the amplification. Insofar as this crude chanting and the messages on the placards solicited murder, we do not think that this was likely to persuade those who witnessed the demonstration in central London, or who saw the television broadcasts of it, to resort to killing, although one cannot be sure of the effect that it might have on those already inclined to terrorist activity.
>
> We have been more concerned to consider the likelihood that the appellants' conduct might have stirred up those taking part in the demonstration to acts of violence. The police who were monitoring the demonstration would have been obvious targets, as might have been the Danish Embassy. The Common Serjeant recorded that police officers had assessed the mood as excitable and that it appeared to be being whipped up into a frenzy by the speakers. The videos that we have seen did not portray the scene that this had suggested to us. While at times the chanting was loud and enthusiastic, the demeanour of the demonstrators did not appear to be violent or threatening. There was a considerable police presence. The police decided that to intervene might provoke disorder and this evaluation may well have been correct.
>
> Having said this, the demonstration took place only six months after the London bombings of 7 July and, at times, both these, the Madrid bombings and the attack of 9/11 were the subject of approbatory chanting. The exhortations on some of the placards and the subject matter of the chanting were offensive in the extreme. They were a demonstration of and an incitement to racial hatred. This must have been apparent to Saleem and we consider that the Common Serjeant was entitled when sentencing him to proceed on the basis that he intended to produce this result.[98]

The court's presumption that the chants led by Saleem were at their core racial was not at all apparent from the court's findings. In the context of the direct participation of the UK and the other named states in invading and occupying one or both of two Islamic countries (lest one forget, Afghanistan and Iraq), the chants could be taken as political rather than racial. To say this is not to downplay the odious violent content – particularly given that it took place only months after a bombing in that very city, which killed 52 victims – but rather to question the *racial* nature of the content. Supporters of the Irish Republican Army, for instance, were not convicted of incitement to racial hatred for similar seditious activities against the UK government, yet they did not always bother to distinguish between 'British' and 'British government'. The convictions depoliticised the actions of the participants.

It is, of course, hardly unusual for governments – and sometimes courts – to suppress political activity in times of terrorist violence. The measures that were used to silence even the most mannerly dissent at the height of the conflicts in Northern Ireland were breathtaking. The young and those with short memories would do well to read Larry Grant's discussion of the trial of pacifist Pat Arrowsmith for incitement to disaffection after she distributed leaflets in public, informing soldiers on how to leave the army.[99] The full text of the leaflet is reproduced in Grant's article and it appears, to modern eyes, almost laughably mild and polite. Denial of the political element of violent activism is not unusual either. What is worrying here is the apparent weakness of the justification offered for Saleem's conviction by the court for that particular offence. We are left with the fear that the breadth of the racial hatred legislation, which lacks any need for proof of specific intent, resulted in an inappropriate decision. The outcome suggests, as Lord Lester, the architect of the revised English Part 3A, recently said, that Parliament 'extended the race hate speech provisions very broadly indeed — perhaps too broadly'.[100]

Heinze's fears about the consequences of overly broad legislation, then, can be challenged but in the light of *Saleem* they are not to be casually dismissed. England, Wales and Northern Ireland may have managed to implement incitement to racial hatred legislation that has been of little threat to freedom of expression for many years. *Saleem*, however, threatens (from the available evidence) to be the harbinger of a new and repressive direction.

The question of how to protect rights and yet preserve a usable form of legislation is nevertheless no easy one. At the moment Members of Parliament and free speech campaigners may be congratulating each other for preventing the incitement to religious and sexual orientation hatred provisions from being so broad that they might threaten a reasonable degree of freedom of expression. It would be simple to suggest that the incitement to racial hatred provisions should be revised to achieve the same effect. But the decision may prove less popular if extremist groups contest the English Part 3A and find that they can design a thousand loathsome ways to escape it.

Little may be achieved, too, if a free hand is left to the daily print media. I carried out a newspaper search for reports and commentaries in UK local and national newspapers on the progress of the Bill to revise the English Part 3A. The great majority took a negative tone towards the Bill in its original format, contrasting it with 'free speech', which was always implicitly assumed to be achieved by minimum interference rather than by regulation. Most gave some space to arguments in favour of the Bill – but usually not before the last paragraph. A few were neutral in tone; these mostly appeared when the Bill was first announced. Only a handful were predominantly positive, two referring to the Bill 'which faces being blocked' and to 'unbridled free speech'. One turned out to be a *Daily Mail* piece dealing not with the incitement provisions but with separate Scottish proposals – and which had a twist in the tail, claiming that the proposals were causing a 'fierce backlash' among Scottish Muslims.[101]

The tone of the reports was not as negative as those which had covered the previous incitement to religious hatred proposals. There was also a great deal less hyperbolic rhetoric claiming that everyday critique and humour would be silenced. The underlying implication remained, however, that a group was receiving undeserved special treatment. This problem of a media meta-discourse that undermines groups through subtler attacks is difficult to tackle.[102]

Here there is a surprising but important point to be made about the reporting of prosecutions for incitement to hatred, and it suggests a direction for some interesting research to test it out. It is often argued that such prosecutions give the oxygen of publicity to small extremist groups. However, the prosecutions are generally reported with considerable distaste for the views of the groups on trial. Far from providing unhealthy publicity, they could be seen as providing some of the few occasions in which the media give significant attention to the deleterious effects of unregulated speech.

Conclusion

It should be apparent that no consensus on hate speech bans is about to be reached, and so I can only conclude with my own observations. I believe that there is room for restricted (but not unenforceable) incitement to hatred law where good evidence shows there is a history of hatred against specific minorities for the law to address. As Rumney points out, some extremist groups are secretive and isolationist, uninterested in dialogue. Incitement to hatred laws have been more successful than many assume in limiting the impact of extremist activities in the UK.[103]

Another necessary element is more intelligent political strategy. Malik describes the amended English Part 3A as 'a welcome sign of the commitment to take a zero tolerance approach to homophobic hate speech' but also emphasises that non-legal solutions are more important because the most serious source of hate speech is mainstream public discourse.[104] She focuses on abuse of Muslims, but her arguments are applicable more widely. She has also argued that the more useful approach in extremist cases may be informed political engagement with the illiberal groups where the groups are willing to take part, even if in some cases the motives of the groups are at first opportunistic. What must come first, though, is developing more sophisticated principles for debate.[105]

I doubt whether any of this is enough without stronger UK enforcement of sanctions against media abuse of freedoms. Though newspapers and broadcasters like to present themselves as champions of freedom of expression, most belong to private, profit-seeking corporations and all depend to some extent on audience figures. To pretend otherwise is cant, and their claim to a single noble motive should not be unquestioningly indulged. I have dealt here only with the print media, which occupy a shrinking sector of the market, but the bestselling newspapers are still powerful enough to shape public discourse and their excesses need to be controlled.

Finally, we have to consider the contradictory records of successive UK governments themselves. Government policies and communications to the public come with many voices and some have consistently appeased bigoted sentiment.[106] In a briefing to Parliament for an early and failed attempt to create an offence of incitement to religious hatred, Liberty made the following acid observation:

> Liberty is aware of the dangerous rise and promotion of anti-Muslim sentiment and hysteria over the last three years in this country. The Government would be wise to look to their own rhetoric and discriminatory and unjust policies before passing further criminal law.[107]

Acknowledgements

I am much indebted to Phil C.W. Chan for his generous and tireless efforts in improving the most intricate details of my paper. I would like to express my gratitude for his enthusiasm and professionalism, and his exceptional intellectual commitment to this special double issue. I also wish to thank Eric Heinze and the three anonymous reviewers for their helpful and insightful comments on an earlier version of this paper.

Notes

1. Wolfenden Committee, *Report of the Committee on Homosexual Offences and Prostitution*, Cmnd. 247 (London: HMSO, 1957); among other things the report recommended decriminalisation in restricted circumstances of some sexual acts between men not below the age of 21.
2. HC Deb., col. 1454–5, 29 June 1960.
3. Ibid., col. 1499.
4. See the material provided by Ben Summerskill of Stonewall to the Public Bill Committee examining the Criminal Justice and Immigration Bill, HC Deb., col. 75, 16 October 2007.
5. New Northern Ireland Assembly member Iris Robinson, wife of the Northern Irish First Minister, http://news.bbc.co.uk/1/hi/northern_ireland/7482263.stm (accessed 23 August 2008).
6. Sexual Offences (Amendment) Act 2000 (c. 44), s. 1. Note that the age of consent in England, Wales and Scotland is 16 but it is 17 in Northern Ireland. A controversial draft Sexual Offences (Northern Ireland) Order 2007 has been proposed to reduce the age of consent in Northern Ireland to 16.
7. Sexual Offences Act 2003 (c. 42), s. 140 and Sch. 7.
8. The distinction was widely debated in the UK in academic writing: for a useful introduction, see the special issue of *Law and Policy* 26, no. 1 (2004). See also the critical discussion by Kristen Walker on the demerits of same-sex marriage: 'The Same-Sex Marriage Debate in Australia', *International Journal of Human Rights* 11, nos 1–2 (2007): 109.
9. Civil Partnership Act 2004 (c. 33).
10. It was previously possible for a gay man or lesbian to adopt as an individual but not as part of a same-sex couple. It is a complex area of law, but see in particular the Adoption and Children Act 2002 (c. 38), and section 30 of the Adoption and Children (Scotland) Act 2007, asp 4, in relation to same-sex couples. Consultation has been taking place in Northern Ireland on the possibility of similar legislation.
11. See, in particular, Employment Equality (Sexual Orientation) Regulations 2003/1661; Equality Act 2006 (c. 3); and a forthcoming comprehensive Equality Bill tabled to be introduced to Parliament in 2009.
12. See, e.g., *Hate Crime: Delivering a Quality Service* (London: Association of Chief Police Officers and Home Office Police and Partnership Standards Unit, 2005), ch. 2.
13. See Criminal Justice Act 2003 (c. 44), s. 146; Criminal Justice (Scotland) Act 2003, asp 7, s. 74; and Criminal Justice (No. 2) (Northern Ireland) Order 2004/1991 (NI 15), Art. 2. These provide for enhanced sentencing where it is proved that an offence was aggravated by hostility (in Scotland, 'malice and ill-will') related to sexual orientation.
14. Neil Bartlett, *Skin Lane* (London: Serpent's Tail, 2007), 204–5, 250.
15. United Kingdom Department for Children, Schools and Families, *Sex and Relationship Education Guidance*, DfEE 0116/2000, 12–13. Note that the guidance covers England, Wales and Northern Ireland only (Scotland deals with these matters separately under the devolution settlement) and does not apply to independent schools; parents may also withdraw their children in state schools from these lessons.
16. To be precise, the English legislation creates several offences under one umbrella, as does the Northern Irish. For the sake of clarity, though, I will refer to each as if there were a single offence in each jurisdiction.
17. All references in this paper to 'English law' or 'English Part 3A' also encompass Wales.
18. See the revised section 29A in Part 3A of the Public Order Act 1986 (c. 64), as amended by the Criminal Justice and Immigration Act 2008 (c. 4), s. 74 and Schs 16 and 28, Part 5. My thanks to Santiago Alonso for correcting my misunderstanding of these.
19. Part 3 (Articles 8–17) of the Public Order (Northern Ireland) Order 1987 (NI 7), as amended by Article 3 of the Criminal Justice (No. 2) (Northern Ireland) Order 2004/1991 (NI 15), which came into force on 28 September 2004.
20. See statement of Maria Eagle, Parliamentary Under-Secretary of State for Justice, to the House of Commons Public Bills Committee discussing the Criminal Justice and Immigration Bill on 29 November 2007. A LexisNexis search I carried out for this paper also did not uncover any Northern Irish case law on the subject.
21. The United Kingdom Parliamentary Joint Committee on Human Rights noted that evidence so far indicated that the kinds of incidents experienced by transgender individuals tended to be covered by the existing criminal law, and that there was currently no evidence of incitement

to hatred against them as a group. It concluded, however, that 'urgent' research should be carried out. *Fifteenth Report*, March 2008, HMSO, paras 2.18–2.20.

22. Thanks to Ian McLeod for raising this point.

23. See, e.g., sections 4, 4A and 5 of the Public Order Act 1986 (c. 64), covering a range of offences involving threatening, abusive or insulting words or behaviour where these are likely or intended to cause harassment, alarm and distress. The Protection from Harassment Act 1997 (c. 40) covers an extensive range of behaviours amounting to harassment. Other offences attract enhanced sentencing under several statutory provisions (general and specific) where there is evidence of motivation or demonstrated hostility related to sexual orientation.

24. This was originally a matter for the common law of incitement to crime: now see Serious Crime Act 2007 (c. 27), Part 2, on encouraging or assisting crime, which covers England, Wales and Northern Ireland. Note that conspiring or soliciting to commit murder is covered by section 4 of the Offences Against the Person Act 1861 (c. 100).

25. These are also to be found in Part 3A, and pre-date the amendment.

26. Where they extend to Scotland – which is the case only with incitement to racial hatred – the equivalent law officer is the Advocate General.

27. See the cases discussed in Geoffrey Bindman, 'Incitement to Racial Hatred', *New Law Journal* (March 1982): 299.

28. B.A. Hepple, 'Race Relations Act 1965', *Modern Law Review* 29 (1966): 314.

29. See discussion in A.T.H. Smith, *Offences against Public Order* (London: Sweet & Maxwell, 1987), 157.

30. Public Bill Committee examining the Criminal Justice and Immigration Bill, HC Deb, col. 75, 16 October 2007.

31. See the leading case of *Brutus* v. *Cozens* [1973] AC 854; see also Smith, *Offences against Public Order*, 42–3, 151–2.

32. Readers from outside the UK may be unfamiliar with the term 'saving'. A saving is a provision 'the intention of which is to narrow the effect of the enactment to which it refers so as to preserve some existing legal rule or right from its operation': F.A.R. Bennion, *Bennion on Statutory Interpretation: A Code*, 5th edn (London: Butterworths, 2008), 725.

33. *Fifth Report*, January 2008, HMSO, para. 1.64: the Committee stated that the provisions as introduced provided in their view 'an appropriate degree of protection for human rights'.

34. HL Debs, *passim*, 7 May 2008. On the amendments regarding incitement to religious hatred in the original Bill creating Part 3A, see Ivan Hare, 'Crosses, Crescents and Sacred Cows: Criminalising Incitement to Religious Hatred', *Public Law* (2006): 520; Kay Goodall, 'Incitement to Religious Hatred: All Talk and No Substance?', *Modern Law Review* 70 (2007): 90.

35. Public Order Act 1986, (c. 64), s. 29J.

36. Atkinson had also campaigned against the earlier failed proposals to introduce the offence. A speculative search of LexisNexis Butterworths News on 18 July 2008, covering all UK regional and national newspapers, simply on the search terms 'Rowan Atkinson', 'religious hatred' and 'law', brought up 510 citations. It should be noted that some of these are duplicates, but it remains evident that the press coverage was substantial.

37. Human Rights Act 1998 (c. 42), s. 3.

38. Ibid., s. 2.

39. Ibid., s. 12.

40. These include Articles 2–12 and 14, and Articles 1 to 3 of the First Protocol and Articles 1 and 2 of the Sixth Protocol, as read with Articles 16 to 18 of the Convention: see section 1 and Schedule 1.

41. As F.A.R. Bennion notes: 'On the presumption that Parliament does nothing in vain, the court must endeavour to give significance to every word of an enactment': *Bennion on Statutory Interpretation: A Code*, 5th edn (London: Butterworths, 2008), 1157. Surplusage is therefore to be avoided.

42. Stonewall did not object to the possibility of such a saving being introduced when it was initially posited at the Public Bill Committee examining the Criminal Justice and Immigration Bill, HC Deb, col. 75, 16 October 2007.

43. Eric Heinze, 'Cumulative Jurisprudence and Human Rights: The Example of Sexual Minorities and Hate Speech', *International Journal of Human Rights* 13, nos 2–3 (2009): 193, 194.

44. The doctrine of margin of appreciation as developed in the jurisprudence of the European Court of Human Rights and associated bodies is a recognition that the Convention is

implemented in states parties with different economic, political and cultural histories and distinctive legal systems. In the area of freedom of expression, the Court discussed this doctrine in *Handyside* v. *United Kingdom* (1976) 1 EHRR 737.

45. Public Bill Committee examining the Criminal Justice and Immigration Bill, 18 October 2007, cols 127 and 129–30.

46. Protocol No. 12 to the Convention for the Protection of Human Rights and Fundamental Freedoms, *Explanatory Report*, Council of Europe. The justificatory restriction derives from Convention jurisprudence: see Robert Wintemute, 'Filling the Article 14 "Gap": Government Ratification and Judicial Control of Protocol No 12 ECHR', *European Human Rights Law Review* (2004): 485.

47. See also *Abdulaziz et al.* v. *United Kingdom*, 28 May 1985, Series A, No. 94, (1985) 7 EHRR 471, where an applicant was permitted to rely on Protocol 4, which the UK had not ratified.

48. As regards the UK, see, e.g., the informed discussion in David I. Hosking, 'A High Bar for EU Disability Rights', *Industrial Law Journal* 36 (2007): 28.

49. Sandra Fredman, *Discrimination Law* (Oxford: Oxford University Press, 2002), ch. 6. Such rights focus on broadening the context of institutional responsibility, for instance imposing a positive duty on an organisation requiring it to be proactive in monitoring recruitment and progress of members of disadvantaged groups within the organisation. This can be compared with a more traditional reactive responsibility that only requires organisations to respond to individual allegations of discrimination as they occur.

50. Sir William Macpherson, *The Stephen Lawrence Inquiry*, Cmnd. 4262-I (London: HMSO, 1999).

51. J.H. Goldthorpe, 'Globalisation and Social Class', *West European Politics* 25, no. 3 (2002): 1.

52. Heinze, 'Cumulative Jurisprudence and Human Rights', 201.

53. In *DPP* v. *Green* [2004] EWHC QB 1225, the court at first instance held that the repeated use of the word 'Paki' accompanied by several expletives did not in this case indicate racist hostility, but rather was in the context of use as a 'racial name' that appeared to mean a neutral label. The decision was criticised and overturned on appeal, although the appellate court observed, citing *R.* v. *Woods* [2002] EWHC 85 (Admin), that there can be cases that have a racially neutral gravamen but nonetheless with demonstrated hostility based on the victim's membership of a racial group. The appellate court did not offer an opinion on whether the use of the word 'Paki' was capable of falling under this heading.

54. Explanatory Memorandum to Criminal Justice (No. 2) (Northern Ireland) Order 2004, SI 2004 No. 1991 (NI 15), 2004, HMSO, paras 2–3.

55. Sam Dick, *Homophobic Hate Crime: The Gay British Crime Survey 2008* (London: Stonewall, 2008), http://www.stonewall.org.uk/documents/homophobic_hate_crime__final_report.pdf (accessed 19 September 2008).

56. Ibid., 31.

57. For more information, see http://www.homeoffice.gov.uk/rds/bcs-methodological.html (accessed 19 September 2008).

58. Katy Radford, Jennifer Betts and Malcolm Ostermeyer, *Policing, Accountability and the Lesbian, Gay and Bisexual Community in Northern Ireland* (Belfast: Institute for Conflict Research, 2006), 16, http://www.conflictresearch.org.uk/documents/LGB%20book%20 complete.pdf (accessed 19 September 2008). See also Neil Jarman and Alex Tennant, *An Acceptable Prejudice? Homophobic Violence and Harassment in Northern Ireland* (Belfast: Institute for Conflict Research, 2003), http://www.conflictresearch.org.uk/documents/ICR_ Homoph.pdf (accessed 19 September 2008).

59. For a summary of early research in the United States, see Karl Pillemer, 'The Dangers of Dependency: New Findings on Domestic Violence against the Elderly', *Social Problems* 33, no. 2 (1985): 146.

60. See section 146 of the Criminal Justice Act 2003 (c. 44), which provides for increase in sentences for aggravation related to disability or sexual orientation (see also section 145, which covers racial and religious aggravation).

61. Select Committee on Northern Ireland Affairs, *Fifth Report*, 'Hate Crime: The Draft Criminal Justice (Northern Ireland) Order 2004', HC 615, HMSO.

62. Select Committee on Northern Ireland Affairs, *Ninth Report*, 'The Challenge of Diversity: Hate Crime in Northern Ireland', HC 548-I, HMSO, para. 16.

63. See http://news.bbc.co.uk/1/hi/uk/7203232.stm (accessed 19 September 2008).

64. See the United States Supreme Court decision in *Chaplinsky* v. *New Hampshire*, 315 US 568 (1942), and Eric Heinze's discussion of the case in 'Viewpoint Absolutism and Hate Speech', *Modern Law Review* 69 (2006): 543.

65. See, e.g., Clay Calvert, 'Hate Speech and Its Harms: A Communication Theory Perspective', *Journal of Communication* 47, no. 1 (1997): 4.

66. For an interesting and exceptionally informed discussion of this in the context of health, see Nancy Krieger, 'Does Racism Harm Health?', *American Journal of Public Health* 93, no. 2 (2003): 194. For a more sceptical perspective, see Larry Alexander, *Is There a Right of Freedom of Expression?* (New York: Cambridge University Press, 2005). Alexander concludes that justified legislation in this field 'will always be limited, local, and based on hunches about consequences': 193.

67. *Gündüz* v. *Turkey*, 4 December 2003, Application No. 35071/97, 41 EHRR 59, para. 40.

68. Heinze, 'Cumulative Jurisprudence and Human Rights', 201.

69. Readers will probably be familiar with the case of *Jersild* v. *Denmark*, (A/298) (1995) 19 EHRR 1, where the broadcast of foul racist remarks about black people was held by the European Court of Human Rights to be in the light of all the circumstances justified.

70. See the 2008 example of a shadow government spokesperson using the phrase 'nigger in the woodpile' (it appears that this was not simply an uncharacteristic slip): http://www.timesonline.co.uk/tol/news/politics/article4297283.ece (accessed 19 September 2008).

71. The point was repeatedly made during parliamentary debates: for a list of the many occasions on which the Bill was debated (it covered several topics other than the incitement to hatred offence), see http://services.parliament.uk/bills/2007-08/criminaljusticeandimmigration.html (accessed 19 September 2008).

72. Goodall, 'Incitement to Religious Hatred', 112–3. Indeed, Helen Fenwick and Gavin Phillipson have argued that these restrictions are 'a strong and welcome contrast' to the potential breadth of the law on racial hatred: *Media Freedom, Offence, Morality and Hate Speech* (Oxford: Oxford University Press, 2006), 516.

73. Between 1988 and 2007, there were 84 prosecutions and 60 convictions: Parliamentary Joint Committee on Human Rights, *Fifth Report* (2008), HMSO, Appendix 2, para. 10. See also Peter Thornton, *Public Order Law* (London: Gaunt, 1987), 61.

74. Donncha O'Carroll, *Legal Study on Homophobia and Discrimination on Grounds of Sexual Orientation – Ireland, European Union Agency for Fundamental Rights* 2008, para. 33, http://fra.europa.eu/fra/material/pub/comparativestudy/FRA-hdgso-NR_IE.pdf (accessed 19 September 2008). The study deals only with the period of 2000–05, but there is no information suggesting any prosecution before or since.

75. John O'Donoghue, Minister for Justice, Equality and Law Reform, Dáil Debates 541, 3 October 2001, 60–1.

76. See Donncha O'Carroll, *Legal Study on Homophobia*, http://www.fra.europa.eu/fraWebsite/attachments/FRA-hdgso-NR_UK.pdf (accessed 11 March 2009), commissioned by the European Union Agency for Fundamental Rights, Vienna, and also the citation therein of Patricia M. Leopold, 'Incitement to Hatred – The History of a Controversial Criminal Offence', *Public Law* (1977): 389, 401–2. Leopold argues that the absence of prosecutions in Northern Ireland during the period when its incitement to racial hatred laws required specific intent was not due to the wording of the statute but because 'a Northern Irish jury was unable to be objective about a case of incitement'.

77. Northern Ireland Affairs Committee, *Inquiry into Hate Crime in Northern Ireland* (2004), 6.

78. [2002] 1 AC 462, 475. Consider also of course the extensive European Convention on Human Rights jurisprudence on interference with rights in accordance with law.

79. S.H. Bailey, D. Harris, and D.C. Ormerod, *Bailey, Harris & Jones Civil Liberties: Cases and Materials*, 5th edn (London: Butterworths, 2001), 1156. See also Anthony Lester and Geoffrey Bindman, *Race and Law* (London: Penguin, 1972), 371.

80. Philip N.S. Rumney, 'The British Experience of Racist Hate Speech Regulation: A Lesson for First Amendment Absolutists?', *Common Law World Review* 32, no. 2 (2003): 117.

81. Geoffrey Bindman, 'Inciting Hatred', *New Law Journal* 157 (2007): 1086.

82. Kerry Moore, Paul Mason and Justin Lewis, *Images of Islam in the UK: The Representation of British Muslims in the National Print News Media, 2000–2008*, (Cardiff: Cardiff School of Journalism, Media and Cultural Studies, 2008), http://www.cardiff.ac.uk/jomec/resources/08channel4-dispatches.pdf (accessed 19 September 2008).

83.   Peter Oborne, *The Independent*, 7 July 2008, http://www.independent.co.uk/news/media/the-shameful-islamophobia-at-the-heart-of-britains-press-861096.html (accessed 19 September 2008).

84.   United Nations Committee on the Elimination of Racial Discrimination, *Concluding Observations of the Committee on the Elimination of Racial Discrimination*, CERD/C/63/CO/11, 10 December 2003.

85.   Parliamentary Joint Committee on Human Rights, *Tenth Report*, March 2007, para. 366.

86.   Chris Frost, 'The Press Complaints Commission: A Study of Ten Years of Adjudications on Press Complaints', *Journalism Studies* 5, no. 1 (2004): 101, 111–2.

87.   *R.* v. *El-Faisal*, [2004] All ER (D) 107, and *R.* v. *Hamza*, 7 February 2006 (unreported); see Simon Freeman, *The Times*, 7 February 2006. As the defendants also exhorted followers to kill or inflict violence on Jews and others, both were convicted of incitement to murder as well.

88.   *R.* v. *Griffin and Collett*, 2 February 2006 (unreported); see *The Guardian*, 2 February 2006. The defendants were acquitted. Video extracts from BBC recordings of the speeches, in which Griffin said among other things 'any woman that they can take by force or guile is theirs', http://news.bbc.co.uk/1/hi/england/bradford/6135060.stm (accessed 19 September 2008).

89.   *P.F.* v. *Wilson* (Sheriff Court), 24 October 2002 (unreported) (my thanks to the Crown Office for providing a copy of the Sheriff's decision).

90.   *R.* v. *Saleem, R.* v. *Muhid, R.* v. *Javed*, 2007 WL 3130840, [2007] EWCA Crim 2692, [2007] All ER (D) 462.

91.   Nick Davies, *Flat Earth News* (London: Chatto & Windus, 2008), 374.

92.   Frost, 'The Press Complaints Commission'.

93.   See, e.g., *Kühnen* v. *Federal Republic of Germany*, 12 May 1988, Application No. 12194/86, (1988) 56 DR 205, where the European Commission of Human Rights stated that freedom of expression embodied in Article 10 could not be relied upon in order to carry out activities that were aimed at the destruction of other Convention rights as prevented by Article 17.

94.   [2004] EWHC 69 (Admin), [2004] All ER (D) 50.

95.   See http://www.christian.org.uk/rel_liberties/cases/harry_hammond.htm (accessed 17 September 2008).

96.   *R.* v. *Saleem, R.* v. *Muhid, R.* v. *Javed*, 2007 WL 3130840, [2007] EWCA Crim 2692, [2007] All ER (D) 462.

97.   In 2005, Danish newspaper *Jyllands-Posten* published several cartoons depicting the prophet Mohammed. Such depictions offended Muslims greatly, and the paper justified their publication as a contribution to debate about censorship. Reaction to the cartoons (which was intensified by the malicious circulation of more extreme cartoons, in the pretence that they had been published by the same paper) led to Muslim protests worldwide, resulting in arsons and deaths.

98.   *R.* v. *Saleem*, paras 45–7.

99.   Larry Grant, 'Incitement to Disaffection', *Index on Censorship* 3, no. 3 (1974): 3. There are many good works on the broader topic of suppression of freedoms of expression and of association in this context, such as the decades of writings by Keith Ewing, Conor Gearty, Clive Walker and many others, but a short and startling piece from that time is David R. Lowry and Robert J. Spjut, 'The European Convention and Human Rights in Northern Ireland', *Case Western Reserve Journal of International Law* 10 (1978): 297.

100. H.L. Deb., 7 May 2008, col. 598.

101. Graham Grant, 'Muslims' Anger over SNP's Pro-Gay Stance', 21 January 2008.

102. There is a huge literature on this in social psychology in particular; for classic texts, see the work of T.A. van Dijk, and also M. Wetherell and J. Potter, *Mapping the Language of Racism* (London: Harvester Wheatsheaf, 1992).

103. Rumney, 'The British Experience'.

104. Maleiha Malik, 'Speech Control', *Index on Censorship* 36, no. 4 (2007): 21.

105. Maleiha Malik, 'Engaging with Extremists', *International Relations* 22 (2008): 85.

106. On anti-immigrant government discourse, see, e.g., Bill Dixon and David Gadd, 'Getting the Message? "New" Labour and the Criminalization of "Hate"', *Criminology and Criminal Justice* 6 (2006): 309, 312–4; John Solomos, *Race and Racism in Britain*, 3rd edn (London: Palgrave Macmillan, 2003), chs 3 and 4.

107. Serious Organised Crime and Police Bill, Liberty's briefing for second reading in the House of Lords, March 2005, para. 32.

Gay male rape victims: law enforcement, social attitudes and barriers to recognition

Philip N.S. Rumney

Department of Law, University of the West of England, UK

This paper examines the experiences of gay male rape victims. It discusses findings from empirical studies of police attitudes along with an increasing number of studies that have examined the experiences of these victims. It also considers social attitudes to this group of victims and the way in which those attitudes impact legal responses to the problem of male rape. Further, this paper identifies three barriers to the recognition of male rape: denial of the problem, hierarchies of suffering, and victim-blaming. Finally, it concludes by considering two possible strategies for improving the treatment of male sexual victimisation within the criminal justice system in England and Wales.

Introduction

In the last two decades there has been a significant growth in research examining the problem of adult male rape, on such issues as the problem of male sexual victimisation within institutional settings,[1] within the general population[2] and during wartime,[3] and also the nature, dynamics and impact of male victimisation.[4] More recently, there has been a growth in research examining male victims' experiences of the criminal justice system. Such research has challenged many societal myths regarding adult male sexual victimisation and has also highlighted the extent to which misunderstandings regarding male rape influence the attitudes of criminal justice professionals and of the wider community.[5]

Despite claims to the contrary,[6] there exists a significant body of work that examines adult male sexual victimisation. There are, however, specific areas that have received little sustained attention. One of these areas concerns the treatment of gay male rape victims within the criminal justice system. This is a particular problem because a significant number of male rape and sexual assault victims are gay and epidemiological research suggests that homosexuality is a particular risk factor in cases of adult sexual victimisation.[7] Gay men also face physical and sexual assault as part of homophobic attacks[8] and are also targeted for rape within prisons where they tend to appear to receive little protection from authorities.[9] The combination of sexual victimisation and negative societal attitudes towards homosexuality does raise the question of whether gay male rape victims are subjected to a form of double victimisation. After being sexually victimised, do they also face particular difficulties in securing appropriate treatment by the criminal justice system? An examination of social and legal responses to gay male rape victims gives us an insight into the extent to which progress has been made in addressing sexuality-based discrimination, while recognising the difficulties facing male rape victims irrespective of their sexuality.

This paper seeks to draw together existing evidence that examines rapes of gay men as well as the policing of such sexual violence. Further, it will analyse the ways in which negative social attitudes may hinder the reporting of male rape to the police and the enforcement of the criminal law when it is reported.

Social attitudes and rape law enforcement

There is compelling evidence that social attitudes have a negative impact on the enforcement of the criminal law on rape and sexual assault. Temkin and Kraché have recently engaged in a detailed analysis of the impact of social attitudes on rape law enforcement in cases involving female victims. They argue that the treatment of rape cases by the criminal justice system relies upon

> stereotypical beliefs about rape which contain a restrictive and inaccurate understanding of what 'real rape' is. By reducing the range of what is considered a genuine rape complaint, these stereotypes are a contributory factor in the justice gap. Rape stereotypes affect the judgments made by individuals dealing with rape cases, for example as police officers, judges or members of a jury, and thereby shape the understanding of rape as it is represented and dealt with in the criminal justice system.[10]

Myths, stereotypes and negative attributions can be seen as a thread running through social and legal constructions of what constitutes a 'genuine' rape deserving of criminal sanction. It is evident that myths and stereotypes regarding rape that exist within general society are also in evidence in legal responses to rape. This occurs in cases involving both female and male sexual victimisation. However, some negative attitudes may differ in their nature and effect. It seems likely that one of the most distinctive points of departure between female and male rape concerns the issue of sexuality. The issue that arises is the extent to which negative attributions towards homosexuality impact attitudes to male rape and the treatment of such cases by the criminal justice system.

Another aspect of this problem is how negative attitudes are shaped and influenced. Recently, some commentators have linked gay pornography to rape-supportive attitudes in the context of male rape. Kendall has argued that pornography featuring male rape and sexual assault causes real harms to men and promotes a model of sexuality that is 'depicted as hierarchical and rarely compassionate, mutual, or equal'.[11] The author borrows from feminist theory in arguing that gay pornography

> relies on the inequality found between those with power and those without it; between those who are dominant and those who are submissive; between those who are top and those who are bottom; between straight men and gay men; between men and women. From these and other materials, we are told to glorify masculinity and men who meet a hyper-masculine, muscular ideal. The result is such that men who are more feminine are degraded as 'queer' and 'faggots' and subjected to degrading and dehumanizing epithets usually invoked against women, such as 'bitch', 'cunt', and 'whore'. These men are in turn presented as enjoying this degradation ... Insofar as sex equality is concerned, the result is the promotion and maintenance of those gendered power inequalities that reject a non-assimilated gay male sexuality and that ensure that homophobia and sexism remain intact.[12]

Kendall argues that such imagery supports a view of sexuality that encourages rape by a variety of means, including the promotion of myths, for example that men enjoy being raped.[13] In reality, it is difficult to determine what impact, if any, such imagery has in reinforcing the myths to which Kendall refers. What is much clearer, however, is that societal conceptions of male rape are shaped by myths and stereotypes. This paper proceeds by examining the various ways in which these myths and stereotypes impinge on societal and police attitudes towards male rape.

Reporting by gay male rape victims

Since it became first legally recognised in 1994, there has been a significant increase in offences of male rape recorded by the police in England and Wales. In 1995 there were 150 offences of male rape recorded by the police;[14] for 2004–05 the figure was 1135.[15] The most recent figure shows 1150 recorded offences of male rape.[16] This, however, is likely to be a gross underestimate of the actual prevalence of male rape given the level of under-reporting. Early small-scale domestic studies of male rape and sexual assault suggested that between 12%[17] and 20%[18] of victims reported to the police. In an epidemiological study of 2474 males Coxell et al. found that '[d]ata from 37 of the 40 men who reported having had non-consensual sex with men showed that ... only two men reported their experiences to the police'.[19] Abdullah-Khan recently found a reporting rate of between 8% and 44%.[20] Men give many reasons for not reporting to the police. The 2002 Her Majesty's Crown Prosecution Service Inspectorate/Her Majesty's Inspectorate of Constabulary (HMCPSI/HMIC) joint inspection report noted that in the year 2000, of the 586 callers to the support group for victims of male rape, Survivors UK, only 11% had reported to the police.[21] Based on research from Survivors UK, the report suggested various reasons for non-reporting by males, including 'not knowing that it is a crime', 'fear of not being believed' and 'concerns that sexuality may become an issue'.[22] Sivakumaran explains the link between sexuality and why some male victims fail to report: 'The fact that survivors of male/male rape question their sexuality and that society considers them homosexual would not be a reason for non-reporting were it not for society's treatment of homosexuals.'[23] There is also some British evidence that gay male rape victims are less likely to report to the police than heterosexual male victims.[24] Finally, in the most recently published research on the subject, Abdullah-Khan surveyed those who counsel male victims. Counsellors provided a number of reasons for male rape victims' non-reporting to the police: 'Challenges to sexuality and homophobia were frequently mentioned, along with the macho-type organisation that the police service is, which suggests that the police would challenge survivors' masculinity, be unsympathetic and uncaring.'[25]

Interestingly, Abdullah-Khan also found in her study that a minority of police officers suggested that gay men may be *more* willing to report rape than heterosexual males. Some of the reasons given, however, are revealing in that they include negative attributions towards gay male rape victims:

> Homosexuals are promiscuous by nature and are more likely to report. Heterosexuals are less likely as they may be thought of as homosexual.[26]

> Homosexuals would report more rapes as they (a) more likely to be raped (b) enjoy the attention and drama (c) may be antipolice regarding police as homophobic.[27]

Other officers identified problems facing heterosexual male victims, including their fear that they might be deemed as gay. One officer argued that men may be less willing to report rape than female victims because of '[s]ocial stigma – feeling of perhaps being labelled homosexual when heterosexual'.[28] It is evident from victims and those who counsel victims that what has been termed the 'taint of homosexuality'[29] impacts perceptions of male rape and may therefore influence men's willingness to report.

A further factor that may impact reporting is the reluctance of men to view their experience of non-consensual sex as rape. In her interviews with male rape victims, Allen found that 'homosexual men generally had more fluid definitions of their experiences of sexual violence and the processes by which they came to define their experiences as rape were more complicated than for heterosexual men'.[30] This resulted from a range of factors that made it less likely that gay male rape victims would, initially at least, name their experiences as rape. For example, some gay men found it difficult to distinguish between situations 'where they had been "forced" or "persuaded" to have intercourse'.[31] A previous sexual relationship between victim and offender resulted in men not tending to initially regard their experiences as rape. For others there was a belief that sex with partners was obligatory, which again hindered the recognition of non-consensual sex as rape.[32]

Given concerns that some male victims have in disclosing their victimisation to the police it is likely that similar concerns may well apply to disclosures to friends and family. In her study, Abdullah-Khan found that two of the 16 men did not disclose their rapes to anyone. Part of the reason for their non-disclosure was that 'they feared that they would be labelled as homosexual or that they "asked for it"'.[33] There is also potentially another problem that impacts specifically gay male rape victims. That is, the reactions of other gay men to their experiences of rape. Funk argues that

> [a]lthough there does seem to be some room for men to discuss their experiences and obtain support from certain aspects of the queer community when discussing being raped as part of a gay bashing, these resources are, in fact, limited and 'ghettoized'. Men who are raped by a date or spouse often do not receive support from within the community, but often are explicitly told not to talk about the incident or are threatened with being removed from the community. The queer male community seems both extremely reticent to discuss the issues and all but unwilling to offer supports [*sic*] to gay and bi men who are sexually assaulted.[34]

Such negative responses suggest that victims may not risk further disclosures to anyone, including the police. Isely has noted that

> [male victims] often feel safer suffering in silence and are reluctant to be revictimized by an unsympathetic legal system or disbelieving treatment professionals ... Those who do report a sexual attack often experience hostile and isolating reactions from the very service providers that are available to provide help. Too often, seeking assistance in dealing with the trauma that can follow a rape too often becomes a humiliating experience in which feelings of depression, anger, guilt, sexual confusion, and anxiety are reinforced in survivors as they become revicti-mized by the police, community agencies, and bewildered friends.[35]

The experience of men who report

For those men who do decide to report to the police, the existing literature indicates that there are significant differences in men's individual experiences. Some measures of their experiences have been somewhat crude and limited. Early research conducted by support group Survivors UK found that, of the 62 men seen at the Wharfside Clinic at St Mary's Hospital Paddington in 1993, seven reported to the police, with three reporting a positive response and four a negative response. In 1992, 70 men were seen at the clinic, eight reported to the police, with six indicating a positive response and two reporting a 'very negative' response.[36] In a study involving 115 male victims of rape and sexual assault, King and Woollett found that only 17 of them reported to the police: 'In 8 cases the police's reaction was reported as helpful, whereas in 5 it was perceived as negative. Seven men were glad (for 3 of whom the assailant had been apprehended) that they had reported to police.'[37] Hillman et al. found that only two out of the 12 males were satisfied with their contact with the police.[38] A feature of the current literature indicates that sexuality and negative attitudes towards homosexuality characterise the experiences of some men who reported. In a study of 40 British male rape victims, Walker and colleagues found that five reported to the police. The authors noted that

[o]f those who did report, only one man said that the police were responsive and helpful. The other four found the police to be unsympathetic, disinterested, and homophobic. They felt that their complaint was not taken seriously and all four regretted their decision to tell the police.[39]

Some caution must be had when considering whether these specific findings prove a continuing problem in police responses to male rape. According to Walker et al., the 'mean time between the assault and participation in the study was 10 years'.[40] Consequently, we do not know when the five men reported. Clearly, a male reporting rape[41] that occurred 10 or 15 years ago might have received very different treatment from one who reported a recent rape. This point is also made in recent research on men and women's experiences of reporting same-sex domestic abuse to the police. Researchers found that victims 'got a mixed response': 'Some had a sympathetic response but no follow through in terms of applying the law to the abusive partner ... A small number had very unhelpful responses from the police though these said this had happened a long time ago.'[42] Indeed, in the most recently published research, Abdullah-Khan found that of the seven men who reported to the police six were satisfied with their treatment.[43]

Research from the United States suggests that negative police reactions are reported as common. Scarce notes that

[o]f those survivors I interviewed who reported their rape to authorities, all but one had an intensely negative experience. The one survivor who was the exception had only a neutral interaction – neither helpful nor overtly detrimental. The most common complaints I have heard from male survivors who I interviewed and have worked with professionally have been disbelief, mockery, homophobia, or a combination of all three from police officers.[44]

There is evidence to suggest that negative reactions may be a particular problem with respect to male rape victims who are gay or who are presumed to be gay. Such men appear to have their experience of rape taken less seriously. For example, in a British study of prison sexual violence, Banbury cites the experience of one male victim thus: 'When I tried to report [a sexual assault], one of the [prison] officers laughed and just said "come on mate, you're gay, hows [sic] that gonna sound?" I had basically been told to forget the incident because I was gay and hence "I wanted it" and the incident was not reported.'[45] Similarly, a study of prison sexual assault in the United States found that 'gay inmates, or those perceived as gay, often face great difficulties in securing relief from abuse. Unless they show obvious physical injury, their complaints tend to be ignored and their requests for protection denied.'[46] Likewise, on the basis of research involving the completion of questionnaires by police officers and by male rape victims, Lees found that

[v]ictim feedback suggested that gay men are treated less sensitively and sympathetically by the police than heterosexual men. Some police officers seem to believe that rape is less traumatic for gay men. Analysis of both police and victim questionnaires shows that police officers

are more likely to regard the testimony of homosexual victims as 'unreliable' – ether to assume that the sex was consensual or that the complaint was malicious.[47]

Isely found that their disclosures of being victims of sexual assault had been met with negativity: 'Members shared personal stories about the negative responses of significant others when the rape was disclosed. Frequently, the men had encountered reactions such as hysterical laughter and assumptions about how "gay men would want to be raped".'[48] Similarly, Jim, who had been sexually assaulted while homeless, told *The Big Issue*, 'I was kipping on the Strand one night and woke up to find a man with his hand inside my sleeping bag. He had his hand between my legs. It really shook me up. But when I confided in my friends they were just embarrassed and laughed.'[49]

Collectively, these findings are troubling. While some men do report a positive response, some police officers and other criminal justice professionals appear to attach to gay men or those they perceive as gay highly questionable assumptions regarding credibility, trauma and truthfulness. This suggests some degree of crossover in police attitudes towards female rape, where some officers make similar assumptions regarding credibility based on highly suspect criteria.[50]

One of the male complainants interviewed by the author for previous research suggests that issues of sexuality and other problems exist in police attitudes to male rape complainants. 'Steve' recollected that he was disappointed by the treatment he received when he reported to the police. He stated: 'One of the officers told me that in these types of cases it was virtually impossible to get a conviction. I thought he was trying to put me off. Do the police only prosecute [*sic*] if you're attacked by a stranger?' Despite being heterosexual, Steve felt that homosexuality was an issue as he was asked questions about his sexuality. In addition, he described himself as being upset by one officer's reaction to other disclosures, which he interpreted as disbelieving:

> I had to tell them that he'd tried to masturbate me during the attack and that I'd got a bit of an erection. One of the officers just went, hang on, how was that? You know, what he meant was how was that possible if you're saying you didn't want it?[51]

Steve's experience was also characterised by a classic example of a police officer second-guessing the reactions to a complaint at later stages of the criminal justice process, by suggesting the difficulty of securing a conviction. Studies involving female victims have shown that officers do sometimes warn complainants of such difficulties. Harris and Grace note that '[i]n warning complainants about the difficulty of securing a conviction, the police might put complainants off pursuing their case without meaning to'.[52] This was clearly Steve's reaction and contributed to his negative experience in reporting. The apparent reaction to the disclosure that Steve had experienced an erection is particularly serious given that we know significant numbers of male victims experience erections during rape and sexual assault.[53]

Some victims of male rape and sexual assault have reported aggressive questioning by the police. In the United States, the experience of Christopher Smith, who was raped at gunpoint by a stranger, gives an indication of the sense of despair that some male victims experience and the way in which unskilled questioning can have a negative impact on a victim's ability to accurately recall a traumatic event. He recounts his experience with the police:

> Then I told the story again. Then again. They asked questions. They interrupted. They told the story back to me, but changed things. They inserted information that I did not provide. Questions sprayed at me from every direction like bullets from a machine gun. Everything became so cloudy and confused.

The officers also asked a series of questions that he found distressing. In addition, the issue of sexuality also arose, but in a context that made little sense:

> Do you have any friends who are gay? ... Why didn't you just run? He wouldn't have shot at you, it's hard to hit a moving target. I would have just started running. Why didn't you run? ... After being degraded and humiliated in so many different ways, I had reached the lowest point ever, I was convinced I was a terrible person. I didn't even feel recognized as a human being.[54]

Finally, an interesting perspective on the treatment of male victims comes from Abdullah-Khan's survey of police officers. She asked participating officers how the treatment of male victims compared with that of female victims, and found that 58 officers suggested that the treatment was similar, four claimed that men received better treatment and 17 that men received worse treatment than female victims.[55] Some officers in the latter group pointed to a lack of training and awareness of male victimisation[56] and Abdullah-Khan describes their view of police responses thus: 'many officers are unsympathetic and do not take male rape seriously'.[57] While such statements reflect obvious concerns in the treatment of male rape by the police, one should show caution about suggesting that men or women receive preferential treatment within the English legal system.[58] On the current evidence, it is simply not possible to make a resilient argument in favour of preferential treatment of either male or female complainants.[59]

Barriers to recognition and law enforcement

Negative social attitudes towards male rape manifest themselves in the denial of male victimisation, victim-blaming and a range of other negative attributions. Collectively, these negative social attitudes operate as barriers to recognition of the problem and have the potential to influence decision-making by the police and the wider criminal justice system. This section analyses several examples of barriers to recognition.

Minimising the problem and denying the possibility of male sexual victimisation

The minimising or denial of male rape as a problem takes many forms. At its worst such attitudes suggest that male rape is physically impossible. Recent research by Anderson and Doherty involving focus group discussions found one participant who expressed such a view when discussing a scenario involving an alleged male rape. The participant 'Mike' stated:

> I was a bit suspicious when it was the one man who raped him because I think that unless this chap who was allegedly raped, and he was enormously weaker than the other guy, there's no go considering the muscularness of like where he was raped, there's no-one going in there like unless he wants it, like.[60]

Scepticism regarding the possibility of men being raped has a long history. In his study of law and sex in late imperial China, Sommer notes that

> the judiciary was highly skeptical that a man could be raped at all: if sodomy had been consummated with an adult male, then it must have been consensual. Only a powerless male could be penetrated against his will – and the most unambiguous form of male powerlessness was youth ... We should not conclude that older males were never in fact raped, but rather that there existed a strong judicial bias against accepting an older male as a rape victim.[61]

Within the scholarly community there is evidence of a tendency to dismiss the importance of male rape as an issue worthy of analysis by criticising any attention it receives. This has included responding to a large-scale study of male rape as a 'matter for concern' because a similar study was not being conducted of female victims.[62] More recently, Novotny has argued that media coverage of the sexual abuse of boys by a number of Roman Catholic clergymen was 'hardly newsworthy'.[63] In some sources, the dismissive treatment is less forthright, and surely unintended. In his study of the Auschwitz concentration camp, Rees discusses the rape and sexual exploitation of women by SS guards at Auschwitz, as well as the experiences of women working in a brothel within the camp.[64] His characterisation of most of these experiences is unsurprisingly negative – he discusses the rape of these women, as well as the 'suffering' of those working in the brothel 'who were forced to have sex'.[65] Yet by contrast, on the basis of the testimony of one inmate, who refers to adolescent boys working for 'prominent' inmates and a 'sexual relationship [that] would often develop between them'.[66] There is no suggestion by Rees that these 'relationships' might have involved coercion. We know, however, from other sources that unsurprisingly such 'relationships' could involve sexual victimisation.[67]

In the context of police attitudes, a particular method of denial is to suggest that the problem of male rape is exaggerated. In her survey of attitudes to male rape held by London Metropolitan Police officers, Abdullah-Khan found two respondents who questioned the extent of male rape as a social and legal problem:

> I think the homosexual lobby in this country is increasingly vociferous and my perception that male rape is growing problem might just be an indication of the success of this lobby.[68]

> I think there may be a perception that it has been overblown by the gay lobby, to get attention and resources.[69]

Within the police service another means of potentially denying the problem of male rape is through the recording of rape allegations. The London Metropolitan Police recently published statistics on the recording of allegations of male and female rape: of the 677 allegations of rape reported in London between April and June 2005, 511 (75.5%) were recorded as crimes, with 32 (4.7%) being 'no crimes' and 134 (19.8%) recorded as 'not crime'.[70] This study also found that '[w]hilst only 23% (143) of female complainants' allegations were recorded as "No Crime"/"Not Crime", 41% (24) in cases of male complainant allegations [were] recorded as "No Crime"/"Not Crime".' In cases involving male victims, charges were more likely to be reduced from rape to a lesser offence and 'a higher number of false complaints linked to mental health issues were recorded with male complainants'.[71] The linkage of mental illness to 'no crime' is also a striking feature of studies involving female complainants.[72] One of the questions raised by these findings is the extent to which the use of the 'no crime'/'not crime' designation is generally appropriate. For example, are men and women with mental health problems more likely to make false allegations or are the police inappropriately labelling reports by these persons as false?[73] A further question that arises is what other factors may influence police treatment and recording of male rape allegations. Abdullah-Khan's survey of police officers found a range of views on the level of false reporting of male rape. Among some officers who thought the false reporting rate was high, the following were described as being sources of false complaints: 'Rent boys, blackmail, vagrant on vagrant revenge' and 'Again promiscuous homosexuals'.[74]

Hierarchies of suffering

It is a well-established finding within the research literature that, in social and legal attitudes to female rape, distinctions are made between the seriousness with which differing types of rape are viewed.[75] It is also becoming increasingly apparent that distinctions are made between male victims based, in part at least, on their sexuality. In a survey of victims and police officers Lees found that '[s]ome police officers seem to believe that rape is less traumatic for gay men [and are] more likely to regard the testimony of homosexual victims as "unreliable"'.[76] In attitude surveys it has been found that students attribute more blame to heterosexual female and gay male victims of rape than to lesbian and heterosexual male victims.[77] White and Kurpius found that students attributed *inter alia* more blame to male than to female rape victims and more blame to gay and lesbian victims than to heterosexual victims.[78] Similarly, Mitchell and Hirschman found that students were prepared to attribute more blame and pleasure and less trauma to a male rape victim who is gay than one who is heterosexual.[79] More recent empirical research provides further evidence of such hierarchies. In their focus group research, Anderson and Doherty found that in discussions involving male rape a 'hierarchy of suffering is established whereby rape is judged to be worse (more "horrible", "disgusting", "shocking", ... "destructive", ... "traumatic") ... for heterosexual men than it is for women or gay men'.[80] Similar findings have been found by Abdullah-Khan in her research involving police officers.[81]

It is worth noting, however, that there is evidence of other 'hierarchies of suffering' within the literature. Bourke has found evidence of nineteenth-century feminists denigrating the trauma of male sexual victimisation. She notes that in the context of young males coerced into prostitution, those feminists suggested that the harm suffered by young women was greater than that suffered by their male counterparts.[82] Similarly, Hite, writing in 1981, suggested that certain forms of sexual assault could not be humiliating to a male victim.[83] Recourse to hierarchies of suffering has also been evident within the parliamentary process. During the parliamentary debates over the legal recognition of male rape in England and Wales, Lord Swinfen stated:

> Non-consensual buggery for a homosexual man would be an extremely traumatic experience. For a heterosexual man it would be an even greater trauma. However, if it happens to a woman it could be more distressing still because not only is she being violated, but her total femininity is being destroyed at the same time as she would not be used in a natural manner that one might expect.[84]

Here again, the trauma suffered by gay male rape victims is seen as less serious than that by heterosexual males. However, unlike some of the other hierarchies, female rape is seen as the most traumatic. Another trauma hierarchy in evidence within the literature is the suggestion that no trauma should result from male rape. Pelka, who has written about his experience of being raped, recounts being told the following by a police officer: 'The good cop told me how upset he'd seen "girls" become after being raped. "But you're a man, this shouldn't bother you."'[85] This is an assertion that appears to be based on a notion of masculine strength and invulnerability to physical and psychological harm. This is a recurrent theme in the literature and will be discussed in the later section in the context of physical resistance to rape.

What is the reasoning behind the assertion that rape of gay men is less traumatic than of heterosexual men? Anderson and Doherty argue that 'victims constructed as "heterosexual" are likely to be judged to have genuinely suffered, principally on the grounds that they are assumed to have experienced a sexual act that is foreign to them'.[86] Such views are problematic for two reasons. First, it is based on the mistaken assumption that all gay men have anal sex. Second, this reasoning is akin to that contained in judicial decisions that suggest that a woman who is raped by her husband is less traumatised than if she were raped by a stranger, because of the previous consensual sexual contact with her assailant. Such a view confuses the crucial distinction between consensual and non-consensual penetrative sex acts and shows little understanding of the impact of sexual victimisation.[87]

Victim-blaming, negative attributions and expectations of resistance

Since the 1970s we have seen the development of a vast literature that illustrates the ways in which female victims of rape may be blamed for their own victimisation. Negative social judgments are made regarding such things as 'inappropriate' behaviour prior to a rape[88] as well as complainants failing to react as expected during and following rape.[89] Collectively, these and other attitudes serve to excuse, minimise, justify or deny rape in cases involving female victims. It is becoming increasingly apparent that similar attitudes are in evidence in the context of male rape.

In their focus group research, Anderson and Doherty asked students to consider a vignette featuring a male, previously a victim of rape, who was walking in an area where previous rapes had occurred when he was allegedly attacked again.[90] The response of some students was to 'project "subconscious" homosexual desires onto the alleged victim as a way of making sense of and dismissing the rape claim in the vignette'.[91] Further, participants described the victim as 'extremely stupid' and referred to him as 'very stupid or more probably he was asking for it, or hoping it would happen'.[92] Repeated references were made to the victim 'wanting' to be raped:

Tony: Yes, it is, it is very odd, I mean either he's very naïve or he's making something up or he wants to be raped, or hoping that it would happen.[93]

Fiona: Maybe he was sub-consciously, he wanted it . . .[94]

Tony: Maybe he's homosexual and he's really embarrassed about his sexuality and er, hoping that some guy comes on to him at 9.30 on the campus, no, I'm serious, maybe he actually was hoping it happened, maybe he's really interested and curious and excited by it.[95]

Blaming victims of male rape who are gay is a consistent feature of the literature on attitudes to male rape. In her study of correctional officers, Eigenberg found that, of the 166 correctional officers surveyed, 46.4% 'believe that inmates deserve rape if they have consented to participate in consensual acts with other inmates'.[96] In a recent review of the existing literature on attitudes towards male rape, Davies and Rogers observe that

[a]ll, without exception, and regardless of the assault situation, have found that gay victims are judged to be more at fault or to blame than heterosexual victims are. It is reasoned that the homosexual (albeit non-consensual) nature of male rape inspires homophobic attributions that result in victim blame and other negative attributions towards male victims.[97]

A further belief that impacts the recognition of male rape concerns an expectation of victim resistance. Sommer notes that in late imperial China the penetrated male suffered great social stigma.[98] While legal codes recognised that young males could be victims of rape perpetrated by older males, outside of this situation '[m]ales were not expected to be weak . . . They were not supposed to be penetrable at all, but rather penetrators, subjects rather than objects of action. Even so, Qing law acknowledged that males could be raped, and that they might consent to sodomy. But for this penetrability to make sense, the male had to be somehow less than male.'[99] He observes that in 'late imperial China, common sense held that to be penetrated would profoundly compromise a male's masculinity; for this reason, powerful stigma attached to a penetrated male'.[100] Indeed, Sommer found that the stigma of being penetrated was also shared by family members and that sometimes 'such shame provoked family members to violent acts against the penetrated male himself'.[101] The shared sense of shame created by male rape is also in evidence in more recent literature. In his prison memoir *A Sense of Freedom*, Jimmy Boyle recounts that young or young-looking prisoners were gang-raped by a particular group of prisoners led by an inmate who became known as 'The Poof'. Boyle notes that some prisoners would 'have a go at him', but says 'I felt deeply humiliated that another prisoner could allow himself to be "used" in this way by [the gang].'[102] Boyle's sense of shame is clearly based on an assumption that an inmate should resist gang rape and anything short of physical resistance constitutes a prisoner allowing himself to be raped.

Assumptions regarding the ability of men to protect themselves and prevent sexual victimisation are also in evidence among some police officers, as the following quotes indicate:

It is difficult for officers to see how an adult male can let himself get into a situation where he can get raped and be unable to physically protect himself.[103]

There is a definite problem with this male issue. A man is a man and should be able to look after himself. This is how I feel policemen see it. Therefore little sympathy.[104]

In the United States, a civil case was brought against prison officials who allegedly failed to adequately protect an inmate, Roderick Johnson. He claimed to have been repeatedly raped by a prison gang, but prison officials disputed his claims of victimisation on questionable grounds:

In pretrial testimony, Jimmy Bowman, another defendant, explained that Mr. Johnson's account was not credible because he had failed to resist the men he said raped him. 'Sometimes an inmate has to defend himself', Mr. Bowman said. 'We don't expect him not to do anything.'[105]

This quote illustrates the strength of the belief that men should resist their attackers. Roderick Johnson claimed to have been the victim of repeated acts of rape and the trial testimony indicated he was, in effect, owned by a prison gang and subjected to threats and violence.[106] In such circumstances, it is difficult to see how someone could resist. The problem with the expectation of resistance is that it fails to show an understanding of the way in which male victims react to rape. Some men verbally and physically resist their attackers. But there is also a consistent finding within the literature that 'men are either too afraid to resist or fight back, or [freeze] with fear' and that 'contrary to widely held beliefs that "real men fight back", men often do not or cannot fight back'.[107]

The question of course for this paper is whether such beliefs relating to victim resistance pose a particular problem for gay men. As already noted, Anderson and Doherty's focus group discussions appeared to centre on the issue of homosexuality and there was also a suggestion that 'victimisation only happens to effeminate individuals who are, necessarily, less than "real men"'.[108] It may be the case that in some instances an association is made between lack of resistance and consent and if there is consent then the victim is, by definition, gay. This might be a particular problem in the case of so-called 'effeminate' men who may be seen as unmanly and therefore more likely to be gay.

Themes and possible explanations

Many of the attitudes discussed in this paper represent a view of masculinity as strong and invulnerable. The result is a reluctance to acknowledge the existence of male sexual victimisation and to treat the penetrated male as in some way devalued, as less of a man, for allowing 'himself to be used in this way', as suggested by Boyle. The difficulty some people have in acknowledging male rape is reflected by comments in which criminal justice professionals and others have trouble understanding why a man cannot resist an attack by a rapist, the suggestion that a man cannot be physically penetrated against his will or that a man should not be traumatised by rape. Challenging such views requires acknowledgment that 'each and every body is permeable and appropriable'.[109]

A further issue is why homophobic attitudes arise in the context of male rape. One of the reasons may be the equation of men being anally penetrable with being gay and therefore less masculine. In their interviews with gay men who engaged in anal intercourse, Kippax and Smith noted that for some of the participants there was an 'incompatibility between being masculine *and* receptive' and for some '[r]eceptivity is automatically associated here with being gay and feminine, suggesting one is more or less gay according to whether or not one engaged in "feminine" sexual practices'.[110] A similar point is made by McGhee: 'male homosexuality and female sexuality are presented in legal discourse and practices in terms of passivity and receptivity to an active and penetrating "heterosexualised" male anatomy and sexuality'.[111]

The association of anal intercourse with homosexuality can also be linked to attitudes that blame gay male rape victims for their own victimisation, but, of course, it goes further. This linkage also reinforces the assumption that, by being anally penetrable (and therefore less masculine), male rape victims *must* be gay. Anderson and Doherty note that 'the projection of a gay identity onto an alleged victim (and this may happen to any victim, regardless of his sexual identity) results in reframing the depicted rape as a consensual sexual encounter'.[112] Thus, it cannot be assumed that the issue of homosexuality only arises in the context of gay male rape victims. Another explanation for the linkage of male rape and homosexuality is that it serves as a form of 'distancing'; as Anderson observes, 'close association between male rape and homosexuality/homophobia may be one way for participants to express their disgust at this act . . . for male participants, male rape perception may be linked to a combination of hegemonic masculinity . . . and emotionally defensive/distancing factors'.[113]

Conclusion: future directions in law and policy

This paper has shown that one of the emerging features of societal and legal attitudes to male rape is the influence of negative perceptions of the crime and its victims. These views, to varying degrees, are held by members of the public and criminal justice professionals. Negative judgments regarding homosexuality seemingly impact not only men who are gay but also heterosexual men. Attitudes towards homosexuality are combined with other beliefs regarding trauma, victim resistance and victim blame. Consequently, some male victims face significant difficulties when seeking help following rape.

A crucial question, therefore, is how such problems should be addressed so as to afford gay male rape victims equal protection under the law without discriminatory treatment. From a human rights perspective, one possible strategy relates to positive obligations of the state to secure the rights of its citizens. It has recently been argued that the incorporation of Article 3 of the European Convention on Human Rights[114] into UK law, through the enactment of the Human Rights Act 1998, places on the state a number of positive obligations concerning the treatment of rape complainants, including the existence of effective laws against rape and effective investigation of rape allegations.[115] Allegations of male rape that are incompetently investigated[116] or influenced by myths and victim-blaming might fall within such a legal framework. Furthermore, in conjunction with Article 3, it might also be the case that Article 14 of the Convention that has for long been accepted as prohibiting sexual orientation discrimination may be invoked where ineffective investigations result from such factors as homophobia.[117]

A further strategy to address the problem of male rape is to challenge ignorance, myths and stereotypes that impact criminal justice responses to male sexual victimisation. This requires the training of criminal justice professionals. In the context of the police, Abdullah-Khan notes that some officers are well informed about male rape, but also observes that for other officers there is a 'huge gap in information about male rape, a gap which respondents themselves readily acknowledge'.[118] In a recent British study involving interviews with gay and lesbian victims of domestic sexual and physical abuse, researchers found that the response of agencies was mixed. The study found that voluntary and statutory agencies have no

> coordinated responses for responding to domestic abuse in same sex relationships . . . Many of the problems lie in agencies being governed by a domestic abuse model that is heterosexual and it is this that often prevents an appropriate response because of assumptions made about who might be the survivor/perpetrator.[119]

Clearly, raising awareness of rape outside of the male/female paradigm is crucial in improving service responses. But improving criminal justice responses to male rape requires a wider response than just the training of professionals. Negative social attitudes inform legal responses and there is, thus, a need to address myths and stereotypes within wider society. Recognition of the need for greater education has resulted in a number of projects that are currently being run to educate schoolchildren regarding the law of rape and related issues.[120] In addition, there have also been education campaigns involving the media.[121] Given the ingrained nature of negative beliefs towards gay men and ignorance regarding male rape, inclusion of this form of sexual victimisation in educational programmes would be helpful. But these programmes cannot be seen as a quick fix and it is only through sustained education in society and within the criminal justice system that myths and stereotypes can be properly challenged.

Acknowledgements

I would like to express my sincere gratitude to Phil C.W. Chan for inviting me to contribute to this special double issue and for his excellent editorial work on this paper.

Notes

1. S. Banbury, 'Coercive Sexual Behaviour in British Prisons as Reported by Adult Ex-prisoners', *Howard Journal* 43 (2004): 113; I. O'Donnell, 'Prison Rape in Context', *British Journal of Criminology* 44 (2004): 24.
2. A. Coxell, M. King, G. Mezey, and D. Gordon, 'Lifetime Prevalence, Characteristics and Associated Problems of Non-consensual Sex in Men: Cross Sectional Survey', *British Medical Journal* 318 (1999): 846.

3. S. Sivakumaran, 'Sexual Violence against Men in Armed Conflict', *European Journal of International Law* 18 (2007): 253.
4. See, e.g., G.C. Mezey and M.B. King, *Male Victims of Sexual Assault*, 2nd edn (Oxford: Oxford University Press, 2000); S. Allen, 'Male Victims of Rape: Responses to a Perceived Threat to Masculinity', in *New Visions of Crime Victims*, ed. C. Hoyle and R. Young (Oxford: Hart, 2002), 23; J. Walker, J. Archer, and M. Davies, 'Effects of Rape on Men: A Descriptive Analysis', *Archives of Sexual Behavior* 34 (2005): 69; J. Walker, J. Archer, and M. Davies, 'Effects of Male Rape on Psychological Functioning', *British Journal of Clinical Psychology* 44 (2005): 225.
5. See most recently N. Abdullah-Khan, *Male Rape: The Emergence of a Social and Legal Issue* (Basingstoke: Palgrave Macmillan, 2008).
6. It has recently been claimed that there is 'a small amount of research literature on male victimization': R. Graham, 'Male Rape and the Careful Construction of the Male Victim', *Social & Legal Studies* 15 (2006): 187, 188. Graham's analysis of our current understanding of male rape and its representation in the scholarly literature is poorly researched and ignores work in the fields of law, history, psychology, and medicine. As a result, many of her observations and conclusions rest on outdated research and are either open to doubt or plainly wrong. For analysis of some of her claims, see P.N.S. Rumney, 'Policing Male Rape and Sexual Assault', *Journal of Criminal Law* 71 (2008): 67, 81–2.
7. In a national British study of 2474 males Coxell et al., 'Lifetime Prevalence', found that men who had experience of consensual sex with other men were six times more likely to have been raped or sexually assaulted as adults than males who had not. In an earlier British study of 930 gay men, F.C.I. Hickson, P.M. Davies, A.J. Hunt, P. Weatherburn, T.J. McManus, and A.P.M. Coxon found that a significant number were victims of non-consensual sex. Of those surveyed it was found that 257 (27.6%) men reported that they had been 'subjected to nonconsensual sex at some point in their lives'. Of these, it was found that 45.2% (99) had been anally penetrated, and in another 11 cases (5%) there had been an unsuccessful attempt at anal penetration; 'Gay Men as Victims of Nonconsensual Sex', *Archives of Sexual Behavior* 23 (1994): 281. In a survey of 287 gay men in Vancouver one-third 'had been forced to have sex against their will at least once in their lives'. However, it is not clear from this study whether all these instances of victimisation occurred during adulthood: D.V. Janoff, *Pink Blood: Homophobic Violence in Canada* (Toronto: University of Toronto Press: 2005), 25.
8. See, e.g., Human Rights Watch and International Gay and Lesbian Human Rights Commission, *More than a Name: State-Sponsored Homophobia and its Consequences in Southern Africa* (New York: Human Rights Watch, 2003); Janoff, *Pink Blood*; S. Hodge and D. Cantor, 'Victims and Perpetrators of Male Sexual Assault', *Journal of Interpersonal Violence* 13 (1998): 222, 234.
9. See, e.g., Human Rights Watch, *No Escape: Male Rape in U.S. Prisons* (New York: Human Rights Watch, 2001); Banbury, 'Coercive Sexual Behaviour'.
10. J. Temkin and B. Kraché, *Sexual Assault and the Justice Gap: A Question of Attitude* (Oxford: Hart, 2007), 209.
11. C.N. Kendall, 'Gay Male Pornography and Sexual Violence: A Sex Equality Perspective on Gay Male Rape and Partner Abuse', *McGill Law Journal* 49 (2004): 877, 905.
12. Ibid., 902.
13. Ibid., 908, 915.
14. Home Office, *Crime in England and Wales 2001/2002* (London: Home Office, 2002).
15. S. Nicholas et al., *Crime in England and Wales 2004/2005* (London: Home Office, 2005), Table 7.01.
16. S. Nicholas et al., *Crime in England and Wales 2006/07* (London: Home Office, 2007), 36. Of these offences, 413 involved males aged 16 and over. Additional forms of male sexual victimisation are covered by a range of other sexual offences: ibid., 37.
17. R.J. Hillman, N. O'Mara, D. Taylor-Robinson, and J.R. Harris, 'Medical and Social Aspects of Sexual Assault of Males: A Survey of 100 Victims', *British Journal of General Practice* 40 (1990): 502, 503.
18. G. Mezey and M. King, 'The Effects of Sexual Assault on Men: A Survey of 22 Victims', *Psychological Medicine* 19 (1989): 205, 207.
19. Coxell et al., 'Lifetime Prevalence'.
20. Abdullah-Khan, *Male Rape*, 189.

21. HMCPSI/HMIC, *A Report on the Joint Inspection into the Investigation and Prosecution of Cases Involving Allegations of Rape* (London: HMCPSI/HMIC, 2002), para. 6.20. In a survey by M. King and E. Woollett, men 'found it difficult to give reasons why they had not reported to police. Six were too ashamed, 2 were trying to forget the assault, 2 were too frightened, 1 could not talk about it, and 1 saw no point in reporting', 'Sexually Assaulted Males: 115 Men Consulting a Counselling Service', *Archives of Sexual Behavior* 26 (1997): 579, 585.

22. *HMCPSI/HMIC Report*, ibid. See also P.L. Huckle, 'Male Rape Victims Referred to a Forensic Psychiatric Service', *Medicine, Science, Law* 35 (1995): 187, 190; M. Scarce, *Male on Male Rape: The Hidden Toll of Stigma and Shame* (New York: Insight Books, 1997).

23. S. Sivakumaran, 'Male/Male Rape and the "Taint" of Homosexuality', *Human Rights Quarterly* 27 (2005): 1274, 1291.

24. Hodge and Cantor, 'Victims and Perpetrators of Male Sexual Assault', 231.

25. Abdullah-Khan, *Male Rape*, 189. It was suggested, ibid., 190, by one counsellor that some gay male rape victims may not report their rapes because they feared being arrested 'for the activity that led to the rape as outdoor sex in groups and toilets is illegal for men.'

26. Ibid., 148. While the suggestion that male rape is less reported than female rape is made elsewhere (see Sivakumaran, 'Male/Male Rape', 1289–90), there is no compelling statistical evidence to support such a claim.

27. Abdullah-Khan, *Male Rape*, 150.

28. Ibid., 147.

29. Sivakumaran, 'Male/Male Rape'.

30. Allen, 'Male Victims of Rape', 35.

31. Ibid., 32.

32. Ibid., 32–4.

33. Abdullah-Khan, *Male Rape*, 215.

34. R.E. Funk, 'Queer Men and Sexual Assault: What Being Raped Says about Being a Man', in *Gendered Outcasts and Sexual Outlaws: Sexual Oppression and Gender Hierarchies in Queer Men's Lives*, ed. C. Kendall and W. Martino (New York: Routledge, 2006), 131, 138.

35. P.J. Isely, 'Adult Male Sexual Assault in the Community: A Literature Review and Group Treatment Model', in *Rape and Sexual Assault III: A Research Handbook*, ed. A.W. Burgess (New York: Garland, 1991), 161, 164.

36. Private correspondence from Survivors UK, 8 November 1994 (on file with author).

37. King and Woollett, 'Sexually Assaulted Males, 584.

38. Hillman et al., 'Medical and Social Aspects', 503.

39. Walker et al., 'Effects of Rape on Men', 74.

40. Ibid., 72.

41. Prior to the enactment of section 142 of the Criminal Justice and Public Order Act 1994 (c. 33), non-consensual penile–anal intercourse was classed as buggery, not rape.

42. C. Donovan, M. Hester, J. Holmes, and M. McCarry, *Comparing Domestic Abuse in Same Sex and Heterosexual Relationships* (Bristol: University of Bristol, 2006), 21. The passage of time is clearly an important factor, and in recent years there have been attempts made by the police to improve responses to male rape and sexual assault.

43. Abdullah-Khan, *Male Rape*, 211. This was a positive finding although, as with many other studies, the small numbers make it difficult to draw general conclusions.

44. Scarce, *Male on Male Rape*, 216.

45. Banbury, 'Coercive Sexual Behaviour', 126.

46. Human Rights Watch, *No Escape*, 152.

47. S. Lees, *Ruling Passions: Sexual Violence, Reputation and the Law* (Buckingham: Open University Press, 1997), 94. J. Gregory and S. Lees note the following reason given by a police officer for regarding a male rape victim as unreliable: 'He is described by his friends as very promiscuous', *Policing Sexual Assault* (London: Routledge, 1999), 126.

48. P.J. Isely, 'Adult Male Sexual Assault', 171–2.

49. L. Johnston, 'Homeless Sex Scandal', *Big Issue*, 11–17 September 1995, 11, 15.

50. See, e.g., L. Kelly et al., *A Gap or a Chasm? Attrition in Reported Rape Cases* (London: Home Office, 2005), 293; J. Temkin, 'Reporting Rape in London: A Qualitative Study', *Howard Journal of Criminal Justice* 38 (1999): 17; J. Temkin, 'Plus Ça Change: Reporting Rape in the 1990s', *British Journal of Criminology* 37 (1997): 507.

51. It is not clear from Steve's disclosures why the officer stated that 'in these types of cases it was virtually impossible to get a conviction'.

52. J. Harris and S. Grace, *A Question of Evidence? Reporting Rape in the 1990s* (London: Home Office, 1999), 20–2.

53. There is research showing that males can experience an erection and even ejaculation during sexual assaults by male or female assailants. In their study of 11 males sexually assaulted by women either as children or adults, P.M. Sarrel and W.H. Masters found that 'men or boys have responded sexually to female assault or abuse even though the males' emotional state during the molestations has been overwhelmingly negative – embarrassment, humiliation, anxiety, fear, anger, or even terror', 'Sexual Molestation of Men by Women', *Archives of Sexual Behavior* 11 (1982): 117, 118. See also King and Woollett, 'Sexually Assaulted Males', 587: 'Just under 20% of the men were stimulated by their assailants until they ejaculated.' In a small-scale study of male rape victims and offenders, A.N. Groth and A.W. Burgess found that '[a] major strategy used by some offenders in the assault of males is to get the victim to ejaculate. This effort may have several purposes. In misidentifying ejaculation with orgasm, the victim may be bewildered by his physiological response to the offense and thus discouraged from reporting the assault for fear his sexuality may become suspect. Such a reaction may serve to impeach his credibility in trial testimony and discredit his allegation of nonconsent. To the offender, such a reaction may symbolize his ultimate and complete sexual control over his victim's body and confirm his fantasy that the victim really wanted and enjoyed the rape. This fantasy is also prominent in the rape of females', 'Male Rape Offenders and Victims', *American Journal of Psychiatry* 137 (1980): 806, 809.

54. Scarce, *Male on Male Rape*, 191–2.

55. Abdullah-Khan, *Male Rape*, 133–7.

56. Ibid., 135.

57. Ibid., 134.

58. See Rumney, 'Policing Male Rape and Sexual Assault', 80–5.

59. On a related matter, an examination of arrest patterns in 19 US states found *inter alia* differing arrest rates for male and female same-sex domestic violence, noting that '[t]he offense need not be very serious for an arrest to be made in cases of female same-sex violence', but 'it appears that the commission of a serious offense is needed to make some police officers treat an incident involving a male same-sex couple as a serious criminal matter': A. Pattavina, D. Hirschel, E. Buzawa, D. Faggiani, and H. Bentley, 'A Comparison of the Police Response to Heterosexual Versus Same-Sex Intimate Partner Violence', *Violence against Women* 13 (2007): 374, 388.

60. I. Anderson and K. Doherty, *Accounting for Rape Psychology: Feminism and Discourse Analysis in the Study of Sexual Violence* (London: Routledge, 2008), 97.

61. M.H. Sommer, *Law, Sex, and Society in Late Imperial China* (Palo Alto, CA: Stanford University Press, 2000), 133–4.

62. T. Gillespie, 'Rape Crisis Centres and "Male Rape": A Face of the Backlash', in *Women, Violence and Male Power: Feminist Activism, Research and Practice*, ed. M. Hester, L. Kelly, and J. Radford (Buckingham: Open University Press, 1996), 161.

63. P. Novotny, 'Rape Victims in the (Gender) Neutral Zone: The Assimilation of Resistance?', *Seattle Journal for Social Justice* 1 (2003): 743, 745. For a critical review of this and other claims made by Novotny, see P.N.S. Rumney, 'In Defence of Gender Neutrality within Rape', *Seattle Journal for Social Justice* 6 (2007): 481.

64. L. Rees, *Auschwitz: The Nazis and the Final Solution* (New York: Knopf, 2005), 236–53.

65. Ibid.

66. Ibid., 252.

67. See, e.g., L. Smith, *Forgotten Voices of the Holocaust* (London: Ebury Press, 2005), 178.

68. Abdullah-Khan, *Male Rape*, 123.

69. Ibid., 131.

70. Deputy Commissioner's Command, Directorate of Strategic Development and Territorial Policing, Project Sapphire, *A Review of Rape Investigations in the MPS* (London: Metropolitan Police Service, 2005), para. 4.3. For definitions of 'no crime' and 'not crime', see ibid., 40.

71. Ibid., para. 4.6.

72. See P.N.S. Rumney, 'False Allegations of Rape', *Cambridge Law Journal* 65 (2006): 128, 156.

73. There are a number of questions that arise in the interpretation of these data. It is not possible to know whether the cases that are classified as 'no crime/not crime' are appropriately labelled. Research that examines the 'no crime' of rape complaints suggests that police officers often apply the criteria inappropriately; see Rumney, ibid.
74. Abdullah-Khan, *Male Rape*, 68.
75. See, e.g., D. Finkelhor and K. Yllo, *License to Rape: Sexual Abuse of Wives* (New York: Free Press, 1985), ch. 8; P.N.S. Rumney, 'Progress at a Price: The Construction of Non-Stranger Rape in the *Millberry* Sentencing Guidelines', *Modern Law Review* 66 (2003): 870.
76. Lees, *Ruling Passions*, 94.
77. A. Wakelin and K.M. Long, 'Effects of Victim Gender and Sexuality on Attributions of Blame to Rape Victims', *Sex Roles* 49 (2003): 477, 483.
78. B.H. White and S.E.R. Kurpius, 'Effects of Victim Sex and Sexual Orientation in Perceptions of Rape', *Sex Roles* 46 (2002): 191.
79. D. Mitchell and R. Hirschman, 'Attributions of Victim Responsibility, Pleasure and Trauma in Male Rape' *Journal of Sex Research* 36 (1999): 369. See also K. Doherty and I. Anderson, 'Making Sense of Male Rape: Constructions of Gender, Sexuality and Experience of Rape Victims', *Journal of Community and Applied Social Psychology* 14 (2004): 85.
80. Anderson and Doherty, *Accounting for Rape Psychology*, 95.
81. Abdullah-Khan, *Male Rape*, 143–5. The author found that '[s]eventeen officers felt that male victims suffer greater trauma than female victims, 2 believed males suffer less trauma, 52 believed the trauma levels are the same ... 18 officers were undecided': ibid., 143.
82. J. Bourke, *Rape: A History from 1860 to the Present* (London: Virago, 2007), 240–1.
83. S. Hite, *The Hite Report on Male Sexuality* (London: Optima, 1981), 749.
84. *Hansard* (HL), 20 June 1994, col. 66.
85. F. Pelka, 'Raped: A Male Survivor Breaks His Silence', in *Rape and Society: Readings on the Problem of Sexual Assault*, ed. P. Searles and R.J. Berger (Boulder, CO: Westview Press, 1995), 252.
86. Anderson and Doherty, *Accounting for Rape Psychology*, 103.
87. See Rumney, 'Progress at a Price'.
88. For discussions of the impact of intoxication on judgments made by mock jurors, see E. Finch and V.E. Munro, 'Breaking Boundaries? Sexual Consent in the Jury Room', *Legal Studies* 26 (2006): 303; P.N.S. Rumney and R.A. Fenton, 'Intoxicated Consent in Rape: *Bree* and Juror Decision-Making', *Modern Law Review* 71 (2008): 279.
89. Negative judgments regarding victim credibility are sometimes a result of the complainant not resisting her attacker or showing little emotion when recounting her victimisation; see Rumney, 'False Allegations of Rape'; Temkin and Kraché, *Sexual Assault and the Justice Gap*.
90. Anderson and Doherty, *Accounting for Rape Psychology*, 62.
91. Ibid., 100.
92. Ibid.
93. Ibid.
94. Ibid., 101.
95. Ibid.
96. H. Eigenberg, 'Male Rape: An Empirical Examination of Correctional Officers' Attitudes toward Rape in Prison', *Prison Journal* 69 (1989): 39, 48–50.
97. M. Davies and P. Rogers, 'Perceptions of Male Victims in Depicted Sexual Assaults: A Review of the Literature', *Aggression and Violent Behaviour* 11 (2006): 367, 371. Recent research suggests evidence of 'erroneous and mythical thinking' about male rape, along with 'some evidence' of homophobia: I. Anderson, 'What is a Typical Rape? Effects of Victim and Participant Gender in Female and Male Rape Perception', *British Journal of Social Psychology* 46 (2007): 225.
98. Sommer, *Law, Sex, and Society in Late Imperial China*, 148–51.
99. Ibid., 132.
100. Ibid., 117–8.
101. Ibid., 150.
102. J. Boyle, *A Sense of Freedom* (London: Pan Books, 1977), 196.
103. Abdullah-Khan, *Male Rape*, 131.
104. Ibid., 135.

105.   A. Liptak, 'Inmate was Considered "Property" of Gang, Witness Tells Jury in Prison Rape Lawsuit', *New York Times*, 25 September 2005, http://www.njbullying.org/Inmate WasConsideredPropertyofGangWitnessTellsJuryinPrisonRapeLawsuit-NewYorkTimes.htm (accessed 11 March 2009).

106.   A former gang member testified that if Johnson refused to comply 'You'll be beaten until you say yes ... He'd be beaten, stabbed, whatever.'

107.   Abdullah-Khan, *Male Rape*, 208.

108.   Anderson and Doherty, *Accounting for Rape Psychology*, 100.

109.   Bourke, *Rape*, 247.

110.   S. Kippax and G. Smith, 'Anal Intercourse and Power in Sex between Men', *Sexualities* 4 (2001), 413, 420, 418 (emphasis in original).

111.   D. McGhee, *Homosexuality, Law and Resistance* (London: Routledge, 2001), 75.

112.   Anderson and Doherty, *Accounting for Rape Psychology*, 104.

113.   Anderson, 'What is a Typical Rape?', 241–2.

114.   Article 3 prohibits *inter alia* the infliction of inhuman and degrading treatment.

115.   P. Londono, 'Positive Obligations, Criminal Procedure and Rape Cases', *European Human Rights Law Review* (2007): 158.

116.   For an example, see Independent Police Complaints Commission, *Report into a Complaint by Geoffrey Vincent Cole against South Wales Police Regarding the Initial Police Actions Following His Alleged Rape and Serious Sexual Assault on 18 October 2005*, Executive Summary, 3–5, 10, http://www.ipcc.gov.uk/coleexecutive_summary_3_7_07.pdf (accessed 17 November 2008).

117.   For a discussion of Article 14 as a freestanding right (which, however, requires ratification by the United Kingdom of Protocol 12 to the European Convention on Human Rights), see P.C.W. Chan, 'Same-Sex Marriage/Constitutionalism and their Centrality to Equality Rights in Hong Kong: A Comparative–Socio-Legal Appraisal', *International Journal of Human Rights* 11, nos 1–2 (2007): 33, n. 62.

118.   Abdullah-Khan, *Male Rape*, 226.

119.   Donovan et al., *Comparing Domestic Abuse*, 20–1.

120.   Carol Withey, Senior Lecturer in Law at the University of Greenwich, has created a 'School Project' in which university students go into school classes to explain the law of rape and help pupils better understand the legal consequences of sexual violence.

121.   Temkin and Kraché, *Sexual Assault and the Justice Gap*, ch. 5.

Criminal law, public health, and governance of HIV exposure and transmission

Alana Klein

Faculty of Law, McGill University, Montreal, Canada

This paper argues that the principal human rights and policy concerns that have been raised over criminalisation of HIV exposure or transmission since the early days of the epidemic cannot be neatly addressed within the traditional criminal law framework. Public health structures may be better placed, in terms of both their mandate and their structure, to incorporate lessons from the public health and human rights movement. This paper critically explores the potential of emerging models of structured coordination between public health and criminal law actors with a view to a more targeted, human-rights-sensitive application of criminal law to the sexual behaviours of people living with HIV. Finally, it assesses these emerging approaches from new governance and restorative justice perspectives.

Introduction

Since the early days of the HIV/AIDS epidemic in the 1980s, scholars and activists have been preoccupied with the question of whether people should be held criminally liable for engaging in risky sexual behaviour without disclosing their HIV-positive status.[1] Now, in most jurisdictions that have considered the issue, the basic question of criminal liability appears to have been settled: the precise requirements for conviction vary, but as a general rule people living with HIV may be prosecuted under certain circumstances for consensual sex that transmits, or risks transmitting, HIV.[2] This paper argues that the principal human rights and social policy concerns that have been raised around criminalisation time and again over the past 20 years cannot be easily addressed within traditional criminal law theory and doctrine. Emerging responses from public health authorities to those who fail to disclose have the potential to better incorporate lessons from health-and-human-rights-based approaches to the epidemic. More context-sensitive, flexible interventions emerging within public health branches of government may interact with the criminal justice system to create what can be understood as a new type of alternative justice system, one that may more capably serve the goals of protecting the public's health and singling out moral wrongdoing than do traditional criminal justice approaches.

The focus of academic and policy discussions to date of the criminalisation of HIV exposure and transmission has largely been on whether and how criminal law statutes and doctrines should develop to cover sexual activities that create a risk of HIV transmission. Some have agreed with a general judicial and legislative consensus that the application of the criminal law is appropriate: society should impose criminal sanctions on those who knowingly expose others to the risk of a fatal, incurable disease – to express societal disapproval to punish offenders for their wrongdoing, to prevent the person from repeating the conduct, and to deter others from similar conduct.[3] Others have argued that the net will inevitably be cast too wide, punishing those who do not rightly deserve to be punished, and that criminalisation will interfere with public health objectives by stigmatising people living with HIV, driving the epidemic further underground and sending to the community the message that the law will protect them from the virus. Instead, caution in extending the criminal law to this area is suggested.[4]

Less attention has been paid, however, to other legal and quasi-legal orders that may affect the operation of the criminal law in practice. Public health authorities, which have an obvious interest and obligation in addressing sexual behaviour that gives rise to the risk of HIV transmission, can play a role in mitigating the bluntness of criminal law in an area like this one by providing more targeted, complex, contextually informed intervention. These interventions, if appropriately conceived, can provide police and prosecutorial authorities with a basis for principled deference in order to ensure better-targeted application of the criminal law where legislation and criminal law doctrine may not be amenable to more precise tailoring. Together, the operation of public health and criminal justice authorities can create an opportunity for collaborative or coordinated governance that may address, in a more nuanced way than the criminal law viewed and acting in isolation, the behaviour of those who engage in sexual activity without disclosing their HIV-positive status to their sex partners.

This paper proceeds as follows. It first traces the debate over criminalisation of HIV exposure and transmission, with reference to the laws of the United Kingdom, the United States, and Canada, and demonstrates that many of the policy and human rights objections around criminalisation of HIV exposure and transmission can be addressed from within criminal law doctrines only incompletely. It then examines how appropriately conceived public health interventions can supplement and even supplant formal criminal law in an area such as this, by providing a basis for principled deference to police and prosecutorial authorities to help screen cases that may be less appropriate for criminal justice solutions. Finally, it places the coordination of criminal law and public health interventions in theoretical context, with reference to 'new governance' and alternative or restorative justice literature. It concludes that, conceived properly, collaboration between the formal criminal justice system and neighbouring legal and quasi-legal orders may mitigate some of the bluntness of criminal law narrowly conceived and guide a more rational conception of the interrelationship between the formal criminal justice system and the other legal orders around which it operates.

The criminal law debate

The debate over criminalisation of HIV exposure and transmission has scarcely changed since 1988 when Kathleen Sullivan and Martha Field published the first major law journal article setting possible legal bases for criminalisation and arguing that it would be a mistake to enact criminal measures to deal with the problem of HIV transmission.[5] Over the years that have followed, Sullivan and Field's concerns have been echoed and elaborated by academics and human rights activists.[6] Meanwhile, courts and legislatures across jurisdictions have, for the most part, determined that the criminal law prohibits people with HIV having sex that risks transmitting or actually transmits the virus without disclosing to their partners in advance that they are HIV-positive.[7]

For some, exposing others to risk of a fatal disease is morally indefensible conduct that merits sanction both to punish obviously dangerous behaviour and to deter others from engaging in similar conduct.[8] Others maintain that criminal law is too blunt an instrument to deal with a matter as complex as HIV exposure and transmission; Burris sets out this orientation:

> [Sex] is a complex behavior, psychologically and morally; disclosure and safe sex are negotiated non-verbally and contextually; risks vary according to the behavior, and are often not as significant as they are portrayed in lurid news reports; a person who practices safe sex or disclosure most or even some of the time represents a public health success.[9]

On this latter view, criminalisation of exposure or transmission provides no assistance to governments trying to prevent the spread of HIV. Opponents of criminalisation point to the vast body of public health literature on the kinds of interventions that promote testing, safer sex, and disclosure[10] and note that there are no studies that demonstrate the effectiveness of criminal justice approaches.[11] Rather, they contend, criminalisation will perpetuate the stigma associated with the disease, which is harmful in itself and also hinders public health efforts that depend on stigma reduction. A number of more precise concerns about how criminalisation in its different forms may undermine public health programmes are also raised. Finally, concerns about justice and the coherence of criminal law often figure in critiques. This section begins with a summary of legal bases for criminal liability for HIV exposure or transmission in the United Kingdom, the United States, and Canada. It then traces the principal concerns and tensions around criminalisation as they arise in these jurisdictions, with reference to emerging scientific understandings about HIV transmission.

The state of the law

In the majority of jurisdictions where courts or legislatures have explicitly considered the issue, people who are HIV-positive can be prosecuted for certain kinds of behaviour that may expose or transmit the virus to a sex partner. A minority of states in the United States have adopted HIV-specific statutes that criminalise certain sexual activities of people who are HIV-positive;[12] in the remaining US states[13] as well as in the United Kingdom[14] and Canada,[15] laws of general application that existed prior to the epidemic have been used to prosecute individuals who engage in unprotected sex without disclosing their HIV-positive status. Although it is difficult to track the precise number of prosecutions, as many convictions are unreported, prosecutions appear to be taking place in a broader range of circumstances and are, it seems, increasingly frequent.

a. United Kingdom

In Scotland in 2001, Stephen Kelly became the first person in the UK to be convicted for HIV transmission under the Scots common law offence of recklessly causing injury to another.[16] Two years later, Mohammed Dica was convicted for HIV transmission in England.[17] Dica was found to have violated section 20 of the Offences Against the Person Act 1861, which applies throughout the UK save Scotland.[18] The provision states that '[w]hosoever shall unlawfully and maliciously wound or inflict grievous bodily harm upon any person, either with or without any weapon or instrument, shall be found guilty of [an offence]'. To date, there have been 14 convictions for sexual HIV transmission in the UK.[19]

The primary distinguishing feature of the UK approaches is that, thus far, they have concerned themselves only with HIV *transmission*; there have been no convictions for

HIV exposure alone.[20] It should also be noted that the mens rea requirement is one of intention or recklessness. To prove recklessness, the prosecution must establish that at the time of the offence the defendant was aware of the risk that some degree of bodily harm might be caused by his or her act or omission and nonetheless ran that risk.[21]

b. United States

Every US state has criminal laws that apply to conduct exposing others to HIV.[22] In 1990, the federal government encouraged the criminalisation of knowingly exposing others to HIV when it passed the Ryan White Comprehensive AIDS Resources Emergency (CARE) Act. The law provided funds for AIDS treatment and care, but required states to demonstrate that their criminal laws were 'adequate to prosecute any HIV infected individual' who knowingly exposed another to HIV through donation of blood, semen, breast milk, sexual activity, or needle-sharing.[23] By 2000, all states had certified that they had laws addressing knowing HIV exposure and the requirement was repealed.[24] It was possible to meet the requirement without enacting HIV-specific offences by demonstrating that criminal laws of general application were sufficient to prosecute knowing HIV exposure. Nonetheless, as of 2008, 18 states have adopted HIV-specific statutes creating a separate crime for knowing sexual exposure to HIV.[25] Some states have public health statutes criminalising exposure or transmission of sexually transmitted infections including HIV,[26] but a 2002 study found that there were no cases in which these laws had been applied in the HIV context.[27] The remaining states may use laws of general application, including murder, attempted murder, manslaughter, reckless endangerment, and assault. Moreover, some prosecutors rely on such laws of general application even where HIV-specific statutes are available.[28]

It is difficult to ascertain how many people have been successfully prosecuted for HIV exposure or transmission in the United States in the context of consensual sexual activity. Researchers typically rely on case reports and newspaper articles and therefore likely underestimate the number of prosecutions. One study, however, showed that between 1986 and 2001 there were 84 prosecutions, 64 of which resulted in convictions, for HIV exposure through consensual sexual activity in the United States. In addition, 40 prosecutions arose in the context of prostitution, 22 of which resulted in convictions.[29] All but 12 states and the US territory of Puerto Rico had at least one reported prosecution.[30]

c. Canada

In Canada, sexual exposure of HIV may be prosecuted under general criminal laws, most frequently the laws of assault and sexual assault and, sometimes, common nuisance.[31] Charges for criminal negligence causing bodily harm may also be brought where there is actual transmission.[32] In 1998, in the seminal case of R. v. Cuerrier the Supreme Court of Canada pronounced on the issue for the first time, holding that that a person may be found guilty of sexual assault for having unprotected sex without disclosing known HIV-positive status, even if the virus is not transmitted.[33] The rationale is that unprotected sex with an HIV-positive person presents a 'significant risk of serious bodily harm'[34] and that non-disclosure of that risk rises to the level of fraud and thus vitiates any consent to sexual activity.

Since the first successful prosecution in 1989,[35] at least 43 people have been convicted for HIV exposure or transmission through otherwise consensual sexual activity in Canada. More than one-third of known convictions occurred between 2005 and 2008.[36]

Concerns about criminalisation

A number of preoccupations drive the criticisms of criminalisation in this context. One is that the very association of HIV transmission with criminality will reinforce stigma against people who are HIV-positive, stigma that governments have an interest in fighting for both human rights and public-health-related reasons.[37] Another is that the criminal justice system cannot be tailored to reliably distinguish behaviour that is both truly risky and morally blameworthy. Relatedly, there is a concern that notions of reasonableness that triers of fact are likely to bring to their determinations in this area may be so divorced from the realities of people who are HIV-positive that standards of behaviour will be unfair. These concerns can be identified in the more precise objections to criminalisation that have been reiterated time and again over the years.

a. Setting wrong incentives and undermining public health programmes

From the earliest days of the debate, critics have asserted, generally without direct empirical evidence, that recourse to the criminal law would interfere with and undermine the fight against the HIV/AIDS epidemic.[38] Encouraging voluntary testing and frank discussion of HIV status remains a central part of most HIV/AIDS prevention strategies, as people who know their status tend to be less likely to engage in high-risk behaviours.[39] There is a concern that people may shy away from testing for fear of exposing themselves to criminal liability for *knowingly* exposing or transmitting HIV.[40] The court in *Cuerrier* considered and rejected this concern about testing, simply stating that '[t]hose who seek testing basically seek treatment. It is unlikely that they will forego testing because of the possibility of facing criminal charges should they ignore the instructions of public health workers'.[41]

Partner notification schemes could also be adversely affected. Throughout the United Kingdom, the United States, and Canada, public health policies include programmes for partner notification which rely on those who have tested HIV-positive to voluntarily disclose the names of sex partners who may have been infected.[42] These partner notification schemes generally try to maintain the anonymity of the tested individual. However, individuals notified may nevertheless be able to deduce that person's identity. As a result, people who test HIV-positive may not want to cooperate in partner notification, fearing that the information may be used against them. Without patient cooperation, public health officials cannot conduct effective partner notification.[43]

In cases where people living with HIV may have engaged in risk-taking behaviour that is unplanned or inadvertent, they should advise their sexual partners that they may want to use post-exposure prophylaxis, that is, a course of antiretroviral drugs which is thought to reduce the risk of seroconversion after exposure to the virus. However, where HIV exposure is a criminal offence, this would be tantamount to admitting to a crime. Some may thus prefer to not disclose and instead to rely on the probability that there has been no transmission or hope that the behaviour will go unnoticed by the law.[44]

Finally, there is an inconsistency in approach between a criminal law that would punish every act of unprotected sex without disclosure and the view, prevalent among scientists, that learning to practise safer sex is a complex social and psychological process.[45] One review has noted that for a variety of reasons a sizeable percentage (in some studies as high as 56%) of people living with HIV continue to have unprotected sex without disclosing their HIV status.[46] The comment of Ekstrand et al. reflects a scientific consensus:

> It is important that people who occasionally engage in unprotected ... intercourse are not blamed for their behaviors. Relapse into unsafe sex may simply reflect the normal process

of any behavior change. Once new behaviors have been acquired, whether they involve a new diet, a new exercise regimen, or condom use, many individuals need and want additional assistance in maintaining this behavior change over time. We do not believe that this struggle should be a stigmatized condition, but simply perceived as a human one.[47]

The recent conviction of a Québec woman is illustrative.[48] The woman, D.C., claimed that she had had sex with her partner only once before disclosing her HIV status, and that a condom had been used. Following the initial encounter, she consulted with her doctor about the risk of transmission if a condom broke, and was advised to disclose her HIV status to her partner.[49] She did so. The couple went on to practise safe sex for four years before the complainant brought charges against D.C. based on the initial encounter. The trial judge found that no condom was used the first time the couple had sex, and convicted D.C. of sexual assault. From a public health point of view, D.C.'s overall behaviour should be reinforced as a successful adoption of safer sex practices through medical consultation. Where every act of unsafe sex without disclosure is stigmatised as criminal, however, the capacity for frank discussion and support through a process of moving towards safer sex practices may be compromised.

b. Undermining notions of shared responsibility

Another longstanding objection to imposition of criminal sanctions in this area, and one that likewise has not been empirically tested, is that imposing criminal liability only on the HIV-positive partner undermines the notion that both partners are equally responsible for the practice of safe sex. Correspondingly, regular recourse to the criminal law may create a 'false sense of security' leading people to believe that the law protects them from being exposed to or contracting HIV.[50]

A shared-responsibility approach, in which consent to sexual activity is understood to include consent to all attendant risks, would obviate the application of the criminal law in this area altogether. That said, self-protection may not always be equally available to sexual partners; a woman may risk abuse from her sexual partner if she asks for condoms, and a married person may have a greater reason to assume fidelity from her or his partner. In these contexts, it may be sensible to impose a duty of disclosure on the more powerful partner.

It is difficult to conceive of a legal standard that is appropriately context sensitive. Placing criminal responsibility for unsafe sex only on the HIV-positive partner is consistent with a view that one may assume, unless told otherwise, that unprotected sex does not carry a risk of infection. In practice, however, this assumption may not always be reasonable. Thus, for example, the outcry among HIV/AIDS activists when a Vancouver street-based sex worker was charged with having unprotected sex with a client without disclosing her HIV status was that the client ought to be understood to have assumed a risk of transmission.[51]

As a matter of criminal law doctrine, courts and criminal law scholars consider the issue of allocation of responsibility through the lens of consent: does a person who consents to having unprotected sex also consent to the risks of sexually transmitted infections? In answering this question, courts have rejected a shared-responsibility approach, in which any consent to sexual activity is understood to include consent to all attendant risks. Courts have also tended to avoid any contextual weighing of responsibility by rejecting any argument of implied consent. Instead, the conclusion has been that the person who is aware of the heightened risk – invariably the HIV-positive partner – bears the primary responsibility to inform her or his partner. Justice Cory of the Supreme Court of Canada expressed the view sharply in *Cuerrier*:

> It is true that all members of society should be aware of the danger and take steps to avoid the risk. However, the primary responsibility for making the disclosure must rest upon those who are aware they are infected. I would hope that every member of society no matter how 'marginalized' would be sufficiently responsible that they would advise their partner of risks. In these circumstances it is, I trust, not too much to expect that the infected person would advise his partner of his infection. That responsibility cannot be lightly shifted to unknowing members of society who are wooed, pursued and encouraged by infected individuals to become their sexual partners.[52]

The Court of Appeal of England and Wales in *Dica* was more nuanced, recognising that different kinds of relationships carry different assumptions about sex:

> At one extreme, there is casual sex between complete strangers, sometimes protected, sometimes not, when the attendant risks are known to be higher and at the other, there is sexual intercourse between couples in a long-term and loving and trusting relationship, which may from time to time also carry risks.[53]

Nevertheless, the context of the sexual encounter was not treated as relevant to the question of whether a person accepts the risk of harm simply by agreeing to have unprotected sex with someone whose HIV status is unknown. Consent to the risk of harm would require *knowledge*, and not mere suspicion, that a sexual partner had HIV.

In *Konzani* the Court of Appeal of England and Wales recognised certain limited circumstances in which a complainant's knowledge of her or his partner's HIV-seropositivity may be imputed:

> By way of example, an individual with HIV may develop a sexual relationship with someone who knew him while he was in hospital, receiving treatment for the condition. If so, her informed consent, if it were indeed informed, would remain a defence, to be disproved by the prosecution, even if the defendant had not personally informed her of his condition. Even if she did not in fact consent, this example would illustrate the basis for an argument that he honestly believed in her informed consent. Alternatively, he may honestly believe that his new sexual partner was told of his condition by someone known to them both. Cases like these, not too fanciful, may arise.[54]

The suggestion here was clearly not that consent to risk of infection may be implied by a person's general knowledge about the risks of unprotected sex with a partner whose HIV status was unknown; rather, the court pointed to specific indications that would lead a person to know that their particular sexual partner was in fact HIV-positive.

An expanded, context-sensitive exception to the requirement of explicit disclosure may allow for more nuanced, contextualised analyses of shared responsibility, but at the risk of stereotyping and moralising. A court might determine, for example, that a man who has had anonymous sex in a gay bathhouse consented to the risk of exposure and transmission, or that an HIV-positive man in the circumstance had an honest belief in such consent.[55] Should the man in the gay bathhouse, absent disclosure, be entitled to less protection than a woman whose husband unbeknownst to her has been unfaithful and is carrying the virus? On one hand, such an approach by triers of fact could be a good thing if it more fairly reflects shared responsibility in some circumstances. On the other hand, there is a risk of discrimination if triers of fact determine when assumptions of risk should be implied based on stereotypes or moral evaluations of gay sex or sex outside traditional unions.

c. Vagueness and criminalisation of lower-risk and risk-free activities

The reach of the criminal law may not track the real likelihood of HIV transmission reflected in scientific research for a number of reasons. Legislators creating HIV-specific statutes setting out prohibited acts may fail to attend to real levels of risk. For example, HIV-specific statutes in Michigan and Arkansas prohibit sexual penetration by an infected person without disclosure, with sexual penetration defined to include 'any other intrusion, however slight, of a part of a person's body or of any object into the genital or anal openings of another person's body'.[56] Activities that do not pose any risk of transmission – such as penetration by sterile sex toys, for example – are clearly encompassed by this definition. Legislative oversight may be to blame for the language of these provisions: the definition seems to have been adopted without modification from rape and sexual assault statutes.[57] For other US states, the reasons for poorly tailored drafting are unclear. Missouri, South Carolina, and Virginia laws include oral intercourse, along with vaginal or anal intercourse, in their definitions of sexual HIV-exposure offences,[58] and Missouri's legislation in particular explicitly states that the 'use of condoms is not a defense'.[59]

Where statutes and the general criminal law leave it to judges and juries to determine whether a risk of HIV transmission is significant enough to attract criminal sanction,[60] boundaries between criminal and non-criminal sexual acts may not be drawn consistently and based on clear and identifiable principles. First, it can be difficult to determine with certainty the HIV transmission risks of any particular sexual act. Whether HIV is transmitted during a given sexual encounter will depend in part on the particular sexual act involved, but also on a number of other factors, which are the subject of ongoing scientific inquiry, as set out below. The consistent and correct use of condoms has been found to reduce the risk of transmission by 90 to 95%,[61] but condom use is never perfect.[62] Recent research reveals that viral load,[63] the presence of other sexually transmitted infections,[64] as well as circumcision[65] also affect transmission risk.[66] Second, even if risk levels could be clearly ascertained, given that risk is relative, there is no obvious way to determine the point at which a risk becomes high enough to attract criminal sanction. In these circumstances, social values can be expected to play an important role and may lead to convictions based on lower-risk or no-risk activities.

Leaving the line-drawing exercise to triers of fact may result in uncertainty about which acts are criminal.[67] The Court of Appeal of England and Wales in *Dica* and the Supreme Court of Canada in *Cuerrier* were somewhat equivocal about the availability of a 'condom defence'.[68] Although there do not appear to have been any convictions in the UK arising from intercourse protected by condoms, lower courts in Canada have come to varying conclusions. In *R. v. Edwards*, a British Columbia Supreme Court judge directed a jury that '[t]here is no legal duty on [the accused] to disclose his HIV status if he used condoms at all times', as there was no evidence at trial of any significant risk of serious bodily harm if he had been using condoms.[69] On the other hand, a Manitoba trial court judge recently convicted Clato Lual Mabior on numerous counts of aggravated sexual assault for not disclosing that he was HIV-positive prior to engaging in sexual intercourse with six females even though condoms had been used with at least two of the complainants.[70] The judge accepted expert evidence at trial that condoms were only 80% reliable.[71] The judge also accepted that 'there was a very high probability that the accused was not infectious, i.e., could not have transmitted HIV',[72] when his HIV viral load was undetectable. Based on these findings, the judge concluded that only 'the combination of an undetectable viral load and the use of a condom would serve to reduce the risk below what would be considered significant risk of serious bodily harm'.[73] On this standard,

Mabior was convicted of aggravated sexual assault against two females where he used a condom but his viral load remained detectable; against one female where the viral load was undetectable and he used a condom that broke; and against three females where there was neither disclosure nor condom use. The case, which is currently on appeal, appears to be the first conviction in Canada where the accused was found to have used a condom. Of note is that at the time of the assaults in question a number of the females were minors, were in the care of child protection authorities, or were given drugs or alcohol by Mabior prior to sexual intercourse.

The ambiguity about 'significant risk' in *R.* v. *Cuerrier* has also left room for some questionable guilty pleas, such as that of an Ontario woman who pleaded guilty to aggravated sexual assault after she had had sexual relationships with two men.[74] The defendant had had unprotected oral sex as well as protected and unprotected vaginal intercourse with the first complainant. With the second complainant, she had had unprotected oral sex and vaginal intercourse with a condom that broke. Both men later tested negative for HIV. It appears that that conviction was based only on the unprotected sexual intercourse with the first complainant,[75] but the sentencing judge ordered the defendant to stay away from both complainants. The court did not discuss the relative sexual risk of oral sex or the implications of the broken condom, nor did it consider relative risk levels of male to female exposure versus female to male exposure. The case was the first case and the only published decision in which a woman in Canada was convicted for HIV exposure. There have been several other charges laid against women for exposure, and in only one of those cases did the complainant later test positive.[76]

UK law requires actual transmission (rather than mere exposure) for a conviction for causing grievous bodily harm under section 20 of the Offences Against the Person Act or reckless transmission under Scots law. Given the limited scope for prosecution for exposure in the UK, the relevance of any condom defence in the UK has been rather limited. Nevertheless, the Crown Prosecution Service in England and Wales has indicated that it would be 'highly unlikely' that the facts would support prosecution for recklessness absent a 'sustained course of conduct during which the defendant ignores current scientific advice regarding the need for and the use of safeguards, thereby increasing the risk of infection to an unacceptable level'.[77] Likewise, in Scotland, which has its own system of criminal prosecution, there has been recognition of the availability of a 'condom defence'. Although the finding of fact in *HM Advocate* v. *Mola* was that the defendant had not used a condom, the trial judge deferred (if somewhat hesitantly) to instructions to Mola from medical practitioners that disclosure was not required if the defendant wore a condom at all times.[78]

Chalmers suggests that criminalising only transmission and not exposure 'appears to accord to chance an unduly prominent role in the attribution of criminal responsibility'.[79] In Chalmers' view, the level of control of the non-discloser over the possibility of transmission is so low that it 'seems proper to treat the transmission as a matter of luck, at least as far as his own culpability is concerned'.[80] However, given the criminal justice system's failures – and perhaps inability – to carefully assess the risk of a particular sexual act given the multitude of factors involved, Chalmers may be overstating the point. Criminalising only actual transmission may go some way towards making up for the fact that judges and juries tend to do a less-than-perfect job in determining which activities pose a sufficient risk as to warrant being considered 'reckless'.

It may be unprincipled to rely on actual transmission as a proxy for assessing the level of risk of a particular sexual behaviour;[81] a better answer would be to call on judges and juries to accurately determine levels of risk for particular sexual activities and draw consistent lines about when that risk is significant. However, as discussed, such assessment may not precisely accord with developing understandings of the level of risk involved. Properly assessing risk may present evidentiary problems and draw the courts into difficult-to-ascertain factual territory. (Was there enough lubrication? Was it rough sex? Slow sex?) Judges may prefer to continue to rely on assumptions that treat all risky activity alike; at best, they may clearly delineate broad but clear categories of risk behaviour that will remain arbitrary.

Both policy- and justice-related concerns are raised if lower-risk activities may be prosecuted. There is a disjuncture with public health policy that emphasises knowledge of *relative* risk in the sexual behaviour of people living with HIV. The concept of 'safer sex' was developed by gay men in the 1980s as a short-term response to an immediate health crisis, and has continued to develop in light of the recognition that consistent condom use may be difficult for a wide variety of psychological and social factors.[82] Today, the term is generally understood to mean using a condom for anal (or vaginal) sex, but not necessarily for oral sex; it appears that many gay men are indeed having more oral sex and less anal sex than in the past.[83] Although public health strategies do not universally explicitly endorse the safer-sex message, scientific researchers suggest that realistic understandings of actual risk levels of different activities will help individuals make effective and sustainable changes in behaviour.[84] Criminal laws that set unrealistic standards of behaviour or fail to distinguish levels of risk may undermine the development of risk reduction strategies and result in poor public health consequences. It also appears unjust to prohibit behaviour that creates little or no risk of harm. This concern may be particularly acute given the tendency for people living with or at risk of HIV to belong to marginalised or stigmatised groups, including those who use intravenous drugs, sex workers, members of ethnic minorities, and gay men.[85]

d. Potential for discriminatory application

The possibility that laws will be disproportionately applied to ethnic minorities or other marginalised groups raises justice and fairness concerns. It also raises public health concerns if criminalisation drives already vulnerable populations, such as migrants or ethnic minorities, further underground and away from public health services. Evidence on this point is equivocal. The National AIDS Trust in the UK observed in 2006 that four of the six convictions in England at that time had been of migrants, three from Africa and one from Portugal,[86] although a recent update suggests that white males are overrepresented among heterosexuals charged with HIV transmission in England and Wales.[87] It is difficult to determine the ethnic patterns in US and Canadian prosecutions, where there have been substantially more convictions and where the media have not always reported demographic information about those charged or convicted. However, a number of authors have suggested that discriminatory application is likely, even taking into account the higher rates of HIV among certain already marginalised groups.[88]

The parallel with the differential impact of drug control laws in the US is not difficult to draw: African-Americans comprise some 15% of people who use drugs,[89] a figure roughly proportionate to their representation in the general US population,[90] but their rates of arrest, conviction and, incarceration remain higher than those *of* white Americans: African-Americans comprise some 44% of those arrested[91] and 39% of those incarcerated[92] for drug-related offences. Such patterns may be replicated in prosecutions for HIV exposure or transmission, particularly given the low number of prosecutions compared with the number of HIV-positive people who engage, whether regularly or occasionally, in behaviours that the law would appear to prohibit.[93] What seems to determine who gets prosecuted is the 'accident of being caught and brought to the attention of a willing prose-cutor'.[94] Prosecutorial discretion may be suggested as a backstop to the potential negative public health impact of criminalisation; yet it is precisely prosecutorial discretion that could lead to discriminatory application of the law over time.

Further opportunities for discrimination and stereotyping can arise where offenders may include not only those who were aware that they were HIV-positive when they had unpro-tected sex, but also those who 'ought to have known'. In the vast majority of prosecutions thus far, the accused had previously tested positive for HIV. However, judges in the UK, the US, and Canada have left open the possibility that a person may be convicted where one was aware of a *risk* that she or he was HIV-positive even if never actually tested positive.[95] Indeed, the notion of recklessness as unjustified risk-taking seems to warrant prosecution of a person who, for example, was experiencing symptoms known to be consistent with HIV-seropositivity, had shared needles with another person who they knew was HIV-positive, and yet continued to practise unsafe sex without disclosure of the risk. However, a rule that someone 'ought to have known' that he or she was HIV-positive may invite stereoty-pical reasoning and disproportionate convictions against men who have sex with men, people who use illegal drugs, aboriginal people, or people from endemic countries who may, simply by virtue of belonging to those groups, be considered to have more reason to suspect HIV-seropositivity. There is little scope for an argument that the complainant assumed any risk of exposure or transmission given the general rule that a person cannot be considered to have consented to a risk of HIV infection simply by virtue of having sex with another person in an elevated risk group. A recent civil case in which each partner alleged that the other had 'brought HIV into the relationship' is illuminating: based on the 'ought to have known' standard for determining liability, a California court authorised discovery (where one party compels the other to produce relevant information for preparations for trial) of every circumstance in which the husband had had sexual relations with other men during the course of his life to determine whether he should have recognised that he was at risk of HIV infection.[96]

Prevailing national HIV/AIDS strategies tend to prioritise reaching vulnerable popu-lations and tailoring responses to the needs of specific populations. The Canadian Federal Initiative on HIV/AIDS, for example, identifies eight separate at-risk populations and commits to developing distinct approaches based on the need for 'evidence-based, culturally appropriate responses that are better able to address the realities that contribute to infection and poor health outcomes for the target groups'.[97] Discriminatory application of the criminal law and perpetuation of negative stereotypes run contrary to such programmes.

Justifying criminalisation in light of policy concerns

Criminal law theory generally offers five primary justifications for punishment: incapacita-tion, general and specific deterrence, rehabilitation, retribution and denunciation.[98] As is reflected in the above analysis, the first three justifications – those that rely on positive consequences of criminalisation – tend to be the most vigorously disputed in relation to criminalisation of HIV exposure and transmission.

Some note that criminal law serves to incapacitate those who continue to endanger others.[99] In response, it has been pointed out that prisons are increasingly becoming the venues where high-risk behaviour is common[100] and that those serving sentences will eventually be released into the community.[101] Others note that given the low number of prosecutions, to have an appreciable effect on HIV rates in broad population terms, 'incapacitation would seem to require far more people being prosecuted and jailed than current practice exhibits'.[102] However, on an individual basis, separation of a given persistent non-discloser from the general population could protect individuals with whom the persistent non-discloser might have gone on to have unprotected sex. Even opponents of criminalisation have conceded that a given individual's behaviour can significantly affect local HIV rates.[103] However, they dispute that HIV-specific criminal laws or the general criminal law remains the only way to address those rare cases.

One could imagine that imprisonment would serve rehabilitative functions. However, most people living with HIV who have unsafe sex without disclosing their HIV status fail to disclose or avoid risky conduct for a complex set of psychosocial reasons.[104] There is no empirical evidence supporting the proposition that criminal sanctions lead individuals to learn to disclose and/or practise safer sex in the future; there is, however, evidence of effectiveness of other tools such as counselling and support addressing the underlying reasons for disclosure difficulties and practising unsafe sex.[105]

Deterrence claims tend to figure more prominently in judicial decisions, generally as assertions and without empirical support.[106] For example, Justice Cory stated in *Cuerrier*, 'If ever there was a place for the deterrence provided by criminal sanctions it is present in these circumstances.'[107] Noting rising rates of new HIV infections in Canada and low condom use (particularly for women), he determined that 'public education alone has not been successful in modifying the behaviour of individuals at risk of contracting AIDS. It follows that if the deterrence of criminal law is applicable it may well assist in the protection of individuals and it should be utilized.'[108] Finally, Justice Cory concluded that '[i]t is right and proper for Public Health authorities to be concerned that their struggles against AIDS should not be impaired. Yet the Criminal Code does have a role to play. Through deterrence it will protect and serve to encourage honesty, frankness and safer sexual practices.'[109] In *R. v. Nduwayo*, a British Columbia Supreme Court judge similarly asserted that 'others who might be inclined to emulate such actions must not be allowed to gain any impression that they can pursue such a deplorable course of conduct without risking sanctions. The consequences are too grave for society not to take every means at its disposal to curb such conduct and the court has a duty to protect the public accordingly.'[110]

Part of the challenge here is that there has been very little *direct* empirical evidence about the impact of the criminal law on HIV risk behaviour. One recent study – apparently the first attempt to directly assess the impact – failed to find that that the existence of HIV-specific laws and people's knowledge of criminalisation had any significant effect on their sexual practices. That is, people who believed that the law required disclosure or condom use did not practise safer sex any more than those who did not.[111]

A second difficulty relates to the way in which deterrence is understood in criminal law doctrine. Policymakers and judges have recognised that the deterrent effects of the criminal law are uncertain,[112] and this recognition has guided, for example, liberal interpretation of Canada's conditional sentencing regime as an alternative to incarceration.[113] A wide body of criminological and criminal law scholarship seeks to understand the reality of deterrent effects of criminal sanctions.[114] However, there does not appear to be any fundamental criminal law norm requiring any *demonstrable* deterrent effect of the criminal law to justify imposing criminal liability for behaviour that may cause physical harm at the individual level.

Retributive and denunciation arguments do not rely on any individual or public health consequences of criminalisation. Instead, they posit that the purpose of imposing criminal sanctions is to punish offenders and express society's disapproval for conduct that is deemed morally blameworthy.

Opponents of criminalisation note the difficulty of defining moral blameworthiness in the context of HIV. If the requisite mens rea remains recklessness or negligence – as is generally the case in the UK, the US, and Canada[115] – behaviour is measured against that expected of the ordinary, reasonable person. This may leave little room for consideration of the complex social-scientific factors that may underlie failures to disclose. This standard may be difficult to conceive and apply without bias to risk-taking in the context of HIV/AIDS. As Dalton observes,

> Concepts like *recklessness* and *negligence* assume a common psychology, a common set of concerns, a common way of viewing the world. However, one of the realities spotlighted by the HIV epidemic is that we don't always identify successfully with one another, or comprehend the lived experience of people very different from ourselves. Especially when sexual risk-taking is at issue, there is palpable risk that jurors will bring to the evaluative process pre-existing images and attitudes towards the groups most closely identified with AIDS ... There is a risk that jurors will be predisposed to see HIV-positive defendants as *abnormal*, *deviant*, and *reckless*.[116]

Burris raises a similar point. Noting that risky behaviour and non-disclosure are not uncommon in the context of HIV infection, he argues that '[a]s we move to behaviour that is more contextually "normal", and throw in the complexities of sexual norms, expectations, forms of disclosure and gradations of risk, it gets harder to find consensus on what, precisely, is bad and so harder for the criminal law to draw clear moral lines that make sense to all stakeholders'.[117]

In individual cases, however, retributivist and denunciatory justifications continue to figure heavily. Indeed, opponents of criminalisation accept that at least some of the time retribution and denunciation may be called for. The difficulty lies in fashioning a legal rule that can guide that determination, and in deciding when an unverified but potential harm at the population level should weigh more heavily than the value of denunciation or retribution at the individual level.

Given the low number of charges relative to the likely number of cases that may meet the legal requirements for prosecution, it would seem that police and prosecutorial discretion play a significant though under-examined role in shaping the application of the criminal law in the context of HIV.[118] In the next section, I suggest that collaboration among prosecutors, police, public health authorities, and community members, through police and prosecutorial discretion, can create possibilities for a more rational and nuanced role for the criminal justice system than previous analyses have reflected.

The public health alternative

Public health authorities in the UK, the US, and Canada possess statutory powers that allow them to use coercive measures against people, including those who are HIV-positive, whose behaviour may represent a threat to public health.[119] With historical roots in the power of quarantine, the use of coercive measures by public health authorities against people living with HIV was controversial from the outset, and for many of the same reasons reflected in the criminalisation debate. However, as the following analysis reflects, public health systems enjoy some kinds of flexibility that criminal justice systems do not. Moreover, public health authorities may be motivated and able to engage more deeply with some aspects of the relationship between HIV/AIDS and human rights than the criminal justice system. Thus, I argue that public health authorities may be better equipped to integrate lessons from health-and-human-rights approaches to HIV/AIDS prevention.

One of the most remarkable consequences of the HIV/AIDS epidemic is that it fundamentally changed the way public health researchers and policymakers looked at disease; it led them to consider the relationship between disease and broad social factors in greater depth and in new ways, with human rights as a central guidepost.[120]

At the outset of the epidemic, human rights were viewed largely as a legal and moral constraint on policymaking, limiting, for example, forced testing, treatment, or quarantine.[121] By the late 1980s, however, public health experts came to recognise human rights violations as themselves a driver of the HIV/AIDS epidemic. Jonathan Mann, who popularised the health-and-human rights movement as the founder and director of the World Health Organisation's Global Programme on AIDS, noted that in every society, regardless of how HIV entered the community, the epidemic evolved along predictable lines: members of groups who before HIV were marginalised, stigmatised, and discriminated against came over time to bear the brunt of the epidemic. He argued that policies that further marginalised those groups and undermined their human rights would likely undermine efforts to curb the epidemic. For instance, when rumours were spread that HIV testing facilities were providing lists of HIV-positive people to governments, participation in HIV testing programmes declined. Yet where anonymous testing facilities were made available, participation of at-risk individuals in HIV testing and counselling programmes rose.[122]

This public health rationale for the protection of human rights found support in public health scholarly and policymaking circles where a shift in theoretical approach was underway. While traditional public health approaches considered diseases as dynamic events occurring within an essentially static context, newer approaches were beginning to look into the 'structural factors' or social determinants of epidemic diseases. These include political, social, cultural, and economic considerations that drive health outcomes. The human rights framework, Mann argued, 'offers a more coherent, comprehensive, and practical framework for analysis and action on the societal root causes of vulnerability than any other framework inherited from traditional public health or biomedical science'.[123]

Human rights have now come to occupy a central place as a set of organising principles for effective public health policy, rather than simply a limit on what governments may do for the public good. Although rights-based strategies have by no means been universal, it is now generally accepted by public health policymakers that, because those who are infected with HIV or at risk of infection are socially vulnerable and fear agencies of the state, every effort should be made to engage with, rather than threaten, them.

The new health and human rights consensus has not resulted in a wholesale abandonment of coercive approaches to public health. For example, calls for mandatory HIV testing have resurfaced among public health experts in recent years over objections of human rights organisations.[124] However, the new public health and human rights consensus has meant a recognition among public health experts of the limits of coercive practices as a means to effect behavioural change; the result is that individual-rights-promoting strategies are increasingly at the centre of public health approaches to HIV/AIDS.[125]

The shifts in culture among public health experts can be observed in the history of attitudes towards whether and how public health laws may be used to address the spread of the virus. During the mid-1980s, as the debate over criminalisation was gaining momentum, there were calls for renewed use of public health laws left over from earlier epidemics[126] to restrict the behaviour of people living with HIV whose actions might endanger others. Initial discussion focused on quarantine powers. There was little support for quarantining people based on HIV-positive status alone.[127] However, for those who remained unwilling or unable to disclose their HIV status, opinions varied. Concerns over the use of public health powers largely mirrored those over criminalisation. Some believed that these laws could contribute to the prevention of the spread of the epidemic by isolating those who persisted in behaviours linked to the spread of HIV.[128] For others, such as Sullivan and Field, the risk of overly broad or discriminatory application to members of vulnerable groups was too great to justify its application, particularly when it would do 'pathetically little to curb the broader problem of AIDS transmission'.[129] Parmet agreed that laws providing for the quarantine of those who refuse or are unable to conform to medical or behavioural guidelines could conceivably be modernised to contain appropriate due process protections and be tailored to meet the goals of public health protection.[130] Like Sullivan and Field, however, Parmet remained doubtful of public health authorities' ability to predict future dangerous conduct and questioned whether procedural safeguards in even a revamped public health law could match those of a criminal trial,[131] such as the heightened burden of proof and enhanced discovery rights.

By the late 1980s, it appeared that the quarantine option, along with other coercive measures like broad-scale mandatory testing, had been rejected.[132] By this point, in line with the health-and-human rights consensus described above, coercive public health measures were seen as likely to undermine the community trust necessary for governments to deal effectively with the epidemic.[133] Through the 1990s, however, times began to change: public health officials began to reassert their professional dominance over infectious disease, and a return to the use of some traditional public health powers, including partner notification mandatory reporting and limited mandatory testing, became more common.[134]

The result has been the renewed use of public health laws to structure and restrict the behaviour of people living with HIV who are considered to pose risks to public health, particularly in the US and Canada,[135] but with a new awareness of the contextual value of human-rights-based approaches to addressing the epidemic. In the 1980s, in some US jurisdictions, public health laws were amended, or new laws enacted, with the HIV epidemic in mind.[136] In Canada, public health laws remain largely unchanged from earlier epidemics but are drafted in sufficient generality to be applied to people living with HIV, either through regulatory definitions or through discretion of public health officials. In contrast, in the UK, legislation has provided only a narrow scope for the use of coercive public health measures. Legislation and regulations in England, Wales, and Northern Ireland require that a person be 'suffering from' AIDS in order to justify detention for failure to take 'proper precautions'; HIV infection alone would not suffice to warrant public health intervention;[137] Scots public health law seems to make no mention of HIV/AIDS.[138] As a result, confinement of people with HIV under public health laws seems to have been rare in the UK.[139]

Applicable public health laws draw on a variety of mechanisms, including treatment and counselling orders,[140] isolation and hospitalisation,[141] and orders to refrain or desist from conduct that may infect others.[142] Generally, those who fail to follow these orders could face confinement[143] or charges for contempt of court.[144]

Some scholarly and judicial attention has been paid to these public health laws – notably to determine whether they contain sufficient procedural safeguards, are capable of correctly identifying threats to public health, and conform to legal and public health principles including the principle of least restrictive means.[145]

Less attention, however, has been given to *how* public health authorities make use of these laws in practice. In the US, Bayer and Fairchild-Carrino in a 1993 survey found that the power to quarantine under newly created public health statutes had been used 'very rarely'.[146] They found that many states did not have formal public health mechanisms for dealing with people living with HIV who persistently failed to follow medical or legal instructions about risk behaviours or took no action upon receiving reports of risky practices. This was so even in states that had revised public health statutes permitting such mechanisms. In only 18 cases across the United States had state public health authorities responded to reports of recalcitrant behaviour with counselling, and in 15 cases 'cease and desist' orders were issued requiring individuals to modify their behaviour or face further criminal sanctions, indicating a 'complex interplay between public health law and criminal law in the effort to impose social control on those deemed a public health threat'.[147] In three of those 15 cases, the result was eventual confinement in a psychiatric facility.[148]

The most interesting aspect of Bayer and Fairchild-Carrino's study, however, was the more complex institutional responses of five states – Colorado, Indiana, Minnesota, Missouri, and Washington. Those states accounted for only 4% of people living with HIV in the United States at the time but documented more cases of people engaging in HIV risk behaviours than the remaining 45 states and the District of Columbia combined – some 450, with 350 found to warrant further action.[149] In Missouri, Bayer and Fairchild-Carrino reported, authorities responded to reports of recalcitrant behaviour first with counselling followed by access to support services, and finally with referral to a local prosecutor for criminal prosecution. The remaining four states followed the model of issuing cease and desist orders backed by the possibility of confinement. In no cases was there resort to criminal sanctions; authorities resorted to the use of confinement powers five times, and only in one state, Indiana.

A more recent model of how public health authorities limit their own use of coercive public health measures can be observed in Calgary, Alberta. As in most Canadian provinces and territories, the Alberta Public Health Act permits the issuance of public health orders and eventual confinement of those who fail to comply with conditions to limit the spread of disease.[150] The legislation does not require efforts to use less restrictive measures before resort is had to public health orders and confinement. In practice, however, the Calgary Health Region has used a graduated approach that begins by addressing the psychosocial factors that mediate non-disclosure, before moving towards public health orders restricting behaviour, temporary apprehension orders, isolation orders, and, finally,, criminal charges under either public health or criminal laws.[151] The model, developed in conjunction with community organisations, the police, and prosecutors, is premised on the belief that the vast majority of HIV non-disclosure cases may be traced to a lack of coping skills, mental health issues, insecure housing, and coercion from others.[152] Since the implementation of the model, the only criminal convictions for non-disclosure have been of individuals who entered guilty pleas and who seemed to have escaped the attention of public health authorities altogether.[153]

Why did public health officials so seldom resort to coercive measures under these models? According to Bayer and Fairchild-Carrino, authorities came to recognise coercion as not particularly useful for public health purposes and that behavioural change would be more likely to be achieved through programme initiatives that would not provoke profound opposition.[154] In other words, although legislation may allow for coercive measures, the health-and-human-rights consensus did not favour maximalist use of coercive sanctions.

Understanding coordination between criminal justice and public health and its potential to mitigate limitations of the criminal law

Successful operation of the public health alternatives such as those outlined above requires, whether formally or informally, police and prosecutorial deference to and coordination with public health authorities. Such deference and coordination may be understood to be a partial response to uncertainties about the effects of the criminal law. In this section, I argue that changes in both the way the criminal law is conceived, along with the health and human rights consensus outlined earlier, have opened up space for what can be understood as a novel form of governance.

The criminal justice system increasingly reflects the fact that issues of individual wrong-doing have significant social and heath-related aspects.[155] As faith in the courts' abilities as an objective, value-neutral arbiter comes under question, and as disciplines of law and health and social services become more attuned to each other, we are seeing an unprecedented number of experimental collaborations between criminal justice and other social institutions, such as drug courts, family violence courts, youth courts, and even informal police and prosecutorial deference to community organisations.

At the same time, as discussed, public health organisations, particularly with regard to HIV/AIDS, have recognised the need to address underlying root causes of risk behaviour, and to enlist the expertise and insider knowledge of people living with HIV if they are to devise successful prevention and response programmes. This is in part due to early activism from the gay community and the credit the gay community has received for curbing the epidemic with the help of contextually appropriate responses.

The upshot is that we can understand police and prosecutorial deference to public health interventions to deal with non-disclosure as setting conditions for a kind of bottom-up, non-legislated diversion programme that can go some way towards reshaping the way the criminal justice system views the limits of its own role. Because it takes into account changing understandings of what constitutes a contextually appropriate response, a system like the Calgary Health Region's may be understood as inviting the participation of interested parties at a local level – public health authorities, police, prosecutors, lawyers, and people living with HIV (a number of whom presumably were infected through non-disclosing sex partners) – in setting up what essentially amounts to a vetting system for criminal prosecution. The terms of vetting – that is, the understanding of what psychosocial factors impede disclosure or the practice of safer sex – will vary with new evidence.

In some ways, this programme may appear unremarkable – an ordinary health or social work approach to dealing with non-disclosure, a support-then-enforcement type of approach. Yet it has some distinct features. First, it was designed through the empowered collaboration of a broader range of actors, so that it is not merely the imposition of a public health solution in place of a criminal justice solution. Rather, by attending to conflicting values, it facilitates more explicit negotiation of boundaries between the criminal law and neighbouring orders. It does a better job than the criminal law alone at attending to what the HIV/AIDS community and public health experts think or know will work in practice.

Second, a programme like Calgary Health Region's, operating as it does alongside a principled independent prosecutorial discretion as to whether to initiate prosecution, must demonstrate its effectiveness in terms of reducing incidents of exposure or singling out truly morally culpable behaviour in order to retain the fragile legitimacy it enjoys in the eyes of criminal law advocates. If the programme fails to play this preventive role, criminal law actors may see little point in deferring, and the call to resort to the criminal law for deterrence or retributive purposes may prove difficult to resist. The interesting result in practice is that these kinds of programmes could create a record of performance that could supply the criminal justice system with a richer and more nuanced understanding of the rational actor, and thus a richer and more nuanced understanding of the appropriate conditions of criminal liability in the context of people living with HIV.

New governance theorists suggest that in circumstances where certain decision makers' (including courts') capacities and legitimacy in dealing with complex social issues are challenged, ongoing deliberation with participation from the most affected parties is a more legitimate and effective mechanism for setting and enforcing behavioural norms.[156] Participatory, accountable, and transparent deliberative governance are increasingly being suggested as a way of dealing with complex criminal[157] and also sexual[158] behaviours. New governance theorists will argue that a programme like the Calgary Health Region's enjoys some legitimacy, despite the fact that it operates without explicit statutory authority. An open call to all truly interested actors to participate in rule-making may be no less democratic than judges interpreting ambiguous legal text on the basis of a notably decontextualised concept of the rational legal subject. Likewise, the programme may gain legitimacy to the extent that it reduces incidents of exposure and more coherently identifies wrongdoing. If police, prosecutors, and judges are to defer to the solutions reached through such governance structures, those structures must provide some form of record or account of their successes and failures (although it is currently unclear whether they do or do not). In a number of reported cases, judges have referred to the breakdown of positive public health responses to justify imposition of criminal sanctions.[159]

The public health and criminal law hybrid model seems to offer a richer answer to criminal law theorists who may be dissatisfied with traditional criminal justice approaches. Consequentialist theorists take seriously concerns that criminalisation of HIV exposure and transmission will deter testing, interfere with efforts to encourage less risky activities, and stigmatise people with HIV with the result that disclosure actually becomes harder. As discussed above, these potential negative effects are raised time and again but are notoriously difficult to ascertain through empirical studies. The collaborative public health and criminal law hybrid model cannot test these empirical questions, but at least it can give policymakers an opportunity to consider them when they make policy choices about which kinds of interventions in fact make disclosure easier. This offers an advantage over the leading law and social norms literature, which relies on abstract law-and-economics analysis to try to guess at what some contextualised version of the rational actor would do in response to different legal pressures.[160] It also offers something to retributivists by providing better information for determining and understanding what kind of behaviour really is morally blameworthy in context: for example, it eliminates the need to regard a person who does not disclose for fear that disclosure will leave them homeless as someone who is similarly situated as the exceptional worst-case actor who simply does not care about the health of their sex partners.[161]

Finally a criminal law and public health hybrid governance system can respond more satisfactorily to particular preoccupations within the alternative and restorative justice literature, particularly with regard to reforming social conditions that lead to crime. The restorative justice school shares much common ground with new governance theory, most clearly in how it favours deliberative civic participation in defining and punishing crime, rather than mere populism.[162] Unlike the traditional criminal justice system from which it deviates, theories of restorative justice take more seriously the political community's responsibilities for social exclusions that lead to crime. Thus, Duff states,

> [i]f criminal punishment is to be justified even in the tentatively doubtful way I am suggesting here, what is minimally required is both a serious collective commitment to reform the content and operations of the penal system, and a serious collective commitment to begin to remedy the kinds of exclusion that undermine the preconditions of criminal liability and punishment.[163]

Where social exclusion has been so clearly linked with vulnerability to criminal prosecution, as is the case for HIV transmission and exposure, a criminal law experiment that seeks to link social support with responses to potentially criminal behaviour more directly seems particularly suitable.

One important concern is that the blending or coordination of criminal law and public health functions through a programme like Calgary's could do more harm than good.[164] Under the kinds of hybrid governance model discussed here, the police, prosecutors, and policymakers retain discretion whether to continue to defer to public health authorities or to favour criminal sanctions. At present only a very small percentage of potential cases are pursued through the criminal justice system, usually depending on the initiative of members of the public reporting cases to the police. If public health and criminal orders became more closely linked, information gathered by public health actors could be used for any number of ends, including expansion of the reach of the criminal law. Thus, in a similar system operating in the prostitution context, transparency requirements have raised awareness of the sheer number of youth involved in prostitution, resulting in the expansion of coercive state approaches to youth prostitution.[165] Similarly, there is a risk here that, for those who fail to get in line quickly enough, criminal sanctions will be even harsher. Likewise, this kind of coordinated system has the potential to bring all aspects of a person's behaviour – not just risky sex – under scrutiny: suddenly, the law may be looking at whether a person attends counselling sessions, manages to live in stable conditions, even stays off drugs – all with the possibility of criminal sanctions in the background.

This reveals that when it comes to the promise of reconceiving the idealised rational actor posited by the criminal justice system, hybrid public health/criminal law governance models may offer promise for a new understanding, but it is an understanding that is still in its infancy. These models may well accommodate a greater range of rational actors – accepting the legitimacy of not disclosing when it would mean risking abuse (as long as one does one's best, under the circumstances, to get out of the situation) or substituting less risky oral sex for riskier activities. But ultimately they may yet again justify coercion against those who fail to fit the modified profile of the rational actor. Does it really get us that much further ahead to say that a woman who may risk abuse or neglect for disclosure should only be exposed to criminal sanctions for failing to disclose her HIV-positive status if she has already been offered housing and counselling?

Like all governance models, therefore, these programmes must address assumptions of power parity within the governance system. Importantly, the emergence of psychosocial support models that underlie graduated response approaches in the first place requires empowerment of the HIV/AIDS community, at the very least to promote the view that public health intervention efforts should be designed with careful consideration of the points of view of the most-affected actors. If the model is to avoid simply redistributing existing oppression, careful attention must be paid to ensuring that weaker parties are continually empowered to prevent system manipulation by the stronger parties, either through agreed-upon features of institutional design or through support external to the governance system by, for example, continued government funding and support for groups at risk of or living with HIV.

Conclusion

This paper has considered how greater attention to how public health and criminal law orders operate alongside one another can give rise to a more complete understanding of how the criminal law operates in practice. It has also shed light on some promising avenues for limiting the reach of the criminal law more rationally now that it seems that criminalisation is more a fact to be dealt with than a development to oppose. However, public health governance models should not be viewed merely as technocratic solutions to blind spots within the criminal justice system. They may well be driven by concerns about impacts, outcomes, and the criminal law's capacity to take proper account of the contexts in which HIV exposure or transmission occurs. But this quest for solutions that work opens up new possibilities for the collaborative exercise of the agency of people living with or at risk of HIV in an ongoing and on-the-ground project of legal reform. The modest hope is that appropriately conceived coordination between criminal law and public health actors will give rise to new opportunities for community members, particularly those who are least understood, to have a more meaningful role in defining and shaping the legal systems that affect them.

Acknowledgements

The author gratefully acknowledges the support and contributions of members of the Faculties of Law at McGill University and the University of Ottawa, participants at conferences including the McGill/ Queen's University Junior Scholars' Conference and the University of British Columbia's 'Standard Margins, Contemporary Issues in Law and Sexuality in Canada' conference, as well as the groups of individuals living with HIV/AIDS in Montreal and Toronto who provided useful feedback on earlier versions of this paper. Individual acknowledgements are owed to Gerald Neuman, Richard Elliott, Glenn Betteridge, Richard Pearshouse, Sandra Ka Hon Chu, Alison Symington, Edwin J. Bernard, Robert James, Matthew Weait, and Catherine Hanssens as well as the anonymous reviewers who provided invaluable comments on this article. Special thanks go to Megan Howatt and Anne Merminod for their exceptional research assistance, and Phil C.W. Chan for his infinite patience and detailed editing.

Notes

1. See, e.g., S. Bronitt, 'Spreading Disease and the Criminal Law', *Criminal Law Review* 21 (1994): 22; J. Chalmers, 'The Criminalization of HIV Transmission', *Journal of Medical Ethics* 28, no. 3 (2002): 160; J.M. Dwyer, 'Legislating AIDS Away: The Limited Role of Legal Persuasion in Minimizing the Spread of HIV', *Journal of Contemporary Health Law and Policy* 9 (1993): 167; R. Elliott, *Criminal Law and HIV/AIDS: Final Report* (Montreal: Canadian HIV/AIDS Legal Network and Canadian AIDS Society, 1997); Z. Lazzarini, S. Bray, and S. Burris, 'Evaluating the Impact of Criminal Laws on HIV Risk Behavior', *Journal of Law, Medicine and Ethics* 30 (2002): 239; J.R. Spencer, 'Liability for Reckless Infection: Part 1', *New Law Journal* (March 2004): 384; J.R. Spencer, 'Liability for Reckless Infection: Part 2', *New Law Journal* (March 2004): 448; K.M. Sullivan and M.A. Field, 'AIDS and the Coercive Power of the State', *Harvard Civil Rights–Civil Liberties Law Review* 23 (1988): 139, 197; M. Weait, 'Criminal Law and the Sexual Transmission of HIV: *R. v. Dica*', *Modern Law Review* 68 (2002): 121; M. Weait, 'On Being Responsible', in *Sexuality and the Law*, ed. V.E. Munro (London: Routledge-Cavendish, 2007), 19; L.E. Wolf and R. Vezina, 'Crime and Punishment: Is There a Role for Criminal Law in HIV Prevention Policy', *Whittier Law Review* 25 (2004): 821, 848.
2. See generally H. Worth, C. Patton, and M. T. McGehee, 'Legislating the Pandemic: A Global Survey of HIV/AIDS in Criminal Law', *Sexuality Research and Social Policy* 2, no. 2 (2005): 15.
3. See, e.g., W.H. Holland, 'HIV/AIDS and the Criminal Law', *Criminal Law Quarterly* 36 (1994): 279, 288; Spencer, 'Reckless Infection: Part 1'; idem, 'Reckless Infection: Part 2'.
4. Sullivan and Field, 'AIDS and the Coercive Power of the State'; Chalmers, 'The Criminalization of HIV Transmission'; Dwyer, 'Legislating AIDS Away'; Lazzarini et al., 'Evaluating the Impact of Criminal Laws on HIV Risk Behavior'; Weait, 'Criminal Law and the Sexual

Transmission of HIV'; Weait, 'On Being Responsible'; Elliott, *Criminal Law and HIV/AIDS*; Wolf and Vezina, 'Crime and Punishment'.

5. Sullivan and Field, 'AIDS and the Coercive Power of the State'.
6. See sources cited in note 1.
7. See Worth et al., 'Legislating the Pandemic'; A. Mears, 'The Criminalisation of HIV Transmission in England and Wales: A Brief Review of the Issues Arising', *Current Opinions in Infectious Diseases* 20 (2007): 47.
8. Spencer, 'Reckless Infection: Part 1'; idem, 'Reckless Infection: Part 2'; Holland, 'HIV/AIDS and the Criminal Law'.
9. S. Burris, L. Beletsky, J.A. Burleson, P. Case, and Z. Lazzarini, 'Do Criminal Laws Influence HIV Risk Behavior? An Empirical Trial', *Arizona State Law Journal* 39 (2007): 467, 469.
10. See generally, e.g., J.D. Auerback and T.J. Coates, 'HIV Prevention Research: Accomplishments and Challenges for the Third Decade of AIDS', *American Journal of Public Health* 90, no. 7 (2000): 1029; Centers for Disease Control and Prevention, 'Advancing HIV Prevention: New Strategies for a Changing Epidemic – United States, 2003', *Journal of the American Medical Association* 289, no. 19 (2003): 2493; G. Marks, S. Burris, and T.A. Peterman, 'Reducing Sexual Transmission of HIV From Those Who Know They Are Infected: The Need for Personal and Collective Responsibility', *AIDS* 13, no. 3 (1999): 297.
11. Z. Lazzarini and R. Klitzman, 'HIV and the Law: Integrating Law, Policy, and Social Epidemiology', *Journal of Law, Medicine and Ethics* 30 (2002): 533, 535.
12. See note 25 below.
13. Wolf and Vezina, 'Crime and Punishment', 857–9.
14. Chalmers, 'The Criminalization of HIV Transmission', describes the conviction of Stephen Kelly for the offence of recklessly causing injury to another person by transmitting HIV to a sexual partner to whom he failed to disclose his HIV-positive status before having unprotected sex.
15. *R. v. Cuerrier* [1998] 2 SCR 371.
16. *BBC News*, 'HIV Case Man Jailed for Five Years', 16 March 2001, http://news.bbc.co.uk/2/hi/uk_news/scotland/1223845.stm (accessed 30 November 2008).
17. *R. v. Dica* [2004] QB 1257.
18. Section 78 of the Offences Against the Person Act 1861 (c.100) provides that the Act does not apply in Scotland.
19. See Mears, 'The Criminalisation of HIV Transmission in England and Wales', 49. The author lists the convictions of Stephen Kelly (2001), Mohammed Dica (2003), Kouassi Adaye (2004), Feston Konzani (2005); Paulo Matias (2005), an anonymous Welsh woman (2005), Derek Hornett (2005), Mark James (2006), and Sarah Porter (2006). There have been four additional convictions since: see E.J. Bernard, 'Ninth English HIV Transmission Conviction for Merseyside Man', *AIDSMAP News*, 27 September 2006, http://www.aidsmap.com/en/news/9F020C62-89BF-47FA-97AD-88AC2FDE32EB.asp (accessed 12 June 2008); E.J. Bernard, 'Bournemouth Man Pleads Guilty in Tenth Successfully Prosecuted Reckless HIV Transmission Case in England and Wales', *AIDSMAP News*, 18 January 2007, http://www.aidsmap.com/en/news/320C5148-995E-4175-8BAF-5502DEA49930.asp (accessed 10 June 2008); *HM Advocate v. Mola*, 2007 SCCR 124, www.scotcourts.gov.uk (accessed 30 November 2008); *BBC News*, 'Man Jailed for Passing HIV Virus', *BBC News*, 21 November 2008, http://news.bbc.co.uk/2/hi/uk_news/england/lancashire/7743159.stm (accessed 10 December 2008.
20. According to at least one author, there is a theoretical possibility that prosecution could be brought under Scots law for the offence of reckless endangerment; see J. Chalmers, 'Sexually Transmitted Diseases and the Criminal Law', *Juridical Review* (2001): 266. In England and Wales, prosecution for exposure would not be possible unless one had acted with the intention of transmitting HIV: see National AIDS Trust, 'Criminal Prosecution of HIV Transmission: NAT Policy Update', August 2006, http://www.nat.org.uk/document/185 (accessed 16 May 2008).
21. *R. v. Savage*; *R. v. Parmenter* [1992] 1 AC 699 (House of Lords).
22. For a summary of US state criminal statutes, see American Civil Liberties Union, 'State Criminal Statutes on HIV Transmission – 2008', http://www.aclu.org/hiv/gen/34228res20080211.html (accessed 30 November 2008).
23. US Code, Title 42, s. 300ff-47 (2000).

24. Ryan White Comprehensive AIDS Resources Emergency (CARE) Act Amendments of 2000, Public Law No. 106-345, s. 301(a), 114 Stat. 1319.

25. Arkansas Code Annotated, §. 5, 14, 123; California Health and Safety Code, s. 120291; Florida Statutes Annotated, s. 384.24; Georgia Code Annotated, s. 165-60(c); Idaho Code, ss. 39-608 and 720; Illinois Compiled Statutes, 5/1216.2; Indiana Code Annotated, s. 35-42-1-7; Iowa Code, s. 709C; Louisiana Revised Statutes, s. 3435; Maryland Health Code Annotated Health-General, s. 18-601.1; Michigan Compiled Laws, s. 333.5210; Missouri Revised Statutes, 191.677; Nevada Revised Statutes, s. 21-205; New Jersey Statutes, s. 2C:34-5; North Dakota Century Code Annotated, s. 12; Oklahoma Statutes, 1192.1; 18 Pennsylvania Consolidated Statutes, s. 2703; South Carolina Code Annotated, s. 4429-145; South Dakota Codified Laws, s. 22-18-31; Tennessee Code Annotated, s. 39-13-109; Virginia Code Annotated, s. 18.2-67, 4:1

26. See, e.g., Alabama Code Annotated, s. 22-11A21(c); California Health and Safety Code, ss. 120290–1; Kansas Statutes Annotated, s. 21-3435; Montana Code Annotated, s. 50-18-112; New York Public Health Law, s. 2307; Tennessee Code Annotated, s. 68-10-107.

27. Lazzarini et al., 'Evaluating the Impact of Criminal Laws on HIV Risk Behavior', 241.

28. See, e.g., A. Waldman, 'Guilty Plea in an HIV Exposure Case', *New York Times*, 19 February 1999, B3. The articles reported that Nushawn Williams pleaded guilty to reckless endangerment.

29. Lazzarini et al., 'Evaluating the Impact of Criminal Laws on HIV Risk Behavior', 245.

30. Ibid.

31. See, e.g., *R.* v. *Hollihan* [1998] NJ No. 176 (Newfoundland Provincial Court); *R.* v. *Kreider* (1993) 140 AR. 81 (Alberta Provincial Court).

32. See, e.g., *R.* v. *Mercer* (1993) CCC (3d) 41 (Newfoundland Court of Appeal).

33. *R.* v. *Cuerrier*.

34. Ibid., para. 128.

35. See, e.g., *R.* v. *Wentzell*, unreported, 8 December 1989, Nova Scotia County Court, file no. CR-10888.

36. Canadian HIV/AIDS Legal Network, *Prosecutions for HIV Transmission and Exposure 1989–2008* (on file with author).

37. See S. Gruskin, A. Hendriks, and K. Tomasevski, 'Human Rights and Responses to HIV/AIDS', in *AIDS in the World II: Global Dimensions, Social Roots, and Responses*, ed. J.M. Mann and D.J.M. Tarantola (New York: Oxford University Press, 1996), 326.

38. See, e.g., Dwyer, 'Legislating AIDS Away'; Lazzarini et al., 'Evaluating the Impact of Criminal Laws on HIV Risk Behavior'; Weait, 'Criminal Law and the Sexual Transmission of HIV'; Weait, 'On Being Responsible'; Elliott, *Criminal Law and HIV/AIDS*.

39. Wolf and Vezina, 'Crime and Punishment', 870.

40. See, e.g., Lazzarini al., 'Evaluating the Impact of Criminal Laws on HIV Risk Behavior'; cf. Holland, 'HIV/AIDS and the Criminal Law'.

41. *R.* v. *Cuerrier*, para. 143.

42. See, e.g., J.G. Hodge and L.O. Gostin 'Handling Cases of Willful Exposure through HIV Partner Counseling and Referral Services', *Women's Rights Law Reporter* 23, no. 1 (2001): 45 (describing New York's and California's partner notification laws and pointing out the tension resulting from the need to respect an HIV-positive individual's privacy so that she or he will participate in public health efforts and the need to warn those who are at risk of being HIV-positive after being exposed to the virus, which despite efforts to maintain the anonymity of the individual may nonetheless result in the individual's identity being deduced).

43. Lazzarini and Klitzman, 'HIV and the Law', 537.

44. National AIDS Trust, 'Criminal Prosecution of HIV Transmission'.

45. See, e.g., J. Holland, C. Ramazanoglu, S. Scott, S. Sharpe, and R. Thomson, 'Risk, Power, and the Possibility of Pleasure: Young Women and Safer Sex', *AIDS Care* 4, no. 3 (1993): 273.

46. G. Marks, S. Burris, and T.A. Peterman, 'Reducing Sexual Transmission of HIV from Those Who Know They Are Infected: The Need for Personal and Collective Responsibility', *AIDS* 13, no. 3 (1999): 297.

47. M. Ekstrand, R. Stall, S. Kegeles, R. Hays, M. DeMayo, and T. Coates, 'Safer Sex among Gay Men: What Is the Ultimate Goal?', *AIDS* 7, no. 2 (1993): 281, 281.

48. *R.* v. *D.C.* (14 February 2008), Longueuil 505-01-058007-051 (Court of Québec, unreported).

49. Ibid., paras 130–1.

50. G. Marks, N. Crepaz, J.W. Senterfitt, and R.S. Janssen, 'Meta-analysis of High Risk Sexual Behavior in Persons Aware and Unaware They Are Infected with HIV in the United States: Implications for HIV Prevention Programs', *Journal of Acquired Immune Deficiency Syndromes* 39 (2005): 446: those who do not know they are HIV-positive are more likely to engage in risky sexual practices.

51. M. Mills, 'Who's Really the Victim here', *XTRA! West*, 31 October 2006, http://www.xtra.ca/public/Vancouver/Whos_really_the_victim_here-2053.aspx (accessed 30 November 2008).

52. *R. v. Cuerrier*, para. 144.

53. *R. v. Dica*, para. 59.

54. *R. v. Konzani* [2005] 2 Cr App R 198, para. 44.

55. M. Weait and Y. Azad, 'The Criminalization of HIV Transmission in England and Wales: Questions of Law and Policy', *HIV/AIDS Policy and Law Review* 10, no. 2 (2005): 5, 9.

56. Arkansas Code Annotated, s. 5-14-123; Michigan Compiled Laws Annotated, s. 333.5210.

57. Wolf and Vezina, 'Crime and Punishment', 851.

58. Missouri Revised Statutes Annotated, s. 191.677; South Carolina Code Annotated, s. 44-29-145; Virginia Code Annotated, s. 18.2-67.4:1.

59. Missouri Revised Statutes Annotated, s. 191.677.

60. This may be the case where general criminal laws are used to prosecute exposure or transmission or where statutes explicitly leave risk determination to juries. For example, Tennessee law prohibits people with HIV knowingly engaging in 'intimate contact', defined as 'bodily contact which exposes a person to the body fluid of the infected person in any manner that presents a significant risk of HIV transmission', Tennessee Code Annotated, s. 39-13-109; South Dakota's and Oklahoma's laws prohibit 'conduct reasonably likely to result in the transfer of the person's own blood, semen or vaginal secretions into the bloodstream of another person', Oklahoma Statutes Annotated Title 21, s. 1192.1; South Dakota Codified Laws s. 22-18-32.

61. K.K. Holmes, R. Levine, and M. Weaver, 'Effectiveness of Condoms in Preventing Sexually Transmitted Infections', *Bulletin of the World Health Organization* 82, no. 6 (2004): 454.

62. S.D. Pinkerton and P.R. Abramson, 'Effectiveness of Condoms in Preventing HIV Transmission', *Social Science and Medicine* 44, no. 9 (1997): 1303.

63. T.C. Quinn, M.J. Wawer, N. Sewankambo, D. Serwadda, C. Li, F. Wabwire-Mangen, M.O. Meehan, T. Lutalo, and R.H. Gray, 'Viral Load and Heterosexual Transmission of Human Immunodeficiency Virus Type 1', *New England Journal of Medicine* 342, no. 12 (2000): 921. One recent study of 593 sero-discordant couples in Spain found that 8.3% of the initially HIV-negative partners whose partners were not taking anti-retroviral therapy became infected during the study period, whereas no partner was infected where her or his HIV-positive partner was treated with highly active anti-retroviral therapy (HAART): J. Castilla, J. del Romero, V. Hernando, B. Marincovich, S. Garcia, and C. Rodriguez, 'Effectiveness of Highly Active Antiretroviral Therapy in Reducing Heterosexual Transmission of HIV', *Journal of Acquired Immune Deficiency Syndromes* 40, no. 1 (2005): 96.

64. See, e.g., A. Wald and K. Link, 'Risk of Human Immunodeficiency Virus Infection in Herpes Simplex Virus Type 2-Seropositive Persons: A Meta-analysis', *Journal of Infectious Diseases* 185, no. 1 (2002): 45.

65. R.H. Gray et al., 'Male Circumcision for HIV Prevention in Men in Rakai, Uganda: A Randomised Trial', *The Lancet* 369, no. 9562 (2007): 657; R.C. Bailey et al., 'Male Circumcision for HIV Prevention in Young Men in Kisumu, Kenya: A Randomised Controlled Trial', *The Lancet* 369, no. 9562 (2007): 643.

66. There have been efforts to determine the per-act risk of transmission for various sex acts. UK guidelines put a woman's risk of contracting the virus through receptive vaginal sex with a man at 1 in 500 to 1 in 1000; a man's risk of contracting HIV through penetrative vaginal or anal intercourse at 1 in 1666; a receptive partner's risk of contracting the virus through anal sex at 1 in 500; and a person's risk of contracting HIV by performing oral sex at negligible to 1 in 2500. The likelihood of contracting HIV from receiving oral sex is not considered a significant transmission risk: M. Fisher et al., 'UK Guideline for the Use of Post-exposure Prophylaxis for HIV Following Sexual Exposure', *International Journal of STD & AIDS* 17 (2006): 81.

67. Thus, the constitutionality of HIV criminalisation laws in the US has been challenged, unsuccessfully, as vague and thus in violation of the fundamental principle of *nulum criminem sinem lege* (that people ought to be able to know what the law is at the time they are said to violate it).

See, e.g., *Illinois* v. *Russell*, 630 N.E.2d 794 (Illinois 1994); *Iowa* v. *Keene*, 629 N.W.2d 360 (Iowa 2001); *Missouri* v. *Mahan*, 971 S.W.2d 307 (Missouri 1998); *Guevara* v. *Superior Court (California):* 73 Cal. Rptr. 2d 421 (App. 6th Dist. 1998); *Louisiana* v. *Gamberella*, 633 So. 2d 595 (La. App. 1st Cir. 1993); *Washington* v. *Stark*, 832 P.2d 109 (Wash. App. 1992). Similar arguments were raised and rejected in *R.* v. *Cuerrier*, para. 139, and *R.* v. *Dica*, para. 55.

68. For example, the Supreme Court of Canada stated in *R.* v. *Cuerrier*, para. 129, that 'the careful use of condoms might be found to so reduce the risk of harm that it could no longer be considered significant'. See, similarly, the Court of Appeal of England and Wales in *R.* v. *Dica*, para. 11.

69. *R.* v. *Nduwayo* [2006] BCJ, no. 3396, original instructions to jury, 12 December 2005 (unreported) (British Columbia Supreme Court).

70. *R.* v. *Mabior* (2008) 78 WCB (2d) 380 (Manitoba Queen's Bench).

71. Ibid., para. 116

72. Ibid., para. 72.

73. Ibid., para. 117.

74. *R.* v. *J.M.* [2005] OJ No. 5649 (Ontario Superior Court of Justice).

75. Ibid., para. 2.

76. See Canadian HIV/AIDS Legal Network, *Prosecutions for HIV Transmission and Exposure.*

77. See Crown Prosecution Service, 'Policy for Prosecuting Cases Involving the Intentional or Reckless Sexual Transmission of Infection', http://www.cps.gov.uk/publications/prosecution/sti.html (accessed 30 November 2008).

78. *HM Advocate* v. *Mola.*

79. Chalmers, 'The Criminalization of HIV Transmission', 161, citing generally A. Ashworth, 'Belief, Intent, and Criminal Liability', in *Oxford Essays in Jurisprudence: Third Series*, ed. J. Eekelaar and J. Bell (Oxford: Clarendon Press, 1987), 16.

80. Ibid.

81. S.H. Kadish, 'The Criminal Law and the Luck of the Draw', *Journal of Criminal Law and Criminology* 84 (1994): 679. Proving actual transmission also raises evidentiary problems: see E.J. Bernard et al., *The Use of Phylogenetic Analysis as Evidence in Criminal Investigation of HIV Transmission* (London: NAM, 2007).

82. J. Elford, 'Changing Patters of Sexual Behaviour in the Era of Highly Active Antiretroviral Therapy', *Current Opinion in Infectious Diseases* 19, no. 1 (2006): 26.

83. T. Schacker et al., 'Clinical and Epidemiologic Features of Primary HIV Infection', *Annals of Internal Medicine* 125 (1996): 257.

84. B. Varghese et al., 'Reducing the Risk of Sexual HIV Transmission: Quantifying the Per-Act Risk for HIV on the Basis of Choice of Partner, Sex Act, and Condom Use', *Sexually Transmitted Diseases* 29, no. 1 (2002): 38.

85. See generally J.M. Mann and D.J.M. Tarantola, 'Societal Vulnerability: Contextual Analysis', in *AIDS in the World II: Global Dimensions, Social Roots, and Responses*, ed. J.M. Mann and D.J.M. Tarantola (New York: Oxford University Press, 1996), 444. See also UNAIDS, *2008 Report on the Global HIV/AIDS Epidemic* (Geneva: Joint United Nations Programme on HIV/AIDS, 1998).

86. National AIDS Trust, 'Criminal Prosecution of HIV Transmission, 12.

87. R. James, Y. Azad, and M. Weait, 'Are the People Prosecuted for HIV Transmission in the Criminal Courts Representative of the UK Epidemic?' (National AIDS Trust, 2007) (on file with author).

88. See, e.g., Sullivan and Field, 'AIDS and the Coercive Power of the State'; Wolf and Vezina, 'Crime and Punishment'.

89. Substance Abuse and Mental Health Services Administration, *National Household Survey on Drug Abuse: Summary Report 1998* (Rockville, MD: Substance Abuse and Mental Health Services Administration, 1999), 13, http://www.oas.samhsa.gov/NHSDA/98SummHtml/NHSDA98Summ-03.htm#P230_21832 (accessed 18 August 2008).

90. Around 12.5% of the US population are African-Americans: US Bureau of the Census, *Profile of General Demographic Characteristics: 2000* (Washington: US Bureau of the Census, 2000), Table DP-1, http://censtats.census.gov/pub/Profiles.shtml (accessed 18 August 2008).

91. T. Kykelhahn and T.H. Cohen, *Felony Defendants in Large Urban Counties, 2004*, (Washington: Bureau of Justice Statistics, 2006), 2, http://www.ojp.usdoj.gov/bjs/pub/html/fdluc/2004/fdluc04st.htm (accessed 20 December 2008).

92. T. Hughes, *New Court Commitments to State Prison, 2000* (Washington: National Corrections Reporting Program, Bureau of Justice Statistics), www.ojp.usdof.gov/bjs/dtdata.htm (accessed 30 November 2008).

93. Marks et al., 'Meta-analysis of High Risk Sexual Behavior'.

94. Lazzarini et al., 'Evaluating the Impact of Criminal Laws on HIV Risk Behavior', 247.

95. In *R.* v. *Williams* [2003] 2 SCR 134, para. 28 (Supreme Court of Canada): Justice Binnie stated obiter that '[o]nce an individual becomes aware of a *risk* that he or she has contracted HIV, and hence that his or her partner's consent has become an issue, but nevertheless persists in unprotected sex that creates a risk of further HIV transmission without disclosure to his or her partner, recklessness is established'. (emphasis original). At least one of the convictions in the UK to date involved a man who had never taken an HIV test but had been diagnosed with other sexually transmitted diseases, had been warned that he was at risk of HIV infection, and failed thereafter to attend an appointment for testing; see C. Dodds et al., *Grievous Harm? Use of the Offences Against the Person Act 1861 for Sexual Transmission of HIV* (London: Sigma Research, 2005), 26, www.sigmaresearch.org.uk/downloads/report05b.pdf (accessed 10 December 2008), discussing the case of Kouassi Adaye, who pleaded guilty to inflicting grievous bodily harm for HIV transmission despite never having actually taken an HIV test.

96. *John B.* v. *Superior Court*, 2006 WL 1805955 (3 July 2006) (California Supreme Court).

97. Public Health Agency of Canada, 'Federal Initiative to Address HIV/AIDS in Canada', http://www.phac-aspc.gc.ca/aids-sida/populations_e.html (accessed 30 November 2008).

98. See, e.g., J.G. Murphy, 'Introduction', in *Punishment and Rehabilitation*, ed. J.G. Murphy (Belmont, CA: Wadsworth, 1995), 2.

99. Holland, 'HIV/AIDS and the Criminal Law', 288–9.

100. See R. Jürgens, *HIV/AIDS in Prisons: Final Report* (Montreal: Canadian HIV/AIDS Legal Network & Canadian AIDS Society, 1996).

101. See Elliott, *Criminal Law and HIV/AIDS*, 61.

102. Burris et al., 'Do Criminal Laws Influence HIV Risk Behavior?', 505.

103. Ibid., 510, quoting Wolf and Vezina, 'Crime and Punishment', 824: 'Williams was ultimately alleged to have exposed forty-eight young women in Jamestown, and an additional fifty to seventy-five young women in New York City.'

104. C.J. de Rosa and G. Marks, 'Preventive Counseling of HIV Positive Men and Self Disclosure of Serostatus to Sex Partners: New Opportunities for Prevention', *Health Psychology* 17 (1998): 227.

105. Ibid.

106. See, e.g., *Cuerrier, R.* v. *Cuerrier*, para. 147: 'It is right and proper for public health authorities to be concerned that their struggles against AIDS should not be impaired. Yet the Code does have a role to play. Through deterrence it will protect and serve to encourage honesty, frankness and safer sexual practices.'

107. Ibid., para. 142.

108. Ibid., para. 146.

109. Ibid., para. 147.

110. *R.* v. *Nduwayo*, original instructions to jury,; *R.* v. *Nduwayo*, 2006 BCSC 1972, para. 7.

111. Burris et al., 'Do Criminal Laws Influence HIV Risk Behavior?', 501.

112. See, e.g., Canadian Sentencing Commission, *Sentencing Reform: A Canadian Approach: Report of the Sentencing Commission* (Ottawa: Minister of Supply and Services, 1987), 136–7.

113. *R.* v. *Gladue* (1999) 133 CCC (3d) 385, 409; *R.* v. *Proulx* (2000) 140 CCC (3d) 449, para. 57; *R.* v. *Wismayer* (1997) 115 CCC (3d) 18, paras 36, 38 and 40.

114. See, e.g., D.M. Kahan, 'Between Economics and Sociology: The New Path of Deterrence', *Michigan Law Review* 95 (1997): 2477.

115. Only California's law is limited to deliberate exposure: California Health and Safety Code, s. 120291.

116. H.L. Dalton, 'Criminal Law', in *AIDS Law Today: A New Guide for the Public*, ed. S. Burris et al. (New Haven: Yale University Press, 1993), 242, 250.

117. Burris et al., 'Do Criminal Laws Influence HIV Risk Behavior?', 510. See also Weait, 'On Being Responsible'.

118. Lazzarini et al., 'Evaluating the Impact of Criminal Laws on HIV Risk Behavior', 247.

119. See, e.g., Public Health (Control of Disease) Act 1984 (c. 22) (UK); Public Health (Infectious Disease) Regulations 1988 (UK). For a review of US state legislation, see W. Parmet, 'AIDS and Quarantine: The Revival of an Archaic Doctrine', *Hofstra Law Review* 14 (1985): 53.
120. S. Burris and L.O. Gostin, 'The Impact of HIV/AIDS on the Development of Public Health Law', in *Dawning Answers: How the HIV Epidemic Has Helped to Strengthen Public Health*, ed. R.O. Valdisseri (Oxford: Oxford University Press, 2003), 96.
121. J.M. Mann, 'Human Rights and AIDS: The Future of the Pandemic', in *Health and Human Rights: A Reader*, J.M. Mann et al. (New York: Routledge, 1999), 216, 217.
122. Ibid.
123. Ibid., 223.
124. *Kaiser Daily Health Report*, 'Human Rights Watch Criticizes Countries for Proposing, Applying Coercive HIV Testing: Calls on WHO, UNAIDS to Update Guidelines', 11 August 2006, http://www.kaisernetwork.org/daily_reports/rep_index.cfm?hint=4&DR_ID=39092 (accessed 10 December 2008).
125. G.M. Oppenheimer, R. Bayer, and J. Colgrove, 'Health and Human Rights: Old Wine in New Bottles?', *Journal of Law, Medicine and Ethics* 30 (2002) 522; S.R. Bagenstos, 'The Americans with Disabilities Act as Risk Regulation', *Columbia Law Review* 101 (2001): 1479; Burris and Gostin, 'The Impact of HIV/AIDS on the Development of Public Health Law'.
126. These laws had generally fallen into desuetude since the mid twentieth century when antibiotics rendered quarantine redundant in most contexts; see Parmet, 'AIDS and Quarantine.
127. See R. Bayer, *Private Acts, Social Consequences: AIDS and the Politics of Public Health* (New York: Free Press, 1989), explaining why early calls for quarantine were rejected.
128. N.L. Ford and M.D. Quam, 'AIDS Quarantine: The Legal and Practical Implications', *Journal of Legal Medicine* 8 (1987): 353.
129. Sullivan and Field, 'AIDS and the Coercive Power of the State', 154–5.
130. Parmet, 'AIDS and Quarantine', 82–90.
131. Ibid., 86.
132. W.E. Parmet, 'Quarantine Redux: Bioterrorism, AIDS and the Curtailment of Individual Liberty in the Name of Public Health', *Health Matrix* 12 (2003): 85.
133. Ibid., 96.
134. R. Bayer, 'Public Health Policy and the AIDS Epidemic: An End to HIV Exceptionalism?', *New England Journal of Medicine* 324, no. 21 (1991): 1500; K.M. DeCock and A.M. Johnson, 'From Exceptionalism to Normalisation: A Reappraisal of Attitudes and Practice around HIV Testing', *British Medical Journal* 316 (1998): 290.
135. See R. Friedman, 'The Application of Canadian Public Health Law to AIDS', *Health Law in Canada* 9, no. 1 (1988): 49; Burris and Gostin, 'The Impact of HIV/AIDS on the Development of Public Health Law'; Parmet, 'AIDS and Quarantine', 59. L.O. Gostin, S. Burris, and Z. Lazzarini, 'The Law and the Public's Health: A Study of Infectious Disease Law in the United States', *Columbia Law Review* 59 (1999): 101.
136. R. Bayer and A. Fairchild-Carrino, 'AIDS and the Limits of Control: Public Health Orders, Quarantine, and Recalcitrant Behavior', *American Journal of Public Health* 83, no. 10 (1993): 1472.
137. Public Health (Control of Disease) Act 1984 (c.22), ss. 35–7; Public Health (Infectious Diseases) Regulations 1985 (UK) SI 1985/434 ss. 36–7; Public Health (Infectious Diseases) Regulations 1988 (UK) SI 1988/546.
138. Public Health etc. (Scotland) Act 2008 (asp. 5).
139. R.M. Martin, 'The Exercise of Public Health Powers in Cases of Infectious Disease: Human Rights Implications', *Medical Law Review* 14, no. 1 (2006): 132, 139.
140. For the United States, see, e.g., Colorado Revised Statutes Annotated, s. 25-4-1406; Delaware Code, ss. 16-703 and 704; Florida Annotated Statutes, s. 384.27; Illinois Compiled Statutes,, 410 I.L.C.S. 325, s. 6; Maine Revised Statues, ss. 22-250-807 and 812; Michigan Compiled Laws, s. 333-5205; Montana Code Annotated, s. 50-18-107; Texas Statutes, ss. 81.082 and 81.174; Utah Code, s. 26-6-4; Vermont Statutes, s. 1096; Code of Virginia, ss. 32.1-43 and 32.1-48.02; Wyoming Statutes, s. 35-4-133; For Canada, see, e.g., Public Health Act, RSA 2000, c. P-37, ss. 40 and 43 (Alberta); Public Health Act, 1994, SS 1994, c. P-37.1, s. 38 (Saskatchewan); Public Health Act, CCSM c. P210, s. 19 (Manitoba); Health Promotion and Protection Act, RSO 1990, c. H-7, ss. 22 and 35 (Ontario); Public Health Act, RSQ, ch. S-22, ss. 88 and 106 (Québec); Public Health Act, SNB 1998, c. P-22.4, ss. 33(4) and

36(2) (New Brunswick); Health Protection Act, SNS 2004, c.4, s. 32(3) (Nova Scotia); Communicable Disease Act, RSNL 1990, c. C-26, s. 15 (Newfoundland).

141. For the United States, see, e.g., Code of Alabama, ss. 22-11a-3 and 22-11-21; General Statutes of Connecticut, ss. 19a-131c; Delaware Codes, s. 16-1704; Florida Annotated Statutes, s. 384.28; Hawaii Revised Statutes, ss. 325-8 and 325-9; Illinois Compiled Statutes, 410 ILCS 325, s. 6; Iowa Code, s. 139A.9; Mississippi Annotated Code, s. 41-23-2; Montana Code Annotated, s. 50-18-107; South Carolina Code Annotated, s. 44-4-530; Texas Statutes, s. 81.082; Utah Code, s. 26-6-4. For Canada, see, e.g., Public Health Act, RSA 2000, c. P-37, ss. 40 and 45 (Alberta); Public Health Act, 1994, SS 1994, c. P-37.1, s. 38 (Saskatchewan); Public Health Act, CCSM c. P210, s. 19 (Manitoba); Health Promotion and Protection Act, RSO 1990, c. H-7, s. 35 (Ontario); Public Health Act, R.S.Q., ch. S-22, s. 106 (Québec); Health Protection Act, SNS 2004, c.4, s. 32(3) (Nova Scotia); Public Health and Safety Act, RSY 2002, c. 176, s. 2 (Yukon); Communicable Disease Regulation, RRNWT 1990, c. P-13, s. 14(1) (Northwest Territories).

142. For the United States, see, e.g., Colorado Revised Statutes Annotated, s. 24-4-1406; Delaware Code, s. 16-1704; North Dakota Century Code Annotated, s. 23-07.4-01. For Canada, see, e.g., Public Health Act, 1994, SS 1994, c. P-37.1, s. 38 (Saskatchewan); Public Health Act, CCSM c. P210, s. 19 (Manitoba); Health Promotion and Protection Act, RSO 1990, c. H-7, ss. 22 and 35 (Ontario); Public Health Act, RSQ, ch. S-22, s. 106 (Québec); Public Health Act, SNB 1998, c. P-22.4, s. 33(4) (New Brunswick); Health Protection Act, SNS 2004, c.4, ss. 32(3) and 38(1) (Nova Scotia); Public Health Act, RSPEI 1988, c. P-30, s. 5(4) (Prince Edward Island).

143. For the United States, see, e.g., Arkansas Annotated Code, s. 20-15-1704; California Health and Safety Code, s. 120280; General Statutes of Connecticut, ss. 19a-131c, Delaware Code, s. 16-1705; Maine Revised Statutes, s. 22-250-810; Michigan Compiled Laws, s. 333-5205; New York Annotated Code, s. 2120; North Dakota Century Code Annotated, s. 23-07.4-02; Texas Statutes, ss. 81.161–7; Code of Virginia, s. 32.1-48.011; West Virginia Code, ss. 16-4-12 and 16-4-14; Wisconsin Statutes, s. 252.11. For Canada, see, e.g., Public Health Act, 1994, SS 1994, c. P-37.1, s. 45.1(1) (Saskatchewan); Public Health Act, CCSM c. P210, s. 22.7 (Manitoba); Health Promotion and Protection Act, R.S.O. 1990, c. H-7, s. 35 (Ontario); Public Health Act, SNB 1998, c. P-22.4, ss. 36(1) and (2) (New Brunswick); Health Protection Act, SNS 2004, c. 4, ss. 38(1) and 46 (Nova Scotia); Public Health Act, R.S.P.E.I. 1988, c. P-30, s. 5(4) (Prince Edward Island).

144. For the United States, see, e.g., Florida Code, s. 384.34; Iowa Code, s. 139A.25; Mississippi Annotated Code, s. 41-23-2; Nebraska Code, s. 71-506; South Carolina Code Annotated, s. 44-4-530; Code of Virginia, s. 32.1-48.014; West Virginia Code, s. 16-4-27; Wisconsin Statutes, s. 252.25. For Canada, see, e.g., Public Health Act, 1994, SS 1994, c. P-37.1, s. 60 (Saskatchewan); Public Health Act, SNB 1998, c. P-22.4, s. 52(3) (New Brunswick); Public Health Act, RSPEI 1988, c. P-30, s. 5(4) (Prince Edward Island); Communicable Disease Act, RSNL 1990, c. C-26, s. 15 (Newfoundland); Public Health and Safety Act, RSY 2002, c. 176, s. 22 (Yukon).

145. The principle of least restrictive means is an ethical principle in public health: see, e.g., American Public Health Association, *Public Code of Ethics*, http://www.apha.org/codeofethics/ethics.htm (accessed 30 November 2008), as well as a legal principle requiring the use of less coercive means, such as education and, arguably, social resources necessary for compliance such as safe housing, before the state may resort to more coercive approaches such as detention: L.O. Gostin, 'The Resurgent Tuberculosis Epidemic in the Era of AIDS: Reflections on Public Health, Law and Society', *Maryland Law Review* 54 (1995): 110. On whether public health detention legislation meets the least restrictive means principle, see Bayer and Fairchild-Carrino, 'AIDS and the Limits of Control'; R. Martin, 'Law as a Tool in Promoting and Protecting Public Health: Always in Our Best Interests?', *Public Health* 121 (2007): 846. For a judicial treatment of the principle in the context of detention orders for non-compliance with behavioural orders to prevent HIV transmission, see *Enhorn* v. *Sweden* [2005] 41 EHRR 30 (European Court of Human Rights).

146. Bayer and Fairchild-Carrino, 'AIDS and the Limits of Control', 1475.

147. Ibid., 1473.

148. Ibid., 1474.

149. Ibid. See also D.E. Woodhouse et al., 'Restricting Personal Behavior: Case Studies on Legal Measures to Prevent the Spread of HIV', *International Journal of STDs and AIDS* 4, no. 2 (1993): 114.

150. RSA 2000 c. P-37, ss. 29 and 39ff.

151. The model is described in R. Bessner, 'Persons Who Fail to Disclose Their HIV/AIDS Status: Conclusions Reached by an Expert Working Group', *Canada Communicable Disease Report* 31, no. 5 (2005): 53.

152. Gordon Kliewer (former HIV designated nurse for the Calgary Health Region) in discussion with author, 13 April 2008.

153. See *R.* v. *Booth* (2005) 71 WCB (2d) 363 (Alberta Provincial Court).

154. Bayer and Fairchild-Carrino, 'AIDS and the Limits of Control', 1475.

155. W.N. Renke, 'Criminal Justice and Public Health', in *Public Health Law & Policy in Canada*, ed. T.M. Bailey, T. Caulfield, and N.M. Reis (Toronto: Butterworths, 2005), 429.

156. For a description of the current state of discussion of new governance approaches, see O. Lobel, 'The Renew Deal: The Rise and Fall of Regulation and the Rise of Governance in Contemporary Legal Thought', *Minnesota Law Review* 89 (2004): 342.

157. See, e.g., M.C. Dorf and C.F. Sabel, 'Drug Treatment Courts and Emergent Experimentalist Government', *Vanderbilt Law Review* 53 (2000): 829.

158. J.L. Cohen, *Regulating Intimacy: A New Legal Paradigm* (Princeton: Princeton University Press, 2002).

159. See, e.g., *R.* v. *Cuerrier*, para. 142.

160. R. Weisberg, 'Norms and Criminal Law, and the Norms of Criminal Law Scholarship', *Journal of Criminal Law and Criminology* 93, nos 2–3 (2003): 467.

161. Cf. Weait, 'On Being Responsible', noting that the criminal law, rooted as it is in classic Western liberal traditions, posits a decontextualised subject when it measures all actors' behaviours against an idealised reasonable person.

162. See, e.g., J. Braithwaite and P. Pettit, *Not Just Deserts: A Republican Theory of Criminal Justice* (Oxford: Oxford University Press, 1990); A.W. Dzur and R. Mirchandani, 'Punishment and Democracy: The Role of Public Deliberation', *Punishment and Society* 9, no. 2 (2007): 151.

163. R.A. Duff, *Punishment, Communication, and Community.* (Oxford: Oxford University Press, 2001), 200.

164. This paper, for example, does not discuss in detail many of the due process safeguards that appear to be absent in much public health legislation.

165. J. Phoenix, 'Governing Prostitution: New Formations, Old Agendas', *Canadian Journal of Law and Society* 22, no. 2 (2007): 73.

Shared values of Singapore: sexual minority rights as Singaporean value

Phil C.W. Chan

Faculty of Law, National University of Singapore, Singapore

For scholars of comparative constitutional law and human rights, Singapore offers an exceptional platform in terms of the number and diversity of issues that require and excite discussions. A human rights issue less discussed is the legal situation affecting persons belonging to sexual minorities in Singapore, where consensual sexual activity between male adults continues to be a crime. The Singapore government opposes sexual minority rights development on the basis of a Singapore 'culture' that revolves around certain 'shared values'. Persons belonging to sexual minorities in Singapore must therefore overcome a formidable hurdle in order to realise their right of equality, and the legal situation affecting them provides useful insight into the development of human rights and governance in Singapore in general. This paper first examines the Singapore government's position on human rights by deconstructing Singapore 'culture'. It then deconstructs the relevant laws affecting persons belonging to sexual minorities in Singapore and, finally, explores whether and how Singapore may develop its own jurisprudence on sexual minority rights under the framework of legitimate constitutional comparativism.

Introduction

For scholars of comparative constitutional law and human rights, Singapore offers an exceptional platform in terms of the number and diversity of issues that require and excite discussions. A former British colony and high-income country with a gross national income by purchasing power parity of US$48,520 per capita for 2007 (ninth in the world and second in Asia after oil-exporting Brunei Darussalam),[1] Singapore has a population of 3,642,700 who hold Singapore citizenship or permanent residency (and another 1,196,700 who hold neither), of which 74.7% are ethnic Chinese, 13.6% ethnic Malays, 8.9% ethnic Indians, and 2.8% 'Others'.[2] Reflecting Singapore's historical lineage with Malaysia, the Constitution of Singapore stipulates Malay as the national language[3] while English remains the medium of official communications.[4] The Constitution also provides for the special position of Malays as 'the indigenous people of Singapore'[5] and for the special regulation of Islam.[6] Singapore's economic success and multiracial character[7] are, however, not the characteristics for which the country is most famed. The penal law of Singapore, including its reversal of the burden of proof and, in many cases, imposition of mandatory death penalty for drug[8] and weapon offences[9] and mandatory caning for a large number of offences ranging from gang robbery[10] to unauthorised affixing of a poster on a public wall (on second conviction);[11] the various government policies that discriminate against women; and restrictions on freedom of expression including through initiations of defamation proceedings by the government or by a number of senior politicians in their personal capacity against opposition parties and foreign newspapers have been subjects of criticism by local rights groups, foreign governments, and international and non-governmental rights bodies.[12]

A human rights issue less discussed, however, is the legal situation affecting persons belonging to sexual minorities in Singapore, where consensual sexual activity between male adults continues to be a crime.[13] While calls for decriminalisation have been made, the government has argued that the 'shared values' (also known as 'Asian values', particularly in transnational discourse) of Singapore that emphasise Confucian notions of responsibilities over rights require a communitarian approach towards human rights and preclude the libertarian approach that the government has argued is suitable (if ever) only in Western countries. Persons belonging to sexual minorities in Singapore must therefore overcome a formidable hurdle in order to realise their right of equality, and the legal situation affecting them provides useful insight into the development of human rights and governance in Singapore in general. As Baden Offord has observed, 'any kind of sexuality which does not conform to the dominant ideological orientation is silenced and made invisible ... the issue of homosexuality is an issue that foregrounds the whole dilemma of citizenship, identity and control in Singapore'.[14]

In this paper, I argue that while human rights ought indeed to be developed from within, the juridical insights and experiences other jurisdictions have garnered provide useful resources for Singapore courts – and Parliament of Singapore – to examine whether and how sexual minority rights, and human rights in general, may be developed in Singapore as Singaporean rights and a Singaporean value. As Abdullahi Ahmed An-Na`im discerns, 'the possibilities of cultural reinterpretation and reconstruction through internal cultural discourse and cross-cultural dialogue, as a means to enhancing the universal legitimacy of human rights', ought to be explored.[15] I am mindful that this task is pregnant with political, social and emotional factors and I am after all a foreigner in Singapore – albeit from a place (i.e. Hong Kong) with which Singapore shares the greatest historical, economic, social, cultural and juristic affinities;[16] one where homosexuality was decriminalised by legislature in 1991[17] and the differentiation in the ages of consent for different-sex and male/male sexual activity declared by the judiciary to be unconstitutional in 2005;[18] one where, as in Singapore, recourse to 'Asian values' alongside Confucian ethics and religious concepts (with predominant if not exclusive focus on Christian concepts) continues to pervade debates on sexual minority rights;[19] and thus one against which the prevailing situation in Singapore may be tested. Much encouraged by Professor Thio Li-ann's call for an honest debate[20] on Singapore's continued criminalisation of consensual male/male sexual activity notwithstanding her staunch opposition as a Nominated Member of Parliament[21] to decriminalisation,[22] this paper first examines the Singapore government's position on human rights by deconstructing the 'shared values' and 'culture' of Singapore that the government has proclaimed. It then deconstructs the relevant laws affecting persons belonging to sexual minorities in Singapore and, finally, explores whether and how Singapore may develop its own jurisprudence on sexual minority rights under the framework of legitimate constitutional comparativism.

Shared values of Singapore: a critique of the Singapore School on human rights

In putting forward a 'culture' in order to override fundamental rights and freedoms, the state must first define what that culture is, in order to discern whether such a culture in fact exists.

Sally Engle Merry has explained convincingly that culture must not be seen as static, rigid, and isolated within a polity: 'Its boundaries are fluid, meanings are contested, and meaning is produced by institutional arrangements and political economy. Culture is marked by hybridity and creolization rather than uniformity or consistency.'[23] Furthermore, as An-Na`im reminds us, in the construction of culture, 'powerful individuals and groups tend to monopolize the interpretation of cultural norms and manipulate them to their own advantage'.[24] One must, in addition, explore whether and why that culture should have such controlling normative force capable of overriding fundamental rights and freedoms.

A colony of the United Kingdom since 1819, Singapore achieved self-government in 1959 and joined the Federation of Malaysia in 1963, from which it was expelled in 1965 due to conflicts arising from the Kuala Lumpur government's insistence on affirmative action for Malays and Singapore's substantial Chinese population.[25] While Singapore has upon independence retained Westminster-style unicameral parliamentary government and the common law legal system, it is essentially a dominant-party state with the People's Action Party (PAP) dominating all aspects of governance.[26]

With an all-encompassing survivalist mentality constructed on the basis of Singapore's small size and population juxtaposed against its large and populous neighbours, its lack of natural resources and its multiracial character, the Singapore government has adopted an authoritarian approach to governance.[27] Singapore has not acceded to major international human rights treaties such as the International Covenant on Civil and Political Rights[28] and the International Covenant on Economic, Social and Cultural Rights[29] that would oblige Singapore to follow internationally agreed human rights norms and subject itself to international monitoring mechanisms,[30] while Singapore courts, as will be seen, have maintained that when interpreting the Singapore Constitution and statutes and developing Singapore common law, they should look within the 'four walls' of the Constitution where legal developments in other jurisdictions have little value. The Constitution contains eight clauses on fundamental liberties, guaranteeing the liberty of the person,[31] prohibiting slavery and forced labour,[32] protecting against retrospective criminal laws and double jeopardy,[33] and guaranteeing freedom of movement,[34] freedoms of speech, assembly, and association,[35] freedom of religion,[36] rights in respect of education,[37] and the right of equality[38] under which discrimination 'on the ground only of religion, race, descent or place of birth' is specifically prohibited save otherwise expressly permitted by the Constitution.[39] Notwithstanding the normatively binding Universal Declaration of Human Rights[40] and the Vienna Declaration and Programme of Action adopted by consensus by 171 States including Singapore at the 1993 United Nations World Conference on Human Rights where it was recognised that '[a]ll human rights are universal, indivisible and interdependent and interrelated',[41] the Singapore government has staunchly argued that not all human rights are universal nor are the modes of implementation of those human rights that (the Singapore government regards) are: instead, human rights are subject to the historical, political, economic, social and cultural particularities of each State. The 'Singapore School' on human rights was epitomised in the 1993 Bangkok Declaration on Human Rights, in which all Asian governments except those of Japan and the Philippines[42] stated that 'while human rights are universal in nature, they must be considered in the context of a dynamic and evolving process of international norm-setting, bearing in mind the significance of national and regional particularities and various historical, cultural and religious backgrounds'.[43]

In critiquing the Singapore School on human rights, it is important that the school of thought is not dismissed *a priori* simply because it disagrees with the universality of human rights proclaimed in various international human rights treaties and resolutions, particularly as the suppression or denial of many of the human rights to which every human being should normatively be entitled is perpetuated by the very fact that they are not explicitly guaranteed by international human rights treaties, or domestic human rights legislation, that purport to protect human rights.[44] It is essential, thus, to explore the Singapore School on human rights from within.

Singapore, Simon Tay notes, 'has no mythic, pre-colonial civilization on which to base a unique Asian identity'[45] and '[i]f the nation is an imagined community . . . the basis of the Singaporean imagination of nationhood must depend on things other than a deep connection with the territory or the people's ancient and common ancestry.'[46] Tham Seong Chee stresses that '[v]alues shaped merely by existential circumstances or [that] are the emanations of a struggle for survival to be effective in the long term need to be validated and rationalized by recourse to a shared historical–cultural past both real and imagined.'[47] Tham finds that Singapore's survivalist mentality 'entails two interrelated parameters: one the institutionalization of a value-system that maintains national unity and promotes common purpose and the other the institutionalization of a value-system that motivates economic attainment'.[48] Thus, the Singapore government has been determined to construct and inculcate a Singapore 'culture' within the populace. Here, it is useful to take note of Annette Marfording's observation that, contrary to Adamantia Pollis' finding of a distinctive Japanese culture in which democracy and fundamental rights are formally enshrined while asserting or advocating them is socially disfavoured,[49] the Japanese's aversion to rights assertion and advocacy has been the result not of an indigenous culture but of long-standing state indoctrination, through education and institutional barriers, of dogmas adopted from Western countries with the aim of preserving the status quo.[50] Marfording argues that in deconstructing a particular process of enculturation, one must not overlook the role of government policies, not in the autonomous determination of cultural values, but in the imposition of a cultural ideology that is not indigenous to the populace. The Singapore government's pursuit of a cultural ideology and its desire to inculcate that cultural ideology in Singaporeans could not have been made more explicit as Singapore President Wee Kim Wee stated in his parliamentary opening address in January 1989 – which formed the basis of the subsequent 'shared values' consultation and discourse in Singapore – the importance of which warrants detailed quotation:

> Singapore is wide open to external influences. Millions of foreign visitors pass through each year. Books, magazines, tapes, and television programmes pour into Singapore every day. Most are from the developed countries of the West. The overwhelming bulk is in English. Because of universal English education, a new generation of Singaporeans absorbs their contents immediately, without translation or filtering.
>
> This openness has made us a cosmopolitan people, and put us in close touch with new ideas and technologies from abroad. But it has also exposed us to alien lifestyles and values. Under this pressure, in less than a generation, attitudes and outlooks of Singaporeans, especially younger Singaporeans, have shifted. Traditional Asian ideas of morality, duty and society which have sustained and guided us in the past are giving way to a more Westernised, individualistic, and self-centred outlook on life.
>
> Not all foreign ideas and values are harmful. We cannot shut out the outside world, and turn inwards on ourselves. As Singapore develops, we must adapt our customs and traditions to suit new circumstances.
>
> However, the speed and extent of the changes to Singapore society is worrying. We cannot tell what dangers lie ahead, as we rapidly grow more Westernised.
>
> What sort of society will we become in another generation? What sort of people do we want our children to become? Do we really want to abandon our own cultures and national identity? Can we build a nation of Singaporeans, in Southeast Asia, on the basis of values and concepts native to other peoples, living in other environments? How we answer these questions will determine our future.

If we are not to lose our bearings, we should preserve the cultural heritage of each of our communities, and uphold certain common values which capture the essence of being a Singaporean. These core values include placing society above self, upholding the family as the basic building block of society, resolving major issues through consensus instead of contention, and stressing racial and religious tolerance and harmony.

We need to enshrine these fundamental ideas in a National Ideology. Such a formal statement will bond us together as Singaporeans, with our own distinct identity and destiny. We need to inculcate this National Ideology in all Singaporeans, especially the young. We will do so through moral education and by promoting the use of the mother tongue, by strengthening the teaching of values in schools, and through the mass media, especially the newspapers and television.[51]

However, the nature of history is that it cannot be erased or treated as if non-existent or alterable. It is an irreversible fact that Singapore was colonised by the United Kingdom for 140 years and colonial enculturation, epitomised by Singapore's post-colonial retention of Westminster-style parliamentary government and predominant use of English in official communications, has coloured and *is* part and parcel of Singapore culture and, consequently, of any Singaporean national ideology. It is not tenable to argue that Singapore culture consists only of Confucian ethics (whether or not in conjunction with Islamic, Hindu, and Christian beliefs and values), just as contemporary Chinese culture is not solely guided by Confucian, communist, or socialist-market teachings. As will be seen, those who oppose sexual minority rights in Singapore have justified their position through a myriad of arguments based on self-selected and self-interpreted 'Asian values', Confucian ethics, and Western/Christian religious concepts. As Hussin Mutalib observes in relation to the formation of Singapore national identity:

Identity-formation is often fluid and ever-changing, and there is a strong overlap between past historical experiences of a people and their present socio-political circumstances. Different ethno-religious groups in a country may also relate to the state with varying intensities; so too individuals within particular ethnic groups, given their socio-economic status and friendships with out-groups, may exhibit different degrees of attachment to the country from their own ethnic groups.[52]

I have argued elsewhere that opposition to sexual minority rights in Hong Kong has stemmed from such cultural schizophrenia that the Hong Kong government has been unable to put forward a coherent argument as to why sexual minority rights are incompatible with Hong Kong 'culture', as it sought to justify laws against gay men that had been adopted during British colonial times and continues to stonewall sexual minority rights development through recourse to self-selected and self-interpreted 'Asian values', Confucian ethics, and religious (exclusively Christian) concepts.[53] *En passant*, to argue that Christianity, with its presence in all parts of the world, is now a religion transcending all national cultures and is no longer a purely Western religion is a fallacious attempt to disguise the ultimate foundation of the religion in Europe (inclusive of Jerusalem and Constantinople). The argument also discredits the central thesis of the Singapore School that human rights are a concept that emanates from Western countries and, for that reason alone, are essentially inapplicable in Singapore.

Furthermore, as Beng-Huat Chua has pointed out, the Singapore government's endeavours to construct and inculcate a Singapore culture around Confucian ethics have taken place only since the 1980s; until then 'rugged individualism' had been encouraged in Singapore.[54] Indeed, Lee Kuan Yew, then Prime Minister and now Minister Mentor of Singapore, once remarked to an audience in the United States in 1967 that 'I am no more a Chinese than President Kennedy was an Irishman.'[55] Neil Englehart has observed that venues where Confucian traditions could have been fostered, such as traditional Chinese schools, 'were systematically destroyed by the [People's Action Party] in the 1970s, ostensibly because they were hotbeds of communism. This reflected a change in educational policy designed to encourage Chinese Singaporeans to become fluent in English. It was thought at the time that this would help attract international capital to Singapore. This policy also had the convenient effect of removing a set of institutions that might have been used to organize an opposition to the PAP among their core Chinese constituency.'[56] Englehart notes that '[b]y the time the PAP decided to launch the Confucian Ethics campaign in the 1980s, the Chinese schools, which could have promoted a Confucian revival among Chinese Singaporeans, had been eliminated. The government, therefore, was free to construct a Confucian campaign from the ground up.'[57]

The Confucian Ethics campaign was nevertheless unsuccessful. Despite the disproportionate resources allocated to Confucian Ethics *vis-à-vis* the other four religions[58] from which secondary school students could choose for the compulsory Religious Knowledge course,[59] only 17.8% of students enrolled in Confucian Ethics as opposed to 44.4% in Buddhist Studies and 21.4% in Bible Knowledge.[60] It is also telling that the curriculum design for Confucian Ethics was assisted by eight American and Taiwanese scholars on Confucianism[61] because, the Singapore Ministry of Education explained, 'Confucian ethics was a field which we were not familiar with and ... we wanted to insure that the right approach was used to teach the subject.'[62] With the Confucian Ethics campaign receiving little fanfare even among Chinese Singaporeans, the Religious Knowledge programme was abandoned in 1990.[63] Englehart notes that the Confucian Ethics campaign failed because 'minority groups perceived it as an attempt to impose Chinese culture on them, while Chinese Singaporeans themselves resisted. Chinese women in particular saw the campaign as an attempt to subjugate them with an archaic and patriarchal code of conduct, while the English-educated Chinese class whose development the PAP had encouraged in the 1970s noticed the authoritarian political implications of the campaign.'[64]

The government then launched the 'shared values' consultation in 1991 in order to placate the unease of ethnic and religious minority groups. In the *White Paper on Shared Values*, which Benedict Sheehy argues enjoys quasi-constitutional status in Singapore,[65] the government stated that '[a] major difference between Asian and Western values is the balance each strikes between the individual and the community. The difference is not so stark as black and white, but one of degree. On the whole, Asian societies emphasise the interests of the community, while Western societies stress the rights of the individual.'[66] It concluded that five core values should guide Singapore society: 'nation before the community and society above self', 'family as the basic unit of society', 'regard and community support for the individual', 'consensus instead of contention', and 'racial and religious harmony'.[67] While the government expressly stated in the *White Paper* that the five core values were shared by all ethnic and religious groups in Singapore and did not simply revolve around Confucian ethics which 'cannot be so shared',[68] Confucian ethics as selected and interpreted by the government permeated the *White Paper* (while Islamic and Hindu beliefs and values bore scant attention), as the government stated that '[m]any Confucian ideals are relevant to Singapore'[69] and 'the Chinese community can draw upon Confucian concepts which form part of their heritage, to elaborate the abstract Shared Values into concrete examples and vivid stories'.[70] In particular, the government referred to the Confucian principle of governance by honourable men (*junzi*) to whom the people, for the sake of good society, entrust the ultimate decision-making capacity.[71] The government also laid emphasis on the 'sanctity of the family unit',[72] which it found to be universal across cultures[73] and 'the fundamental building block out of which larger social structures can be stably constructed'.[74] Yet, family was defined again only in Confucian terms, however 'modified':[75]

> Traditional Confucian family relationships are strictly hierarchical. Sons owe an absolute duty of filial piety and unquestioning obedience to fathers. Males take precedence over females, brothers over sisters, and the first born over younger sons. But in Singapore, the parent–child relationship is more one of respect rather than absolute subordination. Sons and daughters are increasingly treated equally. The relationship between older and younger siblings is less authoritarian. In all these aspects Singaporean practices must continue, without eroding cohesion and loyalty within the family unit.[76]

The fact that the notion of family in Singapore remains stratified in terms of age and gender and the imposition of the Confucian notion of family upon Singapore's multiracial society are best exemplified by the enactment of the Maintenance of Parents Act in 1995 – which enables any person 'domiciled and resident in Singapore who is of or above 60 years of age and who is unable to maintain himself adequately' to apply to the Tribunal for the Maintenance of Parents so created by the legislation for an order that his children maintain him financially[77] – and by a myriad of family and educational policies that discriminate against women.[78]

It is important to observe that the Confucian notion of family, in conjunction with the Confucian notion of *junzi*, assists in complementing and facilitating authoritarian rule in Singapore, as its central precept, filial piety, provides and constitutes the framework against which authority in all generalities is to be understood and observed, and the Chinese, including Chinese Singaporeans, have always regarded the family as a microscopic state. Thus, when deconstructing Singapore 'culture', the 'shared values' of Singapore, and the Singapore School on human rights, one should take note of Thio's caution thus:

> the danger arises when government-articulated collective interests in the name of culture and community become synonymous with state interests. Society and state become conflated. Where this manoeuvre is accomplished, any criticism of government immediately becomes criticism subversive of the state and, thereby, the community's interests. We must be wary when the government (which controls the apparatus of the artificial entity known as the 'state') purports to speak on behalf of the entire community because, even in formal democracies, the interests of minority groups or other sectors of a heterogeneous society may not be perfectly represented in legislative bodies.[79]

As Pollis has argued generally, '[b]y controlling the state structures, and often ignoring the gap between themselves and those over whom they rule, the elites set national goals while simultaneously claiming to represent their societies' cultural values.'[80] While Thio agrees with Pollis that 'the crucial question'[81] is 'whether modern states adhere to the values that they claim inhere in their cultures, or whether the modern state, with its capacity to repress, exploits the language of cultural relativism to justify and rationalize its own repressive actions in the government elites' drive to consolidate or to hold on to political power',[82] there are at least three equally, if not more, fundamental questions that ought to be explored: Does adherence to one's proclaimed values *ipso facto* justify repressive actions by the state? Are adherence to one's proclaimed values and state repression mutually exclusive? *Should*, and if so *why* should, the state at all adhere to its proclaimed values?

This paper will now deconstruct the relevant laws affecting persons belonging to sexual minorities in Singapore with a view to discerning whether the proclaimed values of Singapore in relation to homosexuality and sexual minority rights development are indeed Singaporean values and, if they are, whether and why they should or should not be adhered to. In the process of exploration, it must be borne in mind that no matter one's position on sexual minority rights in Singapore, in order for his or her position to be valid, one must not simply dismiss *a priori* and must understand and critically assess the alleged incompatibility between sexual minority rights and Singapore culture. For the same reason, one must also explore and explain whether and how sexual minority rights may in fact and in law be developed under the Singapore Constitution as Singaporean rights and a Singaporean value.

Deconstructing laws affecting persons belonging to sexual minorities in Singapore

Clare Hemmings has observed that '[f]or national spokesmen for a range of African and Asian nation-states, among others, homosexuality is ... framed as a betrayal in two ways: as a failure of appropriate gendered and sexual citizenship, and as a marker of Western influence. By suturing nation to heterosexuality through positing "gayness ... as a polluting foreign influence", state representatives can deny any history of same-sex practice in the national context at stake, and dismiss global sexual rights movements as straightforwardly imperialistic.'[83] As one of the foremost Confucian filial obligations is to continue the ancestral (male) line, the inability of a person to procreate with another person who is of the same sex, together with the purported exclusivity of biological naturalness in penile–vaginal intercourse,[84] renders the homosexual, as it is generally portrayed, to be thus a role that only a 'specialized, despised, and punished'[85] soul would be willing to assume. Amid depictions of homosexuality as a Western-oriented 'choice',[86] historical evidence that homosexuality permeated imperial China[87] is either entirely ignored or, on the rare occasions that it is acknowledged, simply dismissed as 'wild'.[88] However, the fact remains that the criminalisation of consensual male/male sexual activity in Singapore was implanted as part of British colonial rule and is not indigenous to Singapore society. As Kenneth Paul Tan has observed:

> In colonial Bugis Street, the ah qua[89] was sexually exploited as an object of the illicit desires of tourists and foreign (mostly Caucasian) troops in Singapore. This sexually deviant subject – consumed for pleasure, then 'ridiculed, condemned, and made a spectacle of' – was the grotesque embodiment of the languor and effeminacy associated with the colonized Asian native. As an expression of the complexities of colonial power, the ah qua was more than just the exaggerated eroticized subject of colonial desire. Under British colonial administration, homosexuality was (and today continues to be) against the law. The ah qua, a highly visible and sexualized Asian native, represented the anarchic and destructive tendencies of erotic energies that civilization – in the historic form of colonial domination – needed ... to repress in the name of progress. Laws against the ah qua were laws against (the seductiveness of) moral degeneracy and the ruination of civilization, and therefore served as a broader justification for colonial practices.[90]

Corresponding to section 61 of the Offences Against the Person Act 1861 in the United Kingdom,[91] section 377 of the Penal Code of Singapore stated that '[w]hoever voluntarily has carnal intercourse against the order of nature with any man, woman or animals, shall be punished with imprisonment for life, or with imprisonment for a term which may extend to 10 years, and shall also be liable to fine.'[92] While section 377 has since been repealed and replaced, section 377A of the Penal Code of Singapore, corresponding to section 11 of the Criminal Law Amendment Act 1885 in the United Kingdom[93] (since repealed),[94] continues to prescribe that '[a]ny male person who, in public or private, commits, or abets the commission of, or procures or attempts to procure the commission by any male person of, any act of gross indecency with another male person, shall be punished with imprisonment for a term which may extend to 2 years.'[95] Consent is immaterial to a section 377A prosecution.[96] In his Singapore High Court decision in *Ng Huat* v. *Public Prosecutor,*[97] an appeal against conviction and sentence arising from a prosecution for gross indecency under section 377A – which I argue should have been initiated for assault outraging the modesty of the person under section 354 of the Penal Code as the male victim had not provided informed consent to and had at least once explicitly refused the examination by the appellate radiographer, who was married with two children,[98] of his penis and buttocks for his wrist injury[99] – Chief Justice Yong Pung How stated that '[w]hat amounts to a grossly indecent act must depend on whether in the circumstances, and the customs and morals of our times, it would be considered grossly indecent by any right-thinking member of the public.'[100] The Chief Justice acknowledged *per curiam* that prosecution could be laid under section 377A against a person who had been a victim of male/male sexual assault, but nevertheless did 'not see any real cause for concern':[101]

> My sympathies lie with those perfectly respectable gentlemen who may well be innocent 'victims' of a grossly indecent act. It is true that they may find themselves named within the charge as persons 'with' whom the offence of gross indecency has been committed. Nevertheless, I do not see any real cause for concern. If they did have any homosexual tendencies, they would almost invariably have been charged with the offence as well. The very fact that they are not similarly charged can only attest to their innocence of the act. No aspersions are being cast on their sexual proclivities. Technically, of course, as consent is not an element of the s 377A offence, they could also be charged with the offence, but I am confident that the judicious exercise of prosecutorial discretion will prevail to ensure that such travesties of justice do not occur. There will be no distress or embarrassment, much less any injustice, as long as the law is understood and enforced on a clear and unambiguous basis.[102]

The possibility that a person with or without any homosexual tendencies may have been placed under duress or simply forced into committing gross indecency was not explored.[103] Thus, from *Ng Huat*, if the Chief Justice's reasoning is to be understood literally, it would appear that any person with any homosexual tendencies would be denied the attribute of innocence and ascribed the attribute of guilt in a transaction of gross indecency under section 377A. The circumstances in *Ng Huat* were particularly telling: if the victim had had *or had been suspected of having* any homosexual tendencies (information on which was not provided in the case report), he might well have found himself prosecuted for gross indecency. As Philip Rumney and Oliver Phillips demonstrate, such attributes of guilt and innocence have serious repercussions for all male victims, including gay male victims, of sexual assault[104] and for human agency and rights development generally.[105]

While the sexual minority rights debate in Singapore now largely focuses on section 377A, the Singapore government should also consider amending section 354, which prohibits 'assault or use of criminal force to a person with intent to outrage modesty'[106] and which Meredith Weiss finds to have been commonly used in cases of police entrapment of gay men,[107] insofar as it penalises consensual male/male sexual activity as assault.[108] Lastly, note should be taken of section 19 of the Miscellaneous Offences (Public Order and Nuisance) Act, which prohibits solicitation in a public place whether with or without physical contact.[109] Not unlike in the United Kingdom, consensual female/female sexual activity has never been explicitly criminalised in Singapore.[110]

Those who oppose sexual minority rights in Singapore do not regard it inherently contradictory to premise their arguments on laws implanted by the United Kingdom during colonial times, self-selected and self-interpreted 'Asian values', Confucian ethics, and religious, particularly Christian, concepts simultaneously. Indeed, Weiss has argued that 'Singapore's homophobic opposition is now (somewhat perversely) global rather than local: the shrillest condemnation has been not from, for example, Confucian scholars, but from evangelical Christians – and evangelical Christianity is a relatively recent and marginal Western import.'[111] In response to then Prime Minister and now Senior Minister Goh Chok Tong's interview in June 2003 with the *Time* magazine in which he stated that the Singapore civil service had adopted a policy of employing gay men and lesbians so long as they disclosed their sexual orientation,[112] the National Council of Churches of Singapore, which represents about 150 Anglican, Methodist, and Presbyterian churches in Singapore,[113] issued a statement urging the government 'to maintain: (a) current legislation concerning homosexuality [which at the time included section 377 of the Penal Code]; (b) its policy of not permitting the registration of homosexual societies or clubs; (c) its policy of not allowing the promotion of homosexual lifestyle and activities',[114] Subsequently, in his National Day Rally speech in August 2003, Prime Minister Goh, as he then was, clarified his position thus:

> As for my comments on gays, they do not signal any change in policy that would erode the moral standards of Singapore, or our family values. In every society, there are gay people. We should accept those in our midst as fellow human beings, and as fellow Singaporeans. If the public sector refuses to employ gays, the private sector might also refuse. But gays too, need to make a living.
>
> That said, let me stress that I do not encourage or endorse a gay lifestyle. Singapore is still a traditional and conservative Asian society. Gays must know that the more they lobby for public space, the bigger the backlash they will provoke from the conservative mainstream. Their public space may then be reduced.
>
> I am glad that conservative Singaporeans and religious leaders have made known their views on the matter, clearly but responsibly. I hope we will now move on and focus on more urgent challenges.[115]

Again, one ought to ask, if Singapore is essentially a Confucian polity, why should the National Council of Churches of Singapore that represents Anglican, Methodist, and Presbyterian churches have such influence on governance in Singapore as was apparently reflected in Prime Minister Goh's speech? Also, must a Singaporean be conservative in order to have his or her view heard and taken note of? What attributes must a Singaporean have in order to be considered conservative? Are the views of a conservative Singaporean always correct?

This conjunction, or rather confusion, among 'Asian values', Confucian ethics, and religious/Christian concepts was best epitomised by a parliamentary speech Professor Thio delivered as a Nominated Member of Parliament in October 2007, in which she staunchly opposed decriminalising consensual male/male sexual activity in Singapore. Thio, a leading constitutional law and human rights scholar at the National University of Singapore who was educated at Oxford, Harvard, and Cambridge, and a devout Christian,[116] made a plethora of arguments against decriminalisation in Singapore which can largely be found in similar debates in other jurisdictions.[117] While she was adamant that Singapore was a conservative and communitarian polity with its unique Asian family values and that Singaporeans should debate the issues without foreign or neo-colonial interference or dogmas, she referred to numerous Western religious and philosophical assertions in her denunciation of homosexuality and her rejection of the notion that 'sexual minorities', a term that she found to be devoid of legal meaning, have rights for who they are and what they do in their sexual relations with other persons of the same sex.[118] As Emma Henderson discerns, '[p]arliamentary debates are an important and effective form of social "education" – an arena in which complicated power relations between social groups lead to explicit declarations of competing and often contradictory "truth claims" or "ideologies".'[119] This is particularly the case with Thio's parliamentary speech, given her capacity as a leading legal and human rights scholar and as an independent Nominated Member of Parliament to lay claims to truth and objectivity.[120]

Sexual minority rights as Singaporean value: the role of constitutional comparativism

As discussed above, the core argument of the Singapore School on human rights and the Singapore government's opposition to sexual minority rights lies in the alleged communitarianism/individualism divide in the modes of governance largely inferred from Singapore and Western countries. Judicial and legislative decisions that have been reached in Western countries in support of sexual minority rights, the argument goes, are thus of little value to Singapore jurisprudentially or normatively.

Not surprisingly, foreign judicial decisions have found lukewarm reception in Singapore, whose constitutional jurisprudence has prescribed that Singapore courts should look within the 'four walls' of the Singapore Constitution and resulting Singapore case law when interpreting the Singapore Constitution and statutes and developing Singapore common law. For example, in *Chan Hiang Leng Colin and Others* v. *Public Prosecutor*,[121] the Singapore High Court dismissed the relevance of United States jurisprudence on freedom of religion for the sole reason that United States jurisprudence did not touch upon the local conditions of Singapore: Chief Justice Yong Pung How stated that '[t]he social conditions in Singapore are, of course, markedly different from those in the United States. On this basis alone, I am not influenced by the various views as enunciated in the American cases cited to me but instead must restrict my analysis of the issues here with reference to the local context.'[122] Interestingly, however, the four walls doctrine in Singapore constitutional jurisprudence in fact emanated from the Malayan decision in *Government of the State of Kelantan* v. *Government of the Federation of Malaya and Tunku Abdul Rahman Putra Al-Haj*,[123] where Chief Justice Thomson of the Federation of Malaya stated that the Malayan Federal Constitution 'is primarily to be interpreted within its own four walls and not in the light of analogies drawn from other countries such as Great Britain, the United States of America or Australia'.[124] In turn, the Malayan decision followed[125] the judgment of the Judicial Committee of the Privy Council in *Adegbenro* v. *Akintola*[126] on appeal from the Federal Supreme Court of Nigeria, where Viscount Radcliffe, delivering the judgment of the Judicial Committee, maintained:

> it must be remembered that ... the British Constitution 'works by a body of understandings which no writer can formulate'; whereas the Constitution of Western Nigeria is now contained in a written instrument in which it has been sought to formulate with precision the powers and duties of the various agencies that it holds in balance. That instrument now stands in its own right; and, while it may well be useful on occasions to draw on British practice or doctrine in interpreting a doubtful phrase whose origin can be traced or to study decisions on the Constitutions of Australia or the United States where federal issues are involved, it is in the end ... the wording of the Constitution itself that is to be interpreted and applied, and this wording can never be overridden by the extraneous principles of other Constitutions which are not explicitly incorporated in the formulae that have been chosen as the frame of this Constitution.[127]

When the Judicial Committee was still the court of last resort for Singapore[128] and Hong Kong[129] (among other jurisdictions), it strongly objected to Singapore and Hong Kong courts resorting to foreign and international legal materials (save, of course, English legal materials) in the interpretation of the various individual rights provisions in the Singapore Constitution and the Hong Kong Bill of Rights Ordinance, respectively. In the Singapore case of *Ong Ah Chuan* v. *Public Prosecutor*,[130] Lord Diplock stated:

> their Lordships are of opinion that decisions of Indian Courts on Part III of the Indian Consti-
> tution should be approached with caution as guides to the interpretation of individual articles in
> Part IV of the Singapore Constitution; and that decisions of the Supreme Court of the United
> States on that country's Bill of Rights, whose phraseology is now nearly two hundred years old,
> are of little help in construing provisions of the Constitution of Singapore or other modern
> Commonwealth constitutions which follow broadly the Westminster model.[131]

Caution, however, does not equal outright dismissal. Constitutional comparativism, provided that it is consistent and principled, has intrinsic values and advantages as a juridical enterprise and engine for thoughtful judicial, and even legislative, decisions with carefully discerned insights and experiences from other jurisdictions. By exploring the constitutional, legal and social developments in other jurisdictions, Singapore courts as well as Parliament of Singapore may be better informed and better positioned to discern for Singapore society whether and how an individual right, such as sexual orien-tation equality, may be developed in Singapore under the Singapore Constitution as a Singaporean right and a Singaporean value. As Thio argues on the basis of the Federal Court of Malaysia decision in *Loh Kooi Choon* v. *Government of Malaysia*,[132] which like *Government of the State of Kelantan* followed the Judicial Committee of the Privy Council decision in *Adegbenro* v. *Akintola*, 'it is permissible "to look at other Constitutions to learn from their experiences, and from a desire to see how their progress and well-being is ensured by their fundamental law", while bearing in mind that "[e]ach country frames its constitution according to its genius and for the good of its own society".'[133] A flexible approach supported by coherent reasoning should be adopted such that Singapore courts, as well as Parliament of Singapore, may make use of juridical insights and experiences from beyond Singapore's boundaries. As Lord Diplock in *Ong Ah Chuan* explained:

> In a constitution founded on the Westminster model and particularly in that part of it that
> purports to assure to all individual citizens the continued enjoyment of fundamental liberties
> or rights, references to 'law' in such contexts as 'in accordance with law', 'equality before
> the law', 'protection of the law' and the like, in their Lordships' view, refer to a system of
> law which incorporates those fundamental rules of natural justice that had formed part and
> parcel of the common law of England that was in operation in Singapore at the commencement
> of the Constitution. It would have been taken for granted by the makers of the Constitution that
> the 'law' to which citizens could have recourse for the protection of fundamental liberties
> assured to them by the Constitution would be a system of law that did not flout those funda-
> mental rules. If it were otherwise it would be misuse of language to speak of law as something
> which affords 'protection' for the individual in the enjoyment of his fundamental liberties, and
> the purported entrenchment (by Article 5) of Articles 9(1) and 12(1) would be little better than a
> mockery.[134]

Conversely, outright dismissal of foreign judicial decisions and juridical discourses does not at all benefit Singapore's development of its own jurisprudence and juridical discourse, which, akin to and as part of Singapore culture, is not static in time or in form. As Thio has noted, '[c]ulture is used "negatively" to repel foreign influences by characterising them as alien or inappropriate. It is used "positively" as a major lens through which the process of constitutional adjudication should take place.'[135] Thio argues that Singapore courts ought to explore the differences between the circumstances of a Singapore case and a foreign judicial decision that may possibly be relevant, its reasoning and its underlying context and circumstances, and that 'perfunctory waiving away of foreign cases on the basis of "we're different" is undesirable. A focused elaboration of the different social conditions of these countries would aid in assessing their relevance to the matter at hand.'[136] By participating in 'transnational judicial conversations',[137] Singapore courts, I argue, will benefit greatly the development of Singapore's own jurisprudence and juridical discourse, and may well influence foreign courts and their nations to follow suit. As Sujit Choudhry maintains:

> In cases of constitutional difference, if the court rejects foreign assumptions and affirms its own, the value of this exercise has been to heighten its awareness and understanding of constitutional difference, which in turn will shape and guide constitutional interpretation. Conversely, in cases of constitutional similarity, if similarity once identified is embraced, dialogical interpretation grounds the legitimacy of importing comparative jurisprudence and applying it as law . . . . in cases of constitutional similarity a court may reject shared assumptions and stake out a new interpretive approach proceeding from radically different premises.[138]
> . . .
> Dialogical interpretation probably wins on the dimension of legitimacy, because it makes no normative claims regarding comparative jurisprudence. It uses comparative case law instrumentally, as a means to stimulate constitutional self-reflection. Thus understood, dialogical interpretation is more a legal technique than a theory of constitutional interpretation. Comparative materials are not asserted to be true or right; rather they reflect a particular way of articulating underlying values and assumptions.[139]

The quintessence of colonialism and neo-colonialism is where transnational conversations, within and without courts, are wanting, where values and assumptions are imposed – or self-imposed – upon a polity. It is not neo-colonialism for an independent country to consider, for itself and its own good, the merits and demerits of insights and experiences from other countries, and, as Alison Dundes Renteln has pointed out, 'relativism in no way precludes the possibility of cross-cultural universals discovered through empirical research'.[140] Conversely, by deliberately preventing itself from fulfilling its potential as a valid and equal participant in transnational conversations, Singapore, in the words of Edward Saïd, 'participates in its own Orientalizing'.[141]

Lastly, one must not forget that our world consists of more than Singapore, Asian countries, and Western countries, and that, notwithstanding the convenience of 'Asian values' arguments, Asian countries share much more dissimilarity than similarity *inter se* – religiously, politically, economically, socially, culturally, and jurisprudentially.[142] Singaporeans need look no further than to their Malay neighbours (both in Malaysia and in Singapore) to find that they may share more similarity with many citizens of Western countries.[143] As Amélie Oksenberg Rorty discerns:

> Sometimes there is unexpectedly subtle and refined communication across radically different cultures . . . . sometimes there is insurmountable bafflement and systematic misunderstanding between relatively close cultures. For the most part, however, we live in the interesting intermediate grey area of partial success and partial failure of interpretation and communication. The grey area is to be found at home among neighbors as well as abroad among strangers.[144]

Thus, mindful of the Singapore School on human rights, I suggest that, in relation to sexual minority rights, Singapore may consider taking note of the legal developments in two non-Western jurisdictions – Hong Kong[145] and South Africa[146] – where sexual orientation equality has achieved constitutional and judicial recognition and protection.

The Singapore Constitution states unequivocally that '[a]ll persons are equal before the law and entitled to the equal protection of the law.'[147] Through the Singapore Constitution as an 'enabling tool',[148] Singapore courts, Thio has observed, have agreed that 'rights should be construed in a purposive, generous manner to avoid what Lord Wilberforce termed "the austerity of tabulated legalism" and so as to ensure that individuals receive the "full measure" of fundamental liberties',[149] and it ought to be borne in mind, as Justice Karthigesu in his Singapore High Court decision in *Taw Cheng Kong* v. *Public Prosecutor*[150] stated, that '[c]onstitutional rights are enjoyed because they are constitutional in nature. They are enjoyed as fundamental liberties – not stick and carrot privileges. To the extent that the constitution is supreme, those rights are inalienable.'[151] As Seth Kreimer argues, 'the most constructive use of comparative constitutional law is not as an alternative store of constitutional software, but a challenge to us to reexamine the resources in our own system'.[152] It is to be remembered that the four walls doctrine 'does not require an exclusive reliance on domestic legal sources',[153] and the four walls of Singapore constitutional jurisprudence are expandable and renovatable so that individuals within them may have more room for better and more fulfilling lives. Equally, communitarianism does not at all mean that all voices outside the community's boundaries must be dismissed *a priori*; otherwise, the community is not a community of morality, but a perpetual prison of one's soul.

Conclusion

At the heart of the 'shared values' discourse within Singapore and the 'Asian values' debate transnationally, the fundamental question Singaporeans ought to ask is what kind of society they want their country to be, in relation not just to sexual minority rights, but to all aspects of governance. In this self-exploration, foreigners, be they foreign academics, foreign courts, foreign governments, or international human rights bodies (with the need for state ratification of particular human rights treaties and continuing state co-operation, and these bodies' general lack of enforcement powers), have a very limited role other than to offer insights and experiences that they have themselves discerned and endured. It is of course true that every country is different and that those countries whose legislatures and/or judiciaries have reached decisions in support of sexual minority rights have their own continual dilemmas regarding the oppression and protection of sexual minorities, and it would be presumptuous and silly for anyone to think that they are utopias for sexual minorities. The meaning of deciding one's own destiny perforce embodies one's decision to follow a particular, or to refuse to follow anyone else's, path, be it good or bad, but to dismiss insights and experiences garnered in other countries in the course of their own struggles merely because those insights and experiences were assembled by foreigners about their own foreign countries deprives oneself of valuable opportunities to engage with other life perspectives, however disagreeable, such that one's own life perspectives may be better understood and enhanced. As Thio maintains, in the interpretation of the Singapore Constitution and statutes and the development of individual rights in Singapore, 'the mere citing of "local conditions" as a basis for rejecting foreign jurisdiction cases is not enough – these local conditions must be articulated and elaborated upon so that their "localness" or applicability or cogency may be open for assessment'.[154] Indeed, Victor Ramraj argues that the spirit of transnational conversations inhered in the *White Paper on Shared Values*, 'the stated aim of which is "to evolve and anchor a Singaporean identity", to the extent that it seeks to find common values in varied cultural traditions – a project which ostensibly has identified a considerable intersection of values.'[155]

To live a life the modes and meanings of which are dictated by someone else, however convenient or affluent such a life, is to forgo a true and meaningful life in which one's own thoughts and actions have autonomous meanings. Nor is such a model of governance wise, as it deprives the country of true and meaningful participation and input by its citizenry – the underlying purpose of education rooted in both Confucianism and the Western Enlightenment. It therefore falls upon Singaporeans, and Singaporeans alone, to decide whether and how they should uphold the Confucian ideal to advise the government, gently but dutifully, by meaningfully asking themselves, and their government, what path, or paths, they wish for their country and their society, and it neither is selfish nor undermines the 'shared values' of Singapore for Singaporeans to meaningfully ask themselves, and their government, what path, or paths, they wish for themselves and their future generations.[156] This paper, thus, cannot be better concluded than by adopting Thio's words of wisdom in full:

> I speak, at the risk of being burned at the stake by militant activists. But if we don't stand for something, we will fall for anything. I was raised to believe in speaking out for what is right, good and true, no matter the cost. It is important in life not only to have a Brain, but a Spine.
> One of my favourite speeches by PM Lee [Hsien Loong], which I force my students to read, is his Harvard Club speech 2 years ago where he urged citizens not to be 'passive bystanders' in their own fate but to debate issues with reason and conviction. I took this to heart. To forge good policy, we need to do our homework and engage in honest debate on the issues. Let us also speak with civility, which cannot be legislated, but draws deep from our character and upbringing. Before government can govern man, man must be able to govern himself.
> Sir, let speaking in the public square with reason, passion, honesty, civility, even grace, be the mark of a Citizen of Singapore.[157]

Acknowledgements

I wish to thank Andrew Harding for his support throughout the course of research and writing of this paper and him as well as Simon Chesterman, Paul Serfaty, and Andrew Simester for their valuable observations on earlier versions. All views expressed and any errors or omissions in this paper are mine alone.

Notes

1. World Bank, World Development Indicators database, revised 10 September 2008, http://sitere sources.worldbank.org/DATASTATISTICS/Resources/GNIPC.pdf (accessed 5 October 2008).
2. Singapore Department of Statistics, *Monthly Digest of Statistics Singapore*, September 2008, http://www.singstat.gov.sg/pubn/reference/mdssep08.pdf (accessed 5 October 2008), 3–4.
3. Constitution of the Republic of Singapore, 1999 Rev. Edn, Art. 153A(2). Article 153A(1), ibid., stipulates Malay, Mandarin, Tamil, and English as official languages in Singapore.
4. For a discussion of the politics of English in Singapore, see Chua Beng Huat, 'Multiculturalism in Singapore: An Instrument of Social Control', *Race & Class* 44, no. 3 (2003): 58, 71–3.
5. Constitution of the Republic of Singapore, 1999 Rev. Edn, Art. 155(2).
6. Ibid., Art. 153.
7. For discussions of the purposes and effects of multiracial policies in Singapore, see, e.g., Chua, 'Multiculturalism in Singapore'; Giok Ling Ooi, 'The Role of the Developmental State and Interethnic Relations in Singapore', *Asian Ethnicity* 6, no. 2 (2005): 109; Brenda S.A. Yeoh, 'Cosmopolitanism and its Exclusions in Singapore', *Urban Studies* 41, no. 12 (2004): 2431.
8. See Misuse of Drugs Act 1973 (Cap. 185), 2008 Rev. Edn.
9. See Armed Offences Act 1973 (Cap. 14), 2008 Rev. Edn; Corrosive and Explosive Substances and Offensive Weapons Act (Cap. 65), 1985 Rev. Edn.
10. Penal Code 1871 (Cap. 224), 2008 Rev. Edn, ss. 391 and 395.
11. Vandalism Act 1966 (Cap. 341), 1985 Rev. Edn, ss. 2(a)(ii) and 3.

12.   See, e.g., Human Rights Watch, 'Singapore: End Efforts to Silence Opposition: Defamation
      Suits Put Party at Risk of Bankruptcy', 22 October 2008, http://www.hrw.org/en/news/
      2008/10/22/singapore-end-efforts-silence-opposition (accessed 15 December 2008);
      Singapore Democratic Party, 'Singapore: SDP Writes to International Bar Association about
      its Conference in Singapore', 15 February 2007, http://www.ahrchk.net/statements/mainfi-
      le.php/2007statements/930/ (accessed 15 December 2008); United Nations Committee on
      the Elimination of Discrimination against Women, *Concluding Comments of the Committee
      on the Elimination of Discrimination against Women: Singapore*, CEDAW/C/SGP/CO/3, 10
      August 2007, esp. paras 11–37; United Nations Committee on the Rights of the Child, *Con-
      cluding Observations: Singapore*, CRC/C/15/Add.220, 27 October 2003, esp. paras 23–9,
      32–5, 44–5; United Nations Office at Geneva, 'UN Rights Expert Calls on Singapore Not
      to Carry out Execution', 25 January 2007, http://www.unog.ch/80256EDD006B9C2E/
      (httpNewsByYear_en)/E7E258697043C2C6C125726E003A3E23?OpenDocument (accessed
      15 December 2008); United States Department of State, *Country Reports on Human Rights
      Practices 2007: Singapore* (Washington, DC: United States Department of State, 2008),
      http://www.state.gov/g/drl/rls/hrrpt/2007/100537.htm (accessed 15 December 2008).
13.   Penal Code 1871 (Cap. 224), 2008 Rev. Edn, s. 377A.
14.   Baden Offord, 'The Burden of (Homo)Sexual Identity in Singapore', *Social Semiotics* 9, no. 3
      (1999): 309, 313.
15.   Abdullahi Ahmed An-Na`im, 'Introduction', in *Human Rights in Cross-Cultural Perspectives:
      A Quest for Consensus*, ed. Abdullahi Ahmed An-Na`im (Philadelphia: University of
      Pennsylvania Press, 1992), 1, 3.
16.   For a discussion of the similarity and dissimilarity between the Singapore and Hong Kong
      legal systems, see Andrew B.L. Phang, 'Convergence and Divergence – A Preliminary
      Comparative Analysis of the Singapore and Hong Kong Legal Systems', *Hong Kong Law
      Journal* 23, no. 1 (1993): 1.
17.   Crimes (Amendment) Ordinance 1991. For a discussion of the debates on decriminalisation of
      consensual male/male sexual activity in Hong Kong, see Phil C.W. Chan, 'The Gay Age of
      Consent in Hong Kong', *Criminal Law Forum* 15, no. 3 (2004): 273.
18.   *Leung T.C. William Roy* v. *Secretary for Justice* [2005] 3 HKLRD 657 (Hong Kong Court of
      First Instance), unanimously upheld by the Hong Kong Court of Appeal in *Secretary for
      Justice* v. *Leung T.C. William Roy* [2006] 4 HKLRD 211. The government did not lodge a
      further appeal to the Hong Kong Court of Final Appeal within the prescribed time limit.
      However, although invalidated by the courts, the four relevant provisions of the Crimes
      Ordinance have not yet been repealed by legislature and continue to remain on the statute
      book. For a discussion of the age of consent litigation in Hong Kong, see Phil C.W. Chan,
      'Male/Male Sex in Hong Kong: Privacy, Please?', *Sexuality & Culture* 12, no. 2 (2008): 88.
19.   For discussions of arguments raised in sexual minority rights debates in Hong Kong, see Phil
      C.W. Chan, 'The Lack of Sexual Orientation Anti-Discrimination Legislation in Hong Kong:
      Breach of International and Domestic Legal Obligations', *International Journal of Human
      Rights* 9, no. 1 (2005): 69; Phil C.W. Chan, 'Same-Sex Marriage/Constitutionalism and
      their Centrality to Equality Rights in Hong Kong: A Comparative–Socio-Legal Appraisal',
      International Journal of Human Rights 11, nos 1–2 (2007): 33; Phil C.W. Chan, 'Stonewal-
      ling through Schizophrenia: An Anti-Gay Rights Culture in Hong Kong?', *Sexuality & Culture*
      12, no. 2 (2008): 71.
20.   As noted by Kenneth Paul Tan, 'Sexing up Singapore', *International Journal of Cultural
      Studies* 6, no. 4 (2003): 403, 410; Kenneth Paul Tan with Gary Lee Jack Jin, 'Imagining
      the Gay Community in Singapore', *Critical Asian Studies* 39, no. 2 (2007): 179, 180; and
      Meredith Weiss, 'Who Sets Social Policy in Metropolis? Economic Positioning and Social
      Reform in Singapore', *New Political Science* 27, no. 3 (2005): 267, 281, the Singapore
      government has continued to refuse applications for permission to hold public forum discus-
      sions on homosexuality and sexual minority rights or for registration of People Like Us, the
      main local sexual minority rights lobby group in Singapore, under the Societies Act 1966
      (Cap. 311), 1985 Rev. Edn. For discussions of what it means to be a person belonging to a
      sexual minority in Singapore, see Joseph Lo and Huang Guoqin, eds, *People Like Us:
      Sexual Minorities in Singapore* (Singapore: Select Publishing, 2003).
21.   Under Articles 39(1)(c) and 44(1) of the Constitution of the Republic of Singapore, 1999 Rev.
      Edn, in conjunction with the Fourth Schedule to the Constitution, up to nine persons may be

appointed by the President of Singapore on a two-and-a-half-year term as Nominated Members of Parliament. Article 3(2) of the Fourth Schedule to the Constitution stipulates that '[t]he persons to be nominated shall be persons who have rendered distinguished public service, or who have brought honour to the Republic, or who have distinguished themselves in the field of arts and letters, culture, the sciences, business, industry, the professions, social or community service or the labour movement; and in making any nomination, the Special Select Committee shall have regard to the need for nominated Members to reflect as wide a range of independent and non-partisan views as possible.' For a discussion of the evolution and structure of Singapore's parliamentary system, see Thio Li-ann, 'The Post-Colonial Constitutional Evolution of the Singapore Legislature: A Case Study', *Singapore Journal of Legal Studies* (1993): 80.

22. See full transcript of Thio Li-ann's speech to Parliament of Singapore as a Nominated Member of Parliament during Singapore's Parliamentary Debates on Penal Code Revisions, 22–3 October 2007, http://www.straitstimes.com/STI/STIMEDIA/pdf/20071023/ThioLeeAnn.pdf (accessed 21 October 2008).

23. Sally Engle Merry, 'Human Rights Law and the Demonization of Culture (and Anthropology along the Way)', *Political and Legal Anthropology Review* 26, no. 1 (2003): 55, 67. See also Neil A. Englehart, 'Rights and Culture in the Asian Values Argument: The Rise and Fall of Confucian Ethics in Singapore', *Human Rights Quarterly* 22, no. 2 (2000): 548; Ann-Belinda S. Preis, 'Human Rights as Cultural Practice: An Anthropological Critique', *Human Rights Quarterly* 18, no. 2 (1996): 286.

24. Abdullahi Ahmed An-Na`im, 'Toward a Cross-Cultural Approach to Defining International Standards of Human Rights', in *Human Rights in Cross-Cultural Perspectives: A Quest for Consensus*, ed. Abdullahi Ahmed An-Na`im (Philadelphia: University of Pennsylvania Press, 1992), 19, 27–8.

25. For a history of Malaysia and Singapore, see N.J. Ryan, *A History of Malaysia and Singapore*, 5th edn (Kuala Lumpur and London: Oxford University Press, 1976).

26. See, e.g., Thio, 'Post-Colonial Constitutional Evolution'; Thio Li-ann, 'The Right to Political Participation in Singapore: Tailor-Making a Westminster-Modelled Constitution to Fit the Imperatives of "Asian" Democracy', *Singapore Journal of International and Comparative Law* 6 (2002): 181; Thio Li-ann, '"Pragmatism and Realism Do Not Mean Abdication": A Critical and Empirical Inquiry into Singapore's Engagement with International Human Rights Law', *Singapore Year Book of International Law* 8 (2004): 41; Thio Li-ann, 'Taking Rights Seriously? Human Rights Law in Singapore', in *Human Rights in Asia: A Comparative Legal Study of Twelve Asian Jurisdictions, France and the USA*, ed. Randall Peerenboom, Carole J. Petersen, and Albert H.Y. Chen (London: Routledge, 2006), 158.

27. See Tham Seong Chee, 'Values and National Development in Singapore', *Asian Journal of Political Science* 3, no. 2 (1995): 1.

28. Adopted and opened for signature, ratification and accession by UN GA Res. 2200A(XXI) of 16 December 1966 and entered into force on 23 March 1976.

29. Adopted and opened for signature, ratification and accession by UN GA Res. 2200A(XXI) of 16 December 1966 and entered into force on 3 January 1976.

30. Singapore in 1995 did accede to the Convention for the Elimination of All Forms of Discrimination against Women, adopted and opened for signature, ratification and accession by UN GA Res. 34/180 of 18 December 1979 and entered into force on 3 September 1981. For a discussion of the potential impact of the Convention on governance in Singapore, see Thio Li-ann, 'The Impact of Internationalisation on Domestic Governance: Gender Egalitarianism & the Transformative Potential of CEDAW', *Singapore Journal of International and Comparative Law* 1 (1997): 278.

31. Constitution of the Republic of Singapore, 1999 Rev. Edn, Art. 9.

32. Ibid., Art. 10.

33. Ibid., Art. 11.

34. Ibid., Art. 13.

35. Ibid., Art. 14.

36. Ibid., Art. 15.

37. Ibid., Art. 16.

38. Ibid., Art. 12(1).

39. Ibid., Art. 12(2).

40. Adopted and proclaimed by UN GA Res. 217A(III) of 10 December 1948. For discussions of the legal status and ethical significance of the Universal Declaration of Human Rights, see, e.g., Chris Brown, 'Universal Human Rights: A Critique', *International Journal of Human Rights* 1, no. 2 (1997): 41; Thomas Pogge, 'The International Significance of Human Rights', *Journal of Ethics* 4, nos 1–2 (2000): 45; Bruno Simma and Philip Alston, 'The Sources of Human Rights Law: Custom, Jus Cogens, and General Principles', *Australian Year Book of International Law* 12 (1992): 82; Louis B. Sohn, 'The New International Law: Protection of the Rights of Individuals rather than States', *American University Law Review* 32, no. 1 (1982): 1.

41. Vienna Declaration and Programme of Action, adopted by acclamation at the United Nations World Conference on Human Rights on 25 June 1993, UN Doc. A/CONF.157/24 (Part I), 32 ILM 1661 (1993), para. 5. For discussions of the Vienna Declaration and Programme of Action, see, e.g., Philip Alston, 'The UN's Human Rights Record: From San Francisco to Vienna and Beyond', *Human Rights Quarterly* 16, no. 2 (1994): 375; Kevin Boyle, 'Stock-Taking on Human Rights: The World Conference on Human Rights, Vienna 1993', *Political Studies* 43, no. 1 (1995): 79; Christina M. Cerna, 'Universality of Human Rights and Cultural Diversity: Implementation of Human Rights in Different Socio-Cultural Contexts', *Human Rights Quarterly* 16, no. 4 (1994): 740; Markus G. Schmidt, 'What Happened to the "Spirit of Vienna"? The Follow-up to the Vienna Declaration and Programme of Action and the Mandate of the U.N. High Commissioner for Human Rights', *Nordic Journal of International Law* 64, no. 4 (1995): 591.

42. Adamantia Pollis, 'Cultural Relativism Revisited: Through a State Prism', *Human Rights Quarterly* 18, no. 2 (1996): 316, 333, n. 43.

43. Bangkok Declaration on Human Rights, adopted by the ministers and representatives of Asian States meeting at Bangkok from 29 March to 2 April 1993 pursuant to UN GA Res. 46/116 of 17 December 1991 in the context of preparations for the World Conference on Human Rights, Vienna, para. 8; excerpted in Lynda S. Bell, Andrew Nathan, and Ilan Peleg, eds, *Negotiating Culture and Human Rights* (New York: Columbia University Press, 2001), Appendix B.

44. For a discussion of how international human rights law perpetuates the suppression and denial of sexual minority rights, see Eric Heinze, 'Sexual Orientation and International Law: A Study in the Manufacture of Cross-Cultural "Sensitivity"', *Michigan Journal of International Law* 22, no. 2 (2001): 283. Cf. Eric Heinze, *Sexual Orientation: A Human Right* (Dordrecht: Martinus Nijhoff, 1995).

45. Simon S.C. Tay, 'Culture, Human Rights and the Singapore Example', *McGill Law Journal* 41, no. 4 (1996): 743, 762.

46. Ibid., citing Benedict Anderson, *Imagined Communities: Reflections on the Origin and Spread of Nationalism* (London: Verso, 1983).

47. Tham, 'Values and National Development in Singapore', 6.

48. Ibid., 2.

49. Pollis, 'Cultural Relativism Revisited', 332–4.

50. Annette Marfording, 'Cultural Relativism and the Construction of Culture: An Examination of Japan', *Human Rights Quarterly* 19, no. 2 (1997): 431.

51. As quoted in Government of Singapore, *White Paper on Shared Values*, Cmd. 1 of 1991 (Singapore: National Printers, 1991), para. 2.

52. Hussin Mutalib, 'National Identity in Singapore: Old Impediments and New Imperatives', *Asian Journal of Political Science* 3, no. 2 (1995): 28, 29.

53. Chan, 'Lack of Sexual Orientation Anti-Discrimination Legislation'; Chan, 'Same-Sex Marriage/Constitutionalism'; Chan, 'Stonewalling through Schizophrenia'.

54. Beng-Huat Chua, *Communitarian Ideology and Democracy in Singapore* (London: Routledge, 1995): 23–5.

55. As quoted in Englehart, 'Rights and Culture in the Asian Values Argument', 555.

56. Ibid., 556.

57. Ibid.

58. It ought to be noted, however, that Confucianism is not a religion and is at its core 'thoroughly secular': William K. Gabrenya, Jr, and Kwang-Kuo Hwang, 'Chinese Social Interaction: Harmony and Hierarchy on the Good Earth', in *The Handbook of Chinese Psychology*, ed. Michael Harris Bond (Hong Kong: Oxford University Press, 1996), 309, 310.

59. Michael Hill, '"Asian Values" as Reverse Orientalism: Singapore', *Asia Pacific Viewpoint* 41, no. 2 (2000): 177, 187.

60. Englehart, 'Rights and Culture in the Asian Values Argument', 557.

61. Hill, '"Asian Values" as Reverse Orientalism', 187.

62. As quoted in Englehart, 'Rights and Culture in the Asian Values Argument', 556. Englehart, ibid., aptly puts it: 'In other words, the Confucians did not know their Confucius.'

63. Ibid., 557.

64. Ibid., 557–8.

65. Benedict Sheehy, in 'Singapore, "Shared Values" and Law: Non East versus West Constitutional Hermeneutic', *Hong Kong Law Journal* 34, no. 1 (2004): 67, 73, argues that the *White Paper* 'is a quasi-Constitution because it sets out fundamental principles suitable for organising many aspects of a society such as those found usually in the preamble of a constitution. A constitutional preamble is particularly important because it sets out the governing hermeneutical principles which are to guide the interpretation of all the constitutional articles that follow. The importance of this quasi-Constitutional document, the *Shared Values*, in communicating to the Singaporean community and the world at large can be seen in its ubiquity: it has been integrated into all the Governmental ministries.'

66. *White Paper on Shared Values*, para. 24.

67. Ibid., para. 52.

68. Ibid., para. 40.

69. Ibid., para. 41.

70. Ibid., para. 40.

71. Ibid., para. 41.

72. Ibid., para. 12.

73. Ibid.

74. Ibid.

75. Ibid., para. 43.

76. Ibid., para. 44.

77. Maintenance of Parents Act 1995 (Cap. 167B), 1996 Rev. Edn, s. 3(1). For a discussion of the legislation, see Wing-Cheong Chan, 'The Duty to Support an Aged Parent in Singapore', *Pacific Rim Law and Policy Journal* 13, no. 3 (2004): 547.

78. Gender equality, like sexual orientation equality, is not expressly enshrined in the Singapore Constitution, and women in Singapore suffer discrimination in many facets of their lives directly or indirectly as a result of a myriad of government policies: see, e.g., Michelle M. Lazar, 'For the Good of the Nation: "Strategic Egalitarianism" in the Singapore Context', *Nations and Nationalism* 7, no. 1 (2001): 59; William Keng Mun Lee, 'Gender Inequality and Discrimination in Singapore', *Journal of Contemporary Asia* 28, no. 4 (1998): 484; Lenore Lyons, 'The Limits of Feminist Political Intervention in Singapore', *Journal of Contemporary Asia* 30, no. 1 (2000): 67; Lenore Lyons, 'A Politics of Accommodation: Women and the People's Action Party in Singapore', *International Feminist Journal of Politics* 7, no. 2 (2005): 233; Lenore Lyons, 'A Curious Space "in-between": The Public/Private Divide and Gender-Based Activism in Singapore', *Gender, Technology and Development* 11, no. 1 (2007): 27; Eugene K.B. Tan, 'A Union of Gender Equality and Pragmatic Patriarchy: International Marriages and Citizenship Laws in Singapore', *Citizenship Studies* 12, no. 1 (2008): 73; Teo You Yenn, 'Inequality for the Greater Good: Gendered State Rule in Singapore', *Critical Asian Studies* 39, no. 3 (2007): 423; Thio, 'Impact of Internationalisation on Domestic Governance'; Thio Li-ann, 'Recent Constitutional Developments: Of Shadows and Whips, Race, Rifts and Rights, Terror and *Tudungs*, Women and Wrongs', *Singapore Journal of Legal Studies* (2002): 328.

79. Thio Li-ann, 'An "i" for an "I"? Singapore's Communitarian Model of Constitutional Adjudication', *Hong Kong Law Journal* 27, no. 2 (1997): 152, 155.

80. Pollis, 'Cultural Relativism Revisited', 329.

81. Thio, 'An "i" for an "I"', 156.

82. Pollis, 'Cultural Relativism Revisited', 320.

83. Clare Hemmings, 'What's in a Name? Bisexuality, Transnational Sexuality Studies and Western Colonial Legacies', *International Journal of Human Rights* 11, nos 1–2 (2007): 13, 16, quoting Peter A. Jackson, 'Pre-Gay, Post-Queer: Thai Perspectives on Proliferating Gender/Sex Diversity in Asia', *Journal of Homosexuality* 40, nos 3–4 (2001): 1, 8.

84.   It is one of many arguments Thio proffered in her opposition to decriminalising consensual
      male/male sexual activity in Singapore: see full transcript of Thio's speech to Parliament of
      Singapore (note 22 above). However, it appears that her argument had been pre-empted by
      the Singapore Court of Appeal decision in *Public Prosecutor* v. *Kwan Kwong Weng* [1997]
      1 SLR 697, where the definition of 'carnal intercourse against the order of nature' in
      section 377 of the Penal Code 1871 (Cap. 224), since repealed and replaced, in the context
      of fellatio between a man and a woman was in issue. While following the Indian decision
      in *Lohana Vasantal Devehand and Others* v. *State* [1968] Cr LJ 1277, where it was stated,
      ibid., 1279–80, that 'it could be said without any hesitation that the orifice of mouth is not,
      according to nature, meant for sexual or carnal intercourse. Viewing from this aspect it
      could be said that the act of putting a male organ in the mouth of a victim for the purposes
      of satisfying his sexual appetite, would be an act of carnal intercourse against the order of
      nature' (as quoted in *Kwan Kwong Weng*, 703), Justice Karthigesu managed nonetheless to
      make an allowance for 'foreplay' prior to consensual sexual intercourse between a man and
      a woman. In His Honour's opinion: 'As between a man and a woman and from a biological
      point of view, that being the only sensible point of view to take, sexual intercourse in the
      order of nature is the coitus of the male and female sexual organs. Whether that coitus is
      for the purposes of procreation or not in our view is quite immaterial. Any other form of
      sexual intercourse would, it must follow, be carnal and against the order of nature. We use
      the word "carnal" in the sense that it is lustful ... So, prima facie, fellatio between a man
      and a woman would be carnal intercourse against the order of nature. However, it is a fact
      of life, in humans as well as in animals, that before the act of copulation takes place there
      is foreplay to stimulate the sex urge. ... when couples engaged in consensual sexual inter-
      course willingly indulge in fellatio and cunnilingus as a stimulant to their respective sexual
      urges, neither act can be considered to be against the order of nature and punishable under s
      377 of the Penal Code. In every other instance the act of fellatio between a man and a
      woman will be carnal intercourse against the order of nature and punishable under s 377'
      (ibid., 705). I argue that from a biological point of view male/male anal intercourse or fellatio
      is no more unnatural than fellatio or cunnilingus engaged in between a man and a woman.
85.   Mary McIntosh, 'The Homosexual Role', in *Queer Theory/Sociology*, ed. Steven Seidman
      (Cambridge, MA: Blackwell, 1996), 33, 35.
86.   It is another argument Thio proffered in her opposition to decriminalising consensual male/
      male sexual activity in Singapore: see full transcript of Thio's speech to Parliament of
      Singapore (note 22 above). However, as I have argued elsewhere in relation to the United
      Nations Convention on the Rights of the Child, adopted and opened for signature, ratification
      and accession by UN GA Res. 44/25 of 20 November 1989 and entered into force on 2
      September 1990, and sexual minority identity, opponents of sexual minority rights fail or do
      not regard it necessary to explain the logical corollary that if homosexuality is a choice, then
      so is heterosexuality, and 'heterosexuals who flaunt their heterosexuality while at the same
      time enthusiastically dismissing sexual minority adolescents' (and individuals') sexual orien-
      tations by alleging that sexual orientation is merely a choice may ask themselves when they
      chose to become heterosexuals and remind themselves that if such a choice was ever made,
      their chosen heterosexuality is perforce susceptible to intense volatility. Not surprisingly, this
      is a foremost reason why those who seek to repress other people's sexual orientations have
      first to repress their very own': Phil C.W. Chan, 'No, it is not just a Phase: An Adolescent's
      Right to Sexual Minority Identity under the United Nations Convention on the Rights of the
      Child', *International Journal of Human Rights* 10, no. 2 (2006): 161, 170. Judge Posner of
      the United States Court of Appeals for the Seventh Circuit, writing extra-judicially, has also
      pointed out that '[g]iven the personal and social disadvantages to which homosexuality
      subjects a person in our society, the idea that millions of young men and women have
      chosen it or will choose it in the same fashion in which they might choose a career or a
      place to live or a political party or even a religious faith seems preposterous': Richard
      A. Posner, *Sex and Reason* (Cambridge, MA: Harvard University Press, 1992), 296–7.
      Indeed, according to Thio, one of her two 'homosexual' friends – both of whom were
      Americans and her use of the term 'homosexual' was deliberate to signify 'a degree of
      choice' in homosexuality – 'never came out and struggles with it': Thio's interview with Li
      Xueying, 'A Fiery NMP Gets her Baptism of Fire', *The Straits Times*, 2 November 2007,
      Insight, 30, http://law.nus.edu.sg/news/archive/2007/ST021107.pdf (accessed 2 November

2008). If homosexuality were a choice, why, one may ask, was Thio's friend struggling? The other 'homosexual' friend of Thio's was equally telling, as according to Thio he had '"left" the community' (presumably the sexual minority community, or homosexuality): Thio's interview with Li Xueying, 'A Fiery NMP Gets her Baptism of Fire'. If one can so easily 'leave' homosexuality, why had Thio's friend who was struggling not done likewise? Her friend's 'leaving' homosexuality also attests to my argument in 'No, it is not just a Phase' that if homosexuality is merely a choice that can be discarded, then heterosexuality is an equally volatile choice equally discardable.

87.   See Fang-fu Ruan, 'China', in *Sociolegal Control of Homosexuality: A Multi-Nation Comparison*, ed. Donald J. West and Richard Green (New York: Plenum Press, 1997): 57; Matthew Harvey Sommer, *Sex, Law, and Society in Late Imperial China* (Palo Alto, CA: Stanford University Press, 2000).

88.   Quoted from full transcript of Thio's speech to Parliament of Singapore (note 22 above).

89.   According to Russell Heng Hiang Khng, 'Tiptoe out of the Closet: The Before and After of the Increasingly Visible Gay Community in Singapore', *Journal of Homosexuality* 40, nos 3–4 (2001): 81, 81, ah qua is 'a Chinese Fujian dialect term particular to Singapore – which became a widely used pejorative term for all gay men'.

90.   Tan with Lee, 'Imagining the Gay Community in Singapore', 185, quoting Laurence Wai-Teng Leong, 'Singapore', in *Sociolegal Control of Homosexuality: A Multi-Nation Comparison*, ed. Donald J. West and Richard Green (New York: Plenum Press, 1997), 127, 134. See also Heinze, 'Sexual Orientation and International Law', 283, 307, where it is argued generally that '[t]he notion of minority sexual orientation as "un-African" or "un-Asian" is the embodiment of European-style racism, for it does exactly what Europeans were accused of doing: it ignores the histories of thousands of *different* African and Asian peoples, throughout thousands of years of history, each with their own changing patterns of social and sexual norms. It perpetuates the distinctly colonial idea that Africans or Asians are all alike, that their pre-colonial existence was frozen in time' (emphasis in original).

91.   The provision substituted the death penalty mandated by the 1533 Buggery Act (25 Henr. VIII c. 6) with life imprisonment as the maximum sentence for consensual male/male anal intercourse in the United Kingdom, and has since been repealed: Sexual Offences Act 2003 (c. 42), s. 140 and Sch. 7. According to H. Montgomery Hyde, *The Other Love: An Historical and Contemporary Survey of Homosexuality in Britain* (London: Heinemann, 1970), 40, the Buggery Act was repealed in 1553 by Queen Mary I (1 Mar. c. 1), who was Roman Catholic and restored the powers of ecclesiastical courts which the Buggery Act had removed (indeed the removal was the primary reason for the statute, as Henry VIII severed England from the ultimate authority and jurisdiction of the papacy in order to divorce Catherine of Aragon and marry Anne Boleyn), but was reinstated in 1563 by Queen Elizabeth I (5 Eliz. I c. 17), who was Protestant.

92.   Penal Code 1871 (Cap. 224), s. 377 (since repealed and replaced); as quoted in Lynette J. Chua Kher Shing, 'Saying No: Sections 377 and 377A of the Penal Code', *Singapore Journal of Legal Studies* (2003): 209, 214. Section 377 of the Penal Code 1871 (Cap. 224), 2008 Rev. Edn, in its current form concerns and prohibits sexual penetration of a corpse.

93.   Criminal Law Amendment Act 1885 (c. 69), s. 11.

94.   Sexual Offences Act 2003 (c. 42), s. 140 and Sch. 7.

95.   Penal Code 1871 (Cap. 224), 2008 Rev. Edn, s. 377A.

96.   *Lim Hock Hin Kelvin* v. *Public Prosecutor* [1998] 1 SLR 801 (Singapore Court of Appeal).

97.   [1995] 2 SLR 783.

98.   Ibid., 793.

99.   Ibid., 785–6.

100.   Ibid., 792.

101.   Ibid., 791.

102.   Ibid.

103.   Interestingly, however, Chief Justice Yong Pung How took into account the possibility that 'the appellant will be placed in a precarious position by an extended term of imprisonment within a confined male environment, bearing in mind the nature of the offence for which he has been convicted' among other mitigating factors in his decision to substitute the original sentence of ten months' imprisonment imposed by the magistrate with a sentence of three months' imprisonment: ibid., 794.

104.   Philip N.S. Rumney, 'Gay Male Rape Victims: Law Enforcement, Social Attitudes and Barriers to Recognition', *International Journal of Human Rights* 13, nos 2–3 (2009): 233.

105.   Oliver Phillips, 'Blackmail in Zimbabwe: Troubling Narratives of Sexuality and Human Rights', *International Journal of Human Rights* 13, nos 2–3 (2009): 345.

106.   Section 354(1) of the Penal Code 1871 (Cap. 224), 2008 Rev. Edn, states that '[w]hoever assaults or uses criminal force to any person, intending to outrage or knowing it to be likely that he will thereby outrage the modesty of that person, shall be punished with imprisonment for a term which may extend to 2 years, or with fine, or with caning, or with any combination of such punishments.'

107.   Weiss, 'Who Sets Social Policy in Metropolis?', 274.

108.   In his Singapore High Court decision in *Tan Boon Hock* v. *Public Prosecutor* [1994] 2 SLR 150, a section 354 prosecution arising from an undercover police operation against gay men, Chief Justice Yong Pung How substituted on appeal a fine of SG$2000 for the initial sentence of four months' imprisonment and three strokes of the cane. *Per curiam*, the Chief Justice found that '[i]t is disquieting that an accused arrested as a result of a police operation (where, as far as the homosexual accused could discern, there would appear to be little question of consent being forthcoming from the other man who then turned out to be a police officer in disguise) should be charged with . . . the offence of outraging another's modesty': ibid., 150. The Chief Justice, however, did not examine the issue as the defendant had pleaded guilty and appealed only his sentence (although it ought to be noted here that the court had the inherent jurisdiction to examine the issue *proprio motu*).

109.   Section 19 of the Miscellaneous Offences (Public Order and Nuisance) Act 1906 (Cap. 184), 1997 Rev. Edn, states that '[e]very person who in any public road or public place persistently loiters or solicits for the purpose of prostitution or for any other immoral purpose shall be guilty of an offence and shall be liable on conviction to a fine not exceeding $1,000 and, in the case of a second or subsequent conviction, to a fine not exceeding $2,000 or to imprisonment for a term not exceeding 6 months or to both'.

110.   Nicholas Bamforth, in *Sexuality, Morals and Justice: A Theory of Lesbian and Gay Rights Law* (London: Cassell, 1997), 25, explains that '[t]he reasons for the UK's gender-specific approach remain ambiguous, but are probably connected with the fact that when the relevant provisions were drafted, public acknowledgement of female sexuality would have been unthinkable in English society. Sexual acts between men were unmentionable in polite company, but their existence was at least recognized at the level of public policy, although they were perceived as the product of sinfulness or mental illness rather than a stable sexual orientation; they were therefore legislated against and punished, albeit under oblique names such as "gross indecency". Sexual acts between women were simply ignored.'

111.   Weiss, 'Who Sets Social Policy in Metropolis?', 285. Weiss notes, ibid., n. 128, that 10.1% of Singapore's population self-identified as Christian in the 1980 census, 12.7% in 1990, and 14.6% in 2000, and argues that Christian opposition has particular potency in the sexual minority rights debate in Singapore as Christianity is the fastest-growing religion in Singapore besides Buddhism and, as Robbie B.H. Goh observes, the religion 'most strongly associated with the indices of socioeconomic progress and upwardly mobile class status' ('Deus Ex Machina: Evangelical Sites, Urbanism, and the Construction of Social Identities', in *Postcolonial Urbanism: Southeast Asian Cities and Global Processes*, ed. Ryan Bishop, John Phillips, and Wei Wei Yeo (New York: Routledge, 2003), 305, 307–8). I argue that the general correlation between adoption of Christianity as one's religion and higher socio-economic status in Singapore accords Christians who oppose sexual minority rights in Singapore credibility in the Confucian sense of *junzi* as the only persons wise enough to form an opinion then taken as perforce authoritative.

112.   See Simon Elegant, 'The Lion in Winter', *Time*, 30 June 2003, http://www.time.com/time/asia/covers/501030707/sea_singapore.html (accessed 2 November 2008).

113.   Tan with Lee, 'Imagining the Gay Community in Singapore', 196.

114.   National Council of Churches of Singapore, 'Statement on Homosexuality', 29 July 2003, para. 5, http://www.nccs.org.sg/statement.html (accessed 2 November 2008).

115.   Quoted from Goh Chok Tong, 'From the Valley to the Highlands', National Day Rally speech, 17 August 2003, http://www.gov.sg/nd/ND03.htm (accessed 2 November 2008).

116.   In her interview with Li Xueying of the *The Straits Times* ('A Fiery NMP Gets her Baptism of Fire'), Thio related that she converted from a 'very, very arrogant' atheist to a devout Christian

after she attended a Christian Union talk in October 1987 at the University of Oxford where she was a law student. She recounted that as she was about to leave the talk early she was 'stopped' by a voice and 'basically had a sense that God was talking to me'. According to the interview, Thio studied Bible Knowledge for her O-level Religious Knowledge course, in which she scored an A1. I argue that Thio is an example of the failure of the government's Confucian Ethics campaign and its construction of Singapore 'culture' as essentially Confucian, and of the central role of some Christians in the opposition to homosexuality and sexual minority rights in Singapore and the inconsistency of the opposition which makes use of self-selected and self-interpreted 'Asian values', Confucian ethics, and religious, particularly Christian, concepts simultaneously.

117. For discussions of similar arguments raised in the context of Hong Kong, see Chan, 'Gay Age of Consent'; Chan, 'Lack of Sexual Orientation Anti-Discrimination Legislation'; Chan, 'Same-Sex Marriage/Constitutionalism'; Chan, 'Stonewalling through Schizophrenia'; Chan, 'Male/Male Sex in Hong Kong'.

118. Although Thio's arguments against decriminalising consensual male/male sexual activity in Singapore can largely be found in similar debates in other jurisdictions, she did raise an argument that was rather uncommon in sexual minority rights debates and one that was particularly pertinent to 'filial' Singapore – namely, the correlation, negative as she alleged, between 'sexual minority rights' and women's rights. According to Thio, '[t]o slouch back to Sodom is to return to the Bad Old Days in ancient Greece or even China where sex was utterly wild and unrestrained, and homosexuality was considered superior to man–women relations. Women's groups should note that where homosexuality was celebrated, women were relegated to low social roles; when homosexuality was idealized in Greece, women were objects not partners, who ran homes and bore babies. Back then, whether a man had sex with another man, woman or child was a matter of indifference, like one's eating preferences. The only relevant category was penetrator and penetrated; sex was not seen as interactive intimacy, but a doing of something to someone. How degrading': quoted from full transcript of Thio's speech to Parliament of Singapore (note 22 above). However, it is generally accepted that women's rights and sexual minority rights are substantially and substantively linked and mutually reinforcing: see, e.g., Davina Cooper, 'An Engaged State: Sexuality, Governance, and the Potential for Change', *Journal of Law and Society* 20, no. 3 (1993): 257; He Xiaopei, 'Chinese Queer (*Tongzhi*) Women Organizing in the 1990s', in *Chinese Women Organizing: Cadres, Feminists, Muslims, Queers*, ed. Ping-Chun Hsiung, Maria Jaschok, and Cecilia Milwertz, with Red Chan (Oxford: Berg, 2001): 41; Susie Jolly, '"Queering" Development: Exploring the Links between Same-Sex Sexualities, Gender, and Development', *Gender and Development* 8, no. 1 (2000): 78; Oliver Phillips, 'A Brief Introduction to the Relationship between Sexuality and Rights', *Georgia Journal of International and Comparative Law* 33, no. 2 (2004): 451; David A.J. Richards, *Women, Gays, and the Constitution: The Grounds for Feminism and Gay Rights in Culture and Law* (Chicago: University of Chicago Press, 1998); Rachel Rosenbloom, ed., *Unspoken Rules: Sexual Orientation and Women's Human Rights* (London and New York: Cassell, 1996). It is therefore very interesting that Thio, the leading women's rights legal scholar in Singapore, considered society's acceptance of homosexuality to be a direct and controlling factor in society's subordination of women. It is to be recalled that gender equality, like sexual orientation equality, is not expressly enshrined in the Singapore Constitution, and women in Singapore suffer discrimination in many facets of their lives directly or indirectly as a result of a myriad of government policies: see, e.g., Lazar, 'For the Good of the Nation'; Lee, 'Gender Inequality and Discrimination in Singapore'; Lyons, 'The Limits of Feminist Political Intervention in Singapore'; Lyons, 'A Politics of Accommodation'; Lyons, 'A Curious Space "in-between"'; Tan, 'A Union of Gender Equality and Pragmatic Patriarchy'; Teo, 'Inequality for the Greater Good'; Thio, 'Impact of Internationalisation on Domestic Governance'; Thio, 'Recent Constitutional Developments'. Contrary to Thio's position, I argue that the status of persons belonging to sexual minorities in Singapore is positively correlated with the status of women in Singapore and that developing sexual minority rights in Singapore will at the same time enhance women's rights and, as importantly, rights consciousness in Singapore, as oppression of women and oppression of persons belonging to sexual minorities, including lesbian women, have always come from the same source – the male heterosexual state. As Nancy Kim reminds us, '[t]he label "culture" has obscured the power-play involved in the evolution of "traditional"

practices that affect women. ... "culture" is often composed of different "subcultures" that may or may not conform to the expectations and norms of the broader society. ... The culture of which anthropologists speak is the dominant culture within society – the culture of society's power elite. Culture, thus distilled, leaves out rebels, misfits, and the disempowered. ... In almost every society, the power elite is comprised overwhelmingly of men. Because most cultures are male-dominated, how and what women choose to accept or reject as part of their culture is often ignored or suppressed', 'Toward a Feminist Theory of Human Rights: Straddling the Fence between Western Imperialism and Uncritical Absolutism', *Columbia Human Rights Law Review* 25, no. 1 (1993): 49, 88–90. The correlations between the statuses and oppressions of women and of persons belonging to sexual minorities in Singapore, and how women and persons belonging to sexual minorities in Singapore may work together to enhance greater general equality in Singapore, warrant a paper of its own. *En passant*, Thio's correct acknowledgment in her parliamentary speech that homosexuality was common in China helped discredit the alleged incompatibility between homosexuality and Confucian ethics as cultural values encompassing all Chinese – traditional Confucian ethics do not metamorphose into something else at Singapore's, or any, borders. Also, in the context of Thio's argument that sexual minority rights development undermines the status of women, one must keep in mind that 'man–*women* relations' in Singapore, Chinese, Christian, Hindu, or Islamic culture – whether Thio's use of the plural form was deliberate or inadvertent – used to be polygamous consisting of one man and more than one woman, and that the celebrated definition of civil marriage in common law – 'as understood in Christendom ... the voluntary union for life of one man and one woman, to the exclusion of others' – emanated from the English decision in *Hyde* v. *Hyde and Woodmansee* (1866) 1 LR P & D 130, 133, which concerned not homosexuality but polygamous marriage. Indeed, the Biblical provision, that 'Let a woman learn in silence with full submission. I permit no woman to teach or to have authority over a man; she is to keep silent. For Adam was formed first, then Eve; and Adam was not deceived, but the woman was deceived and became a transgressor. Yet she will be saved through childbearing, provided they continue in faith and love and holiness, with modesty' (1 Timothy 2:11–15), formed the basis for the centuries-long suppression and disenfranchisement of women in society, which South African Supreme Court of Appeal Judge Farlam, who is also Chancellor of the Anglican Church of the Province of Southern Africa, in *Fourie* v. *Minister of Home Affairs*, Case CCT 232/03, 30 November 2004, para. 121, cited as one reason why same-sex marriage had not and could not have been recognised in South Africa, since as 'the principle of legal equality between the spouses was not enshrined in our law there were many rules forming part of our law of matrimonial relations which put the husband in a superior position and the wife in an inferior one. The law could thus not easily accommodate same-sex unions because, unless the partners thereto agreed as to who was to be the "husband" and who the "wife", these rules could not readily be applied to their union.' It is therefore crucial when reflecting on human rights or governance issues to keep in mind that '[i]f people are not aware of the historical and contextual nature of human rights and not aware that human rights become realized only by the struggles of real people experiencing real instances of domination, then human rights are all too easily used as symbolic legitimizers for instruments of that very domination': A. Belden Fields and Wolf-Dieter Narr, 'Human Rights as a Holistic Concept', *Human Rights Quarterly* 14, no. 1 (1992): 1, 5.

119.   Emma Henderson, 'Of Signifiers and Sodomy: Privacy, Public Morality and Sex in the Decriminalisation Debates', *Melbourne University Law Review* 20, no. 4 (1995–6): 1023, 1024.

120.   As Thio stated in her interview with Li Xueying of *The Straits Times* ('A Fiery NMP Gets her Baptism of Fire'), '[t]here was an overwhelming sense of relief that I had said what I had said. So maybe one of the functions of the NMP is because we are not so much weighted by considerations of political niceties because we have no constituency. Our constituency is to our conscience and our truth and our own reputations in putting forth what we hope will be considered credible arguments.'

121.   [1994] 3 SLR 662.

122.   Ibid., 681.

123.   [1963] MLJ 355.

124.   Ibid., 358.

125.   Ibid.

126.   [1963] 3 WLR 63.
127.   Ibid., 73–4.
128.   Appellate recourse to the Judicial Committee of the Privy Council as the court of final resort for Singapore was first restricted in 1989 when Parliament of Singapore enacted the Judicial Committee (Amendment) Act 1989 (No. 21 of 1989) whereby an appeal to the Judicial Committee would thenceforth be allowed only if, in a civil case, all the parties to the proceedings agreed to such an appeal prior to the Singapore Court of Appeal hearing the case or, in a criminal case, if the proceedings involved the death penalty and the presiding judges of the Singapore Court of Criminal Appeal, since merged with the Singapore Court of Appeal in 1993 by the Supreme Court of Judicature (Amendment) Act 1993 (No. 16 of 1993), could not come to a unanimous decision. Subsequently, the Constitution of the Republic of Singapore was amended in 1994 and the Judicial Committee (Repeal) Act 1994 (No. 2 of 1994) enacted to the effect that as of 8 April 1994 all appeals to the Judicial Committee were disallowed and the Singapore Court of Appeal constituted thenceforth the court of final resort for Singapore. For a discussion of the evolution of the legal system of Singapore, see Kevin Y.L. Tan, *The Singapore Legal System*, 2nd edn (Singapore: Singapore University Press, 1999).
129.   In *Attorney General of Hong Kong* v. *Lee Kwong-kut* [1993] 3 HKPLR 72, 100, Lord Woolf insisted that Hong Kong courts ought to determine the question of inconsistency between a statutory provision and the Hong Kong Bill of Rights Ordinance (Cap. 383) through literal examination of the statutory provision alone. A too generous approach to the interpretation of the Ordinance, His Lordship surmised, would only lead to injustice: 'While the Hong Kong judiciary should be zealous in upholding an individual's rights under the Hong Kong Bill, it is also necessary to ensure that disputes as to the effect of the Bill are not allowed to get out of hand. The issues involving the Hong Kong Bill should be approached with realism and good sense, and kept in proportion. If this is not done the Bill will become a source of injustice rather than justice and it will be debased in the eyes of the public. In order to maintain the balance between the individual and the society as a whole, rigid and inflexible standards should not be imposed on the legislature's attempts to resolve the difficult and intransigent problems with which society is faced when seeking to deal with serious crime. It must be remembered that questions of policy remain primarily the responsibility of the legislature.' For a discussion of constitutional comparativism and its implications for rights development in Hong Kong, see Phil C.W. Chan, 'Keeping up with (which) Joneses: a critique of constitutional comparativism in Hong Kong and its implications for rights development', *International Journal of Human Rights* 13, nos 2–3 (2009): 307–28. In line with the transfer of sovereignty over Hong Kong from the United Kingdom to China, the Hong Kong Court of Final Appeal, established by Article 81 of the Basic Law of the Hong Kong Special Administrative Region of the People's Republic of China, 29 ILM 1519 (1990), adopted by the Seventh National People's Congress at its Third Session on 4 April 1990 in pursuance of the 1984 Joint Declaration of the Government of the United Kingdom of Great Britain and Northern Ireland and the Government of the People's Republic of China on the Question of Hong Kong, 23 ILM 1366 (1984), and the Hong Kong Court of Final Appeal Ordinance (Cap. 484), replaced the Judicial Committee of the Privy Council as of 1 July 1997 as the court of final resort for Hong Kong. See, however, Article 82 of the Basic Law of Hong Kong, which states that '[t]he power of final adjudication of the Hong Kong Special Administrative Region shall be vested in the Court of Final Appeal of the Region, which may as required invite judges from other common law jurisdictions to sit on the Court of Final Appeal', and Article 158 of the Basic Law of Hong Kong, which states that '[t]he power of interpretation of this Law shall be vested in the Standing Committee of the National People's Congress. The Standing Committee of the National People's Congress shall authorise the courts of the Hong Kong Special Administrative Region to interpret on their own, in adjudicating cases, the provisions of this Law which are within the limits of the autonomy of the Region. The courts of the Hong Kong Special Administrative Region may also interpret other provisions of this Law in adjudicating cases. However, if the courts of the Region, in adjudicating cases, need to interpret the provisions of this Law concerning affairs which are the responsibility of the Central People's Government, or concerning the relationship between the Central Authorities and the Region, and if such interpretation will affect the judgments on the cases, the courts of the Region shall, before making their final judgments which are not appealable, seek an interpretation of the relevant provisions from the Standing Committee

of the National People's Congress through the Court of Final Appeal of the Region. When the Standing Committee makes an interpretation of the provisions concerned, the courts of the Region, in applying those provisions, shall follow the interpretation of the Standing Committee. However, judgments previously rendered shall not be affected. The Standing Committee of the National People's Congress shall consult its Committee for the Basic Law of the Hong Kong Special Administrative Region before giving an interpretation of this Law.' For a discussion of the judicial and political autonomy of Hong Kong, see Phil C.W. Chan, 'Hong Kong's Political Autonomy and its Continuing Struggle for Universal Suffrage', *Singapore Journal of Legal Studies* (2006): 285.

130. [1981] 1 MLJ 64.
131. Ibid., 70.
132. [1977] 2 MLJ 187.
133. Li-ann Thio, 'Beyond the "Four Walls" in an Age of Transnational Judicial Conversations: Civil Liberties, Rights Theories, and Constitutional Adjudication in Malaysia and Singapore', *Columbia Journal of Asian Law* 19, no. 2 (2005–6): 428, 431–2, quoting *Loh Kooi Choon*, 189.
134. *Ong Ah Chuan*, 71.
135. Thio, 'An "i" for an "I"', 177.
136. Ibid., 176.
137. See, e.g., Vicki C. Jackson, 'Comparative Constitutional Federalism and Transnational Judicial Discourse', *International Journal of Constitutional Law* 2, no. 1 (2004): 91; Christopher McCrudden, 'A Common Law of Human Rights?: Transnational Judicial Conversations on Constitutional Rights', *Oxford Journal of Legal Studies* 20, no. 4 (2000): 499; Anne-Marie Slaughter, 'Judicial Globalization', *Virginia Journal of International Law* 40, no. 4 (1999–2000): 1103; Thio, 'Beyond the "Four Walls"'.
138. Sujit Choudhry, 'Globalization in Search of Justification: Toward a Theory of Comparative Constitutional Interpretation', *Indiana Law Journal* 74, no. 3 (1998–9): 819, 858.
139. Ibid., 892.
140. Alison Dundes Renteln, 'Relativism and the Search for Human Rights', *American Anthropologist* 90, no. 1 (1988): 56, 56.
141. Edward W. Saïd, *Orientalism* (New York: Vintage Books, 1978), 325.
142. See Yash Ghai, 'Human Rights and Governance: The Asia Debate', *Australian Year Book of International Law* 15 (1994): 1.
143. As Thio has pointed out in 'Recent Constitutional Developments', 368, Singapore and Malaysia, the two most vocal countries asserting the potency, legitimacy and immediacy of an 'Asian values' approach to human rights, share *inter se* divergent perspectives on the 'Asian values' they propound, which 'demonstrates how this school is not a singular set of values. An important point of differentiation is that Malaysia advocates the need for a revived religious public culture. Singapore, in espousing a principle of secularity framing State–Religion relations when it seceded from Malaysia, where Islam is the official religion of the Federation, does not.'
144. Amélie Oksenberg Rorty, 'Relativism, Persons, and Practices', in *Relativism: Interpretation and Confrontation*, ed. Michael Krausz (Notre Dame, IN: University of Notre Dame Press, 1989), 418, 418.
145. *Leung T.C. William Roy* v. *Secretary for Justice* [2005] 3 HKLRD 657 (Hong Kong Court of First Instance); *Secretary for Justice* v. *Leung T.C. William Roy* [2006] 4 HKLRD 211 (Hong Kong Court of Appeal). Article 22 of the Hong Kong Bill of Rights Ordinance (Cap. 383), modelled upon and implementing Article 26 of the International Covenant on Civil and Political Rights, states that '[a]ll persons are equal before the law and are entitled without any discrimination to the equal protection of the law. In this respect, the law shall prohibit any discrimination and guarantee to all persons equal and effective protection against discrimination on any ground such as race, colour, sex, language, religion, political or other opinion, national or social origin, property, birth or other status.' The International Covenant on Civil and Political Rights shall remain in force in Hong Kong even if the Hong Kong Bill of Rights Ordinance is repealed, as Article 39 of the Basic Law of Hong Kong states that '[t]he provisions of the International Covenant on Civil and Political Rights, the International Covenant on Economic, Social and Cultural Rights, and international labour conventions as applied to Hong Kong shall remain in force and shall be implemented through the laws of the Hong Kong Special Administrative Region. The rights and freedoms enjoyed by Hong Kong

residents shall not be restricted unless as prescribed by law. Such restrictions shall not contravene the provisions of the preceding paragraph of this Article.' Note should also be taken of Article 25 of the Basic Law of Hong Kong, which states unequivocally that '[a]ll Hong Kong residents shall be equal before the law.'

146. *National Coalition for Gay and Lesbian Equality* v. *Minister of Justice*, 1999 (1) SA 6 (Constitutional Court of South Africa); *National Coalition for Gay and Lesbian Equality* v. *Minister of Home Affairs*, 39(4) ILM 798 (2000) (Constitutional Court of South Africa); *Fourie* v. *Minister of Home Affairs*, Case CCT 232/03, 30 November 2004 (Supreme Court of Appeal of South Africa); *Minister of Home Affairs* v. *Fourie*, Case CCT 60/04, 1 December 2005 (Constitutional Court of South Africa). The Constitution of the Republic of South Africa as promulgated in 1996 is the first national constitution in the world that expressly protects against sexual orientation discrimination, Article 9(3) of which states that '[t]he state may not unfairly discriminate directly or indirectly against anyone on one or more grounds, including race, gender, sex, pregnancy, marital status, ethnic or social origin, colour, sexual orientation, age, disability, religion, conscience, belief, culture, language and birth.' Article 9(4) of the Constitution goes on to prohibit unfair discrimination by any person on the any of the grounds specified in Article 9(3) and mandate enactment of national legislation to prevent or prohibit such unfair discrimination. Article 10 of the Constitution, in the most unequivocal manner, affirms that '[e]veryone has inherent dignity and the right to have their dignity respected and protected.'

147. Constitution of the Republic of Singapore, 1999 Rev. Edn, Art. 12(1).
148. Phillips, 'A Brief Introduction to the Relationship between Sexuality and Rights', 453.
149. Thio, 'Beyond the "Four Walls"', 438, citing *Constitutional Reference, No. 1 of 1995* [1995] 2 SLR 201 (Constitution of the Republic of Singapore Tribunal), and quoting *Minister of Home Affairs* v. *Fisher* [1980] AC 319, 329 (Judicial Committee of the Privy Council, on appeal from the Court of Appeal for Bermuda).
150. [1998] 1 SLR 943.
151. Ibid., 965.
152. Seth F. Kreimer, 'Invidious Comparisons: Some Cautionary Remarks on the Process of Constitutional Borrowing', *University of Pennsylvania Journal of Constitutional Law* 1, no. 3 (1998–99): 640, 650.
153. Thio, 'Beyond the "Four Walls"', 431.
154. Thio, 'An "i" for an "I"', 174.
155. Victor V. Ramraj, 'Comparative Constitutional Law in Singapore', *Singapore Journal of International and Comparative Law* 6 (2002): 302, 327, quoting *White Paper on Shared Values*, para. 1.
156. See Joseph Chan, 'A Confucian Perspective on Human Rights for Contemporary China', in *The East Asian Challenge for Human Rights*, ed. Joanne R. Bauer and Daniel A. Bell (Cambridge: Cambridge University Press, 1999), 212.
157. Quoted from full transcript of Thio's speech to Parliament of Singapore (note 22 above).

Keeping up with (which) Joneses: a critique of constitutional comparativism in Hong Kong and its implications for rights development

Phil C.W. Chan

Faculty of Law, National University of Singapore, Singapore

This paper explores Hong Kong courts' recourse to foreign and international legal materials in the interpretation of the two most important rights instruments governing Hong Kong, the Basic Law of Hong Kong and the Hong Kong Bill of Rights Ordinance, both generally and in two specific cases concerning freedom of expression and the age of consent for male/male sexual activity. It discusses how Hong Kong courts within the confines of political realities continue to allow themselves to be overridden by foreign courts in matters concerning Hong Kong. Constitutional comparativism as has been practised in Hong Kong, this paper argues, merely serves to allow for and perpetuate unpredictable judicial reasoning and the lingering effects of Hong Kong's colonial past, and is in need of a consistent and reasoned approach for its legitimate application and, ultimately, the protection of human rights, including sexual minority rights, and the rule of law in Hong Kong.

Introduction

Those outside Hong Kong often wonder whether and how much the political, socio-economic and cultural landscape of Hong Kong has changed since its return to Chinese sovereignty after 155 years of British colonial rule. China's resumption of sovereignty, they generally believe, must have resulted in *some* negative outcomes for Hong Kong, and if Hong Kong had remained under British colonial rule the city would have been better off.

However, what the people of Hong Kong ought to ask is whether they finally have a definitive say, as permitted by the confines of political realities, in matters concerning Hong Kong or in fact continue to allow themselves to be overridden by what other people think is best. As a legal scholar, I must leave the complex task of analysing the political, socio-economic and cultural effects of China's resumption of sovereignty to political scientists, economists, and cultural anthropologists. Instead, this paper explores Hong Kong courts' recourse to foreign and international legal materials in the interpretation of the two most important rights instruments governing Hong Kong: the Basic Law of the Hong Kong Special Administrative Region of the People's Republic of China (hereinafter referred to as the Basic Law of Hong Kong), promulgated in 1990 by China's National People's Congress as a Chinese national law under Article 31 of the Constitution of the People's Republic of

China in pursuance of the 1984 Sino-British Joint Declaration,[1] and the Hong Kong Bill of Rights Ordinance, enacted in June 1991 by Hong Kong's colonial legislature in response to the Tiananmen Massacre in Beijing in June 1989. The two rights instruments have since become the core of Hong Kong's public law persona where the development of its own identity and destiny lies.

In his keynote address to the annual meeting of the American Society of International Law in 2003, United States Supreme Court Justice Stephen Breyer referred to his colleague Justice Ruth Ginsburg as she stated extra-judicially that 'comparative analysis emphatically is relevant to the task of interpreting constitutions and enforcing human rights'.[2] However, does constitutional comparativism in post-colonial Hong Kong merely serve to allow for and perpetuate the lingering effects of Hong Kong's colonial past? Indeed, Wiktor Osiatynski asks, 'is the continuation of a model of the former colonial power synonymous with borrowing?'[3] As Roger Alford explains, comparative law concerns the central development of a constitutional theory in a particular jurisdiction with comparativism as an interpretive paradigm.[4] 'The legitimacy of constitutional comparativism', Alford argues, 'should be determined by constitutional theory. Comparativism is not a constitutional theory; it is a methodology that is employed depending on a judge's particular theory.'[5]

Thus, this paper first explores the debate within the Hong Kong judiciary (including the Judicial Committee of the Privy Council up to 30 June 1997) on whether, why and how to approach foreign and international legal materials in the interpretation of the Hong Kong Bill of Rights Ordinance (from June 1991) and the Basic Law of Hong Kong (from July 1997). It then examines two specific Hong Kong human rights cases: *Ng Kung Siu* v. *HKSAR*,[6] which concerned the criminalisation of desecration of the Chinese national and Hong Kong regional flags in Hong Kong within the confines of freedom of expression, and *Leung T.C. William Roy* v. *Secretary for Justice*,[7] which concerned the higher age of consent for male/male sexual activity in the light of an individual's right of equality and his right to privacy. The two decisions are chosen as they illustrate how constitutional comparativism as has been practised in Hong Kong may be capable of both undermining and augmenting the protection of fundamental rights and freedoms guaranteed by the Basic Law of Hong Kong and the Ordinance, and in both instances the Hong Kong courts' approaches were problematic. Constitutional comparativism as has been practised in Hong Kong, this paper argues, is in need of a consistent and reasoned approach for its legitimate application and, ultimately, the protection of human rights, including sexual minority rights, and the rule of law in Hong Kong.

Hong Kong courts' general approaches to constitutional comparativism

A constitution, as the *grundnorm* of a polity, ought to be the embodiment of the polity's values, beliefs, and self-identification. As a legally binding instrument consisting of norms antecedent to and governing the polity, a constitution both empowers and constrains the legislative, executive and judicial branches of government. A constitution, furthermore, enshrines and preserves the political compromises leading to its promulgation.

While the Basic Law of Hong Kong was imposed upon Hong Kong under an agreement between the United Kingdom and China and the Hong Kong Bill of Rights Ordinance was enacted by Hong Kong's colonial legislature, the two rights instruments seek to enshrine, guarantee and protect the interests of Hong Kong and its people within the confines of political realities, and a study of constitutional comparativism in Hong Kong will be an immediate misadventure if it is not informed by an understanding of the two instruments. The Preamble to the Basic Law of Hong Kong, first and foremost, states:

> Upholding national unity and territorial integrity, maintaining the prosperity and stability of Hong Kong, and taking account of its history and realities, the People's Republic of China has decided that upon China's resumption of the exercise of sovereignty over Hong Kong, a Hong Kong Special Administrative Region will be established in accordance with the provisions of Article 31 of the Constitution of the People's Republic of China, and that under the principle of 'one country, two systems', the socialist system and policies will not be practised in Hong Kong.[8]

The substantive provisions of the Basic Law of Hong Kong then provide the following general safeguards for the autonomy of post-colonial Hong Kong:

(1) Hong Kong is authorised 'to exercise a high degree of autonomy and enjoy executive, legislative and independent judicial power, including that of final adjudication'.[9]

(2) The socialist system and policies practised in China will not extend to post-colonial Hong Kong, whose 'previous capitalist system and way of life shall remain unchanged for 50 years'.[10]

(3) 'The laws previously in force in Hong Kong, that is, the common law, rules of equity, ordinances, subordinate legislation and customary law shall be maintained, except for any that contravene this Law, and subject to any amendment by the legislature of the Hong Kong Special Administrative Region.'[11]

(4) In addition to Chinese, English may be used as an official language by the three branches of government in Hong Kong.[12]

In addition, the Basic Law of Hong Kong indicates and guarantees in 18 separate provisions such fundamental rights and freedoms as may continue to be enjoyed in Hong Kong as of 1 July 1997.[13] Article 39 of the Basic Law of Hong Kong, in particular, guarantees the continued application in post-colonial Hong Kong of the International Covenant on Civil and Political Rights (ICCPR),[14] the International Covenant on Economic, Social and Cultural Rights,[15] and International Labour Organisation conventions previously applicable.[16] The Basic Law of Hong Kong also establishes a Hong Kong Court of Final Appeal, replacing the Judicial Committee of the Privy Council as of 1 July 1997 as the court of final resort for Hong Kong.[17] The Hong Kong Court of Final Appeal, which may recruit judges from other common law jurisdictions,[18] is vested with the power of final adjudication.[19] However, in cases involving the interpretation of the Basic Law of Hong Kong concerning 'affairs which are the responsibility of the Central People's Government, or concerning the relationship between the Central Authorities and [Hong Kong], and if such interpretation will affect the judgments on the cases, the courts of [Hong Kong] shall, before making their final judgments which are not appealable, seek an interpretation of the relevant provisions from the Standing Committee of the National People's Congress'.[20]

As will be seen, the debate within the Hong Kong judiciary about the correct approach in the interpretation of the two rights instruments has, however, lain to a lesser extent with the Basic Law of Hong Kong than with the Hong Kong Bill of Rights Ordinance, as the Basic Law of Hong Kong was not in force until 1 July 1997 and the Judicial Committee of the Privy Council, the court of final resort for Hong Kong up to 30 June 1997, played a pivotal role in the debate, which soon became settled as the Hong Kong Court of Final Appeal assumed the role of the Judicial Committee and pronounced its opinion on the matter.

The Hong Kong Bill of Rights Ordinance is the municipal legislation implementing the ICCPR in Hong Kong and its substantive rights provisions are closely modelled upon those of the Covenant. Section 2(3) of the Ordinance stated that in 'interpreting and applying this Ordinance, regard shall be had to the fact that the purpose of this Ordinance is to provide for the incorporation into the law of Hong Kong of provisions of the International Covenant on Civil and Political Rights'.[21] Yash Ghai maintains that the provision was 'undoubtedly an invitation to the judiciary to consider the interpretations of the ICCPR by the Human Rights Committee as well as of other international bodies dealing with analogous provisions. This internationalises the rights issue in a manner which upsets China, which prefers to see rights as determined by the specific historical and economic circumstances of a particular state.'[22] Thus, it was not surprising that section 2(3), together with three other provisions of the Ordinance, was specifically not adopted by the Standing Committee of the National People's Congress on 23 February 1997 as part of the law of Hong Kong as of 1 July 1997 in accordance with Article 160 of the Basic Law of Hong Kong.[23] The reason for the Standing Committee's refusal to adopt the provisions probably lay in China's unease with international human rights law and the ICCPR having an explicit direct effect on the interpretation and application of a domestic law, that is, the Hong Kong Bill of Rights Ordinance and consequently all domestic laws of Hong Kong. Ghai, Peter Wesley-Smith, and Johannes Chan all argue that the Standing Committee's refusal nevertheless had no legal effect on the continuing operation of the ICCPR, as judges may rely on the preamble, long title and substantive provisions of the Ordinance all of which make reference to the ICCPR and its incorporation into the law of Hong Kong.[24] Chan further argues that the repeal of any statutory provision found to be inconsistent with the Ordinance took effect on the commencement of the Ordinance, that is, 8 June 1991, and it matters neither when the impugned statutory provision was enacted nor when the inconsistency was discovered: any such impugned statutory provision cannot be 'laws previously in force in Hong Kong' under Article 8 of the Basic Law of Hong Kong and thus cannot have been adopted as part of the law of Hong Kong as of 1 July 1997.[25]

It must be pointed out, however, that neither the United Kingdom government nor Hong Kong's colonial government desired a bill of rights in Hong Kong but for the Tiananmen Massacre in Beijing in 1989[26] which caused public and foreign investors' confidence in the Hong Kong government and the future of Hong Kong to sink 'to an all-time low'[27] as well as an influx of emigration and outflow of capital from Hong Kong. Meanwhile, the Chinese government opposed a bill of rights in Hong Kong as it considered the Basic Law of Hong Kong to be sufficient to protect the rights the ICCPR guarantees. According to Ghai, 'China interprets the expression as "applied to Hong Kong" [in Article 39 of the Basic Law of Hong Kong] to mean as already provided for under domestic law, a stance which the Chinese claim Britain earlier promoted as a way to persuade it to include the ICCPR in the Joint Declaration.'[28] While the Chinese government refrained from refusing to adopt the Bill *in toto* as part of the law of Hong Kong as of 1 July 1997, it did refuse to adopt certain provisions of the Ordinance which expressly incorporated the ICCPR into the law of Hong Kong, as has been noted.[29]

In any case, did the Hong Kong judiciary take up the invitation Ghai saw before it was too late? In *R.* v. *Sin Yau-ming*,[30] Hong Kong Court of Appeal Vice-President Silke observed that 'the glass through which we view the interpretation of the Hong Kong Bill is a glass provided by the Covenant. We are no longer guided by the ordinary canons of constructions of statutes nor with the dicta of the common law inherent in our training. We must look, in our interpretation of the Hong Kong Bill, at the aims of the Covenant and give "full recognition and effect" to the statement which commences that Covenant.'[31]

His Lordship suggested the sources of law that Hong Kong courts should refer to when interpreting the Ordinance:

> While this court is, in effect, required to make new Hong Kong law relating to the manner of interpretation of the Hong Kong Bill and consequentially the tests to be applied to those laws now existing and, when asked, those laws yet to be enacted, we are not without guidance in our task. This can be derived from decisions taken in common law jurisdictions which contain a constitutionally entrenched Bill of Rights. We can also be guided by decisions of the European Court of Human Rights ... and the European Human Rights Commission ... Further, we can bear in mind the comments and decisions of the United Nations Human Rights Committee ... I would hold none of these to be binding upon us though in so far as they reflect the interpretation of articles in the Covenant, and are directly related to Hong Kong legislation, I would consider them as of the greatest assistance and give to them considerable weight.[32]

The two-stage approach of the Supreme Court of Canada in *R.* v. *Oakes*[33] to interpreting the Canadian Charter of Rights and Freedoms[34] then became the yardstick for Hong Kong courts in their interpretation of the Ordinance when determining if a particular statutory provision conflicted with it. Its impact on Hong Kong jurisprudence warrants that it be quoted in detail:

> Two central criteria must be satisfied to establish that a limit is reasonable and demonstrably justified in a free and democratic society. First, the objective to be served by the measures limiting a *Charter* right must be sufficiently important to warrant overriding a constitutionally protected right or freedom. The standard must be high to ensure that trivial objectives or those discordant with the principles of a free and democratic society do not gain protection. At a minimum, an objective must relate to societal concerns which are pressing and substantial in a free and democratic society before it can be characterized as sufficiently important. Second, the party invoking s.1 must show the means to be reasonable and demonstrably justified. This involves a form of proportionality test involving three important components. To begin, the measures must be fair and not arbitrary, carefully designed to achieve the objective in question and rationally connected to that objective. In addition, the means should impair the right in question as little as possible. Lastly, there must be a proportionality between the effects of the limiting measure and the objective – the more severe the deleterious effects of a measure, the more important the objective must be.[35]

Nevertheless, as Ghai notes, while both enshrine and guarantee certain fundamental rights and freedoms, the Ordinance and the Charter also share marked dissimilarity:[36] the Ordinance does not have a general limitation clause, unlike the Charter that contains a notwithstanding clause[37] that the Canadian federal or provincial legislatures may invoke to override a judgment dispositive of the issue. There is also no reference in the Ordinance to a 'free and democratic society' as there is in the Charter[38] from which the Supreme Court of Canada deduced the *Oaks* approach to give effect to the Charter's 'overarching values and purposes',[39] and which, with universal suffrage continuing to be wanting in Hong Kong,[40] simply cannot be analogised to apply in Hong Kong.

The Judicial Committee of the Privy Council, however, took issue with Hong Kong courts referring to foreign and international legal materials (save, of course, English legal materials). In *Attorney General of Hong Kong* v. *Lee Kwong-kut*,[41] Lord Woolf insisted that Hong Kong courts ought to abandon the *Oakes* approach and instead determine the question of inconsistency between a statutory provision and the Hong Kong Bill of Rights Ordinance through literal examination of the statutory provision alone. A too generous approach to the interpretation of the Ordinance, His Lordship surmised, would only lead to injustice:

While the Hong Kong judiciary should be zealous in upholding an individual's rights under the Hong Kong Bill, it is also necessary to ensure that disputes as to the effect of the Bill are not allowed to get out of hand. The issues involving the Hong Kong Bill should be approached with realism and good sense, and kept in proportion. If this is not done the Bill will become a source of injustice rather than justice and it will be debased in the eyes of the public. In order to maintain the balance between the individual and the society as a whole, rigid and inflexible standards should not be imposed on the legislature's attempts to resolve the difficult and intransigent problems with which society is faced when seeking to deal with serious crime. It must be remembered that questions of policy remain primarily the responsibility of the legislature.[42]

Following Lord Woolf's demand for judicial restraint, Hong Kong courts' receptiveness to foreign and international legal materials notably subsided. In *Kwan Kong Company Limited* v. *Town Planning Board*,[43] Hong Kong High Court Justice Waung held that in interpreting the Hong Kong Bill of Rights Ordinance, recourse to foreign and international legal materials ought to be avoided if possible, as 'other domestic and international instruments are the product of very different circumstances and situations',[44] and common law rules of interpretation would suffice:

From the judgments of *Attorney General* v. *Lee Kwong-Kut* and *Ex parte Lee Kwok Hung*,[45] I can detect the common law asserting its good sense requiring that proper interpretation of the human rights Articles in the Hong Kong Bill of Rights ... be subjected to the common law rules of interpretation with its concentration on the text of the statute rather than by resorting to the complex, uncertain and huge volumes on foreign jurisprudence importing in the guise of 'autonomous meanings' foreign concepts which run contrary to the normal meaning of words under a Hong Kong statute.[46]

Recourse to European Convention on Human Rights (ECHR) jurisprudence, according to Justice Waung, was particularly inappropriate, for '[i]n Hong Kong, with our common law tradition and our special eastern situations, we are not equipped to properly understand, appreciate, analyze, apply or develop this foreign jurisprudence',[47] and 'unless something overwhelming and compelling can be shown in any particular European authority, the Hong Kong Court should very wisely decline to be seduced by the seemingly inexhaustible literature from the European Court of Human Rights'.[48] It should be noted, however, that Justice Waung's view that the Hong Kong Bill of Rights Ordinance was not a quasi-constitutional instrument and should not be given a generous interpretation was rejected on appeal.[49]

Interestingly, in *Ming Pao Newspapers* v. *Attorney General of Hong Kong*[50] which was adjudicated during the same period, both the Hong Kong Court of Appeal and the Judicial Committee of the Privy Council made use of ECHR jurisprudence. In particular, the Judicial Committee invoked the doctrine of margin of appreciation, found only in ECHR jurisprudence, to justify deference to Hong Kong's legislature; Lord Jauncey stated:

The position is accordingly this. First, the Legislative Council has decided that notwithstanding the provisions of the Bill s.30(1) is necessary to preserve the integrity of investigations into corruption. This is a policy decision that cannot be described as 'so unreasonable as to be outside the State's margin of appreciation' (*James* v. *United Kingdom* (1986) 8 EHRR 123 at 154). Indeed, it appears to their Lordships to be a decision which was eminently sensible and by no means disproportionate to the important objectives sought to be achieved. Secondly, the court with its knowledge of local conditions in Hong Kong has endorsed the decision. In these circumstances their Lordships could see no reason to interfere.[51]

As Chan points out, the Judicial Committee's recourse to the doctrine of margin of appreciation *was* inappropriate, as the doctrine developed in response to the fact that the (currently) 47 Council of Europe members states have among them differing legal, political, economic, social and cultural conditions and their national legislatures should be able to formulate policies without heavy scrutiny by the European Court of Human Rights on which members states confer jurisdiction and powers through ratification of and continued participation in the ECHR.[52] The doctrine 'is not apposite in the domestic context of a particular State'.[53] Furthermore, the margin varies depending on the particular circumstances of the case and the Strasbourg court retains the ultimate supervisory role regarding compatibility with the ECHR[54] by which Hong Kong has never been bound. How such a purely European doctrine can be extrapolated into Hong Kong was left unexplained by the Judicial Committee.

Finally, as it assumed the role of the Judicial Committee in Hong Kong as of 1 July 1997, the Hong Kong Court of Final Appeal pronounced its opinion on whether constitutional comparativism was acceptable in post-colonial Hong Kong in *Tang Siu Man* v. *HKSAR*.[55] Justice Bokhary, while acknowledging that decisions of the House of Lords ceased to have binding authority over Hong Kong courts as of 1 July 1997,[56] stated that if the reasoning of a particular decision of the House was cogent then it ought to be followed, as in order to 'develop our own jurisprudence to greatest advantage, it is appropriate for us to tap the best available wisdom of other jurisdictions'.[57] His Lordship also indicated that decisions from other common law jurisdictions were of persuasive authority as Hong Kong courts adjudicated cases.[58] In *Ng Ka Ling and others* v. *Director of Immigration*,[59] Chief Justice Li stated that the Basic Law of Hong Kong 'is an entrenched constitutional instrument to implement the unique principle of "one country, two systems". As is usual for constitutional instruments, it uses ample and general language. It is a living instrument intended to meet changing needs and circumstances.'[60]

Hong Kong courts' approaches to constitutional comparativism in specific cases

The fact that the Hong Kong Court of Final Appeal has stamped its seal of approval on constitutional comparativism in Hong Kong nevertheless does not resolve the fundamental question of whether Hong Kong courts' recourse to foreign and international legal materials in the interpretation of the Basic Law of Hong Kong and the Hong Kong Bill of Rights Ordinance is consistent, principled and, ultimately, legitimate. In other words, is it possible that Lord Woolf and Justice Waung may have been *correct* in rejecting such recourse in the interpretation of Hong Kong laws?

Most English laws and judicial decisions were adapted or followed in Hong Kong before July 1997. In two separate surveys, Wesley-Smith finds that both between 1974 and 1983 and between 1972 and 1997, approximately 74% of cases cited by Hong Kong courts were English cases while 20% were Hong Kong cases.[61] The signing of the Sino-British Joint Declaration in 1984, the enactment of the Hong Kong Bill of Rights Ordinance in 1991 and the impending handover of sovereignty in 1997 little moved the attitudes of the judiciary and the legal profession on the question of what constituted laws of Hong Kong as they continued to rely heavily on English judicial decisions.[62] Indeed, the practice of following English judicial decisions has since been endorsed by the Hong Kong Court of Final Appeal.[63] Recourse to judicial decisions from Western common law jurisdictions such as Australia, Canada, New Zealand and the United States, as well as decisions of bodies established under an international or regional agreement such as the United Nations Human Rights Committee[64] and the European Court of Human Rights,[65] also has continued.

However, in so doing Hong Kong courts generally do not take cognisance of the circumstances or the *ratio decidendi* of, or the constitutional or legislative framework governing, the particular foreign case and, ultimately, the particular foreign constitution. As South African Constitutional Court Justice Kriegler in *Bernstein* v. *Bester*[66] maintained, '[f]ar too often one sees citation by counsel of, for instance, an American judgment in support of a proposition relating to our Constitution, without any attempt to explain why it is said to be in point. Comparative study is always useful, particularly where Courts in exemplary jurisdictions have grappled with universal issues confronting us. ... But that is a far cry from blithe adoption of alien concepts or inappropriate precedents.'[67] Meanwhile, it is significant that recourse to judicial decisions from common law jurisdictions that are predominantly inhabited by non-Caucasians, such as most of the Caribbean countries, India, Malaysia and Singapore, and the mixed legal system that is South Africa's (whose constitutional jurisprudence is particularly rich and discerning) is rarely seen in a Hong Kong court judgment. In the process, foreign laws and judicial decisions may become part of the law of Hong Kong without going through and satisfying Hong Kong's legislature and legislative procedures (however undemocratic they may be – two wrongs do not make a right), while Chinese national laws in order to become part of the law of Hong Kong must be added to Annex III to the Basic Law of Hong Kong through an elaborate and politically controversial procedure.[68]

Chan has sought to explicate such incoherence on the grounds that foreign legal materials from non-Caucasian common law jurisdictions are inaccessible, unfamiliar to lawyers and judges trained in the common law, and difficult to be extrapolated into Hong Kong's legal system.[69] However, the inaccessibility or unfamiliarity of particular foreign legal materials is not sufficient or normative justification for their exclusion or for Hong Kong courts' incoherent and unprincipled approach, and Caribbean, Indian, Malaysian, Singaporean and South African legal materials are no more inaccessible than those from Australia, Canada, New Zealand and, indeed, England and Wales. Legal materials from the Caribbean countries, India, Malaysia, Singapore and South Africa also are no more unfamiliar to a Hong Kong lawyer or judge than the vast and complex jurisprudence that is the United States', where criminal law and family law, to name but two, are primarily matters for the 50 individual states constrained by specific federal laws and regulations, and where federal constitutional oversight must accord the state constitutions and laws of the 50 states deference if not exclusivity and is available and prescribed only where specific criteria and procedures are met. Lastly, the nature of things dictates that *all* foreign legal materials, including English legal materials, must suffer some difficulty in being extrapolated into another legal system.

Indeed, one must ask, why is it so alarming and adverse to Hong Kong's judicial and political autonomy if and when a provision of the Basic Law of Hong Kong, a Chinese national law that derives authority from Article 31 of the Constitution of the People's Republic of China, is interpreted by the Standing Committee of the National People's Congress – a legislative body of China of which Hong Kong now forms a part – or if and when a Chinese law is adopted in Hong Kong through amendment to Annex III to the Basic Law of Hong Kong, when all the while recourse to foreign and international legal materials, including in particular English judicial decisions, is taken as good wisdom, good practice and general enhancement of Hong Kong's laws and legal system? One may argue that as Hong Kong continues to operate under a common law legal system and with recourse to judicial decisions from other common law jurisdictions being a chief characteristic of the common law tradition, it is only natural that Hong Kong courts make use of jurisprudence and legal materials from other common law jurisdictions. The argument, however, implies that common law jurisdictions operate as a league or under a general umbrella, which is certainly not the case, and it overlooks a fact of great juridical importance: it is *Hong Kong common law* – common law is devoid of meaning if not aligned with a particular *locus* – under which Hong Kong is governed. It also ought to be noted that the common law legal system, implanted in if not imposed upon Hong Kong by the British, is favourably regarded by the local population, with 'common law' sometimes used as a demonstration slogan and synonym of Hong Kong's autonomy, primarily because China adopts the civil law legal system and anything China adopts *must* be inferior if not simply dangerous. Sin Wai Man and Chu Yiu Wai argue that Hong Kong courts' unquestioned recourse to foreign judicial decisions stems from a desire for 'linkage with the ideal Occident' – ideal in the sense that the laws and judicial reasoning adopted by Western countries must be flawless and must be preferred to those that originate locally – 'portrayed as so important that firstly the application of the standards of the Occident to local situations is viewed as unproblematic, and, secondly, the possibility of the development of a locally based common law is perceived as unimportant'.[70] Hong Kong courts' unquestioned recourse to foreign and international legal materials, this paper argues, is diminutive not only of China's sovereignty over Hong Kong, but also of Hong Kong's autonomy over itself. Indeed, as will be seen, in *Ng Kung Siu* v. *HKSAR*, a case that concerned freedom of expression, the Hong Kong Court of Final Appeal did not hesitate to premise its unanimous and concurring judgments on the basis of judicial decisions, legislation and quasi-legal materials from various civil law jurisdictions ranging from Germany, Italy, Japan, Norway to Portugal, and to completely ignore United States jurisprudence which places freedom of expression in a sacrosanct position in the American legal system and the American psyche.

Thus, constitutional comparativism as has been practised in Hong Kong suffers want of objectivity, consistency and principle, as judges and lawyers rely on their own choosing as to which jurisdictions to make use of in a particular case, and neglect or dismiss those jurisdictions with which they are not familiar or are simply in disagreement. The danger underlying such an approach lies not so much in the courts' incomprehension of or disagreement with foreign jurisdictions, as in the fact that the rule of law itself is thereby placed in a vulnerable position, as judges may now engage in an unpredictable exercise through which they self-select foreign laws and their meanings as part of the law of Hong Kong. Anthony Lester argues that only cases that will directly and most benefit one's arguments should be cited to the court.[71] Such an approach, with respect, derails not only the normative determination of the particular issue and the particular case, but also the normative development of the common law (again, Hong Kong common law) and, ultimately, the rule of law in Hong Kong. As United States Supreme Court Justice Scalia in *Roper* v. *Simmons*[72] maintained, '[t]o invoke alien law when it agrees with one's own thinking, and ignore it otherwise, is not reasoned decision-making, but sophistry.'[73]

This paper now explores how the problem revealed itself in two specific Hong Kong human rights cases, namely, *Ng Kung Siu* v. *HKSAR* and *Leung T.C. William Roy* v. *Secretary for Justice*. The two decisions are chosen as they illustrate how constitutional comparativism as has been practised in Hong Kong may be capable of both undermining and augmenting the protection of fundamental rights and freedoms guaranteed by the Basic Law of Hong Kong and the Hong Kong Bill of Rights Ordinance, and in both instances the Hong Kong courts' approaches were problematic.

Ng Kung Siu v. HKSAR

Ng Kung Siu v. *HKSAR* concerned the criminalisation of desecration of the Chinese national and Hong Kong regional flags in Hong Kong notwithstanding freedom of expression. As Raymond Wacks has noted, '[a] country's flag is a potent emblem of its nationhood. It therefore evokes both reverence and, for those who oppose the state's policies, abhorrence. For the latter of course it provides a graphic demonstration of protest. A picture of a burning flag is worth a thousand words – especially on the evening news.'[74] In their political demonstration against the lack of democracy in China and in Hong Kong, the two appellants in the case marked the Chinese national and Hong Kong regional flags with 'shame' prominently in Chinese characters.[75] They were convicted of desecrating the Chinese national flag and the Hong Kong regional flag by publicly and wilfully defiling them, contrary to section 7 of the National Flag and National Emblem Ordinance[76] and section 7 of the Regional Flag and Regional Emblem Ordinance.[77] The appellants, each sentenced to be bound over to keep the peace in his own recognisance for a period of 12 months, appealed their convictions, arguing that the provisions were inconsistent with their freedom of expression guaranteed by Article 19 of the ICCPR[78] and thus with Article 39 of the Basic Law of Hong Kong which guarantees the continued application of the Covenant in post-colonial Hong Kong (arguments on Article 27 of the Basic Law of Hong Kong[79] and Article 16 of the Hong Kong Bill of Rights Ordinance,[80] both of which guarantee freedom of expression as *a Hong Kong freedom*, were nonetheless not raised). The government, in reply, argued that restriction on freedom of expression may be justified for the protection of public order, and that it was in this case. It was noted that no violence occurred in the course of the appellants' political demonstration.[81]

The Hong Kong Court of Appeal allowed their appeals that had been directed from the Hong Kong Court of First Instance. In its brief unanimous judgment, two United States authorities on freedom of expression under the First Amendment to the United States Constitution, *Texas* v. *Johnson*[82] and *United States* v. *Eichman*,[83] where the United States Supreme Court ruled that the criminalisation of desecration of the United States national flag was inconsistent with the First Amendment, were the only judicial authorities referred to, and relied upon, substantively.[84] The court also accepted the argument of the defence that 'none of the leading common law jurisdictions criminalise the defacing of the national flag'.[85]

The Hong Kong Court of Final Appeal unanimously disagreed. The court found that the criminalisation of desecration of the Chinese national and Hong Kong regional flags in Hong Kong 'is not a wide restriction of the freedom of expression. It is a limited one. It bans one mode of expressing whatever the message the person concerned may wish to express, that is the mode of desecrating the flags. It does not interfere with the person's freedom to express the same message by other modes.'[86] (Does freedom of expression not encompass freedom to choose *the* expression and *how*?)

Interestingly, in its unanimous judgment the court entirely cast aside United States jurisprudence in allowing the government's appeal and restoring the convictions of the appellants, despite the sacrosanct importance of freedom of expression in the American legal system which the Hong Kong Court of Appeal had acknowledged. Instead, the court referred only to one foreign decision, an advisory opinion by the Inter-American Court of Human Rights under the American Convention on Human Rights,[87] on the meaning of 'laws' in the context of restrictions on rights and freedoms.[88]

Justice Bokhary in his concurring opinion was less reserved. His Lordship first referred to the Australian High Court decision in *Levy* v. *Victoria*[89] – the circumstances of which

His Lordship admitted were different, as the Australian court ruled that restrictions on the appellant's entry into a duck-shooting area in order to protest against laws permitting the shooting of birds and the illegal shooting of protected species did not contravene freedom of expression – to support his view that the criminalisation of desecration of the Chinese national and Hong Kong regional flags in Hong Kong affected only the mode and not the substance of freedom of expression.[90] His Lordship then addressed the question of which foreign judicial decisions should *not* be followed, and they were, no less, the two United States Supreme Court decisions in *Texas* v. *Johnson* and *United States* v. *Eichman* which the Hong Kong Court of Appeal had found dispositive of the issue and which the Hong Kong Court of Final Appeal in its unanimous judgment entirely ignored. Justice Bokhary found that neither of the American decisions was unanimously decided as each was decided by a bare majority of five to four[91] (which, itself, showed unfamiliarity with United States Supreme Court jurisprudence, that many cases before it were decided by a five-to-four majority). Adamant that laws criminalising desecration of the Chinese national and Hong Kong regional flags in Hong Kong were not incompatible with freedom of expression and the ICCPR, *ipso facto* because many jurisdictions that were signatories to the Covenant also had such laws, His Lordship discerned that instead of the two American authorities, Hong Kong courts should look to decisions 'upholding the constitutionality of laws which protect the national flag and render breaches punishable'.[92] His Lordship found a German decision and an Italian one to be particularly useful, as both Germany and Italy were signatories to the ICCPR and their laws criminalising desecration of the national flag were upheld by Germany's Federal Constitutional Court and Italy's Supreme Court of Cassation, although their relevant contexts, laws or judicial reasoning were not at all examined in Justice Bokhary's concurring opinion.[93] His Lordship indicated that further guidance may be obtained by looking at Norway, '*about which we have been supplied information*'[94] and which, according to His Lordship, had no law criminalising desecration of the Norwegian national flag but one criminalising public insult to foreign flags,[95] which His Lordship found to be the same in Japan.[96] Lastly, His Lordship relied on a letter of the Procurator-General of Portugal on the relevant law of Portugal pointing to criminalisation.[97] His Lordship took comfort in the fact that the Portuguese law '[appeared] to criminalize a considerable number of things which our own flag and emblem protection laws do not criminalize'.[98] Thus, His Lordship concluded, the criminalisation of desecration of the Chinese national and Hong Kong regional flags in Hong Kong was not inconsistent with freedom of expression, particularly as 'the only restriction placed is against the desecration of objects which hardly anyone would dream of desecrating even if there was no law against it'[99] – which was patently untrue, for otherwise there would have been no need for such legislative provisions to be enacted so urgently by the Provisional Legislative Council of Hong Kong, the formation of which was itself a constitutional controversy,[100] or for the prosecutions in question. It is also precisely the meaning of freedom of expression that one may choose to *not* desecrate the Chinese national and Hong Kong regional flags.

Why should Hong Kong laws on a matter that threatened freedom of expression in the infancy of the Hong Kong Special Administrative Region and its ultimate rule by China, a country known to suppress such a freedom, reflect the particular opinions of the Germans, Italians, Norwegians, Japanese and Portuguese, and not the vast and vigorous jurisprudence of the United States? What did the other 180 or so countries have to say about their national flags? Also, it could not have escaped Justice Bokhary's attention that Germany, Italy, Norway, Japan and Portugal are all civil law and not common law jurisdictions. As His Lordship referred to Norway and Japan on their criminalisation of desecration of foreign flags but not of national flags, Justice Bokhary failed to explain why that was the case. As for the Portuguese law supported by a letter of the Procurator-General of Portugal, the fact that it was more wide-ranging in its criminalisation of desecration of the national flag did not at all answer and was wholly irrelevant to the constitutionality of the criminalisation in Hong Kong. Furthermore, the notion that just because a country is a signatory to the ICCPR its laws must be compatible with it rids violation of an international human rights treaty of its very meaning. Lastly, even if German, Italian, Norwegian, Japanese and Portuguese laws on the matter were compatible with the ICCPR, Hong Kong courts must, and failed to, explain why and how similar Hong Kong laws were equally reconcilable, as symmetry in dissimilar contexts may and does lead to dissimilar outcomes.

Instead of following a handful of foreign laws and judicial decisions (let alone quasi-legal materials) without proper inquiry as to why they were chosen and why others were not, and why and how they might be relevant in justifying the criminalisation of desecration of the Chinese national and Hong Kong regional flags within the confines of freedom of expression in Hong Kong, Hong Kong courts ought to have engaged in their own analysis as to why, as a matter of Hong Kong law, such criminalisation was justified in Hong Kong, particularly given Hong Kong's unique circumstances as a special administrative region of China and, against this context, its legislative and (China's) treaty commitments to freedom of expression. The courts may, indeed must, explain why and how particular foreign and international legal materials may and may not be relevant, and explore whether those particular foreign and international legal materials were indicative of a normative consensus or constituted persuasive reasoning. Finally, the courts ought to have taken the opportunity to elucidate judicially whether and how the ICCPR may continue to have an impact on Hong Kong laws as a result of Article 39 of the Basic Law of Hong Kong which guarantees the continued application of the Covenant in post-colonial Hong Kong.

Leung T.C. William Roy v. *Secretary for Justice*

Leung T.C. William Roy v. *Secretary for Justice* was an application for judicial review challenging the higher age of consent for male/male sexual activity in the light of an individual's right of equality and his right to privacy. The applicant, a 20-year-old man self-identified as a homosexual since puberty, alleged that sections 118C,[101] 118F(2)(a),[102] 118H[103] and 118J(2)(a)[104] of the Crimes Ordinance discriminatorily impinged upon his ability to form and develop a mutually consensual and loving relationship with another man as he was subjected to the threat of criminal prosecution and imprisonment for expressing his affection through sexual intimacy and intercourse.[105] Thus, although hitherto not the subject of any criminal prosecution,[106] the applicant argued that the continuing existence of the four legislative provisions violated his right to privacy under Article 29 of the Basic Law of Hong Kong and Article 14 of the Hong Kong Bill of Rights Ordinance and constituted discrimination against him on grounds of sexual orientation in violation of his right of equality under Article 25 of the Basic Law of Hong Kong and Article 22 of the Ordinance.[107]

After concluding that the act of buggery between males was a form of sexual intercourse[108] and elucidating the equality guarantees in Hong Kong,[109] the Hong Kong Court of First Instance stated that '[t]here can be no doubt that gay men have been historically disadvantaged by being perceived to belong to a group marked by stereotyped capacities. The Nazis, for example, had no difficulty in recognising homosexuals as a class, the status being bestowed in order to degrade them as a class. Much of our human rights jurisprudence today springs from the need to protect against such discrimination.'[110]

The court referred to the views of the United Nations Human Rights Committee in *Toonen* v. *Australia*[111] and the judgment of the European Court of Human Rights in *Salguiero da Silva Mouta* v. *Portugal*, where it was concluded, respectively, that Articles 2(1) and 26 of the ICCPR and Article 14 of the ECHR protected an individual against discrimination on grounds of sexual orientation. The court, thus, held that Article 22 of the Hong Kong Bill of Rights Ordinance similarly protected against discrimination on grounds of sexual orientation.[112] In establishing jurisdiction over the matter, the court took note of the Hong Kong Court of Final Appeal decision in *Ng Ka Ling*, where the highest court stated that as 'a matter of obligation, not of discretion' the judiciary must examine whether a particular legislative provision in Hong Kong alleged to violate a fundamental right or freedom was compatible with the Basic Law of Hong Kong or the Hong Kong Bill of Rights Ordinance and, if not, to have it declared unconstitutional and invalid to the extent of its inconsistency,[113] and referred to Article 35(1) of the Basic Law of Hong Kong which states that 'Hong Kong residents shall have the right to . . . access to the courts . . . for timely protection of their lawful rights and interests . . . and to judicial remedies.'[114] Interestingly, instead of referring to the European Court of Human Rights decision in *Norris* v. *Ireland*[115] as the Hong Kong Court of Appeal subsequently did,[116] the court referred to the decision of the European Court of Justice in *Union de Pequerios Agricultores* v. *Council of the European Union*,[117] alongside a number of English, one Canadian and one South African decisions on the general nature of judicial review,[118] to conclude that the continuing existence of the four legislative provisions under challenge and their continuing effect on the applicant was sufficient to enable him to have the necessary *locus standi* to challenge the provisions and have his application for judicial review entertained.[119]

As the government conceded the unconstitutionality of sections 118F(2)(a), 118H and 118J(2)(a) of the Crimes Ordinance,[120] the court indicated that 'it is important, in my opinion, to have regard not to each of the sections challenged by the applicant in isolation but instead to view them together as a legislative scheme'.[121] In finding that section 118C discriminatorily targeted gay men and infringed their right of equality, the court relied[122] particularly on the Ontario Court of Appeal decision in *R.* v. *M. (C.)*.[123] The Hong Kong court also relied on the European Commission of Human Rights decision in *Sutherland* v. *United Kingdom*[124] (although it mistook the decision as 'a watershed case in the European Community'[125] which should in fact be the Council of Europe) and held that '[d]enying persons of a minority class the right to sexual expression in the only way available to them, even if that way is denied to all, remains discriminatory when persons of a majority class are permitted the right to sexual expression in a way natural to them. During the course of submissions, it was described as "disguised discrimination". It is, I think, an apt description. It is disguised discrimination founded on a single base: sexual orientation.'[126] Thus, the court held, the four provisions of the Crimes Ordinance under challenge constituted grave and continuing interference with the applicant's private life and violated his right of equality.[127] In September 2006, the Hong Kong Court of Appeal unanimously upheld the judgment of the Hong Kong Court of First Instance.[128] The government did not lodge a further appeal to the Hong Kong Court of Final Appeal within the prescribed time limit. However, although invalidated by the courts, the four provisions of the Crimes Ordinance have not yet been repealed by legislature and continue to remain on the statute book.

While it is commendable that both the Hong Kong Court of First Instance and the Hong Kong Court of Appeal embraced constitutional protection of equality in Hong Kong on grounds of sexual orientation, it must be pointed out that while the courts relied on Canadian and European judicial decisions, they failed to take cognisance of the laws and judicial decisions of more than 100 jurisdictions that condemned consensual same-sex sexual activity (Iran to public hanging and Saudi Arabia to public decapitation). As Alford argues:

> If at its bottom [constitutional comparativism] is a process-oriented approach, it will sacrifice core individual rights for the sake of thoroughgoing comparative methodology. ... If on the other hand, a comparative theory is at its essence a substantive ideal, it must illuminate the selective nature of that ideal. That is, it must explain why certain universally recognized norms are constitutionally cognizable, while other foreign practices that are less solicitous to individual rights are not. If international norms are the substantive ideal without such distinctions, then a convincing case must be made not only for internalizing those norms to enhance individual rights, but also for internalizing those norms to diminish certain rights that are currently enjoyed at an enhanced level...[129]

In particular, as the government referred to the case of Zimbabwe and a decision of the Supreme Court of Zimbabwe to support its argument that the judiciary should defer to the legislature in matters of social policy, the Hong Kong Court of First Instance merely noted that no evidence was laid to demonstrate 'what today − if it can be ascertained − is the prevailing view of the Hong Kong community towards matters of homosexual activity carried out consensually and in private. In a cosmopolitan society like Hong Kong "social norms and values" change, often rapidly.'[130] Was the court suggesting then that if the Hong Kong community did predominantly view homosexuality and sexual minorities along the same lines as Zimbabweans (or, more accurately, what the Zimbabwean government purported to be *the* Zimbabwean view[131]), the applicant's constitutional right of equality and his constitutional right to privacy under the Basic Law of Hong Kong and the Hong Kong Bill of Rights Ordinance should no longer be protected? The court, this paper argues, ought to have explained whether and why, as a matter of Hong Kong law, protection provided for in the Basic Law of Hong Kong and the Hong Kong Bill of Rights Ordinance against discrimination must encompass protection against sexual orientation discrimination irrespective of the views of the Hong Kong general public. Instead, what the court was saying amounted in essence to this: 'We have no idea what Hong Kong people think, and frankly we don't care, as we must agree with the Canadians and Europeans (and ignore the Zimbabweans, who are just not quite the same as us to warrant our attention).'

With English courts out of the picture (the issue was decided by Parliament in Westminster through legislation in 2000 and 2003[132]), why, one ought to ask, should an Ontario appellate court decision (*R. v. M. (C.)*), which did not receive subsequent scrutiny by the Supreme Court of Canada, on a provision of the Canadian Charter of Rights and Freedoms which unlike the Hong Kong Bill of Rights Ordinance is not premised upon and does not purport to implement the ICCPR, a European Court of Human Rights decision under the ECHR (*Salguiero da Silva Mouta*) to which Hong Kong was not a party, or a European Commission of Human Rights decision under the ECHR which was subsequently settled out of court (*Sutherland*) carry such influential, in this case determinative, weight in, indeed over, Hong Kong judicial reasoning? Either out of pure overlooking or in order to avoid having to engage in a similar vigorous debate and face similar criticism in terms of comparative methodology, both Hong Kong courts sidestepped a discussion of the United States Supreme Court case of *Lawrence* v. *Texas*[133] decided (by a 6−3 majority) only two years before. In addition, the Hong Kong Court of First Instance's reliance on a decision by the European Court of Justice which is not based on and does not enforce a human rights treaty but a series of treaties aiming solely at European economic integration (even if the European Union has subsequently encompassed a broader political integration 'founded on the principles of liberty, democracy, respect for human rights and fundamental freedoms, and the rule of law'[134]) – notwithstanding the availability of more suitable authorities such as the European Court of Human Rights decision in *Norris* v. *Ireland* that over almost identical facts and arguments held in favour of jurisdiction – evidenced only too clearly Hong Kong courts' incoherent and unprincipled, if not also uninformed, approach to foreign and international legal materials when interpreting the Basic Law of Hong Kong and the Hong Kong Bill of Rights Ordinance. Last but not least, considering the pervasive disdain in Hong Kong for Chinese laws, for reasons noted above, it was not surprising that neither the Hong Kong Court of First Instance nor the Hong Kong Court of Appeal examined the legal status in China of homosexuality and equality and privacy rights in the context of sexual orientation – which, considering that in China there were no laws at all against homosexuality,[135] might well have been dispositive of the case summarily in favour of the applicant.

Again, instead of blindly following self-selected foreign and international legal materials, the Hong Kong courts ought to have engaged in their own analysis as to why, as a matter of Hong Kong law, protection against discrimination in Hong Kong must encompass protection against sexual orientation discrimination, and why and how particular foreign and international legal materials may and may not be relevant. As part of sound constitutional comparativism and judicial reasoning, the courts must provide reasons, under and in the context of Hong Kong laws, for their reflexive application of laws and judicial decisions of Western countries and their reflexive neglect or dismissal of legal materials from countries such as Zimbabwe. Finally, of course, the courts ought to have explored the disparity between Hong Kong and Chinese laws in respect of consensual male/male sexual activity to discern whether and how colonial laws against an individual on the basis of sexual orientation now stood in post-colonial Hong Kong. As Michael Ramsey maintains, if the ultimate commonality among different jurisdictions lies not in the interpretation of constitutional texts but in the determination of whether criminalisation of or a discriminatory age of consent for consensual same-sex sexual activity is morally and socially justifiable, then 'the intuitive authority of the [European Court of Human Rights], as compared to billions of individuals and entities worldwide that might also have a philosophical opinion on the matter, is greatly diminished. The [European Court of Human Rights], as a court, may be of persuasive source of *legal* reasoning, but it is not necessarily a better moral and social decision maker than the multitude whose opinions we are not invited to study.'[136] The argument that jurisprudence from developing countries carries less value in an affluent and cosmopolitan jurisdiction such as Hong Kong is jurisprudentially unsound, as 'this seems to revive the discredited nineteenth-century concept of "civilized" and "uncivilized" nations, and subconsciously to endorse a Eurocentrism that would be indefensible if argued overtly'.[137] Indeed, without even the most basic civil right of universal suffrage, by which even the government of such a politically and economically unstable jurisdiction as Zimbabwe is formally elected, is Hong Kong really so developed?

Conclusion

This paper does not agree with Lord Woolf's or Justice Waung's wholesale dismissal of constitutional comparativism in the interpretation of the Hong Kong Bill of Rights Ordinance and, by extension, the Basic Law of Hong Kong, as constitutional comparativism has its intrinsic values and advantages. In particular, constitutional comparativism offers Hong Kong courts and jurists, as well as the Hong Kong people and government, informed reflection on and understanding of Hong Kong laws and society and how post-colonial Hong Kong's legal, political and social systems may proceed.

However, this paper also does not agree with Hong Kong courts' approach hitherto to constitutional comparativism. Indeed, it is a cause for worry that Hong Kong courts' recourse to foreign and international legal materials – in particular their almost automatic application of English judicial decisions – is incoherent and unprincipled. Furthermore, the fact that an English court must now take into account ECHR jurisprudence in its decision when an ECHR right is involved[138] means that a Hong Kong court may on one occasion rely on an English judicial decision because it was enlightened by ECHR jurisprudence and yet on another occasion refuse to follow an English judicial decision because it was tainted by jurisprudence under a treaty by which Hong Kong has never been bound. As a result, Hong Kong laws are rendered unpredictable, and the rule of law in Hong Kong undermined. It is trite to say that '[a] constitutional theory that advances the rule of law promotes legal certainty, efficacy, stability, supremacy, and impartiality.'[139] Richard Posner, a judge of the United States Court of Appeals for the Seventh Circuit, warns extra-judicially of constitutional comparativism as it invites individual judges to 'troll deeply in the world's *corpus juris*' which they may then use to support an essentially politically desired or otherwise pre-determined outcome.[140] Such an approach does not advance the rule of law or protection of fundamental rights and freedoms, for '[a] comparative theory must be able to make the case as to why its preferred set of rights are superior to other sets of rights, and the theory must do so consonant with political democracy and the rule of law.'[141] Otherwise, all sets of rights, depending on the views of particular judges and their choice of foreign authorities, will be at risk, at any time, of disfavour and demise.

Perhaps Hong Kong courts may desire to (be seen to) lay the same kind of emphasis as United States Supreme Court Justice O'Connor did on a 'good impression', that recourse to foreign and international legal materials 'may not only enrich our own country's decisions; it will create that all-important good impression. When [Hong Kong] courts are seen to be cognizant of other judicial systems, our ability to act as a rule-of-law model for other nations [(read: China)] will be enhanced.'[142] While it is understandable that Hong Kong courts may endeavour to show to the Hong Kong people and overseas audiences that, despite the transfer of sovereignty, they remain an independent and enlightened judiciary that observes and guarantees the rule of law in Hong Kong, the irony is that by seeking to give such a 'good impression' through incoherent and unprincipled recourse to foreign and international legal materials, *they* are undermining the rule of law in Hong Kong. While it is equally understandable that Hong Kong courts may endeavour to differentiate Hong Kong's laws and legal system as much as possible from those of China in order to avoid the ultimate amalgamation (including amalgamation in appearance) between Hong Kong and Chinese laws and legal systems, recourse to foreign and international legal materials without proper inquiry and only on the supposed basis that they enlighten Hong Kong laws *simpliciter* is not justified. Such recourse is diminutive not only of China's sovereignty over Hong Kong, but also of Hong Kong's autonomy over itself.

'[T]he most constructive use of comparative constitutional law', Seth Kreimer discerns, 'is not as an alternative store of constitutional software, but a challenge to us to reexamine the resources in our own system.'[143] As Justice O'Connor in the United States Supreme Court case of *Planned Parenthood of Southeastern Pennsylvania* v. *Casey*[144] maintained, '[t]he Court's power lies ... in its legitimacy, a product of substance and perception that shows itself in the people's acceptance of the Judiciary as fit to determine what the Nation's law means and to declare what it demands. ... the Court's legitimacy depends on making legally principled decisions under circumstances in which their principled character is sufficiently plausible to be accepted by the Nation.'[145] As time goes on and as China continues to influence Hong Kong thinking (it would be naïve to think that it is not doing so), Hong Kong courts in the future may well decide to resort to constitutional comparativism *against* protection of fundamental rights and freedoms in Hong Kong – if they have not already done so (as in *Ng Kung Siu*). Constitutional comparativism as has been practised in Hong Kong, thus, 'threatens to undermine the integrity of both constitutional law and comparative law'[146] in Hong Kong.

Acknowledgements

I wish to thank Asia-Pacific College of Diplomacy, Australian National University, for inviting me as a Visiting Fellow between September and December 2006, during which I was able to attend Vicki Jackson's Geoffrey Sawer Lecture 'Transnational Challenges to Constitutional Law: Convergence, Resistance, Engagement' (2 November 2006) and to conduct research for this paper which her lecture inspired. I am much grateful also to Faculty of Law, University of Ottawa; Asian Institute, Munk Centre for International Studies, University of Toronto; and Institut für Öffentliches Recht, Albert-Ludwigs-Universität Freiburg, for enabling the writing of this paper during my extended academic visits in 2007; to Simon Evans, Michael Palmer, and Paul Serfaty for their valuable comments on earlier versions of this paper; to Eileen Lam and Susanne Nagel for their administrative assistance; and to Eric Heinze and School of Law, Queen Mary, University of London, for enabling my views to be tested in an engaging guest seminar (16 April 2008). Any error or omission in this paper is mine alone.

Notes

1. Basic Law of the Hong Kong Special Administrative Region of the People's Republic of China, 29 ILM 1519 (1990), adopted by the Seventh National People's Congress at its Third Session on 4 April 1990 in pursuance of the 1984 Joint Declaration of the Government of the United Kingdom of Great Britain and Northern Ireland and the Government of the People's Republic of China on the Question of Hong Kong, 23 ILM 1366 (1984). Article 31 of the Constitution of the People's Republic of China states that '[t]he state may establish special administrative regions when necessary. The systems to be instituted in special administrative regions shall be prescribed by law enacted by the National People's Congress in the light of the specific conditions.'
2. Stephen Breyer, 'Keynote Address', *American Society of International Law Proceedings* 97 (2003): 265, 265, quoting Ruth Bader Ginsburg and Deborah Jones Merritt, 'Affirmative Action: An International Human Rights Dialogue', *Cardozo Law Review* 21 (1999): 253, 282.
3. Wiktor Osiatynski, 'Paradoxes of Constitutional Borrowing', *International Journal of Constitutional Law* 1 (2003): 244, 248.
4. Roger P. Alford, 'In Search of a Theory for Constitutional Comparativism', *UCLA Law Review* 52 (2005): 639, 644.
5. Ibid., 641.
6. [1999] 1 HKLRD 783 (Hong Kong Court of Appeal); [1999] 3 HKLRD 907 (Hong Kong Court of Final Appeal).
7. [2005] 3 HKLRD 657 (Hong Kong Court of First Instance); [2006] 4 HKLRD 211 (Hong Kong Court of Appeal).
8. Basic Law of Hong Kong, Preamble.
9. Ibid., Art. 2.
10. Ibid., Art. 5.
11. Ibid., Art. 8.
12. Ibid., Art. 9.
13. Ibid., Arts 24–41.
14. Adopted and opened for signature, ratification and accession by UN GA Res. 2200A(XXI) of 16 December 1966 and entered into force on 23 March 1976.
15. Adopted and opened for signature, ratification and accession by UN GA Res. 2200A(XXI) of 16 December 1966 and entered into force on 3 January 1976.

16. Article 39 of the Basic Law of Hong Kong states that '[t]he provisions of the International Covenant on Civil and Political Rights, the International Covenant on Economic, Social and Cultural Rights, and international labour conventions as applied to Hong Kong shall remain in force and shall be implemented through the laws of the Hong Kong Special Administrative Region. The rights and freedoms enjoyed by Hong Kong residents shall not be restricted unless as prescribed by law. Such restrictions shall not contravene the provisions of the preceding paragraph of this Article.'

17. Ibid., Art. 81.

18. Ibid., Art. 82.

19. Ibid.

20. Ibid., Art. 158.

21. Hong Kong Bill of Rights Ordinance (Cap. 383), s. 2(3).

22. Yash Ghai, 'Sentinels of Liberty or Sheep in Woolf's Clothing? Judicial Politics and the Hong Kong Bill of Rights', *Modern Law Review* 60 (1997): 459, 461.

23. Article 160 of the Basic Law of Hong Kong states that '[u]pon the establishment of the Hong Kong Special Administrative Region, the laws previously in force in Hong Kong shall be adopted as laws of the Region except for those which the Standing Committee of the National People's Congress declares to be in contravention of this Law. If any laws are later discovered to be in contravention of this Law, they shall be amended or cease to have force in accordance with the procedure as prescribed by this Law. Documents, certificates, contracts, and rights and obligations valid under the laws previously in force in Hong Kong shall continue to be valid and be recognized and protected by the Hong Kong Special Administrative Region, provided that they do not contravene this Law.' By Decision of the Standing Committee of the National People's Congress on the Treatment of the Laws Previously in Force in Hong Kong in Accordance with Article 160 of the Basic Law of the Hong Kong Special Administrative Region of the People's Republic of China (Cap. 2206), adopted at the 24th Session of the Standing Committee of the Eighth National People's Congress on 23 February 1997, the following provisions of the Hong Kong Bill of Rights Ordinance were not adopted as part of the law of the Hong Kong Special Administrative Region as of 1 July 1997:

> Section 2(3): In interpreting and applying this Ordinance, regard shall be had to the fact that the purpose of this Ordinance is to provide for the incorporation into the law of Hong Kong of provisions of the International Covenant on Civil and Political Rights as applied to Hong Kong, and for ancillary and connected matters.
> Section 3(1): All pre-existing legislation that admits of a construction consistent with this Ordinance shall be given such a construction.
> Section 3(2): All pre-existing legislation that does not admit of a construction consistent with this Ordinance is, to the extent of the inconsistency, repealed.
> Section 4: All legislation enacted on or after the commencement date shall, to the extent that it admits of such a construction, be constructed so as to be consistent with the International Covenant on Civil and Political Rights as applied to Hong Kong.

24. Yash Ghai, 'The Continuity of Laws and Legal Rights and Obligations in the SAR', *Hong Kong Law Journal* 27 (1997): 136; Peter Wesley-Smith, 'Maintenance of the Bill of Rights', *Hong Kong Law Journal* 27 (1997): 15; Johannes Chan, 'The Status of the Bill of Rights in the Hong Kong Special Administrative Region', *Hong Kong Law Journal* 28 (1998): 152.

25. Chan, 'Status of the Bill of Rights', 152–4.

26. Ghai, 'Sentinels of Liberty or Sheep in Woolf's Clothing?', 460.

27. Norman J. Miners, *The Government and Politics of Hong Kong*, 5th edn (Hong Kong: Oxford University Press, 1991), 27.

28. Ghai, 'Sentinels of Liberty or Sheep in Woolf's Clothing?', 461.

29. See text in note 23 above.

30. [1992] 1 HKCLR 127.

31. Ibid., per Silke V.-P., 141.

32. Ibid.

33. [1986] 1 SCR 103.

34. Canadian Charter of Rights and Freedoms (Part I, Constitution Act 1982, S.C. 1982, c. 79; Canada Act 1982, c. 11 [United Kingdom]).

35.   *Oakes*, per Dickson C.J., 138–9.
36.   Ghai, 'Sentinels of Liberty or Sheep in Woolf's Clothing?', 468.
37.   Section 33 of the Canadian Charter of Rights and Freedoms states that '(1) Parliament or the legislature of a province may expressly declare in an Act of Parliament or of the legislature, as the case may be, that the Act or a provision thereof shall operate notwithstanding a provision included in section 2 or sections 7 to 15 of this *Charter*. (2) An Act or a provision of an Act in respect of which a declaration made under this section is in effect shall have such operation as it would have but for the provision of this *Charter* referred to in the declaration. (3) A declaration made under subsection (1) shall cease to have effect five years after it comes into force or on such earlier dates as may be specified in the declaration. (4) Parliament or the legislature of a province may re-enact a declaration made under subsection (1). (5) Subsection (3) applies in respect of re-enactment made under subsection (4).'
38.   Section 1, ibid., states that '[t]he *Canadian Charter of Rights and Freedoms* guarantees the rights and freedoms set out in it subject only to such reasonable limits prescribed by law as can be demonstrably justified in a free and democratic society.'
39.   David Beatty, 'The Canadian Charter of Rights: Lessons and Laments', *Modern Law Review* 60 (1997): 481, 483.
40.   For a discussion of Hong Kong's political autonomy and its struggle for universal suffrage, see Phil C.W. Chan, 'Hong Kong's Political Autonomy and its Continuing Struggle for Universal Suffrage', *Singapore Journal of Legal Studies* (2006): 285.
41.   [1993] 3 HKPLR 72.
42.   Ibid., per Lord Woolf, 100.
43.   [1995] 5 HKPLR 261 (Hong Kong High Court); [1996] 6 HKPLR 237 (Hong Kong Court of Appeal).
44.   Ibid., per Waung J., 300 (Hong Kong High Court).
45.   *R.* v. *Securities and Futures Commission*, ex parte *Lee Kwok Hung* [1993] 3 HKPLR 39 (Hong Kong Court of Appeal).
46.   *Kwan Kong Company Limited*, 300 (Hong Kong High Court).
47.   Ibid., 315.
48.   Ibid., 316.
49.   *Kwan Kong Company Limited*, per Litton V.-P., paras 43–4 (Hong Kong Court of Appeal).
50.   [1995] 5 HKPLR 13 (Hong Kong Court of Appeal); [1996] 6 HKPLR 103 (Judicial Committee of the Privy Council).
51.   Ibid., per Lord Jauncey, 111–12 (Judicial Committee of the Privy Council).
52.   Johannes M.M. Chan, 'Hong Kong's Bill of Rights: Its Reception of and Contribution to International and Comparative Jurisprudence', *International and Comparative Law Quarterly* 47 (1998): 306, 319.
53.   Ibid.
54.   *Sunday Times* v. *United Kingdom* (1979) 2 EHRR 245.
55.   [1998] 1 HKLRD 350.
56.   Ibid., per Bokhary P.J., 378.
57.   Ibid., 377.
58.   Ibid.
59.   *Ng Ka Ling (an infant)* v. *Director of Immigration, Tsui Kuen Nang* v. *Director of Immigration, Director of Immigration* v. *Cheung Lai Wah (an infant)* [1999] 1 HKC 291.
60.   Ibid., per Li C.J., 339.
61.   Peter Wesley-Smith, 'The Legal System, the Constitution, and the Future of Hong Kong', *Hong Kong Law Journal* 14 (1984): 137; Peter Wesley-Smith, 'The Geographical Sources of Hong Kong Law', *Hong Kong Law Journal* 29 (1999): 1.
62.   Wesley-Smith, 'The Geographical Sources of Hong Kong Law', 1.
63.   *Tang Siu Man* v. *HKSAR* [1998] 1 HKLRD 350.
64.   On the powers and functions of the United Nations Human Rights Committee, see ICCPR, Arts 28–45.
65.   Convention for the Protection of Human Rights and Fundamental Freedoms (ETS No. 005), opened for signature on 4 November 1950 and entered into force on 3 September 1953. The Convention was amended by Protocol No. 11 (ETS No. 155) to the Convention, opened for signature on 11 May 1994 and entered into force on 1 November 1998, to the effect that the supervisory mechanism consisting of a European Court of Human Rights and

a European Commission of Human Rights be replaced with a single and permanent European Court of Human Rights. For an account of the theory and practice of the European Convention on Human Rights, see P. van Dijk and G.J.H. van Hoof, *Theory and Practice of the European Convention on Human Rights*, 3rd edn (The Hague: Kluwer, 1998).

66.   1996 (2) SA 751.
67.   Ibid., per Kriegler J., para. 133.
68.   See Basic Law of Hong Kong, Art. 18 and Annex III.
69.   Chan, 'Hong Kong's Bill of Rights', 309.
70.   Sin Wai Man and Chu Yiu Wai, 'Whose Rule of Law? Rethinking (Post-)Colonial Legal Culture in Hong Kong', *Social & Legal Studies* 7 (1998): 143, 151.
71.   Anthony Lester, 'Human Rights Advocacy in Practice', in *The Hong Kong Bill of Rights: A Comparative Approach*, ed. Johannes Chan and Yash Ghai (Hong Kong: Butterworths Asia, 1993), 201, 208–10.
72.   125 S Ct 1183 (2005).
73.   Ibid., per Scalia J., 1228.
74.   Raymond Wacks, 'Our Flagging Rights', *Hong Kong Law Journal* 30 (2000): 1, 1.
75.   *Ng Kung Siu*, per Stuart-Moore J.A., 786 (Hong Kong Court of Appeal).
76.   Section 7 of the National Flag and National Emblem Ordinance (Cap. 2401) states that '[a] person who desecrates the national flag or national emblem by publicly and wilfully burning, mutilating, scrawling on, defiling or trampling on it commits an offence and is liable on conviction to a fine at level 5 and to imprisonment for 3 years.'
77.   Section 7 of the Regional Flag and Regional Emblem Ordinance (Cap. 2602) states that '[a] person who desecrates the regional flag or regional emblem by publicly and wilfully burning, mutilating, scrawling on, defiling or trampling on it commits an offence and is liable (a) on conviction on indictment to a fine at level 5 and to imprisonment for 3 years; and (b) on summary conviction to a fine at level 3 and to imprisonment for 1 year.'
78.   Article 19(2) of the ICCPR states that '[e]veryone shall have the right to freedom of expression; this right shall include freedom to seek, receive and impart information and ideas of all kinds, regardless of frontiers, either orally, in writing or in print, in the form of art, or through any other media of his choice.' Freedom of expression, however, may be restricted, as Article 19(3), ibid., states that '[t]he exercise of the rights provided for in paragraph (2) of this article carries with it special duties and responsibilities. It may therefore be subject to certain restrictions, but these shall only be such as are provided by law and are necessary (a) for respect of the rights or reputations of others; (b) for the protection of national security or of public order (ordre public), or of public health or morals.'
79.   Article 27 of the Basic Law of Hong Kong states that 'Hong Kong residents shall have freedom of speech, of the press and of publication; freedom of association, of assembly, of procession and of demonstration; and the right and freedom to form and join trade unions, and to strike.'
80.   Paragraphs (2) and (3) of Article 16 of the Hong Kong Bill of Rights Ordinance are worded identically to paragraphs (2) and (3) of Article 19 of the ICCPR quoted in note 78 above.
81.   *Ng Kung Siu*, per Stuart-Moore J.A., 786 (Hong Kong Court of Appeal).
82.   491 US 397 (1989).
83.   496 US 310 (1990).
84.   *Ng Kung Siu*, per Stuart-Moore J.A., 791 (Hong Kong Court of Appeal).
85.   Ibid.
86.   *Ng Kung Siu*, per Li C.J., 921 (Hong Kong Court of Final Appeal).
87.   On the powers and functions of the Inter-American Court of Human Rights based in San José, Costa Rica, see American Convention on Human Rights, signed at San José on 22 November 1969 and entered into force on 18 July 1978, Arts 33(b) and 52–69.
88.   *Ng Kung Siu*, per Li C.J., 924–5 (Hong Kong Court of Final Appeal).
89.   (1997) 189 CLR 579.
90.   *Ng Kung Siu*, per Bokhary P.J., 929–30 (Hong Kong Court of Final Appeal).
91.   Ibid., 930.
92.   Ibid., 931.
93.   Ibid.
94.   Ibid. (emphasis added).
95.   Ibid.
96.   Ibid.

97. Ibid.
98. Ibid., 932.
99. Ibid., 933.
100. For a discussion of the constitutional controversy surrounding the Provisional Legislative Council of Hong Kong, see Johannes M.M. Chan, 'The Jurisdiction and Legality of the Provisional Legislative Council', *Hong Kong Law Journal* 27 (1999): 374.
101. Section 118C of the Crimes Ordinance (Cap. 200) states that '[a] man who (a) commits buggery with a man under the age of 21; or (b) being under the age of 21 commits buggery with another man, shall be guilty of an offence and shall be liable on conviction on indictment to imprisonment for life.'
102. Section 118F(1), ibid., states that '[a] man who commits buggery with another man otherwise than in private shall be guilty of an offence and shall be liable on conviction on indictment to imprisonment for 5 years.' Section 118F(2) states that '[a]n act which would otherwise be treated for the purposes of this section as being done in private shall not be so treated if done (a) when more than 2 persons take part or are present; or (b) in a lavatory or bathhouse to which the public have or are permitted to have access, whether on payment or otherwise.'
103. Section 118H, ibid., states that '[a] man who (a) commits an act of gross indecency with a man under the age of 21; or (b) being under the age of 21 commits an act of gross indecency with another man, shall be guilty of an offence and shall be liable on conviction on indictment to imprisonment for 2 years.'
104. Section 118J(1), ibid., states that '[a] man who commits an act of gross indecency with another man otherwise than in private shall be guilty of an offence and shall be liable on conviction on indictment to imprisonment for 2 years.' Section 118J(2) states that '[a]n act which would otherwise be treated for the purposes of this section as being done in private shall not be so treated if done (a) when more than 2 persons take part or are present; or (b) in a lavatory or bathhouse to which the public have or are permitted to have access, whether on payment or otherwise.'
105. *Leung T.C. William Roy*, per Hartmann J., para. 5 (Hong Kong Court of First Instance). For a discussion of the age of consent debates in Hong Kong, see Phil C.W. Chan, 'The Gay Age of Consent in Hong Kong', *Criminal Law Forum* 15 (2004): 273.
106. *Leung T.C. William Roy*, ibid., para. 7.
107. Ibid., para. 8. Article 29 of the Basic Law of Hong Kong states that '[t]he homes and other premises of Hong Kong residents shall be inviolable. Arbitrary or unlawful search of, or intrusion into, a resident's home or other premises shall be prohibited.' Article 14(1) of the Hong Kong Bill of Rights Ordinance states that '[n]o one shall be subjected to arbitrary or unlawful interference with his privacy, home or correspondence, nor to unlawful attacks on his honour and reputation.' Article 14(2), ibid., states that '[e]veryone has the right to the protection of the law against such interference or attacks.'
108. *Leung T.C. William Roy*, ibid., paras 17–20.
109. Ibid., paras 34–42.
110. Ibid., para. 44.
111. 1(3) IHRR 97 (1994).
112. *Leung T.C. William Roy*, per Hartmann J., paras 43–6 (Hong Kong Court of First Instance).
113. *Ng Ka Ling*, per Li C.J., 322.
114. Basic Law of Hong Kong, Art. 35(1).
115. (1991) 13 EHRR 186.
116. *Leung T.C. William Roy*, Ma C.J.H.C., para. 42 (Hong Kong Court of Appeal).
117. [2003] QB 893.
118. *Leung T.C. William Roy*, Hartmann J., paras 62–79 (Hong Kong Court of First Instance)
119. Ibid., paras 58–9.
120. Ibid., para. 12.
121. Ibid., para. 133.
122. Ibid., paras 137–9.
123. (1995) 98 CCC (3d) 481.
124. (1997) 24 EHRR CD22.
125. *Leung T.C. William Roy*, per Hartmann J., para. 142 (Hong Kong Court of First Instance).
126. Ibid., para. 141.
127. Ibid., para. 147.

128. *Leung T.C. William Roy* (Hong Kong Court of Appeal).
129. Alford, 'In Search of a Theory for Constitutional Comparativism', 711–2.
130. *Leung T.C. William Roy*, per Hartmann J., para. 142 (Hong Kong Court of First Instance). For discussions of arguments raised in sexual minority rights debates in Hong Kong, see Phil C.W. Chan, 'The Lack of Sexual Orientation Anti-Discrimination Legislation in Hong Kong: Breach of International and Domestic Legal Obligations', *International Journal of Human Rights* 9, no. 1 (2005): 69; Phil C.W. Chan, 'Same-Sex Marriage/Constitutionalism and their Centrality to Equality Rights in Hong Kong: A Comparative–Socio-Legal Appraisal', *International Journal of Human Rights* 11, nos. 1–2 (2007): 33; Phil C.W. Chan, 'Stonewalling through Schizophrenia: An Anti-Gay Rights Culture in Hong Kong?', *Sexuality & Culture* 12 (2008): 71.
131. For an illustrative discussion of the struggles facing persons belonging to sexual minorities in Zimbabwe, see Oliver Phillips, 'Blackmail in Zimbabwe: Troubling Narratives of Sexuality and Human Rights', *International Journal of Human Rights* 13, nos. 1–2 (2009): 345.
132. Sexual Offences (Amendment) Act 2000 (c. 44), s. 1; Sexual Offences Act 2003 (c. 42), s. 140 and Sch. 7.
133. 539 US 558 (2003). In *Leung T.C. William Roy*, para. 140, the Hong Kong Court of First Instance referred to the *obiter dictum* of Justice O'Connor's concurring opinion (not majority opinion as the Hong Kong court stated) in *Lawrence* v. *Texas* and did not discuss the United States Supreme Court's majority opinion delivered by Justice Kennedy. The Hong Kong Court of Appeal did not at all mention the American case.
134. Consolidated Versions of the Treaty on European Union and of the Treaty Establishing the European Community, *Official Journal of the European Union*, C 321 E/1, 29 December 2006, Art. 6(1).
135. In imperial China homosexuality 'was considered neither a crime nor immoral behaviour': Fang-fu Ruan, 'China', in *Sociolegal Control of Homosexuality: A Multi-Nation Comparison*, ed. Donald J. West and Richard Green (New York: Plenum, 1997), 57, 57. Matthew Harvey Sommer, in *Sex, Law, and Society in Late Imperial China* (Palo Alto, CA: Stanford University Press, 2000), 114, points out that 'it is only in the Qing [dynasty] that lawmakers included such acts in the venerable criminal category of "illicit sexual intercourse" (*jian*)'. In republican China, homosexuality has never been explicitly classified as an offence, with the communist (now socialist-market) government in particular refusing to acknowledge that there are any persons belonging to sexual minorities within its territory. The offence of hooliganism, which the communist/socialist-market Chinese government used to suppress homosexuality alongside political dissent, was repealed in 1997: Ruan, 'China', 63–5.
136. Michael D. Ramsey, 'International Materials and Domestic Rights: Reflections on *Atkins* and *Lawrence*', *American Journal of International Law* 98 (2004): 69, 74 (emphasis in original).
137. Ibid., 81.
138. Human Rights Act 1998 (c. 42), ss. 1–3.
139. Alford, 'In Search of a Theory for Constitutional Comparativism', 708.
140. Richard Posner, 'No Thanks, We Already Have Our Own Laws', *Legal Affairs* (July–August 2004): 40, 42.
141. Alford, 'In Search of a Theory for Constitutional Comparativism', 711.
142. Sandra Day O'Connor, 'Remarks at the Southern Center for International Studies', 28 October 2003, http://www.southerncenter.org/OConnor_transcript.pdf (accessed 25 April 2008). See also Vicki C. Jackson, 'Transnational Discourse, Relational Authority, and the U.S. Courts: Gender Equality', *Loyola of Los Angeles Law Review* 37 (2003): 271, 358–9, where the jurist argues that 'constitutions do not function solely as a charter of self-government, or an expression of unique national identity . . . . Constitutions are thus adopted, and interpreted, not only with an eye to the internal demands of the polity but also with an eye on the stature and position of the nation state in the international arena'.
143. Seth F. Kreimer, 'Invidious Comparisons: Some Cautionary Remarks on the Process of Constitutional Borrowing', *University of Pennsylvania Journal of Constitutional Law* 1 (1999): 640, 650.
144. 505 US 833 (1992).
145. Ibid., per O'Connor J., 865–6.
146. Ramsey, 'International Materials and Domestic Rights', 82.

Sexual minorities and human rights in Japan: an historical perspective

Mark McLelland[a] and Katsuhiko Suganuma[b]

[a]School of Social Sciences, Media and Communication, University of Wollongong, Australia;
[b]Centre for International Education and Research, Oita University, Japan

Contemporary Japan maintains longstanding and well-documented traditions of same-sex eroticism and yet the terminology for describing these traditions as well as the contexts and identities through which they have been expressed have changed greatly since Japan's opening to the West at the end of the nineteenth century. These changes have been most striking in the post-war period, when new rights-centred discourses concerning issues of sexual identity and sexual citizenship began to develop alongside enduring Japanese notions situating sexual expression in the private realm of personal interest or play. Taking a broad historical view, this paper shows that it is only since the mid-1980s that a voluble discourse linking same-sex sexual activity and human rights has gained mainstream attention. The factors that led to this paradigm shift are outlined as are the current and future challenges facing a range of sexual minorities in Japan.

Introduction

Japan has one of the most enduring and best-documented traditions of same-sex eroticism in the world and yet the terminology for describing this tradition as well as the contexts and identities through which it has been expressed have changed greatly over the course of the last century.[1] These changes have been most striking in the post-war period, when new rights-centred discourses concerning issues of sexual identity and sexual citizenship have developed alongside enduring Japanese notions situating sexual expression in the private realm of personal interest (*shumi*) or play (*asobi*).[2]

It is only since the mid-1980s that a voluble discourse linking same-sex sexual activity and human rights has gained public attention. In part this is because in contemporary Japan neither cross-dressing nor same-sex sexual behaviours have been branded illegal and so the police surveillance and harassment of sexual minorities, both male and female, which has continued to be a significant motivating factor for lesbian and gay activism elsewhere, especially in the United States, has been largely absent. Likewise, there has been no powerful moral authority such as the Roman Catholic Church singling out homosexuality as a sin. It has therefore been more difficult for individuals in Japan who experience same-sex desires to imagine that they share a common predicament, let alone an agenda for activism and reform.[3]

In the United States, like African-Americans and women who also faced entrenched discrimination, sexual minorities were empowered by the emergence in the late 1960s of a counter-culture that, as Humphreys notes, 'was an essential condition for the gay revolution'.[4] The late 1960s saw the rapid emergence of national and international alliances among sexual minorities who decided to fight back against the 'statutory oppression'[5] that, deriving from Judaeo-Christian ethics, underlay the legal codes of most Western countries. In Japan, however, where the expression of private sexual practice has tended to be overlooked by both state and religious authorities,[6] the 1960s counter-culture had little impact on same-sex-desiring individuals and communities.

Consequently, we did not see in the 1970s in Japan the birth of a national lesbian and gay movement similar to that in the West. The politicisation of homosexuality did take place to a lesser extent, taking hold among lesbians earlier than gay men, largely because of the politicising influence of the feminist movement and the fact that women were so obviously disenfranchised in Japanese society. However, the mainstream feminist movement's lack of interest in lesbian issues[7] and the precarious financial and social situation of many lesbians meant that lesbian activism had little visibility or effect outside of specific communities in the 1970s. It was not until the mid-1980s that a new generation of 'gay' men emerged and began to employ modes of organisation and activism similar to those that had been pioneered by lesbian and gay organisations in the West,[8] with the mainstream media beginning to deal with lesbian and gay issues outside of the entertainment paradigm that had dominated the discussion in the post-war period.[9]

Taking an historical perspective, this paper looks at a variety of factors that led to the development of a politicised sense of lesbian, gay and transgender consciousness in Japan (as yet there has not been a bisexual movement in Japan or much awareness of bisexuality). We also consider enduring cultural assumptions about the nature of sexuality as well as the influence of modern anti-identitarian influences that have made it difficult in Japan to organise a mass movement for social reform along sexual identity lines.

The pre-modern background to Japan's queer cultures

In Japan, searching for a history of 'sexual minorities' is problematic given that same-sex sexuality, particularly as practised between men, has only recently come to be considered unusual and been consigned to the pathological side of a 'normal'/'abnormal' divide. During the Edo period (1603–1867) no normative connection was made between gender and sexual preferences because all men, whether samurai, priest or commoner, were able to engage in both same- and opposite-sex affairs. At the time, men's same-sex sexual relationships were governed by a code of ethics described as *nanshoku* (male eroticism) or *shudō* (the way of youths) in the context of which elite men were able to pursue boys and young men who had not yet undergone their coming-of-age ceremonies, as well as transgender males of all ages from the lower classes who worked as actors associated with the kabuki theatre. As well as being a conspicuous social reality, these relationships were widely represented in the culture of the period in art, in literature and on stage.[10]

Significantly, while *nanshoku*, made up of the characters for 'man' and 'eroticism', was a general term covering a variety of forms of love practised between men, the parallel term *joshoku*, made up of the characters for 'woman' and 'eroticism', actually referred to love relationships between men and women. It was the case that no concept existed at the time which referred in a general sense to women's same-sex love and, consequently, there was no way of cognitively linking male and female 'homosexuality'. Although there are some literary and artistic references to sexual acts taking place between women during pre-modern times, frequently involving male onlookers, women's same-sex love was not accorded the same level of moral seriousness as that between men. This does not mean that such relationships were not widespread at a time when women, like men, were limited in their interactions with the other sex, but simply that the cultural mechanisms to ensure their remembrance were not in place.[11]

The development of sexological perspectives

It so happened that sexology, which added 'scientific' criticisms to legal and religious disapproval of same-sex sexual relationships, was developing in European medical circles at precisely the same time as Japan opened itself to Western influence during the Meiji period (1867–1912). This was a time when numerous Japanese intellectuals and experts travelled to the West for knowledge and insight. The influence of German medicine was particularly strong and Japanese doctors who returned from centres of medical expertise such as Berlin were the main conduits through whom new categories devised by German sexologists such as Krafft-Ebing were disseminated into Japanese. These new medical perspectives on sex had a wide impact on culture, the early twentieth century being a time when *seiyoku* (sexual appetite or desire) was beginning to be elucidated as a factor behind character development in Japanese fiction. Mori Ōgai's novel, *Vita Sexualis*, published in 1909, was one of the first to take the 'sexuality' of its protagonist as its central theme and this elaboration of a space of sexual interiority in literature fuelled popular discussions concerning normal (*seijō*) and perverse (*ijō*) forms of sexuality and, accordingly, persons.[12]

It can be argued that Meiji-period sexology was largely the province of an intellectual elite, but growing literacy led to a more proletarian readership in the Taisho period (1912–25) which saw what has been described as a *hentai* (queer or perverse) 'boom', the first of several explosions of interest in 'queer sexuality' (*hentai seiyoku*) that were to occupy the Japanese media over the next half-century. This widespread interest is best understood in relation to a cultural fad known as *ero-guro nansensu* or 'erotic grotesque nonsense' which was prominent in the popular culture of the late 1920s.[13] It was during this period that *dōseiai* (same-sex love) emerged as the most popular of a handful of terms approximating a translation of the European concept of 'homosexuality'.[14] For the first time in Japanese a category became available within which a variety of female/female same-sex romantic and physical relationships could be grouped, and through which it became possible to speak of male and female same-sex desires as dimensions of the same phenomenon.[15]

In the early twentieth century, several prominent Japanese women writers wrote publicly about their relationships with other women, among whom, Yuasa Yoshiko,[16] a Japanese-Russian translator, had at one time or another romantic relationships with other members of the 'Blue Stocking' feminist society. Although the word *rezubian* was not a commonly acknowledged term in the pre-war period, in an interview late in her life Yuasa affirmed that she was indeed a *rezubian*, thus indicating that educated elite women, at least, were able to resist the narrative of perversion.

Queer culture during the Pacific War

Whereas sexual matters were fairly openly debated in the press in the 1920s, Japan's descent into militarism in the early 1930s saw the government tighten its hold on sexual discourse and practice.[17] Despite the fact that the ideology of the period was relentlessly hetero-normative and pronatal, as Japan's regional conflicts progressed, actual social organisation became increasingly homo-social. Throughout the 1930s, greater numbers of men were drafted into the military, thus delaying the marriage of bachelors and separating married men from their wives, thereby encouraging the development of greater intimacy between men. At the same time, unmarried women moved to take the place of these men in the factories. One of the results of this separation between the sexes was what has, in relation to the cinema of the period, been referred to as 'the death of romance'—since romantic love between a man and a woman was seen as incompatible with the heroic masculinity demanded by the war effort.[18] Accordingly, in popular culture at least, men's romantic love for women tended to be displaced by images of homo-social brotherhood. There were, for instance, many media accounts of 'love between comrades' (*sen'yūai*) where male homo-social bonding was shown to have encouraged feats of great chivalry, self-sacrifice and valour on the battlefield. Of course, these official narratives contained no mention of more physical relationships, since, due to the severe censorship exercised, among other ways, through the government's control over paper rations there were few opportunities to discuss sexuality outside of the reproductive paradigm endorsed by the state.

However, accounts published in the early post-war years do suggest that relationships between senior soldiers and young recruits sometimes had a sexual element.[19] One text dated 1952 and entitled *Homosexuality on the Battlefront* noted that 'veteran officers choose for their orderlies soldiers who are beautiful youths [*bishōnen*]' and that these boys were used as a 'substitute for women' and an 'outlet for sexual desire' (*seiyoku no hakeguchi*) on the front line.[20]

During the Pacific War, the category 'the homosexual' was not imagined or invoked as a threat to the Japanese war effort in the way it was within the Allied forces (who regularly purged 'sexual deviants' – male and female – from their ranks).[21] To an extent, in Japan same-sex sexual behaviour was still seen as a potential shared by men in general and an understandable consequence of sex segregation. Thus, while Japan's militarism did not in itself contribute to the development of fixed gay identities (unlike, arguably, the Allied war effort), there is considerable evidence, albeit circumstantial, suggesting that homoeroticism and, in certain contexts, explicit same-sex sexual interaction were encouraged by the process of sex segregation which accelerated as Japan's position in the war gradually deteriorated.

The rapid development of a post-war queer culture

The immediate post-war period witnessed a loosening of traditional sex and gender ideologies, resulting in an endorsement of 'curiosity-seeking' (*ryōki*) in sexual matters and a less judgmental attitude towards homosexuality and other non-procreative acts in the popular press.[22] For instance, a great detail of information about sexual practices framed as 'sex education' for married couples was disseminated through magazines such as *Modern Couple* which significantly extended the repertoire of sexual acts beyond the procreative paradigm recommended in pre-war sex advice. Practices such as kissing, necking and petting were given detailed coverage and pamphlets describing these terms newly transliterated into the *katakana* script were often included as free inserts in these magazines.[23]

From the early 1950s, a range of magazines that had much in common with the 1920s fad for publications specialising in 'erotic, grotesque nonsense' appeared. Sporting titles such as *Sexual Morals Science* and *Sexual Morals Storybook*, these magazines courted a readership of 'intellectuals' and 'cultured persons' who were interested in analysing and accounting for the apparently sudden proliferation of 'queer' or perverse desires (*hentai seiyoku*) after the war. The 'experts' consulted by these magazines were as likely to be professors of French literature (since French authors such as de Sade, Gide and Proust were considered to deal with perversion) as they were to be doctors or Freudian psychologists. Furthermore, the fact that readers often wrote letters and contributed longer descriptive pieces about their own 'perverse desires' meant that pathologising medical and psychoanalytic theories did not establish such a firm hold on the popular discourse on queer desires in Japan as was the case in American popular writings. Indeed, many of the experts consulted seemed to have more than a professional interest in the topics they were analysing and given that the magazines relied on contributions from readers for a substantial percentage of their contents, there were many rather upbeat accounts of non-heterosexual interests and practices. These upbeat accounts are most evident in a number of roundtable discussions staged for the magazines in which queer individuals such as cross-dressing male prostitutes (*danshō*), homosexual (*homo*) bar goers and female homosexuals (*josei no homo*) discussed their lives, often contradicting or qualifying the opinions of the 'experts'.[24]

These early 'queer' magazines offer invaluable insight into the social organisation of a range of non-hetero-normative communities and identities in the first post-war decade. For instance, we learn from accounts in these magazines that immediately after the war the first homosexual drinking places were referred to as *danshoku kissaten*, that is, 'male eroticism coffee shops', and those meeting there were referred to by a wide range of terms, both modern and more traditional, including *sodomia* (sodomite), *homo* (homosexual) and *danshokuka* (conjoining the nominalising suffix -*ka* or '-ist' to the Edo-period term for male/male eroticism). However, by the mid-1950s, the newly imported term *gei*, which had been introduced during the US occupation, was being deployed as a trendy term to refer to homosexual nightspots and the professional young men who worked there (but not the customers). Since many of the 'boys' working in these establishments exhibited transgender characteristics, *gei* came to represent a group of professional bar workers who engaged in transgender and other performances to entertain a clientele of more gender-normative customers referred to as *homo* – an important distinction within the subculture that was to remain in place until the early 1980s.

However, where men with same-sex desires were concerned, the bar world was not the only means of socialisation. The magazines mentioned above contained personals columns that facilitated men, particularly those living outside the major cities, to network, and a number of organisations were established, ostensibly for the 'study' of male/male sexuality, including cross-dressing. The earliest and most long-lived of these groups was the Adonis Club, which published a newsletter and held regular meetings between 1952 and 1962. The group's newsletter was a mixture of highbrow essays (often concerning homosexuality among historical figures), personal ads, and erotic fiction and illustrations. Although it had a small circulation confined to club members, it was an important prototype for the commercial *homo* magazines that developed in the 1970s.

While in the early 1950s the main focus of sexual 'curiosity seeking' was on male/male desires, with a large number of articles dedicated to male homosexuality and cross-dressing, women's same-sex sexuality was not entirely overlooked. As mentioned, 'female same-sex love' (*joshi dōseiai*) had been regularly discussed in the *ero-guro* press of the 1920s and, although the term 'lesbian' was not itself used, there was some discussion of 'Lesbos love' (*resubosu ai*) in the early post-war press. Yet, just as there was less written about female homosexuality, there were far fewer descriptors referring to women with same-sex desires, and they were in some texts simply referred to as *josei no homo* or 'female homos'. Indeed, in the early 1950s, discussion of female homosexuality, it seems, was included very much as an afterthought.[25]

It was not until the 1960s that there was a more widespread media interest in the women's same-sex love subculture. For instance, numerous media reports appeared regarding the bar Yume no Shiro (Castle of Dreams,) which was founded in 1961 to take advantage of the popularity of the all-female Shōchiku Kagekidan, an acting troupe that featured many beautiful actresses in male 'trouser roles'. As increasing numbers of women moved to the cities, seeking an independent life supported by remunerated employment, the number of such bars expanded throughout the 1960s and it became possible for some women with the money and the leisure (who were themselves often employed in the entertainment trade) to socialise in a world organised according to butch (*tachi*) and femme (*neko*) gender roles – a paradigm that owes more to traditional transgender performance in the Japanese theatre than to parallel developments in the United States' lesbian subculture of the time.[26]

So far no evidence has come to light of the existence of 'Lesbos' publications or organisations for women similar to those that developed for *homo* men in the 1950s and 1960s. However, all this was to change in response to the impact of second-wave feminism that hit Japan at the end of the 1960s. During this period, there developed a broader consciousness of *rezubian* (lesbian) issues as part of the women's liberation discourse and the early 1970s saw the rise of a range of women's groups and publications around *rezubian* identity and desire.

The development of queer activism

Significantly, in the early 1970s it was the term *rezubian*, not *gei*, that first began to be deployed with political connotations and it was Japanese lesbians, not gay men, who were the first to build community ties based on politics and not just sexual attraction. On the whole, lesbian and gay activism in Japan has developed independently. Men and women with same-sex desires socialised in different environments, there was never any organised police persecution and, given the absence of sodomy and unequal age-of-consent laws, there were no issues of common concern that might have brought gay men and lesbians together. Hence, there have never been any commercial publications in Japan seeking, in a sustained manner, to offer a wider queer perspective that might act as a bridge between gay men's and lesbians' communities.

The founding of the lesbian group Wakakusa no Kai (Young Grass Club) in Tokyo in 1971 is often spoken of as a turning point in lesbian community-building in Japan.[27] While some women who attended its meetings were looking for partners rather than a community, others wanted to engage in a more political manner. Despite the fact that mainstream Japanese feminism has long been criticised for overlooking lesbian issues, all-women feminist spaces did create fertile environments for the experience and expression of female same-sex intimacy. Gay men, who were not discriminated against *as men*, did not have the same motivation to agitate for political change and there were no attempts to develop a broader coalition with lesbian women as was the case in the early years of the gay rights movement in the United States.

The most enduring of Japanese lesbian organisations has been Regumi, a group founded in the late 1980s, consisting of a loose alliance of lesbians, from the bar world or involved in feminist activities. The group's name was made up of *re* which stood for *rezubian* and the character *gumi* or 'group'. *Regumi tsūshin* (Regumi News) is a newsletter published since 1985 and includes information about lesbian literature, various support and discussion groups and a telephone information line. However, it was not until May 1995 that *Phryne*, the first commercial magazine aimed at lesbian and bisexual women, was released. Despite initial optimism that the magazine would reach a crossover audience of heterosexual feminist women, *Phryne* folded after only its second issue. The next year saw another attempt at publishing a commercial magazine for lesbian and bisexual women – *Anise*. Seven issues were published between 1996 and 1997 before lack of funds led to the temporary suspension of publication. However, gradual sales of back numbers enabled the magazine to recommence publication in 2001, although it has once more folded since.

Contrary to the difficult experience of sustaining politically oriented lesbian feminist publications, erotic publications aimed at gay men have had a more successful history. Commencing with *Barazoku* (Rose Tribe) in 1971, there has been a constant stream of commercially successful men's magazines, some of which lasted for several decades, with circulations of up to 40,000. However, since the late 1990s, when the easy availability of pornographic material and networking spaces on the Internet cut into their sales, these magazines have subsided, with *Barazoku* virtually ceasing publication in 2004 after more than 30 years.

Despite the prevalence of more erotic media directed at gay men, it would be mistaken to assume that the politics of sexuality have not been of interest to some. Indeed, an explicit connection between Japan's hetero-normative (as opposed to patriarchal) social system and the oppression of sexual minorities was made by Tōgō Ken as early as 1971. Tōgō founded the political party Zatsumin no Kai (Miscellaneous People's Party) which brought together a wide range of individuals who were socially disenfranchised on account of their various 'failures' to live in accordance with received notions of family life and relationships. From the early 1970s onwards, Tōgō ran many times for a seat in Japan's parliament, the National Diet, and although unsuccessful he continued his campaigning over the following 20 years.[28]

It is problematic, however, to identify Tōgō as Japan's first 'gay' activist, since he deliberately used the indigenous term *okama* to describe himself. Technically a term for a large pot for cooking rice, *okama* has been used since at least the Edo era as a slang term for buttocks and by association for effeminate gay men (who are assumed to engage in passive anal sex). It is hence a troubling term for many gay men who dislike its connotations of effeminacy and passivity. Tōgō, however, insisted on recuperating the term, much as the lesbian and gay movements in the United States was to do with 'queer' in the early 1990s, and insisted that to counter homophobia in the Japanese context it was necessary to engage with local Japanese terms for sexual difference. Tōgō was, however, a controversial figure, and was unable to galvanise widespread support among gay men (or within the other communities he canvassed).[29] During the late 1970s other figures had more impact, such as Ōtsuka Takashi, the first activist to begin to use the loanword *gei* (gay) in a more political manner in his weekly segment on the popular underground radio programme *The Snake Man Show*.[30]

Although by the late 1970s pioneers such as Ōtsuka Takashi had begun to utilise *gei* as an identity category, Japanese activists still had few connections with lesbian and gay movements outside Japan. This is not surprising, since, unlike the more politicised term *rezubian*, *gei* was only just beginning to be articulated as a subject position. In the minds of many, *gei* was still a term associated with professional bar workers and the entertainment trade. This situation began to change in 1983, however, when a foreign journalist researching an article on homosexuality in Japan published an interview with Minami Teishirō, editor of the *homo* magazine *Adon* (not to be confused with the earlier *homo* newsletter *Adonis*). This brought Minami to the attention of the International Lesbian and Gay Association (ILGA), which, as well as offering support to developing lesbian and gay organisations around the world, also lobbied national governments and international organisations such as the United Nations to ensure protection of rights of sexual minorities. Minami agreed to be the representative of ILGA in Japan and also travelled to overseas ILGA conferences and workshops as a representative of Japanese sexual minorities.

One of ILGA Japan's most conspicuous successes was the organisation of the first Tokyo Lesbian and Gay Parade in August 1994, which attracted over 1000 participants. This success was repeated the following year when participation more than doubled. However, participation in the 1996 parade fell back to just over 1000, since many people were unhappy with the parade's organisers, who were accused of being too controlling.[31] The disagreements were not easily resolved and as a consequence rates of attendance at the 1997 event were even lower, plummeting to fewer than 100. Lesbians, who felt they were excluded from the decision-making process in earlier parades, refused to participate at all, preferring to stage their own *daiku* (dyke) march.[32] These disagreements drew attention to the particular difficulty in Japan of establishing a shared agenda for gay men and lesbians.

Frequent disputes over the parades are evidence that ILGA Japan has never been able to establish itself as a broad and representative group for sexual minorities in Japan. Minami found that gaining any kind of consensus among queer communities on issues such as coming out, HIV prevention measures and the need for public activism was extremely difficult. As an older man erring perhaps on the side of conservatism, Minami found that younger members were impatient with his leadership and in 1986 an inevitable split took place, younger members of the group leaving to found OCCUR, also known in Japanese as Ugoku Gei to Rezubian no Kai (Organisation for Moving Gays and Lesbians). OCCUR has consistently taken a more proactive stance than earlier groups towards the media and professional and government organisations.[33] One of its key strategies has been to deploy the notion of *tōjisha* or 'persons [directly] concerned'. Originally a legal term referring to the 'parties concerned' in litigation, *tōjisha* is now widely used among minority and civil rights groups to insist on their right to self-representation and self-determination.[34] The association of the term *tōjisha* with sexual minorities and particularly transgender persons helped the public at large to conceive of individuals with and expressing a range of sexual minority identities and desires as *sexual minorities* (*seiteki mainoritī*) and, as such, having rights akin to other disadvantaged groups in society.

As part of its insistence on *tōjisha* agency, OCCUR has been involved in lobbying the Japan Society of Psychology and Neurology to have homosexuality declassified as a mental illness and has lobbied the publishers of Japan's major dictionaries and encyclopaedias to have definitions of homosexuality rewritten in line with modern understandings of gay men and lesbians as members of a sexual minority. OCCUR has also worked with the Tokyo metropolitan government to have sexual minorities included under the city's human rights charter, and it was involved in prolonged litigation with the Tokyo municipal government concerning equal access for sexual minority groups to public conference and recreational facilities. These initiatives resulted in the translation and promulgation of a range of new vocabularies for discussing queer identities and desires, such as *seiteki shikō* or 'sexual orientation', bringing discussions of minority sexualities in Japan in line with Western paradigms. This paradigm shift has not, however, been welcomed by all sexual minority individuals in Japan,[35] particularly transgender persons working within the entertainment industry, some of whom have argued that the shift to 'normalise' queer desires detracts from the potential of queer perspectives to interrogate and hold to account some of the negative effects of Japan's overtly patriarchal and hetero-normative social system.

The surge of political activism by sexual minority groups themselves, especially those representing gay men, from the mid-1980s through the beginning of the 1990s, can in large part be understood as a response to the HIV/AIDS panic in Japan.[36] At the initial stage of the epidemic in Japan, the majority of individuals who contracted the HIV virus were patients who had received non-sterilised blood products for haemophilia. However, the AIDS surveillance guidelines produced by the Ministry of Health and Welfare from

1985 to 1993 together with the AIDS Prevention Law passed by the government in 1988 identified 'male homosexuality' itself as one of the fundamental routes for HIV infection.[37] Given the fact that the government itself was responsible for disseminating the contaminated blood products among Japanese pharmaceutical companies, it is not unreasonable to speculate that the government targeted male homosexuals as a scapegoat in order to ward off criticism by the public. In fact, although the Ministry of Health and Welfare was well aware of HIV infections among patients with haemophilia, in 1985 it publicly announced that a Japanese gay man who had been living abroad was the first patient to develop AIDS – not the same as contracting HIV, of course – in the country. Through negative publicity on the part of the government, representations of homosexuality, and in particular gay men, were strongly conflated with negative perceptions of promiscuity, the supposedly 'decadent' sexuality of the West, and imported foreign disease. It was this social milieu that prompted many gay activists, including Minami and OCCUR, to challenge such negative stereotypes through public campaigns that drew upon previous successful strategies developed by gay activists during the AIDS panic in Western countries.

The 1990s was also an important decade for the development of what might be termed local or indigenous takes on queer theory. During the decade two theorists in particular, Fushimi Noriaki and Kakefuda Hiroko,[38] rose to prominence, although the latter found the strain of public scrutiny too enervating and has since retired from public life. Fushimi initially gained attention during Japan's 'gay boom', a period in the early 1990s when mainstream media suddenly became interested in gay lifestyles and issues. His 1991 book *Private Gay Life* opened with a 'queer' (*hentai*) declaration in which he disavowed any interest in being 'normal', since he felt that this term was always already discriminatory (in that 'normal' needs to discover and position itself against the 'abnormal' in order to be intelligible). Hence, Fushimi's approach was strategically different from the minoritising perspective adopted by OCCUR and others. Fushimi was not interested in normalising sexual minority desires but in critiquing and ultimately dismantling what he termed the 'hetero-system'. Fushimi has gone on to write numerous books, including a novel that won the prestigious Bungei prize. He remains Japan's most articulate and influential gay intellectual.

Another key intellectual figure who contributed to the formulation of queer studies in Japan was Kakefuda Hiroko, whose 1992 book *On Being 'Lesbian'* impacted on lesbian and feminist debates throughout the 1990s. Like Fushimi, she avoids a minoritising approach to lesbian identity which posits a clearly defined group of 'lesbians' as separate and distinct from 'heterosexual women', rather arguing that 'lesbians' are produced through the othering effects of the dominant hetero–homo binary embedded in the patriarchal family system. As a construct, a product of social othering, Kakefuda argues that it was impossible to constitute oneself as a lesbian subject in Japan, hence the scare quotes surrounding the term in the title of her book. Kakefuda goes on to argue that in Japan's patriarchal order women in general are denied agency and the means of self-representation, irrespective of the object of their desires. For a period of about two years after the publication of her book, Kakefuda was a prominent voice in both lesbian and mainstream media but by 1995 the strain of being asked to speak as a lesbian (despite the fact that her book disavowed this possibility) took its toll and she retired from public life.

In the decade since Kakefuda's groundbreaking publication, much has changed for lesbians in Japan. As discussed above, there have been a series of commercial lesbian publications, including ten issues of the erotic magazine *Carmilla*, which did much to help women visualise and take control of their same-sex desires.[39] Perhaps a key indicator of these changes has been the election to public office of a woman asserting a lesbian identity (albeit she came out after she took office). In 2003 Otsuji Kanako was elected to the Osaka Prefectural Assembly and in 2005 published her autobiography in which she came out as a lesbian, making her the first (successful) openly sexual minority politician in Japan. She subsequently campaigned for a number of pro-sexual-minorities policies, including the right for same-sex couples to access Osaka's public housing. She did not stand for re-election in 2007 but became instead a Democratic Party candidate for a seat in the national House of Councillors in the July 2007 elections. Yet, despite largely positive media coverage both at home and abroad, Otsuji's attempt to enter national politics was unsuccessful. Indeed, much to her campaign team's surprise, she received an unexpectedly small number of votes nationwide, despite the fact that the Democratic Party won the overall election against the ruling Liberal Democratic Party with a significant margin. In retrospect, the tactic of politicising the issue of human rights for sexual minorities failed to resonate with the Japanese public as well as with sexual minorities themselves.[40]

Although Otsuji did not publicly declare her orientation at the time of her being elected, another campaigner, male-to-female transgender activist Kamikawa Aya, who ran for office in the Tokyo Municipal Council, did go public about her transgender status during her 2003 campaign. Needless to say she attracted a lot of media attention and it is encouraging that she polled very well and was elected, despite the fact that on official election papers her gender was still listed as male. It was not until 2004 that, under strict conditions, some transgender individuals were granted a right to change their registered biological sex on identity documents. Kamikawa was successfully re-elected in 2007.

Transgender culture

As outlined earlier, transgenderism has long been conspicuous in Japanese theatres and also in the 'floating world' of clubs and bars in the post-war period. The *gei* subculture of the bar world which rapidly took off in the 1950s remained strongly associated in the public mind with effeminacy and cross-dressing. Masculine women, often associated with the 'trouser role' players in all-women theatre troupes, were also able to socialise at certain bars in Tokyo specifically catering to them, although such bars were never as extensive as those for gay men (unlike the situation in the United States, gay men and lesbians did not socialise in the same venues).

Female-to-male transgender persons seem not to have developed as extensive a subculture as have male-to-female transgender persons. As early as 1955 there were already small organisations set up for the 'study' of cross-dressing, which attracted a membership of male-to-female cross-dressers and produced newsletters for circulation among members. It was not until 1980, however, that the first commercial magazine aimed at male-to-female cross-dressers, *Queen*, was published. *Queen* was closely aligned with the Elizabeth Club, a relatively large on-venue male-to-female cross-dressing club founded in 1979 which subsequently opened branches in several suburbs of Tokyo as well as in other cities. *Queen* pitched itself as an amateur hobby magazine for recreational cross-dressing and was in no sense a vehicle for transgender activism and, thus, continued to frame transgenderism as an aspect of the entertainment world.

Despite the Japanese media's longstanding interest in transgenderism as expressed in the confines of the entertainment world[41] and exemplified by Miwa Akihiro, one of the best-known post-war transgender figures, it was not until the coming out of Torai Masae as a female-to-male transsexual in the mid-1990s that public awareness was focused on the hardship faced by those whose gender identity and sexed body do not coincide. It is significant in this context that it was a female-to-male transgender person who sought to make this connection, thus underlying the fact that it has often been sexually non-conformist women (or in this case a biological woman transitioning to male) who have pioneered in bringing attention to the political dimensions of the sex and gender system.

Subsequently, there were a range of other figures who publicly came out about their transgender status and the newly designated condition of *sei dōitsusei shōgai* (gender identity disorder) was a frequent point of discussion in the popular media at the turn of the century. Since changes to legislation in Japan in 1997, the performance of gender reassignment surgery on those diagnosed by doctors to be suffering from 'gender identity disorder' is now permitted. Since 2004, those having completed the surgery, under certain strict circumstances, are also permitted to change their registered biological sex on official documents. However, the conditions that must be met have been criticised by many in Japan's sexual minority community as being overly pathological. Many feel that the choice of the term *shōgai*, which in Japanese connotes a sense of 'disability' and harm, is overly pathologising and that the problem lies not so much with the individual 'patient' but rather with a rigid binary gender system that does not acknowledge that gender expression can be multiple and varied and is not reducible to simple categories of 'male' or 'female'. Also, many complain that the legislation which allows only unmarried individuals without children to change their registered biological sex is too narrow and is discriminatory against many in the transgender community.[42]

Some observations on future prospects

As we hope this paper has articulated, the different ways in which the discourses, practices and identities of Japan's sexual minorities have been constructed are always historically contingent. In particular, the Meiji era, the immediate post-war decade and the late 1980s AIDS panic were exemplary periods in which Japan's interactions with globally circulating discourses of sexuality, especially those deriving from the West, gave rise to new forms of sexual knowledge and identity. In the modern period, patterns of Japanese sexual identity and practice have always been articulated and reformulated in relation to ideas deriving from foreign cultures. At the same time, precisely because of this translational process, such imported knowledge does not always produce the same effects and outcomes in Japan as in its original locale. Recognising the complexity of this indigenising process has always been one of the greatest challenges facing many sexual minority communities outside the West, including those in Japan.

If we pay attention to the post-AIDS panic era, there have clearly been cases where the deployment of foreign knowledge has proved successful in Japan. As indicated above, although several issues remain unsolved, the legal condition of transgender persons who wish to have sex reassignment surgery in Japan has been much improved since the 1997 reform which relied upon the medico-scientific discourses of gender identity disorder adopted from the United States. Moreover, increasing social recognition has been accorded Japanese transgender persons as exemplified by the successful political career of Kamikawa Aya as well as the recent positive media attention given to transgender persons.[43]

Yet, despite these positive developments, the current legislation for people with gender identity disorder is still designed strictly to enable 'patients' to 'fix' or 'normalise' their gender identity. Not much imagination is necessary to figure out that the current system grants legal rights only to those transgendered persons who conform to the traditional gender economy. It is not surprising then that human rights for gay men and lesbians are less likely to be recognised in Japanese society precisely because their demands for inclusion pose a more radical threat to traditional modes of organising gender and sexuality.

The positive steps that Japanese transgender activism has made notwithstanding, there has not been much progress in relation to gay men and lesbians in the legal domain recently. Otsuji's unsuccessful political campaign shows that the centripetal force necessary for lesbians and gay men to mobilise for legal reform in Japan seems to be lacking. Such a tendency can also be seen in the fact that Ishikawa Wataru, a Japanese gay activist, lost in the election for the Tokyo Municipal Council in 2007. These failures suggest that openly gay candidates have problems even in mobilising the gay vote.

The problem of galvanising a collective identity that might advance lesbian and gay identity politics in this new millennium is difficult to fathom. However, we offer here several explanations. First, unlike in the United States, where the gay rights movement has a much longer history – dating back well into the 1950 – within the last two decades Japanese lesbian and gay identity politics has developed in tandem with recently emergent deconstructive perspectives, such as postmodernism and queer theory, that have problematised identity politics. During the initial stage of the AIDS panic, the insistence on identity politics came to the surface because there was an urgent need to establish a viable subjectivity for sexual minorities in reaction to the stigmatisation of mainstream society. However, in recent years, such overt social discrimination that might compel gay men and lesbians to collectively resist public demonisation has been a relatively rare occurrence. On the other hand, for transgender persons with gender identity disorder, mundane life can often be a site of perpetual struggle and stress, which gives them a viable impetus to act, to seek change.

Second, as the recent troubles faced by lesbian and gay publication businesses indicate, the Internet has taken over and now assumed the role as the primary communication device between and among many Japanese sexual minorities and their members. This medium has encouraged further diversification among Japan's sexual minorities, making it not only possible to create new linkages among sexual minorities but also more difficult to sustain the collective identity necessary to mobilise politics. Furthermore, due to this rapid exchange of information and knowledge brought about by the Internet, national boundaries are becoming ever more permeable and elusive. Although many of these cross-cultural and transnational exchanges, not only with the West, but also with non-Western cultures, especially with neighbouring Asian countries, are invaluable, such interactions simultaneously invite the possibility of generating ever more compartmentalised senses of belonging which are not reducible to traditional sets of identity categories, such as those based on region, religion, nationality, ethnicity or race. These deconstructive tendencies underline the difficulties that the various actors within the Japanese lesbian and gay liberation movements have faced in articulating a viable collective identity that can push for change.

One might ask the question from a human rights perspective: 'How can the situation for sexual minorities in Japan be improved?' This is an open question to which we do not have any clear answers. Certainly we do not feel optimistic about any nostalgic return to a classic (male) form of same-sex identity politics, which would be an anachronism in the Japan of the new millennium. Nor would we wish to claim that the contemporary situation for Japanese sexual minorities is one in which individuals are emancipated from the strains of identitarian labelling. As Foucault's canonical writing on the relationship between modernity and sexuality convincingly explains, the discourse and knowledge constituting sexuality in any historical context always reflect the contours of modernity within which subjectivities are contextualised.[44] That is, the 'bio-power' with which sexual subjectivities are complicit is not a trans-historic or trans-cultural apparatus, but rather always historically and socially contingent. Therefore, when we try to understand the contemporary situations facing Japan's sexual minorities, it is a mistake to interpret the situations as either 'backward' or 'advanced' in relation to Western points of reference. Instead, the situations facing Japanese gay men, lesbians and transgender persons are best understood in the wider context of Japanese society in the new millennium.

While there is no doubt that efforts to create international coalitions among organisations for sexual minorities are invaluable and must continue to be pursued, international human rights campaigning also needs to pay close attention at the same time to the diversity and complexity of the different cultural and historical situations of the peoples concerned. With this in mind, international sexual minority rights campaigning can continue to contribute to the better understanding of the social conditions of Japanese sexual minorities and their cultures as we come to a more nuanced understanding of the different trajectories taken by sexual minority communities across the world's societies.

Notes

1. For detailed accounts of this history in English, see G. Pflugfelder, *Cartographies of Desire: Male–Male Sexuality in Japanese Discourse, 1600–1950* (Berkeley, CA: University of California Press, 1999); M. McLelland, *Queer Japan from the Pacific War to the Internet Age* (Lanham, MD: Rowman & Littlefield, 2005); M. McLelland, K. Suganuma and J. Welker, eds, *Queer Voices from Japan: First-Person Narratives from Japan's Sexual Minorities* (Lanham, MD: Lexington Press, 2007); S. Chalmers, *Emerging Lesbian Voices from Japan* (London: RoutledgeCurzon, 2002); J. Welker, 'Telling Her Story: Narrating a Japanese Lesbian Community', *Japanstudien* 16 (2004): 119. In Japanese, see N. Fushimi, ed., *Dōseiai nyūmon* [Introduction to Homosexuality] (Tokyo: Potto shuppan, 2003); N. Fushimi, *'Gei' to iu keiken* [The Experience Called 'Gay'] (Tokyo: Potto shuppan, 2002); Y. Hiratsuka, *Nihon ni okeru danshoku no kenkyū* [Research on Male Eroticism in Japan] (Tokyo: Ningen no kagakusha, 1994).
2. For detailed discussions of traditional Japanese notions of sexual expression, see M. McLelland, *Male Homosexuality in Modern Japan: Cultural Myths and Social Realities* (London: RoutledgeCurzon, 2000); W. Lunsing, *Beyond Common Sense: Negotiating Gender and Sexuality in Japan* (London: Kegan Paul, 2001). In Japanese, see N. Fushimi, *Puraibēto gei raifu* [Private Gay Life] (Tokyo: Gakuyō shobō, 1991).
3. We acknowledge that these observations rely on a rather stark and simplistic contrast between Japan and 'the West' and so run the risk of re-inscribing a simplistic binary. However, in this paper we wish to make Japanese sexuality and culture intelligible within a cross-cultural perspective. For an astute analysis of the strategic employment of a binary paradigm, see K. Vincent et al., *Gei Sutadīzu* [Gay Studies] (Tokyo: Seidosha, 1997), 154; K. Suganuma, 'Associative Identity Politics: Unmasking the Multi-layered Formation of Queer Male Selves in 1990s Japan', *Inter-Asia Cultural Studies* 8 (2007): 485.
4. L. Humphreys, *Out of the Closets: The Sociology of Homosexual Liberation* (Englewood Cliffs, NJ: Prentice Hall, 1972), 113.
5. M. Gould, 'Statutory Oppression: An Overview of Legalized Homophobia', in M. Levine, ed., *Gay Men: The Sociology of Male Homosexuality* (New York: Harper & Row, 1979), 51.
6. See H. Taniguchi, 'The Legal Situation Facing Sexual Minorities in Japan', *Intersections* 12 (2006), http://intersections.anu.edu.au/issue12/taniguchi.html (accessed 1 March 2008); Fushimi, *Puraibēto gei raifu.*
7. V. Mackie, 'Women's Groups in Japan: An Overview of Major Groups', *Feminist International* 2 (1980): 106. On the invisibility of lesbian issues prior to the early 1990s, see H. Kakefuda *'Rezubian' de aru to iu koto* [On Being 'a Lesbian'] (Tokyo: Kawade shobō, 1992).
8. See H. Sunagawa, 'Japan's Gay History', *Intersections* 12 (2006), http://intersections.anu. edu.au/issue12/sunagawa.html (accessed 1 March 2008).
9. On the enduring connection between same-sex sexuality and transgenderism in Japanese popular culture, see M. McLelland, 'Japan's Original Gay Boom', in *Popular Culture and Globalization in Japan*, ed. M. Allen and R. Sakamoto (London: Routledge, 2006), 159.
10. Pflugfelder, *Cartographies of Desire.*
11. G. Leupp, '"The Floating World is Wide..." Some Suggested Approaches to Researching Female Homosexuality in Tokugawa Japan (1603–1868)', *Thamyris* 5 (1998): 1.

12. For a discussion of the effect of new sexological perspectives on the Japanese literary traditions, see J. Reichert, *In the Company of Men: Representations of Male–Male Sexuality in Meiji Literature* (Palo Alto, CA: Stanford University Press, 2006).

13. D. Roden, 'Taisho Culture and the Problem of Gender Ambivalence', in *Japanese Intellectuals during the Inter-war Years*, ed. J.T. Rimer (Princeton, NJ: Princeton University Press, 1990), 37. For an accessible Japanese source reproducing original accounts, see T. Shimamura, *Ero guro nansensu: Modan toshi bunka* [Erotic, Grotesque Nonsense: Modern City Culture] (Tokyo: Yumani shobō, 2005).

14. M. Takeuchi, 'Deviants of Modern Society: The Self-Realization of Male Homosexuals as Seen from Magazine Postings in Taisho Japan', *Gender and Sexuality* 3 (2008): 77.

15. P. Wu, 'Performing Gender along the Lesbian Continuum: The Politics of Sexual Identity in the Seitō Society', *US–Japan Women's Journal English Supplement* 22 (2002): 64; M. Furukawa, 'The Changing Nature of Sexuality: The Three Codes Framing Homosexuality in Modern Japan', trans. A. Lockyer, *US–Japan Women's Journal English Supplement* 7 (1994): 98.

16. See 'A Visit with Yuasa Yoshiko, a Dandy Scholar of Russian Literature', in *Queer Voices from Japan: First-Person Narratives from Japan's Sexual Minorities*, ed. M. McLelland, K. Suganuma and J. Welker (Lanham, MD: Lexington Press, 2007), 31.

17. S. Frühstück, *Colonizing Sex: Sexology and Social Control in Modern Japan* (Berkeley, CA: University of California Press, 2003); T. Hasegawa, *Waisetsu shuppan no rekishi* [History of Obscene Publications] (Tokyo: Sanichi shobō, 1978).

18. M. Suzuki, 'Sensō ni okeru dansei sekushuaritī' [Men's sexuality during war], in *Nihon no otoko wa doko kara kite doko e iku?*, ed. H. Asai, S. Itō and Y. Murase (Tokyo: Jūgatsusha, 2001), 98; I. Standish, *Myth and Masculinity in the Japanese Cinema: Towards a Political Reading of the 'Tragic Hero'* (London: Curzon, 2000).

19. See 'My Career in Danshoku: Notes on Sodomy' and 'Nostalgia for My Time in the Army: Concerning Male Nudity', in *Queer Voices from Japan: First-Person Narratives from Japan's Sexual Minorities*, ed. M. McLelland, K. Suganuma and J. Welker (Lanham, MD: Lexington Press, 2007), 41, 51.

20. S. Asakura, 'Sensen ni okeru dōseiai' [Homosexuality on the battlefront], *Kitan kurabu* (June 1952): 137.

21. A. Berube, *Coming out under Fire: The History of Gay Men and Women in World War Two* (New York: Free Press 1990).

22. R. Hasegawa and T. Takagi, 'Senzen sengo ero sesō ōdan' [Cross-section of pre- and post-war erotic conditions], *Amatoria* (April 1953): 159.

23. M. McLelland, 'Kissing Is a Symbol of Democracy: Dating, Democracy and Romance in Japan under the Occupation', *Journal of the History of Sexuality* (2009): forthcoming.

24. See 'Grand Sodomia Conference: A Discussion of the Joys and Agonies of Homosexuality' and 'Roundtable: Female Homos Here We Go', in *Queer Voices from Japan: First-Person Narratives from Japan's Sexual Minorities*, ed. M. McLelland, K. Suganuma and J. Welker (Lanham, MD: Lexington Press, 2007), 81, 139.

25. M. McLelland, 'From Sailor Suits to Sadists: "Lesbos Love" as Reflected in Japan's Postwar "Perverse Press"', *US–Japan Women's Journal* 27 (2004): 27.

26. J. Robertson, *Takarazuka: Sexual Politics and Popular Culture in Modern Japan* (Berkeley, CA: University of California Press, 1998).

27. There are as yet no comprehensive Japanese lesbian historical studies tracing these events in Japanese or English. Regarding the comparative lack of lesbian studies in Japanese academia, see C. Maree, 'The Un/state of Lesbian Studies: An Introduction to Lesbian Communities and Contemporary Legislation in Japan', *Journal of Lesbian Studies* 11 (2005): 291. For Japanese sources, see the essays and discussions in *Aniisu 'Komyunitī no rekishi 1971–2001: nenpyō to intabyū de furikaeru* [Community history 1971–2001: Reflecting back with timelines and interviews], Summer 2001; see also the essays in *Bessatsu Takarajima, Onna wo ai suru onnatachi no monogatari* [Stories of Women Who Love Women] (Tokyo: JICC Shuppankyoku, 1987).

28. See 'Tōgō Ken, the Legendary Okama: Burning with Sexual Desire and Revolt', in *Queer Voices from Japan: First-Person Narratives from Japan's Sexual Minorities*, ed. M. McLelland, K. Suganuma and J. Welker (Lanham, MD: Lexington Press, 2007), 263. In Japanese, see K. Tōgō, *Jōshiki wo koete: okama no michi 70-nen* [Beyond Common Sense: 70 Years on the *Okama* Path] (Tokyo: Potto shuppan, 2002).

29. See the discussions of Tōgō's impact in N. Fushimi, K. Oikawa, K. Noguchi, K. Matsuzawa, N. Kurokawa and T. Yamanaka, eds, *Okama wa sabetsu ka: 'Shūkan Kin'yōbi' no sabetsu jiken* [Is *Okama* Discriminatory? The *Shūkan Kin'yōbi* Discriminatory Expression Incident] (Tokyo: Potto Shuppan, 2002).

30. See Ōtsuka Takehi, 'True Tales from Ni-chōme', in *Queer Voices from Japan: First-Person Narratives from Japan's Sexual Minorities*, ed. M. McLelland, K. Suganuma and J. Welker (Lanham, MD: Lexington Press, 2007), 247.

31. See Hideki Sunagawa's account in 'Reflections on the Tokyo Lesbian and Gay Parade 2000', in *Queer Voices from Japan: First-Person Narratives from Japan's Sexual Minorities*, ed. M. M. McLelland, K. Suganuma and J. Welker (Lanham, MD: Lexington Press, 2007), 281.

32. See K. Suganuma, 'Festival of Sexual Minorities in Japan', *Intersections* 12 (2006), http://intersections.anu.edu.au/issue12/katsuhiko.html (accessed 1 March 2008).

33. See the contributions from OCCUR members in B. Summerhawk, C. McMahill and D. McDonald, eds, *Queer Japan: Personal Stories of Japanese Lesbians, Gays, Bisexuals and Transsexuals* (Norwich, VT: New Victoria, 1998).

34. S. Nakanishi and C. Ueno, *Tōjisha shuken* [The Sovereignty of the *Tōjisha*] (Tokyo: Iwanami shoten, 2002).

35. For discussions of tensions among various lesbian and gay groups in the 1990s, see W. Lunsing, 'Lesbian and Gay Movements: Between Hard and Soft', in *Soziale Bewegungen in Japan*, ed. C. Derichs and A. Oziander (Hamburg: Mitteilungen der Vereinigung fur Natur und Volkenkunde, 1998), 280; W. Lunsing, 'Japan: Finding Its Way?', in *The Global Emergence of Gay and Lesbian Politics: National Imprints of a Worldwide Movement*, ed. B. Adam et al. (Philadelphia: Temple University Press, 1999), 293.

36. On the history of HIV/AIDS in Japan, see H. Hasegawa, 'AIDS and the Gay Community in Japan', *Intersections* 12 (2006), http://intersections.anu.edu.au/issue12/hasegawa1.html (accessed 9 March 2008).

37. For more details of this account, see T. Kazama, 'Bio-power and Death: On the Representation of Male Homosexuals in the Era of AIDS', *Kaihō shakaigaku kenkyū* 17 (2003), 33.

38. K. Suganuma, 'Fushimi Noriaki's and Kakefuda Hiroko's Continuing Relevance to Japanese Lesbian and Gay Studies and Activism', *Intersections* 14 (2006), http://intersections.anu.edu.au/issue14/suganuma.htm (accessed 1 March 2008).

39. On the history of *Carmilla*, see J. Welker and K. Suganuma, 'Celebrating Lesbian Sexuality: An Interview with Inoue Meimy, Editor of Japanese Lesbian Erotic Lifestyle Magazine *Carmilla*', *Intersections* 12 (2006), http://intersections.anu.edu.au/issue12/welker2.html (accessed 1 March 2008).

40. Otsuji came in 29th among the 35 proportional representational candidates officially endorsed by the Democratic Party.

41. J. Mitsuhashi, 'Seitenkan no andāguraundoka to hōdō: 1970~90 nendai zenhan wo chūshin ni' [The underground-isation of sex-change in the media: from the 1970s to the first half of the 90s], in *Sengo Nihon josō/dōseiai kenkyū*, ed. M. Yajima (Tokyo: Chūō daigaku shuppanbu, 2006), 473; J. Mitsuhashi, 'The Transgender World in Contemporary Japan: The Male to Female Crossdressers' Community in Shinjuku', *Inter-Asia Cultural Studies* 7 (2006): 202.

42. The 'no-child' policy was mitigated in June 2008 when the House of Councilors voted in favour of a Bill that proposed allowing gender identity disorder (GID) patients with children to change their sex registration in their family registries. However, this was conditional on their children being adults at the time of the change: 'Diet Set to Let Parents Change Sex on Registry', *Japan Times*, 4 June 2008, http://search.japantimes.co.jp/member/member.html?mode=getarticle&file=nn20080604a5.html (accessed 4 June 2008).

43. For instance, post-operative male-to-female transgender singer-songwriter Nakamura Ataru has recently drawn much media attention by appearing in several Japanese TV programmes. For more details, see V. Mackie, 'How to Be a Girl: Recent Japanese Media Portrayals of Transgendered Lives', *Asian Studies Review* 32 (2008): 411. It is also significant that Nakamura participated as a transgender singer in one of the highest-rating TV programmes in Japan, NHK's New Year's Eve singing contest *Kōhaku Uta Gassen*, in 2007.

44. M. Foucault, *The History of Sexuality, Vol 1: An Introduction*, trans. R. Hurley (New York: Pantheon, 1978). For a concise summary of Foucault's idea of the discursive construction of sexuality, see E. Probyn, 'Michel Foucault and the Uses of Sexuality', in *Lesbian and Gay Studies: A Critical Introduction*, ed. A. Medhurst et al. (London: Cassell, 1997), 132.

Blackmail in Zimbabwe: troubling narratives of sexuality and human rights

Oliver Phillips

School of Law, University of Westminster, London, UK

Through analysis of a challenging scenario of blackmail of a gay man in Zimbabwe, this paper highlights the significance of the discursive and rhetorical realm in which law operates. Drawing on historical and contemporary sexual politics in Zimbabwe, it situates the practice of blackmail within its local context and considers how the active sexual agency of the victims, combined with their respective racial and sexual identities, pre-empted their representation as 'innocent', and restricted their access to legal or discursive exculpation. It shows how the ascendant narratives that emerge from the blackmail scenario obscure the victims' 'truth', render them perpetually 'guilty', and reinscribe conventional sexual hierarchies. This paper illustrates how the advance of sexual rights is inhibited by a tension between our idealisation of innocence in making rights claims and our aspiration to agency in developing sexual equality.

Introduction

Blackmail has been the steady companion of laws prohibiting same-sex sexual acts across jurisdictions,[1] in an association so pervasive that such laws have been labelled 'a blackmailer's charter'.[2] Zimbabwe is no exception to this, as even its Director of Public Prosecutions conceded that the law against homosexual acts is 'the easiest, clearest and surest way of blackmail'.[3] Vulnerability to blackmail, however, is not the exclusive preserve of homosexuals and while, 'in practice, many prosecutions concern the betrayal or threatened revelation of sexual secrets'[4] the leverage that enables the exertion of a menacing demand can be gained or manufactured through a wide variety of (non-sexual) means. Peter Alldridge suggests that one might usefully distinguish a threat to do something harmful from a threat to disclose some discreditable information.[5] In relation to this latter threat, he draws attention to the key conjunction of information and power that underlies blackmail: 'The power of a secret rests with its potential revelation. Blackmail, which threatens guilt with shame by the revelation of a secret, provides an axis in the relationship between information and power.'[6]

The main case of blackmail discussed in this paper is one where threats of both 'harm' and 'discreditable disclosure' were combined to exert maximum leverage for the extortionists, and yet despite the use of violence and the threat of further 'harm', as well as concerted resistance to their threats, it was the discreditable disclosure that prevailed throughout the entire scenario, as it was supported by so many conventional markers of guilt. This is because the victims were engaged in sexual relationships that were not only between two persons of the same sex but also transgressed conventional boundaries of race, class, and age. Fuelled with political rhetoric and received through the prism of post-colonial memories, the symbolic significance of these transgressions was so great as to render it impossible for the victims to represent their relationships in a redeeming narrative. Their effect was to exclude any claim the victims might make to 'innocence', as they cast the victims outside particular and multiple definitions of belonging in the context of the Zimbabwean state, and demonstrated how blackmail, while complicit in disguising deviance, actually relies on and reinforces conventional social relationships and sexual hierarchies.

In this paper, I am attempting neither an exegesis of the criminal law of blackmail nor a comprehensive examination of the limited data available on cases of extortion.[7] Rather, I focus selectively on an actual scenario to illustrate the representational dynamics that frame the articulation of sexual relationships into the realm of law. I touch on other accounts of blackmail to consider the extent to which both the criminal law and the surrounding socio-political context facilitate vulnerability to blackmail, and relate them to the scenario in considering how they all preclude the identification of particular sexual agents as victims entitled to access to justice. Clear normative parameters emerge from intersections of sexuality, race, gender, and class to shape Zimbabwean notions of desert and victimisation and to determine the attribution of guilt and innocence to sexual agency. The deliberate selection of sexual relationships that challenge conventional boundaries thus obliges us to consider whether this same tension between sexual agency and the attribution of guilt and innocence inhabits the narratives that frame access to the remedial power of human rights in general. The delivery of greater sexual agency to those subordinated or marginalised in gendered and sexual hierarchies is a precondition of equality and of effective engagement with other problems (such as the transmission of HIV, the exploitation of sex workers, violence against women, etc.). This paper therefore aims to examine the way this tension operates, by considering how their identification as active sexual agents effectively deprives of their rights those marginalised and most in need of recognition and enforcement of those very same rights.

A challenging scenario

Joe, a white professional expatriate of about 35 years old, had been living in Harare, Zimbabwe, for about seven years, working for an international development organisation and in receipt of a good salary. For about six months he lived together with a 22-year-old black Zimbabwean man named Farai. Farai was reasonably educated, occasionally employed, and, as he earned far less than Joe, he quite clearly gained materially and substantially from their cohabitation. The huge disparity in their wealth being typical of economic relations both within Zimbabwe and, in the broader global context, between their two countries of origin (Joe was from a former colonial power), they openly acknowledged it to be a factor whose difficult negotiation had brought them together.[8] They explicitly contrasted this with the manner in which both class and race ordinarily served to separate Zimbabweans from one another. Frustrated with the racial segregation so endemic to social existence in Harare, Joe was delighted that Farai could introduce him to a Zimbabwean culture that most white people living in Zimbabwe never experienced and in which they rarely had direct participation, and similarly Farai was intrigued to learn about a European culture that was not English. In interviews they described these differences of class and race as fuelling their intimate relationship; they represented the exchanges (economic and cultural) obliged by these differences as continual investments in their mutual social and intellectual capital. They shared many other more ordinary matters of fun and friendship and their relationship was one of mutual enjoyment, so that while they were not about to swear oaths of lifelong fidelity they had fun together until they parted amicably in February/March of 1996.

On 8 May 1996, South Africa promulgated its new constitution, including its prohibition of sexual orientation discrimination. This, along with other provisions, put South Africa in the vanguard of the global recognition of sexual rights. That this is distinctive and unprecedented within a regional context was emphasised by a series of events that began for Joe and Farai that very same day in Zimbabwe. Joe opened his front door in Harare to find Farai beaten and bleeding on his doorstep. He had a deep gash in his forehead, his eyes were glazed, and heavy bruising had caused his neck and cheeks to swell. He would not look directly at Joe. Farai was not alone, but was with two men who claimed to be his brothers, though Joe had seen only one of them before. Farai did not say anything. The 'brothers' asked for money to take Farai to the hospital, which Joe, genuinely concerned, unhesitatingly gave. He wanted to accompany them, but they insisted it was not necessary and politely suggested that it might be better if he did not. A day later, the two men returned without Farai, asking for money to take Farai out of town because he was in danger, giving an elaborate story involving witchcraft, gruesome physical harm, and a lack of money. Joe refused, as they were asking for a lot of money, and he suspected that he was being deceived in some way. Two hours later, a man carrying a 'press card', identifying him as a journalist working for a local press agency, visited Joe. He did not want to give Joe too many details but claimed that Farai had told him 'a story about Joe and Farai' that he was going to publish in the national press and that he wanted to check a few details with Joe. He made it clear that he expected Joe to pay him some money. Joe took the 'journalist's' name and card number, threatened to sue him if he published any unfounded material, reminded him that blackmail was against the law, and demanded the name of his superior at the newspaper. Later, two other men visited Joe, making numerous threats to his physical safety, and Joe refused to talk to them. On this occasion, Joe's references to lawyers and human rights organisations and his stubborn resistance kept the extortionists at bay, but he nevertheless spent the following months anxious that they might reappear and fearful for the well-being of Farai, who seemed to have disappeared without trace. Farai's family disapproved strongly of his homosexuality and Joe suspected that one of the men involved was actually a relative of Farai's, so it was unlikely that he would seek shelter with them. In fact, Farai had managed to escape his captors and take refuge in another part of the country. He decided it was safer not to stay in touch with Joe, and he only reappeared in Harare two years later, by which time Joe's contract was over and he had left the country.

Meanwhile, some months after this initial incident, Joe met another young man called Tendai – they established a relationship gradually and Tendai came to live with Joe. However, in May 1997, they both found themselves caught up in the middle of a second attempt to extort money from Joe. It comprised essentially the same elements, but this time there was considerably more violence, serious damage to property (at both Joe's home and, to the alarm of his colleagues, at the office), and the antagonists included a couple of policemen rather than a journalist. This also meant that Tendai and Joe each spent some time being held in a police station – Tendai being physically pressured to provide evidence against Joe, who in turn was threatened with charges for homosexual offences entailing imprisonment. They both had the clear impression that the initial intention was not to put either of them in jail but to extort as much money as possible from the situation, to indulge a fairly straightforward desire to kick the inherently dissident queers about, and a more historically rooted desire to invert the usual racial power dynamics by causing fear and pain to a relatively rich white man. Ironically, the involvement of the police, while initially more intimidating, provided Joe with an opportunity to draw on more formal structures and resources. He contacted the legal representative of the Gays and Lesbians of Zimbabwe (GALZ), whose considerable experience in dealing with these matters meant that slowly and gently he managed to extricate both Joe and Tendai from the situation. Such a clear-cut conclusion was unusual, and was in reality attributable to their refusal to confess to any illegal activities and Joe's access to good legal, material, and political resources on account of his social and economic capital.

While details of this account are accurate, names have been changed to protect the identity of those involved. I have chosen to focus on this particular scenario because some of the parties involved confided in me over the entire course of its unfolding, and because its details bring to the fore the key axes of information/power/narrative and sexuality/rights/innocence that are the subject of this paper. Furthermore, it will become clear that while no homosexual relationship can have conventional legitimacy in the Zimbabwean government's prescriptive cultural scenario,[9] the relationships of Joe, Farai, and Tendai also challenge assumptions of suitability in terms of race, economic class, and, to some extent, age, and so preclude exculpatory narratives of innocence on multiple grounds. For Joe, his access to resources (including a highly educated articulacy) could not overcome one dynamic that he experienced as a great source of frustration for some time afterwards: his inability, within the Zimbabwean discursive field, to represent these relationships as worthy of respect rather than censure. In interviews with the author, he repeatedly expressed great frustration at the impossibility of narrating these stories without invoking signifiers that determinedly attributed blame and censure to himself, Farai, or Tendai, or all three of them (depending on the listener). To understand this fully, and to analyse the scenario properly, it is necessary to locate the key discursive signifiers that produced this effect, through an overview of pertinent elements of the cultural and socio-political context.

Sex, power, and an invitation to blackmail

Our ability to resist the intrusion of public structures and assert the pleasure of our own desire or, more pertinently, our ability to reject an uninvited proposition tends to be a crude but effective measure of our broader social power. It is this which locates sex and pleasure within the realm of political struggle, whether articulated in terms of class, race, or gender, as has been highlighted in recent years by failed attempts to prevent the transmission of HIV.[10] Young women in Southern Africa are disproportionately vulnerable to HIV/AIDS as their cultural and socio-economic powerlessness become key vectors of infection.[11] It has become clear that the capacity to negotiate safe sex is a key factor among other economic and social conditions determining vulnerability to infection.[12] And just as our ability to negotiate safe sex depends on access to power within our intimate relationships, so are our capacities to fulfil desires and experience sexual pleasure, or to resist pressure and refuse sexual advances, all mediated by our access to power in broader social relationships.[13]

Clear illustrations of the way in which sexual relations are symbolic of broader social relations abound in both colonial historiographies and post-colonial narratives of sexual relations. The Ndebele rebellion in Southern Rhodesia in 1896 and the Zulu rebellion in 1906 both included explicit grievances about the British treatment of Ndebele and Zulu women,[14] but soon thereafter the 1906 Immorality Act in Southern Rhodesia imposed serious penalties for any sexual contact between a black man and a white woman. Both parties were subject to punishment, including the death penalty for rape or attempted rape, but there was no legal constraint at all on white men's relations with black women and it is clear that the colonial authorities declined to prosecute white men known to be forcing their attentions on black women.[15] Not for the first time, women's bodies served as the terrain on which specific hierarchies of sexuality and race were mapped out. Such overt privileging of race and gender combined with other legal and historical developments in the colonial context to produce a particular post-colonial legacy. Zimbabwean women's challenges to patriarchal structures have thus led feminism to be characterised by the ruling party as a 'new form of cultural imperialism'[16] with sexuality, hetero-normativity, and gendered identity being increasingly invested as determinants of national culture.[17] In building a national identity, culture's explicitly historical and social construction is concealed and it is instead reified through dogmas and then romanticised to serve this ideological function more effectively.[18] Such dogmatic proclamations of 'traditional culture' aim to pre-empt critical attempts to historicise 'culture' and invariably serve to corroborate the conceit that culture has an organic origin whose definition is untouched by political interference.[19] They also mask the real difficulties that beset the Zimbabwean state's approach to culture and that arise out of a particular post-colonial dynamic. This dynamic consists of a tension between asserting, on one hand, a 'traditional' lineage-based culture that prioritises interests presented as collective and is invoked through claims to group rights and ethnic sovereignty, and, on the other hand, the political culture of a 'modern' nation-state where individual autonomous citizens are entitled to rights of equality that are construed as universal and guaranteed by numerous international conventions that the state has ratified.[20] John Comaroff explains that the continuing prevalence of these contradictory registers of *primal sovereignty* and *radical individualism* derives from the colonial discourse of rights, which created 'ethnic subjects, racinated and recast in an often antagonistic dialectic of construction and negation'.[21]

Early initiatives by the colonial state to protect young girls from marriage and prohibit marriage without consent began a shift from lineage membership to state regulation, giving women's rights 'priority over the rights of the lineage [and] usurping the rights of family heads to control the sexual choices of members of their households and lineages'.[22] However, arguably the most significant shift from the power of the patriarch to the rights and obligations of an individual citizen was the enactment of the 1982 Legal Age of Majority Act by the post-colonial government. This conferred the possibility of legal personhood on all Zimbabweans upon reaching the age of 18, so that black women were no longer to be perpetual minors constantly under the guardianship of a man (unless they chose to remain so). Yet since then the government's commitment to gender equality has been demonstrably inconsistent, vacillating between first empowering and then restraining women, between a devotion to traditional family structures of customary law and the pressure to recognise citizens as individuals with rights in relation to the state.[23] Zimbabwean contests around sexuality and gender therefore serve as a direct reflection of this ambivalence towards the contradictory registers of primal sovereignty and radical individualism. A woman's ability to choose her partner goes to the heart of this, for under customary law marriage entails the transfer of a bridewealth payment (*lobola*) from the groom to the bride's male guardian (father, brother, uncle, etc.). Thus, if a woman declares herself to be a lesbian who will not marry and gain *lobola*, her brothers will have fewer resources with which to secure the wives whom they themselves desire. A woman's declaration of lesbianism therefore represents a challenge to the normative patriarchal structures of lineage, to the economic base of reproductive culture, and to the status of those men to whom she is supposed to owe allegiance. It is not just a symbolic challenge but a declaration that has significant economic and social consequences. At the same time, it is clear that a woman's ability to choose her partner and have autonomous ownership of her sexuality is fundamental to her recognition as a fully entitled legal subject.

It is this real conflict that allows homosexuality to be so convincingly characterised as contrary to Zimbabwean culture. But it is also the static notion of a reified culture functioning as ideology and the recognition of sexual relations as an indicator of social power that are manifest in the rhetoric of Robert Mugabe and other senior government officials when they have repeatedly defined homosexuality as anti-Zimbabwean and 'whitewashed' it as a 'sickness' imported by white settlers.[24] Mugabe has frequently referred to homosexuality as a threat to the moral fabric of society; he berated 'sodomists' for 'behaving worse than dogs and pigs'[25] and proclaimed a return to 'traditional' culture, saying, 'We have our own culture, and we must rededicate ourselves to our traditional values that make us human beings.'[26]

This vituperation is evidence of attempts to reject homosexual behaviour as extrinsic to Zimbabwean culture, relying on the notion that it 'is mainly done by whites and is alien to the Zimbabwean society in general'.[27] This was amplified through repeated use of the metaphor of homosexuality as a white man's disease infecting the African nation's virtuous heterosexual inclination. This portrayal of such a confluence of racial and sexual degeneration was intended to carry the twin implications that, first, white Western 'culture' is depraved, as it corrupts other cultures with the 'evil' practice of homosexuality, and, second, homosexuals must be white, as they are, by definition, 'depraved'. Thus, the signifier of homosexuality is used to denounce 'white culture', and the colouring of homosexuals as white is used to denounce them as non-Zimbabwean.[28] This emphatic approach has the effect of sublimating the fluidity of the performative identities that characterise the post-colonial and reinforcing artificial but rigid boundaries of difference through the rhetoric of anti-imperialism.

Homosexuality has been represented as a danger that is specifically anti-Zimbabwean and anti-African to the extent that Zimbabweans have been incited to arrest homosexuals 'and hand them over to the police'.[29] The danger that homosexuals represent is realised in the social proximity of black Zimbabweans who identify as gay or lesbian. Their self-declared presence in Zimbabwean civil society signifies that the 'other' is now an 'insider' and highlights the artificiality of government's emphatic boundaries of culture and difference.[30] More directly, having homosexuals 'inside' local culture suggests a threat to traditional structures of power, as they make moral demands for respect and equality and thereby expose the supposedly 'natural' confluence of sexuality and race, as well as the boundaries of culture, to be constructed and challengeable. This challenge to normative assumptions of familiarity and difference supplies the foundation for the development of what Gail Mason appropriately terms a 'collective hate' of the dangerous homosexual.[31]

The much-repeated invective against homosexuality has arguably served as an invitation for patriotic Zimbabweans to intervene in the intimate relationships of anyone suspected of being a homosexual. It has given licence to any plan for enrichment gestating in the mind of a potential extortionist, and in the 1990s it seemed clear that it had produced real effects. As well as calling for their apprehension, Mugabe proclaimed that homosexuals should not 'have any rights at all'[32] and his ministers have supported him by, among other things, calling homosexuals 'the festering finger' to be 'eradicated', 'chopped off', and 'kept separate'.[33] These (and other similar) public statements were all made in 1995 and 1996, and in the years following there appears to have been a marked increase in incidents of extortion and blackmail aimed at persons on account of their sexual orientation.[34] This is despite the fact that extortion is treated as a more serious offence in Zimbabwean law than consensual homosexual acts.[35] It suggests that these comments were understood by some

Zimbabweans as an invitation to find ways of harassing and excluding the homosexual from the social body, while they were internalised by others as confirmation that any homosexual tendency, as the embodiment of treason, must be excluded from oneself.

Arguably, the rhetoric of politicians merely provides a pretext for acts of extortion that are essentially motivated by greed and opportunism, as a genuinely homophobic nationalism may well lead protagonists to violence but would also oblige them to hand their victims over to the state. However, a successful blackmailer requires their threat of disclosure to remain as a threat, and to profit from their act they must collude with the victims to keep their relationship secret, thereby allowing them to remain within the collective body and participating (for profit) in the intimacy that so dangerously threatens the nation. This should mean that blackmail cannot be legitimised as a service to the integrity of the Zimbabwean state and the preservation of its distinct moral order. Yet cases of blackmail did appear to increase subsequent to the rhetorical flourishes of Mugabe and his government, suggesting that their vocal homophobia served at least as a pretext for opportunists, and at most as a justificatory device that had particular post-colonial resonance. Moreover, this surge in blackmail suggests that theoretical constructs of consistency and ideology have less individual purchase than expedience and opportunism in a context where money is in demand and wanting. The additional involvement of police in this context supports the suggestion by Les Moran that 'the blackmailer takes up the position of the agent of the law in order to better realize the law's concerns: to unleash a terror against that which is forbidden and to punish that which is forbidden in the name of good order [and to] mimic the legitimate use of terror as a practice through which to produce a particular social order'.[36] In fact, these shared motivations can also obscure the distinction between law's legitimate authority and the illegitimate terror of the blackmailer, particularly for those police officers who choose to extract money while simultaneously claiming to secure national purity. Even if limited to a single officer acting unofficially, any suggestion of police support for the blackmailer brings far closer the immediate terror of legal threat, delivering a corresponding growth in authority and pressure, which is possibly why there are so many accounts of police complicity in blackmail across many jurisdictions.[37] Evidence in Zimbabwe suggests that the complicity of police in blackmail schemes has in the past been sporadic rather than predictable, as there are officers who have tried on occasion to be helpful, but it is also clear that in other situations they have themselves been implicated in the process of extortion.[38]

Blackmail in general

In Zimbabwe the readiness of certain police officers to profit from a case of extortion that comes to their attention means that victims are reluctant to report the offence, as to do so significantly increases the likelihood of their own arrest and may compound the pressure on them to hand over even more money. There are numerous instances where the police have become actively involved in the extortion, often seeking to displace the original extortionist or to obtain a share of the money being extorted.[39] In some cases, the police have actively sought out gay men and lesbians on their own initiative for the purpose of extortion. Extortion can also take place obliquely in instances where gay men or lesbians are the victims of theft or violence, and the perpetrator threatens to allege the commission of a homosexual offence if a complaint of theft or violence is made against him or her to the police. In numerous instances where the victims did make reports to the police, notwithstanding these threats, the gay or lesbian victims were arrested on the basis of the perpetrators' allegations and held in custody despite a lack of evidence. Some attempts were dropped where lawyers intervened, and the presence of a lawyer experienced in dealing with blackmail appears to offer the best possibility of extrication for the victim, but few in Zimbabwe can afford access to legal representation. In 2003, an average of one case of extortion per month was brought to the attention of the Gays and Lesbians of Zimbabwe, and the police were actively involved in approximately half of these either in collaboration with the extortionist or on their own account.[40]

What makes these attempts at extortion particularly difficult to challenge is the fact that they involve intimate sexual relationships that are against the law and their unacceptability is being constantly and publicly reiterated. Regardless of whether the allegations levelled against him are false or not, the victim accused of a homosexual act is therefore discredited from the beginning and invariably has to start from a position where his guilt is presumed. But the burden of all the baggage that such an accusation carries goes beyond the lack of a presumption of innocence to undermine the victim's credibility in general. Prosecutions for either extortion or for homosexual sex frequently rely on the conflicting testimony of the parties involved, and thus often come down to the question of which witness is the most credible in a scenario where the truth has no place; the truth will invariably be contrary to the needs of all those involved – blackmailer, victim, and profiteering police officer – ensuring that it is excluded from all accounts. In many cases, the extortionist claims to be a heterosexual who was propositioned or seduced by a homosexual.[41] Such a claim automatically invests the extortionist with the innocence of a victim whose 'normal' life is interrupted by the predatory homosexual, who in turn is positioned as both interfering stranger and 'offender': 'The sexual stranger is feared as the potential *perpetrator* of unimaginable crimes ... but the hatred generated by this fear means that it is the same "stranger" who ultimately becomes the victim of discrimination, abuse and violence ... because he/she is unknown, unknowable, and, hence, dangerous.'[42] Homosexuality is thus construed as good justification for extortion, and while the courts might eventually dismiss the charges for lack of evidence the procedures leading up to trial present individual police officers, prosecutors, and the initial extortionists with plenty of opportunities to intimidate the target and relieve him or her of money or goods.

Evidence from Zimbabwe makes clear that those who are open about their sexual orientation continue to be subject to, and may even become more visible targets for, blackmail, especially when the law continues to prohibit the acts of which extortionists might (even spuriously) accuse them. The removal of secrecy does not diminish the possibilities for blackmail,[43] as, actively identifying as the 'dangerous outsider', the victim 'is imbued with a collective familiarity that allows him/her to be recognized by the perpetrator as a suitable target in the first place'.[44] Similarly, decriminalisation of consensual homosexual acts might be expected to remove the vulnerability to blackmail of homosexuals, but this is not easy to establish with any reliability. Alldridge suggests that blackmail and its contribution to the growth of criminality was 'a principal reason for the enactment of the Sexual Offences Act 1967' in England, and, recognising that decriminalising consensual homosexual acts between adults might be expected to engender an increase in the reporting of blackmail to the police, he surmises that the exceptional decline in reported instances of blackmail in the year following decriminalisation is 'something of a vindication'.[45] However, research by Donald West suggests that any such decline was countered by the continuation of police strategies to obtain confessions of guilt based on harassment and intimidation of gay men, including the failure to investigate their complaints of criminal victimisation, and threats to disclose their sexual orientation to family or employer.[46] Furthermore, Les Moran presents evidence from as late as the 1990s to show that blackmail persists in England 'in forms similar to those practiced before the Wolfenden review'.[47] The failure of English law reform in 1967 to ensure these practices disappeared is undoubtedly related to the fact that the reform was limited to decriminalising consensual sexual acts in private between men over the age of 21. Maintaining an unequal age of consent and the restriction to private space immediately limited the remit of the reform, such that a number of gay men still found themselves in conflict with the law. This incomplete decriminalisation therefore failed to provide any complete obliteration of recorded instances of blackmail, and, although those limits to reform have since been overcome,[48] the particular sensitivities of blackmail will always make it difficult to establish accurately its reduction let alone extinction. It is trite to say that blackmail will be most inviting where there are *both* a criminally prohibited act *and* an interpersonal need for secrecy, but it is precisely this conjunction of criminality and secrecy that makes blackmail an offence so notoriously difficult to report or record, and so impossible to reflect with any accuracy in statistics. Nevertheless, one might logically expect that where there is neither a criminal act nor an element of secrecy, there should be some diminution in the possibilities for blackmail. The fact that this diminution is not so complete as to render blackmail obsolete for homosexuals is arguably a reflection of the broader, more social (as opposed to legal) limits to same-sex rights and equality which constitute discourses of sexual difference and exclusion. Blackmail therefore appears to attach itself most commonly to deviance that invites either social censure or criminal sanction, and preferably both. In Zimbabwe the context is considerably ripened by representations of homosexuality as 'dangerous', as well as a lack of police accountability and a corruption so endemic that police operate easily outside the constraints of the law.

Furthermore, despite the underlying motivation of greed, falling victim to extortion is not the preserve of the wealthy, as is made clear by the small amount of some of the sums extorted. Arguably, it is a victim's social vulnerability that makes him or her most susceptible to exploitation. While victims with less economic or social capital cannot give a large payment, they may well be more amenable to smaller pressures to pay or to deliver alternative services on a more regular basis. Accounts from Zimbabwe certainly suggest that wealth is more likely to provide victims with the resources (such as legal advice) required to protect themselves from threats of extortion, compared with those with fewer resources, who have fewer options but to succumb. Indeed, the pressure can be disproportionately greater, and more acutely manipulated, where there are fewer resources with which to negotiate a release. This makes it clear that it is fallacious to consider blackmail or extortion as revolutionary, and it is untenable to suggest that it may have some excusable merit as an exercise in redistribution where disparities of wealth are unjust. Similarly, Alldridge argues against the suggestion that laws against blackmail operate 'to protect a particular class of people (people with money, who care about their reputations) from those whom in the normal course of events their privileged position makes them immune', as it cannot account for the range of victims or the linguistic and historical dynamics of blackmail's legal prohibition.[49] Far from inverting structured relationships of economic power, it explicitly relies on them and ultimately works to reinforce them through the need to sustain the non-disclosure of secrets.

The number of black homosexuals who have fallen victim to extortion also makes clear that the government's attempts to '*white*wash' homosexuality have not precluded their victimisation; instead they become pivotal in signifying the danger that 'outsiders' represent to 'insiders'. The accusation that they are adopting 'white' or 'Western' identities that have no place in Zimbabwe remains common, along with the presumption that black homosexuals must have been corrupted by a white person. Indeed, where an inter-racial same-sex couple is identified, it is invariably assumed that the white partner has bought the love and attention of the black partner, who is only in the relationship for material gain. This is directly attributable to the discourse of homosexuality as a 'white disease', as it fails to allow for any real same-sex desire on the part of the black partner and suggests a callous power manipulation on the part of the white partner. It offers an explanation whose credibility is rooted in long histories of racial disparities in wealth, sexual exploitation, and relationships of labour wherein black Zimbabweans lacked agency. These memories produce particular discursive tropes that dominate the representation of the relationships between Joe and Farai and Tendai, as they are forced to tell the story of their relationships in terms other than their own, contradicting their own perceptions of what they have developed together. Their intimacy must now be described and explained for the public audience, in terms that match audience expectations. The scripts of the participants, the exigencies of the desires that formed the basis of the relationships, become rapidly invisible, and their own definitions of their relationships are eclipsed. Their intimacy is, in fact, overpowered, as its narration automatically divests it of the quality that makes it intimate.

Ascendant narratives and the denial of innocence

Intimacy may well be defined as the point at which one attempts to isolate the private from the public.[50] Simon and Gagnon dissect the interaction of private and public as refracted across three levels:

> Cultural scenarios are the instructional guides that exist at the level of collective life ... as systems of signs and symbols through which the requirements and practice of specific roles are given ... The possibility of a lack of congruence between the abstract scenario and the concrete situation must be resolved by the creation of interpersonal scripts. This is a process that transforms the social actor from being exclusively an actor to being a partial scriptwriter or adapter shaping the materials of relevant cultural scenarios into scripts for behaviour in particular contexts. Interpersonal scripting is the mechanism through which appropriate identities are made congruent with desired expectations.

> Where complexities, conflicts, and/or ambiguities become endemic at the level of cultural scenarios, much greater demands are placed on the actor than can be met by interpersonal scripts alone ... intrapsychic scripting creates fantasy in a rich sense of that word: the symbolic reorganization of reality in ways to more fully realize the actor's many-layered and sometimes multi-voiced wishes. Intrapsychic scripting becomes a historical necessity, as a private world of wishes and desires that are experienced as originating in the deepest recesses of the self must be bound to social life: individual desires are linked to social meanings. Desire is not reducible to an appetite, an instinct; it does not create the self, rather it is part of the process of the creation of the self.[51]

Along with Simon and Gagnon's interpersonal scripts, intimacy might be seen as the process through which we attempt to negotiate a balance of our private feelings, with the intrusion of public institutions, and the way we represent this all to the world at large. Consequently, it is situated in the same axis of information and power that Alldridge identifies as the location of blackmail, for both intimacy and blackmail engage in the trading of secrets and the power and prerogative of their revelation. The particular way in which blackmail 'provides an axis in the relationship between information and power'[52] in the scenario of Joe, Farai, and Tendai both relies on and reinforces the disparities between their intrapersonal scripts and the cultural scenario.

The first thing to note about the blackmailing of Joe, Farai, and Tendai is that the cultural scenario rendered it impossible to inscribe innocence into the narratives of their interpersonal scripts. They were targeted because, according to the Zimbabwean cultural scenario, Farai and Tendai could not claim to be innocent unless they represented the nature of their relationship with Joe in such a way as to describe Joe as the rich white older man who had taken advantage of their naiveté and poverty. Such a representation would not only reaffirm Mugabe's characterisation of homosexuality as imperialist corruption, but would also confirm that Farai and Tendai were not really homosexuals who threatened to corrupt the integrity of the nation, but were true Zimbabweans who had been corrupted on account of their youth and the economic disadvantages that are the legacy of colonialism. On one hand, the blackmailers' greed is rationalised as extending the redistributive economic benefits beyond Farai or Tendai to a wider circle of people who are intervening to prevent the continuing corruption. On the other hand, this representation of Farai and Tendai serves to simultaneously recall and distance the danger of the homosexual threat, reaffirming that it is still present but locating it outside the bounds of culture and the nation, so that it is both excluded and without any claim to moral proximity. This is reaffirmed by Joe's representation as the European man who has to buy the cooperation of young local men with his wealth. But despite its offer of repentance, and perhaps because of the rationalisation it offered the blackmailers, this was a representation that both Tendai and Farai resisted vehemently.

This also illustrates how the description and understanding of the relationships were altered when their intimacy was interrupted by the extortionists. First Farai and Joe, and then Tendai and Joe lost control of the narrative, the ability to define what it was that they had, and so, in many ways, ownership of the relationship, since it came to be defined by others. The public signifiers of difference (age, class, race) that had been integral to their desire now became a means of defining their relationship as problematic and impossible. Both Farai and Tendai are of Shona ethnicity, and Joe had been specifically interested in this aspect of their identity; an explicit part of the attraction was that he was gaining close experience of Shona culture, about which most white people in Zimbabwe remain ignorant even though it is the pre-dominant ethnicity in Zimbabwe. He was learning a lot from Farai and Tendai about Zimbabwe and what it meant to live as a Zimbabwean, rather than just how to live as a white expatriate, in isolated bourgeois splendour. This was very important to him, and it was an explicit part of his interest in Farai and Tendai. They in turn were openly drawn to Joe's whiteness (rendered more exotic by the fact that he was not English), his wealth, his open challenge to conventional politics and relations of race, sex, and class, and the prestige of his lifestyle, which was still youthful enough to include all the trappings of a global gay youth culture – music, fashion, designer labels, technology, and electrical boys' toys. This is not as superficial as it may at first seem, as these are the accessories of a lifestyle that included the possibility of travelling out of Zimbabwe, broadening the general parameters of their horizons, networking with other well-resourced people, and continually investing in their own intellectual, social, and political capital. While these were important factors in their relationships, there was also a more basic physical desire and camaraderie that cannot be easily quantified, but which was fuelled by the exceptionality of inter-racial homosexual relationships in Zimbabwe. All of these are the sort of things negotiated in establishing the interpersonal scripts of many intimate relationships in any context, as they constitute the fabric through which two persons establish that they share a commonality, that there is compatibility, that they are interested enough in one another to invest in exploring their bond further.

However, once the relationship is being discussed in the public domain, the cultural scenario through which their relationship is judged obscures these interpersonal scripts, and it is defined by collective understandings of how race, sex, class, and gender intersect. A colonial history redolent with the unpunished sexual exploitation of Zimbabwean men and women as well as the more general manipulation of disproportionate economic power determines a definition of inter-racial sex as exploitation from which Farai and Tendai seem powerless to escape.[53] Furthermore, the homosexuality of their relationship ensures that any discussion in public fora will have as initial reference points the definitions and castigations handed down by Mugabe and other Zimbabwean public figures, which represent the specific character-istics of this relationship as the epitome of cultural and moral danger, both individual and national. Any violence or even profiteering directed at this relationship can then be easily rationalised as justifiable and, indeed, an honourable service in defence of the post-colonial state. And while honourable service in defence of the purity of the post-colonial state might theoretically require the delivery of homosexuals to the police, evidence clearly suggests that in practice this does not preclude the simultaneous handing over of money, the police often colluding to place additional pressures on the victims.

The homophobic context that facilitates these incidents and the cultural scenario through which their interpersonal scripts are distorted have the effect of regularly and repeatedly undermining the self-esteem of gay men and lesbians living within it, regardless of their class and race. It is a complex entanglement of internalisation, resistance, desire, denial, and abuse that surrounds and structures the relationships, and then makes them dif-ficult to sustain, even within race or class. Some accounts of extortion, whether detailed in Human Rights Watch's reports[54] or discussed with this author, do not involve a third party but are often suggested to be the result of disagreements within a relationship, or the act of someone unsure or ambivalent about or even disturbed by their sexual orientation. The emotional and psychological damage that is incurred simply by living in such a virulently homophobic context is evident in the difficulties that many encounter in developing trust and maintaining intimate relationships.[55] It is this insecurity that allows extortionists to prosper and is in turn cultivated and magnified by their activities, for extortion simul-taneously draws upon and reinforces a social order where secrecy and invisibility thrive and where these characteristics come to embody a vulnerability that is psychological, phys-ical (violence and injury), and physiological (HIV and greater risk of infection). The inability to articulate consensual intimate relationships in a narrative that has public credibility is the basis not only for extortion, but also for ignorance. This interferes with work done to prevent transmission of HIV, as there is strong disincentive to identify one's own behaviour to be homosexual and even greater disincentive to then identify oneself as homosexual.[56] Further-more, we have seen how the secrecy on which blackmail depends is reinforced by the silen-cing that a perceived absence of innocence foists upon its victims. This silencing renders ever more audible the legitimating discourse of blackmailers, thereby lending credence to their claim to be 'punishing the forbidden in the name of good order',[57] while it renders ever more secretive the victims' own intrapsychic and interpersonal scripts, obscuring them further beneath the prescriptive narrative of the cultural scenario.

Thus, the noisy rhetoric that licenses anti-homosexual violence produces a nexus of information and power that emphasises the homosexual's 'guilt' and reinforces their vulnerability to blackmail, while simultaneously rendering impossible the representation of interpersonal homosexual scripts as plausible or acceptable, making them once more 'unspeakable'. Blackmail works to silence the homosexual at two levels. First, blackmail inhibits sexual activity, as it aims to terrorise the disruptive body of the homosexual into an acquiescent silence. Second, through amplifying those narratives that signify shame and disorder, the homosexual's agency in representing his or her own negotiated intimacy is increasingly constrained, and ultimately silenced:

> At best the silence that is connected to the homosexual in order to make its sense and nonsense
> is a requirement and an effect of the technologies of its production. This silence forms a part of

the very mechanics of incitement and production that generate the homosexual in law. This requirement of silence is a prerequisite, generating a requirement to speak about the male genital body. As such, silence is indispensable to the proliferating economy of the discourse on this homosexual of the law. Through the principle of silence (and invisibility) that is installed in the machinery of policing is made the necessity of elaborate police practices and procedures to extract the truth of sex through the technique of surveillance and confession ...

So those police practices formally dedicated to diminishing homosexual practices have been implicated in producing their increased social visibility.[58]

As an axis of information and power, blackmail filters narratives and silence to produce a particular 'truth' about the homosexual, whereby law's agents (whether accredited or self-appointed) reaffirm the key signifiers of the cultural scenario by revealing the homosexual's supposed inner core, that which is represented as a secret self, and by implication a 'true' identity. But when a relationship becomes subject to scrutiny through the threat of blackmail, its 'truth' is primarily represented through strategic negotiation rather than confession on the part of the victims, and interpolation by others. This means that the 'truth' of its secrets is actually obscured, as the threats and contesting narratives remove it ever farther from the real experience and control of the person or persons supposedly at its heart. While extortion threatens to expose the secretive, it actually aims to preserve it through reinvention. Extortion prioritises the public structures of identity over any personal investment in intimacy which the partners in the relationship may have made, reaffirming those structures through the carefully managed (non-)disclosure of significantly interpolated 'secrets'.

Conclusion: the relevance of rights

The centrality of sex makes it extremely difficult to describe these relationships in such a way that the narrative can offer up the clearly identifiable 'victims' and 'offenders' that are of strategic value in a petition for human rights. Carole Vance and Alice Miller have suggested that making claims around specifically sexual rights is exceptionally difficult, as claims to human rights tend to rely on narratives that invoke representations of innocence and victimisation, and accounts of sex outside marriage invariably contradict conventional notions of innocence.[59] It is clear that the ideal candidate for a rights test case is someone whose 'innocence' is indisputable and whose situation is beyond reproach. Yet 'innocence' is clearly a tag that has specifically gendered application, such that women's active sexual agency tends to preclude its attribution. In some contexts 'innocence' does not even extend to women exercising sexual agency within marriage, but more commonly it precludes women's sexual agency outside marriage; whereas men's sexual agency tends to be valorised regardless of marriage, and tends to invite censure when its threat to hetero-normative structures is not contained (invisibly) within the private realm.[60] These are broad generalisations, but it remains the case that the further one gets from Gayle Rubin's charmed circle of 'Good, Normal, Natural, Blessed' behaviour that represents the pinnacle of sexual hierarchies, the more remote is the conventional ascription of 'innocence'.[61]

Relationships of intimacy necessarily involve the strategic balancing of private desires and public structures. They are therefore partly constituted through the exercise of discretion as to when to disclose which secrets and to whom (whether to each other or to others). Such decisions reflect the paradox of an autonomy that is inherently relational, and remind us that the task of drawing these difficult boundaries between private prerogative and public proscription attaches to any rational, rights-bearing legal subject in a social setting, as it is a key aspect of agency. However, this becomes considerably more complicated in the very difficult scenarios that frequently lie behind extortion, as they rarely invoke a simple bipolar narrative of victim and abuser. The key elements of power and vulnerability in sexual black-mail invariably arise from complex relationships that breach such moulds of convention as orientation, fidelity, or legality possibly in conjunction with the transgressing of other social divisions (such as race and class in the case of Joe, Farai, and Tendai). It is the location of these relationships outside of marriage and procreation that initially deprives them of a notional innocence and a measure of control over the narratives that claim to speak their 'truth' in the proliferating discourse of sex. And just as sexuality has come to represent an inner truth in a post-colonial society dependent on an ever-narrowing construction of national identity, so blackmail serves to castigate anew the dissident queer.[62] It completes the homosexual's exclusion from the realm of dignity, a concept that arguably underlies rights and equality but which simultaneously threatens to reproduce the social respectability that adheres to Rubin's 'charmed circle' dominating the landscape of sexual hierarchies.[63] Yet, Justice Albie Sachs of the Constitutional Court of South Africa clearly associates dignity with substantive equality:

> The manner in which discrimination is experienced on grounds of race or sex or religion or disability varies considerably – there is difference in difference. The commonality that unites them all is the injury to dignity imposed upon people as a consequence of their belonging to certain groups. Dignity in the context of equality has to be understood in this light. The focus on dignity results in emphasis being placed simultaneously on context, impact and the point of view of the affected persons. Such focus is in fact the guarantor of substantive as opposed to formal equality.
>
> ... In the case of gays, history and experience teach us that the scarring comes not from poverty or powerlessness, but from invisibility. It is the tainting of desire, it is the attribution of perver-sity and shame to spontaneous bodily affection, it is the prohibition of the expression of love, it is the denial of full moral citizenship in society because you are what you are, that impinges on the dignity and self-worth of a group.[64]

Blackmail does bring about precisely these effects – it taints desire and removes dignity. It frequently leaves the victim of the extortion feeling guilty, as they believe that they have precipitated this threat through their own stupidity or recklessness, and that they are there-fore to blame. Yet blackmail inevitably removes dignity and clarity because by necessity it must involve situations that are messy, that contain moral ambivalence, that are drawn from a complicated history of desire and betrayal in which there are no angels. As life is without angels, this messy complexity is unavoidable. It does, however, mean that it is not possible to gloss over the difficulties, to resolve the issue by marking out an innocent person for sal-vation and a villain for penitence, before delivering up some comforting moral absolutes. For this lack of a clear solution and a clean resolution is symptomatic of the almost total subjugation of 'truth' in the strategic narratives that arise in response to the threat of harm or disclosure, and in response to the disruption of the interpersonal scripts of the people involved, and as a result of the manipulation of information and power in order to simply extract value, rather than produce something anew.

This analysis of blackmail therefore highlights a tension that exists between our treat-ment of sexuality and our treatment of rights. However implicit or explicit, the expectation of innocence in the narrative of rights claims confronts us with immediate practical difficul-ties, as it demands that we start from a seriously disabling position, for, as suggested by Vance and Miller, the propriety associated with conventional definitions of innocence tends to preclude the exercising of sexual agency and autonomy.[65] Publicly articulating and then exercising sexual desires, particularly outside marriage, brings private sexual relations into the public sphere and makes it very hard to claim innocence, thereby obstructing an easy claim to rights.

It is unlikely and probably undesirable that we should be able to detach sexuality from any notion of innocence and guilt, but we do need to reconfigure the relationship so that innocence/guilt attaches to issues of harm and autonomy rather than morality or social value. We need to be clear that sex does not inherently besmirch innocence and that sex is not in itself corrupting, in order to develop a relationship between sexuality and rights that values equality and autonomy as suitable frames for agency. This critical reconfiguration of sexuality and notions of guilt/innocence establishes a more effective platform from which to combat sexual violence and the transmission of HIV; being alert to issues of agency and autonomy, it should also foster the experience of sexuality as pleasure. The specific limitations that restrain the development of sexual rights in the international sphere suggest that this conventional requirement of innocence involves an implicit refusal of sexual agency which is a key obstacle to the association of rights and sexuality in many cultural contexts.[66]

It is therefore unsurprising that law reform in any part of the world cannot on its own stop the practice of blackmail. So long as there is still shame and indiscretion to pave its way the decriminalisation of homosexuality in Zimbabwe or elsewhere is unlikely to extinguish sexual minorities' vulnerability to extortion. The incidents that I have described here came to our knowledge because the victims identified as homosexual in as open a manner as was possible in a context where same-sex sexual acts were and remain criminal. It is the law that produced their initial vulnerability while the accompanying rhetoric then advertised the opportunities to profit from that vulnerability. Proper application of rights due Zimbabwean citizens under international law prohibits criminalisation of consensual sexual conduct between males[67] and might pre-empt the law's initiatory role in this opportunism. This suggests that an appropriate way to start challenging this situation is for homosexuals in Zimbabwe to claim the human rights due them, but that can only be the start. Whatever the practical obstacles of making such a claim (including the question of making the Zimbabwean government responsive to a finding against them), it seems unquestionable in principle that those Zimbabweans targeted for extortion on account of consensual same-sex sexual conduct should be able to rely on a context that recognises human rights as fostering some protection. Yet, the evidence in this paper suggests that the reality of extortion is far more complicated, making this possibility seem ever more remote, and reminding us of the limits of law as an instrument for securing agency. Rather, the law represents one terrain through which broader discursive battles might be fought – so that while the realm of law might be an initial platform for producing or challenging extortionate practices, it is only one part of a far bigger discursive realm in which these relations are given life.

Notes

1. Some indication of the ubiquity of this association of prohibition and vulnerability is offered in D.J. West and R. Green, eds, *Socio-legal Control of Homosexuality: A Multi-nation Comparison* (New York, Plenum, 1997), where blackmail by individuals and extortion by police are identified directly or indirectly as problems for sexual minorities in Austria (284), Bolivia (101) England (216), Syria, Lebanon, Islamic countries in North Africa (116), the Netherlands (302), Pakistan (120), Russia (239), Singapore (141), South Africa (24 and 26), and Zimbabwe (49, 52). See also A. Gupta, 'Section 377 and the Dignity of Homosexuals', *Economic and Political Weekly*, 18 November 2006, 4815, 4821, for an incisive analysis of the implications of criminalisation of homosexuals in India, including a discussion of blackmail.

2. 'The Rt Hon. Earl Jowitt, Lord Chancellor of England from 1945 to 1952, made the surprising declaration that when he became attorney general in 1929 he was impressed with the fact that

"A very large percentage of blackmail cases, nearly ninety per cent of them – were cases in which the person blackmailed had been guilty of homosexual practices with an adult person". The Wolfenden Report stated that of seventy-one cases of blackmail reported to the police in the years 1950–3, thirty-two were connected with homosexual activities' (D.J. West, *Homosexuality* [London: Penguin, 1968], 100). Thus, in its 1957 report, the Wolfenden Committee was able to note that the provision criminalising homosexual acts 'was frequently referred to as "the blackmailer's charter"' (L.J. Moran, *The Homosexual(ity) of Law* [London: Routledge, 1996], 52).

3. Interview with Yunnus Omerjee, Director of Public Prosecutions, Harare, January 1993. The interview was one of many conducted as part of the research for this author's PhD thesis: 'Sexual Offences in Zimbabwe: Fetishisms of Procreation, Perversion and Individual Autonomy' (University of Cambridge, 1999).

4. A. Ashworth, *Principles of Criminal Law*, 5th edn (Oxford: Oxford University Press, 2006), 390.

5. P. Alldridge, '"Attempted Murder of the Soul": Blackmail, Privacy and Secrets', *Oxford Journal of Legal Studies* 13, no. 3 (1993): 370.

6. Ibid., 368.

7. There is very little published research on blackmail in Zimbabwe, but Human Rights Watch, in *More than a Name: State-Sponsored Homophobia and Its Consequences in Southern Africa* (New York: Human Rights Watch, 2003), 92–102, offers some detailed affidavits and accounts of specific cases, while more historical but general information is offered by M. Epprecht in *Hungochani: The History of a Dissident Sexuality in Southern Africa* (Montreal: McGill-Queen's University Press, 2004) and by Gays and Lesbians of Zimbabwe (GALZ) in *Unspoken Facts: A History of Homosexualities in Africa* (Harare, 2008). This paper draws from these sources, from confidential formal and informal interviews carried out with gay men in Harare during the years 1990–2000, and from personal observation and extensive communications with both the GALZ director and GALZ legal representative. The evident limits of these few authoritative sources and the self-selected nature of the interviews means that this research is far from a comprehensive overview of blackmail in Zimbabwe. Many of the interviews were conducted in confidentiality, and the names of those interviewees are withheld by mutual agreement.

8. While the names of those concerned have been changed, the details of the scenarios described here have not been altered and are drawn from a series of informal interviews with 'Joe', 'Farai', and 'Tendai' conducted in Harare between 1995 and 1997. Additional commentary is informed by my own observations of the unfolding events, email correspondence with 'Joe', and interviews of other gay men in Harare between 1991 and 1997. I also draw on the information in Human Rights Watch, *More than a Name*, 92–102.

9. Traditional culture actually allows far more space and possibilities for same-sex sexual relations than is reflected in the absolutist statements of Mugabe and other senior Zimbabwean politicians. Their vehement adherence to a binary conception of homo/heterosexuality is a further importation of the Western conceptualisations of sexuality that came with colonial law and Christianity to supplant the 'traditional' cultural regulation of sexual behaviours: see O. Phillips 'Constituting the Global Gay: Individual Subjectivity and Sexuality in Southern Africa', in *Sexuality in the Legal Arena*, ed. C. Stychin and D. Herman (London: Athlone Press, 2000), 17; S. Murray and W. Roscoe, *Boy Wives and Female Husbands: Studies in African Homosexualities* (New York: St Martin's Press, 1998). Marc Epprecht's *Humgochani* makes clear that the history of same-sex sexual relations in Zimbabwe is far more complex, accommodating, and fluid than simply prohibitory; see also GALZ, *Unspoken Facts*.

10. See A. Akeroyd 'Coercion, Constraints and "Cultural Entrapments": A Further Look at Gendered and Occupational Factors Pertinent to the Transmission of HIV in Africa', in *HIV & AIDS in Africa: Beyond Epidemiology*, ed. E. Kalipeni, S. Craddock, J. Oppong, and J. Ghosh (London: Blackwell, 2004), 89.

11. E. Kalipeni, S. Craddock, and J. Ghosh, 'Mapping the AIDS Pandemic: The Geographical Progression of HIV in Eastern and Southern Africa', in *HIV & AIDS in Africa: Beyond Epidemiology*, ed. E. Kalipeni, S. Craddock, J. Oppong, and J. Ghosh (London: Blackwell, 2004), 58; B.G. Schoepf, 'AIDS in Africa: Structure, Agency, and Risk', in *HIV & AIDS in Africa: Beyond Epidemiology*, ed. E. Kalipeni, S. Craddock, J. Oppong, and J. Ghosh (London: Blackwell, 2004), 121.

12. P. Lurie, P. Hintzen, and R. Lowe, 'Socioeconomic Obstacles to HIV Prevention and Treatment in Developing Countries', in *HIV & AIDS in Africa: Beyond Epidemiology*, ed. E. Kalipeni, S. Craddock, J. Oppong, and J. Ghosh (London: Blackwell, 2004), 209.

13. Schoepf, 'AIDS in Africa'.

14. R. Hyam, 'Empire and Sexual Opportunity', *Journal of Imperial and Commonwealth History* 14 (1986): 36.

15. See Phillips, 'Sexual Offences in Zimbabwe', 111–32; see also D. Jeater, *Marriage, Perversion and Power: The Construction of Moral Discourse in Southern Rhodesia 1894–1930* (Oxford: Clarendon Press, 1993), 90; J. Pape, 'Black and White: "The Perils of Sex" in Colonial Zimbabwe', *Journal of Southern African Studies* 16, no. 4 (1990): 699.

16. G. Seidman, 'Women in Zimbabwe: Post-independence Struggles', *Feminist Studies* 10, no. 3 (1984): 432.

17. See O. Phillips, 'Zimbabwean Law and the Production of a White Man's Disease', *Social & Legal Studies* 6, no. 4 (1997): 471; N. Hoad, 'Tradition, Modernity, and Human Rights: An Interrogation of Contemporary Gay and Lesbian Rights' Claims in Southern African Nationalist Discourses', *Development Update* 2, no. 2 (1998): 32; see also J. Alexander, 'Not Just (Any) Body Can Be a Citizen: The Politics of Law, Sexuality and Postcoloniality in Trinidad and Tobago and the Bahamas', in *Sexualities and Society: A Reader*, ed. J. Weeks, J. Holland, and M. Waites (Cambridge, UK: Polity Press, 2003), 174.

18. M. Aarmo, 'How Homosexuality Became "Un-African": The Case of Zimbabwe', in *Female Desires: Same-Sex Relations and Transgender Practices Across Cultures*, ed. E. Blackwood and S. Wieringa (New York: Columbia University Press, 1999), 255.

19. For a critical conceptualisation of the role of 'tradition' in culture, see E. Hobsbawm and T. Ranger, eds, *The Invention of Tradition* (Cambridge, UK: Canto Press, 1991); for work that draws on Hobsbawm and Ranger to examine the interaction of 'tradition' and 'sexuality' in Zimbabwe, see Phillips, 'Sexual Offences in Zimbabwe'; idem, 'Constituting the Global Gay'.

20. The international instruments that Zimbabwe has ratified include the African Charter on Human and Peoples' Rights, the International Covenant on Civil and Political Rights, the International Covenant on Economic, Social and Cultural Rights, the Convention on the Elimination of All Forms of Discrimination against Women, the Convention on the Rights of the Child, and the Convention on the Elimination of All Forms of Racial Discrimination.

21. J. Comaroff, 'The Discourse of Rights in Colonial South Africa: Subjectivity, Sovereignty, Modernity', in *Identities, Politics and Rights*, ed. A. Sarat and T.R. Kearns (Ann Arbor: University of Michigan Press, 1997), 234.

22. Jeater, *Marriage, Perversion and Power*, 81.

23. See O.C. Phillips, '(Dis)Continuities of Custom in Zimbabwe and South Africa: The Implications for Gendered and Sexual Rights', *Health and Human Rights* 7, no. 2 (2004): 82.

24. See Phillips, 'Zimbabwean Law and the Production of a White Man's Disease'.

25. *The Herald* (Harare), 12 August 1995.

26. *The Citizen* (Johannesburg), 12 August 1995.

27. Robert Mugabe in *GALZ Newsletter* 11 (1994): 13.

28. Phillips, 'Zimbabwean Law and the Production of a White Man's Disease'.

29. Robert Mugabe in C. Dunton and M. Palmberg 'Human Rights and Homosexuality in Southern Africa', *Current African Issues*, 2nd edn (Uppsala, Sweden: Nordiska Afrika Institut, 1996), 12–13.

30. H.K. Bhabha, ed., *Nation and Narration* (London: Routledge, 1990); J. Dollimore *Sexual Dissidence: Augustine to Wilde, Freud to Foucault* (Oxford: Clarendon Press, 1991).

31. G. Mason, 'Being Hated: Stranger or Familiar?', *Social & Legal Studies* 14, no. 4 (2005): 586.

32. Robert Mugabe, Opening Speech and Press Conference, Zimbabwe International Book Fair (ZIBF), Harare, 1 August 1995.

33. Mudariki MP, Chigwedere MP, and Gezi, MP, 'The Evil and Iniquitous Practice of Homosexualism and Lesbianism', Zimbabwe Parliamentary Debates, *Hansard*, 28 September 1995, 2779.

34. The experience of the legal representative of GALZ as well as the Director of GALZ was that the number increased (D. Matyzsak and K. Goddard, personal communication). It is impossible to ever know the exact number of incidents, as the nature of extortion is such that it operates most effectively on those who are most reluctant to tell anyone of their predicament, so there are likely to be a significant number of incidents that have not come to the attention of GALZ officers.

35. Section 134 of the Criminal Law Codification and Reform Act stipulates that blackmail carries a level 13 fine (the second-highest tariff) or twice the value of the property extorted or a maximum of 15 years' imprisonment. Section 73(1) of the Sexual Offences Act 2006 stipulates that any consensual sexual acts between men (up to and including anal penetration) carry a level 14 fine (the highest tariff) but one year's imprisonment.

36. Moran, *The Homosexual(ity) of Law*, 56.

37. Ibid., 52, stresses that this was the subject of numerous submissions to the Wolfenden Committee; see also West and Green, *Socio-legal Control of Homosexuality*, 126–8; H.M. Hyde *The Other Love: An Historical and Contemporary Survey of Homosexuality in Britain* (London: Heinemann, 1970), 255. For examples of police complicity in other jurisdictions, see T. Wright and R. Wright, 'Bolivia: Developing a Gay Community – Homosexuality and AIDS', in *Socio-legal Control of Homosexuality: A Multi-nation Comparison*, ed. D.J. West and R. Green (New York, Plenum, 1997), 101; S. Murray and B. Khan 'Pakistan', in *Socio-legal Control of Homosexuality: A Multi-nation Comparison*, ed. D.J. West and R. Green (New York, Plenum, 1997), 120; I. Kon, 'Russia', in *Socio-legal Control of Homosexuality: A Multi-nation Comparison*, ed. D.J. West and R. Green (New York, Plenum, 1997), 239.

38. For detailed affidavits of extortion and accounts of police complicity, see Human Rights Watch, *More than a Name*, 92–102.

39. In a typical case described to this author (confidential interview), the police refused to assist a victim who had money and a mobile phone extracted from him under threat of physical violence (the victim had refused to yield to the threat of a false accusation of demanding oral sex at gunpoint). The threats took place in the presence of the police, and the extortionist demanded that a total of Z$70,000 be paid to him (about US$100 at the time of the original incident). Initially a police officer sought to 'negotiate a sum' between the two parties, but when the victim refused to part with any money a police case file ('docket') was opened against the victim, who was then threatened with arrest for homosexual activities.

40. D. Matyszak, legal representative of GALZ, personal communication.

41. Human Rights Watch, *More than a Name*, 92–102.

42. Mason, 'Being Hated', 590.

43. This is clear from my own interviews with many Zimbabwean gay men over the years, but also see Human Rights Watch, *More than a Name*, 92–102.

44. Mason, 'Being Hated', 600.

45. Alldridge, '"Attempted Murder of the Soul"', 376.

46. D.J. West, *Sexual Victimization: Two Recent Researches into Sex Problems and their Social Effects* (London: Gower, 1987), 126–7.

47. Moran, *The Homosexual(ity) of Law*, 58.

48. The Sexual Offences (Amendment) Act 2000 (c. 44) finally brought into law an equal age of consent of 16 years old for homosexual and heterosexual acts.

49. Alldridge, '"Attempted Murder of the Soul"', 373.

50. In the South African Constitutional Court case of *National Coalition for Gay and Lesbian Equality* v. *Minister of Justice*, CCT 11/98, this approach was explicitly adopted by Justice Albie Sachs in his ruling that the offence of sodomy in South Africa was unconstitutional because it violated a person's rights to equality, dignity, and privacy (para. 30), stating that '[p]rivacy recognises that we all have a right to a sphere of private intimacy and autonomy which allows us to establish and nurture human relationships without interference from the outside community. The way in which we give expression to our sexuality is at the core of this area of private intimacy' (para. 32).

51. W. Simon and J.H. Gagnon, 'Sexual Scripts', in *Culture, Society and Sexuality: A Reader*, ed. R. Parker and P. Aggleton, 2nd edn (New York and London: Routledge, 2007), 31.

52. Alldridge, '"Attempted Murder of the Soul"', 368.

53. For more on this history of sexual exploitation in colonial Zimbabwe, see Jeater, *Marriage, Perversion and Power*; Phillips, 'Sexual Offences in Zimbabwe'; Pape 'Black and White'.

54. Human Rights Watch, *More than a Name*, 92–102.

55. GALZ, *Unspoken Facts*, 4, 213.

56. O.C. Phillips, 'The Invisible Presence of Homosexuality: Implications for HIV/AIDS and Rights in Southern Africa', in *HIV & AIDS in Africa: Beyond Epidemiology*, ed. E. Kalipeni, S. Craddock, J. Oppong, and J. Ghosh (London: Blackwell, 2004), 155; see also C.A.

Johnson, *Off the Map: How HIV/AIDS Programming Is Failing Same-Sex Practicing People in Africa* (New York: International Gay and Lesbian Human Rights Commission, 2007).

57. Moran, *The Homosexual(ity) of Law*, 56.

58. Ibid., 166–7

59. Carole Vance and Alice Miller first suggested this at a panel on 'Sexuality and Rights: Questions, Challenges, and Ways Forward' at the 16th World Congress of Sexology, Havana, 10–14 March 2003. For more on this, see A. Miller and C. Vance, 'Sexuality, Human Rights and Health', *Health and Human Rights* 7, no. 2 (2004): 5; A. Miller, 'Sexuality, Violence against Women, and Human Rights: Women Make Demands and Ladies Get Protection', *Health and Human Rights* 7, no. 2 (2004): 16.

60. For a further exploration of this gendered regulation of sexuality and hetero-normative space, see J. Millbank, 'A Preoccupation with Perversion: The British Response to Refugee Claims on the Basis of Sexual Orientation 1989–2003', *Social & Legal Studies* 14, no. 1 (2005): 115; see also E. Henderson '"I'd Rather Be an Outlaw": Identity, Activism and Decriminalisation in Tasmania', in *Sexuality in the Legal Arena*, ed. C. Stychin and D. Herman (London: Athlone Press, 2000), 35.

61. For a full explanation of this hierarchical model of sexual behaviours and their social regulation, see G. Rubin, 'Thinking Sex: Notes for a Radical Theory of the Politics of Sexuality', in *Pleasure and Dange: Exploring Female Sexuality*, ed. C. Vance (London: Routledge & Kegan Paul, 1984), 267.

62. In 1999, Keith Goddard, the openly gay convenor of GALZ, found himself subjected to blackmail attempts. Having successfully liaised with the Zimbabwe Republic Police (ZRP) in the past, he took all three of the threatening letters to the ZRP so that they could carry out a proper investigation. While they did arrest the blackmailer, who was convicted of extortion, the police also charged Goddard with 'forcible sodomy', even though there was no evidence to support such a charge and the allegations were so implausible as to be patently spurious. In 2004, the Attorney General finally conceded that the charges were baseless, but the police continued to threaten spurious prosecution as a means to intimidate the organisation and to pressure the administrator of GALZ. Thus, despite the evident fabrication of the threatening narrative, it prevails in the introduction of the issue into law, persistently infringing Goddard's dignity.

63. For more on Rubin's 'charmed circle' and sexual hierarchies, see Rubin, 'Thinking Sex'. But on the place of 'dignity' in human rights see R.E. Howard, 'Dignity, Community, and Human Rights', in A. A. An-Na'im, ed., *Human Rights in Cross-Cultural Perspectives: A Quest for Consensus* (Philadelphia: University of Pennsylvania Press, 1992), 81. Howard argues that the concept of dignity is often achieved through conformity and adherence to social values and customs; in other words, it reflects the moral worth of a person living in an unequal and hierarchical society, whereas human rights are an egalitarian means for allocating membership in a collectivity to each individual regardless of status. Howard argues that human rights are modern, individualist, and liberal while concepts of dignity and justice can be traced through all societies; she suggests that they can be used to buttress human rights but should not be confused with human rights.

64. *National Coalition for Gay and Lesbian Equality* v. *Minister of Justice*, CCT 11/98, per Sachs J., paras 126–7.

65. Miller and Vance, 'Sexuality, Human Rights and Health'; Miller, 'Sexuality, Violence against Women and Human Rights'.

66. A useful illustration of this is the South African Constitutional Court's unanimous decision that the continued prohibition of sex work was consistent with the constitutional rights to privacy, dignity, freedom, security of the person, and economic activity, and that the decriminalisation thereof was a matter for the legislature rather than the Constitutional Court (*S* v. *Jordan*, 2002 [11] BCLR 1117 [SC]). Insofar as the Court's denial of sex workers' rights reaffirmed their criminality and vulnerability, it also marked out the acceptable limits of sexual agency and failed to dislodge a discourse of morality for one of harm reduction and workers' rights. The Court's exceptionally cautious and restrained approach towards its law-making role and the unanimity of its decision suggested that sex-workers' 'innocence' was so remote that even this august rights-oriented body could not bridge their divide from legitimate entitlement.

67. In May 1991, Zimbabwe acceded to the International Covenant on Civil and Political Rights binding on the country since August 1991. *Toonen* v. *Australia*, 1(3) IHRR 97 (1994), made

clear that laws prohibiting consensual sexual conduct between male adults violate Article 26 of the Covenant. The United Nations Human Rights Committee specifically requested that Zimbabwe reverse its treatment of homosexual conduct with appropriate legislation in its *Consideration of Reports Submitted by States Parties under Article 40 to the Covenant*, CCPR/C/74/Add.3, HRI/CORE/1/Add.55, 26 March 1998.

Lost in transition: transpeople, transprejudice and pathology in Asia

Sam Winter

Faculty of Education, University of Hong Kong, China

Asia (particularly South and Southeast) is home to large numbers of transpeople: persons who are gender identity variant in that they present and identify in a gender other than that matching the gender assigned to them at birth. Many make a gender category transition early in life. Access to competent and transfriendly medical support services within the established health system is often difficult, and alternatives are risky. Regardless of physical transition, transpeople are often denied opportunities to change the gender recorded on key identification documents. The result is that transpeople wanting to live in stealth are frustrated in their attempts to do so. They become easy targets for transprejudice and discrimination, many being pushed towards work at society's margins (for example sex work). Where transpeople are denied the right to change documents specifying their legal gender status, they are also denied legal recognition for mixed-gender partnerships they enter into (i.e. the right to marry, as well as associated family rights, including adoption of children). Recent evidence suggests that psychiatry may exacerbate transprejudice by pathologising gender identity variance. The current debate in Western countries on de-pathologisation is therefore highly important for the future welfare of transpeople in Asia.

Introduction

This paper[1] is about the lives of transgender people or, more informally, 'transpeople' in Asia. It begins with some observations regarding transgender experiences across the continent, and then focuses on one key aspect of the experiences: transprejudice and associated discrimination. It ends with a reflection upon what is, in the opinion of this author, an important factor supporting such prejudice and discrimination, the idea that transpeople suffer from a mental disorder. The emphasis throughout is upon transwomen in South and Southeast Asia. The reason for this is that their lives have been more thoroughly researched than those of transwomen elsewhere in Asia or of transmen across the continent.[2] However, it seems reasonable to assume that many challenges facing transwomen in South and Southeast Asia apply to those other groups as well.

Before beginning I need to make my own use of key terms clear. In this paper I mean by 'transpeople' persons who present and identify in a gender category other than that matching the gender category assigned to them (usually on the basis of genital anatomy) at birth, adopting the appearance and social roles associated with that gender category. They may be described as 'gender identity variant'. The period of time during which the individual progressively moves towards an alternative gender presentation and/or identity is called 'gender transition'. Gender variant individuals who are not gender identity variant (for example some transvestites and cross-dressers) are not discussed in this paper. It should be noted, however, that they encounter much of the prejudice and discrimination (discussed later in this paper) that gender identity variant people do. In Western literature some trans-people are often called 'transsexual'.[3] This term is problematic. First, it is often used to refer only to those who have undergone or intend to undergo sex reassignment surgeries (called SRS) involving (for transwomen) the construction of a vagina and clitoris, or (for transmen) the construction, by one means or another, of a penis.[4] For many gender identity variant people in developing countries these surgeries are simply not part of their life agenda. Second, the term carries unfortunate connotations of mental disorder, being a diagnostic label employed in the Tenth Revision of the *International Statistical Classification of Diseases and Related Health Problems* (ICD-10) published by the World Health Organis-ation. For some time in Western countries there has been an increasingly vocal debate on the pathologisation of gender identity variance. For these reasons I avoid using the term 'trans-sexual' in this paper, preferring to employ 'transpeople', and substituting the term where other authors have used the term 'transsexuals'. Within that group called transpeople 'trans-women' are those assigned to the male gender category at birth who present in a non-male gender. One might otherwise call them 'gender identity variant men'. Similarly 'transmen' are those individuals designated female at birth who present and perhaps identify as non-female, individuals who might otherwise be called 'gender identity variant women'.

Three aspects of the terms and definitions offered deserve special comment. First, the use of 'non-male' for transwomen and 'non-female' for transmen. In some cultures, includ-ing many in Asia, a sexual and gender cosmography exists that is more varied than the two categories 'male' and 'female' with which research in Western countries is familiar. Although many 'gender identity variant men' may indeed present as women (or at least as a sub-set of women) others may identify as a blend of male and female or as a third sex or gender. To this extent the terms 'transwomen' and 'transmen', products of a binary male–female sexology, are imperfect. I use them for three reasons. First, they keep things simple: as will be evident, there is a plethora of culture-specific terms for describing transpeople in Asia,[5] many so broad in meaning that they also denote individuals who are not gender identity variant. Second, they keep things respectful: many indigenous terms are derogatory. Third, they are preferable to 'gender identity variant men' and 'gender identity variant women': however else they may identify and present, 'gender identity variant men' by their nature do not present, and seldom identify, as men; the corresponding point applies to 'gender identity variant women'.

Second, the term 'transpeople', as used here, refers to those who have undergone, or are undergoing, a gender transition. The challenges of gender transition, including but not limited to the stigma attached to being recognised as a transperson, not only can make lives difficult for those transitioning, but also can discourage others from following suit. In that sense individuals reluctant to make a gender transition may be victims of stigma as much as those who have already made it.

A note is also needed on the sexual preferences and sexual behaviours of transpeople. Terms such as 'homosexual' and 'heterosexual' (and 'gay', 'lesbian', 'bisexual', etc.) are Western conceptions. Many Asians are unfamiliar with them, there being no easy trans-lation into their native languages or sexological worldviews. However, I take the opportu-nity to put on record that I consider an androphilic transwoman (i.e. one sexually attracted to men) to be heterosexual because of her attraction to a member of another gender and a gynephilic transwoman (i.e. one attracted to women) as homosexual because she has a same-gender preference. My usage is contrary to much Western literature (particularly medical), which persists in referring to androphilic transwomen and gynephilic transman as homosexual (indeed as homosexual transsexual males and females, respectively).

Much of the (largely Western) research in social sciences and the humanities on transpeople's lives documents stigma, prejudice, discrimination and social and economic marginalisation, much of which impacts on transpeople's mental and physical health and well-being[6] as it does on homosexuals'.[7] Indeed, the website *Remembering Our Dead*, which currently lists around 350 transpeople, most of whom died violent deaths, bears testimony to the hostile extremes to which antipathy towards transpeople can extend.[8] This leads me to two final terms: 'transphobia' and 'transprejudice'. 'Transphobia' refers to a broad antipathy towards transpeople; negative attitudes and beliefs that (expressed by family members, students and teachers, employers and co-workers, and through institutions, services, government agencies and legal systems) often frame transpeople's experiences.[9] Transphobia corresponds to a better established term used in relation to homosexuals: 'homophobia', meaning 'the dread of being in close quarters with homosexuals – and in the case of homosexuals themselves, self-loathing'.[10] However, the term transphobia, like homophobia, may be a misnomer, wrongly implying that fear underlies the stigma, discrimination, marginalisation and violence that sexual minority groups suffer. King and his colleagues have recently argued for the term 'transprejudice'.[11] It is the term used in this paper and is defined as the negative valuing, stereotyping and discriminatory treatment of individuals whose appearance and/or identity does not conform to the current social expectations or conventional conceptions of gender. Note that the term embraces discriminatory behaviours as well as the attitudes and beliefs that give rise to such behaviours. In practice it may sometimes be useful to distinguish between prejudice (which is about attitudes and beliefs) and discrimination (which is about behaviour). I refer to them separately in this paper.

The challenge for transpeople in Western countries has been, and remains, to secure the right to gender expression (a right that implies others treating them as members of the gender in which they wish to present), the right of equality of access to goods and services (especially in relation to health, education and employment); the rights to marriage and family life consistent with their gender presentation; and the right to privacy.[12] Much of the same challenge faces transpeople in Asian countries, although, as will be evident, their life circumstances sometimes call for priorities different from their Western counterparts'.

The key premises of this paper are as follows. First, across Asia (particularly South and Southeast) there are large numbers, indeed communities, of transpeople, often transitioning early in life, and often socially visible in their societies. Second, access to high-quality, competent and transfriendly gender healthcare within the established health systems is often difficult, and alternatives are risky. Third, regardless of gender transition, transpeople are often denied opportunities to change the gender markers recorded on key documents used for identification. Fourth, the healthcare and documentation issues combine to frustrate attempts by transpeople who wish to live in 'stealth' actually to do so. They therefore become easy targets for transprejudice and discrimination. Fifth, transprejudice and discrimination are widespread across Asia. Employment presents a particular problem, with many transpeople pushed towards work at society's margins (for example sex work). Where transpeople are denied the right to change documents that specify legal gender status, they are in effect denied legal recognition for any mixed-gender partnership they enter into. Unable to marry within a mixed-gender partnership, they are denied associated family rights, including adoption of children. Finally, recent evidence suggests that modern psychiatry may exacerbate transprejudice by pathologising gender identity variance. The implication is that the current debate in Western countries on the de-pathologisation of gender identity variance is highly important for the future welfare of transpeople in Asia.

A note is needed here about rights. In any given society, rights, whether enjoyed or denied, exist in a broad context. Across Asia as a whole, part of that context is that a human rights culture is not as well developed as in, for example, Europe. Indeed, international human rights treaties such as the International Covenant on Civil and Political Rights and the International Covenant on Economic, Social and Cultural Rights have been portrayed by some in Asia as Western neo-colonial impositions in conflict with 'Asian values'. It is fair to say that a few Asian governments ride roughshod over the rights of their majorities (let alone any of their minorities), displaying little tolerance for any social activism aimed at securing those rights. In these countries transpeople are arguably only one of the groups who are oppressed. But their situation is exacerbated by the fact that international human rights law, which is interpreted and enforced through domestic laws, is silent on matters of sexuality. The exclusion of sexuality from the United Nations human rights agenda has been criticised for perpetuating the view that sexuality is a 'complex, even mysterious' case in matters of human rights and its exclusion from that agenda.[13] The effect is that even among those countries that have signed or ratified the International Covenant on Civil and Political Rights and/or the International Covenant on Economic, Social and Cultural Rights the position of transpeople under the instruments' 'any other status' provisions remains unclear.[14]

Asia is a vast and culturally diverse continent, home to about 60% of the world's population, and perhaps a similar percentage of the world's transpeople. Given its immensity and diversity it is difficult to make generalisations about any Asian context for transpeople's lives. For one thing, concepts of sex, gender and sexual preference and behaviour differ widely across Asia: in any one place they reflect ways of thinking, and are expressed in language, unfamiliar not only to Westerners but also to Asians elsewhere.[15]

Until recently the lives of transpeople in Asia were not a popular research topic. When in 2002 I researched the English-language humanities and social sciences literature on transpeople and gender identity variance, I found that only 7% originated from or concerned Asia. The research literature (print and web based) has significantly grown in the past few years. The TransgenderASIA Centre carries (as of 29 April 2008) a bibliography of around 200 works, over a quarter of which are post-2002.[16] The research coverage is patchy. Across Asia, transmen remain under-researched, and even for transwomen most of the available English-language research has focused on a broad band of 18 countries in South, Southeast and East Asia (less than half the total of Asian countries yet accounting for around 95% of the Asian literature).[17] These 18 countries are a highly diverse group, historically, culturally, economically and politically. Nevertheless, some general observations can be made about the prevalence and social visibility of transpeople; issues of healthcare, documentation and stealth; and transprejudice and discrimination. All these observations carry implications for transpeople's lives.

High prevalence and social visibility

Transpeople are a highly visible feature of some Asian cultures; as the subject of magazine articles and documentaries, portrayed as characters in soap operas, taking part in beauty contests (which in some places are televised), and evident in urban centres as well as in villages. They often form distinct communities. The few reports examining numbers mainly concern transwomen. They suggest that in some Asian cultures, at least, transpeople seem far more common than in much of North America or Europe, where most research has hitherto been done. There may be between 50,000 and 100,000 Malaysian transwomen (*maknyah*) (around 1:75 to 1:150 birth-assigned males aged 15 and above).[18] In India there are an estimated 500,000 Indian transwomen (*hijra*) (about 1:600).[19] In Thailand there are perhaps 300,000 transwomen (*phuying khaam phet*) (around 1:300).[20] High prevalences are not entirely limited to South or Southeast Asia. In one town in Oman in the 1970s an estimated one in 60 birth-assigned men were living as *xanith* transwomen.[21] These prevalence figures far exceed the most commonly cited Western prevalence figures for 'male-to-female transsexualism': around 1:30,000 (birth-assigned) adult men and 1:100,000 women in Europe.[22] The discrepancy almost certainly results from the fact that figures in Western countries represent those who attend medical clinics or are diagnosed as 'gender identity disordered' (or 'transsexual'), and have been approved for SRS or have undergone it. In contrast, estimates in Asian countries have generally included all transwomen; 'pre-op' (pre-operative) and 'non-op' (non-operative) as well as 'post-op' (post-operative). As has been pointed out elsewhere, transpeople who approach clinics may represent a small minority of transpeople overall.[23] This is most certainly the case for Asian societies.[24]

Interestingly, several Asian reports provide figures based on clinic-based counting methodologies of the sort common in Western studies, that is, counting the number of transpeople seeking or undergoing SRS. Two examples are offered here. For Iran, official statistics suggest 15,000 to 20,000 transpeople nationwide.[25] Even at 15,000, this represents around 1:3300 of Iran's approximately 50 million people aged 15 and above. For Singapore, estimated prevalence is 1:2900 for transwomen.[26] Again, both are well above commonly quoted figures in Western countries.[27] Obviously, the more transpeople there are in a community, the more potential victims of stigma, prejudice and discrimination there are. But there are other implications. It may be especially hard for any transperson who wants to live in stealth actually to do so when it is commonly known that the gender identity variant community is large in that society.

The high numbers of transpeople in some Asian cultures should be seen in the light of pre-modern traditions and beliefs that drew on themes of gender identity variance in the arts, religion and history to an extent not found in the Judaeo-Christian West[28] and without portraying it as a disorder.[29] Many pre-modern Asian cultures afforded transpeople well-respected social roles, often as spirit mediums and healers or as actors, singers and dancers. [30] Over the past few centuries these traditional social roles have eroded in the face of modernisation (or Western colonisation, Christianisation, urbanisation) only to be replaced by less prestigious roles such as beauty and hair salon work, dance and mime performances for tourists, and, in many societies, begging and (for transwomen) sex work.[31] The involvement of transwomen in sex work begs a paper of its own. Briefly put, transwomen in some pre-modern societies provided a sexual outlet, enabling men to bypass strict limits on access to women outside the institution of marriage, for example in Oman, India and Thailand.[32] It is possible that contemporary transwomen, deprived of some of the roles previously available, drawn into the money economy and deprived of other employment opportunities, have increasingly pursued a sexual outlet role in the context of sex work. The nature of their work places gender identity variant sex workers at particular risk of HIV/AIDS over and above other sex workers.

But how many gender identity variant individuals are there who do not make a transition, for example because of fear of family rejection or of not being able to get a job? Locating them is perforce difficult, yet it holds the prospect of enabling an estimate of the upper bound for the number of transpeople in a culture: the number of transpeople there would be were it not for the stigma involved in transitioning and the accompanying prejudice, discrimination and social and economic marginalisation. A study by Cruz and

Rogando-Sasot drew on data from a nationwide study of 15- to 27-year-old Filipinos in 2002 and suggested that around 2% of birth-assigned males reported that they would, if they could, choose to be female, *because they felt female.*[33] If these figures provide any guide to other countries, it appears that gender identity variance is a common phenomenon.

Lastly, in many Asian cultures it is not only the numbers of transpeople that are striking; it is also the age at which they transition (during childhood and adolescence, rather than adulthood). Indeed in much of Southeast and East Asia early transition seems to be the norm. This impression is confirmed by community-based research on transwomen in Thailand, the Philippines, Laos, Malaysia, Singapore, South Korea and Japan and by clinic-based studies in Singapore and Japan involving transwomen and transmen.[34] In some cultures young people engaged in gender transition typically benefit from support and guidance from older people in the transcommunity, in turn offering support to those who come after them.[35] The availability of this social networking likely increases the chance that gender identity variant individuals actually transition rather than attempt to suppress their predisposition in the hope that it will fade away and they may have a 'normal life', a strategy that would be familiar to many Western transpeople.

Healthcare issues

In much of Asia gender transition is facilitated by the easy availability of hormones. Southeast Asia is a case in point. In Laos various products are available, costing around US$1 for a month's supply. In the Philippines many transwomen report obtaining contraceptive drugs at their local reproductive health centres. In Thailand up to 20 products containing cross-sex hormones are available over the counter at major pharmacies.

The situation for surgery is more mixed. In Thailand SRS can cost as little as 50,000 baht (about US$1580 at April 2008 exchange rates), breast implants from 40,000 baht (US$1260).[36] Even in terms of average Thai income these prices are low (around ten weeks and eight weeks of average income, respectively). Until recently, castration surgery (removal of the testicles) provided an even cheaper route to emasculation (at US$125). Some 16,000 clinics were offering the service (incidentally providing an indication of the number of people engaged in gender transition). The Medical Council of Thailand, concerned about the numbers undergoing this surgery, has now banned the practice.[37]

Elsewhere in Asia, surgery can be prohibitively expensive, low quality or illegal. A recent article concerning the Philippines quoted at least US$2100 for breast implants and US$6300 for SRS.[38] More current figures indicate that charges have risen, with breast implant surgery apparently now costing at least US$2800 and SRS surgery at least US$7100.[39] These figures represent 10 months and 26 months of average income, respectively. Facing such costs, many transwomen in Asia turn to cheaper alternatives: injected silicone (a procedure particularly common in the Philippines) and simple castration (now banned in Thailand but available elsewhere). In India, SRS as understood in Western countries is hardly available at all. Instead many transwomen in *hijra* (and related) communities undergo a crude procedure involving both castration and penectomy, but not construction of a vagina.[40] Few of those who perform the operations have any recognised medical qualification.[41] In Malaysia, since 1983 SRS involving Muslim patients or surgeons has been banned on religious grounds.[42] The Muslim population is of course the majority in Malaysia, and would otherwise be expected to provide most of the patients and surgeons.

Notwithstanding cross-national variations in the availability of transition-related medical procedures, it is clear that many adolescents in Asia are taking cross-sex hormones and undergoing some form of genital surgery.[43] The effects of cross-sex hormones are sometimes permanent, the side effects numerous and sometimes dangerous. Surgery is often irreversible, most clearly in the case of genital surgery. Surgical procedures themselves (particularly castration, penectomy and silicone injection performed by medically untrained personnel) can be risky. Reports of subsequent ill-health or death are common. Transpeople who have undergone surgery sometimes express regret. Yet gender identity variant adolescents commonly take hormones or undergo surgery without independent professional advice regarding potential consequences, suitability or, in the case of cross-sex hormones, knowledge of what distinguishes use from abuse. Failure to consult a medical professional often stems from a perception that personnel in the public health system (where there is one) are unsympathetic. Private doctors, on the other hand, are often too expensive. Fellow transpeople, though not always medically knowledgeable, are generally sympathetic, and free. They often become the major source of medical advice for their peers.

My own research confirms the scale of unsupervised hormone use. In three separate studies (in Laos, Thailand and the Philippines, each with local co-researchers) I found that transpeople hardly ever consulted medical professionals about the use of cross-sex hormones, either before or while taking them.[44] Not surprisingly, all three studies revealed disturbing patterns of hormone (ab)use. Many participants appeared to consume whatever their friends recommended. When they had money they ingested doses well above recommended levels. When they had no money, they ingested none at all. They were largely ignorant of health risks involved in prolonged hormone use, many failing to take the most obvious precautions against ill-effects (such as desisting from smoking). Not surprisingly, many of those who took hormones eventually desisted through health complications. In the Lao study, around half had stopped taking hormones within six years, nine out of ten citing health problems. The Thai and Philippine studies yielded similar figures. Predictably, a recent Thai study revealed that transpeople taking hormones had a poorer overall quality of life than those who did not.[45]

Accessible, affordable, approachable and competent trans-healthcare is a goal for transpeople of all ages. It is particularly urgent for those transitioning during adolescence and even pre-adolescence, who may be poorly informed and most easily swayed by the advice of uninformed older mentors. One way forward is by way of community education programmes that inform not only the mentees but also the mentors. Beyond these issues, consent and confidentiality are important matters concerning gender identity variant minors. Also important is the issue of alternative treatment choices. Puberty-delaying hormones are a good example. Available to minors in some parts of Europe and the United States, they are entirely reversible, making it possible for doctors, parents and perhaps the young transitioning person to avoid some of the soul-searching when less reversible procedures are being considered. Yet, I have not come across their use anywhere in Asia.

Documentation issues

In many Western countries, 'post-op' transpeople may now change their legal status. Some countries extend this right to 'pre-op' and 'non-op' transpeople (those who have not undergone SRS or do not intend to do so).[46] Few countries in Asia recognise this as a right, even for 'post-op' people. Transpeople therefore remain unable to change their birth certificates, family register or other legal documentation designating their gender.[47] Indeed, in many Asian countries transpeople are not able to amend any personal identification documentation at all.

Turning first to the Asian countries that allow a change in legal gender status (as evident in a person's marriage rights): this right currently appears available only in Japan, South Korea, China (though perhaps limited to certain provinces), Singapore and, according to informal reports, Indonesia[48] and Iran.[49] A favourable decision by a Kuwaiti court in 2004 was overturned on appeal within a few months.[50] Similarly, transpeople in the Philippines, who were until recently able to petition their regional courts for a new birth certificate, now find that practice thrown into doubt by a Supreme Court ruling.[51] In all Asian jurisdictions that allow changes in legal gender status the right is conditional not only on the transperson concerned having reached a relevant minimum age, but also upon him or her having undergone SRS. This latter requirement can be quite onerous, since many transpeople may not want or be able to afford the operation (or indeed operations, in the case of transmen). Another common condition, in the absence of provisions allowing for same-sex marriage, is that the person concerned should not already be married. Notwithstanding the conditions imposed, the impact of the opportunity to change legal status can be substantial for individual transpeople: it means that they will be able to enter mixed-gender marriages (i.e. heterosexually: a transwoman to a man, a transman to a woman). The numbers of transpeople potentially affected are substantial. Research across the region confirms that most transpeople are heterosexual.[52] Legal status as spouse, *inter alia*, enables mutual inheritance and insurance rights and, where one partner is hospitalised and unable to consent to medical procedures, the right to do so on his or her behalf. Where agencies regulating child adoption require the adopting couple to fit the hetero-normative mould, marriage makes it possible for a gender identity variant partner to be an adopting parent.

Two things are worth underlining here. First, apart from the six countries listed (the Philippines and Kuwait presently excluded), all other countries in Asia currently deny transpeople the right to change legal gender status. This is regardless of how long they have lived in another gender role, how well they 'pass' or how many procedures (pharmaceutical and surgical) they have undergone. All the rights that stem from changed legal gender status are also denied them. Indeed, in all but the six countries a transwoman in Asia is legally able to marry only another (legally defined) woman, and a transman another (legally defined) man. In view of the reluctance of so many Asian countries currently to recognise same-sex unions, this is somewhat ironic. Second, even in those six countries the right to change legal gender status is denied transpeople who have not undergone SRS or choose not to undergo it. That such central importance is placed upon one particular surgical procedure, which is only one of many steps that (some) transpeople undergo during what may be a long process of gender transition, is something I have described elsewhere as being a bizarre 'anatomania'.[53]

My own home, Hong Kong, is a paradox with respect to documentation issues. The government funds SRS for transpeople once they have gone through a standard diagnostic and monitoring procedure. It also allows those who have undergone SRS to change their personal documentation (ID card, driving licence, passport). On the other hand, it denies them the opportunity to change their birth certificates, the document that determines legal gender status.[54] The effect is that one branch of government facilitates gender transition while another branch hinders it, an irony not lost on transpeople and transactivists. The result has been described as a sort of legal limbo.[55]

Finally, Thailand, often thought of as progressive in matters relating to transpeople, presents a sad case. Home to a large number of transpeople (estimated at around 300,000)[56] of whom as many as one in three have undergone SRS,[57] the government does not allow changes in transpeople's legal gender status or the gender marked on personal documentation. The effect is that for a wide range of daily tasks it is impossible, regardless of ability otherwise to pass, for transpeople to maintain privacy in respect of their gender identity variance.

Stealth issues

Healthcare issues outlined above – absence of information on hormones, dosages and side effects, absence of easy access to affordable quality surgery, and easy availability of sub-standard substitutes – all combine to reduce transpeople's ability to pass in informal social situations (as well as pose health risks). Documentation issues – absence of gender affirmative documentation carried about the person and to determine legal gender status – combine to reduce the ability to pass in more formal situations involving bureaucracies and the law. Figures from Thailand, the Philippines and Laos reveal how commonly transpeople are 'read', with five to eight out of every ten transwomen revealing that strangers know them to be transwomen 'most of the time' or 'all the time'.[58]

I do not suggest that living in stealth is the highest priority for all transpeople in Asia. Indeed, many appear quite comfortable with being recognised for who they are. Substantial numbers of transwomen in places such as Thailand, the Philippines and Laos claim that they prefer to be transwomen (rather than birth-assigned women) and that they would prefer to be transwomen in their next life (or in the case of Philippine society, which is predominantly Christian, if given a chance to start life again).[59] It seems highly unlikely that stealth is the highest priority for these individuals. Notwithstanding, for those who *would* prefer to live in stealth, health and documentation issues make life more difficult (indeed often render privacy impossible).

Transprejudice and discrimination

I have already noted the indications of transprejudice and discrimination in Asia. Unsympathetic health workers may act as a barrier to effective trans-healthcare, in turn reducing transpeople's chances to transition successfully, and therefore to retain privacy over their gender identity variance. Unsupportive government policies on documentation have a similar effect. Restrictive government policies on change in legal gender status impose limitations upon one's privacy as well as family life. Throughout Asia transprejudice runs far wider and deeper. It is often expressed in attitudes and beliefs that have the effect of stigmatising transpeople, and in discriminatory behaviours involving gender coercion, social and economic marginalisation and even actual violence. It is commonly found at all levels of society, and in all aspects of life (interpersonal and institutional).

Within the family, where across Asia harmony is highly valued,[60] transpeople often endeavour not to express their gender identity variance. Those who do express it may be rejected by their families, subjected to abuse and violence in their homes and/or thrown out from their homes. They may be taunted, ostracised and abused by peers at school and subjected to gender coercion by school authorities and drop out of education accordingly. Some, especially those drifting into the city with little education or few contacts, may find getting a job difficult. Driven to the fringes of society, living on the streets and on their wits, some (particularly transwomen) drift into sex work, where they risk harassment, abuse and violence. Gender identity variant sex workers are faced with a reality that is grim (even in comparison with the usual standards of sex work). Faced with pressures to take bar fines and have sex with customers, they are left vulnerable to risks arising from the unwillingness of many customers to use condoms, as well as the increased risk that comes from being the receptive participant in anal intercourse.

For those working on the street, police harassment is an additional problem; one that serves to discourage the carrying of condoms and lubricant. Migrants from the countryside, often less educated and informed than their urban counterparts, may be particularly at risk. Drug and alcohol use, quite common among those involved in sex work, exacerbate the problem of unsafe sex. Impotence drugs used by customers add to the problem, raising the risk of anal abrasions. Government failure (or outright refusal) to enact anti-discrimination legislation on grounds of gender identity to protect transpeople puts them at risk of further marginalisation and the state at odds with its international obligations.[61] Laws against homosexuality, common across Asia, put heterosexual transpeople at risk of prosecution. Worst of all, in some societies the very government agencies that are charged with protecting the weakest fail to do so. Police abuse is common, is often systematic, is sometimes violent, and is in many places all of these (as the recent cases of Bangladesh,[62] Nepal[63] and Karnataka state in India have shown)[64] and is often initiated or justified on the basis of ill-defined vagrancy and public decency laws that effectively criminalise cross-dressing.

Together with other researchers I recently undertook a detailed examination of transprejudice in Asia.[65] Our 30-item questionnaire examined attitudes and beliefs about transwomen and was completed by 841 undergraduate students in seven societies: five Asian (Hong Kong, the Philippines, Thailand, Singapore and Malaysia) and two Western (the United Kingdom and the United States). Transprejudice was evident in all seven. Although it is difficult to draw firm conclusions from cross-societal comparisons in this study, it is worth noting that the Malaysian and US samples (from Kedah and Arkansas, specifically) tied for the highest overall levels of transprejudice. Slightly lower levels were found in Hong Kong and Singapore, followed by Thailand and the Philippines. The UK sample (largely from London) expressed least transprejudice.

Transprejudice was most evident in those items that focused directly on transwomen's rights. The item 'transwomen should be allowed to marry men' provides a good illustration. Among Malaysian respondents 63% disagreed with the proposition (higher than the 50% found in the United States). Even among the otherwise comparatively accepting Filipinos, 53% of the respondents rejected that transwomen should be so enabled. The item 'transwomen should be allowed to work with children' provides another illustration. Among Malaysian respondents 33% disagreed with the proposition, as did 14% of Filipinos. On this matter Thais were most supportive of transpeople's rights, but even then 13% of the respondents disagreed that they should have the right to work with children. Transpeople in Asia intending to enter teaching (or even to apply for a place in training college) would take little comfort from these figures.

At this point it is worth considering a few societies in more detail, taking first Malaysia (a comparatively transprejudiced society) then Thailand and the Philippines (more transfriendly), then briefly reviewing six other (widely differing) societies (Hong Kong, Kuwait, Pakistan, Nepal, India and Bangladesh).

A comparatively transprejudiced society: Malaysia

In our study of undergraduates' attitudes and beliefs about transwomen, we found many Malaysian participants who believed transwomen (*maknyah*) to be mentally disordered (49% of respondents), sexually perverted (46%), weak in character (46%), in some way unnatural (61%) or displaying unstable personalities (72%). Few could accept a son becoming a transwoman (16%) or a friend becoming one (24%). Few believed that they should be allowed to marry men (18%, against the 63% who opposed), while 31% believed that they should be allowed to work with children (33% opposed).

The transprejudice evident in these responses is echoed throughout Malaysian society, leading to discrimination so systematic and encompassing that it merits the word 'oppression'; an oppression perpetrated by law-makers, bureaucrats and academics. Transpeople are unable to change their legal gender status (and for Muslim transpeople not even their ID cards). Indeed, the 1955 Minor Offences Act criminalises cross-dressing and has led to many arrests. A 1983 fatwa (religious edict) has reinforced the ban on cross-dressing and has banned SRS, at least for transpeople and surgeons who are Muslims.[66] The fatwa is somewhat difficult for an outsider to understand, in view of the liberal attitudes towards SRS in a much stricter Islamic society, Iran.[67] The subsequent absence of Muslim surgeons in this area has had an effect on all Malaysian transpeople, making SRS less easily available than hitherto. A group of academics recently published a book on the problem of 'effeminacy' in men, proposing ways of preventing it and stamping it out when it occurs.[68] Inspired by the same problematising stance on gender identity variance, politicians in one part of the country have proposed a programme of forced rehabilitation for 'cross-dressers'.[69] At least one marriage has been nullified after it was found, subsequent to the marriage, that one of the spouses was gender identity variant.[70]

Predictably, many transwomen report difficulties in obtaining employment. Teh reported that 62% encountered difficulties, adding that 54% of her sample were actively involved in sex work (although estimates elsewhere have been as high as 65%).[71] Whether engaged in sex work or not, transwomen are harassed by the police and, if they are Muslims, the powerful Islamic Religious Authority. Many have been arrested and charged with indecent behaviour, the most common offence being cross-dressing. Those taken to police stations were often forced to strip and then to dress as male, a humiliating experience. Some reported being beaten.[72] In one particularly egregious case, the police were reported to have beaten a middle-aged transwoman (in full view of witnesses) on the grounds that she was cross-dressing in a public place, and then later sought the names of any persons visiting the victim in hospital. The incident prompted Amnesty International to issue a call for action.[73] Oppression at this level can be expected to have an impact on transpeople's mental health. Teh found that 14% of her sample had attempted suicide at least once. Intriguingly, the figure is lower than that those found in Thailand and the Philippines, a finding that may reflect the particularly negative view Islam takes towards suicide.[74]

Two comparatively transfriendly societies: Thailand and the Philippines

Transprejudice is evident even in more transfriendly societies such as Thailand and the Philippines, where transwomen once enjoyed social status (often as spirit mediums or healers). In both countries nowadays family members commonly frown upon gender identity variance in their children. In a recent study around 21% of Thai transwomen (*phuying kham phet*) and 40% of Filipina transwomen (*transpinay*) reported paternal rejection when transitioning.[75] In the Philippines school authorities often put great pressure on gender identity variant students to conform, with some schools known to rate students on masculinity and then append the ratings to the school reports they send to the post-secondary colleges to which the students have applied. The ratings can sabotage a young gender identity variant student's entry to a college of choice.

In both countries transwomen encounter difficulties in obtaining employment, all the more because many of them are already well into gender transition by the time they try to do so. Like their Malaysian counterparts their chances of employment are undermined by the documentation they hold that records their birth-assigned gender regardless of their gender transition. The consequence is that many nowadays are employed outside mainstream employment in 'trans-ghetto' jobs. These include work as beauticians (for example, the Filipina *salonistas*), cabaret performers and entertainment and sex workers (in bars, on the Internet or on the street). Such difficulties extend to graduates from prestigious universities, many of whom are forced to conceal their gender identity variance during working hours (presenting as best they can as male: in effect 'in drag') and to revert to their female self afterwards.[76]

The Thai and Philippine governments provide no effective legal protection against discrimination on grounds of gender identity. Indeed, they actually perpetrate some of the most debilitating discrimination. As has been noted, Thai transpeople legally remain members of their birth-assigned gender regardless of how long or successfully they have presented in another gender or how much they have modified their bodies. Thai transpeople's ID cards (which, like all their compatriots, they are obliged to carry at all times) as well as school certificates and passports all present to employers, service providers and government officials a legal gender contrary to their gender presentation. Transwomen (being legally men) are summonsed at the age of 20 for military service (along with all other men of that age who have not already done military training at high school). Some, particularly those who have not undergone breast surgery, run the risk of being humiliated in a group physical examination. Those relieved of military service receive discharge papers (the so-called 'SorDor 43') denoting 'mental disorder'. They must produce their discharge papers when applying for any job. The documentary evidence that they have a 'mental disorder' is highly likely to deter any potential employer from offering them employment. The Thai military have announced that the phrase 'mental disorder' will be replaced in future with 'belonging to the third category'. It remains uncertain whether this will affect the many SorDor 43s issued in previous years.

Notwithstanding progress on the SorDor 43 issue and a recent move to amend the law on rape to include (legally) male victims, it is not surprising that 17% of Thai transwomen reported Thai society to generally reject transpeople.[77] A recent study by Liselot Vink and myself found that many transwomen believed that their gender identity variance made them more susceptible to verbal abuse (14%), sexual harassment (15%), violence (16%) or being treated as sinful (20%), sexually perverted (22%) or sick (17%); made it more difficult to consult a doctor (10%) or receive proper treatment (9%); and made them generally more vulnerable to human rights abuse (15%). Around 22% reported having attempted suicide on one or more occasions.[78]

The situation in the Philippines seems more progressive, although there have been recent steps backward. Until recently a Filipino transperson who had undergone SRS, paid the legal costs, tolerated the public attention, waited the months or years involved and risked an unfavourable decision was able to petition a regional court for a new birth certificate. The only allowable grounds for such a change was that a mistake was made on the original certificate. The courts seemed ready in most cases to accept that one had been made. The costs involved in obtaining SRS (which, as noted earlier, are extremely high in the Philippines) and hiring a lawyer to represent oneself effectively made a change in legal gender status beyond the means of most transpeople. Worse still, the Attorney-General, in response to a family values backlash, mounted a successful appeal. The Supreme Court of the Philippines recently overturned a key decision favourable to a transgender person, leaving other favourable decisions at risk of being similarly overturned.[79] Not surprisingly, there is dismay in the gender identity variant community.[80] Thus, it is not surprising that 30% of Filipina transwomen feel that society generally rejects transpeople.[81] Winter and Vink found that many transwomen believed that their gender identity variance made them more susceptible to verbal abuse (29%), sexual harassment (35%), violence (30%) or being treated as sinful (40%), sexually perverted (40%) or sick (46%); made it more difficult to consult a doctor (8%) or get the right treatment (5%); and made them generally more vulnerable to human rights abuse (15%). Around 16% reported having attempted suicide on one or more occasions.[82]

Six other societies

So much for Malaysia, Thailand and the Philippines (respectively, predominantly Islamic, Buddhist and Christian). We turn now to Hong Kong, a relatively secular society that portrays itself as progressive and liberal (under the official banner of 'Asia's world city'). Transpeople encounter rejection within the family and beyond, and find it difficult to obtain employment. In the local language (Cantonese) they are often called *yan yiu* ('human monsters'), although more moderate alternatives exist. The media, sensationalistic when covering transgender issues, employ the word *yan yiu* with little compunction. In 2008 I and others made a complaint to the Broadcasting Authority regarding a television programme that used the phrase around 20 times within ten minutes. The basis of our complaint was the word's inherent offensiveness. The Authority rejected our complaint as unfounded. In 2003 a magazine reporter stalked a transwomen through an Internet chat room, discovered the place where she worked (a beauty salon), took photos of her at work and ran a sensationalist pictorial on her (headed 'The man who wears a bra'). She lost her job. The following year she committed suicide.[83]

The Hong Kong government adopts an ambivalent stance towards transpeople. While the Hospital Authority subsidises SRS, the Security Bureau dismisses requests (even after SRS) for change in legal gender status. The government thus facilitates medical transition but prohibits legal transition. It has also continued to forestall any legislation that would protect transpeople, alongside members of other sexual minorities, against discrimination and harassment.

In less progressive Asian societies conditions are even tougher: Kuwait, Pakistan, Nepal, India and Bangladesh illustrate the point. In Kuwait, 14 transpeople were arrested within the space of a few weeks for cross-dressing (specifically, on the grounds that they were violating a law that criminalised 'impersonation of the other sex' and set custodial sentences of up to one year). They were reportedly abused both psychologically and physically by police officers while detained.[84] As noted earlier, a Kuwaiti court ruling that allowed a transwoman (who had undergone SRS in another country) to change her legal gender status was recently overturned on appeal.[85] In Pakistan a newly married couple were separated, charged, found guilty and incarcerated, on the grounds that the groom (who it turned out is a post-op transman and was known to be one by his bride) had lied by presenting as a man at the wedding. In any case, it was alleged, the SRS he had undergone was not done properly.[86] In Nepal transwomen (*meti*) have been mocked, threatened, chased, arbitarily detained, stripped, raped and/or assaulted (in some cases almost to the point of death) by the police in a series of incidents described by some human rights activists as a programme of 'sexual cleansing'.[87] In India, a 2003 report detailed widespread violations against the *hijra* and *kothi* in the state of Karnataka in southern India. The incidents encompassed harassment at home as well as police harassment, entrapment and abuse including rape.[88] In Bangladesh abuses of this sort appear widespread, involving not only the police but also *mastans* (violent gang members acting as musclemen for political parties in exchange for the parties' tolerance of their racketeering and other criminal activities).[89]

In short, transprejudice is widespread across Asia, leading to discriminatory behaviours at both interpersonal and institutional levels, in turn leading to limitations on opportunities and to social and economic marginalisation, even exclusion. Discrimination is sometimes so debilitating and systematic that it merits the word 'oppression'. Gender-coercive schools deprive transpeople of education directed at the full development of their personality; unwilling employers deprive them of opportunities to work and to have an adequate standard of living; governments deprive them of privacy as well as family life, and effective protection against discrimination and harassment. Transpeople are consequently put at risk of poor mental and physical health. In extremis, oppression can be so severe that it leads to de facto deprivation of the right to life. All these represent a barrier to one's exercise of freedom of expression, including gender expression, enshrined in various international human rights treaties which roughly half of Asian governments have ratified or acceded to. In some jurisdictions many of these rights and freedoms are also enshrined in domestic law (such as, in the case of Hong Kong, through the Hong Kong Bill of Rights Ordinance[90]).

The way forward for transpeople in Asia is not easy. Strategies include local organising as well as alliances among transgender rights groups and with other local and international human rights lobbies, and campaigns pressuring governments not only to promote public education about transpeople and their rights but also to more directly effect their rights such as by changing their legal status and legislating against discrimination and harassment on grounds of gender identity. The 'any other status' clause in various international human rights treaties should be extended to transpeople. Beyond this, education is necessary in the family and at school (places where transpeople first encounter transprejudice) but also in the workplace and wider society. In this respect, legislation serves as the most powerful educational tool. Finally, it is essential that action be taken in the world of medicine – specifically psychiatry. It is to this point that I now turn.

The role of psychiatry in fuelling transprejudice

Gender identity variance is widely viewed in Western countries as symptomatic of a mental disorder, and transpeople as mentally ill. The *Diagnostic and Statistical Manual* (DSM-IV) published by the American Psychiatric Association describes their condition as 'gender identity disorder'. ICD-10, the manual published by the World Health Organisation, describes it as 'transsexualism'.

The diagnoses, and their underlying rationale, have become increasingly controversial.[91] Criticisms have been laid on the technical aspects of the diagnostic process, including diagnostic criteria, information upon which clinicians make a diagnosis and the absence of an 'exit clause' by which transpeople (once transitioned) may be free of a diagnosis. More fundamental criticisms have focused on the nature and consequences of pathologisation, including the idea that pathologisation is a tool of social control, stemming from restrictive ideologies of sex, gender and sexuality; perpetuates an essentialism that sees the transwoman as a man and the transman as a woman, undermining a person's gender self-identification; encourages ethically questionable 'reparative' treatment while undermining the legitimacy of effective medical procedures that enhance transpeople's lives; and contributes to unfavourable court decisions for transpeople. It has also been argued that gender identity variance in itself involves no pathology, any mental disturbance experienced by transpeople being the result of intolerance and stigma, and that pathologisation merely exacerbates intolerance and stigma and does so more than many other psychiatric diagnoses because it involves pathologisation of one's identity. These last criticisms suggest that, in a gender identity variant person, pathologisation may bring about pathology.

Psychiatry is Western dominated. Across Asia psychiatrists are connected with developments in psychiatry through organisations such as the Washington-based American

Psychiatric Association and the Geneva-based World Psychiatric Association.[92] Thus, it is inevitable that psychiatric orthodoxy on gender identity variance will undermine long-standing local views of gender identity variance as an aspect of human diversity rather than a mental disorder.

In a seven-society study of attitudes and beliefs regarding transwomen we conducted a factor analysis on the pooled data. [93] This was to identify the core attitudes and beliefs underlying our data. Five factors were identified, namely, the belief that transwomen suffered from a mental disorder; the belief that transwomen were not women, should not be treated as such and should not be afforded their rights; rejection of social contact with transwomen in a range of situations, including among family members and teachers; rejection of social contact with transwomen within one's peer group; and, finally, the belief that transwomen were sexually motivated to do what they do, were promiscuous and engaged in sexually deviant behaviour. Together, the five factors accounted for 51% of variance.

Importantly, these factors were inter-correlated. Strong and consistent across the seven countries were links between, on one hand, the belief that transwomen suffered from a mental disorder and, on the other hand, refusal to regard or treat them as women or to afford them rights as women (with a correlation coefficient of 0.55) as well as unwillingness to accept the idea of any social contact with them, either within the family (with a correlation coefficient of 0.50) or among peers (with a correlation co-efficient of 0.64). These correlations were statistically highly significant, suggesting that they were extremely unlikely to be due to chance. They raised the possibility that the view of gender identity variance as mental disorder may support and encourage key transprejudicial attitudes.

This possibility is worrying. As has been discussed, transprejudice and discrimination impair mental health and well-being. If pathologisation of transpeople (on the basis of their gender identity variance) reinforces and perpetuates transprejudice, then the result is a self-fulfilling prophecy in which transpeople, regarded by others as mentally disordered, do indeed encounter mental health problems, but largely, perhaps only, as a result of being so regarded. When I have expressed this concern elsewhere,[94] I have been accused of over-stating or oversimplifying the case. My answer is that, in my experience, transpeople whose gender identity variance has been accepted by significant others within and outside the family are generally well-adjusted individuals, free from any distress or disability associated with their self-identification. It therefore seems to me that there may be no 'gender identity disorder', except the inability or unwillingness of transprejudiced people to accept transpeople. True, psychiatric diagnosis *has* offered transpeople in some more affluent parts of the world the hope or expectation of subsidised gender healthcare. My fear is that many transpeople in Asia, with different priorities and other health needs, are paying the price.[95]

Concluding thoughts

In this paper I have described the difficulties transpeople in Asia encounter regarding their gender healthcare needs and gender-identifying documentation and argued that such difficulties reduce these people's ability to make a successful gender transition and (if they wish) to live in stealth. Consequently, transpeople are left especially vulnerable to any transprejudice and discrimination in their societies. I have presented evidence suggesting that transprejudice and discrimination of varying sorts and degrees is evident in all Asian societies. Across Asia transprejudice is prompted or supported by the belief that transpeople are mentally ill. Given the impact that prejudice is known to have upon minority group individuals' mental health and well-being, a self-fulfilling prophecy may be at work.

I do not suggest that every person in Asia reads psychiatric diagnostic manuals – there is no such need. Psychiatric thinking percolates into mainstream society in many ways, especially through the media. There are other vehicles for dissemination. For example, we have seen how in Thailand many transpeople are designated 'mentally disordered' when relieved of military service and how their SorDor 43 discharge papers depict to all potential employers their 'mentally disordered' status.

Nor do I suggest that transprejudice arises solely out of the 'mental disorder' view of transpeople or that it would wane overnight if gender identity variance were de-pathologised. Religion sometimes supports transprejudice; for example the Roman Catholic and other church faiths in the Philippines teach that androphilic transwomen are homosexual (and therefore sinful) men, and Muslim clerics in Malaysia teach that transpeople are un-Islamic. Indeed, if the history of homosexuality is anything to go by, de-pathologisation may only lead to a reinvigoration of the inclination of the religious right (Christian or Islamic) to portray transpeople as sinful. Rather, pathologisation is *one* factor that prompts and supports transprejudice. It is, in my view, a notion that is scientifically bankrupt, and socially disastrous for the gender identity variant person.

De-pathologisation may not erase overnight the stigma that transpeople are mentally ill; there remain to this day those who regard homosexuals as mentally disordered more than 30 years after the American Psychiatric Association removed homosexuality from its *Diagnostic and Statistical Manual*. But de-pathologisation is a start. With the Association gearing up to produce a fifth revision of its manual in the next few years, it is time to proclaim, more loudly than ever, that transpeople represent human diversity rather than defect and that the world is richer for their presence. This is more than an American affair. In my view, this is a matter of human rights central to the lives of transpeople worldwide, including the lives of transpeople in Asia.

Notes

1. This paper draws on nine years of communications with many transpeople in Asia (including activists for transpeople's rights), and from more formal research work (my own, my students' and that of my collaborators associated with the TransgenderASIA Centre). My own most recent work has been to collect autobiographies (oral and written, delivered in English or translated from local languages into English) of transpeople as part of the 'Trans Lives: Asian Voices' project funded by the University of Hong Kong.
2. The TransgenderASIA Centre publishes a bibliography of relevant English-language materials drawn from the humanities and social sciences: http://web.hku.hk/~transgenderASIA/index.htm (last accessed at 1 December 2008).
3. Stephen Whittle, Lewis Turner and Maryam Al-Alami, 'Engendered Penalties: Transgender and Transsexual People's Experiences of Inequality and Discrimination', 2007, http://archive.thecabinetoffice.gov.uk/equalitiesreview/upload/assets/www.theequalitiesreview.org.uk/transgender.pdf (accessed 14 October 2008).
4. Stephen Whittle, *Respect and Equality: Transsexual and Transgender Rights* (London: Cavendish, 2002).
5. There are a startling variety of names, with several sometimes available in just one language. Examples for 'transwomen' include: *kathoey* (Thailand, Laos), *pumia, pumae, phet tee sam; sao, phuying praphet song* (Thailand); *acault* (Myanmar/Burma); *bayot, bayog, babyalan, asog, bantut, bakla, binabae* (the Philippines); *maknyah* (Malaysia); *waria* (throughout Indonesia); *banci* (old Batavia); *calabai* (Bugis); *kedie* (Java and Bali); *kawekawe* (Makassar and Bugis); *wandu* (Java); *yen yiu* (China); *yirka-la-ul-va-irgin, ne-uchica* (northern Siberia); *khanith* and *xanith* (Oman); *hijra* and *kothi* (India); *chokka* and *meti* (Nepal); *aravani* (Tamil Nadu); *khusra* and *zanana* (Pakistan); *donme* (Turkey); and *ah kua* (Singapore). Many of these terms are imprecise and (at least as used nowadays) demeaning, and are thus often ill-suited to the tasks of rights activism on behalf of the communities concerned. Consequently,

some rights groups have started to construct their own vocabulary of gender identity variance. Filipino transactivists have introduced the Tagalog–English compound terms *babaeng* (or *lalaki*) *transgender* for transgender woman or man (Sass Rogando-Sasot, email communication with author, 3 July 2007), and more recently *transpinay* and *transpinoy*, literally 'trans Filipino woman' and 'man', respectively (Society for Transsexual Women of the Philippines, press release, 4 May 2008). In Thailand activists have recently introduced the terms *khon* (or *phuying, phuchaai*) *khaam phet* ('a person/woman/man who has crossed sex'), *khon* (or *phuying, phuchaai*) *plaeng phet* ('a person/woman/man who has changed sex') (Krisana Mamanee, Nada Chaiyavit and Prempreeda Pramoj Na Ayutthaya, email communications with author, 5 May 2008, 16 May 2008 and 26 November 2008, respectively). Attempts to construct a vocabulary that conveys both dignity and precision may be an essential first step for transpeople to achieve recognition as a distinct community able to promote its members' interests and press for their rights.

6. See, e.g., Jay Harcourt, 'Current Issues in Lesbian, Gay, Bisexual, and Transgender (LGBT) Health: Introduction', *Journal of Homosexuality* 51, no. 1 (2006): 1; Arnold H. Grossman and Anthony R. D'Augelli, 'Transgender Youth: Invisible and Vulnerable', *Journal of Homosexuality* 51, no. 1 (2006): 111; Kristen Clements-Nolle, Rani Marx, Robert Guzman and Mitchell Katz, 'HIV Prevalence, Risk Behaviors, Health Care Use, and Mental Health Status of Transgender Persons: Implications for Public Health Intervention', *American Journal of Public Health* 91 (2001): 915.

7. See, e.g., Eric R. Wright and Brea L. Perry, 'Sexual Identity Distress, Social Support, and the Health of Gay, Lesbian and Bisexual Youth', *Journal of Homosexuality* 51, no. 1 (2006): 81; Ilan H. Meyer and Laura Dean, 'Patterns of Sexual-Behavior and Risk-Taking among Young New-York-City Gay Men', *AIDS Education and Prevention* 7, no. 5 (1995): 13; Jeanne Abelson et al., 'Factors Associated with Feeling Suicidal: The Role of Sexual Identity', *Journal of Homosexuality* 51, no. 1 (2006): 59.

8. See http://www.gender.org/remember/ (accessed 1 December 2008).

9. See, e.g., Wing Foo Tsoi, 'Male and Female Transsexuals: A Comparison', *Singapore Medical Journal* 33, no. 2 (1992): 182; Jody Norton, '"Brain Says You're a Girl, but I Think You're a Sissy Boy": Cultural Origins of Transphobia', *International Journal of Sexuality and Gender Studies* 2, no. 2 (1997): 139; Darryl Hill and Brian Willoughby, 'The Development and Validation of the Genderism and Transphobia Scale', *Sex Roles* 53, nos 7–8 (2005): 531.

10. George Weinberg, *Society and the Healthy Homosexual* (New York: St Martin's Press, 1972), 4.

11. Mark King, Sam Winter and Beverley Webster, 'Contact Reduces Transprejudice: A Study on Attitudes towards Transgenderism and Transgender Civil Rights in Hong Kong', *International Journal of Sexual Health* 22, no. 1 (2009): 17–34.

12. See, e.g., Whittle et al. 'Engendered Penalties'; Ontario Human Rights Commission, 'Policy on Discrimination and Harassment because of Gender Identity', http://www.ohrc.on.ca/en/resources/Policies/PolicyGenderIdent/pdf (accessed 29 April 2008); International Conference on Transgender Law and Employment Policy, 'The International Bill of Gender Rights', http://www.pfc.org.uk/node/275/print (accessed 24 April 2008); International Lesbian and Gay Association/Europe, 'Transgender Working Party Platform', http://www.ilga-europe.org/europe/notice_board/resources/transgender_working_party_platform (accessed 29 April 2008); Murray Couch et al., *Transnation: A Report on the Health and Wellbeing of Transgendered People in Australia and New Zealand* (Melbourne: Australian Research Centre in Sex, Health and Society, La Trobe University, 2007); Anti-Discrimination Board of New South Wales, 'Transgender Discrimination', http://www.lawlink.nsw.gov.au/lawlink/adb/ll_adb.nsf/pages/adb_transgender (accessed 29 April 2008).

13. See Eric Heinze, 'Sexual Orientation and International Law: A Study in the Manufacture of Cross-Cultural "Sensitivity"', *Michigan Journal of International Law* 22 (2001): 283.

14. Article 2 of the International Covenant on Civil and Political Rights states that '[e]ach State Party to the present Covenant undertakes to respect and to ensure to all individuals within its territory and subject to its jurisdiction the rights recognised in the present Covenant, without distinction of any kind, such as race, colour, sex, language, religion, political or other opinion, national or social origin, property, birth or other status'. Article 2 of the International Covenant on Economic, Social and Cultural Rights contains very similar wording, although Yvonne Klerk argues that it requires enforcement that is even more immediate than under the International Covenant on Civil and Political Rights: 'Working Paper on Article 2(2) and

Article 3 of the International Covenant on Economic, Social and Cultural Rights', *Human Rights Quarterly* 9 (1987): 250, 260. Article 26 of the International Covenant on Civil and Political Rights states that '[a]ll persons are equal before the law and are entitled without any discrimination to the equal protection of the law. In this respect, the law shall prohibit any discrimination and guarantee to all persons equal and effective protection against discrimination on any ground such as race, colour, sex, language, religion, political or other opinion, national or social origin, property birth or other status'; see, in particular, the views of the United Nations Human Rights Committee in *Toonen* v. *Australia*, 1(3) IHRR 97 (1994); *Young* v. *Australia*, United Nations Human Rights Committee, Communication No. 941/2000, CCPR/C/78/D/ 941/2000, 6 August 2003 (cf., however, *Joslin* v. *New Zealand*, United Nations Human Rights Committee, Communication No. 902/1999, CCPR/C/75/D/902/1999, 17 July 2002).

15. Southeast Asia is interesting in this respect. Michael Peletz, in 'Transgenderism and Gender Pluralism in Southeast Asia since Early Modern Times', *Current Anthropology* 47, no. 2 (2006): 309, argues that 'gender pluralism' was evident across the region in pre-modern times. Gender variant individuals enjoyed legitimacy, even social status. Peletz remarks that gender pluralism has waned in more modern times, though remnants are still evident. It is true that even nowadays sex, gender and sexual preference and behaviour (and their inter-relationships) are perceived across the region in a way unfamiliar even in other parts of Asia. The conceptual division between 'sex' and 'gender' provides an example. In Thailand and the Philippines, there is one word for both (*phet* and *kasarian*, respectively), a situation similar to that in pre-twentieth-century Europe; for more detail of the increased use of 'gender' in Western countries, see David Haig, 'The Inexorable Rise of Gender and the Decline of Sex: Social Change in Academic Titles, 1945–2001', *Archives of Sexual Behavior* 33, no. 2 (2004): 87. The absence of any convenient vocabulary for distinguishing between sex and gender can sometimes confuse any sensible debate on the rights of transpeople. Scholars and activists across Asia nowadays find it sometimes necessary to invent terms to distinguish the two (for example the recently developed terms *phet phawa*, *phet saphap* and *phet saphawa* [all meaning 'sex condition/status' in Thai]: Peter Jackson, email communication with author, 5 November 2008). Furthermore, some Asian cultures seem (from a Western point of view) to conflate sex/gender with sexual preference and behaviour. In Thailand, for example, a person's status as a man or a woman may be defined not so much by his or her biology (genital anatomy), but more in terms of what he/she does with it, and with whom he/she does it. Simply put, the act of being penetrated connotes femininity. The corollary is that the act of penetrating connotes maleness. A man who penetrates other men does so without undermining his claim to maleness, especially if he also penetrates birth-assigned women. Indeed he can even enhance his status as a male by letting it be known that he penetrates both men and women: Preempreeda Pramoj na Ayutthaya, 'Sexual Fluidity within Bisexuality in Thailand', paper presented at 10th International Conference of Thai Studies, Bangkok, 9–11 January 2008. In contrast, the biological man who is habitually penetrated by other men forfeits his claim to maleness, since he has abandoned the orthodox male sexual role. The male-identi-fying gay 'bottom' here becomes the emasculated man. Defined as other than a 'real man', it is understood that he may adopt a generalised non-male social role, as a member of a third gender (*phet thee sam*) or as a woman of the second kind (*phuying praphet song*), identifying as such (or even identifying as *phuying jing*, a 'real woman'). See also Serena Nanda's discussion of multiple genders in Indian culture in 'Hijra and Sadhin: Neither Man nor Woman in India', in *Gender Diversity: Cross-Cultural Variations*, ed. Serena Nanda (Long Grove, IL: Waveland Press, 2000), 27. Finally, it is common in Western countries to conceptualise sex and gender as fixed, transwomen for example often claiming that throughout their lives they have possessed a feminine essence (for example as a 'woman of transgender experience', etc.). Once a gender transition has been made, it is rare for steps taken to be retraced (i.e. gender reversion). However, in some Asian cultures it is relatively common to see this sort of thing take place: a birth-assigned male who once identified and presented as female may later reclaim presen-tation as male. Some may choose this gender reversion freely. Others are pressed to do so by the daily difficulties of leading a translife. In recent Thai, Lao and Philippine studies we found that 11%, 13% and 21% of our participant transwomen, respectively, anticipated presenting as men by the time they were 50 years old. For detail on these studies, see Sam Winter, 'Thai Transgenders in Focus: Demographics, Transitions and Identities', *International Journal of Transgenderism* 9, no. 1 (2006): 15; Sam Winter and Serge Doussantousse, 'Gender

Identity Variance in Laos' (under review); Sam Winter, Sass Rogando-Sasot and Mark King, 'Transgendered Women of the Philippines', *International Journal of Transgenderism* 10, no. 2 (2007): 79. For some transwomen in Asia, reversion to maleness involves adopting a male sexual role, perhaps even by marrying a woman: see, e.g., the *xanith* in Oman as discussed in Unni Wikan, *Behind the Veil in Arabia: Women in Oman* (Chicago IL: University of Chicago Press, 1991). We see, then, in the relationship between sexual behaviour and sex/gender the possibility for a gender fluidity that contradicts the relatively fixed genders constructed in Western discourse. Many transwomen in Asia have told me about their transgender friends who later reverted to presenting as men or, somewhat aghast, how they came across former boyfriends who were now presenting as female. The point here is that this is a worldview of multiple and fluid sexes/genders based as much on behaviour as on biology. Legal systems that conceive gender as binary (male or female), biologically based (in practice based on genitalia) and fixed for life (notwithstanding that a few Asian jurisdictions accept change in legal gender status after SRS) are typically incapable of accommodating such sexual cosmographies.

16. Key work covers Buddhist and Buddhist-influenced societies like Thailand, Laos, Myanmar/Burma, Cambodia and Vietnam; Shinto Japan; Islamic societies such as Pakistan, Bangladesh, Oman, Indonesia, Turkey and Malaysia; Hindu societies such as India and Nepal; Confucian societies such as China, Hong Kong, Taiwan and Singapore; and the Philippines, a society that is predominantly Christian.

17. The 18 countries are Turkey, Pakistan, India, Nepal, Bangladesh, Myanmar/Burma, Laos, Cambodia, Vietnam, Thailand, Malaysia, Singapore, Indonesia, the Philippines, China (including Hong Kong), Taiwan, South Korea and Japan. The figure of 95% is based on a count I made using the bibliography published on the TransgenderASIA website.

18. See, e.g., Jeswan Kaur, 'Transgender: Mak Nyah Cry for Compassion', 6 November 2008, http://www.sgbutterfly.org/index.php?name=News&file=article&sid=218 (accessed 11 October 2008); Farid Jamaludin, 'Transsexuals: Declare Us as Women', *The Star*, 21 January 2001, http://ai.eecs.umich.edu/people/conway/TS/MalaysianTS.html (accessed 5 March 2009).

19. Nanda, 'Hijra and Sadhin'.

20. Sam Winter, 'Counting *Kathoey*', http://web.hku.hk/~sjwinter/TransgenderASIA/paper_counting_kathoey.htm (accessed 22 October 2008).

21. Wikan, *Behind the Veil in Arabia*.

22. American Psychiatric Association, *Diagnostic and Statistical Manual of Mental Disorders: DSM-IV* (Washington: American Psychiatric Association, 1994).

23. Femke Olyslager and Lynn Conway, 'On the Calculation of the Prevalence of Transsexualism', paper presented at First Biennial Symposium of the World Professional Association for Transgender Health, Chicago, 5–8 September 2007. This article was subsequently re-published in the refereed journal *Tijdschrift voor Genderstudies* in 2008. See Femke Olyslager and Lynn Conway, 'Transseksualiteit komt vaker voor dan u denkt. Een nieuwe kijk op de prevalentie van transseksualiteit in Nederland en België' [Transsexualism is more common than you think. A new look at the prevalence of transsexualism in the Netherlands and Belgium], *Tijdschrift voor Genderstudies* 11, no. 2 (2008): 39.

24. In a recent Lao study, only one of 214 participating transwomen had undergone SRS: Winter and Doussantousse, 'Gender Identity Variance in Laos'. In a corresponding Philippine study it was found that only one out of 147 participants had and 29% indicated they had no desire to do so: Winter et al., 'Transgendered Women of the Philippines'. Even among Thai transpeople, for whom SRS is more easily affordable and available, only 28% of a sample of 195 transwomen had undergone an operation, and 12% had no desire to do so: Winter, 'Thai Transgenders in Focus'.

25. Robert Tait, 'Sex Change Funding Undermines No Gays Claim', *The Guardian*, 26 September 2007, http://www.guardian.co.uk/world/2007/sep/26/iran.gender (accessed 5 May 2008).

26. Wing Foo Tsoi, 'The Prevalence of Transsexualism in Singapore', *Acta Psychiatrica Scandinavica* 78, no. 4 (1988): 501.

27. Iran may pose an interesting case. Homosexual sexual conduct is a capital offence yet the possibility exists for subsidised SRS and change in legal gender status for people diagnosed as transsexual. It has been suggested that some who undergo SRS may simply be homosexual men and women attempting to bypass the criminalisation of their sexual preferences: Megan Stack, 'Iran Warms up to Sex Changes, but Still Shuns Homosexuality', *Los Angeles Times*, 30

January 2005; Tait, 'Sex Change Funding Undermines No Gays Claim', http://web.hku.hk/~sjwinter/TransgenderASIA/iran.pdf (accessed 5 March 2009). The situation in Singapore is somewhat similar in that gay men are liable for criminal prosecution and incarceration yet transpeople who have undergone SRS are able to change their legal gender status and to marry.

28.   References encompass the arts, literature, religion, folklore and superstitions. Examples include aesthetic traditions valuing androgyny in Japan: Junko Saeki, 'Beyond the Gender Dichotomy: The Cross-Dressing Tradition in Japanese Theatre', *Intersections* 16 (2008), http://intersections.anu.edu.au/issue16/saeki.htm (accessed 11 November 2008); cross-dressing (sometimes apparently gender identity variant) actors and/or actresses in imperial China and Japan (ibid.); Brett Hinsch, *Passions of the Cut Sleeve: The Male Homosexual Tradition in China* (Berkeley, CA: University of California Press, 1990); Sophie Volpp, 'Gender, Power and Spectacle in Late-Imperial Chinese Theatre', in *Gender Reversals and Gender Cultures: Anthropological and Historical Perspectives*, ed. Sabrina Petra Ramet (London: Routledge, 1996), 138; gender-bending Hindu deities and Buddhist bodhistavas: Nanda, 'Hijra and Sadhin'; Burkhard Scherer, 'Gender Transformed and Meta-gendered Enlightenment: Reading Buddhist Narratives as Paradigms of Inclusiveness', *Revista de Estudos da Religião* 3 (2006): 65; beliefs about salvation through gender modification in Hindu and Buddhist cultures: Cynthia Humes, 'Becoming Male: Salvation through Gender Modification in Hinduism and Buddhism', in *Gender Reversals and Gender Cultures: Anthropological and Historical Perspectives*, ed. Sabrina Petra Ramet (London: Routledge, 1996), 123; creation myths involving three sexes in Thailand: Rosalind Morris, 'Three Sexes and Four Sexualities: Redressing the Discourses on Gender and Sexuality in Contemporary Thailand', *Positions* 2, no. 1 (1994): 15; and cross-dressing in order to ward off widow ghosts, also in Thailand: Mary Beth Mills, 'Attack of the Widow Ghosts: Gender, Death, and Modernity in Northeast Thailand', in *Bewitching Women, Pious Men: Gender and Body Politics in Southeast Asia*, ed. Aihwa Ong and Michael Peletz (Berkeley, CA: University of California Press, 1995), 244.

29.   Possibly reflecting this cultural history, an international study of attitudes towards transwomen found that while 49% of Malaysians regarded transwomen as mentally disordered, 13%, 21% and 15% shared this view in Thailand, Singapore and the Philippines, respectively. In the latter three countries transwomen were much more commonly regarded as 'normal, just different' (54% of Thais, 66% of Singaporeans and 82% of Filipinos). However, many saw their condition as a physical disorder (12% of Thais, 24% of Singaporeans and 18% of Filipinos regarding transwomen as 'women in the wrong body'): Sam Winter et al., 'Transpeople, trans-prejudice and pathologisation: a seven-county factor analytic study', *International Journal of Sexual Health* 21, no. 2 (2009) 96–118.

30.   Examples include Oman, India, Burma, Thailand, the Philippines, Indonesia, China, South Korea, Japan and the island of Okinawa, and Siberia. For detail, see Matthew Allen, 'Being Male in a Female World: Masculinity and Gender in Okinawan Shamanism', in *Genders, Trans-genders and Sexualities in Japan*, ed. Mark McLelland and Raj Dasgupta (London: Routledge, 2005); Marjorie Balzer, 'Sacred Genders in Siberia: Shamans, Bear Festivals, and Androgyny', in *Gender Reversals and Gender Cultures: Anthropological and Historical Perspectives*, ed. Sabrina Petra Ramet (London: Routledge, 1996), 164; Carolyn Brewer, 'Baylan, Asog, Trans-vestism, and Sodomy: Gender, Sexuality and the Sacred in Early Colonial Philippines', *Inter-sections* 2 (1999), http://wwwsshe.murdoch.edu.au/intersections/issue2/carolyn2.html (accessed 10 November 2008); Eli Coleman, Philip Colgan and Louis Gooren, 'Male Cross-Gender Behavior in Myanmar (Burma): A Description of the Acault', *Archives of Sexual Behavior* 21, no. 3 (1992): 313; Hyung Ki Choi et al., 'South Korea', in *International Encyclopedia of Sexuality*, http://www2.hu-berlin.de/sexology/IES/southkorea.html (accessed 10 November 2008); Hinsch, *Passions of the Cut Sleeve*; Serena Nanda, 'Transgendered Males in Thailand and the Philippines', in *Gender Diversity: Cross-Cultural Variations*, ed. Serena Nanda (Long Grove, IL: Waveland Press, 2000), 71; Peletz, 'Transgenderism and Gender Pluralism in Southeast Asia since Early Modern Times'.

31.   See, e.g., Serge Doussantousse and Bea Keovongchith, 'Male Sexual Health: Kathoeys in the Lao PDR, South East Asia – Exploring a Gender Identity', http://web.hku.hk/~sjwinter/TransgenderASIA/paper_doussantousse.htm (accessed 28 June 2006); Barbara Earth, 'Diversi-fying Gender: Male to Female Transgender Identities and HIV/AIDS Programming in Phnom Penh, Cambodia', *Gender and Development* 14 (2006): 259; Adnan Hossain, 'They Swing

between Both Sexes; Hijras as "Asexual Others"", http://web.hku.hk/~sjwinter/Transgender-ASIA/paper_swinging.htm (accessed 5 September 2006); Serena Nanda, 'The Hijras of India', in *A Queer World: The Center for Lesbian and Gay Studies Reader*, ed. Martin Duberman (New York: New York University Press, 1997); Yik Koon Teh, *The Mak Nyahs: Male to Female Transsexuals in Malaysia* (Singapore: Eastern Universities Press, 2002); Winter, 'Thai Transgenders in Focus'; Winter et al., 'Transgendered Women of the Philippines'. In some cases the forces of change were abrupt. Invaders and colonists (who were usually Europeans from a Judaeo-Christian tradition and less favourably disposed towards gender variance, and indeed gender identity variance, than the indigenous cultures concerned) attempted to stamp out what they thought was perverse and sinful behaviour. The case of the Philippines is a well-documented example. Nanda, 'Transgendered Males in Thailand and the Philippines', describes the '"sexualising" and masculinising of Filipino culture' by successive Arab, Spanish and American domination and details its effects on gender variant people (and on relationships, both mixed and same sex, in general). Brewer, 'Baylan, Asog, Transvestism, and Sodomy', has written in detail on the role played by the Spanish, remarking on early colonists' reports of cross-gender *bayog*, *bayoc* and *asog* shamans and *babaylan* ritual facilitators, all of whom offended the sensibilities of the newcomers. The author (para. 14) quotes the Jesuit Brother Francisco Ignacio Alcina, who wrote in 1668, 'The fact is the Asog considered themselves more like women than like men in their manner of living, or going about, or even in their occupations. Some of them applied themselves to women's tasks, like weaving and cultivating, etc. In dress, although they did not wear petticoats (these were not worn by women in ancient times either) they did wear some Lambon, as they are called here. This is a kind of long skirt down to the feet, so that they were recognised even by their dress.' It may be that Alcina's use of the past tense when referring to these people, just 80 years after the arrival of Spanish Governor Miguel Lopes de Legaspi, attested to the success of the Spanish in eradicating gender variance. 'Modernising' forces may not always have been detrimental to the quality of life enjoyed by transpeople; they may have sometimes enhanced their lives. In Thailand, for example, 19th-century reforms of dress and appearance (to fend off colonisation by making Thais appear 'less barbaric' in the eyes of potential Western colonists) may have resulted in new opportunities for expressions of gender variance (and indeed gender identity variance). Twentieth-century reforms of names (requiring that all be gender specific) may have had the same effect: Peter Jackson, 'Performative Genders, Perverse Desires: A Bio-history of Thailand's Same-Sex and Transgender Cultures', *Intersections* 9 (2003), http://wwwsshe.murdoch.edu.au/intersections/issue9/jackson.html (accessed 7 September 2005). More recently, easy access to hormones (with up to 23 products available over the counter in some pharmacies in Thailand) and relatively inexpensive SRS often of a high standard (even attracting trans-patients from overseas) have arguably further enhanced the ability of transpeople to express their gender identity variance more fully than at any time in the history of Thai culture.

32. See, e.g., Wikan, *Behind the Veil in Arabia*; Richard A. Jenkins and Bryan Kim, 'Cultural Norms and Risk: Lessons Learned from HIV in Thailand', *Journal of Primary Prevention* 25, no. 1 (2004): 17; Nanda, 'Transgendered Males in Thailand and the Philippines'.

33. Sass Rogando-Sasot, email communication with author, 14 March 2008. A second study was conducted by a team involving myself (Winter et al., unpublished report available from author) which examined gender satisfaction among 526 university undergraduate students from four Asian societies (Hong Kong, Malaysia, Singapore and Thailand). Respondents completed the seven-item questionnaire anonymously. Two items touched clearly upon gender disaffection. Among men 1.4% reported feeling 'uncomfortable being a member of this sex' 'all the time'; among women 2.8%. Among men, 2.1% wished they 'had not been born into this sex' 'all the time'; among women 2.8%. While some of the respondents may have expressed gender dissatisfaction because of the social conditions they face in their cultures (among women gender inequality, among men the burden of being family breadwinners), it seems likely that some of the dissatisfaction we observed was a result of a more fundamental gender dysphoria. Interestingly, we obtained broadly similar figures for a sample of 193 undergraduate students in the United Kingdom and the United States.

34. Turning first to community-based samples, a study of 195 Thai *phuying khaam phet* revealed that half of them felt 'not male' by the age of 11, half of those who took hormones doing so by 16 and half of those who were cross-dressing doing so full-time by 18: Winter, 'Thai Transgenders in Focus'. Broadly similar results were found in a Philippine sample of 147 *transpinay*;

the corresponding mean ages were 10, 17 and 18: Winter et al., 'Transgendered Women of the Philippines'. In a comparable Lao study involving 214 *kathoey* the corresponding mean ages were 11, 17 and 13: Winter and Doussantousse,, 'Gender Identity Variance in Laos'. Teh, *The Mak Nyahs*, reported that 71% of her sample of 507 Malaysian *maknyah* 'thought they were female when they were children' and 14% were cross-dressing by 11, 82% by 20. In a sample of 43 South Korean transwomen, Tae-Suk Kim et al. found a mean onset of gender dysphoria by 11 and cross-dressing by 18: 'Psychological Burdens Are Associated with Young Male Transsexuals in Korea', *Psychiatry and Clinical Neurosciences* 60, no. 4 (2006): 417. All of these studies were community based (involving sampling based on social networks within the respective communities of transwomen). Turning now to clinic-based studies: from Singapore a study involving 200 transwomen and 100 transmen found that by the age of 12 74% of the transwomen and 80% of the transmen had begun to identify as the other gender. By 18 the figures rose to 99% for both transwomen and transmen. By 12 60% of the transwomen and 84% of the transmen had begun to cross-dress. By 18 the figures rose to 92% of the transwomen and 94% of the transmen; by the same age 38% of transwomen had started taking hormones (the figure appeared much lower for transmen): Wing Foo Tsoi, 'Developmental Profile of 200 Male and 100 Female Transsexuals in Singapore', *Archives of Sexual Behavior* 19, no. 6 (1990): 595. From Japan, a study involving 349 transwomen and 230 transmen reported that by the time they entered elementary school 28% of the transwomen and 70% of the transmen reported discomfort with their gender identity. Another 28% of the transwomen and 23% of the transmen were experiencing gender discomfort by the end of elementary schooling. For detail, see Nobuyuki Okabe et al., 'Clinical Characteristics of Patients with Gender Identity Disorder at a Japanese Gender Identity Disorder Clinic', *Psychiatry Research* 157 (2008): 315.

35.   In the case of Thailand, see, e.g., LeeRay M. Costa and Andrew Matzner, *Male Bodies, Women's Souls: Personal Narratives of Thailand's Transgendered Youth* (Binghampton, NY: Haworth, 2006); Richard Totman, *The Third Sex: Kathoey, Thailand's Ladyboys* (London: Souvenir Press, 2003).

36.   Nuttawut Udomsak, email communication with author, 28 April 2008.

37.   *International Herald Tribune*, 'Thai Health Ministry Issued Temporary Ban on Castrations for Non-Medical Purposes', 2 April 2008, http://www.iht.com/bin/printfriendly.php?id= 11620629 (accessed 2 October 2008).

38.   Winter et al., 'Transgendered Women of the Philippines'.

39.   Sass Rogando-Sasot, email communication with author, 30 April 2008.

40.   See Nanda, 'Hijra and Sadhin'.

41.   Ibid., 33, provides a vivid description of the operation: 'The surgery is (ideally) performed by a *hijra*, called a "midwife". The client is seated in front of a picture of the goddess [Bahuchara Mata] and repeats Bahuchara's name over and over, which induces a trancelike state. The midwife then severs all or part of the genitals (penis and testicles) from the body with two diagonal cuts with a sharp knife. The blood from the operation, which is considered part of the male identity, is allowed to flow freely; this rids the person of their maleness. The resulting wound is healed by traditional medical practices and a small hole is left open for urination.'

42.   Teh, *The Mak Nyahs*.

43.   See Winter, 'Thai Transgenders in Focus: Demographics, Transitions and Identities'; Winter et al., 'Transgendered Women of the Philippines'; Sam Winter and Serge Doussantousse, 'Transpeople, Hormones and Health Risks: A Lao Study', *International Journal of Sexual Health* 21, no. 1 (2009): 35–48.

44.   In the Lao study we found that 60 of the 112 transwomen reported taking hormones at some point in their lives. Only two had ever consulted a doctor about hormone use, with four consulting other medical professionals. In contrast, four out of five had consulted other transwomen: Winter and Doussantousse, 'Transpeople, Hormones and Health Risks'. More recent studies of hormone use in Thailand and the Philippines have found much the same pattern of advice-seeking. Of the 150 Thai transwomen, 139 reported taking cross-sex hormones at some point in their lives, 43 consulting a doctor and/or a nurse and 120 consulting transgender friends before doing so. The advice-seeking after beginning hormone use was hardly more balanced; 70 consulted a doctor and/or a nurse and 101 consulted other transwomen: Sam Winter, Ling Li and Chayada Lertraksakun, report in preparation. Of the 150 Filipina transwomen, 132 reported taking cross-sex hormones at some point in their lives, only 68 consulting

a doctor and/or nurse and 114 consulting transgender friends: Sam Winter and Brenda Alegre, report in preparation.

45. Somchai Suja, Sasiraporn Sutanyawatchai and Supawinee Siri, *Quality of Life in Male to Female Transsexuals Using and Not Using Female Hormone Therapies* (Chiang Mai, Thailand: Chiang Mai University, 2005).

46. For example, any transperson (pre-op, post-op or non-op) may change legal gender status, under strictly controlled circumstances, in the United Kingdom. The Gender Recognition Act 2004 (c. 7) enables transpeople to change their birth certificates (the document that designates legal gender status) if they satisfy a panel of professionals that they have been living in their preferred gender for some time, intend to do so permanently and are not already married (this last provision designed to avoid creation of a same-sex marriage).

47. In some Asian jurisdictions legal gender status is designated on the birth certificate (e.g. the Philippines and Hong Kong). In others it is on a family register entry (e.g. Japan and South Korea). In Singapore the ID card has since 1996 performed the function of legal gender status designation: Waipang Au, 'Singapore: A Woman with a Past', July 2005, http://www.yawningbread.org/arch_2005/yax-457.htm (accessed 24 March 2008).

48. Dede Oetomo, email communication with author, 22 February 2008.

49. See Tait, 'Sex Change Funding Undermines No Gays Claim'.

50. *BBC News*, 'Kuwaiti Sex-Change Case Overturned', 12 October 2004, http://news.bbc.co.uk/2/hi/middle_east/3734336.stm (accessed 10 December 2008).

51. Decision in the Case of *Rommel Jacinto Dantes Silverio* v. *Republic of the Philippines*, Supreme Court of the Philippines 19 October 2007, http://elibrary.supremecourt.gov.ph/decisions.php?doctype=decisions%20/%20signed%20resolutions&docid=a45475a11ec72b843d74959b60fd7bd6476b8ef08b258 (accessed 10 December 2008).

52. Almost all research hitherto conducted in this area concerns transwomen, for whom a heterosexual sexual preference (androphilia, i.e. attraction to men) appears most common. Consider the research from Malaysia, Singapore, South Korea, Thailand, the Philippines, Laos and Japan. In Malaysia, Teh, *The Mak Nyahs*, reported that 97% of her *maknyah* participants were attracted to men when they were younger and had a male as their first date. A similar figure (largely the same participants we can assume) had never been attracted to women. In Singapore, Tsoi, 'Developmental Profile of 200 Male and 100 Female Transsexuals in Singapore', found that all the transwoman participants in his study were androphilic. In South Korea, around 98% of transwomen in Kim et al.'s study, 'Psychological Burdens Are Associated with Young Male Transsexuals in Korea', reported attraction to men. My own research findings in Southeast Asia echo these generally high figures for androphilia among transwomen. In five independent samples of between 147 and 225 participants in Thailand, the Philippines and Laos, my colleagues and I have obtained prevalence rates for exclusive androphilia ranging from 76 to 92%: see Winter, 'Thai Transgenders in Focus; Winter et al., 'Transgendered Women of the Philippines'; Sam Winter and Liselot Vink, 'Predictors of Mental Health in a Sample of Transwomen in Thailand' and 'Predictors of Mental Health in a Sample of Transwomen in the Philippines' (both in preparation); Winter and Doussantousse, 'Gender Identity Variance in Laos'. Given the tendency of some Asian cultures to confer femaleness on any birth-assigned male who habitually adopts the 'penetratee' role, the generally high levels of findings of heterosexuality in samples of transwomen may not be entirely surprising. The only major exception to this picture of overwhelming heterosexuality is in a Japanese sample of transwomen, only 40% of whom were attracted to men (a further 14% appeared to be bisexual): Okabe et al., 'Clinical Characteristics of Patients with Gender Identity Disorder at a Japanese Gender Identity Disorder Clinic'. What about the sexual preferences of transmen in Asia? Tsoi's Singapore study indicated that a majority may be heterosexual (gynephilic, i.e. erotically attracted to women), although on this matter Tsoi's figures appear somewhat unclear. In Japan, Okabe et al. reported that 92% of transmen were gynephilic. How do these figures compare with Western countries? The most reliable research in this respect is a study of 113 transwomen referred to a Dutch gender identity clinic, which identified 61 (54.5%) who were exclusively androphilic, a figure well below most of the figures in Asian countries cited above; see Yolanda L.S. Smith et al., 'Transsexual Subtypes: Clinical and Theoretical Significance', *Psychiatry Research* 137, no. 3 (2005): 151.

53. Sam Winter, 'Language and Identity in Transgender: Gender Wars and the Thai *Kathoey*', in *Problematising Identity: Everyday Struggles in Language, Culture and Education*, ed. A. Lin (Mahwah, NJ: Lawrence Erlbaum, 2008), 119.

54. The Director of Immigration, who acts on such matters for the Security Bureau, made clear the government's position in a reply letter dated 7 August 2002 to Robyn Emerton of TEAM (Transgender Equality and Acceptance Movement). The letter was headed 'Position of Post-operative Transsexuals: Immigration Issues Government of Hong Kong', and stated that in the Director of Immigration's opinion the relevant Hong Kong law (i.e. Births and Deaths Registration Ordinance (Cap. 174)) allowed changes only where the original certificate contained an error (a condition, it was implied, not applicable to transpeople).

55. See Robyn Emerton, 'Time for Change: A Call for the Legal Recognition of Transsexual and Other Transgender Persons in Hong Kong', *Hong Kong Law Journal* 34, no. 3 (2004): 515; Robyn Emerton, 'Neither Here nor There: The Current Status of Transsexual and Other Transgender Persons under Hong Kong Law', *Hong Kong Law Journal* 34, no. 2 (2004): 245.

56. Winter, 'Counting *Kathoey*'.

57. See Winter, 'Thai Transgenders in Focus'.

58. Recent research in Laos, the Philippines and Thailand (sample sizes 214, 158 and 225, respectively) reveals how common it is for transwomen to be read. Asked how many strangers, in their experience, were aware that they were transwomen, 47.4, 56.5 and 84%, respectively, answered 'most' or 'all' (as opposed to 'some' or 'none'). Asked how often, at a distance and wearing make-up, they were thought by strangers to be birth-assigned women, 14.8, 7.8 and 14.8%, respectively, answered 'never' (as opposed to 'some', 'most' or 'all' of the time): Winter and Doussantousse, 'Gender Identity Variance in Laos'; Winter and Vink, 'Predictors of Mental Health in a Sample of Transwomen in Thailand' and 'Predictors of Mental Health in a Sample of Transwomen in the Philippines'.

59. Among 147 Filipina transwomen 20% reported preferring to be a transwoman (rather than a birth-assigned woman), and 10% reported wanting to be a transwoman if they were given a chance to start life again: Winter et al., 'Transgendered Women of the Philippines'. Among 195 Thai transwomen 15% preferred to be a transwoman (rather than a birth-assigned woman), and 11% expressed a desire to again be gender identity variant in their next life: Winter, 'Thai Transgenders in Focus'. Among 214 Lao transwomen the figures were 43 and 20%: Winter and Doussantousse, 'Gender Identity Variance in Laos'.

60. Erick Laurent, 'Sexuality and Human Rights: An Asian Perspective', *Journal of Homosexuality* 48, nos 3–4 (2005): 163.

61. See, e.g., Phil C.W. Chan's criticism of the Hong Kong government's position and approach in 'The Lack of Sexual Orientation Anti-discrimination Legislation in Hong Kong: Breach of International and Domestic Legal Obligations', *International Journal of Human Rights* 9, no. 1 (2005): 69.

62. Human Rights Watch, *Ravaging the Vulnerable: Abuses against Persons at High-Risk of HIV Infection in Bangladesh* (New York, 2003).

63. Human Rights Watch, *World Report* (New York, 2006).

64. People's Union for Civil Liberties–Karnataka, *Human Rights Violations against the Transgender Community* (Bangalore, 2003).

65. Winter et al., 'Transpeople, transprejudice and pathologisation'.

66. Teh, *The Mak Nyahs*.

67. Fereydoon Mehrabi, Mehrdad Eftekhar Ardebili and Nahaleh Moshtagh Bidokhti, 'Sexual Experience and Fantasies of Homosexuals and Transsexuals in Iran', paper presented at First World Congress for Sexual Health: Achieving Health, Pleasure and Respect, Sydney, 15–19 April 2007.

68. Mohd Noor Noraini et al., *Sexual Identity: Effeminacy among University Students* (Kuala Lumpur: International Islamic University Malaysia, 2005).

69. *New Straits Times*, 'Rehabilitation Centre for Cross-Dressers', 12 April 2007.

70. For detail, see Yik Koon Teh, 'Give Transsexuals Room to Live', *The Sun*, 2 April 2007, http://www.sun2surf.com/article.cfm?id=17470 (accessed 23 April 2007). It is noted that cases such as this are not unknown in Western countries. For instance, in the United Kingdom there were the two leading cases of *Corbett* v. *Corbett (otherwise Ashley)*, [1970] 2 All ER 33, and *R.* v. *Tan and others* [1983] 2 All ER 12, both of which denied any possibility of change in legal gender status, even for post-operative transpeople and for the purposes of the criminal law. The Gender Recognition Act 2004, representing a substantial step forward in the recognition and development of transpeople's rights, now enables a gender identity variant person to change his or her legal gender status, even where surgery has not taken place.

71. See Teh, *The Mak Nyahs*; Yik Koon Teh and Slamah Khartini, *Maknyahs (Male Transsexuals) in Malaysia* (Kuala Lumpur: Ministry of Science, Technology and Environment of Malaysia, 2000).
72. Teh, *The Mak Nyahs*.
73. Amnesty International, 'Malaysia: Fear for Safety/Torture or Ill-Treatment', 3 August 2007, http://web.amnesty.org/library/Index/ENGASA280022007 (accessed 20 August 2007).
74. M. Aamer Sarfraz and David Castle, 'A Muslim Suicide', *Australasian Psychiatry* 10, no. 1 (2002): 437.
75. See Winter et al., 'Transgendered Women of the Philippines'; see also Winter, 'Thai Transgenders in Focus'.
76. Winter and Vink examined the impact of being gender identity variant upon the lives of trans-women in Thailand ('Predictors of Mental Health in a Sample of Transwomen in Thailand') and found that 22% of Thai transwomen believed that being a transgender person reduced their chances of obtaining employment and 29% believed that it reduced the choices of jobs available. In a similar study conducted by Winter and Vink in the Philippines ('Predictors of Mental Health in a Sample of Transwomen in the Philippines') the figures were somewhat lower, 12% and 15%, respectively. The authors of the two studies believe the figures to be underestimates of the extent of the problems transpeople face in obtaining employment, even in these two comparatively tolerant societies. The reason is that in contacting participants we relied on social networks within the gender identity variant community. Those in full-time studies or already in employment were more readily drawn into our samples. Transpeople not in employment were less likely to learn of our study and to join our sample accordingly. Yet these transpeople are likely those who had had the most direct experience of transprejudiced hiring practices. Had the jobless (particularly the chronically jobless) been better represented in our sample, our figures for the impact of being a transgender person upon obtaining employment would probably be more alarming.
77. Winter, 'Thai Transgenders in Focus'.
78. Winter and Vink, 'Predictors of Mental Health in a Sample of Transwomen in Thailand'.
79. *Rommel Jacinto Dantes Silverio* v. *Republic of the Philippines*.
80. Filipino transpeople's dismay has recently been heightened by the Supreme Court of the Philippines' overturning of a lower court's favourable decision over a petition by an intersex person for a new birth certificate: Decision in the case of *Republic of the Philippines* v. *Jennifer B. Cagandahan*, Supreme Court of the Philippines, 12 September 2008. http://elibrary.judiciary.gov.ph/decisions.php?doctype=Decisions%20/%20Signed%20Resolutions&docid=12218055 63131007007 (accessed 9 March 2009). In important respects her case was identical to that of a transgender person, with the one difference that she was able to point to a physical disorder underlying her gender dysphoria (congenital adrenal hyperplasia); also, unlike transwomen, she was seeking a birth certificate designating her as male.
81. Winter et al., 'Transgendered Women of the Philippines'.
82. Winter and Vink, 'Predictors of Mental Health in a Sample of Transwomen in the Philippines'.
83. For detail, see Robyn Emerton, 'Finding a Voice, Fighting for Rights: The Emergence of the Transgender Movement in Hong Kong', *Inter-Asia Cultural Studies* 7, no. 2 (2006): 243.
84. Human Rights Watch, 'Kuwait: Repressive Dress-Code Law Encourages Police Abuse: Arrests Target Transgender People', 16 January 2008, http://hrw.org/english/docs/2008/01/17/kuwait17800.htm (accessed 5 May 2008).
85. 'Kuwaiti Sex-Change Case Overturned'.
86. *BBC News*, 'Pakistan "Same-Sex" Couple Held', 22 May 2007, http://news.bbc.co.uk/2/hi/6679733.stm (accessed 5 May 2008).
87. See, e.g., Human Rights Watch, 'Nepal: Police on "Sexual Cleansing" Drive: Transgender People Routinely Subjected to Physical and Sexual Abuse', 11 January 2006, http://www.hrw.org/en/news/2006/01/11/nepal-police-sexual-cleansing-drive (accessed 10 December 2006); Sunil Pant, *Social Exclusion of Sexual and Gender Minorities: Final Report* (Kathmandu: Blue Diamond Society, 2005).
88. People's Union for Civil Liberties–Karnataka, *Human Rights Violations against the Transgender Community*.
89. Human Rights Watch, *Ravaging the Vulnerable*.
90. Article 22 of the Hong Kong Bill of Rights Ordinance (Cap. 383), modelled upon and implementing Article 26 of the International Covenant on Civil and Political Rights, states that '[a]ll persons are equal before the law and are entitled without any discrimination to the

equal protection of the law. In this respect, the law shall prohibit any discrimination and guarantee to all persons equal and effective protection against discrimination on any ground such as race, colour, sex, language, religion, political or other opinion, national or social origin, property, birth or other status.' See *Leung T. C. William Roy* v. *Secretary for Justice* [2005] 3 HKLRD 657 (Hong Kong Court of First Instance); *Secretary for Justice* v. *Leung T. C. William Roy* [2006] 4 HKLRD 211 (Hong Kong Court of Appeal).

91. Criticisms have been numerous, varied and prolonged. The earliest were by Justin Richardson, Richard Isay and Shannon Minter: Justin Richardson, 'Setting Limits on Gender Health', *Harvard Review of Psychiatry* 4, no. 1 (1996): 49, followed by a response to his critics in Justin Richardson, 'Response: Finding the Disorder in Gender Identity Disorder', *Harvard Review of Psychiatry* 7, no. 1 (1999): 43; Richard Isay, 'Remove Gender Identity Disorder in DSM', *Psychiatric News* 32, no. 9 (1997): 13; Shannon Minter, 'Diagnosis and Treatment of Gender Identity Disorder in Children', in *Sissies and Tomboys: Gender Nonconformity and Homosexual Childhood*, ed. Matthew Rottnek (New York: New York University Press, 1999), 9. Since then criticisms have gathered pace, including Nancy H. Bartlett, Paul L. Vasey and W.M. Bukowski, 'Is Gender Identity Disorder in Children a Mental Disorder?', *Sex Roles* 43, nos 11–12 (2000): 753; Stuart Chen-Hayes, 'Counseling and Advocacy with Transgendered and Gender-Variant Persons in Schools and Families', *Journal of Humanistic Counseling, Education and Development* 40 (2001): 34; Darryl B. Hill et al., 'Gender Identity Disorders in Childhood and Adolescence a Critical Inquiry', *Journal of Psychology & Human Sexuality* 17 (2006): 7; Andrea James, 'A Defining Moment in Our History: Examining Disease Models of Gender Identity', http://www.tsroadmap.com/info/gender-identity.pdf (accessed 5 July 2006); Susan J. Langer and James I. Martin, 'How Dresses Can Make You Mentally Ill: Examining Gender Identity Disorder in Children', *Child and Adolescent Social Work Journal* 21, no. 1 (2004): 5; Arlene Lev, 'Disordering Gender Identity Disorder in the DSM-IV-TR', *Journal of Psychology and Human Sexuality* 17, nos 3–4 (2005): 35; Paul L. Vasey and Nancy H. Bartlett, 'What Can the Samoan "Fa'afafine" Teach Us about the Western Concept of Gender Identity Disorder in Childhood?', *Perspectives in Biology and Medicine* 50, no. 4 (2007): 481; Anne Vitale, 'Rethinking the Gender Identity Disorder Terminology in the Diagnostic and Statistical Manual of Mental Disorders IV', paper presented at Conference of Harry Benjamin International Gender Dysphoria Association, Bologna, 6–9 April 2005; Ian Wilson, Chris Griffin and Bernadette Wren, 'The Validity of the Diagnosis of Gender Identity Disorder (Child and Adolescent Criteria)', *Clinical Child Psychology and Psychiatry* 7, no. 3 (2002): 335; Sam Winter, 'Transphobia: A Price Worth Paying for "Gender Identity Disorder"?', paper presented at First Biennial Symposium of the World Professional Association for Transgender Health, Chicago, 5–8 September 2007; Kelley Winters, 'Gender Dissonance Diagnostic Reform of Gender Identity Disorder for Adults', *Journal of Psychology & Human Sexuality* 17 (2006): 71; Madeleine H. Wyndzen, 'A Personal and Scientific Look at a Mental Illness Model of Transgenderism', *APA Division 44 Newsletter* (Spring 2004): 3.

92. As of 14 December 2008 the senior officers of the World Psychiatric Association (WPA) were overwhelmingly from Western countries; only two of the 20 positions in the WPA Executive Committee and Council were held by members from Asia (Hong Kong and Israel, respectively).

93. Winter et al., 'Transpeople, transprejudice and pathologisation'.

94. Winter, 'Transphobia'.

95. Presumably subsidies for healthcare for transpeople would remain even if transpeople were regarded as experiencing a physical disorder, a re-conceptualisation that would conform to the subjective experience of many transpeople (i.e. 'I feel I was born into the wrong body'); be logically consistent with the only effective treatment for transpeople (i.e. medical treatment designed to bring one's body in harmony with one's identity); and be less stigmatising than a mental disorder. Finally, this view of transpeople would accord with recent research on biologically based brain gender that suggests that gender identity variance may indeed have a physical basis: Terry Reed et al., 'Atypical Gender Development – a Review', *International Journal of Transgenderism* 9, no. 1 (2006): 29; thus, it may best be regarded as a form of intersexualism.

From discretion to disbelief: recent trends in refugee determinations on the basis of sexual orientation in Australia and the United Kingdom

Jenni Millbank

Faculty of Law, University of Technology, Sydney, Australia

In *Appellants S395/2002 and S396/2002* v. *Minister for Immigration and Multicultural Affairs*, the High Court of Australia was the first ultimate appellate court to consider a claim for refugee status based upon sexual orientation. By majority the court rejected the notion prevalent in earlier cases that decision-makers could 'expect' refugee applicants to 'co-operate in their own protection' by concealing their sexuality. This paper explores the impact of *S395 and S396* on the refugee jurisprudence of Australia and the United Kingdom five years on. Refugee decision-makers in both countries have been slow to fully appreciate the fact that sexual minorities are secretive about their sexuality and relationships as a result of oppressive social forces rather than by 'choice'. In addition, in Australia there has been a clear shift away from discretion towards disbelief as the major area of contest, with a significant increase in decisions where the applicant's claim to actually being gay, lesbian or bisexual is outright rejected. In an alarming number of cases tribunal members used highly stereotyped and Westernised notions of 'gayness' as a template against which the applicants were judged.

Introduction

In December 2003 the High Court of Australia handed down its decision in *Appellants S395/2002 and S396/2002* v. *Minister for Immigration and Multicultural Affairs*, in which two Bangladeshi gay men were seeking refugee status on the ground of membership of a particular social group.[1] *S395 and S396* was the first decision of an ultimate appellate court anywhere in the world to deal with a claim for refugee status based on sexual orientation, and remains so to date.[2] At issue was the interpretation of persecution: specifically, whether it was lawful for primary decision-makers to consider whether gay, lesbian and bisexual asylum seekers could or should be 'discreet' (or more accurately, *secretive*) in their country of origin so as to avoid or lessen the risk of persecution. 'Discretion' reasoning had appeared very widely in the refugee case law of both Australia and the United Kingdom prior to that point,[3] although it had been consistently rejected by lower-level courts and tribunals in comparable receiving countries such as Canada and New Zealand in earlier years.[4]

By a narrow majority of 4–3, the High Court held that the tribunal decision-maker had erred in dividing the particular social group into two subsets of 'discreet' and 'open' homosexuals and in failing to consider firstly the future-focused question of what would happen if the applicants were in fact discovered to be gay and secondly whether the need to act 'discreetly' to avoid the threat of serious harm *itself* constituted persecution.[5] The majority emphatically rejected the notion that decision-makers could 'expect' or had any jurisdiction to 'reasonably require' refugee applicants to 'co-operate in their own protection' by concealing their sexuality.[6]

This paper explores the impact of the *S395 and S396* decision on the refugee jurisprudence of Australia and the UK five years on through an examination of available tribunal-level determinations and judicial review cases concerning sexual orientation in both countries both before and after the decision. The cases analysed cover the period between 1994 and 2007, comprising 528 Australian cases (made up of 369 decisions from the Refugee Review Tribunal [RRT] and 159 judicial review cases drawn from the Federal Court of Australia, the Federal Magistrates Court and appeals from those courts to the Full Federal Court) and 116 UK decisions (made up of 70 tribunal decisions and 46 judicial review cases drawn from the Queen's Bench and the Court of Appeal of England and Wales).[7]

Given that our earlier research[8] found a very strong correlation between 'discretion' reasoning and negative outcomes for applicants in cases from 1994 to 2003, we anticipated that disapproval of discretion-based reasoning, combined with the clear judicial summons to consider sexuality as a form of identity rather than as mere private sexual behaviour, would lead to a higher level of positive outcomes for gay, lesbian and bisexual asylum seekers from 2004 onwards.[9] Yet this has not eventuated, and in fact the overall success rates for sexual minority applicants improved little over what is now a 14-year timeframe of our study.[10]

We suggest that while *S395 and S396* did have a clear positive impact on the Australian jurisprudence through the direct abolition of a highly discriminatory line of reasoning, the overall impact of the decision has been far more muted, and even arguably thwarted, by the practices of decision-makers at lower levels.[11] This has been for a number of reasons. First, decision-makers in both Australia and the UK have been slow to fully absorb and apply the insight that gay people are secretive about their sexuality and relationships as a result of oppressive social forces rather than by 'choice'. A number of lower-level decision-makers have thus continued to characterise gay men and lesbians as 'naturally' discreet when possible, without actually inquiring into why this has occurred. In a related development, UK decision-makers have resisted seeing S395 and S396 as persuasive and have tended to reframe issues in terms of general UK law on persecution, thus avoiding the question of *why* the applicant shielded their identity from becoming known.

In addition, in Australia there has been a clear shift away from discretion towards disbelief as the major area of contest in decisions since *S395 and S396*, with a significant increase in decisions where the applicant's claim to actually being gay, lesbian or bisexual is outright rejected. Our research found that in an alarming number of cases tribunal members cross-examined applicants using highly stereotyped and Westernised notions of 'gayness' as a template that, when applicants did not fit, led to their claim of sexual identity being rejected. Moreover, both Australia and the UK have severely constricted the grounds of review available for refugee determinations in recent years,[12] such that even highly dubious initial decisions are not overturned if the flaw is characterised as factual (as findings regarding applicants' motivations for secrecy, or the credibility of their membership of the group, almost invariably are).

The applicants from the *S395 and S396* decision itself exemplified this bind: having brought a rare successful claim for judicial review to the ultimate appellate court in Australia, the men had their claim remitted to the tribunal for re-determination, expecting that it would consider whether they faced a real chance of persecution given that this was the issue in dispute at all five levels of adjudication.[13] Yet on remittal the second tribunal decided that they were not gay after all, and this decision was then held to be unreviewable by the courts.[14] This raises an issue of broad significance to refugee determination: the iniquity of cutting off avenues of later review without attempting to remedy the manifest flaws at earlier stages of the decision-making process. Our research also highlights the particular need to provide careful guidance and training on sexuality issues so that primary decision-makers are able to question applicants in a sensitive way and base any determination of their sexual orientation on relevant grounds.

The discretion problem

At its baldest, discretion reasoning entailed a 'reasonable expectation that persons should, to the extent that it is possible, co-operate in their own protection',[15] by exercising 'self-restraint'[16] such as avoiding any behaviour that would identify them as gay;[17] never telling anyone they were gay;[18] only expressing their sexuality by having anonymous sex in public places;[19] pretending that their partner is a 'flatmate';[20] or indeed remaining celibate.[21] This approach subverted the aim of the Refugees Convention – that the receiving state provide a surrogate for protection from the home state – by placing the responsibility of protection upon the applicant: it is he or she who must avoid harm. The discretion approach also varied the scope of protection afforded in relation to each of the five Convention grounds by, for example, protecting the right to be 'openly' religious but not to be openly gay or in an identifiable same-sex relationship.[22]

The appearance of discretion reasoning in a decision strongly correlated to failure for lesbian and gay applicants. In Australia from 1994 to 2003 discretion appeared as an issue in the text of 114 of the tribunal decisions, representing almost 40% of publicly available RRT cases on sexual orientation through that period. When discretion appeared as an issue, applicants had a failure rate of 70% at tribunal level, a figure roughly in line with failure rates for sexual orientation claims in Australia overall.[23] However, where it was clear from the reasoning that discretion was identified as something that was a 'reasonable' expectation or requirement of the applicant, the failure rate rose to 98% at tribunal level.[24] In the UK, discretion was raised almost as often as in Australia, appearing as a consideration in 34% of tribunal-level cases.[25] The impact was even more significant: when discretion was raised at all, applicants had a failure rate of 90% at tribunal level, and this rose to 100% when it was apparent from the reasoning that discretion was an expectation.[26]

The role of discretion in the Australian and UK cases has been extensively critiqued elsewhere,[27] so only a few brief comments will be made here on how it was manifested and the errors of reasoning that it led to. The idea of discretion reflects broader social norms concerning the 'proper place' of lesbian and gay sexuality,[28] as something to be hidden and reluctantly tolerated, a purely private sexual behaviour rather than an important and integral aspect of identity, or as an apparent relationship status. The discretion approach explicitly posited the principle that human rights protection available to sexual orientation was limited to private consensual sex and did not extend to any other manifestation of sexual identity[29] (which has been variously characterised as 'flaunting',[30] 'displaying'[31] and 'advertising'[32] homosexuality as well as 'inviting'[33] persecution). Thus for example in 2001 the Federal Court of Australia held that the Iranian Penal Code prohibiting homosexuality and imposing a death penalty did 'place limits' on the applicant's behaviour; the applicant had to 'avoid overt and public, or publicly provocative, homosexual activity. But having to accept those limits did not amount to persecution.'[34] On appeal, the Full Federal

Court endorsed the view that 'public manifestation of homosexuality is not an essential part of being homosexual'.[35] The discretion approach thus has had wide-reaching ramifications in terms of framing the human rights of lesbians and gay men to family life, freedom of association and freedom of expression as necessarily lesser in scope than those held by heterosexual people.[36]

Discretion reasoning also led to and compounded errors in a range of areas of analysis in the refugee determination process, including the role of internal relocation alternatives, the likelihood of objective risk based on country evidence, and the relationship between the criminalisation of gay and lesbian sex and the unavailability of state protection. Each of these issues will be briefly outlined below.

In making a determination of the likelihood of persecution, decision-makers may consider whether the applicant would be safe elsewhere in his or her country, either because there is less chance of persecution occurs if the threat of harm is itself localised, or because there is greater sufficiency of state protection in some areas.[37] In considering internal relocation, decision-makers also take into account questions of 'reasonableness', considering the individual impact on the applicant of relocation, including whether doing so would isolate them from sources of financial and emotional support.[38] In sexuality cases, internal relocation considerations typically involve asking whether the applicant could move from a rural or remote area where they have been endangered to a larger metropolitan setting,[39] usually the capital city – not uncommonly characterised as having a 'thriving' gay scene – often by reference to listings of social venues drawn exclusively from tourist guides.[40] Discretion reasoning clouded the consideration of internal relocation by implicitly or explicitly assuming that the purpose of relocation was to achieve (re)concealment rather than to move to a place of actual safety and sufficiency of state protection.[41] This was glaringly illustrated by the following exchange drawn from the transcript of an RRT hearing in 2002 in which internal relocation was held to be reasonable:

Applicant: *I tried to approach the police . . .*

Member: *Well you don't need to approach the police now . . . you know that that's useless, your aim now is to stay away from gay bashers . . . and ahm prying family neighbours . . . there must be more anonymous accommodation.*[42]

In short, discretion reasoning led to the assumption that applicants would be safe in a big city because no one would know they were gay (and they can keep it that way), rather than because it actually *was* safe to be gay in a big city.

Discretion reasoning also led to misreading and misrepresentation of general country information on the objective risk of persecution for members of the group. Because this line of reasoning assumed that applicants should and would conform to their culture or government's oppressive regimes in order to avoid harm, decision-makers avoided assessing the magnitude of the harm posed, including harm as serious as the death penalty,[43] and balancing that harm in the assessment of risk. In the Australian tribunal decisions, the assumption of discretion was held to foreclose the question of risk to the extent that on occasion there was literally no assessment at all of the country situation and the risk of harm to someone who *was* identified as gay or lesbian.[44] It also led to some wildly improbable conclusions on country conditions, most notably that Iran was 'tolerant' of homosexuality.[45]

In both Australia and the UK it was notable that discretion reasoning compounded long-standing errors in examining the role of criminal law when assessing likelihood of persecution. Decision-makers routinely dismissed criminal proscriptions on gay and lesbian sex as 'theoretical' and not persecutory if there was insufficient evidence that they were regularly enforced.[46] Embedded in the finding of non-enforcement was the assumption that applicants would not – and could not – alert authorities to their sexuality, thus overlooking the crucial question of what kind of state protection would be available if members of the group experienced sexuality-based violence and police were to characterise them as criminal offenders rather than victims. (Indeed in some cases judges and tribunal members have actually referred to the applicant as a 'potential offender'[47] and to gay sex as 'sexual misconduct'.[48]) Thus discretion reasoning obscured the important connection between formal criminal sanctions, whether or not regularly enforced, and the failure of state protection from harm caused by both state and non-state actors.

In sum, discretion reasoning detracted from the future-focused nature of the well-founded fear test: in effect making it virtually impossible for a claim to succeed unless an applicant could demonstrate past persecution through their sexuality already becoming known in their country of origin.[49]

The end of discretion as we knew it

The High Court decision in *S395 and S396* should have provided a remedy to the numerous flaws of reasoning outlined above. The two majority judgments expressly found that refugee decision-makers could neither assume nor require discretion and held that the assessment of persecution must inquire into both why the applicant concealed their identity and what would occur if it were revealed, as part of the process of identifying whether there was a well-founded fear.[50]

Australian case law from 2004 onwards does demonstrate a positive impact from the judgment. In the 2004–7 period, discretion was raised in 52 cases in Australia, representing 30% of publicly available refugee decisions on sexual orientation. Almost half of these were judicial review decisions, reflecting both an overall rise in the number of judicial review applications in these later years in the pool of Australian cases and the likelihood that the *S395 and S396* decision itself precipitated a number of applications for review.[51] At tribunal level when discretion was raised as an issue in the post-*S395 and S396* period of 2004–7, the failure rate dropped to 27% – almost a mirror reversal of the pre-*S395 and S396* success and failure rates when the issue of discretion appeared.[52] Tribunal decision-makers now commonly accept applicants' claims that they would rather be open about their sexuality (rather than querying the 'reasonableness' or 'right' to do so). So, for example, we see statements from 2004 onwards such as:

> I accept that his situation has changed from that in Bangladesh in that he is now openly gay and he can not hide his sexual feelings now he has lived this lifestyle in Australia. I accept that it would be different for the applicant if he were to return to Bangladesh now. The applicant fears that he would have to hide his true identity and that he would suffer repercussions when his sexuality was revealed.[53]

In a number of recent cases the tribunal also held that concealment of one's sexuality was or would be persecutory.[54]

There were only a small number of UK cases available in the 2004–7 period, probably due to the restriction from April 2005 of tribunal review to points of law only.[55] Yet of the handful of available cases, most did address the issue of discretion and these had a markedly low failure rate compared with the earlier period. Of a total of 16 tribunal cases, 12 raised the issue of discretion – six of which were positive decisions.[56] Although it may be hard to generalise from such a small number of cases, it is still striking that, as in the Australian cases, this represented almost a mirror reversal of success/failure rates from the pre-*S395 and S396* era.

It now appears far more likely that decision-makers in sexual orientation cases in both Australia and the UK properly address the risk of persecution question by weighing the likelihood of exposure to persecutors with the severity of harm posed, rather than simply assuming that the threat, however severe, can be avoided by secrecy.

In addition, the High Court of Australia by majority held in *S395 and S396* that living in a state of fearful concealment could *itself* be found to be so oppressive as to constitute persecution. Justice McHugh and Justice Kirby stated,

> In cases where the applicant has modified his or her conduct, there is a natural tendency for the tribunal of fact to reason that, because the applicant has not been persecuted in the past, he or she will not be persecuted in the future. The fallacy underlying this approach is the assumption that the conduct of the applicant is uninfluenced by the conduct of the persecutor and that the relevant persecutory conduct is the *harm* that will be inflicted. In many – perhaps the majority of – cases, however, the applicant has acted in the way that he or she did only because of the *threat* of harm. In such cases, the well-founded fear of persecution held by the applicant is the fear that, unless that person acts to avoid the harmful conduct, he or she will suffer harm. It is the *threat* of serious harm with its menacing implications that constitutes the persecutory conduct.[57]

They concluded that to 'determine the issue of real chance without determining whether the modified conduct was influenced by the threat of harm is to fail to consider that issue properly'.[58] It is this latter aspect of the judgment that has been less successfully translated into practice in lower-level decision-making, as decision-makers have continued to avoid asking the question: *why* has the applicant lived in secrecy?

Avoiding and undermining *S395 and S396* – no need to inquire into the naturally discreet

A guide to the path that decision-makers would take to avoid fully addressing the implications of *S395 and S396* was provided by the dissenting judgments in that case. In particular the joint dissenting opinion of Justice Callinan and Justice Heydon reinscribed discretion as a 'naturally' occurring state for the applicants specifically and also as a neutral state of social grace that encompassed all people generally without discrimination, including heterosexual people.[59] The dissenting judges placed a clear onus on applicants to bring a claim at first instance demonstrating that their lives of former secrecy were motivated largely – or even solely – through fear of harm.[60] The absence of such proof was taken as demonstrating that a life of secrecy is a matter of 'free choice':

> The question in this case was not, as the appellants contended, whether, absent imposed or enforced discretion as to their homosexuality, they would be likely to be persecuted in their country of origin, *but whether their mode of conduct was voluntarily chosen*, and had and would not provoke persecution of them.[61]

Justice Callinan and Justice Heydon found that the appellants 'were not oppressed',[62] as they were discreet as a matter of 'free choice'.[63] In cases decided since then, tribunal members in both Australia and the UK have held for example that a closeted lesbian relationship 'does not seem to us to be so very different from the conventional married lives of many other couples who neither flaunt their sexuality nor adopt an overtly heterosexual lifestyle';[64] that 'the sexual practices and behaviour of all people, whether heterosexual or homosexual are not matters that are made public';[65] and that 'discretion in their public sexual practices . . . [is] part of the ordinary consensus of civilised mankind'.[66] These remarks indicate a profound and continuing failure to comprehend the hegemonic and naturalised expression of heterosexuality in all cultures. Such a frame of reference renders it possible to avoid the implications of *S395 and S396* by (re)constructing the applicant's fear as an individualised preference or as an expression of their 'natural' personality or character.[67]

The combined effect of these assumptions is to place a heavy onus on applicants to raise the issue of suppression at first instance.[68] A number of recent judicial review decisions in the UK have held that it is the applicant who must raise, and prove, that their life of 'discretion' was largely or solely in response to fear of persecution; the decision-maker has no duty to inquire.[69] In the 2005 UK case of *RG* the court went so far as to find that the applicant had to raise and prove the persecutory nature of suppression as a *distinct* issue in addition to his fear of persecution generally. Evidence was submitted at first instance by a doctor who stated that,

> If [the applicant] is returned to Colombia, it is likely to be highly traumatic for him. Firstly, he would have to immediately try to repress his sexuality and live a double life, living as if he is not homosexual (when I asked him how he would be affected by this, he said: 'For me, it would be to die.') Suppression of his sexual identity is likely to have traumatic effects.[70]

The original adjudicator ignored this report in holding that the applicant would 'regulate his behaviour' to avoid 'unwelcome attention' that would place him in 'danger',[71] such that with 'one or two elementary precautions'[72] he would not be at risk as an HIV-positive gay man in Colombia. Yet on judicial review the Court of Appeal of England and Wales accepted the Home Secretary's argument that there was no error because

> it was RG's case throughout that what he feared was the actual persecution of the death squads, not the consequence to his psychology of trying to avoid them.[73]

It is also notable that UK decision-makers were openly reluctant to see *S395 and S396* as persuasive authority or as contributing something 'new' to its own refugee jurisprudence. English decision-makers responded that *S395 and S396* was not novel because the majority judgment of Justice McHugh and Justice Kirby had cited a decision of the Court of Appeal of England and Wales on political persecution[74] in support of the principle that an applicant was not required to avoid persecution by modifying behaviour if such modification would itself be persecutory.[75] In doing so, English courts either missed or deliberately misread the crucial point that persecution principles had been very differently applied in cases concerning sexuality in contrast to cases on political grounds in *both* countries prior to *S395 and S396*. Thus the UK tribunals and courts considering *S395 and S396* reordered it into their own frame of reference and excluded the most challenging aspect of the decision, which was that, in order to properly address the issue of persecution, there *is* a duty to inquire why applicants have concealed their sexuality.

Using older English cases as the frame of reference allowed an easy slippage back into assumptions of 'natural' discretion informed by stereotyped ideas of sexual identity as a concealable form of sexual behaviour only acceptable in its 'proper place'. This is borne out by the striking fact that the one English case to fully engage with the ideas raised by *S395 and S396*, and to imaginatively and empathically consider the real day-to-day impact of a life of secrecy, did not actually concern a gay applicant or a same-sex relationship. In *HYSI*[76] the applicant was a man from Kosovo of mixed Albanian and Roma ancestry who claimed that once his mother's Roma ancestry was known he would be subject to persecution. At first instance the adjudicator, in an echo of many claims based on sexual orientation, held that the applicant could internally relocate in order to conceal his identity and thus live a 'normal' life. The Court of Appeal of England and Wales in addressing the question of whether this would be 'unduly harsh' in the context of relocation jurisprudence considered that

> this would probably involve the appellant leading a hermit-like existence, indeed without any social intercourse based on trust. As a stranger he is bound to be asked questions. He would presumably have to lie. Even if he could provide some colourable but some untruthful explanation for his arrival in the new location ... he would have to live with that lie ... Moreover, he would thereafter have to avoid letting slip any intimation of his true ethnicity, or his constant lies. He would simply have to continue to lie and conceal his origins, while simultaneously living with the risk that the truth would be suspected or discovered ...
>   More significantly, however, this consideration serves to highlight that continuing deliberate concealment of his identity on relocation carries with it the unavoidable conclusion that this particular son should ignore his mother.[77]

This detailed and textured engagement with what it would actually *mean* to the applicant's sense of self-identity, encompassing both social interaction and the ability to claim a familial relationship, stands in stark contrast to the approach of the UK tribunal in a number of recent cases concerning sexual orientation. The blithe assurance of the tribunal in *AT* in 2005 that a life of secrecy, fear and shame for lesbian and gay people is simply part of the 'ordinary consensus of civilised mankind'[78] may have been tempered in expression in later cases, but the approach it rests upon has continued. In the 2008 case of *JM* the tribunal characterised the secrecy of a gay man in Uganda as him 'being mindful of his society's concepts of good manners and the general social mores'.[79] At the risk of belabouring the point, it is hard to imagine the tribunal characterising, for example, the inability to freely express one's political opinion as 'good manners'.

Disturbingly, in the 2008 case of *HJ* concerning a gay man from Iran, the Home Secretary put forward the circular argument that an applicant having had a past life of secrecy in their home country was *in itself* proof that a life of secrecy is a tolerable state, claiming that

> self-restraint due to fear will be persecution only if it is such that a homosexual person cannot reasonably be expected to tolerate such self-restraint. Where a person does in fact live discreetly to avoid coming to the attention of the authorities he is reasonably tolerating that position.[80]

This argument was largely accepted by the tribunal, which noted that 'Homosexuals may wish to, but cannot, live openly in Iran as is the case in many countries'[81] and held that 'To live a private life discreetly will not cause significant detriment to his right to respect for private life, nor will it involve suppression of many aspects of his sexual identity.'[82] In *HJ* and *JM* it appears that the shift in law from asking whether the applicant 'should' be secretive to asking whether he can 'reasonably be expected to tolerate' secrecy has not materially altered the tribunal's approach to the interpretation of persecution.[83]

Sexual identity as 'an allegation ... easy to make and impossible to disprove'[84]

> The real mischief ... that is likely to be caused by this allowing his appeal is by encouraging a flood of fraudulent Zimbabwean (and no doubt other) asylum-seekers posing as sodomites.[85]

Credibility is very often an issue of significance in refugee determinations; indeed it is common for some or many aspects of a claim to be disbelieved, even in claims that are ultimately successful. In determinations on the basis of sexuality there will rarely be any 'objective' or external markers of the claimant's membership of the group in the way that there will more often be for other grounds such as political opinion. In particular, if the claimant was not open about his or her identity before leaving the country of origin, evidence of membership will largely consist of the claimant's own account of his or her feelings and experiences.

In our study we did not find evidence that *S395 and S396* led to an influx of fraudulent claims.[86] What we did find, however, was a significant increase in the proportion of Australian decisions where the applicant's claim of a gay, lesbian or bisexual identity was specifically doubted or disbelieved, from 16% of available cases prior to *S395 and S396* to 38% of cases in the 2004–7 period.[87] We suggest that there has been a shift in this period from 'discretion' to 'identity disbelief' as the major ground for negative determinations in Australia. It is possible that decision-makers relying upon 'discretion' reasoning to find no risk of persecution felt relieved of the task of making a searching examination of applicant's identity claims, leading to a far greater emphasis on testing identity since *S395 and S396*. The small number of available UK tribunal decisions available during this time, combined with the confinement of tribunal review to points of law, renders it impossible to determine if a similar trend has occurred in that jurisdiction; therefore the following discussion addresses exclusively the Australian cases.

The wide scope for variable determinations as to the veracity of claims to membership of a group based on sexuality is exposed in a particularly glaring fashion when cases are returned to the tribunal for redetermination following a successful application for judicial review; most notably in *S395 and S396* itself. As the Australian tribunal has complete access to, but is not bound by, earlier findings on remittal it is free to make a completely inconsistent (and unreviewable) finding of fact. In the two original delegates' decisions and in the first joint tribunal decision, the two Bangladeshi men in *S395 and S396* were believed on some aspects of their claim of past persecution and disbelieved regarding several other aspects, but were accepted at both stages as being truthful in their claims to be gay and in a long-term relationship with each other. Having brought two unsuccessful applications for judicial review and finally succeeding before the High Court, their applications for refugee status were returned to the tribunal for rehearing in 2005. The tribunal then held, some six years after their first claims in which they had consistently presented and been accepted as a gay couple, that they were not actually gay.[88] In a similar matter the Federal Magistrates Court refused review of a tribunal's belated decision that the claimant was not gay, stating that '[s]exual orientation is essentially a very subjective matter. It is not easily reconciled with the notion of objective proof.'[89] While the cases were replete with references to 'allegations' of gay identity as something easy to make and hard to disprove[90] (in an uncanny echo of the rape mythology that women have faced in the legal system for centuries[91]), it could just as readily be argued based on our research that findings of the falsity of sexual identity in refugee determinations are easy to make and impossible to appeal.

While not suggesting that every claimant who brings a claim based on sexual orientation is truthful,[92] this section of the paper argues that the Australian cases on identity and credibility evince some extremely disturbing trends, not least of all because inquiry into such issues appears to have proceeded without any kind of formal training into culturally appropriate or sensitive methods of eliciting information on the complex and personal questions of sexual identity and experience. As one RRT decision noted, in a rare articulation of anything other than the 'ease' of false claims, it is difficult for applicants to substantiate and for decision-makers to evaluate [claims on sexual orientation]. By their very nature, they involve private issues of self-identity and sexual conduct, and sometimes personal issues for individuals that may be stressful or unresolved. Social, cultural and religious attitudes to homosexuality in an applicant's society may exacerbate such problems.[93]

Yet in numerous cases it appears from the text of decisions that applicants were questioned principally about matters such as the locations and names of gay nightclubs in Sydney and Melbourne to assess their familiarity with the gay 'scene'. Nicole LaViolette has noted that the experience and understanding of one's sexual orientation can vary enormously, 'depending upon their country of origin, gender, culture, social class, education, religion, family background, and socialization. There is no uniform way in which lesbians and gay men recognize and act on their sexual orientation.'[94]

Surely it is an unreasonable expectation of individuals from elsewhere in the world who are attracted to members of the same sex that they should be interested in and attend gay bars and clubs in inner-city locations in Australia as a matter of course upon their relocation here. Yet when applicants responded that they were not familiar with the locations of gay bars, asserted a preference for socialising privately or in other venues or suburbs, or claimed to have gone to mainstream pornography venues for male/male sex, they were disbelieved.[95] (Moreover when applicants did name bars they had attended, some tribunal members took steps such as telephoning the named bars to ask whether the staff remembered them.[96])

In a 2005 tribunal case, a bisexual applicant stated that he had been to a gay sauna and gave an accurate description of its location although he was unable to name it. The tribunal member then peppered the applicant with detailed questions about this sex-on-premises venue, addressing the applicant's experience and recollection of the changing room because, in the tribunal's words, 'what happens after that is potentially sensitive and individual'[97] (although it appears that the tribunal member did in fact ask repeatedly about what occurred 'after your shower'[98]). While the gist of the applicant's claim was that his companion had paid money and received something in return at the entrance, and that the locker-room was dark, the tribunal used a website photo of the venue to decide that the venue could not have been dark and held that it did not 'make sense that patrons would be handed a ticket in a place where people commonly wear only towels and get wet'.[99] On judicial review, the transcript revealed that it was in fact the tribunal member himself who had introduced the idea of a ticket in his questions, the applicant never having mentioned it; yet the decision was not disturbed by the court.[100]

There are numerous other indications that Australian decision-makers are continuing to apply stereotyped ideas of what it means to be gay, or preconceptions as to what a gay identity necessarily entails. For example, in some cases where the applicants indicated (whether or not as part of their claim) that they adhered to a religious faith the tribunal held that this impugned their claim to be gay or lesbian.[101] In a 2003 decision the tribunal stated,

> Having regard to the teachings of the Catholic Church I am firmly of the view that a person of single sex orientation must have at least considered their position in the Church and whether they wished to continue to practise ... Catholicism.[102]

Most unusually this case was overturned in a judicial review decision in which the Federal Magistrates Court not only applied but extended the reach of *S395 and S396*, citing it for the proposition that 'it may be jurisdictional error to expect an applicant to behave in a particular way' and finding that the RRT 'erred by expecting the applicant, if he were truthful, to behave like a "good" Catholic'.[103]

In other cases, tribunal members held that applicants could not be gay because they did not know the legal status of gay sex in their countries of origin,[104] did not know the meaning of words used to identify (very particular kinds of) gay men[105] or appeared from their 'manner towards each other' to be more like friends than lovers.[106] There were also instances in which applicants' unwillingness, or inability, to answer detailed questions about sexual acts or encounters was held to undermine their credibility.[107]

In a 2001 case the tribunal member repeatedly asked the applicant, who was from Iran, about his identification with popular culture in order to determine if he was gay.

> Mr Hardy: *Well I put it to you that this isn't something that you can switch on and off [a reference to the applicant's homosexuality], it's something that, particularly if it isolates you, it can take over your whole life. It can be the lens through which you see the whole world, if you're lonely enough as a result of, or feel isolated enough as a result of being different from other people ... um here, sorry here's an example. Here's an example. If, if say, a famous Egyptian novelist wins the Nobel Prize, but he's also a homosexual who writes about, ah, you know, the love between two men. It mightn't be a big part of his story but it might be an element in the novel, right. Just say he gets banned in Iran, okay. Might not your ears prick up when you hear that that author has been banned in Iran, and you go, oh, yeah, that's another, that's just another case, just another problem.*
>
> The applicant: *I don't understand it. I'm sorry.*[108]

In a passage that needs to be quoted at length to be fully appreciated, the tribunal member listed a series of examples of cultural 'phenomena' and 'icons' that might indicate homosexual orientation:

> The Tribunal asked the Applicant which, if any, art, literature, song lyrics or popular culture icons spoke to him in his isolation from the rest of the society. The Applicant provided not one example. He said he did not understand the question. The Tribunal asked him if his ears pricked, say, when he heard of any famous, perhaps foreign artist, performer or author being banned in Iran for reasons of immorality. In reply, he said he did not understand the question. The Tribunal was not demanding that the Applicant be a leading Gide scholar or even a Marilyn Monroe fan, but it did seem odd that the sexuality he was forced to suppress in Iran did not find expression in any phenomena at all, whether in high culture or low, also considering that he claimed elsewhere to have been alert to what was happening in countries like Australia ...
>
> The Tribunal thus well understands that it should not expect all or any homosexual men in Iran to take an interest, for example, in Oscar Wilde, or in Alexander the Great, or in Naguib Mahfooz, or in Greco-Roman wrestling, or in the songs of Egypt's tragic muse Oum Khalsoum, let alone, say, in the alleged mystique of Bette Midler or Madonna ... However, the Tribunal was surprised to observe a comprehensive inability on the Applicant's part to identify any kind of emotion-stirring or dignity-arousing phenomena in the world around him.[109]

While overtly disclaiming that manifesting an interest in Oscar Wilde et al. was required of an applicant who claimed to be gay, the kind of questioning evinced in the case – which apparently went on to address the applicant's familiarity with the work of Freud (deemed 'negligible'[110]) – together with the tone of the decision appears to suggest just the opposite. Unusually, the applicant was successful in his application for judicial review on the very difficult ground of actual bias, as the Federal Magistrates Court held that the questions revealed 'a pre-formed template into which the Tribunal considered all homosexual males would fit' and a 'completely closed' approach to the issue.[111] The Minister then appealed to the Full Federal Court, which reinstated the tribunal decision and held that it was a 'matter of common sense' and 'perfectly legitimate' to test a claim 'by reference to knowledge or attitudes which members of the relevant religion, social group or political party might be expected to posses'.[112] If the applicant were Catholic, the Full Court reasoned, 'the RRT might test this assertion by enquiring as to the applicant's knowledge of matters of Catholic doctrine, ritual, traditional belief and the like'.[113] While the Full Court appeared blind to the critical absence of a universally known or accepted doctrine (or even standard King James edition) on gay cultural icons, the applicant was eventually granted leave to appeal to the High Court two years later.

The transcript of the leave to appeal hearing reveals that the three sitting High Court members were far less sanguine than the Federal Court had been about the tribunal's manner of establishing that the applicant was gay. Justice Gummow noted that the applicant had only a secondary school level of education and spoke Farsi such that 'one would doubt if he knew anything about famous Egyptian novelists', who 'write in Arabic, presumably',[114] while Justice Kirby repeatedly raised the question of stereotyping[115] and Justice Heydon characterised the tribunal decision as giving the 'impression of nonchalance' and 'a certain amount of sneering'.[116] When counsel for the Minster clung to the argument that the tribunal had claimed it did *not* expect the applicant to take an interest in the named 'icons', Justice Kirby retorted that 'the "not" is a bit undone by what follows when I think Marilyn is thrown in'.[117] Justice Gummow was even more critical of the use of disclaimers in the decision:

Gummow: *What sort of training do these people get in decision making before they are appointed to this body, Mr Solicitor?*

Mr Bennett: *I cannot assist your Honour on that.*

Gummow: *No. Well, whatever it is, what happened here does not speak highly of the results of it.*[118]

Given the tone of these remarks it was not surprising that the Minister consented to remit the matter back to the tribunal prior to the substantive determination of the appeal by the High Court.[119] Unfortunately, however, the remittal by consent ensured the continued absence of a clear judicial overruling of the Full Federal Court's decision in *WAAG* which had expressly validated this kind of 'gay catechism' approach to sexual identity. The Full Federal Court's decision in *WAAG* clearly discouraged judicial review of other ill-founded or illogical tribunal determinations that the applicants were not gay, lesbian or bisexual.[120] It also bodes ill for the system of refugee determination that a decision as plainly troubling as this could be repeatedly defended by the Minister (including initiating an appeal from the Magistrate's judgment which had set it aside) and moreover be upheld by three out of four judges adjudicating it before it was finally set aside by consent some four years after it had been made.[121]

Accepting that the tribunal does validly need to assess the credibility of applicants' claims to be gay, lesbian or bisexual, some suggestions are made in the next section as to how this can be undertaken.

The need for training and guidelines

There is now a considerable body of refugee scholarship which poses credibility assessment as the most critical aspect of the refugee determination process and contends that it is often undertaken inappropriately.[122] While some researchers have emphasised the use of guidelines to structure the decision-maker's approach to the task,[123] many others have argued that transforming institutional culture through avenues such as ongoing training are more important in creating a place for 'critical reflection'[124] in the assessment of truth-telling.

When sexual orientation claims first emerged in Canada in the early 1990s, tribunal members themselves requested training on the issue, as they did not feel equipped to judge whether or not the applicants were members of this particular social group.[125] Nation-wide sexual orientation training was first provided to the Canadian tribunal as long ago as 1995 by an external expert, Nicole LaViolette, and has been regularly updated since then.[126] In addition, the 2003 compendium to the Canadian Gender Guidelines does address, albeit in a limited way, sexual orientation.[127]

LaViolette argues that the 'one aspect of the lives of lesbians and gay men that is universal is the pervasive societal rejection of their sexual orientation ... most lesbians and gay men will struggle with their sexual identity at some point in their lives'.[128] Thus, she con-tends that questions about the personal experience of being gay or lesbian provide the 'strongest basis' for assessing credibility as to group membership. This is not the same, however, as questioning applicants about their sexual activities. Unlike those making claims based on other Convention grounds, applicants who seek refugee status on the basis of sexual orientation often have feelings of shame and self-hating or internalised homophobia[129] and so may find answering questions about their sexuality very difficult, most especially when these questions are sexually explicit and/or when they are being questioned by an authority figure.[130] Additionally, if the translator is a member of the same small community in the receiving country and/or is a member of the opposite sex, the applicant's willingness to make disclosures can be seriously compromised.[131] All of these constraints must be taken into account in the process of eliciting information and in assessing narratives that vary in particulars or are not initially detailed.

LaViolette's Canadian training materials suggest three areas of inquiry: (i) personal and family, (ii) lesbian and gay contacts in both sending and receiving country and (iii) experi-ence/knowledge of discrimination and persecution. Most importantly for our purposes, in this first field, LaViolette suggests a series of open-ended questions that invite the applicant to tell their narratives of how they came to their own self-knowledge or experience of 'difference', how they felt about it and how others reacted, without resorting to intrusive questions about sexual experiences.

In March 2008, the Australian tribunal finally conducted a single external training session for two hours on Sexual orientation issues.[132] This training was undertaken as the result of a federal Senator highlighting the case of a bisexual-identified claimant from Pakistan.[133] Ali Humayan was in a long-term same-sex relationship that had begun during immigration detention yet he was held by the tribunal to be neither gay nor bisexual but rather the 'product of the situation where only partners of the same sex are available'.[134] The case generated intense media interest and significant public criticism.[135] Given this context it is unclear what degree of commitment there is to ongoing training (either in the induction process for new members or update training for existing members) or to incor-porating external input on sexual orientation issues in a systematic way through all levels of the refugee determination process.

There are also no internal or external guidelines available to assist decision-makers in sexual orientation cases in Australia at either tribunal or original minister's delegate level.[136] The Australian gender guidelines, introduced in 1996 and not revised since,[137] do not include any reference to sexual orientation. While the UK tribunal-level gender guidelines introduced in 2000[138] did make numerous references to sexual orientation, including as an integral aspect of gender norms, when the tribunal was abolished and recon-stituted in 2005 the new tribunal determined that it was not bound by its predecessor's guidelines.[139] New gender guidelines brought in by the Home Office in the UK (first issued in 2004 and revised in 2006) to guide determinations at the bureaucratic level are far less comprehensive and do not contain specific material on sexual orientation.[140] In addition, in both Australia and the UK there is evidence that the relevant gender guidelines, however incomplete in their coverage, have been honoured more in the breach than the observance at all levels of the refugee determination process[141] and moreover have been completely ignored in sexual orientation cases.[142] In both countries community groups have begun actively lobbying to generate specific sexual orientation guidelines.[143] UNHCR has recently released a guidance note on the determination of sexual orientation claims which addresses any of the issues raised here.[144] The research outlined in this paper suggests that in addition to the creation of detailed guidelines comprehensive and ongoing training about their use is also needed.

Bearing in mind the extremely restrictive grounds of review for refugee decisions, the importance of high-quality, consistent and factually well-founded decisions at the merits stage is fundamental if the refugee determination system is to sustain any claim to fairness. Failure to address these concerns will ultimately undermine any real gain from *S395 and S396*.

Conclusion

The rejection of 'discretion' reasoning by the High Court in *S395 and S396* was a critical juncture for refugee law in Australia and the UK, marking a definitive break from earlier decisions that had implicitly or explicitly framed the entitlements of refugee claimants on the basis of sexual orientation as lesser than those brought by others. In doing so, *S395 and S396* established the right of refugee claimants to be openly gay, lesbian or bisexual and has improved the likelihood of successful claims based on sexual orientation. The determination also brings refugee jurisprudence in these two countries more closely in line with developments in international human rights jurisprudence, which has expanded in recent years to encompass a far more substantive approach to equality and to private life.[145]

However, the promise of this development has also been undermined, particularly at lower (which are also, increasingly, the final) levels of factual decision-making in the refugee determination process. Our research found a reluctance to fully engage with and implement the findings of *S395 and S396* through ongoing assumptions about the 'naturalness' of secrecy about gay, lesbian or bisexual identity and consequent failure to inquire into the oppressive social and legal conditions that create and perpetuate such secrecy. In addition, we found a distinct shift in the Australian decisions towards outright disbelief in claimants' identity as a major basis for negative determinations. Here again, deeply held assumptions about how gay, lesbian or bisexual identity is, or ought to be, manifested have played a significant role in determining outcomes. In a disturbing number of cases, a finding that the applicant was not a member of the particular social group appeared to result from quite dubious or improper questioning, and indeed on occasion reflected outright stereotyping in the decision-making process.

These recent trends in sexual orientation refugee case law highlight the broader and ongoing need for improved resources earlier in the refugee determination process, as well as the necessity for a return to the greater availability of judicial oversight in order to correct errors when they do occur. The introduction and maintenance of expert external training on sexuality issues and the creation and implementation of guidelines on sexual orientation may not be the answer to every criticism identified in this paper, but they will help to ensure that early-level determinations on sexual orientation claims are both more consistent and more reliable.

Postscript

Since the time of writing the litigation in *S395/2002* has continued. After the second negative tribunal determination discussed in this paper, the applicants failed in their applications for judicial review in 2004 and 2006 but the matter was remitted by consent for a third tribunal hearing in 2008. Both the second and third tribunal determinations in the claim denied refugee status on the basis that the applicants lacked credibility and were not gay men in a relationship with each other. In *NAOX* v. *Minister for Immigration and Citizenship* [2009] FCA 1056 (18 September 2009), the Federal Court held that the third tribunal had acted in bad faith and evinced actual bias in pre-determining that the applicants were not gay men. The Court also made the extraordinary finding that the tribunal had tailored its decision around credibility findings in order to 'bullet proof' its administrative decision from judicial review. The matter was therefore remitted to be heard for a fourth time by the tribunal in 2010. More than ten years have elapsed since the applicants first made their claim for refugee status. The outcome is not known at this time.

Acknowledgements

This study was devised in conjunction with Professor Catherine Dauvergne at the University of British Columbia and I am enormously grateful for her input at every stage of the project. This research was supported by an Australian Research Council Discovery Project Grant. Thanks to Laurie Berg, Katherine Fallah and Marianna Leishman for their invaluable research assistance.

Notes

1. *Appellants S395/2002 and S396/2002* v. *Minister for Immigration and Multicultural Affairs* (2003) 216 CLR 473 (*S395 and S396*).
2. Article 1A(2) of the 1951 Convention Relating to the Status of Refugees, 189 UNTS 150, as amended by the 1967 Protocol Relating to the Status of Refugees, 606 UNTS 267 (hereinafter referred to as 'Convention'), defines a refugee as any person who, 'owing to well-founded fear of being persecuted for reasons of race, religion, nationality, membership of a particular social group or political opinion, is outside the country of his nationality and is unable or, owing to such fear, is unwilling to avail himself of the protection of that country; or who, not having a nationality and being outside the country of his former habitual residence, is unable or, owing to such fear, is unwilling to return to it'. Sexual orientation had been accepted as the basis for a particular social group claim in most major refugee-receiving nations by the mid-1990s: see, e.g., *Re R (UW)* [1991] CRDD No 501 (Quicklaw), IRB Reference *U91-03331* (7 October 1991); *Ward* v. *Attorney-General (Canada)* [1993] 2 SCR 689 (Canada); *Matter of Toboso-Alfonso*, 20 I&N Dec 819 (BIA 1990) (United States); *N93/00593* [1994] RRTA 108 (25 January 1994) (Australia); *Applicant A* v. *Minister for Immigration and Ethnic Affairs* (1997) 190 CLR 225 (Australia); *Vraciu* v. *Secretary of State for the Home Department* [1994] UKIAT 11559 (21 November 1994); *R.* v. *Immigration Appeal Tribunal*, ex parte *Shah* [1999] 2 AC 629 (United Kingdom).
3. See discussions in Catherine Dauvergne and Jenni Millbank, 'Before the High Court: *Applicants S396/2002 and S395/2002*, a Gay Refugee Couple from Bangladesh', *Sydney Law Review* 25 (2003): 97; Jenni Millbank, 'The Role of Rights in Asylum Claims on the Basis of Sexual Orientation', *Human Rights Law Review* 4 (2004): 193.
4. See, e.g., in Canada, *Re XMU* [1995] CRDD No 146 (Quicklaw), IRB Reference T94-06899 (23 January 1995); in New Zealand, *Re GJ* [1995] Refugee Appeal 1312/93 (30 August 1995).
5. *S395/2002 and S396/2002*, per McHugh and Kirby JJ., para. 18. The earlier levels of judicial review were *Kabir* v. *Minister for Immigration and Multicultural Affairs* [2001] FCA 968 (Federal Court, 26 July 2001) and *Kabir* v. *Minister for Immigration and Multicultural Affairs* [2002] FCAFC 20 (Full Federal Court, 22 February 2002). The original tribunal-level decision was RRT decision *N99/28381* and *N99/28382* (unreported, 5 February 2001), but is not publicly available.
6. *S395/2002 and S396/2002*. The two majority judgments are by Gummow and Hayne JJ. jointly and McHugh and Kirby JJ. jointly.
7. The Australian cases were all obtained from the Australasian Legal Information Institute database (http://www.austlii.edu.au), while the UK cases were obtained from the Electronic Immigration Network case database (http://www.ein.org.uk), the Asylum and Immigration Tribunal website (http://www.ait.gov.uk), and LEXIS.

8. The first phase of the study analysed all available Australian and Canadian decisions on sexual orientation and refugee status over the period 1994–2000: see discussions in Catherine Dauvergne and Jenni Millbank, 'Burdened by Proof: How the Australian Refugee Review Tribunal Has Failed Lesbian and Gay Asylum Seekers', *Federal Law Review* 31 (2003): 299; Jenni Millbank, 'Imagining Otherness: Refugee Claims on the Basis of Sexuality in Canada and Australia', *Melbourne University Law Review* 26 (2002): 144. In the second phase of the study these decisions were updated to the end of 2007 and the pool was widened to include all available refugee cases on sexual orientation from the UK and New Zealand.

9. The study counted 'positive' or 'negative' decisions from the perspective of the applicant, even if (as in the case of judicial review and also some UK tribunal outcomes) the decision is one of remittal and reconsideration of the claim rather than an ultimate positive determination of refugee status. This gives an inflated sense of 'positive' outcomes, as we do not have access to the majority of the remittal determinations and some, perhaps many, of these will *ultimately* be negative to the applicant. However, we include the judicial review decisions for the very reason that they are often the only publicly available record of a case, the original negative tribunal determination usually not being released.

10. The success rate for applicants in Australia in the first phase of the research covering 1994–2000 was 22% at tribunal level (and remains 22% when judicial review decisions are also included) and from 2001 to 2007 was 37% at tribunal level (or 28% when judicial review decisions are included). While there was a marked increase in the success rates at RRT level, our conclusion that there has not been a sizable increase in the success rate in Australia is based upon the whole pool including judicial review cases, for two reasons. First, there was a sharp reduction in the proportion of released RRT decisions post-2000 and, second, most of the judicial review determinations arose from RRT decisions that were *not* released; thus we treated the judicial review decisions as proxy for the unreleased RRT decisions in determining an overall success rate. In the UK, the positive decision rate was 50% at tribunal level from 1994 to 2000 (8 of 16 cases, although note that four of these positive decisions led to remittal while four were actual grants of refugee status). The positive rate falls to 23% when the 19 judicial review decisions are included. The positive decision rate was 37% at tribunal level from 2001 to 2007 (20 of 54 decisions, although note that eight of these positives were remittals, while 12 were actual grants of refugee status), the positive rate remaining 37% when judicial review decisions are included.

11. In Australia the original decision on refugee status is taken by a delegate of the Minister for Immigration and Citizenship (also known variously through the period of this study as the Minister for Immigration and Multicultural Affairs and the Minister for Immigration and Multicultural and Indigenous Affairs) and in the UK by a delegate of the Home Secretary, in both countries a fairly low-ranking bureaucratic officer. If this determination is negative, the applicant can apply for a de novo merits review of the decision. In Australia this review is undertaken by the Refugee Review Tribunal (RRT), which sits with a single member. In the UK until April 2005 this review was undertaken by the Immigration Appellate Authority (IAA) in a two-tier system; first, an immigration adjudicator reviewed the decision de novo and then leave could be given to the Immigration Appeal Tribunal (IAT), which until 2002 provided a second level of de novo review and after 2002 was limited to points of law by the Nationality, Immigration and Asylum Act 2002 (c. 41) (UK). From 2005 the two-tier structure was abolished and replaced by the Asylum and Immigration Tribunal (AIT): Asylum and Immigration (Treatment of Claimants, etc.) Act 2004 (c. 19) (UK). The AIT can only grant review based on an error of law.

12. See, e.g., Richard Rawlings, 'Review, Revenge and Retreat', *Modern Law Review* 68 (2005): 378; Catherine Dauvergne, 'Sovereignty, Migration and the Rule of Law in Global Times', *Modern Law Review* 67 (2004): 588.

13. These being the Minister's delegate, the RRT, the Federal Court, the Full Federal Court and the High Court. Note, however, that at the last three levels the review was limited to points of law; the facts as found by the RRT were assumed.

14. See *NAOX* v. *Minister for Immigration and Multicultural and Indigenous Affairs* [2006] FMCA 434 (13 April 2006) (note that the second RRT decision is not publicly available).

15. See *V95/03527* [1996] RRTA 246 (9 February 1996), p. 7 of typescript.

16. See, e.g., *R.* v. *Secretary of State for the Home Department* ex parte *Binbasi* [1989] Imm AR 595, p. 5 of typescript; *Boyd* v. *Secretary of State for the Home Department* [2000] UKIAT 00TH01419 (1 June 2000), p. 2 of typescript.

17. See, e.g., *Jain* v. *Secretary of State for the Home Department* [1999] EWJ No 5243 (6 October 1999), para. 9. See also *T* v. *Special Immigration Adjudicator* [2000] EWJ 3020 (11 May 2000); *Dumitru* v. *Secretary of State for the Home Department* [2000] UKIAT 00TH00945 (3 April 2000); *V99/10346* [2001] RRTA 568 (20 June 2001).
18. See, e.g., *V98/08356* [1998] RRTA 4841 (28 October 1998); *N01/40155* [2003] RRTA 138 (18 February 2003). In an early UK case this was characterised as 'inviting persecution': *R.* v. *Secretary of State for the Home Department* ex parte *Binbasi*, p. 4 of typescript.
19. See, e.g., *V97/06483* [1998] RRTA 27 (5 January 1998); this was also a finding in RRT Reference *N97/20994* (unreported, 4 May 1998) and in RRT Reference *N98/2231* (unreported, 22 September 1998). Cases that have been removed from the Australasian Legal Information Institute database since the first phase of the study are on file with author.
20. See, e.g., *N99/29824* [2001] RRTA 890 (16 October 2001).
21. See, e.g., *V95/02999* [1995] RRTA 897 (26 April 1995); *V97/06802* [1997] RRTA 3846 (30 September 1997).
22. The Convention definition and grounds are outlined in note 2 above. See e.g., 'Freedom of religion is of course a fundamental human right. Furthermore, the public profession of one's religion will normally be an essential part of the practice of one's religion ... so the inability to publicly profess and practice one's religion is a clear violation of freedom of religion. This is not the case with sexuality ... Public manifestation of homosexuality is not an essential part of being homosexual.' *V98/08356*, not disturbed on judicial review: *LSLS* v. *Minister for Immigration and Multicultural Affairs* [2000] FCA 211 (6 March 2000).
23. Over the period of 1994–2003 the failure rate of lesbian applicants before the RRT was 86% and the failure rate of gay male applicants before the RRT was 73%.
24. Sixty-four of the 65 cases in which discretion was expected or required were negative to the applicant. There were a further 11 judicial review cases where discretion was expected or required, of which 10 were negative.
25. There were 61 AIT and IAT cases, 21 of which raised discretion. Of those 21 cases, it was apparent from the decisions that 19 expected or required discretion. These figures are drawn from 1994 until November 2004, as it took several months for the *S395 and S396* decision to become known in the UK.
26. Discretion was also raised in 37 UK judicial review cases through that period. Of those cases it was clear that discretion was expected or required in 13 cases, 12 of which were negative to the applicants.
27. See, e.g., note 3 above; see also Jenni Millbank, '"A Preoccupation with Perversion": The British Response to Refugee Claims on the Basis of Sexual Orientation 1989–2003', *Social & Legal Studies* 14 (2005): 115.
28. This idea is explored in the work of many scholars but see, e.g., Gail Mason, *The Spectacle of Violence: Homophobia, Gender, and Knowledge* (London: Routledge, 2002).
29. For example: 'The right to free expression of sexuality does not extend so far as to a right to publicly proclaim one's sexuality' and it is reasonable to avoid 'overt manifestations of homosexuality such as public embracing', which, while 'irksome and unjust', is 'not an infringement of human rights': *V96/05496* [1998] RRTA 196 (15 January 1998).
30. See, e.g., *V99/10323* [2000] RRTA 456 (14 April 2000).
31. See, e.g., *EK* v. *Secretary of State for the Home Department* [2004] UKIAT 00021, para. 16; *071723892* [2007] RRTA 323 (5 December 2007).
32. See, e.g., *MV* v. *Secretary of State for the Home Department* [2003] UKIAT 00005, para. 11.
33. See, e.g., *V97/06483*, where this term was attributed to the claimant.
34. *Nezhadian* v. *Minister for Immigration and Multicultural Affairs* [2001] FCA 1415 (18 October 2001), para. 12.
35. *WABR* v. *Minister for Immigration and Multicultural Affairs* [2002] FCAFC 124 (10 May 2002), para. 23. The Full Court further held that '[i]t is not appropriate to submit that the ability to proclaim one's sexual preference is an essential right, the denial of which would or could lead to persecution': ibid., para. 19.
36. See, e.g., *Khanmeeri* v. *Minister for Immigration and Multicultural and Indigenous Affairs* [2002] FCA 625 (17 May 2002); *LSLS* v. *Minister for Immigration and Multicultural Affairs*.
37. See, e.g., Guy Goodwin-Gill and Jane McAdam, *The Refugee in International Law*, 3rd edn (Oxford: Oxford University Press, 2007), 123, para. 5.61; James Hathaway and Michelle Foster, 'Internal Protection/Relocation/Flight Alternative as an Aspect of Refugee Status Determination', in Erika Feller, Volker Türk and Frances Nicholson, eds, *Refugee Protection*

in International Law: UNHCR's Global Consultations on International Protection (Cambridge, UK: Cambridge University Press, 2003), 357.

38. See, e.g., *Januzi* v. *Secretary of State for the Home Department* [2006] 2 AC 426 (UK); *Minister for Immigration and Multicultural Affairs* v. *Khawar* (2002) 210 CLR 1 (Australia); *Ranganathan* v. *Canada (Minister of Citizenship and Immigration)* [2001] 2 FC 164.

39. See, e.g., *N02/41697* [2003] RRTA 457 (22 May 2003). Note that this case also held that the inability to live openly with a partner did not constitute 'serious harm' within the definition of persecution in the relevant Act. See also *SZAHV* v. *Minister for Immigration* [2004] FMCA 28 (28 January 2004), where the Magistrate uncritically reproduced the RRT's finding that 'in the larger cities in Ghana, in particular Accra, it seems that there is no real impediment upon homosexuals living an openly gay lifestyle': ibid., para. 31. (The Magistrate in this case did, however, find, based on *S395 and S396*, that the relocation reasoning had been clouded by the assumption of discretion, and remitted the matter for redetermination.)

40. See, e.g., *NAIK* v. *Minister for Immigration and Multicultural and Indigenous Affairs* [2003] FMCA 400 (1 September 2003) (referring to 'independent information in relation to gay bars in Nigeria': ibid., para. 14); *N97/18897* [1998] RRTA 4984 (13 November 1998).

41. See, e.g., *JD (Zimbabwe)* v. *Secretary of State for the Home Department* [2004] UKIAT 00259, where a lesbian from Zimbabwe claimed that she could not maintain a 'cloak of invisibility' because she had been exposed and the IAT held that she could internally relocate and act with discretion in order to 'attain invisibility': ibid., para. 19. In Australia see, e.g., *V99/10323*; *N99/29824*. The assumption of self-concealment continues to be embedded in relocation reasoning in some later decisions: see, e.g., *071263822* [2007] RRTA 115 (13 June 2007).

42. Transcript of an RRT hearing quoted on judicial review upholding the original decision (which also rested on credibility concerns): *NADO* v. *Minister for Immigration and Multicultural and Indigenous Affairs* [2003] FCA 215, para. 24. A further appeal to the Full Federal Court also failed: *NADO* v. *Minister for Immigration and Multicultural and Indigenous Affairs* [2003] FCAFC 169 (8 August 2003).

43. For example in RRT Reference *N98/23955* (unreported, 24 September 1998) the tribunal held that the applicant should be 'able to conduct himself in a manner acceptable to his own society': p. 8 of typescript. The tribunal went on to state, 'Many societies, including our own, are homophobic' (ibid.). The decision was from the first phase of the study and is no longer available on the Australasian Legal Information Institute database but is on file with author.

44. See, e.g., *N01/36734* [2002] RRTA 898 (8 October 2002); *N03/45734* [2003] RRTA 674 (18 July 2003); *N02/44482* [2003] RRTA 1076 (10 November 2003).

45. See, e.g., in Australia, *SAAM* v. *Minister for Immigration and Multicultural Affairs* [2002] FCA 444 (18 April 2002); *Khalili Vahed* v. *Minister for Immigration and Multicultural Affairs* [2001] FCA 1404 (4 October 2001); *SAAF* v. *Minister for Immigration and Multicultural Affairs* [2002] FCA 343 (28 February 2002); *Nezhadian* v. *Minister for Immigration and Multicultural Affairs*; *WABR* v. *Minister for Immigration and Multicultural Affairs*. This conclusion was held unreviewable as a question of fact in *Gholami* v. *Minister for Immigration and Multicultural Affairs* [2001] FCA 1091 (7 August 2001). In the UK see, e.g., *Musavi* v. *Secretary of State for the Home Department* [2002] UKIAT 04050 (30 August 2002), although detailed expert evidence admitted in more recent cases helped to dispel this myth: see, e.g., *HS (Iran)* v. *Secretary of State for the Home Department* [2005] UKAIT 00120 (4 August 2005).

46. See, e.g., in the UK, *Jain* v. *Secretary of State for the Home Department*, and in Australia, *MMM* v. *Minister for Immigration and Multicultural Affairs* (1998) 90 FCR 324; see discussion in Millbank, '"A Preoccupation with Perversion"'.

47. *WABR* v. *Minister for Immigration and Multicultural Affairs*, para. 25. See also *YF (Eritrea)* v. *Secretary of State for the Home Department* [2003] UKIAT 00177 (5 December 2003), para. 18.3 and *Saeed* v. *Secretary of State for the Home Department* [2002] UKIAT 01465 (10 May 2002), para. 6, quoting adjudicator.

48. See *T* v. *Special Immigration Adjudicator*, para. 2.

49. See Dauvergne and Millbank, 'Before the High Court'.

50. *S395/2002 and S396/2002*, per McHugh and Kirby JJ., para. 35; per Gummow and Hayne JJ., paras 80–2.

51. See, e.g., *SZDLD* v. *Minister for Immigration and Multicultural and Indigenous Affairs* [2005] FMCA 113 (18 February 2005). Of the 102 Australian judicial review cases in this period, 16 specifically reference *S395 and S396*.

52. In addition, of the 21 judicial review cases during this period that raised discretion, five were successful.

53. *N04/48689* [2004] RRTA 679 (22 October 2004), p.10 of typescript. Concealment was framed as a 'double life' rather than a 'normal life' in *N05/50670* [2005] RRTA 88 (19 May 2005), and in *071818233* [2008] RRTA 62 (15 February 2008) it was described as a 'façade'. See also *071411578* [2007] RRTA 172 (9 August 2007) for the influence of *S395 and S396*.

54. For example: 'even if he was able to hide his homosexuality to reduce the risk of harm, the Tribunal finds that having to do so would be persecutory in itself given the freedom he has experienced here': *N04/49627* [2005] RRTA 7 (25 February 2005), p. 31 of typescript. See also: *N05/51364* [2005] RRTA 137 (29 July 2005); *V05/18306* [2006] RRTA 67 (22 May 2006); *071676868* [2007] RRTA 260 (17 October 2007); *071818233* [2008] RRTA 62 (15 February 2008).

55. Prior to 2005 there were two levels of tribunal review in the UK. Until 2002 both levels, the adjudicator and the IAT, exercised merits review; from 2002 to 2005, only the adjudicator exercised merits review. See *AIT Review Report*, April 2006, http://www.ait.gov.uk/Documents/AboutUs/AITReviewReport.pdf (accessed 2 May 2008); Asylum and Immigration (Treatment of Claimants, etc.) Act 2004 (c. 19) (UK).

56. Similarly, of the 12 judicial review cases available for this period, seven raised discretion and only three of those seven were negative decisions.

57. *S395/2002 and S396/2002*, para. 43 (emphasis in original).

58. Ibid. Gummow and Hayne JJ. also found the tribunal in error because it 'did not ask *why* the appellants would live "discreetly"': para. 88 (emphasis in original).

59. Ibid. Callinan and Heydon JJ. stated that 'it is clear the appellants did not seek to make a case that they wished to express their homosexuality in other than a discreet, indeed personal way. There may be good reason, divorced entirely from fear, for this': para. 108 They continued, 'in many societies, both heterosexual and homosexual couples regard their domestic and sexual arrangements and activities as entirely private': ibid.

60. This was adopted for example in *RG (Colombia)* where the adjudicator and Court of Appeal on review held that the applicant had to demonstrate that external threat 'was the reason that the pattern of behaviour *forced on him* was different from that which otherwise he would have adopted': *RG (Colombia)* v. *Secretary of State for the Home Department* [2006] EWCA 2528 (20 January 2006), para. 12 (emphasis added).

61. *S395/2002 and S396/2002*, para. 92 (emphasis added). This approach was approved in the IAT decision in *MN (Kenya)* v. *Secretary of State for the Home Department* [2005] UKIAT 0021 (28 January 2005), para. 10.

62. *S395/2002 and S396/2002*, ibid., para. 106.

63. Ibid., para. 110.

64. IAT findings of 20 December 2004, quoted on review in *Amare* v. *Secretary of State for the Home Department* [2005] EWCA Civ 1600 (20 December 2005), para. 6.

65. *N99/28400* [2001] RRTA 846 (26 September 2001), upheld on review in *SZAOD* v. *Minister for Immigration and Multicultural and Indigenous Affairs* [2004] FMCA 89 (19 March 2004) where it was described as 'rather deftly' avoiding error identified in *S395 and S396*.

66. *AT (Iran)* v. *Secretary of State for the Home Department* [2005] UKAIT 00119 (27 July 2005), para. 28. The sentence concluded, 'and still more so of a number of races considered "uncivilised" so far as they still exist.'

67. See, e.g., the following recent Australian cases holding that the applicant was 'naturally' discreet: *SZANS* v. *Minister for Immigration and Multicultural and Indigenous Affairs* [2005] FCAFC 41 (17 March 2005), para. 18, quoting the tribunal (RRT decision of 29 August 2002, not publicly available); *SZATS* v. *Minister for Immigration and Multicultural and Indigenous Affairs* [2004] FMCA 660 (11 November 2004), para. 21, quoting the tribunal (RRT decision of 29 September 2000, not publicly available, upheld on review); *N00/34199* [2002] RRTA 543 (19 June 2002), pp. 7 and 11 of typescript, upheld on review in *SZBSA* v. *Minister for Immigration and Multicultural and Indigenous Affairs* [2005] FMCA 1248 (31 August 2005), para. 6, quoting RRT with approval. In the UK see *Z* v. *Secretary of State for the Home Department* [2004] EWCA Civ 1578 (2 December 2004), para. 17; *Amare* v. *Secretary of State for the Home Department*, para. 4, quoting IAT findings; *EK (Uganda)* v. *Secretary of State for the Home Department* [2004] UKIAT 00021, para. 16. At times the arguments of the relevant government have betrayed the knowledge that this 'free' choice is not so free yet is still presented as a natural one; for example in 2006 the

Home Secretary argued that 'because in Algeria there are no gay rights, there are no opportunities for displaying homosexuality ... and it will be *impossible for him not to be discreet*': *B* v. *Secretary of State for the Home Department* [2007] EWHC 2528, para. 20 (emphasis added, although note that the court did remit the case for redetermination). There have also been some rare examples in Canadian law: see, e.g., *Hussain* v. *Canada (Minister of Citizenship and Immigration)* [2004] RPDD No. 732 (19 March 2004).

68. Including when the first instance determination in fact preceded the *S395 and S396* decision: see, e.g., *S135 of 2003* v. *Minister for Immigration and Multicultural and Indigenous Affairs* [2004] FCA 1521 (16 July 2004).

69. See, e.g., *Z* v. *Secretary of State for the Home Department*, para. 20; *MN (Kenya)* v. *Secretary of State for the Home Department*, para. 27; *XY* v. *Secretary of State for the Home Department* [2008] EWCA Civ 911 (31 July 2008), para. 14; *HJ* v. *Secretary of State for the Home Department* [2008] UKAIT 00044 (18 April 2008), paras 41–2, 45. Some Australian cases implicitly took the same view, see *SZBSA* v. *Minister for Immigration and Multicultural and Indigenous Affairs*.

70. Quoted on review, *RG (Colombia)*, para. 17.

71. Quoted on review, ibid., para. 6.

72. Quoted on review, ibid., para. 7.

73. Ibid., para. 18.

74. *Ahmed* v. *Secretary of State for the Home Department* [2000] INLR 1.

75. 'Although *S395* was presented to the court that granted permission in this appeal as a new departure in refugee law, and for that reason justifying the attention of this court, in truth it is no such thing': *Z* v. *Secretary of State for the Home Department*, para. 16, and quoted in *DW (Jamaica)* v. *Secretary of State for the Home Department* [2005] UKIAT 00168 (28 November 2005), para. 78. See also *J* v. *Secretary of State for the Home Department* [2006] EWCA Civ 1238 (26 July 2006), para. 10. In *Amare* v. *Secretary of State for the Home Department*, the court appeared to prefer the early UK case of *Jain* v. *Secretary of State for the Home Department*. In addition, in *LK (Zimbabwe)* v. *Secretary of State for the Home Department* [2005] UKAIT 00159 (17 November 2005), the Home Secretary unsuccessfully argued on review that the adjudicator had committed a legal error by applying *S395 and S396* instead of inconsistent English tribunal-level authority.

76. *HYSI* v. *Secretary of State for the Home Department* [2005] EWCA Civ 711 (15 June 2005).

77. Ibid., paras 33–4.

78. *AT (Iran)* v. *Secretary of State for the Home Department*, para. 28.

79. *JM* v. *Secretary of State for the Home Department* [2008] UKIAT 00065 (11 June 2008), para. 149. Note also the Secretary of State's argument that 'even if some modification of conduct was required *out of respect for social norms*' this was not persecution: ibid., para. 77 (emphasis added).

80. *HJ* v. *Secretary of State for the Home Department*, para. 10. The case of *HJ* was a redetermination following a successful application for judicial review by the applicant in *J* v. *Secretary of State for the Home Department*. In *J* the Court of Appeal endorsed the approach of *S395 and S396*.

81. *HJ* v. *Secretary of State for the Home Department*, para. 45.

82. Ibid., para. 46.

83. The claimant has been granted leave by the Court of Appeal to apply for judicial review of the decision in *HJ*: email communication with S. Chelvan, 3 October 2008.

84. *Krasniqi* v. *Secretary of State for the Home Department* [2001] UKIAT 01TH02140 (19 June 2001), para. 2.

85. *Z* v. *Secretary of State for the Home Department*, para. 4.

86. In fact there were markedly *fewer* tribunal cases on sexual orientation available in Australia in the years 2005, 2006 and 2007 (down to 12, 9 and 20, respectively, compared with an average of around 30 tribunal decisions per year in preceding years), which could be the result of any or all of the following factors: a smaller number of actual claims, a higher success rate before the Minister's delegate (thus leading to fewer applications for review before the tribunal), or the tribunal selecting fewer cases for release. The Minister does not keep figures on the number or success rates of claims according to ground of claim so we are unable to assess the first two possibilities. However it is clear from the RRT annual reports that in the years 2006–7 and 2004–5 the tribunal released only 8% and 10% of decisions from those years, respectively, rather than its stated target of 20% of decisions: see *Migration Review Tribunal & Refugee*

Review Tribunal Annual Report 2006–2007 (2007), 18; *Migration Review Tribunal & Refugee Review Tribunal Annual Report 2004–2005* (2005), 9. No information is available from the 2005–6 annual report. This leads us to infer that the drop in the number of decisions is more likely to have been a result of this overall release policy rather than to reflect either fewer claims or a higher earlier success rates.

87. Fifty-seven of 351 decisions prior to December 2003 disclosed significant doubts about the claimants' membership of the particular social group, while 67 of 176 cases did so afterwards.

88. The tribunal decision is not publicly available, but its reasoning can be discerned from the application for judicial review arising from it: *NAOX* v. *Minister for Immigration and Multi-cultural and Indigenous Affairs*. Despite the unsuccessful attempt of the applicants to argue both bias and issue estoppel in the case, the Minister subsequently consented to remittal, and the claim was heard for a third time by the RRT in 2008, again resulting in a negative decision that is not publicly available: email communication with Tina Edwards, RRT, 22 October 2008.

89. In the only successful judicial review case concerning discretion prior to *S395 and S396*, *W133/01A* v. *Minister for Immigration and Multicultural Affairs* [2002] FCA 395 (5 April 2002), the Federal Court found an error of law in the tribunal's ruling that discretion was poss-ible because this was inconsistent with another finding that past acts of persecution based on sexual orientation had occurred: *N01/37352* [2001] RRTA 381 (24 April 2001). When the case was remitted to a differently constituted RRT, it was held that the man was not gay after all. That decision (which is not publicly available) was then held to be unreviewable because it was a determination of fact: *WAIH* v. *Minister for Immigration and Multicultural and Indigenous Affairs* [2003] FMCA 40 (4 March 2003), para. 23.

90. See, e.g.: 'This is a claim which is easily made but not easily tested', *N04/48510* [2004] RRTA 367 (17 May 2004), p. 11 of typescript; 'The claim of being homosexual is in many ways an easy one to make, and a difficult one to dispute', *N97/16114* [1998] RRTA 4882 (2 November 1998), p.13 of typescript; *SZIGI* v. *Minister for Immigration and Multicultural Affairs* [2006] FMCA 1800 (20 November 2006), para. 25, quoting the tribunal (8 December 2005, decision not publicly available).

91. See, e.g.: 'I must warn you to be especially careful in considering the evidence in a case where sexual allegations are made . . . It is a very easy allegation to make. It is often very hard to contra-dict . . . It is hard to contradict, and of course, it can be of a very serious and distressing nature': *R.* v. *Johns* (unreported, SA SC, 26 August 1992); this warning was ultimately held to be an error of law on appeal: *Question of Law Reserved on Acquittal Pursuant to Section 350(1A) Criminal Law Consolidation Act (No 1 of 1993) Judgment No 3896* (1993) 59 SASR 214.

92. One case noted a somewhat improbable incident in which six members of a male sporting team that had visited Australia all claimed refugee status on the basis of their homosexuality: *071626698* [2008] RRTA 5 (4 January 2008).

93. *071397909* [2007] RRTA 187 (15 August 2007). The questioning in this case also appeared sensitive, with the decision-maker noting that, '[w]ith these issues in mind, the Tribunal explored with the applicant a wide range of circumstances relevant to its assessment. These included his self-identity; his self-disclosure and others' perceptions of him; his past experi-ences; his knowledge of and association with other homosexuals; his relationships and per-sonal contacts; and incidental evidence': p. 9 of typescript. However, even with careful questioning that is sensitive to such issues, the difficulties introduced by translation may still render the inquiry incomprehensible: see, e.g., transcript quoted in *SZIGI* v. *Minister for Immigration and Multicultural Affairs*, paras 10–14.

94. Nicole LaViolette, 'Coming out to Canada: The Immigration of Same-Sex Couples under the Immigration and Refugee Protection Act', *McGill Law Journal* 49 (2004): 969, 996.

95. See, e.g., *N04/48953* [2005] RRTA 363 (25 January 2005); *N05/50659* [2005] RRTA 207 (17 May 2005); *N03/45493* [2003] RRTA 303 (2 April 2003); *SZIXG* v. *Minister for Immigration and Multicultural Affairs* [2007] FMCA 1331 (30 July 2007) (RRT decision not available); *SZKLN* v. *Minister for Immigration and Citizenship* [2007] FMCA 1407 (8 August 2007) (RRT decision not available); *071494945* [2007] RRTA 276 (19 September 2007). Conversely, when an applicant could establish his familiarity with gay venues in Canberra, the tribunal held that this did not establish that he was gay (although in the same case a lack of familiarity with a local church was held to undermine his claim to be a Christian): *SZJSL* v. *Minister for Immi-gration and Multicultural Affairs* [2007] FMCA 313 (19 February 2007) (RRT decision not available).

96. See, e.g., *SZEOP* v. *Minister for Immigration and Multicultural Affairs* [2006] FMCA 1707 (7 December 2006), para. 13; *N97/16114*, pp. 6 and 7 of typescript.

97. *N05/50659*, p. 11 of typescript.

98. On review the applicant's counsel pointed to a series of passages from the transcript which indicated that this questioning occurred: *SZGNJ* v. *Minister for Immigration and Multicultural and Indigenous Affairs* [2006] FMCA 91 (24 February 2006), para. 3.

99. *N05/50659*, p. 11 of typescript.

100. *SZGNJ* v. *Minister for Immigration and Multicultural and Indigenous Affairs*, para. 80. This was in part because the findings on credibility were characterised as findings of fact, but also because the ground of claim was that of apprehended bias, which requires a very high threshold to satisfy.

101. See, e.g., *SZJSL* v. *Minister for Immigration and Multicultural Affairs*, where the applicant's lack of knowledge that his church condemned homosexuality was held to impugn his claim to being a Christian: RRT decision quoted in FMCA decision, para. 8. See, also, *SZAKD* v. *Minister for Immigration and Multicultural and Indigenous Affairs* [2004] FMCA 78 (19 March 2004).

102. Quoted on review in ibid., para. 7.

103. Ibid., para. 26. The second RRT decision, which is not publicly available, was again negative to the applicant: email communication with Ailsa Wilson, RRT, 24 April 2008.

104. See, e.g., *071494945*; *SZEND* v. *Minister for Immigration and Citizenship* [2007] FMCA 1171 (21 June 2007) (RRT decision not publicly available).

105. See *SZBFO* v. *Minister for Immigration and Multicultural and Indigenous Affairs* [2005] FMCA 207 (2 March 2005), where failure to recognise the word *kothi* led the tribunal to reject the applicant's claim to be gay; upheld on review a second time in *SZGQG* v. *Minister for Immigration and Multicultural and Indigenous Affairs* [2006] FMCA 193 (14 February 2006). *Kothi* is a very class-specific word used by effeminate gay men: see Peoples' Union for Civil Liberties, Karnataka, *Human Rights Violations against the Transgender Community: A Study of Kothi and Hijra Sex Workers in Bangalore, India* (September 2003), 19.

106. *SZKIS* v. *Minister for Immigration and Citizenship* [2007] FMCA 1223 (18 July 2007), para. 31, citing RRT decision of 13 February 2007 (not publicly available). Another common thread was that decision-makers took evidence that the applicant had been married or in an opposite-sex relationship as evidence that they were lying, as it was 'inconsistent' with being gay, rather than as evidence that they were bisexual or had accepted their homosexuality later in life (see e.g., *071204626* [2007] RRTA 146 13 August [2007]; *N05/51729* [2005] RRTA 311 8 November [2005]; *N02/42894* [2006] RRTA 1093 14 November [2003]) though this did not always occur (see, e.g., *N05/50670*).

107. For example: 'The Applicant's evidence also lacks important detail, for example about the nature and type of sexual activity on the video, who was involved in specific activities': *N97/15882* [1997] RRTA 3396 (5 September 1997), p. 7 of typescript; judicial review denied subsequently in *SZEOE* v. *Minister for Immigration and Multicultural Affairs* [2004] FMCA 1096 (16 December 2004) and in *SZEOE* v. *Minister for Immigration and Multicultural Affairs* [2005] FCA 694 (31 May 2005). In *NAIK* v. *Minister for Immigration and Multicultural and Indigenous Affairs*, the applicant was disbelieved because he was 'halting and evasive' when questioned about 'critical issues' in his testimony, which appeared to centre upon being discovered engaged in gay sex (RRT decision not publicly available). See also *071913999* [2008] RRTA 35 (18 February 2008), in which the tribunal member asked the applicant in the course of the hearing to supply his login name and password for the online social networking and dating websites he had joined.

108. Quoted on review in *WAAG* v. *Minister for Immigration and Multicultural and Indigenous Affairs* [2002] FMCA 191 (30 August 2002), para. 12 (RRT decision not publicly available).

109. Quoted on review in ibid., para. 10.

110. This was quoted by both Heydon J. and Gummow J. in the leave to appeal transcript: *WAAG* v. *Minister for Immigration and Multicultural and Indigenous Affairs* [2004] HCA Trans 475, p. 6 of typescript.

111. *WAAG* v. *Minister for Immigration and Multicultural and Indigenous Affairs* [2002], para. 23.

112. *SBAN* v. *Minister for Immigration and Multicultural and Indigenous Affairs* [2002] FCAFC 431 (18 December 2002), para. 65.

113. Ibid.

114. *WAAG* v. *Minister for Immigration and Multicultural and Indigenous Affairs* [2004], per Gummow J., p. 4 of typescript. Gummow J. also noted with characteristic attention to detail, 'They do not look upon Alexander the Great as much of a hero in Iran, I would have thought': p. 10 of typescript.
115. Ibid., pp. 3 and 6 of typescript.
116. Ibid., pp. 10 and 11 of typescript, respectively.
117. Ibid., p. 9 of typescript.
118. Ibid., p. 5 of typescript.
119. See *WAAG* v. *Minister for Immigration and Multicultural and Indigenous Affairs* [2004].
120. 'This court has been criticised before for making comments upon the apparent illogicality of findings by the Tribunal on the question of homosexuality and for that reason will not risk further reprimand': *SZAKE* v. *Minister for Immigration and Multicultural and Indigenous Affairs* [2004] FMCA 138 (4 March 2003), para. 8 (note that this was the same magistrate whose decision was overturned by the Full Federal Court in *WAAG*).
121. On remittal the applicant was ultimately successful in his claim. The redetermination, *N05/52122* (17 November 2005), is not publicly available but was accessed by the author through a Freedom of Information request.
122. See, e.g., Deborah Anker, 'Determining Asylum Claims in the United States: A Case Study on the Implementation of Legal Norms in an Unstructured Adjudicatory Environment', *Review of Law and Social Change* 19 (1992): 433; Michael Kagan, 'Is Truth in the Eye of the Beholder? Objective Credibility Assessment in Refugee Status Determination', *Georgetown Immigration Law Journal* 17 (2003): 367; Gregor Noll, ed., *Proof, Evidentiary Assessment and Credibility in Asylum Proceedings* (Leiden, The Netherlands: Martinus Nijhoff 2005).
123. See, e.g., Brian Gorlick, 'Improving Decision-Making in Asylum Determinations', UNHRC Working Paper No. 119 (2005). Canada has had detailed policy guidelines on credibility assessment for some time, while Australia and the UK have recently introduced brief guidelines: see Refugee Protection Division (Canada), *Assessment of Credibility in Claims for Refugee Protection* (current version 2004); Migration Review Tribunal and Refugee Review Tribunal (Australia), *Guidance on the Assessment of Credibility* (2006, updated 2008); Home Office (UK), *Asylum Instructions on Assessing Credibility in Asylum and Human Rights Claims* (2007). For critique of the increasingly structured approach to negative credibility assessment in legislation, see Robert Thomas, 'Assessing the Credibility of Asylum Claims: EU and UK Approaches Examined', *European Journal of Migration and Law* 8 (2006): 79.
124. François Crépeau and Delphine Nakache, 'Critical Spaces in the Canadian Refugee Determination System: 1989–2002', *International Journal of Refugee Law* 20 (2008): 50. See also Audrey Macklin, who argues for critical self-awareness and self-interrogation, in 'Truth and Consequences: Credibility Determination in the Refugee Context', paper presented at International Association of Refugee Law Judges Conference, Ottawa, 14–16 October 1998.
125. Personal communication with Nicole LaViolette.
126. Ibid. See also Nicole LaViolette, 'Gender-Related Refugee Claims: Expanding the Scope of the Canadian Guidelines', *International Journal of Refugee Law* 19 (2007): 169, n. 173.
127. See Immigration and Refugee Board, *Compendium of Decisions, Guideline 4: Women Refugee Claimants Fearing Gender-Related Persecution*, February 2003 update (although LaViolette, 'Gender-Related Refugee Claims', argues that the gender guidelines have been inadequately utilised to date for sexual orientation claims and recommends that they be revised to more directly address sexual minorities).
128. Nicole LaViolette, 'Sexual Orientation and the Refugee Determination Process: Questioning a Claimant about their Membership in the Particular Social Group', prepared for Immigration and Refugee Board (2004), 5.
129. See, e.g., *N01/37891* [2001] RRTA 889 (16 October 2001), where the tribunal disbelieved that the applicant was gay partly on the basis that he 'only ever referred to his claimed sexuality as a sexual or psychological problem. He showed no sign in his evidence of ever having seen his sexuality as a matter of private right': p. 1 of typescript.
130. More commonly a refugee applicant will be asked questions concerning sexual acts when their claim of persecution under any ground involves sexual assault. While not suggesting that such questioning is always undertaken well, it is one that is addressed by gender guidelines in most jurisdictions.
131. See, e.g., *N01/37352*, where the Iranian applicant had not disclosed his homosexuality in the

first interview because the interpreter was 'an Afghan lady': p. 4 of typescript. See also *N01/37891*, where an Iranian applicant said 'he had been too "shy" to talk about sexuality with the women present at the entry interview': p. 9 of typescript. In 2008 the Australian tribunal amended its credibility guidelines to include sexual orientation as a reason to consider 'whether it would be appropriate for an interpreter of a particular gender to assist with the hearing': Migration Review Tribunal and Refugee Review Tribunal (Australia), *Guidance on the Assessment of Credibility* (2006, updated 2008), para. 4.5.

132. See 'Tribunal Promise', *Sydney Star Observer*, 28 February 2008.

133. Caro Meldrum, 'Refugee Review Tribunal to Develop Sexuality Training', *ABC News Online*, 15 June 2007, http://www.abc.net.au/news/newsitems/200706/s1952753.htm (accessed 23 April 2008).

134. Quoted on review in *SZJSL* v. *Minister for Immigration and Multicultural Affairs*, para. 8 (the tribunal decision in the matter is not publicly available but is on file with the author). Judicial review was denied but the case is currently under review by the Minister as part of a review of all long-term immigration detainees following a change of government at federal level.

135. See, e.g., Eric Jensen, 'Bisexuality a Result of Detention, Detainee Told', *Sydney Morning Herald*, 9 May 2007; Harley Dennett, 'Queer Refugee Fears Own Family', *Sydney Star Observer*, 10 May 2007; see also Meldrum, 'Refugee Review Tribunal to Develop Sexuality Training'.

136. Such guidelines were recommended by Amnesty International in 2001: *Crimes of Hate, Conspiracy of Silence: Torture and Ill-Treatment Based on Sexual Identity* (2001), Recommendation 7. See also Dauvergne and Millbank, 'Burdened by Proof'.

137. See Department of Immigration and Multicultural Affairs, *Guidelines on Gender Issues for Decision Makers*, July 1996, reproduced in *International Journal of Refugee Law* 9 (1997): 195.

138. See Immigration Appellate Authority, *Asylum Gender Guidelines* (2000). These guidelines operated at tribunal level.

139. Asylum Aid, 'Submission of Evidence to the Independent Asylum Commission', 27 July 2007, para. 40.

140. See Home Office, Asylum Policy Instructions, 'Gender Issues in Asylum Claims' (2006). These guidelines operate at the level of border control and decisions taken by the Minister's delegate.

141. The Australian guidelines were originally directed to the Minister's delegate rather than to the tribunal but note that omitting to consider the guidelines at tribunal level was held to constitute a legal error in *Applicants M16 of 2004* v. *Minister for Immigration and Multicultural and Indigenous Affairs* [2005] FCA 1641 (24 November 2005). This approach was affirmed in a case concerning a lesbian from Uganda before the Federal Magistrates Court in *MZXFJ* v. *Minister for Immigration and Multicultural Affairs* [2006] FMCA 1465 (10 October 2006), the only case in our pool to have referred to the guidelines. On the Australian guidelines more broadly, see Susan Kneebone, 'Women within the Refugee Construct: "Exclusionary Inclusion" in Policy and Practice – the Australian Experience', *International Journal of Refugee Law* 17 (2005): 7. On the operation of the UK guidelines generally, see Sophia Ceneda and Clare Palmer, *'Lip Service' or Implementation: The Home Office Gender Guidance and Women's Asylum Claims in the UK*, Asylum Aid Report (2006).

142. Of the 342 RRT decisions in our study decided after the introduction of the gender guidelines in July 1996, including 91 decisions on lesbian claimants, not one referred to the guidelines (although one judicial review case in 2006 did do so: *MZXFJ* v. *Minister for Immigration and Multicultural Affairs*). In the UK none of the 80 tribunal or judicial review cases in our study decided after the introduction of the gender guidelines in November 2000, including 16 decisions on lesbian claimants, referred to the gender guidelines.

143. Community groups in the UK are currently developing their own sexuality documents in an attempt to 'reduce homophobia and ignorance surrounding LGBT individuals seeking asylum': UK Lesbian and Gay Immigration Group, 'Sexual and Gender Identity Guidelines Initiative', http://www.uklgig.org.uk/guidelines.htm (accessed 1 July 2008). In Australia see Ghassan Kassisieh, *From Lives of Fear to Lives of Freedom* (2008), prepared for New South Wales Gay and Lesbian Rights Lobby.

144. UNHCR, Guidance Note on Refugee Claims Relating to Sexual Orientation and Gender Identity (2008).

145. See, e.g., *Karner* v. *Austria* [2003] ECHR 395 (24 October 2003); *EB* v. *France* [2008] ECHR 55 (22 January 2008).

Bisexuals need not apply: a comparative appraisal of refugee law and policy in Canada, the United States, and Australia

Sean Rehaag

Osgoode Hall Law School, York University, Toronto, Canada

This paper offers an analysis of refugee claims on grounds of bisexuality. After discussing the grounds on which sexual minorities may qualify for refugee status under international refugee law, the paper empirically assesses the success rates of bisexual refugee claimants in three major host states: Canada, the United States, and Australia. It concludes that bisexuals are significantly less successful than other sexual minority groups in obtaining refugee status in those countries. Through an examination of selected published decisions involving bisexual refugee claimants, the author identifies two main areas for concern that may partly account for the difficulties that bisexual refugee claimants encounter: the invisibility of bisexuality as a sexual identity, and negative views held by some refugee claims adjudicators towards bisexuality as well as the reluctance of some adjudicators to grant refugee status to sexual minorities who differ from gay and lesbian identities as traditionally understood.

The world is not to be divided into sheep and goats ... It is a fundamental of taxonomy that nature rarely deals with discrete categories. Only the human mind invents categories and tries to force facts into separated pigeon-holes. The sooner we learn this concerning human sexual behavior the sooner we shall reach a sound understanding of the realities of sex.[1]

Introduction

Bisexuality tends to be invisible in human rights practice and discourse, even in areas that are otherwise comparatively sensitive to sexual minority issues.[2] For example, at the time of writing, the *European Human Rights Reports* lists 68 cases that mentioned lesbians or homosexuals, but only four that mentioned bisexuals.[3] Similarly, the Canadian Human Rights Tribunal referred to lesbians or homosexuals in 24 decisions, but to bisexuals in only two decisions.[4] An equally revealing picture of the invisibility of bisexuality is evident in the names of prominent non-governmental organisations fighting for the human rights of sexual minorities. Consider, for example, the International Gay and Lesbian Human Rights Commission,[5] the International Gay and Lesbian Association,[6] the National Gay and Lesbian Task Force,[7] the Gay and Lesbian Rights Lobby,[8] the Lesbian and Gay Equality Project,[9] and Equality for Gays and Lesbians.[10]

In light of such invisibility, this paper aims to bring greater attention to bisexuality in one particular area of international human rights: international sexual minority refugee law.

An individual who is outside his or her country of origin, and who has a well-founded fear of persecution on account of his or her sexual orientation, meets the international legal definition of a refugee and is eligible for refugee status.[11] However, as I will demonstrate in this paper, bisexuals who allege a feared persecution on account of their sexual identity are frequently unable to secure refugee status. I argue that among the primary causes of the difficulties bisexual refugee claimants encounter are negative views held by some refugee claims adjudicators towards bisexuality, as well as the reluctance of some adjudicators to grant refugee status to sexual minorities who differ from gay and lesbian identities as traditionally understood.

My argument will proceed by first providing a brief introduction to international sexual minority refugee law. Then, I will examine the experiences of bisexual refugees in three major host states: Canada, the United States, and Australia. Through both quantitative and qualitative analysis of these experiences, I will demonstrate that bisexual refugee claimants have more difficulty securing refugee status than do other groups of sexual minorities. Finally, I will examine some of the reasons why bisexuals encounter difficulties securing refugee status.

Before turning to my main argument, it is pertinent to first address the terminology used in this paper. Debates regarding appropriate labels for sexual behaviours, sexual identities, and sexual orientations are one of the mainstays of discussions about what human rights have to say about sexual minorities.[12] One source of these debates is that, regardless of which terminology one chooses to embrace, it will inevitably fail to accord with the self-understanding of many of those who are supposed to be covered by the terminology. There have, for example, been sharp disagreements over terms such as MSM (men who have sex with men), WSW (women who have sex with women), 'homosexual', 'gay', LGBT (lesbian, gay, bisexual, and transgender), and 'queer'.[13] Some of the concerns expressed over such terms include whether a term occludes distinct sexual identities and complex intersectional considerations related to gender, class, race, language, religion, physical ability, HIV status, and so on;[14] whether one inappropriately conflates (or bifurcates) sexual behaviours and sexual identities;[15] and whether one excludes particular groups that ought to be included.[16] Moreover, cross-cultural dimensions add a further level of complexity to these debates, because even if one's chosen terminology is accepted within one community, it may be inappropriate in communities located in other regions of the world.[17]

In this paper, I adopt the general term 'sexual minorities'. I choose the term because it has relatively unsettled and imprecise boundaries. This imprecision is helpful, as it allows the term to include all persons seeking protection from persecution on account of hetero-normativity,[18] irrespective of their precise sexual identities or sexual behaviours.[19]

One further terminological matter remains: my use of the term 'bisexuality'. Debates about appropriate labels are, if anything, even more pronounced with respect to bisexuality than to other sexual minority identities.[20] Once again, cross-cultural considerations muddy the waters. Some of those characterised in one locale as 'bisexual' may be viewed in others as 'homosexual' or 'heterosexual'.[21] In the context of this paper, it is necessary to note in particular that a person who would otherwise identify as exclusively homosexual may be coerced into different-sex sexual relations or into adopting bisexual identities through hetero-normative persecution.[22]

This paper attempts to sidestep some of these debates over the definition of 'bisexuality' because my interest is not to set out a particular definition and advocate its use by refugee claims adjudicators. Rather, my interest is to explore how sexual minority refugee claimants whose cases involve allegations of non-gender-exclusive sexuality are treated in the refugee determination systems in several major host states. In this paper, therefore, I use the term 'bisexual' loosely to mean a person whose sexual orientation, sexual identity, or sexual behaviour is not directed exclusively towards persons of one particular sex or gender.[23]

International refugee law and sexual minorities

It is well settled in international refugee law that non-citizens facing persecution abroad on account of their sexual orientations are eligible for refugee status.[24] The 1951 Convention Relating to the Status of Refugees,[25] however, does not explicitly include sexual orientation. The Convention defines a refugee as any person who

> owing to well-founded fear of being persecuted for reasons of race, religion, nationality, membership of a particular social group or political opinion, is outside the country of his nationality and is unable, or owing to such fear, is unwilling to avail himself of the protection of that country.[26]

Some sexual minority refugees have – with varying degrees of success – attempted to argue that their fear of persecution stemmed from their 'political opinion'.[27] The argument has, thus far, proved to be particularly effective for human rights activists who encounter hetero-normative persecution as a result of their efforts to enhance the rights of sexual minorities.[28] Political opinion, however, has been interpreted very broadly in international refugee law to cover 'any opinion on any matter in which the machinery of State, government, and policy may be engaged'.[29] As a result, one could plausibly argue that 'political opinion' covers sexual minorities who face persecution for challenging both traditional gender norms as well as the inevitability of heterosexuality. With respect to the former (i.e. traditional gender norms), the United Nations High Commission for Refugees (UNHCR) *Guidelines on Gender-Related Persecution* state that political opinion 'may include an opinion as to gender roles. It would also include non-conformist behaviour which leads the persecutor to impute a political opinion.'[30] This is significant because persecution targeting sexual minorities often aims to 'foster and maintain "appropriate" gender role behaviour'.[31] Meanwhile, with regard to the latter (i.e. challenging the inevitability of heterosexuality), the argument would find some support in the commonly made claim that the heterosexually structured family is the fundamental socio-economic unit, one that is supported through a variety of state policies.[32] Sexual minorities, by their very existence, may be understood as challenging both the heterosexual family and the state policies that support it. In other words, sexual minorities may have political opinions regarding gender roles and the heterosexual family imputed to them, and may be persecuted on that basis.[33]

One might also plausibly contend that hetero-normative persecution sometimes involves not only persecution on grounds of 'political opinion' but also persecution on grounds of 'religion'.[34] The UNHCR *Guidelines on Gender-Related Persecution*, for example, state that

> [i]n certain States, the religion assigns particular roles or behavioural codes to women and men respectively. Where a woman does not fulfil her assigned role or refuses to abide by the codes, and is punished as a consequence, she may have a well-founded fear of being persecuted for reasons of religion. *Failure to abide by such codes may be perceived as evidence that a woman holds unacceptable religious opinions regardless of what she actually believes.*[35]

Just as women who are persecuted for transgressing gender roles or behavioural codes prescribed by religious dogmas may – irrespective of their actual religious beliefs[36] – be understood as facing persecution on grounds of religion, so too can sexual minorities.[37] Indeed, as Nicole LaViolette notes, many sexual minority refugee claims involve fears of persecution where the claimant's '[h]omosexuality is not only perceived as non-conformity to gender-specific roles but also . . . a crime against religion'.[38] The argument would seem especially warranted where the agents of persecution are in one way or another tied to religious institutions – which is not unlikely given the longstanding hetero-normative traditions in most major world religions. It would also be worth pursuing such an argument in countries where religious and state institutions are not sharply divided.[39]

Although persecution on grounds of either religion or political opinion presents avenues for securing refugee status that are, in principle, open at least to some sexual minorities facing hetero-normative persecution, it is much more common for sexual minority refugee claimants to argue that they meet the refugee definition because they face persecution on grounds of their 'membership in a particular social group'.[40]

One of the leading cases on what exactly constitutes a 'particular social group' is the Canadian Supreme Court decision, *Ward* v. *Canada*.[41] In *Ward*, Justice La Forest explained that there were three distinct types of 'particular social groups' for the purpose of the refugee definition:

(1) groups defined by an innate or unchangeable characteristic;
(2) groups whose members voluntarily associate for reasons so fundamental to their human dignity that they should not be forced to forsake the association; and
(3) groups associated by a former voluntary status, unalterable due to its historical permanence.[42]

Offering examples of each of the three types of social groups, Justice La Forest stated that '[t]he first category would embrace . . . sexual orientation'.[43] In other words, sexual minorities facing persecution qualify for refugee protection as 'particular social groups' because, according to Justice La Forest, sexual orientation is an 'innate or unchangeable personal characteristic'.[44]

This passage has been cited with approval by courts in jurisdictions around the world[45] and by the UNHCR *Guidelines on Social Group Claims*.[46] However, there has been some recent movement away from this approach to sexual minority refugee jurisprudence.

Following *Ward*, a number of commentators have sharply critiqued Justice La Forest's reliance on the purported 'innate or immutable' nature of sexual orientation.[47] According to these commentators, there are both strategic and symbolic benefits in grounding sexual minority refugee protection within the second category of 'particular social groups' identified in *Ward*: groups that associate 'for reasons so fundamental to their human dignity that they should not be forced to forsake the association.'[48] It is worth noting that this second category in *Ward* – which I will call the fundamental human dignity approach – has been given a slightly modified interpretation in subsequent international refugee law, most significantly through the UNHCR *Guidelines on Social Group Claims*.[49] According to these *Guidelines*, the focus of the fundamental human dignity approach is not on whether members of a particular social group actually 'voluntarily associate', but rather on the question of whether the characteristic that the group shares is 'fundamental to identity, conscience or the exercise of one's human rights'.[50]

The strategic advantage of embracing the fundamental human dignity approach is that the approach insulates sexual minority refugee protection from any possible shifts in research in science or social sciences on the 'causes' of sexual orientation. Views on the 'causes' of sexual orientation have long been hotly contested by scientists and social scientists alike. Many researchers suggest that sexual orientation is either related to genetics or to early childhood experiences (or to some combination of the two). Thus, they understand sexual orientation as by and large a fixed psychosocial characteristic.[51] Other researchers, however, suggest that sexual orientation can and does change over time. Admittedly, some of such research is associated with those who controversially assert that homosexuality is a psychological condition that can be 'cured'[52] through so-called 'conversion therapy' or 'sexual reorientation therapy'.[53] As a study on political agendas in conversion therapy notes,

> Current approaches tend to utilize religious and psychodynamic principles that define homosexuality as a 'condition' that results when a child does not receive sufficient love through the attachment to the same-sex parent . . . For the sake of salvation, sexual reorientation programs tend to rely on the power of God and prayer to help the repentant homosexual strengthen willpower, reduce desire, and limit behavior . . . Heterosexual marriage and children are promised, which sexual reorientation therapists consider a healthy adaptation to a hetero-sexual world.[54]

However, some of the research finding that sexual orientation is mutable has emerged from scholars who do not hold disparaging views about homosexuality. Rather, these scholars emphasise the socially contingent and shifting aspects of human sexuality – including hetero-sexuality – and argue that human sexuality is too complex to be fully captured by models that hold that people simply 'are' homosexual or heterosexual (or any other sexual identity).[55] Indeed, one of the primary aims of these scholars – often called 'queer theorists' – is to elucidate the power politics at play in what they view as the processes of social regulation that produce individuals who 'perform' naturalised sexual identities.[56]

What I want to emphasise here is that the debate over the 'immutability' of sexual orientation remains controversial and neither side of the debate has an exclusive claim to represent the views held by sexual minorities. In this context, it seems unwise to use the presumed 'immutability' of sexual orientation as the reason why sexual minorities facing hetero-normative persecution are entitled to refugee status. The risk is that, if the view of sexual orientation advocated by those on the 'mutability' side of the debate becomes dominant, then sexual minorities facing persecution will no longer meet the refugee definition. Nancy Knauer cautions against the risky strategy of tying sexual minority rights to a particular strain of evidence in science or social sciences regarding the nature and causes of sexual orientation:

> By premising their rights claims . . . on assertions of immutable status, pro-gay advocates have entrusted the success of a major social and political movement to the reliability of a few incon-clusive studies concerning, *inter alia*, the size of the hypothalamus in the cadavers of gay men and the inner ears of lesbians.[57]

One strategic advantage, then, of grounding sexual minority refugee claims on the founda-tional principle that no one should be required to change their sexual orientations, rather than on the idea that no one can change their sexual orientations, is that sexual minorities will be able to secure refugee status irrespective of the ebbs and flows of the debates on the 'causes' of sexual orientation.

Just as important as this strategic advantage of the fundamental human dignity approach is that the immutability approach to sexual minority refugee protection carries problematic symbolic implications. To see these implications, let us consider why Justice La Forest attached relevance to whether sexual orientation is an immutable characteristic. It is important to note, in this regard, that Justice La Forest inferred the three types of 'particular social groups' mentioned above from the human rights commitments animating international refugee law.[58] One of these human rights commitments inheres in the basic objection to differential treatment based on characteristics for which human beings cannot normatively be held responsible. If they are not responsible for their sexual orientations – if sexual orientations are, in other words, immutable personal characteristics – then differential treatment based on sexual orientation runs foul of this objection. Yoshino characterises these sorts of arguments as involving what he calls the 'immutability defense'.[59] As Yoshino puts it, '[g]ays often defend their homosexuality by characterizing it as an immutable trait ... Immutability has exonerative force because of the widely held belief that it is abhorrent to penalize individuals for matters beyond their control.'[60]

Compare the message the immutability defence approach sends with that which inheres in the alternative foundation for sexual minority protection, the fundamental human dignity approach, which holds that no human beings should be required to change their sexual orientations. The latter approach sends the message that sexual orientation is so closely connected to a person's fundamental human dignity that persecution aimed at enforcing 'compulsory heterosexuality'[61] and traditional gender norms[62] is a human rights violation of such magnitude as to trigger refugee protection. Rather than presenting sexual minorities as unpopular minorities in need of protection because individuals are not responsible for their sexual orientations, this approach presents hetero-normative persecution as an impermissible trespass upon a person's fundamental human dignity.[63]

In recent years, courts and refugee claims tribunals in several jurisdictions have begun to embrace this alternative approach to sexual minority jurisprudence, perhaps due to its strategic and symbolic advantages. For example, in *Hernandez-Montiel* v. *I.N.S.*,[64] the United States Court of Appeals for the Ninth Circuit held that sexual minorities fell within both the first and second categories of 'particular social groups' identified in *Ward*.[65] That is to say, one reason why sexual minorities persecuted abroad are entitled to refugee status and asylum in the United States is that 'sexual orientation and sexual identity ... are so fundamental to one's identity that a person should not be required to abandon them'.[66] Tribunals in Australia[67] and New Zealand[68] have come to similar conclusions and have refused to consider sexual minority refugee protection solely through the lens of protection for groups defined by innate and unchangeable characteristics.[69]

In principle, then, the ultimate rationale for sexual minority refugee protection appears to be shifting away from the contention that sexual orientation is an immutable characteristic, and towards the view that persecutory enforcement of compulsory heterosexuality and traditional gender norms is an infringement of fundamental human dignity. However, closer attention to case law reveals that sexual minority refugee claims continue in practice to be measured against relatively rigid and immutable understandings of sexual orientations. Nowhere is this clearer than in the experience of bisexual refugee claimants.[70]

The experience of bisexual refugee claimants in selected host states

Bisexual refugee claimants' experience, while varying to some degree across host states, shares two major features: (1) their presence in the host states' refugee jurisprudence is largely invisible and (2) they face extremely low refugee claim success rates. Both these features are evident in the experience of bisexual refugee claimants in three major host states: Canada, the United States, and Australia.

Canada

In Canada, the earliest published case explicitly involving a bisexual refugee claimant was decided in 2000.[71] The decision involved a refugee claimant from Mexico who self-identified as a 'bisexual man who prefers men and being a transvestite'[72] and who had been repeatedly brutalised by the Mexican police.[73] The claimant obtained refugee status, largely on the basis of persuasive country condition evidence involving frequent reports of violence directed towards transvestites in Mexico.[74]

However, in the following years, other bisexual refugee claimants have been largely unsuccessful in obtaining refugee protection. For example, according to a recent study undertaken by the author, no explicitly bisexual refugee claimant was granted refugee status in reported Canadian refugee decisions between 2001 and 2004.[75] In evaluating this figure, it should be noted that the study identified only 11 reported refugee decisions involving bisexuals, out of a total of 115 reported sexual minority refugee decisions.[76] Moreover, it should be borne in mind that only a small fraction of Canadian refugee decisions are published, and those that are published cannot be taken to be a representative sample of all refugee determinations.[77]

To get a clearer picture of how sexual minority refugee claims – including bisexual refugee claims – are actually being decided in Canada, it is possible to use a formal request through the Access to Information Act[78] to obtain data directly from the database of the administrative tribunal responsible for refugee determinations in Canada, that is, the Immigration and Refugee Board (IRB).[79]

According to data acquired through a formal Access to Information request regarding refugee determinations by the IRB in 2006,[80] bisexual refugee claims made up approximately 8% of sexual minority refugee claims decided by the IRB in 2006 (44 out of 577 decisions). The success rate for sexual minority claimants (58%) exceeded the average success rates at the IRB for the year (54%). However, the success rate for bisexual refugee claimants (39%) was significantly lower. It is, moreover, worth noting that while the success rates for gay male and lesbian claimants were virtually identical (60%), cases involving gay men (424) significantly outnumbered cases involving lesbians (100). In cases involving bisexuals, male claimants (33) once again outnumbered female claimants (11), but whereas success rates for gay and lesbian claimants matched closely, success rates for male bisexual claimants (33%) were lower than those for female bisexual claimants (55%).[81]

The author's previous study, which examined all (that is, reported and unreported) sexual minority refugee decisions by the IRB in 2004, came to mostly similar conclusions. According to that study, bisexual refugee claims made up 7% of sexual minority claims (100 out of 1351 decisions). Moreover, the success rate in sexual minority refugee claims (49%) slightly exceeded the average IRB success rates for the year (46%), and far exceeded the success rate in bisexual refugee claims (25%).[82]

It appears then that, notwithstanding the success of the claimant in the first reported refugee decision involving a bisexual in Canada, bisexual refugee claimants have had a difficult time obtaining refugee status in Canada, compared with both refugee claimants in general and sexual minority refugee claimants in particular.[83]

United States

Although *Hernandez-Montiel* v. *INS*, a leading US case, explicitly considered the possibility that framing sexual minority refugee law exclusively in terms of homosexuality and heterosexuality may be 'too restrictive',[84] reported cases involving bisexual applicants for refugee status and asylum in the United States have been rare.[85] Indeed, there has only been one federal court decision explicitly involving a bisexual applicant, and in that case the applicant's bisexuality was mentioned only in passing.[86] Moreover, the first – and thus far only – United States Board of Immigration Appeals case involving an explicitly bisexual applicant for refugee status and asylum currently reported in legal databases was decided in 2007.[87] In that case an HIV-positive bisexual from Mexico was unsuccessful in obtaining refugee status and asylum in the United States.[88]

There are currently no statistics available on unreported average grant rates in refugee applications in the United States involving sexual minorities.[89] However, it is possible to get a sense of what such statistics might reveal by using information obtained from the Asylum Documentation Program (ADP) of the International Gay and Lesbian Human Rights Commission.[90] From 1994 to 2007, the ADP assisted sexual minority refugee claimants, and their advocates, by providing documentation on the conditions faced by sexual minorities in particular countries abroad. When the ADP was contacted for assistance, staff recorded details of their cases in a database. Where possible, the outcomes of the cases in which the ADP provided assistance were also recorded.

According to the ADP's internal database,[91] bisexual cases were rarely reported to the ADP. In fact, bisexual cases represented less than 1% of the cases involving sexual minority refugee claimants in the United States that were reported to the ADP from 1994 to 2007 (38 cases out of 4241). Cases involving bisexual men (35) were more frequently reported than those involving bisexual women (3), just as reported cases involving gay men (3576) were much more common than those involving lesbians (627).

As with the Canadian data, the grant rate for bisexuals (5%) was significantly lower than the rate for gay men and lesbians (17%) in cases where the final outcomes were reported to the ADP. However, caution must be exercised when interpreting these statistics. In particular, the reported grant rates likely significantly understated the actual grant rates in sexual minority refugee claims, in large part because, due to limited resources, the ADP was not able to systematically determine the outcomes of all cases in which they offered assistance.[92] As a result, data regarding refugee claim outcomes are only available in 14% of the cases involving bisexuals, and 21% of the cases involving gay men and lesbians reported to the ADP. Nonetheless, it seems significant that in the data collected by the ADP, whereas the grant rates of gay men (17%) and lesbians (17%) matched closely, the grant rates of gay men and lesbians (17%), on one hand, and bisexuals (5%), on the other, diverge significantly.

Australia

As far back as 1997, Justice Kirby of the High Court of Australia ruled, *obiter*, that 'homosexual and bisexual men and women' qualify for asylum under the category of those who suffer persecution on account of their membership in a particular social group.[93] This passage was then cited with approval by the Australian High Court in its 2003 decision holding that sexual minorities constituted a particular social group for the purposes of refugee law.[94] A subsequent Federal Court decision also explicitly affirmed that 'bisexuals can form a particular social group for the purposes of refugee law'.[95]

Although it is clear, then, that bisexuals facing persecution are in principle eligible for refugee status in Australia, in practice reported refugee claims involving bisexuals appear to have been quite rare. A study of Australian sexual minority refugee determinations from 1994 to 2000,[96] undertaken by Jenni Millbank and Catherine Dauvergne, identified 204 sexual minority refugee determinations, out of which 161 involved men and 43 involved women.[97] In only two of the identified cases[98] 'the claimants self-identified as "bisexual" in their applications'.[99] Moreover, in these two cases the Australian Refugee Review Tribunal (RRT), 'rather than considering bisexuals as a particular social group, assumed the applicants to be homosexual'.[100] The authors of the study also identified two further cases[101] where the applicants were identified by the RRT as either bisexual[102] or ambiguous in their sexuality.[103] In none of these four cases – all of which involved men – did the applicant succeed in securing refugee status. It is worth noting that during the same period the average grant rate in the Australian sexual minority refugee decisions identified by Millbank and Dauvergne was 22%,[104] with gay men (26%) enjoying a significantly higher grant rate than lesbians (7%).[105]

More recently, there have been some Australian cases where bisexual claimants have secured refugee status,[106] or where federal courts have overturned negative RRT decisions involving bisexual claimants.[107] Still – as with the experience of bisexuals in Canada and the United States – these positive decisions remain the exception, rather than the rule.[108]

Analysis of the experience of bisexual refugee claimants

My review of the experience of bisexual asylum claimants in Canada, the United States, and Australia has highlighted that bisexuals are largely invisible in refugee determination systems, and that bisexuals seem to have a more difficult time securing refugee status than other groups of sexual minorities. It is, thus, pertinent to attempt to account for these two central observations.

Bisexual invisibility

There is very little information currently available on bisexual refugee claimants in Canada, the United States, or Australia. To begin with, as we have seen, there are few reported bisexual refugee decisions, that is, decisions published in official law reports. As we have also seen, however, according to data obtained from Canada's IRB, approximately 7–8% of sexual minority refugee claims made in Canada were identified by the IRB as involving bisexuals. There is no reason to think that the proportion of bisexuals among sexual minority refugee claimants in the United States or Australia is any lower. The issue of why there have been few reported bisexual asylum decisions is, therefore, a puzzle to be explored.

While some refugee law scholars have discussed bisexuality within larger analyses of sexual minority refugee claims, there is relatively little scholarship that concentrates exclusively on bisexual refugee claims.[109] One reason why bisexuals have drawn little attention in the area of international refugee law may be due to perceptions that refugee claims involving bisexuals are uncommon because decisions involving such claims have only infrequently been reported. This explanation, however, fails to fully account for the lack of attention to bisexual refugee claims as they arise. After all, the number of lesbian refugee claims is also low compared with the number of claims involving gay men, and yet significant scholarly attention has – quite rightly – been paid to analysing and attempting to improve refugee determinations involving lesbians.[110] Moreover, one of the main preoccupations in the scholarly literature on lesbian refugee claimants is precisely to examine why women are under-represented in sexual minority refugee claims.[111]

In my view, a more persuasive explanation for the lack of attention to bisexual refugee claimants in both reported decisions and in refugee law scholarship relates to a broader social phenomenon identified by scholars who have engaged closely with bisexuality.

That social phenomenon is that bisexuals tend to be invisible in – or actively erased from – both sexual minority and mainstream communities.[112]

Many theorists tie the invisibility of bisexuality to a naturalised conception of human sexuality, in which human beings are understood to be either essentially heterosexual or essentially homosexual.[113] According to Kenji Yoshino, maintaining this naturalised binary understanding of human sexuality serves the interests of heterosexual communities, as heterosexuals inhabit a privileged position in this naturalised binary hierarchy.[114] Gagnon, Greenblat, and Kimmel echo this view, noting that

> Only a few thinkers [have begun] to consider what would happen if *what appeared to be* the most natural of all forms of conduct, the conventionalised sexual relations of women and men, was treated as problematic and the topic of history, anthropology, and sociology rather than biology, psychiatry, and individualist psychologies. To entertain the belief that the sexual desires of the majority are as much the result of a social construction as are the desires of all sexual minorities is a classic example of what is bad (perhaps even intolerable) to think, much less to practice.[115]

It is important to appreciate, however, that this naturalised binary is also useful to many in sexual minority communities.[116] In particular, essentialised homosexual subject positions can form an important site for political mobilisation against heterosexist oppression.[117] Moreover, in many states around the world, sexual minorities have resorted to essentialist accounts of sexual orientations in order to bring constitutional challenges to heterosexist discrimination.[118] It is worth considering, in this regard, a remark by Justice Kirby, the first openly gay Justice of the Australian High Court:

> The advent of the Human Genome Project and the likelihood that, in many cases at least, sexual orientation is genetically determined, make it unacceptable to impose upon those affected unreasonable legal discrimination or demands that they change. It was always unacceptable; but now no informed person has an excuse for blind prejudice and unreasonable conduct. If we are talking about the unnatural, demands that people deny their sexuality or try to change it, if it is part of their nature, are a good illustration of what is unnatural. An increasing number of citizens in virtually every Western democracy are coming inexorably to this realisation.[119]

Now, Justice Kirby did not intend to suggest that human beings are genetically predetermined to be either homosexual or heterosexual, to the exclusion of all other sexual identities. On the contrary, in both court decisions and extra-judicial writings, Justice Kirby regularly refers not only to gay men and lesbians, but also to bisexuals and other groups of sexual minorities.[120] Nonetheless, bisexuality complicates the essentialist – and even biological determinist – account of human sexuality at the heart of the above passage. It is this account of human sexuality that, according to Yoshino, both heterosexual and many sexual minority communities have an interest in maintaining.[121]

Bisexuality challenges the essentialist account of human sexuality in at least two ways. First, many – though by no means all[122] – bisexuals understand their sexual identity as involving some degree of choice, and often a highly politicised choice at that.[123] Liz Highleyman, for example, describes how she came to identify as bisexual in the following terms:

> Some people become radicalised politically because of their oppression as gays, lesbians and bisexuals. Others questions their heterosexuality as a result of their radical politics ... It was within radical political circles, in fact, that I first got to know bisexual, gay and lesbian people. I began to wonder why so many people who shared my political ideals rejected

traditional notions of gender and sexuality, and I started to question many of the assumptions I had grown up with. When I thought about it, it made little sense to rule out the romantic and sexual potential of half of humanity.[124]

Second, many bisexuals report that their sexual identity is fluid and undergoes shifts over time. Marie King, for example, notes that '[h]aving lived my life for a number of years as a heterosexual and then for an equally long period as a lesbian, I have lately arrived at a kind of bisexual synthesis'.[125] Others, such as Dave Matteson, suggest that their sexual identity – or the identity that they present to others – shifts even more frequently in response to social context:

> I made a decision fairly early in my public coming out to frequently use the word gay when speaking to the mainstream heterosexual community. I did not want to have my bisexuality seen as minimizing the side of me that is gay. On the other hand, when doing work in the gay community I have stressed being bisexual, to help fight the prejudice there against bisexuals.[126]

Or, as Starhawk puts it in more colourful terms,

> those of us who are bisexual, and honest, have to admit that our sexual orientation sometimes seems to change with the phases of the moon or the level of pollen in the air, or just with propinquity to whoever happens to be around. I honour the lesbian and gay activists who have made their sexual orientation a cornerstone of their identities, and respect the political need for doing so ... But if I'm honest about my own sexual identity, it has something to do with a deep reluctance to be pinned down.[127]

Taken together, because many in both heterosexual and sexual minority communities have an interest in preserving essentialist understandings of human sexuality, and because bisexuality challenges these understandings, bisexuality is often downplayed, ignored, or even erased. Yoshino calls this phenomenon 'the epistemic contract of bisexual erasure'.[128] The result of this epistemic contract is that bisexuality is largely invisible in both heterosexual and sexual minority communities.[129]

It is worth reflecting on the possibility that the invisibility of bisexuality in the refugee determination systems in Canada, the United States, and Australia, as well as in some of the work of contemporary refugee law scholars, both partakes in and contributes to this epistemic contract of bisexual erasure.

Low grant rates in bisexual refugee claims

Once the invisibility of bisexual refugee claimants is challenged, one of the most pressing issues that needs to be explored is why bisexuals face much lower refugee claim grant rates than those involving gay men and lesbians in Canada, the United States, and Australia.

A full analysis of the low grant rates for bisexual refugee claimants would require an extensive review of unpublished refugee decisions. The methodological challenges involved in such a review render this enterprise beyond the scope of this paper. However, based on the few reported decisions involving bisexual refugee claimants, a few tentative observations can be made.

First and foremost, reported refugee decisions reveal troubling views about bisexuality held by refugee claims adjudicators. Perhaps the most flagrant example can be found in the comments made by an adjudicator at the Australian RRT in a case involving a bisexual refugee claimant from China.[130] In this decision, after accepting that homosexuals constitute a particular social group for the purposes of the refugee definition,[131] the RRT went on to note that,

> by stressing at the hearing that he is bisexual, the Applicant has not satisfied the Tribunal that he is reconciled to homosexual activity, lifestyle or even social association, or that he has any kind of preternatural homosexual identity or tendencies. *It seems to the Tribunal that if this case were about political opinion, it would be as if the Applicant were saying that, at heart, he was a little bit disposed towards democracy but also eager to support authoritarianism; if it were about religion, it would be as if the Applicant, at heart, were a little bit Christian and a little bit atheist.* There is significant equivocation in the Applicant's evidence and it goes against him.[132]

To understand this passage, it is important to emphasise that the RRT went on to note that 'the notion of a group defined as "bisexuals" has been considered insofar as the homosexual side of bisexual[s] ... were an issue'.[133] The RRT, in other words, was prepared to entertain the possibility that bisexuals may meet the refugee definition where they faced persecution because of their 'homosexual side'. However, the RRT simultaneously found that the mere assertion of bisexuality was sufficient evidence to hold that the claimant did not, in fact, have a 'homosexual side' (that is, he was not 'reconciled to homosexual activity, lifestyle or even social association' and did not have 'any kind of preternatural homosexual identity or tendencies').[134] The understanding of homosexuality that animated such a holding is one that sees homosexuality as the absence or antithesis of heterosexual desire. Combined with the notion that bisexuals are only eligible for refugee status to the extent that they will otherwise be persecuted on account of homosexuality, this understanding of homosexuality serves to erase the very possibility that bisexuals may be eligible for refugee status.

This case was admittedly an outlier in that, as we have seen, several refugee tribunals and courts have accepted bisexuality as a basis for refugee claims. However, troubling comments and findings made by adjudicators are not infrequent in refugee claims involving bisexuals. Sometimes the findings made by adjudicators in such claims are so disturbing that even the lawyers representing the governments will distance themselves from them. For example, in a recent Canadian federal court judicial review of a negative refugee determination involving an 18-year-old bisexual from Saint Lucia, 'counsel for the Minister conceded that some of the ... findings were "silly" and that the [adjudicator]'s language was "inappropriate"'.[135] The 'silliest' and most 'inappropriate' of the findings in question related to a purported inconsistency identified by the adjudicator in the claimant's failure to engage in sexual activity in Canada, notwithstanding her previous sexual experiences with both men and women:

> The claimant testified that she has not been sexually active [in Canada]. She [says she] is underage to go to gay clubs and she is busy with going to school. *It is difficult to believe how a person sexually active with a male and two females from the age of 14 is living a celibate life now.*[136]

This comment is disturbing because it closely matches negative stereotypes about bisexuals as sexually voracious or 'pathologically promiscuous'.[137] Indeed, in the cited passage the adjudicator appeared to reject the claimant's asserted bisexual identity merely because the claimant's behaviour (that is, 'celibacy') departed from these stereotypes. This indicates not only that individuals whose sexual identities depart from the stereotypes about human sexuality held by adjudicators may have their refugee claims improperly denied, but also that the underlying understanding of human sexuality held by some adjudicators continues to be premised upon immutability. More specifically, this particular adjudicator was simply unwilling to accept that the claimant's sexual behaviour might change in response to different circumstances; the adjudicator seemed to be saying that if the claimant *really* had sexual relations with both men and women from the age of 14, then she would necessarily continue to do so at the age of 18, irrespective of the very different circumstances in which she now found herself.

Although explicit remarks involving such extremely negative views of bisexuality have been relatively rare in reported refugee decisions involving bisexuals, troubling views of bisexuality were nonetheless frequently implicit in the types of evidence that refugee claims adjudicators cited when assessing the sexual identities of refugee claimants. For example, in a Canadian case involving a woman from Iran, the IRB cited evidence that the claimant intended to marry a man to conclude that the claimant was not, in fact, a bisexual. As the adjudicator put it,

> The claimant arrived in Canada with a male companion ... In response to the question as to whether they were planning to get married, the claimant replied, 'So far there is a commitment but officially we haven't signed a paper or anything.' ... [The claimant's] actions are those of a heterosexual woman.[138]

Similarly, in another Canadian case involving a woman from Hungary, the IRB held that the claimant was not a bisexual, partly based on evidence of prior different-sex sexual conduct:

> The claimant came to Canada because allegedly she was persecuted, among other reasons, on account of her sexual orientation. However ... the evidence shows that since last year she has been living with her boyfriend.[139]

These decisions were seriously problematic, as they failed to understand the reality of bisexual experiences. Indeed, one of the common themes of literature on bisexuality is the challenge of having one's bisexual identity taken seriously when one is in a sexually exclusive long-term relationship. The difficulty bisexuals encounter in this regard is that one's sexual identity is often read with reference to the gender of one's current or recent sexual partner(s). Consider, for example, the frustration expressed by Ruth Colker, a leading bisexual theorist, with being perceived as heterosexual because of her marriage to a man: 'in cases such as mine, most people probably just attach the label "married woman" to me with its assumptions about exclusive heterosexuality without even inquiring about my sexual orientation'.[140] Similarly, as William Burleson notes, 'if a self-identified bisexual woman is in a monogamous relationship with another woman, she is now assumed to be lesbian'.[141]

In order to challenge these views, it is important to emphasise that although some bisexuals have multiple recent or concurrent sexual partners of various sexes/genders,[142] others may be in long-term sexually exclusive relationships.[143] Consider, for example, the following comments by Rifka Reichler:

> I am a 23-year-old married Jewish woman. I have never slept with a woman, nor do I expect to. Yet, I am bisexual ... and participate in the bisexual community. The newspapers and newsletters I read, the conversations I have with friends, the buttons I hang in my study, and the organizations I join all affirm my bisexuality. The term *bisexual* affirms the part of me that loves women, now and in the future, regardless of who I am sleeping with.[144]

If one understands that sexual identity and sexual behaviour are not necessarily perfectly correlated, as the above comments by bisexual authors attest, then it seems unclear in what respect evidence that a refugee claimant maintains a sexually exclusive relationship could plausibly be read as challenging the credibility of his or her asserted bisexual identity. Rather, the fact that adjudicators in bisexual refugee claims cited such evidence suggests that they were actually concerned with establishing, not whether the claimant was bisexual, but rather where the claimant fit into an essentialist hetero/homosexual binary.

A similar point can be made with regard to cases where evidence of same-sex sexual relationships was disregarded in assessing a refugee claimant's sexual minority identity. For example, in a recent Australian bisexual refugee case, the RRT, after noting that the male claimant had previously maintained sexual relationships with women, dismissed evidence regarding the claimant's ongoing sexual relationship with a man while he was in long-term immigration detention.[145] The RRT in particular noted that

> I do not accept that the Applicant is in fact bisexual ... I consider that his relationship with ... [another male immigration detainee] is simply the product of the situation where only partners of the same sex are available and says nothing about his sexual orientation.[146]

In another Australian bisexual refugee case involving a man from Pakistan, the RRT stated:

> The Tribunal accepts that the Applicant might have enjoyed sexual play with other males when he was a teenager ... However, the Tribunal is not prepared to accept on the evidence before it that this was anything but *a transient, youthful phase*.[147]

Again, what is troubling about these remarks is that the adjudicators seemed to be preoccupied with uncovering the claimants' essential and unchangeable 'true' sexual identities. Evidence of same-sex sexual behaviour that the adjudicators understood as being affected by a particular social context – for example, youthful experimentation or sex-segregated incarceration – may therefore be disregarded. Thus, the following remarks by Millbank about the Australian Refugee Review Tribunal are apposite and can be extended to other refugee claims adjudication bodies:

> In situations where the applicant was seen as having some choice, or their sexuality any way fluid or temporary – if they could be seen as bisexual, young, sexually inexperienced generally, or having had only limited same-sex-sexual experiences, the Australian tribunal, in particular, was very reluctant to accept them ... under the social group category.[148]

In the end, if these troubling comments in the few reported cases involving bisexual refugee claimants reflect the overall trend among the unpublished cases, then one possible explanation for the low refugee claim grant rates for bisexuals is that although in principle bisexuals who have a well founded fear of being persecuted for their sexual orientation are eligible for refugee status, in practice at least some refugee claims adjudicators will only grant refugee status to sexual minorities who display more traditionally understood sexual identities that fit within an essentialised homo/hetero binary. As previously mentioned, however, such a hypothesis needs to be tested further by reviewing decisions that were unpublished.

Conclusion

This paper has sought to shed light on an area of international refugee law that seldom attracts much attention: refugee claims made by bisexuals. It has demonstrated that bisexuals outside their countries of origin who have a well-founded fear of persecution on grounds of their sexual orientation in principle meet the refugee definition. However, it has also shown that, at least in Canada, the United States, and Australia, bisexual refugee claimants are much less likely to succeed in securing refugee status than are other groups of sexual minorities. As few decisions involving bisexual refugee claimants are published, further empirical analysis of unpublished decisions should be undertaken to identify the causes of the low success rates in bisexual refugee claims. On the basis of the few decisions that were published, I hypothesise that such research would reveal that among the reasons for the low grant rates include (1) the invisibility of bisexuality and (2) the disparaging views of some refugee claims adjudicators on bisexuality and their willingness to grant refugee status to bisexuals only to such extent as their cases appear to match adjudicators' perceptions of homosexual or lesbian sexual identities.

Ultimately, we must bear in mind that the stakes in refugee determinations are immense. Negative and wrongly decided refugee claims will result in individuals being forcibly repatriated to countries where they will face persecution, torture, or even death. Accordingly, the current treatment of bisexual refugee claimants in Canada, the United States, and Australia provides cause for grave concern.

Acknowledgements

This paper was written while the author was a visiting researcher at the Asylum Documentation Program of the International Gay and Lesbian Human Rights Commission in San Francisco. He would like to thank Dusty Araujo and others at the Program for providing a congenial research environment. He would also like to thank the University of Toronto International Human Rights Program for its generous financial assistance.

Notes

1. Alfred Kinsey, Wardell Pomeroy, and Clyde Martin, *Sexual Behavior in the Human Male* (Philadelphia: W.B. Saunders, 1948), 639.
2. See generally Clare Hemmings, 'What's in a Name? Bisexuality, Transnational Sexuality Studies and Western Colonial Legacies', *International Journal of Human Rights* 11 (2007): 13. See also notes 112–29 and accompanying texts below.
3. These figures were obtained by searching for 'homosexual or lesbian' and 'bisexual', respectively, using Westlaw-Ecarswell's electronic database entitled 'EHR-RPTS'. The search was conducted on 20 May 2008.
4. These figures were obtained by searching for 'homosexual or lesbian' and 'bisexual', respectively, using Quicklaw's electronic database entitled 'Canadian Human Rights Tribunal Decisions'. The search was conducted on 20 May 2008.
5. International Gay and Lesbian Human Rights Commission, http://www.iglhrc.org.
6. International Gay and Lesbian Association, http://www.ilga.org.
7. National Gay and Lesbian Task Force, http://www.thetaskforce.org.
8. Gay and Lesbian Rights Lobby, http://www.glrl.org.au.
9. Lesbian and Gay Equality Project, http://www.equality.org.za.
10. Égalité pour les gais et les lesbiennes, http://www.egale.ca.
11. See notes 24–70 and accompanying texts below. In this paper I use the term 'refugee claim' to cover requests made for protection against deportation to face persecution (i.e. meaning that the refugee claimant is already present in the host state). The term thus covers, for example, what would be considered 'refugee claims' in Canada, as well as what are termed applications for 'asylum' or for 'withholding of removal' in the United States. The issue of requests for

refugee protection or resettlement made from outside host states is beyond the scope of this paper.

12. See generally Judith Butler, *Bodies that Matter: On the Discursive Limits of 'Sex'* (New York: Routledge, 1993), 223–42; Francisco Valdes, 'Queers, Sissies, Dykes, and Tomboys: Deconstructing the Conflation of "Sex", "Gender" and "Sexual Orientation" in Euro-American Law and Society', *California Law Review* 83 (1995): 1; Elivra Arriola, 'Law and the Gendered Politics of Identity: Who Owns the Label "Lesbian"?', *Hastings Women's Law Journal* 8 (1997): 1; Sonia Katyal, 'Exporting Identity', *Yale Journal of Law & Feminism* 14 (2002): 97.

13. For an excellent overview of debates over these terms in sexual minority communities, see 'Symposium on Linguistic Creativity in LGBT Discourse', *World Englishes* 17 (2002): 187.

14. Terms that aim at broad inclusivity – including, for example, 'queer', MSM, and WSW – are frequently critiqued along these lines. See, e.g., Viviane Namaste, *Sex Change, Social Change: Reflections on Identity, Institutions, and Imperialism* (Toronto: Women's Press, 2005), 21 ('"Queer" is quite specific to Anglo-American locations'); Rebecca Young and Ilan Meyer, 'The Trouble with "MSM" and "WSW": Erasure of the Sexual-Minority Person in Public Heath Discourse', *American Journal of Public Health* 95 (2004): 1144.

15. Valdes, 'Queers, Sissies, Dykes, and Tomboys', 161–212.

16. Nancy Knauer, 'Gender Matters: Making the Case for Trans Inclusion', *Pierce Law Review* 6 (2007): 1 ('Lesbian and gay advocacy organizations officially began to incorporate transgender issues in the late 1990s, as signalled by the now ubiquitous "T" that appears at the end of the popular acronym "LGBT". However, the resulting alliance has been an uneasy one and the incorporation has been partial.')

17. See, e.g., Gilbert Herdt, 'Bisexuality and the Causes of Homosexuality: The Case of the Sambia', in *Bisexualities: The Ideology and Practice of Sexual Conduct with Both Men and Women*, ed. Erin Haeberle and Rolf Gindorf (New York: Continuum, 1998), 164 ('Sambia do not have a noun category either for *homosexual* or for *heterosexual*. They do not recognize in their history or culture that someone can be exclusively homosexual in partner selection, or exclusively heterosexual'). See also Sebastian Maguire, 'The Human Rights of Sexual Minorities in Africa', *California Women's International Law Journal* 35 (2004): 1.

18. Throughout this paper I refer to 'hetero-normative' persecution. I choose this terminology, rather than the more common 'homophobic' persecution, as it emphasises that the persecution participates in enforcing compulsory heterosexuality, and is not merely a persecutory reaction to an unpopular minority. Also, 'hetero-normative' persecution is a general term that (partly) encompasses other more specific forms of persecution targeting particular sexual minorities, including homophobia, bi-phobia, trans-phobia, etc.

19. The term, thus, covers not only homosexual, lesbian, bisexual, transsexual, and intersexed individuals, but also others who may be mistreated on the basis of their sexual identity or sexual behaviour. For example, one could argue that the term includes (but is not limited to) sex workers, adulterers, swingers, polyamorists, and sado-masochists. For a discussion of the applicability of international refugee law to some of these sexual minorities, see, e.g., Kristen Walker, 'New Uses of the Refugees Convention: Sexuality and Refugee Status', in *The Refugees Convention 50 Years On*, ed. Susan Kneebone (Aldershot: Ashgate, 2003), 251, 273–7.

20. For an excellent review on debates over the term 'bisexuality' see Kenji Yoshino, 'The Epistemic Contract of Bisexual Erasure', *Stanford Law Review* 52 (2000): 370.

21. Katyal, 'Exporting Identity', 153.

22. In the literature on bisexuality, these individuals are sometimes referred to as 'defence bisexuals': Yoshino, 'The Epistemic Contract of Bisexual Erasure', 371–2.

23. By phrasing my definition this way, I also hope to circumvent the unfortunate binary evoked by the term 'bisexuality', which problematically implies that all people fall into one of two (and only two) genders or sexes. For a critique of binary understandings of gender, see Kate Bornstein, *Gender Outlaw: On Men, Women and the Rest of Us* (New York: Vintage Books, 1994).

24. UNHCR, *Guidelines on International Protection: Gender-Related Persecution within the Context of Article 1A(2) of the 1951 Convention and/or its 1967 Protocol Relating to the Status of Refugees*, UN Doc. HCR/GIP/02/01, 7 May 2002; reproduced in *International Journal of Refugee Law* 14 (2002): 457, paras 15–16. See also James Hathaway, *The Law of Refugee Status* (Toronto: Butterworths, 1991), 163; Jenni Millbank, 'Imagining Otherness:

Refugee Claims on the Basis of Sexuality in Canada and Australia', *Melbourne University Law Review* 26 (2002): 149.

25. 189 UNTS 150, entered into force on 22 April 1954.

26. Ibid., Art.1.A(2) (emphasis added).

27. Erik Ramanathan, 'Queer Cases: A Comparative Analysis of Global Sexual Orientation-Based Asylum Jurisprudence', *Georgetown Immigration Law Journal* 11 (1996): 26.

28. See, e.g., *C.Y.T. (Re)* [1998] CRDD No. 186.

29. Guy Goodwin-Gill and Jane McAdam, *The Refugee in International Law*, 3rd edn (Oxford: Oxford University Press, 2007), 87.

30. UNHCR, *Guidelines on International Protection*, para. 32. For a discussion arguing that gender norm non-compliance is often at the root of persecution experienced by sexual minorities, see Nicole LaViolette, 'Gender-Related Refugee Claims: Expanding the Scope of the Canadian Guidelines', *International Journal of Refugee Law* 19 (2007): 169.

31. Chris Kendall, 'Lesbian and Gay Refugees in Australia: Now that "Acting Discreetly" is No Longer an Option, will Equality be Forthcoming?', *International Journal of Refugee Law* 15 (2003): 718. See also LaViolette, 'Gender-Related Refugee Claims'.

32. See, e.g., International Covenant on Civil and Political Rights, Art. 23(1): 'The family is the natural and fundamental group union of society and is entitled to protection by society and the state.' For a discussion of the heterosexual nature of the types of families recognised under international law, see Kristen Walker, 'Capitalism, Gay Identity and International Human Rights Law', *Australasian Gay and Lesbian Law Journal* 9 (2000): 58, 68–70.

33. Nicole LaViolette, 'The Immutable Refugees: Sexual Orientation in *Canada (A.G.)* v. *Ward*', *University of Toronto Faculty of Law Review* 55 (1997): 29; Kristen Walker, 'Sexuality and Refugee Status in Australia', *International Journal of Refugee Law* 12 (2000): 178; Ramanathan, 'Queer Cases', 26.

34. For a general discussion of the possibilities of framing hetero-normative violence as persecution on account of religion, see Jeffrey Redding, 'Human Rights and Homo-sectuals: The International Politics of Sexuality, Religion, and Law', *Northwestern University Journal of International Human Rights* 4 (2005): 436.

35. UNHCR, *Guidelines on International Protection*, para. 25 (emphasis added).

36. For a persuasive analysis that draws on the UNHCR *Guidelines* to argue that persecution on grounds of religion is an appropriate category through which to assess refugee claims involving repressive gender norms, regardless of the actual religious beliefs of refugee claimants, see Karen Musalo, 'Claims for Protection Based on Religion or Belief', *International Journal of Refugee Law* 16 (2004): 212.

37. See generally LaViolette, 'Gender-Related Refugee Claims', 169–214.

38. Ibid., 202.

39. The UNHCR *Guidelines* note, however, that in such states persecution targeting those who fail to conform to repressive religious norms may be taken as persecution on grounds of religion or as persecution on grounds of political opinion: UNHCR, *Guidelines on International Protection*, para. 26.

40. Arwen Swink, 'Queer Refuge: A Review of the Role of Country Condition Analysis in Asylum Adjudications for Members of Sexual Minorities', *Hastings International and Comparative Law Review* 29 (2006): 254; Walker, 'Sexuality and Refugee Status in Australia', 178 esp. n. 9.

41. *Ward* v. *Canada* [1993] 2 SCR 689. See also Goodwin-Gill and McAdam, *The Refugee in International Law*, 10 (identifying *Ward* as 'one of the leading "social group" cases'); Walker, 'New Uses of the Refugees Convention', 265–6 (discussing the importance of *Ward* in the development of international refugee law).

42. *Ward* v. *Canada*, 739. Note that this definition was drawn in part from an earlier United States Board of Immigration Appeals decision, *Matter of Acosta*, 19 I & N Dec. 211 (BIA 1985), 233.

43. *Ward*, ibid.

44. Ibid.

45. *Hernandez-Montiel* v. *I.N.S.*, 225 F.3d 1084 (9th Cir., 2000), 1093; *Islam* v. *Secretary of State for the Home Department Immigration Appeal Tribunal and Another* [1999] UKHL 20.

46. UNHCR, *Guidelines on International Protection: 'Membership of a Particular Social Group' within the Context of Article 1A(2) of the 1951 Convention and/or Its 1967 Protocol Relating to the Status of Refugees*, HCR/GIP/02/02, 7 May 2002, para. 6.

47. See, e.g., LaViolette, 'The Immutable Refugees'; Walker, 'Sexuality and Refugee Status in Australia', 209.

48. *Ward* v. *Canada*, 739.

49. UNHCR, *Guidelines on International Protection*, para. 11.

50. Ibid. See also European Union Council Directive 2004/83/ED of DATE April 2004, ch. 3, Art.10.1(d): 'a group shall be considered to form a particular social group where in particular ... members of that group share ... a characteristic or belief that is so fundamental to identity or conscience that a person should not be forced to renounce it'.

51. See, e.g., John Bailey, Michael Dunne, and Nicholas Martin, 'Genetic and Environmental Influences on Sexual Orientation and its Correlates in an Australian Twin Sample', *Journal of Personality and Social Psychology* 78 (2000): 524. For a general review of literature in social sciences on the 'causes' of sexual orientation, see Simon LeVay, *Queer Science: The Use and Abuse of Research into Homosexuality* (Cambridge, MA: MIT Press, 1996).

52. Julianne Serovich, Shonda Craft, Paula Toviessi, Rashmi Gangamma, Tiffany McDowell, and Erika Grafsky, 'A Systematic Review of the Research Based on Sexual Reorientation Therapy', *Journal of Marital and Family Therapy* 34 (2008): 227 (noting that conversion therapy aims 'to "cure" homosexuals by transforming them into heterosexuals').

53. For a discussion of conversion therapy, see Robert Spitzer, 'Can Some Gay Men and Lesbians Change their Sexual Orientation? 200 Participants Reporting a Change from Homosexual to Heterosexual Orientation', *Archives of Sexual Behavior* 32 (2003): 403; contra, Kenneth Cohen and Ritch Savin-Williams, 'Are Converts to be Believed? Assessing Sexual Orientation "Conversions"', *Archives of Sexual Behavior* 32 (2003): 427; Gregory Herek, 'Evaluating Interventions to Alter Sexual Orientation: Methodological and Ethical Considerations', *Archives of Sexual Behavior* 32 (2003): 438.

54. Lee Beckstead, 'Cures Versus Choices: Agendas in Sexual Reorientation Therapy', *Journal of Gay and Lesbian Psychotherapy* 5 (2001): 88.

55. For an excellent review of 'social constructivist' scholarship challenging the view of sexual orientation as immutable, see Edward Stein, ed., *Forms of Desire: Sexual Orientation and the Social Constructivist Controversy* (New York: Routledge, 1992). See also Michel Foucault, *The History of Sexuality, Volume I: An Introduction* (New York: Pantheon, 1978).

56. Janet Halley, 'Sexual Orientation and the Politics of Biology: A Critique of the Argument from Immutability', *Stanford Law Review* 46 (1994): 503; Butler, *Bodies that Matter*; Brenda Cossman, 'Sexuality, Queer Theory, and "Feminism after": Reading and Rereading the Sexual Subject', *McGill Law Journal* 49 (2004): 847.

57. Nancy Knauer, 'Science, Identity, and the Construction of the Gay Political Narrative', *Law & Sexuality* 12 (2003): 6.

58. *Ward* v. *Canada*, 739: 'The meaning assigned to "particular social group" in the Act should take into account the general underlying themes of the defence of human rights and anti-discrimination that form the basis for the international refugee protection initiative.'

59. Yoshino, 'The Epistemic Contract of Bisexual Erasure', 405.

60. Ibid.

61. Adrienne Rich, 'Compulsory Heterosexuality and Lesbian Existence', *Signs* 5 (1980): 631.

62. For an argument that hetero-normative persecution is best understood as targeting non-compliance with gender norms, see Kendall, 'Lesbian and Gay Refugees in Australia'.

63. See generally Halley, 'Sexual Orientation and the Politics of Biology'.

64. *Hernandez-Montiel* v. *I.N.S.*

65. The court explicitly cited *Ward* and adopted Justice La Forest's definition of 'particular social groups': ibid., 1093, n. 6. In adopting the Canadian definition the court resolved a previous conflict in American refugee law over whether 'particular social groups' had to involve voluntary association (*Sanchez-Trujillo* v. *INS*, 801 F.2d 1571 (9th Cir. 1986), 1576) or immutable characteristics (*Matter of Acosta*, 19 I. & N. Dec. 211 (BIA 1985), 233).

66. *Hernandez-Montiel* v. *I.N.S.*, 1093.

67. See, e.g., *A* v. *Minister for Immigration and Ethnic Affairs* (1997) 142 ALR 331; *S395/2002 and S396/2002* v. *Minister for Immigration and Multicultural Affairs* (2003) ALR 112.

68. *Refugee Appeal No. 1312/93* (30 August 1995); *Refugee Appeal No. 74665/03* (7 July 2004).

69. Canada is an outlier in this regard. However, there is some support for a shift in this direction to be found in Canadian constitutional jurisprudence on sexual minority rights, particularly in decisions by Supreme Court Justice L'Heureux-Dubé. See, e.g., *Egan* v. *Canada* [1995] 2

SCR 513, per L'Heureux-Dubé J., dissenting (esp. para. 89); *Vriend* v. *Alberta* [1998] 1 SCR 493, per L'Heureux-Dubé J., concurring (esp. para. 186); *Trinity Western University* v. *British Columbia College of Teachers* [2001] 1 SCR 772, per L'Heureux-Dubé J., dissenting (esp. para. 69).

70. There are, in fact, other areas of sexual minority refugee law where rigid understandings of human sexuality continue to influence refugee jurisprudence notwithstanding the dominance of the fundamental human dignity approach. Jenni Millbank, for example, argues that the frequently criticised requirement in the refugee jurisprudence of some jurisdictions – including the United Kingdom – that sexual minorities must try to avoid persecution in violently hetero-normative societies by being 'discreet' is connected to a rigid understanding of human sexuality as a matter that is inherently or 'naturally' private: 'A Preoccupation with Perversion: The British Response to Refugee Claims on the Basis of Sexual Orientation 1989–2003', *Social & Legal Studies* 14 (2005): 115.

71. *BDK (Re)* [2000] CRDD No. 72.

72. Ibid., para. 8.

73. Ibid., paras 2–3.

74. Ibid., para. 7.

75. Sean Rehaag, 'Patrolling the Borders of Sexual Orientation: Bisexual Refugee Claims in Canada', *McGill Law Journal* 53 (2008): 59, 76.

76. Ibid, 69, 76–7.

77. Millbank, 'Imagining Otherness', 149.

78. RSC, 1985, c. A-1.

79. Immigration and Refugee Protection Act, SC 2001, c. 27, s. 170(b).

80. The full data are available online: Sean Rehaag, 'New Refugee Claim Data & IRB Member Grant Rates', http://www.ccrweb.ca/documents/rehaagdata.htm (accessed 1 November 2008). For a description of the methodology used to acquire and compile the data, as well as for a description of the limits to the data set, see Sean Rehaag, 'Troubling Patterns in Canadian Refugee Adjudication', *Ottawa Law Review* 39 (2008): 335.

81. In addition to cases involving gay men, lesbians, and bisexuals, there were nine sexual minority decisions that the Immigration and Refugee Board placed in a category labelled 'Other'. The grant rate in these cases was 56%.

82. Rehaag, 'Patrolling the Borders of Sexual Orientation', 70–1.

83. For a fuller discussion of bisexual refugee claims in Canada, see ibid., 59–102.

84. *Hernandez-Montiel* v. *I.N.S.*, 1093.

85. Jin Park, 'Pink Asylum: Political Asylum Eligibility of Gay Men and Lesbians under U.S. Immigration Policy', *UCLA Law Review* 42 (1995): 1115, n. 5: 'asylum claims based on bisexuality do not appear to be common'.

86. *Ford* v. *Bureau of Immigration and Customs Enforcement's Interim Field Office Dir. for Det. and Removal*, 294 F. Supp. 2d 655 (3d Cir. Pa., 2005), 656–7: 'Petitioner describes himself as bi-sexual with a greater homosexual inclination.'

87. *In Re: Jesus-Jimenez Rodriguez*, 2007 WL 1676897 (BIA, 24 April 2007), No. A71922463.

88. Ibid.

89. For general information about asylum grant rates in the United States, see Jaya Ramji-Nogales, Andrew Schoenholtz, and Philip Schrag, 'Refugee Roulette: Disparities in Asylum Adjudication', *Stanford Law Review* 60 (2007): 295.

90. As of the time of writing, the Asylum Documentation Program is no longer part of the International Gay and Lesbian Human Rights Commission. The Program has now joined the Heartland Alliance (National Immigration Justice Center).

91. The data were produced using a search through the Program database performed by the author at the Program office in San Francisco on 24 September 2007. It should be noted that in addition to the figures presented, the Program also assisted a significant number of refugee claimants (i.e. applicants for asylum or withholding of removal) whose cases raised issues related to transgender oppression or persecution targeting HIV-positive individuals.

92. Dusty Araujo, Asylum Documentation Coordinator, ADP, personal correspondence dated 24 January 2008 (on file with author).

93. *A* v. *Minister for Immigration and Ethnic Affairs*, 390.

94. *S395/2002 and S396/2002*, 126.

95. *VRAW and VRAX* v. *Minister for Immigration and Multicultural and Indigenous Affairs* [2004] FCA 1133, para. 1.

96. Jenni Millbank, 'Gender, Sex and Visibility in Refugee Claims on the Basis of Sexual Orientation', *Georgetown Immigration Law Journal* 18 (2003): 71. See also Catherine Dauvergne and Jenni Millbank, 'Burdened by Proof: How the Australian Refugee Review Tribunal Has Failed Lesbian and Gay Asylum Seekers', *Federal Law Review* 31 (2003): 299.

97. Millbank, 'Gender, Sex and Visibility in Refugee Claims on the Basis of Sexual Orientation', 73, n. 11.

98. *RRT Reference: N95/07313* [1997] RRTA 2438 (27 June 1997); *RRT Reference: N97/15882* [1997] RRTA 3396 (5 September 1997).

99. Millbank, 'Gender, Sex and Visibility in Refugee Claims on the Basis of Sexual Orientation', 93, n. 98.

100. Ibid.

101. Ibid.

102. *RRT Reference: V97/06483* [1998] RRTA 27 (5 January 1998).

103. *RRT Reference: V98/09111* [1999] RRTA 418 (22 February 1999).

104. Millbank, 'Gender, Sex and Visibility in Refugee Claims on the Basis of Sexual Orientation', 73, n. 14.

105. Ibid., 75, n. 19.

106. See, e.g., *RRT Reference: V02/14641* [2004] RRTA 351 (7 May 2004); *RRT Reference: 061020474* [2007] RRTA 25 (7 February 2007).

107. See, e.g., *VRAW and VRAX* v. *Minister for Immigration and Multicultural and Indigenous Affairs*; *SZAKD* v. *Minister for Immigration* [2004] FMCA 78.

108. For examples of negative Australian decisions involving bisexuals, see, e.g., *SZJSL* v. *Minister for Immigration and Multicultural Affairs and Another* [2007] FMCA 313 (19 February 2007); *SZGNJ* v. *Minister for Immigration and Multicultural and Indigenous Affairs and Another* [2006] FMCA 91 (24 February 2006); *SZEHT* v. *Minister for Immigration and Multicultural and Indigenous Affairs* [2005] FCA 1468 (7 October 2005); *SZENG and Another* v. *Minister for Immigration and Multicultural and Indigenous Affairs and Another* [2005] FMCA 1435 (29 September 2005); *SZEOE* v. *Minister for Immigration and Multicultural and Indigenous Affairs* [2005] FCA 694 (31 May 2005); *RRT Reference: N03/45936* [2003] RRTA 709 (31 July 2003); *RRT Reference: N01/37929* [2003] RRTA 567 (20 June 2003); *RRT Reference: N01/38642* [2003] RRTA 285 (31 March 2003); *RRT Reference: N01/36734* [2002] RRTA 898 (8 October 2002).

109. For an example of a refugee law scholar who has addressed bisexuality in some detail, see Walker, 'Sexuality and Refugee Status in Australia', 187–8.

110. See, e.g., LaViolette, 'Gender-Related Refugee Claims'; Victoria Nelson, 'Homosexual or Female? Applying Gender-Based Asylum Jurisprudence to Lesbian Asylum Claims', *Stanford Law and Policy Review* 16 (2005): 417; Swink, 'Queer Refuge'; Millbank, 'Gender, Sex and Visibility in Refugee Claims on the Basis of Sexual Orientation'; Dauvergne and Millbank, 'Burdened by Proof'.

111. See esp. Millbank, 'Gender, Sex and Visibility in Refugee Claims on the Basis of Sexual Orientation'.

112. See, e.g., Clare Hemmings, *Bisexual Spaces: A Geography of Sexuality and Gender* (New York: Routledge, 2002), 82–90; Robyn Ochs, 'Biphobia: It Goes More than Two Ways', in *Bisexuality: The Psychology and Politics of an Invisible Minority*, ed. Beth Firestein (Thousand Oaks, CA: Sage, 1996), 225; Ruth Colker, *Hybrid: Bisexuals, Multiracials and Other Misfits under American Law* (New York: New York University Press, 1996), 15–21; Naomi Mezey, 'Dismantling the Wall: Bisexuality and the Possibilities of Sexual Identity Classification Based on Acts', *Berkeley Women's Law Journal* 10 (1995): 98.

113. Yoshino, 'The Epistemic Contract of Bisexual Erasure'; Halley, 'Sexual Orientation and the Politics of Biology'.

114. 'The Epistemic Contract of Bisexual Erasure', 402–4.

115. John Gagnon, Cathy Greenblat, and Michael Kimmel, 'Bisexuality: A Sociological Perspective', in *Bisexualities: The Ideology and Practice of Sexual Conduct with Both Men and Women*, ed. Erin Haeberle and Rolf Gindorf (New York: Continuum, 1998), 88.

116. Yoshino, 'The Epistemic Contract of Bisexual Erasure', 404–10.

117. Ibid., 407.

118. For an example of an essentialist approach to constitutional sexual minority rights jurisprudence in Canada, see e.g., *Egan* v. *Canada*, 528 (holding that sexual orientation is a constitutionally prohibited ground of discrimination because sexual orientation 'is a deeply personal characteristic that is either unchangeable or changeable only at unacceptable personal costs'). For a persuasive critique of this aspect of *Egan*, see Robert Leckey, 'Chosen Discrimination', *Supreme Court Law Review (2d)* 18 (2002): 445. For a discussion of the role of essentialist arguments in United States constitutional equality jurisprudence involving sexual minorities, see Halley, 'Sexual Orientation and the Politics of Biology'; Kari Balog, 'Equal Protection for Homosexuals: Why the Immutability Argument is Necessary and How it is Met', *Cleveland State Law Review* 53 (2006): 545; Yoshino, 'The Epistemic Contract of Bisexual Erasure', 405.

119. Michael Kirby, 'Sexuality and Australian Law', *Journal of Homosexuality* 48, nos 3–4 (2005): 31, 33.

120. Ibid., 32. See also note 93 and accompanying text above.

121. Yoshino, 'The Epistemic Contract of Bisexual Erasure', 401–2.

122. Joan, 'This Is Me', in *Bisexual Horizon*, ed. Sharon Rose and Cris Stevens (London: Lawrence & Wishart, 1996), 142: '[Bisexuality] is obviously a part of me, how nature made me, and there's no use in trying to fight against it.'

123. Gagnon et al., 'Bisexuality', 99; Simon Scott, 'Politically Bi', in Rose and Stevens, *Bisexual Horizon*, 236.

124. Liz Highleyman, 'Thoughts of a Bisexual Anarchist', in Rose and Stevens, *Bisexual Horizon*, 271.

125. Marie King, 'It Could Be Either', in Rose and Stevens, *Bisexual Horizon*, 105.

126. Dave Matteson, 'Bisexual Feminist Man', in *Bi Any Other Name: Bisexual People Speak Out*, ed. Loraine Hutchins and Lani Kaahumanu (Boston, Alyson, 1991), 47.

127. Starhawk, 'The Sacredness of Pleasure', in *Bisexual Politics: Theories, Queries & Visions*, ed. Naomi Tucker (New York: Hawthorne Press, 1995), 327.

128. Yoshino, 'The Epistemic Contract of Bisexual Erasure', 428–9.

129. This phenomenon goes some distance towards explaining the infrequent references to bisexuality by the human rights tribunals and organisations noted at the beginning of the paper. See notes 2–10 above and accompanying text.

130. *RRT Reference: N95/07313.*

131. Ibid.

132. Ibid. (emphasis added).

133. Ibid.

134. Ibid.

135. *Alternor* v. *Canada*, 2008 FC 570, [2008] FCJ No. 731.

136. *RPD File No. TA6-12910* (18 July 2007) (on file with author), overturned by *Alternor* v. *Canada* (emphasis added). The author would like to thank Richard Odeleye for providing a copy of the decision.

137. Elias Farajajé-Jones, 'Fluid Desire: Race, HIV/AIDS and Bisexual Politics', in *Bisexual Politics: Theories, Queries & Visions*, ed. Naomi Tucker (New York: Hawthorne Press, 1995), 119–20. See also Kirsten McLean, 'Negotiating (Non)Monogamy: Bisexuality and Intimate Relationships', in *Current Research on Bisexuality*, ed. Ronald Fox (Binghamton, NY: Harrington Park Press, 2004), 85; Amanda Udis-Kessler, 'Challenging the Stereotypes', in *Bisexual Horizon*, ed. Sharon Rose and Cris Stevens (London: Lawrence & Wishart, 1996), 45–57 esp. 50.

138. *K.O.C. (Re)* [2003] RPDD No. 420, 11.

139. *Gyorgyjakab* v. *Canada (Minister of Citizenship and Immigration)* [2004] RPDD No. 698, 43.

140. Colker, *Hybrid*, 28.

141. William Burleson, *Bi America: Myths, Truths and Struggles of an Invisible Community* (New York: Harrington Park Press, 2005), 45.

142. Felicity Cade, 'Marriage and Bisexuality', in *Bisexual Horizon*, ed. Sharon Rose and Cris Stevens (London: Lawrence & Wishart, 1996), 114: 'I am a happily married bisexual feminist with other lovers of both genders, and playmates whose gender I would not dare to predict.'

143. See generally Annie Murray, 'Forsaking All Others: A Bifeminist Discussion of Compulsory Monogamy', in *Bisexual Politics: Theories, Queries & Visions*, ed. Naomi Tucker (New York: Hawthorne Press, 1995), 293; Burleson, *Bi America*, 119–23.

144. Rifka Reichler, 'A Question of Invisibility', in *Bi Any Other Name: Bisexual People Speak Out*, ed. Loraine Hutchins and Lani Kaahumanu (Boston, Alyson, 1991), 77.
145. This case was upheld on judicial review: *SZJSL* v. *Minister for Immigration and Multicultural Affairs and Another.*
146. Ibid.
147. *RRT Reference: N05/50659* [2005] RRTA 207 (17 May 2005) (emphasis added).
148. Millbank, 'Gender, Sex and Visibility in Refugee Claims on the Basis of Sexual Orientation', 93.

Independent human rights documentation and sexual minorities: an ongoing challenge for the Canadian refugee determination process

Nicole LaViolette

Faculty of Law, University of Ottawa, Canada

Sexual minorities must meet the same evidentiary burden as all other refugee claimants. Independent country information produced by international human rights organisations plays an important role in meeting this burden. However, in the case of gay, lesbian, bisexual, and transgender claimants, existing country documentation still fails to provide the kind of information refugees need to support their claims. This is due to the continual struggle of human rights organisations to properly document abuses against sexual minorities. Also, the legal questions most relevant to claims based on sexual orientation and gender identity have shifted over the last 15 years. Early cases turned on whether a claimant's fear of persecution was well founded or whether the claimants were able to prove their sexual orientation. Recent cases have focused on the distinction between persecution and discrimination, the availability of state protection, and possible regional contrasts in the treatment of sexual minorities within a country. The shift in legal issues requires evidence that is either not available or is not sufficiently focused or detailed to meet the legal requirements of the Canadian refugee determination process.

Introduction

In May 2008, Gambian President Yahya Jammeh vowed to 'cut off the head' of any homosexual found in his country and announced his intention to introduce legislation that would be 'stricter than those in Iran' with regard to same-sex sexual conduct.[1] For the third year in a row, the 2008 gay pride event in Moscow was marred by violence and municipal authorities refused to authorise the gathering.[2] In April 2008, the police raided a Kyrgyzstan centre for gay, lesbian, bisexual, and transgender communities.[3] In Jamaica, the police failed to protect individuals from a string of homophobic mob attacks that occurred in 2007 and 2008.[4] In June 2008, three Ugandan human rights defenders were arrested after they distributed a press release calling for HIV prevention programmes for members of the gay, lesbian, bisexual, and transgender communities.[5]

The events described above underscore two important facts about the persecution of sexual minorities.[6] First, the human rights situations of sexual minorities around the world continue to be alarming. Many countries maintain severe criminal penalties for consensual sex between persons of the same sex, including the death penalty.[7] Sexual minorities also are frequent targets of hate crimes.[8] In several countries, restrictions have been imposed on freedoms of expression and association of sexual minorities,[9] while in others homosexuality and transexuality are perceived as Western phenomena,[10] anti-revolutionary behaviours,[11] crimes against religion,[12] sexually deviant and immoral behaviours,[13] mental disorders,[14] or unacceptable challenges to gender-specific roles.[15]

The second conclusion to be drawn from a 2008 sample of human rights violations against sexual minorities is that international human rights organisations are now making serious efforts to document abuses against sexual minorities. Indeed, all of the incidents mentioned above were reported by mainstream human rights organisations such as Amnesty International and Human Rights Watch, as well as by organisations devoted to documenting abuses against sexual minorities such as the International Gay and Lesbian Human Rights Commission (IGLHRC). This is a relatively new development; as recently as the early 1990s, abuses against sexual minorities were rarely documented by human rights organisations.

The continued human rights violations against sexual minorities and the increased attention given by human rights organisations to such abuses are of great significance in the context of refugee law. Egregious human rights violations have led some gay, lesbian, bisexual, and transgender people to seek refuge in countries with better human rights protection. This movement has led some states to interpret international norms to extend asylum and refugee protection to women and men fleeing persecution based on their sexual orientation and gender identity. In the last 20 years, decision-makers in countries such as the United States,[16] the United Kingdom,[17] Germany,[18] New Zealand,[19] Australia,[20] Finland,[21] Belgium,[22] and the Netherlands[23] have granted refugee status to individuals who fear persecution based on their sexual orientation or gender identity.[24]

In order to support their claims for refugee status, refugees are generally required to rely on documentary evidence outlining the human rights conditions in their countries of origin. Independent country information thus plays an important role in the refugee determination process. It is used to ascertain the existence of a risk of persecution and to assess a claimant's credibility and the plausibility of the claimant's account of persecution.[25] It is therefore essential that human rights violations against sexual minorities be documented.

This paper examines a specific evidentiary problem facing women and men who make refugee claims based on sexual orientation or gender identity persecution, namely, the extent to which independent country information provides adequate and useful evidence in support of their applications. I will focus on claims submitted by sexual minorities to the Canadian refugee determination system that were adjudicated between 1991 and 2008. Canada is the first reported jurisdiction to accept refugee claims based on sexual orientation and gender identity. Until recently, its administrative tribunal was the only such body to have adjudicator training on these issues and to produce in-house human rights information on the situations of sexual minorities in different countries. As such, Canada's longstanding and comprehensive case law and experience yields interesting conclusions about the use of documentary evidence in refugee cases dealing with sexual minorities.

Two time periods are examined, as distinctive trends have emerged in Canada over the past 17 years in relation to the role of human rights documentation in claims based on sexual orientation and gender identity. I will begin by examining the evidentiary hurdles that confronted sexual minorities in the 1990s when claims were first processed in Canada. It will be seen that when claims based on sexual orientation or gender identity were first presented, both the refugee claimants and the Immigration and Refugee Board of Canada (IRB) were unable to produce what was perceived as acceptable independent country evidence on the situations of sexual minorities in the claimants' countries of origin. A review of cases in the last 10 years reveals that while some of the initial obstacles have been overcome, existing human rights documentation still fails to provide the kind of information sexual minority refugees need to support their claims. The analysis in this paper will demonstrate that problems with independent country information can translate into poor assessments in the refugee hearing room.

Refugee claims based on sexual orientation and gender identity between 1991 and 1998

The refugee determination process in Canada

a. General principles

The international community strengthened international protection for refugees following the massive displacement of populations during and after World War II.[26] The result was the codification of the rights and status of refugees in two international instruments: the 1951 UN Convention Relating to the Status of Refugees (hereinafter referred to as 'Convention'),[27] and the 1967 Protocol Relating to the Status of Refugees (hereinafter referred to as 'Protocol').[28] Canada ratified both the Convention and the Protocol in 1969 and thus accepted the main obligation that flows from the international instruments, embodied in Article 33 of the Convention, that signatory states will not return any individual to a territory where the individual's life or freedom will be threatened. In Canada, the refugee determination process is entrusted to the IRB, an independent tribunal established in 1989. The IRB's Refugee Protection Division (RPD) handles claims brought by persons seeking refugee status and determines whether claimants meet the definition of refugee. Section 96 of the Immigration and Refugee Protection Act states that a refugee is a person who fears persecution by reason of race, religion, nationality, membership in a particular social group, or political opinion, and who cannot obtain the protection of his or her country of nationality or habitual residence.[29]

The notion of persecution is at the heart of the definition of refugee. In order for the feared abuse to be deemed persecution, it must be considered sufficiently serious. Furthermore, a claimant must establish that the persecution is based on the claimant's political opinion, race, religion, nationality, or membership in a particular social group. Finally, refugee protection is conferred on the claimant only if the claimant succeeds in showing that the claimant's country of nationality or habitual residence is unwilling or unable to offer protection.[30] If any person satisfies the definition of refugee, Canada has an international obligation not to return the person to the country where the person may face persecution.[31]

It is generally understood that 'a well-founded fear of being persecuted' contains both a subjective and an objective requirement. This dual criterion was recognised in Canada in *Adjei* v. *Canada*.[32] The Federal Court of Canada held that the fear of persecution is two-fold. On the one hand, the 'fear must be present in the mind of the applicant for the definition of Convention refugee to be met'.[33] On the other hand, this subjective fear must have an objective basis, that is, the 'refugee's fear [must] be evaluated objectively to determine if there is a valid basis for that fear'.[34] It is clear that even the most fervently stated fear of persecution will not be enough if objective evidence tends to deny the existence of risk.[35] The practical result is that objective evidence of a reasonable chance of persecution is a necessary and decisive element in any refugee claim.

In order to meet the requirements of the Convention definition of refugee, a claimant must therefore present supporting evidence at the full hearing. Evidence to support a refugee claim normally consists of testimony of the claimant and general evidence of a country's human rights record. In the absence of evidence of past persecution, a claim may be established by objective evidence that 'persons similarly situated to the claimant are at risk in the state of origin'.[36] The claimant's testimony may constitute the whole of the evidence if it is 'plausible, credible and frank'.[37] Independent country information is typically drawn from governmental, non-governmental, and media reports. Evidence from witnesses, including expert witnesses, may also be introduced in the course of a claim.[38] Both the claimant and the RPD share the responsibility of fact-finding. The RPD may take judicial notice of any facts, information, or opinions within its specialised knowledge.[39] This process is assisted by the IRB's national network of publicly accessible Resource and Documentation Centres, which collect and summarise available sources of relevant information. Finally, as an administrative tribunal, the IRB is not bound by legal or technical rules of evidence.[40] The Immigration and Refugee Protection Act provides that proceedings shall be as informal and expeditious as are consistent with fair treatment.[41] The RPD may base a decision on evidence it considers credible and trustworthy in the circumstances of the particular case.[42]

b. Sexual minorities and the refugee determination process

Sexual minorities have claimed refugee status in Canada since 1991; the first reported sexual orientation claim to be decided by the IRB was dated 7 October 1991.[43] Since then, the RPD has dealt with thousands of claims based on sexual orientation and gender identity. In April 2002 *The Globe and Mail*, a major Canadian newspaper, reported that, '[i]n the past three years, nearly 2,500 people from 75 different countries have sought asylum on the basis of sexual orientation in Canada'.[44] Sean Rehaag found that the RPD decided 1351 sexual-orientation-based claims in 2004.[45] In the same study, Rehaag examines the grant rates in sexual orientation cases and concludes that 'sexual-minority refugee claims are, on average, approximately as successful as traditional refugee claims'.[46]

A review of cases reported between 1991 and 1998 reveals that the majority of sexual orientation and gender identity cases turned almost exclusively on one or a combination of three legal issues. First, when such claims were initially submitted to the RPD, adjudicators debated whether sexual minorities fit any of the grounds set out in the Convention definition of refugee.[47] This question was eventually resolved by a decision of the Supreme Court of Canada, which extended refugee status to sexual minorities primarily because of the persecution individuals feared they would be subjected to as members of a particular social group. In *Ward* v. *Canada*,[48] it was confirmed obiter that sexual orientation constitutes the basis of a particular social group as defined in the Convention.[49] Subsequently, the Federal Court of Canada found that the question of whether sexual orientation can be the basis of a claimant's membership in a particular social group 'has effectively been put beyond doubt by the decision of the Supreme Court of Canada in *Ward*'.[50] The majority of sexual minority refugees have since claimed that their fear of persecution is grounded on their membership in a particular social group, one constituted by individuals with the same sexual orientation or gender identity as their own.[51]

Second, women and men claiming to be homosexuals, bisexuals, or transgendered had to satisfy adjudicators that they were in fact members of a sexual minority.[52] Since sexual minorities claim to be members of a 'particular social group', one of the elements to be satisfied in a refugee claim based on sexual orientation or gender identity is the claimant's membership in that group.[53] Gay, lesbian, bisexual, and transgender claimants, for example, are rarely able to provide conclusive documentary or witness evidence to confirm their sexual orientations, and, therefore, the element most determinative in establishing whether the individual is a member of the particular social group is the claimant's credibility. Assessing the veracity of the claimant's sexual orientation or gender identity is a very difficult, sensitive, and complex task in the context of an administrative or quasi-judicial hearing. In particular, the very private and intimate nature of an individual's sexual orientation or gender identity poses real challenges for adjudicators, who are nonetheless required to engage with claimants about their personal lives and relationships. The RPD acknowledged in 1995 that adjudicators were struggling with this aspect of sexual minority claims.[54] In addition, claimants themselves began to provide supporting evidence of their sexual orientations, including asking their partners, families, or friends to testify at the refugee hearing;[55] providing photographs or videos of partners or activities in the gay, lesbian, bisexual, or transgender communities;[56] submitting letters or proof of membership in gay, lesbian, bisexual, and transgender organisations;[57] and presenting medical and psychological reports.[58] While a case may still turn on the issue of the claimant's sexual orientation,[59] steps have been taken to improve the quality of the inquiry in the refugee hearing room.

The third recurring issue, and the one most relevant to the present inquiry, relates to the absence or reliability of independent documentary evidence on human rights violations against sexual minorities. A refugee claimant is required to show 'a reasonable fear of future persecution through credible, direct, and specific evidence'.[60] In addition, such evidence must outline either the government's participation in the persecution of sexual minorities or the state's unwillingness or inability to provide protection from persecution performed by private actors.[61] Generally, assessments of whether a refugee claim has an objective basis are made by relying on a broad cross-section of official and non-governmental sources in addition to the testimony of the claimants themselves.

When claims based on sexual orientation and gender identity were first presented in the early 1990s, sexual minorities encountered a specific set of problems in the area of fact-finding.[62] First, in many countries, very little information was available on human rights violations against sexual minorities. Governmental and non-governmental organisations were not documenting human rights violations against sexual minorities and thus were not able to provide the independent country information necessary to prove the objective components of the definition of refugee. Second, when available information originated from gay, lesbian, bisexual, and transgender organisations, their evidence was sometimes dismissed as biased and unreliable. I will now examine both of these evidentiary problems.

Independent country information

a. Evidentiary challenges[63]

Several reasons explain the absence of documentary information on human rights violations against sexual minorities in the early 1990s. At that time, only a minority of non-governmental organisations (NGOs) were beginning to document abuses against sexual minorities. Amnesty International, one of the most prominent international human rights organisations, refused until 1991 to document abuses against sexual minorities.[64] Other prominent human rights organisations were also slow in working on behalf of sexual minorities.[65] Many more NGOs continued to maintain that the rights of homosexuals and other sexual minorities were not human rights issues at all.[66] Meanwhile, various intergovernmental institutions also demonstrated a reluctance to legitimise the rights of sexual minorities internationally by inquiring into their status. During its 50-year existence, the UN Commission on Human Rights issued only one report concerning sexual minorities.[67] The Sub-Commission on the Prevention of Discrimination and the Protection of Minorities consistently ignored calls by human rights organisations to appoint a special rapporteur to undertake a comprehensive study of discrimination against sexual minorities.[68] In 1995, the Fourth UN Conference on Women dropped any direct reference to sexual orientation in the final platform document issued from the conference.[69]

The scarcity of human rights documentation, and the serious consequences this had for claimants, was evident in many RPD decisions. In *Re R. (U.W.)*,[70] a gay man from Uruguay was unable to present to the refugee panel any documentary evidence on the treatment of sexual minorities by state officials in Uruguay. This led the panel to conclude that the documentary record did not support the fear of persecution the claimant alleged, and his request for protection was denied. A similar conclusion was reached in a case involving a gay man from Jordan,[71] in which not only did the adjudicators decide that the absence of evidence failed to support the claimant's fear of persecution, but they also considered it an indication that homosexuals as a group were *not* persecuted in Jordan. Claimants from Mexico and Brazil also failed to convince the RPD that their fears of persecution were well founded due to a lack of documentary evidence.[72]

Often, if documentary evidence on the persecution of sexual minorities was found, it was produced by gay, lesbian, bisexual, and transgender organisations that often investigated and compiled human rights documentation because of the refusal of mainstream governmental and non-governmental human rights organisations to consider the plight of sexual minorities. Juan Pablo Ordoñez, a Colombian human rights lawyer, described what a human rights ombudsman had told him: 'the moment a faggot begins hanging around my house [his] human rights are over ... I'd rather have a daughter who's a whore than a faggot son ... [If I were to have a homosexual child] I would treat him like the family dog, just like any other case from my office. I believe I love my dog more than I'd love a faggot.'[73] In Uruguay, the family of a lesbian, who was arrested by the Argentinean military and subsequently disappeared, joined an association for the relatives of disappeared persons. When the woman's sexual orientation became known, the association ignored her family and abandoned all efforts to find her.[74] In the Philippines, a lesbian working for a human rights organisation was fired when the board of directors found out about her sexual orientation.[75] The lack of interest and, in many cases, open hostility to sexual orientation and gender identity issues on the part of human rights organisations convinced many gay, lesbian, bisexual, and transgender organisations to document human rights violations themselves in order to draw international attention.

While sexual minority rights organisations were often the only source of documentary evidence, early decisions of the RPD on sexual orientation and gender identity refugee claims indicated a strong preference for materials from mainstream human rights organisations. The decision in *Re H. (Y.F.)*[76] provides a good illustration of how the absence of evidence of persecution in reports from mainstream and well-known human rights organisations impacted on claimants negatively. In that case, a gay man from Brazil claimed a well-founded fear of persecution because of his membership of a particular social group, namely homosexuals, in Brazil. Despite the presentation of documentary evidence on extra-judicial killings collected by a Brazilian sexual minority rights group, the adjudicator denied the refugee claim, stating,

> if there was a serious possibility that homosexuals, as a particular social group, had a well-founded fear of persecution because of their sexual orientation, the panel is of the opinion that one or more of the human rights publications would cite this as a concern ... [however] [t]he panel was not able to find any reference to such a concern in the recent Amnesty International Report or Human Rights Watch World Report.[77]

This view was repeated in *Re N. (L.X.)*,[78] where one of the adjudicators noted that reports from Human Rights Watch, Lawyers Committee for Human Rights, Amnesty International, and the United States State Department did not identify homosexuals as being at risk of persecution in Argentina.[79] What these decision-makers failed to acknowledge was that those organisations were not mandated to investigate violations against sexual minorities, or had only recently adopted policies to document human rights abuses and had not begun to collect information.

In other cases, the RPD found materials from sexual minority rights organisations to be lacking in credibility. For instance, in *Re N. (L.X.)*, a RPD adjudicator dismissed reports submitted by the gay claimant's counsel because '[m]ost of the documentary evidence is from gay advocacy groups or publications that would understandably highlight and possibly exaggerate the issues of the homosexual community. These publications are in my view one-sided.'[80] In *Re H. (Y.F.)*,[81] documentary evidence, which suggested that gay men, lesbians, and transvestites in Brazil were victims of systematic violence and extrajudicial killings, was dismissed. The source of the evidence was the Grupo Gay da Bahia, one of Brazil's most active sexual minority rights organisations, and the RPD refused to accept their findings as credible without corroboration from other sources such as mainstream newspapers or human rights organisations.[82] In a case involving a gay man from Pakistan, the claimant's counsel objected to the characterisation of documents submitted from sexual minority rights organisations as carrying little or no weight.[83] The panel dismissed his complaints, stating that 'it will give all documents submitted in evidence the appropriate probative weight'.[84]

Many organisations, for instance, those representing international trade unions, journalists, and religious groups, pay particular attention to human rights violations against their members and their observations are regularly accepted as evidence.[85] Often, interested human rights groups have the knowledge, expertise, and connections to best document specific kinds of persecution. This is particularly true of sexual minorities, who, as extremely marginalised members of society, are often difficult to reach. Amnesty International acknowledged this in a letter to sexual minority rights activists in which the human rights organisation stated that

> [a]s with all human rights documentation, the abuses Amnesty investigates are brought to its attention through a wide range of human rights networks. Our work in this area has developed in cooperation with both international and local gay and lesbian groups who have documented abuses by governments in many countries. The work of gay and lesbian groups has been absolutely crucial, since many mainstream human rights organizations have failed to address the violations gay men and lesbians suffer.[86]

In fact, mainstream human rights organisations were relying on sexual minority rights organisations' sources in their own work. Amnesty International's letter cited above was presented to sexual minority rights activists by representatives of the organisation at an international sexual minority conference.[87] The objective was to encourage and recruit gay men and lesbians from around the world to bring to the organisation's attention violations against sexual minorities. The evidence submitted by the claimant in the Brazilian case *Re H. (Y.F.)*[88] regarding the extrajudicial killings of more than 600 gay men, transvestites, and lesbians was included in a publication by Amnesty International (USA),[89] a clear indication that the human rights organisation found the evidence very credible. Moreover, the United States State Department used documentation from the IGLHRC in their annual reports.[90] In a letter to Canadian lawyer El-Farouk Khaki, Human Rights Watch stated that they considered the work of IGLHRC to be credible and trustworthy.[91] Without the groundbreaking work of sexual minority rights organisations, mainstream human rights organisations would have faced an even more difficult task in documenting abuses against sexual minorities.

Criticisms were directed at the RPD for failing to adequately address documentation problems. Several lawyers complained to the RPD about the difficulty in either obtaining documentation or having it deemed credible and trustworthy by refugee claims adjudicators.[92] In 1995, the Canadian Council for Refugees (CCR) adopted a policy statement in which it recommended that the RPD 'research and make widely available information on the culture and human rights status of gay men and lesbians in each part of the world from which claimants come'.[93] Moreover, the CCR specifically called on the RPD to recognise the value and expertise of both the documentation from sexual minority rights groups and the testimony of their members when they appear before the Board as expert witnesses.

b. Overcoming the problems

While the problems with documentary evidence were significant in the early 1990s, both mainstream and sexual minority rights organisations increased their efforts to uncover the most flagrant violations of the human rights of sexual minorities. In the mid- and late-1990s, several mainstream human rights organisations started to produce reports or publicly denounced human rights violations against sexual minorities, including Amnesty International,[94] the Committee to Protect Journalists,[95] the Inter-Church Committee on Human Rights in Latin America,[96] the Lawyers Committee for Human Rights (now known as Human Rights First),[97] and Human Rights Watch.[98] Moreover, as mentioned above, mainstream human rights organisations also began to collaborate with gay, lesbian, bisexual, and transgender rights groups to document human rights abuses. The collaboration produced reports that benefited from the investigative expertise of general human rights organisations and the specific knowledge and resources of groups dedicated to defending the rights of sexual minorities.[99]

The willingness of international human rights organisations to document abuses against sexual minorities translated into an increase in objective documentation available in the refugee hearing room. For example, in granting refugee status to a Cambodian gay man in 1999, the RPD commented that there was 'ample documentary evidence on human rights abuses in Cambodia' to satisfy the RPD that there was an objectively valid basis for fear of persecution.[100] In deciding a case involving a gay man from Belarus, the RPD noted that 'there is considerable evidence regarding the plight of homosexuals in Belarus'.[101]

Moreover, documentation produced by sexual minority rights organisations like IGLHRC began to be cited as reliable and credible sources in refugee claims. In fact, Amnesty International recommended that refugee tribunals and adjudicators use information gathered by sexual minority rights organisations.[102] In describing a documentary source that outlined the status of gay men and lesbians in Mexico, an adjudicator of the RPD stated, 'The panel views this article as reliable given that its author draws upon a variety of sources including reports from Amnesty International, the International Gay & Lesbian Human Rights Commission, various human rights organisations situated in Mexico, and prominent intellectuals in the field of homosexuality and gay rights within and outside Mexico.'[103] In 1995, the RPD granted refugee status to a Russian gay man by relying on reports from both Amnesty International and IGLHRC.[104] In another case, involving a lesbian from the Ukraine, the panel used an IGLHRC report on Russia as documentary evidence, stating that while the report 'does not deal specifically with the Ukraine, the Panel finds it useful by analogy'.[105] In a case involving a Chilean gay man, the claim was accepted in part because of information gathered by a Chilean sexual minority rights group and the IGLHRC.[106] In a decision involving a Bulgarian claimant, the RPD characterised the International Lesbian and Gay Association as 'a credible and trustworthy source'.[107]

In many cases, the best and most reliable sources of documentary evidence are at the local level. In addition to acknowledging international organisations like IGLHRC and the International Lesbian and Gay Association (ILGA) as important sources of information, the RPD has extended the same credibility to information from domestic groups. For instance, information provided by the Gay Enhancement Association of Trinidad and Tobago was referenced in a 1998 claim.[108] Information provided by the Lambda Legal Defense and Education Fund (LLDEF) in the United States was cited in relation to a claim brought forth by an American gay refugee claimant. LLDEF was described as 'a leading gay rights organization that has undertaken substantial research on the U.S. situation'.[109] The group was also described as an 'informed and unbiased [group] with no interest in the outcome of these proceedings'.[110]

Moreover, the RPD took some steps to overcome the difficulties it had in gathering information. The Resource and Documentation Directorate (hereinafter referred to as 'the Directorate') is responsible for meeting the needs of the RPD in 'bringing forth credible and trustworthy information relating to country conditions'.[111] It produces both country information packages and specific responses to requests for information by adjudicators. A review of materials produced by the Directorate between January 1992 and July 1995 indicated that researchers were often unable to locate information when requests for information on the issue of sexual orientation were made by the RPD.[112] Efforts were soon made to overcome this problem. General publications began to include references to the status of gay men and lesbians. For instance, a 1995 chronology of events in Iran makes several references to the criminalisation of homosexuality and the death penalty that attaches to persons convicted of same-sex sexual conduct.[113] In 1996, the division produced its first document specifically on sexual minorities, a bibliography and selection of articles on sexual orientation issues in Latin America.[114] Several more documents on sexual minorities were published in 1999 on Mexico,[115] Poland,[116] and Russia.[117] The Directorate now regularly produces information on the situations of sexual minorities in different countries.[118]

In addition, Refugee Protection Officers (RPOs) began to actively pursue documentary evidence in specific cases. In the Canadian refugee determination process, the RPO assists the refugee determination process by ensuring that all relevant information is laid before the decision-maker responsible for deciding a claim. In a 1999 claim, the adjudicator deciding a case involving a Colombian lesbian noted that the refugee claims officer (RCO) (as they were then called) was of great assistance to the panel and it was '[t]hanks mainly to the tireless efforts of the RCO ... [that] new material was obtained on the situation of lesbians in Columbia'.[119] The material gathered included 'information on the treatment of lesbians by Colombian state authorities and the general public, and on the protection available to lesbians who are physically and/or sexually abused'.[120] In addition, the officer was able to obtain specific information on sexual minority rights groups by communicating directly with activists in Colombia.[121] Evidence produced by RPOs, often gathered from direct communication with NGOs, has also been determinative in other cases.[122]

Documentary evidence in refugee claims based on sexual orientation and gender identity was also an issue addressed in the course of professional development training for RPD adjudicators.[123] The first such training was held in 1995. The IRB specifically requested that the availability and reliability of independent country information on sexual minorities be addressed in the training sessions. An important section of the presentation therefore dealt with these issues.[124] The training sessions examined the human rights work done by both mainstream and sexual minority rights organisations, and it is suggested by some commentators that they have had an impact on the quality of decisions made in the refugee hearing room.[125]

Finally, the difficulty in documenting human rights violations in some countries is at times overcome through a claimant's own evidence. Indeed, the RPD can adduce from the claimant's testimony the information it requires to determine the issue of 'well-founded fear'. In fact, as long as the claimant's testimony is 'plausible, credible and frank, it may constitute the whole of the evidence of objective risk'.[126] In the case of a gay Pakistani claimant, the three-member panel stated that 'the panel reasons that this claimant in the circumstances that led to his flight from Pakistan has told a plausible story which, in the absence of contrary evidence, can be regarded by the panel as trustworthy evidence'.[127] The Federal Court of Appeal has stated that when an 'applicant swears to the truth of certain allegations, this creates a presumption that those allegations are true unless there is reason to doubt their truthfulness'.[128]

Refugee claims based on sexual orientation and gender identity between 1998 and 2008

The preceding discussion has attempted to demonstrate how sexual minority refugee claimants were at a disadvantage when claims were first made in the 1990s. The situation changed quickly as mainstream human right organisations expanded their mandates to include the investigation of discrimination and persecution against sexual minorities. In addition, documentation from sexual minority rights organisations was increasingly regarded as a credible source of information for the refugee determination process in Canada. Finally, the IRB took constructive steps to overcome the problems they encountered in finding documentation. The Board showed a willingness to train decision-makers on the specific nature of evidentiary issues in claims based on sexual orientation or gender identity.

These developments translated into significant progress. Nevertheless, while the developments described above allowed many gay and lesbian refugee claimants to provide some supporting evidence of their well-founded fear of persecution by the late 1990s, documentary challenges remain to this day.

Ongoing problems with the availability of independent country documentation

In 2003, Catherine Dauvergne and Jenni Millbank examined the use of independent evidence in refugee cases based on sexual orientation in both the Canadian and Australian refugee determination processes. Information from human rights organisations such as Amnesty International was referred to in 29% of cases while documentation from groups dedicated to the human rights of sexual minorities was used in 14% of cases.[129] Clearly, the availability of independent country information in 2003 had improved in comparison to the early and mid 1990s.

In addition, an increasing number of mainstream NGOs have expanded their mandates to include the protection of sexual minorities. For instance, International Service for Human Rights and the International Commission of Jurists convened a meeting in 2006 in Yogyakarta, Indonesia, which 'brought together UN experts and others to develop a set of Principles outlining the application of international law to human rights based on sexual orientation and gender identity'.[130] New NGOs have been established: ARC International has been working since 2003 with UN agencies to push for increased attention to violations of the human rights of sexual minorities.[131] UN Special Rapporteurs are increasingly integrating sexual orientation and gender identity issues in their reports.[132] In 2004, the United Nations Commission on Human Rights adopted a 'Resolution on Extra-judicial, Summary or Arbitrary Executions' which called on states to 'investigate promptly and thoroughly all killings committed in the name of passion or in the name of honour, all killings committed for any discriminatory reason, including sexual orientation'.[133] ILGA reports that 'there are altogether 60 countries that have publicly supported sexual orientation as an issue at the United Nations Commission on Human Rights/Human Rights Council since 2003'.[134]

Nevertheless, the extent to which international human rights organisations are able to uncover worldwide abuses against sexual minorities is still limited. Louise Arbour, then UN High Commissioner for Human Rights, declared in 2006 that '[b]ecause of the stigma attached to issues surrounding sexual orientation and gender identity, violence against LGBT persons is frequently unreported, undocumented, and goes ultimately unpunished. Rarely does it provoke public debate and outrage. This shameful silence is the ultimate rejection of the fundamental principle of universality of rights.'[135] An Australian report also describes the current situation:

> Although progress has been made in the past ten years, mainstream organisations continue to struggle to properly document human rights abuses against sexual minorities. Amnesty International highlights that state persecution on the basis of sexual orientation may often be hidden in vaguely-worded charges, such as 'participation in a corrupt gathering' or 'harming others', as has been the case in Iran and Saudi Arabia. Persecution by non-state actors may be even more difficult to document, particularly where directed at women whose stories may be more difficult to access. Examples of this type of persecution include 'therapeutic' practices to 'cure' homosexuality, domestic violence and honour killings.[136]

Clearly, significant barriers continue to prevent the documentation of human rights violations against sexual minorities. This in turn translates into a scarcity of information that can be used to support refugee claims. For instance, the IRB's Research and Documentation Directorate still cannot locate independent country information when requested to do so by the RPD. In a 2007 response to a request for information about Mongolia, the Directorate stated that '[u]p-to-date information on the treatment of homosexuals by authorities and society in general was scarce among the sources consulted by the Research Directorate'.[137] In responding to a request for information about the treatment of homosexuals in the Turkish military, the Directorate relied on a handful of limited sources and admitted that 'additional and more recent information ... could not be found'.[138]

Amnesty International and Human Rights Watch have made sexual orientation and gender identity serious concerns and both organisations publish reports and news releases documenting human rights abuses against sexual minorities. Nevertheless, neither organisation is able to produce information about all countries. Moreover, only a fraction of situations, often the most egregious, make it into their documentation. While both organisations have fully integrated issues related to sexual orientation and gender identity into their overall work, detailed country reports devoted exclusively to human rights violations against sexual minorities are infrequently released.[139] Moreover, the reports that are produced may not investigate countries from which significant numbers of gay men, lesbians, bisexuals, and transgender persons are fleeing. The RPD has dealt with a considerable number of Mexican gay, lesbian, bisexual, and transgender claimants,[140] yet neither Amnesty International nor Human Rights Watch has released a current report on the human rights conditions for sexual minorities in Mexico.

Even NGOs exclusively dedicated to documenting human rights violations against sexual minorities have limited abilities to investigate and publish information. The IGLHRC has published country reports but many of these are now outdated.[141] The most recent country or regional report was published in 2003.[142] Shorter 'action alerts' about human rights developments in different regions and countries are posted on the IGLHRC website but information on many pages appears outdated, suggesting limited resources.[143] ILGA published an annual report of state-sponsored homophobia in 2008 which provides a survey of states with legislation criminalising consensual sexual acts between persons of the same sex.[144] Yet the report is not able to provide any specific information about the ways in which the laws are applied, the number of prosecutions, or the overall repressive impact of the criminal prohibitions. This would require resources and research beyond the means of the organisation. Keeping information current is also difficult for NGOs with limited resources. In *Garcia* v. *Canada (Minister of Citizenship and Immigration)*,[145] the RPD ignored a report by the Mexican Citizen's Commission Against Homophobic Hate Crimes on assassinations that were motivated by homophobic hate, because the study was not current. While the RPD was faulted for ignoring the information altogether, the Federal Court of Canada noted that the report was prepared six years before the claimant's hearing, and, as a result, the RPD could decide not to ascribe much weight to the report.[146]

National human rights associations face the same challenge as international ones; most notably, increased activism is met with attacks on human rights defenders. This has seriously impeded their ability to document violations. The particular risks faced by human rights defenders working on issues of sexual orientation were recognised by the Special Representative of the UN Secretary-General on human rights defenders in 2001:

> Greater risks are faced by defenders of the rights of certain groups as their work challenges social structures, traditional practices and interpretation of religious precepts that may have been used over long periods of time to condone and justify violation of the human rights of members of such groups. Of special importance will be women's human rights groups and those who are active on issues of sexuality especially sexual orientation and reproductive rights. These groups are often very vulnerable to prejudice, to marginalization and to public repudiation, not only by State forces but other social actors.[147]

The UN High Commissioner for Human Rights recognised the problem as well:

> I recognize that many LGBT human rights organizations work in extremely difficult circumstances. They are denied freedom of association when the authorities shut them down, or otherwise prevent them from carrying out their work. They are physically attacked when they organize demonstrations to claim their rights. Many have even been killed for daring to speak about sexual orientation. They are denied access to important fora, including at the international level, where they should be able to have their voices heard.[148]

Increasing the risks is the fact that, according to the *2008 State-Sponsored Homophobia* report, being a gay man or a lesbian risks jail time in 86 countries and the death penalty in seven.[149] Serious risks are therefore involved in investigating, documenting, and reporting human rights violations against sexual minorities, especially if researchers are themselves gay, lesbian, bisexual, or transgender.

The absence of official government reporting increases the challenges of providing reliable information. Most countries do not collect statistics or report publicly on incidents of violence against sexual minorities. For instance, in a recent report on sexual minorities in Turkey, Human Rights Watch cited figures on homophobic violence from a study apparently conducted by the Turkish Ministry of Justice.[150] But, as the study remains unpublished, and the number of subjects and the methodologies unknown, Human Rights Watch were careful to note that while the data were consistent with their findings the 'figures must therefore be treated as inconclusive'.[151] A number of sexual minority rights organisations have tried to monitor reports of violence and incidents of homophobia, and their research and findings have been used by mainstream human rights organisations. For instance, Human Rights First cites surveys conducted by sexual minority rights groups in several countries in their 2007 report *Homophobia: 2007 Hate Crime Survey*.[152] Human Rights First does state, however, that while such surveys offer evidence of the problem of homophobic violence the 'surveys are not always undertaken with scientific precision or cannot claim to be fully representative'.[153]

The absence of reliable independent country information can lead refugee tribunals to use inappropriate sources as substitutes. In 2002, Michael Battista, a refugee lawyer in Toronto, sent a letter to the IRB to complain about material contained in a standard information package prepared by the RPD which was produced for a hearing of a claimant he was representing.[154] According to Battista, the package contained material promoting Mexico's gay tourist and travel industry. This included downloaded information from websites promoting Mexico's gay tourist destinations. Battista claimed that such material was inherently promotional and depicted social conditions in the most palatable light. In addition, the information was unreliable, as sources or authors were not identified. Finally, Battista argued that the material was highly prejudicial, as it relied on stereotypical notions of gay men as primarily interested in socialising, parties, and sexual activity.[155] Dauvergne and Millbank have similarly criticised the Australian Refugee Review Tribunal for relying on the *Spartacus Guide*, a travel guide aimed at gay men, at refugee hearings.[156]

Failure to document abuses can still impact on claimants negatively.[157] In 2000, a gay man from the Bahamas failed to obtain refugee status in part because the RPD concluded that the absence of reports of abuses by Amnesty International meant that 'gays are not persecuted in the Bahamas and that human rights are respected'.[158] In *Canada (Minister of Citizenship and Immigration) v. Shwaba*,[159] the RPD found that there was no documentation on the conditions in Grenada with respect to the alleged persecution of homosexuals except for a document that was ten years old.[160] A gay Thai claimant failed to secure refugee status in Australia because the tribunal concluded that 'if there was a problem with homosexuals being seriously threatened and attacked in Thailand or if police refused to provide adequate state protection to homosexuals ... that this would be reported in independent country information'.[161] Moreover, as the analysis will now show, shortcomings in the availability and specificity of independent country information make it difficult for gay, lesbian, bisexual, and transgender claimants to meet legal specific requirements of the refugee determination process, which can translate into poor assessments in the refugee hearing room.

The challenge of emerging legal issues

As discussed above, claims in the 1991–98 period generally turned on whether sexual orientation or gender identity constituted the basis of a particular social group, whether claimants were able to prove their sexual orientations or gender identities, and on the legitimacy of a claimant's well-founded fear. With regard to the last, the early cases focused almost exclusively on whether a claimant could buttress her or his testimony regarding fear of persecution with objective evidence that human rights abuses against sexual minorities did in fact occur in the claimant's country of origin. Very often, without such evidence, claimants were unsuccessful in gaining protection.

Two developments would change the nature of the inquiry in sexual orientation cases. Information on the nature, scope, and seriousness of human rights abuses against sexual minorities was slowly becoming accessible to refugee claimants and decision-makers. At the same time, increased activism by gay, lesbian, bisexual, and transgender people at both national and international levels was securing modest legal and social achievements for sexual minorities in different countries.

The developments impacted on the refugee determination process in Canada. The inquiry into a claimant's well-founded fear became more layered. Whether a claimant has a well-founded fear of persecution is in fact a complex factual and legal issue. Rather than simply assessing the existence of serious human rights violations against sexual minorities, adjudicators were increasingly interested in determining whether claimants feared discrimination rather than persecution. In addition, since a claimant's fear of persecution could result from a state's failure to protect the claimant, the focus of the hearing began to turn on the availability of state protection and the existence of internal flight alternatives. All three of these issues are linked to objective conditions in the country of origin and therefore require documentation in order to properly evaluate their relevance to a claimant's case. The analysis will look at each issue in turn, and its accompanying evidentiary challenges.

a. Discrimination versus persecution

The notion of persecution is at the heart of the definition of refugee, yet the concept is poorly defined.[162] In *Ward*, the Supreme Court of Canada defined persecution as 'sustained or systematic violation of basic human rights demonstrative of a failure of state protection'.[163] In *Rajudeen* v. *Canada (Minister of Employment and Immigration)*,[164] the Federal Court of Appeal defined persecution as 'acts of harassment, cruelty, punishment, injury or annoyance inflicted in a persistent, systematic or repetitive manner'.[165] In terms of specific acts, tribunal and courts decisions recognise torture, rape, arbitrary arrest and detention, assault, and repeated harassment as forms of persecution.[166] The definition of persecution consequently necessitates that the harm feared be serious and that it be inflicted in a persistent, repetitive, or systematic way.[167]

The requirement that the harm be serious has led to a distinction between persecution, on one hand, and discrimination, on the other. It is true that persecution can be manifested by a series of discriminatory acts; the concept of discrimination is therefore an aspect of persecution. However, refugee law makes an important distinction between discrimination and persecution. According to the *United Nations High Commissioner for Refugees Handbook on Procedures and Criteria for Determining Refugee Status*,[168] while discrimination may amount to a violation of human rights, it will not necessarily amount to persecution. Paragraph 54 of the *Handbook* states,

> Differences in the treatment of various groups do indeed exist to a greater or lesser extent in many societies. Persons who receive less favourable treatment as a result of such differences are not necessarily victims of persecution. It is only in certain circumstances that discrimination will amount to persecution. This would be so if measures of discrimination lead to consequences of a substantially prejudicial nature for the person concerned, e.g. serious restrictions on his right to earn his livelihood, his right to practise his religion, or his access to normally available educational facilities.[169]

Thus, what distinguishes persecution from discrimination is the degree of seriousness of the harm.

Canadian refugee law adopts this important distinction between discrimination and persecution. At the same time, courts have recognised that discrimination may also rise to the level of persecution. The Federal Court of Canada stated, in the case of *Sagharichi v. Canada (Minister of Employment and Immigration)*,[170] that incidents of discrimination may very well amount to persecution. Refugee claimants must demonstrate that incidents cumulatively or singly 'constitute a serious, systematic and repeated violation of core human rights'.[171] Discrimination in itself does not establish persecution, but it may ground a finding if it is very serious. In all cases, it is a mixed question of law and fact.[172] Finally, the distinction between discrimination and persecution rests entirely on the evidence submitted to the RPD.[173]

A few refugee claims based on sexual orientation or gender identity raised the distinction between discrimination and persecution before 1998,[174] but it was really in the last ten years that Canadian decision-makers increasingly evaluated evidence to determine whether a sexual minority claimant would be subjected to persecution or to the less serious harm of discrimination. One reason for the increased relevance of the issue is the fact that in several countries the social, political, and legal situations of sexual minorities has been changing. While some countries continue to seriously repress homosexuality and transexuality, other countries are becoming more accepting of sexual diversity.

The impact of this progress is now often at issue at refugee hearings. According to a refugee lawyer in Toronto, the RPD 'tends to be more sympathetic to claimants from countries such as Pakistan and Iran where homosexuality is illegal'.[175] More tenuous are cases involving claimants from countries that have emerging sexual minority communities and rights organisations and concrete legal reforms, such as Mexico and several Latin American and Eastern European countries.[176] For example, in *Cuesta* v. *Canada (Minister of Citizenship and Immigration)*, the RPD described the situation in Colombia in 2003 thus:

> I note it is very clear from the documents that there is a continuum of an improving situation for persons of the claimant's particular sexual orientation. The situation there is not perfect by any means, but it is clear that there have been improvements, starting in 1980 when consensual homosexuality was decriminalized. Regarding the Constitution of 1991, even his counsel described a very liberal Constitution.[177]

Similar conclusions were drawn in numerous cases, including in a 2004 Brazilian claim where the RPD concluded that '[w]hile the panel accepts that in Brazil, deeply ingrained attitudes against homosexuality continue to exist, there are numerous examples in the documentary evidence that the situation for sexual minorities is improving'.[178] After canvassing the situation in Ghana, the RPD decision-maker in *Titus-Glover* v. *Canada (Minister of Citizenship and Immigration)* stated that '[t]he overall impression I get is that there is definitely discrimination against homosexuals in Ghana but no persecution'.[179] A similar conclusion was reached in a 2006 case relating to South Korea: 'Thus, while it is clear the situation for gays in South Korea is not as good as it is in Canada, I find there is insufficient evidence to show there is systemic and repeated violation of human rights or serious and sustained discrimination and harassment that amounts to persecution of all gays.'[180]

The fact that independent human rights documentation continues to be difficult to obtain for many parts of the world means that assessment of whether a particular country's conditions constitute discrimination rather than persecution is sometimes based on little objective evidence. Moreover, some adjudicators may continue to reason, as they did in the early sexual orientation and gender identity claims, that the scarcity or absence of reports evidences a lack of persecution.[181] This appears to have been the case in a decision reviewed by the Federal Court of Canada, where the RPD had reviewed the independent country information and concluded that,

> if violence against homosexuals was serious and widespread, it would have appeared in the United States' Department of State Report on Human Rights, Amnesty International Reports or the Human Rights Watch World Report. Since violence against homosexuals was not mentioned in any of these three reports, the Board concluded that it was not a serious and widespread problem in Hungary.[182]

Considering the comparatively recent mainstream attention given to persecution based on sexual orientation and gender identity, and the ongoing challenges in documenting human rights abuses, refugee claims adjudicators should be careful to avoid drawing conclusions that no persecution exists without clear positive evidence.[183] Amnesty International warns that 'lesbians and gay men who have experienced torture or ill-treatment may not have access to documented evidence of their personal experiences. Patterns of torture and other abuses facing lesbians and gay men are not well documented in most countries, although some non-governmental organisations have begun to track these abuses.'[184] Adjudicators must 'take into account reasons why reports of persecution may be unavailable'.[185]

The lack of evidence is a challenge for both the claimant and the decision-maker. For instance, in *Zakka* v. *Canada (Minister of Citizenship and Immigration)*,[186] the Federal Court of Canada stated that an applicant cannot simply rely on the existence of a law proscribing homosexual acts to demonstrate risk. The claimant must produce evidence that similarly situated persons were subjected to arbitrary harassment and detention under the law. This was the conclusion also in *Birsan* v. *Canada (Minister of Citizenship and Immigration)*,[187] where the Federal Court held that '[i]t is certainly not unreasonable to conclude that the mere existence of a law prohibiting homosexuality in public cannot prove, if it is not enforced, that homosexuals are persecuted'.[188] In *Oviawe* v. *Canada (Minister of Citizenship and Immigration)*,[189] the absence of persuasive evidence regarding the manner and frequency with which section 214 of the Nigerian Criminal Code, which rendered sodomy punishable by up to 14 years' imprisonment, was enforced resulted in the conclusion that the claimant did not face persecution. As the Federal Court of Appeal in *Sagharichi* pointed out, 'the dividing line between persecution and discrimination or harassment is difficult to establish, the more so since, in the refugee law context, it has been found that discrimination may very well be seen as amounting to persecution'.[190] Thus, in *Inigo Contreras* v. *Canada (Minister of Citizenship and Immigration)*,[191] the documentary evidence, including the *2004 United States Department of State Report*, was far from definitive on the issue of persecution. The evidence suggested the existence of discrimination against homosexuals and acts of persecution, but also pointed to government efforts to fix the situation and to the work of NGOs in trying to improve the treatment of sexual minorities. In *Re J.Q.U.*,[192] the RPD pointed out that previous IRB decisions went both ways in relation to homosexuals from Poland on the issue of discrimination versus persecution. Similarly, while the documentary evidence in a Brazilian claim outlined problems with the treatment of sexual minorities, including that: (1) 'Brazilian cities ... have laws protecting homosexuals from discrimination on the basis of sexual orientation, although their enforcement is sketchy'; (2) '"average" homosexuals ... are viewed as a threat'; (3) '[i]n Rio, there are also antihomosexual hit squads'; (4) '[p]olice not only fail to stop the killings, but also occasionally participate in them without any fear of legal repercussions'; and (5) '[Brazilian] macho culture [creates] an understanding among police and judges that violence and murder of homosexuals does not deserve serious attention',[193] the RPD concluded that 'homosexuals may experience measures of harassment and discrimination and incidents of violence in rare circumstances in Brazil, but are not subject to serious harm amounting to persecution'.[194] This was based on the fact that the same documentary evidence suggested that homosexuality was not illegal; that a public opinion poll showed that 60% of Brazilians of both sexes were in favour of recognition of couples of the same sex; that flamboyant homosexuality was widely accepted; and that a federal human rights official had scheduled meetings with sexual minority rights representatives.[195] The weighing of evidence in this decision on Brazil seems to have inexplicably favoured the minor progress outlined in the independent country information rather than the more serious reports of homophobic violence and impunity.

One of the problems lies in the type of country information that may be available to the adjudicators. In a 1999 case involving two gay men from Uruguay, the RPD concluded that the situation for homosexuals in Uruguay was not perfect but constituted discrimination falling short of persecution.[196] Yet the documentary evidence mentioned in the RPD's reasons focused exclusively on the improved social position of homosexuals. Independent country information, including information from a Uruguayan sexual minority rights group, outlined the existence of some gay groups in the capital city of Montevideo, and the holding of a public parade and workshops, including one event where a psychiatrist held an open panel on homophobia at a town council.[197] However, I argue, this type of documentation does not provide useful assessment of the specific human rights situation of sexual minorities in a particular country. If the independent country information focuses on the mere existence of a sexual minority rights organisation, adjudicators may fail to appreciate that this 'does not reveal much detail about the conditions for that organisation, the size or influence of the organisation and/or any restrictions on its operations'.[198] Adjudicators require a diversity of country information that paints a complete picture of the situation for them to be able to understand 'the nature of homophobic persecution, which is cemented by a complex interaction between legal, political, social, religious and familial spheres'.[199] For instance, in the Uruguayan case, the absence of penal provisions prohibiting homosexuality was mentioned by the RPD. Such absence, however, does not mean that same-sex conduct is legally condoned, especially in public settings. Many Latin American countries have used laws that penalise offences against morality and decency to repress homosexuality.[200]

The fact that much current documentary evidence is often not determinative on the issue of discrimination versus persecution is illustrated by the findings in four Sri Lankan cases decided between 2004 and 2007, in each of which documentary sources suggested that homosexuality was illegal under Sri Lankan law and punishable by up to 12 years' imprisonment; that gay men were subject to harassment, extortion, and blackmail from police; and that gay men were generally treated with aversion. At the same time, evidence pointed to more societal openness; the emergence of support organisations for gay men and lesbians; and the fact that, while a law prohibiting homosexuality remained on the books, it was not being used in practice to prosecute individuals. Similar human rights documentation was introduced at the hearings, yet different conclusions were reached over whether the country conditions constituted persecution or discrimination. In *De Seram* v. *Canada (Minister of Citizenship and Immigration)*, the RPD focused on the improvement in the conditions for sexual minorities to conclude that the claimant would face 'harassment and prejudice' rather than persecution.[201] In *Abdul Hameed* v. *Canada (Minister of Citizenship and Immigration)*, the RPD concluded that 'gays in Sri Lanka, and the claimant, face discrimination and not persecution', even though the decision-maker acknowledged that 'homosexuality is illegal under Sri Lanka law'; that gay men were 'generally being treated with distaste'; and that 'incidents of gay beatings are reported in Sri Lanka'.[202] In contrast, in the third case, the RPD concluded that an accumulation of human rights violations, including risk of blackmail from police and alienation from family and society at large, did amount to persecution.[203] In the last case, the Federal Court of Canada allowed an application for judicial review of the RPD's determination that a claimant's testimony was not credible in light of the documentary evidence that indicated that, although there was a law on the books prohibiting homosexuality in Sri Lanka, the law was not enforced by the police.[204] The Federal Court of Canada concluded that the RPD failed to refer to evidence that sexual minority rights 'organisations are frequent police targets, and that members are physically and verbally abused by the police'.[205] In addition, the Federal Court stated that 'although the law banning sodomy is not enforced, the police often use the existence of the law to blackmail homosexuals'.[206]

b. State protection

International refugee law was designed to reinforce protection individuals may receive from their own countries. Absent a complete breakdown of the state apparatuses or an admission by the state authorities that they are unable to protect the claimant, a claimant must advance clear and convincing evidence of the state's inability to protect him or her. The claimant has the burden of proof and 'must assume his or her legal burden on a balance of probabilities'.[207] The Federal Court of Appeal recently clarified that the evidence adduced must be 'relevant, reliable and convincing'.[208] The Supreme Court of Canada in *Ward* held that such proof may consist of testimony of 'past personal incidents in which state protection did not materialize' or of 'similarly situated individuals who were let down by the state protection arrangement'.[209] The focus of the inquiry is on determining whether there is objective evidence outlining inadequate state protection.[210]

In addition, courts have held that 'where a state is in effective control of its territory, has military, police and civil authority in place, and makes serious efforts to protect its citizens, the mere fact that it is not always successful at doing so will not be enough to justify a claim that the victims of terrorism are unable to avail themselves of such protection'.[211] Further in *Kadenko*, the Federal Court of Appeal stated that the burden of proof was proportional to the degree of democracy within the state in question.[212] The more democratic the state, the more available domestic remedies the claimant must exhaust before claiming refugee protection.

State protection has been a consistent and recurring issue in sexual orientation and gender identity claims in the last ten years.[213] Increasingly, the outcome of claims has depended on whether the claimant has adduced clear and convincing evidence that state authorities cannot or will not protect sexual minorities. The relevance of this inquiry is illustrated by the fact that one of only two decisions to ever be designated as a 'jurisprudential guide' by the IRB is a 2003 case dealing with state protection for sexual minorities in Costa Rica.[214] A jurisprudential guide is designated pursuant to section 159(1)(h) of the Immigration and Refugee Protection Act.[215] Adjudicators are expected to adopt the reasoning in a jurisprudential guide if the facts of the case before them are sufficiently similar. When the RPD received an unusual number of claims from sexual minority claimants from Costa Rica, the RPD decided that these cases turned on the issue of state protection and designated as a jurisprudential guide a decision that concluded that state protection was generally available in Costa Rica.

Several reasons explain the growing relevance of availability of state protection. Availability of state protection has been influenced by the social, political, and legal progress in several countries. Legal reforms include specific measures to protect the human rights of sexual minorities, including remedies such as mechanisms for individual complaints to an ombudsman or human rights commission or measures to counter homophobia within police and state security forces. Refugee claims adjudicators have therefore begun to examine the extent to which a gay man, lesbian, bisexual, or transgender person can seek protection in his or her country of origin rather than obtain refugee protection in Canada.

Another reason the question of state protection is increasingly relevant in sexual orientation and gender identity claims is the fact that a significant number of claims identify private violence as the source of the feared persecution. Violence against sexual minorities is often committed by individuals who do not represent the state. Shannon Minter states that lesbians, like other women, are often victims of violence at the hands of family members. They are forced to marry; subjected to psychiatric treatment against their will; deprived of their children; and are victims of discrimination with respect to housing, employment, education, and health services.[216] Gay male claimants also testify about abuse received at the hands of family members,[217] and the family and social pressures that require them to conform to strict gender-based social roles. Some of the claimants have been forced into marriages of convenience,[218] while others claim to have been pressured to have children.[219] The situation of a Nigerian claimant shows the extent to which family members may become the agents of persecution: 'The claimant's father and his three brothers confronted the claimant while he was at university, broke the information that they had about his homosexuality, horsewhipped him, and mistreated him, whereupon the father involved the village elders in a ritual and gave his son, the claimant, an ultimatum: either get married or be gotten rid of by the father.'[220] In another case, a claimant of Moroccan origin testified about the abuse and torture he was subjected to at the hands of his father.[221] In such cases, where the agents of persecution are private individuals, the availability of state protection becomes a key issue to be determined, as it is presumed that a claimant could turn to the state for protection from family members or other private persecutors.

The fact that human rights organisations still do not provide adequate documentation on many countries has serious consequences for claimants who have the burden of proof when it comes to state protection. It is difficult to rebut the presumption of state protection when human rights documentation is unavailable or provides little information on attitudes and actual practice. While some cases benefit from extensive and wide-ranging human rights documentation,[222] others rely on a relatively small range of sources.

For example, in a 1999 case involving a gay man from Estonia, the RPD noted that the claimant made unsuccessful attempts to obtain documentary evidence about similarly situated persons.[223] He was unable to secure any credible human rights information; rather, according to the RPD, he provided second- or third-hand anecdotal evidence and 'opinions gleaned from TV and newspapers' which were not considered sufficient evidence to rebut the presumption of state protection.[224] The documentary evidence that was available showed that 'Estonia is a democracy that is making serious efforts at protecting its citizens from human rights abuses'.[225] While the RPD acknowledged that the documentary evidence made no mention of sexual minority rights, it concluded that 'there was no evidence that Estonian police are homophobic'[226] and the claim was rejected. Lack of evidence was also an issue in *Re J.M.Y.*[227] While homosexuality was found to be against the law in Jordan, the RPD noted that the 'the claimant provided little evidence that the law was generally enforced'.[228] In another case, the RPD cited a 'Response to Information Request' prepared by the Documentation and Resource Directorate on state protection and remedies available to sexual minorities in Brazil who were victims of physical violence.[229] The adjudicator noted that the document highlighted a public opinion poll that showed that 60% of Brazilians of both sexes expressed support for recognition of couples of the same sex.[230] The adjudicator, however, failed to explain how a favourable public opinion poll may evidence state protection.

An additional concern is the emphasis the RPD sometimes places on human rights documentation that outlines progress in the recognition of the rights of sexual minorities over evidence that may suggest that this has not translated into effective state protection. El-Farouk Khaki described the problem thus: 'We need to look beyond what social advances have been made to the overall human rights situation to see how rights have improved for gay people.'[231] Khaki added that '[m]ost Latin American countries have amazing constitutions, but that doesn't mean [they are] enforced.'[232] As has been noted in the Australian context, 'the absence of criminalising provisions seem[s] to raise overly positive assumptions about the lack of state prosecution or the availability of securing state protection'.[233] Moreover, where laws do criminalise same-sex sexual conduct, further evidence of their enforcement or threat of enforcement is required in order to rebut the presumption of state protection.[234]

The problem, however, is that human rights documentation does not always deal specifically or directly with the availability of state protection for sexual minorities. Take, for instance, a caveat Amnesty International inserted in their recent report on the decriminalisation of homosexuality:

> This paper does not provide a survey of statutes and practices that directly or indirectly criminalize individuals for consensual same-sex practices and, by erroneous association, transgender people irrespective of their sexual orientation. Such a study requires careful research across languages and criminal law, analysing specifically what actions are criminalized; how vague laws are interpreted by law enforcement officials and across the legal system(s); how actual or imputed behaviour, gender expression and claims to sexual or gender identity are differently criminalized for women, men and transgender people; how these practices of criminalization are informed by race and class, and so forth. Such a study would be invaluable but is outside the scope of this overview.[235]

Unfortunately, comprehensive examinations of statutes and practices are rarely conducted. Even the 2008 ILGA report *State-Sponsored Homophobia* does not include an analysis of the scope, impact, and enforcement of laws that criminalise same-sex conduct. What is required is specific information about how criminal sanctions, whether enforced or not, 'reinforce persecutory environments and destroy opportunities for [sexual minorities] to seek protection from state authorities'.[236] An Australian refugee decision made the following observation:

> The exact numbers of LGBT [lesbian, gay, bisexual and transgender] people that are being prosecuted may not be available, but those figures do not necessarily indicate the level of tolerance or acceptance by public authorities. The 'effectiveness' in oppressing LGBT people of legislation criminalising homosexuality is not necessarily reflected in the number of prosecutions. Many LGBT people either abstain from same-sex relationships, or keep occasional social and sexual contacts secret, applying severe restrictions to their social life and personal identity, in order to prevent arrests, harassment or prosecutions. As long as 'open homosexuality' is not allowed, and LGBT people live their life in fear and secrecy, the criminalisation of homosexuality can be said to be 'effective' in its repression, even if this is not reflected in large numbers of prosecutions and/or arrests.[237]

Amnesty International has also recognised that the extent to which a specific law represses sexual minorities goes beyond the direct enforcement of the legislation:

> Such laws, even when not implemented, construct societal attitudes, sending a clear message of, at best, second-class citizenship to people who identify as lesbian, gay, bisexual or transgender, or anyone who engages in any form of consensual same-sex sexual conduct, or

those whose self-defined gender identity or gender expression differs from acceptable 'norms' of gender and sexuality. It is not just the conduct that is denounced by law but the individual who performs it. Such laws encourage private and state acts of violence and fuel impunity for those acts.[238]

Independent country information will be more useful to adjudicators and claimants if the documentation 'look[s] beyond official reports of prosecutions and persecution to cultures of silence which surround human rights abuses against sexual minorities'[239] and examines the reasons why homophobic violence and abuses may be underreported.

Moreover, when objective evidence is available, the RPD sometimes emphasises evidence that describes progress in the social situation of sexual minorities rather than information that suggests problems with state protection.[240] For instance, in *Re D.I.Z.*,[241] the RPD relied on the ILGA *World Legal Survey* to assess state protection for gay men in Bulgaria. The decision focused on the report's description of the social networks that have developed in the gay and lesbian communities:

> In spite of the negative attitude of the society towards gays and the sexual anonymity of most of the gays the situation has changed in the last several years. Several issues of a gay magazine were issued, gay books were published, gay dating agencies were established, several gay bars, clubs, discos, sex shops were opened. The independent private media inform about gay events, the national and the private television cast films with gay themes, and gay movies are shown in the cinema.

It also stated the following on the capital city of Sofia in particular: 'there are as many as four gay clubs in Sofia, along with a "sex shop" known as Flamingo's. The Website further states that Sofia's Orlov Most ("Eagles Bridge") and Vazrazhdane Square are gay cruising areas.'[242] The RPD noted that '[t]he document also refers to discrimination against gays and lesbians and cases of police brutality' but that the report characterised these incidents as 'occasional rather than systematic',[243] and the claim was rejected. In *Pitrowski* v. *Canada (Minister of Citizenship and Immigration)*,[244] the RPD cited a report from a Polish sexual minority rights group,[245] but set aside some of its findings in relation to the high rates of violence against sexual minorities[246] and refusal to report incidents to the police.[247] The RPD emphasised instead evidence indicating that the police were courteous at the Warsaw gay pride parade.[248] The decision concluded thus:

> Given the documentary evidence and notwithstanding the incidents referred to in the LAMBDA Warsaw Association Report (there are two million gay and lesbian persons living in Poland), plus noting the fact that Poland is now a member of the European Union and is still being monitored as such regarding the extent to which it is capable of protecting its citizens, I find that the claimant has not established a well-founded fear of persecution for a Convention ground in Poland.[249]

Such decisions suggest that the RPD will interpret human rights documentation that describes the growing social space achieved by sexual minorities as evidence that state protection exists.

Similar human rights documentation can also lead to different conclusions in relation to the availability of state protection. In *Re B.B.Y.*,[250] the RPD concluded that the documentary evidence supported the gay claimant's case that he could not benefit from state protection in Lebanon. Provisions dealing with homosexuality existed in the penal code that made it an imprisonable offence to engage in homosexual activities. Yet in another decision decided a day earlier the RPD dismissed the importance of the same provisions. Relying on 'gay and lesbian guides' as evidence, the RPD concluded that despite the fact that open homosexual relationships were not allowed and there was no visible support for gay rights, discreet homosexual behaviour was possible and Lebanese authorities did not actively prosecute homosexuals.[251]

Another issue of relevance for sexual minorities is the fact that they have to declare their sexual orientation in order to access state protection. The question becomes whether this is realistic or reasonable;[252] this is an assessment that can benefit from independent country information. For instance, Human Rights Watch published a report on homophobic violence in Jamaica in 2004 and their findings on police authorities are summarised as follows:

> Victims of violence are often too scared to appeal to the police for protection. In some cases the police themselves harass and attack men they perceived to be homosexual. Police also actively support homophobic violence, fail to investigate complaints of abuse, and arrest and detain them based on their alleged homosexual conduct. In some cases, homophobic police violence is a catalyst for violence and serious – sometimes lethal – abuse by others.[253]

The report detailed numerous violent and abusive incidents supporting the conclusion that it would be unreasonable for Jamaican gay men and lesbians to seek state protection.

In *Re V.Z.D.*,[254] the RPD was able to rely on documentation to take into account the impact disclosure of a Mexican woman's sexual orientation would have on her custody dispute with her ex-husband. The RPD concluded thus:

> The panel further took into consideration the consequences for xxxx xxxxxx of such exposure of a police report whereby she would have to disclose her lesbian relationship, given the custody battle between her and her former spouse. The documents indicate that custody could be removed from the custodial parents if moral codes are at issue. The panel finds that in this particular case and circumstances the claimant has established that they are unwilling, due to their fear, to seek the protection of the authorities in Mexico, and that they have provided clear and convincing proof that, given their particular circumstances, the state is therefore unable to protect them.[255]

In another case, the adjudicator found the documentary evidence regarding state protection to be mixed, but nevertheless concluded that the particular circumstances of the claimant made it unreasonable to expect him to come out and declare himself to be a homosexual in order to access state protection.[256] The same conclusion was reached in the case of a Nigerian gay man where the RPD concluded that the claimant would risk his life 'with the exposure of his own alternative lifestyle' to the police.[257]

While the aforementioned cases carefully examined the issue of disclosure to public authorities, and concluded that the refusal to come out was reasonable, the RPD dismissed a similar reluctance to disclose by a Polish gay man in a 2007 claim. The RPD reviewed the documentary evidence on homophobia in Poland submitted by the claimant and stated that 'it is easy to understand why homosexuals in Poland very often hide their sexual orientation and frequently face discrimination at work, in the street and in their own families'. Nevertheless, the adjudicator concluded,

> The fact that he alleged that he did not file a complaint because he was afraid of revealing that he is a homosexual and because he believed that the police sometimes discriminate against homosexuals is not a reasonable excuse for not contacting the authorities, especially when at least some of the aggressors against whom a complaint can be filed can be identified.[258]

The RPD added that the fact '[t]hat some victims are reluctant to take administrative or legal action against the people who assaulted them, because they do not want to reveal that they are homosexual and because they doubt the effectiveness of the recourse in question, is not clear and convincing evidence of the state's inability to protect them, but simply evidence that such protection is not perfect.'[259] Consequently, a claimant's fear of coming out to state authorities needs to be buttressed by human rights reports that specifically detail the consequences of disclosure. While some human rights organisations have begun to include this kind of information, as Human Rights Watch did in the report on Jamaica mentioned above, this is not always the case in other independent country information.

To summarise, in Canadian refugee law, unless the state apparatuses have broken down completely, the state is presumed to be capable of protecting its citizens. Refugee claimants must therefore rebut the presumption of state protection by showing clear and convincing evidence that the state authorities in their countries of origin are unable or unwilling to protect them. This burden is made more difficult for sexual minorities, as independent country information remains hard to find for many parts of the world and because current information is often general and descriptive in relation to state protection rather than specific and evaluative.

c. Internal flight alternative

Claimants have an additional evidentiary burden when making their case for a well-founded fear of persecution. The concept of 'internal relocation alternative', or 'internal flight alternative' (IFA) is an extension of the concept of state protection. In assessing whether a refugee's fear of persecution is well founded, the RPD will determine whether the claimant can avail himself or herself of a safe place in the country of origin. Refugee protection will be denied if a claimant did not exhaust all possibilities of reaching safety in an area within the claimant's own country before seeking international protection. James Hathaway has expressed the concept of IFA as follows: '"internal protection alternative" analysis should be directed to the identification of asylum-seekers who do not require international protection against the risk of persecution in their own country because they can presently access meaningful protection in a part of their own country'.[260]

While the concept of IFA is not mentioned in international legal instruments, in *Rasaratnam* v. *Canada (Minister of Employment and Immigration)*, the Federal Court of Canada held that 'a determination of whether or not there is an IFA is integral to the determination of whether or not a claimant is a Convention refugee'.[261] As outlined in *Rasaratnam* and *Thirunavukkarasu*,[262] the test to be applied in determining whether there is an IFA is two-fold: (1) the Board must be satisfied on a balance of probabilities that there is no serious possibility of the claimant being persecuted in the part of the country where it finds an IFA exists; and (2) conditions in the part of the country considered to be an IFA must be such that it would not be unreasonable, in all the circumstances, including those particular to the claimant, for him or her to seek refuge there.[263]

The IFA rule essentially involves an analysis of the general situation in the country to determine the risks faced by the claimant in the proposed site of relocation. It also involves a consideration of the individual's personal circumstances to assess the claimant's ability to effectively access and integrate into that location. Both of these conditions must be satisfied for a finding that the claimant has an IFA. Finally, while the burden of proof rests upon the claimant once the issue of IFA has been raised, the RPD 'cannot base a finding that there is an IFA, in the absence of sufficient evidence, solely on the basis that the claimant has not fulfilled the onus of proof'.[264]

IFAs are increasingly being assessed in claims based on sexual orientation and gender identity.[265] Social, political, and legal progress is sometimes highly localised in a state; more tolerant destinations may therefore constitute an IFA for gay men, lesbians, bisexuals, or transgender persons. In addition, meaningful protection in a different area of the country may indeed be available to a claimant where he or she is being persecuted by a non-governmental entity acting independently of any governmental control or support. As mentioned above, private persecution is regularly raised in cases brought forth by members of sexual minorities.

As IFAs are an extension of the concept of state protection, many of the problems identified in the previous section apply to the use of independent country information in determining the viability of an IFA for sexual minorities. Similar to the presumption of state protection, the problem associated with IFAs stems from its increasing use to deny refugee status to claimants who cannot produce enough evidence to negate the possibility of an IFA. While some decisions do rely on extensive documentary evidence,[266] many others did not. In many cases, the independent country information did not address the issue of IFAs or the effectiveness of measures that purported to ensure state protection in the alternative location. The concern that independent country information does not probe the actual reality of protection is a constant concern in refugee claims based on sexual orientation and gender identity. For instance, a gay claimant acknowledged that Mexico City had recognised same-sex relationships, in addition to extending inheritance rights and benefits, but he dismissed the reforms: 'But that's paper. I don't need papers in my life, I need reality.'[267] In *Orozco Gonzalez* v. *Canada*, Mexico City was considered a viable IFA on the basis of documentary information that indicated that the capital city had its own annual gay parade; the city government had adopted anti-discrimination legislation; and the police forces had created a preventive policing unit in order to address the issue of homophobia.[268] Nothing in the independent country information addressed the actual implementation of the measures adopted by authorities in Mexico City; in fact, it appears that such an assessment was not available. The claimant, who had the burden of proof, could offer no objective evidence to rebut the suggestion that Mexico City was a viable IFA. He simply described the independent country information as 'crap'.[269] In another case, the RPD dismissed a claimant's attempt to challenge the existence of an IFA on the basis that the documentary evidence was outdated.[270]

The problem with independent country information is in large part due to the fact that an IFA is a highly specific refugee law concept. International and national human rights organisations generally engage in fact-finding in attempts to influence public opinion and international organisations and to shame and stigmatise abusive governments. They are not primarily concerned with gathering information to meet the specific legal needs of asylum seekers and refugee claimants. Therefore, human rights reports rarely compare internal locations to determine whether one part of a country is a safer place for minorities or targeted individuals. In their recent report on Turkey, Human Rights Watch provided a comprehensive picture of the discrimination and repression facing sexual minorities.[271] However, the report did not compare the status of gay men, lesbians, bisexuals, and transgender persons relative to their geographic location within the country. It is therefore unclear how useful the information in the report will be to a refugee claimant trying to counter claims that large cities like Ankara or Istanbul may constitute IFAs.

The unreliability of independent country information in relation to IFAs is evidenced by the RPD's attempt to deal with the issue in relation to Mexican claims. In October 2006, the IRB identified a 2005 decision, *Gutierrez* v. *Canada*,[272] as having persuasive value regarding the availability of an IFA in Mexico for refugee claims on grounds of sexual orientation or gender identity.[273] While persuasive decisions are not binding on adjudicators, they are offered 'as models of sound reasoning that may be adopted in appropriate circumstances'.[274] Adjudicators 'are encouraged to rely upon them in the interests of consistency and collegiality'.[275] In the Mexican case, decided on 24 February 2005, the RPD held that Mexico City constituted an IFA for gay men and lesbians. The finding relied on a national documentation package dated November 2004, although more recent information from 2005 was available at the time.[276] In addition, the viability of Mexico City as an IFA was buttressed by a 2003 report by the World Policy Institute in which the author claimed that strong regional contrasts existed in the treatment of sexual minorities but that substantial gains had been made in such urban centres as Mexico City.[277] Several RPD decisions cited this 2003 human rights report in support of their findings that Mexico City was an IFA for sexual minorities.[278]

The IRB must have felt fairly confident that the decision was reliable to designate it as a persuasive decision in 2006. Yet, less than a year later, RPD adjudicators were calling into question the conclusion that Mexico City was a safe place for sexual minorities. Indeed, even as an IRB spokesperson was quoted in July 2007 as saying that 'there is a persuasive decision that argues homosexual refugee claimants have an in-country flight alternative in Mexico City to escape persecution for their sexual orientation',[279] some refugee claims adjudicators were rejecting the accuracy of the decision. In *Re H.K.T.*, the persuasive decision was characterised as an older case that, having relied on evidence available in 2004, was now pre-empted by evidence available in 2007.[280] The adjudicator concluded that the persuasive decision 'is neither persuasive, nor helpful, for a case to be determined in 2007'.[281] The viability of an IFA in Mexico City was rejected and the claimant was considered to be a person in need of refugee protection on account of his sexual orientation. In another 2007 case, the persuasive decision was also found to be unhelpful because the claimant was already living in Mexico City and the adjudicator held that, 'even in Mexico City, homophobia is still common, and although protective measures exist, they are … ineffective'.[282] Interestingly, both these 2007 decisions used country information packages put together by the Documentation and Research Directorate of the IRB to conclude that the findings of the persuasive decision in relation to Mexico City as an IFA were not in fact persuasive.[283] Finally, in May 2008, the Deputy Chairperson of the RPD issued a notice revoking the persuasiveness of the decision regarding the availability of an internal flight alternative in Mexico, stating that 'over time, the evidence on which the … decisions were based may have become dated and the reasoning in the decisions, based on the evidence, may no longer have persuasive value relevant to more recent claims'.[284]

Conclusion

The preceding discussion has attempted to demonstrate how gay, lesbian, bisexual, and transgender refugee claimants in Canada continue to find themselves disadvantaged when it comes to proving the objective elements of the refugee definitional test. The study reveals that evidentiary challenges have evolved since 1991, when claims based on sexual orientation were first introduced in the refugee determination process in Canada. It is certainly significant that mainstream human rights organisations are no longer reluctant to advocate on behalf of sexual minorities, in contrast to the neglect that existed as recently as the early 1990s. This has resulted in an increase in independent country information on the human rights situations of gay men, lesbians, bisexuals, and transgender people around the world. In addition, the efforts of sexual minority rights organisations to overcome indifference of mainstream human rights organisations by investigating and reporting the most egregious violations are no longer regarded with distrust at refugee hearings.

Despite these developments, assessment of the objective basis of sexual-orientation- or gender-identity-based claims for refugee protection continues to present challenges to both claimants and RPD adjudicators. First, availability of documentation remains a problem. The extent to which mainstream international human rights organisations and sexual minority rights groups are able to uncover worldwide abuses against sexual minorities is still limited. In most countries, stigma continues to attach to issues surrounding sexual orientation and gender identity. This often means that homophobic violence is frequently unreported, undocumented, and ultimately unpunished, making it difficult to investigate the problem. Increased activism has also been met with attacks on gay, lesbian, bisexual, and transgender human rights defenders, which seriously impede their ability to document violations. Resource limitations also hinder the ability of human rights groups to investigate and publish reliable, current, and comprehensive information. Failure to document abuses can still impact claimants negatively and the absence of reliable independent country information has led adjudicators to use inappropriate sources as substitutes.

Second, the legal issues considered determinative of a refugee claim have shifted towards more complex issues of fact and law. The inquiry into a claim based on sexual orientation or gender identity has become increasingly layered. Rather than simply assessing the existence of serious human rights violations against sexual minorities, adjudicators are now interested in determining whether claimants fear discrimination rather than persecution, whether they can access state protection, and the extent to which another internal location can serve as alternative refuge. All three of these issues are linked to objective conditions in the country of origin and therefore require documentation in order to properly evaluate their relevance to a claimant's case. The absence of independent country information that is sufficiently focused or detailed to meet these new issues often translates into poor assessments in the refugee hearing room.

The findings of this study suggest two main paths to improving the evidentiary burden of sexual minority claimants. First, refugee claims adjudicators must take into account the obstacles that continue to impede the production of adequate independent country information. While documentation has increased and improved, significant challenges remain, especially in relation to providing the kind of specific and detailed evidence now required to distinguish persecution from discrimination, and to rebut the presumption of state protection. In the early 1990s, the IRB responded to problems with independent country information by providing training to adjudicators in addition to increasing their own efforts to research human rights situations. Such efforts must be continued, as evidentiary problems facing sexual minorities have not yet disappeared, and adjudicators must understand the scope of ongoing challenges. In addition, research conducted and evaluated by the IRB can often be more specific to the issues raised at refugee determination hearings than general human rights reports may offer.

Second, human rights organisations must take steps to improve the independent country information that ends up being used at refugee hearings. Human rights organisations must explicitly acknowledge that their work is not only used to influence public opinion and to shame abusive governments, but is also a vital piece in the refugee determination process. For instance, country reports produced by human rights organisations should not only direct recommendations to the government of the state under investigation, but data should also be assessed in a way that will be useful to refugee-accepting countries. Increased focus should be given to the distinction between persecution and discrimination, to the availability of state protection as well as to possible regional contrasts in the treatment of sexual minorities within a country. More human rights organisations must research the situations of sexual minorities, and those who already do must augment their work in the area in order to ensure that information is available for all regions of the world. Finally, human rights information must be produced for countries from which significant numbers of sexual minorities are fleeing, as these refugees will in all likelihood require objective evidence to gain refugee protection in another country.

Independent country information plays an important role in the refugee determination process. It is therefore essential for refugees that international human rights organisations continue to document violations against sexual minorities and take into account the specific requirements of the refugee determination process when producing information. Refugee claims adjudicators in turn must keep in mind the cultures of silence which surround human rights abuses against sexual minorities and examine the reasons why homophobic violence and abuses may be under-reported. Should both these developments take place, the refugee determination process in Canada and elsewhere as it applies to sexual minorities will ultimately provide a better guarantee of protection.

Acknowledgements

The author wishes to thank Marie-Clode LaRocque and Stephen Hug for their invaluable research contributions and their meticulous editing assistance. The author gratefully acknowledges the financial support of the Law Foundation of Ontario and the Faculty of Law of the University of Ottawa.

Notes

1. 'Gambia Gay Death Threat Condemned', *BBC News*, 23 May 2008, http://news.bbc.co.uk/2/hi/africa/7416536.stm (accessed 29 November 2008); 'President Plans to Kill off Every Single Homosexual', *Afrik.com*, 19 May 2008, http://en.afrik.com/article13630.html (accessed 29 November 2008); Human Rights Watch, 'Gambia: President Should Disavow Reported Homophobic Threats', http://www.hrw.org/english/docs/2008/06/10/gambia19089.htm (accessed 29 November 2008).
2. Human Rights First, *Homophobia: 2007 Hate Crime Survey* (New York: Human Rights First, 2007), 5–6, http://www.humanrightsfirst.info/pdf/07601-discrim-hate-crimes-web.pdf (accessed 29 November 2008); IGLHRC, 'IGLHRC Condemns the Violence at Moscow's Gay Pride Rally', press release, 30 May 2007, http://www.iglhrc.org/site/iglhrc/section.php?id=5&detail=733 (accessed 29 November 2008); and Kent Coolen, 'Moscow Pride Organizers Outwit Opposition', *Xtra!*, 4 June 2008, http://www.xtra.ca/public/viewstory.aspx?Aff_TYPE=1&STORY_ID=4877&PUB_TEMPLATE_ID=1 (accessed 29 November 2008).
3. Human Rights Watch, 'Kyrgyzstan: Halt Anti-gay Raids', http://hrw.org/english/docs/2008/04/17/kyrgyz18570.htm (accessed 29 November 2008).
4. Human Rights Watch, 'Jamaica: Shield Gays from Mob Attacks', http://hrw.org/english/docs/2008/02/01/jamaic17957.htm (accessed 29 November 2008); Krishna Rau, 'Fleeing for My Life': Jamaican Activist Seeks Refuge in Canada', *Xtra!*, http://www.xtra.ca/public/viewstory.aspx?AFF_TYPE=3&STORY_ID=4387&PUB_TEMPLATE_ID=2 (accessed 29 November 2008).
5. Amnesty International, 'Uganda: Amnesty International Condemns Attacks against Lesbian, Gay, Bisexual and Transgender People', http://www.amnesty.org/en/library/asset/AFR59/004/2008/en/6e4ca521-32e1-11dd-863f-e9cd398f74da/afr590042008eng.pdf (accessed 29 November 2008).
6. The expression 'sexual minority' will be used throughout this paper to refer to those whose minority status is a result of either their sexual or emotional conduct with another person of the same sex or their refusal to conform to social roles tied to their biological sex at birth. Thus, the notion of sexual minorities regroups gays, lesbians, bisexuals, and transgender persons who include transsexuals and transvestites. The author recognises, however, that the expression does not distinguish differences among sexual minorities. The terms 'gay',

'lesbian', 'bisexual', 'transgender', 'homosexual', and 'same-sex' will also be used in a partial attempt to address the inadequacies of the expression 'sexual minority'.

7. For a survey of laws prohibiting same-sex sexual conduct, see Daniel Ottosson, *State-Sponsored Homophobia: A World Survey of Laws Prohibiting Same-Sex Activity Between Consenting Adults* (Brussels: ILGA, 2008), http://www.ilga.org/statehomophobia/ILGA_State_Spon-sored_Homophobia_2008.pdf (accessed 29 November 2008).

8. Human Rights First, *Homophobia: 2007 Hate Crime Survey*, 5.

8. Ibid.

9. *The Guardian*, 'Cuba's First Gay Pride Parade Cancelled', 26 June 2008, http://www.guardian.co.uk/world/2008/jun/26/cuba (accessed 29 November 2008).

10. See Sonia Katyal, 'Exporting Identity', *Yale Journal of Law & Feminism* 14 (2002): 97, 125–32; see also *Re H.F.P.* [1999] CRDD No. 188 ¶ 15 (QL); *Re C.X.S.* [1995] CRDD No. 134 (QL); *Re U.F.S.* [1999] CRDD No. 81 (QL); *Re J.P.R.* [1999] CRDD No. 182 ¶ 9 (QL); *Re M.X.J.* [2006] RPDD No. 113 ¶ 8 (QL).

11. See *Re U.L.X.* [1998] CRDD No. 83 ¶ 2 (QL); *Re C.Y.T.* [1998] CRDD No. 186 ¶ 2 (QL*)*; *Re V. (O.Z.)* [1993] CRDD No. 164 (QL).

12. See *Re C.X.S*; *Re P.L.Z.* [2000] CRDD No. 97 ¶ 12 (QL).

13. See *Re L. (M.D.)* [1992] CRDD No. 328 (QL); *Re P. (E.U.)* [1992] CRDD No. 397 (QL); *Re B.B.Y.* [2003] RPDD No. 29 ¶ 8 (QL).

14. See *Re L.(M.D.)*; *Re G.J.M.* [2002] CRDD No. 71 (QL); see also Marta Falconi, 'Gay Italian Labelled as Disabled Wins Discrimination Case against Gov't', *CBC News*, 14 July 2008, http://www.cbc.ca/cp/Oddities/080714/K071404AU.html (accessed 29 November 2008); *BBC News*, 'Gay Counselling' Call Rejected', 6 June 2008, http://news.bbc.co.uk/2/hi/uk_news/northern_ireland/7439661.stm (accessed 29 November 2008); *News 24*, 'Homo-sexuality Is a Disease', 28 June 2008, http://www.news24.com/News24/World/News/0,,2-10-1462_2348827,00.html (accessed 29 November 2008).

15. See Nicole LaViolette, 'Gender-Related Refugee Claims: Expanding the Scope of the Canadian Guidelines', *International Journal of Refugee Law* 19, no. 2 (2007): 180.

16. IGLHRC, 'First-Ever Asylum Granted to Persecuted Gay Man', media alert, 3 August 1993; and IGLHRC, 'Attorney General Supports Gay Asylum', press release, 17 June 1994.

17. Brent Creelman, 'Gay Iraqis Win Asylum in UK, but Process Still Too Tough for Most', *Xtra!*, 20 September 2007, http://www.xtra.ca/public/viewstory.aspx?AFF_TYPE=1&STORY_ID=3622&PUB_TEMPLATE_ID=1 (accessed 29 November 2008); *BBC News*, 'Gay Iranian Granted Asylum', 21 May 2008, http://news.bbc.co.uk/2/hi/uk_news/7411706.stm (accessed 29 November 2008). For an analysis of UK decisions, see Jenni Millbank, 'A Preoc-cupation with Perversion: The British Response to Refugee Claims on the Basis of Sexual Orientation, 1989–2003', *Social & Legal Studies* 14, no. 1 (2005): 115.

18. Maryellen Fullerton, 'A Comparative Look at Refugee Status Based on Persecution Due to Membership in a Particular Social Group', *Cornell International Law Journal* 26, no. 3 (1993): 505, 531–5.

19. *Re GJ* [1995] Refugee Appeal No. 1312/93 (Refugee Status Appeals Authority), where the New Zealand Appeals Authority granted asylum to a gay man from Iran.

20. David Tuller, 'Political Asylum for Gays?', *The Nation* 256, no. 15 (19 April 1993): 520; Christopher N. Kendall, 'Lesbian and Gay Refugees in Australia: Now that "Acting Discreetly" Is No longer an Option, Will Equality Be Forthcoming?', *International Journal of Refugee Law* 15, no. 4 (2003): 715.

21. IGLHRC, *International Asylum*, Fact Sheet, 20 April 1995.

22. Ibid.

23. Human Rights Watch, 'Netherlands: Asylum Rights Granted to Lesbian and Gay Iranians', press release, 19 October 2006, http://hrw.org/english/docs/2006/10/19/nether14428.htm (accessed 29 November 2008); *Gay Times*, 'Dutch Government Grants Asylum to Gay and Lesbian Refugee', April 1993.

24. For a general survey of countries that grant asylum to sexual minorities, see European Council on Refugees and Exiles, 'ELENA Research Paper on Sexual Orientation as a Ground for Rec-ognition of Refugee Status', http://www.ecre.org/resources/research_paper/350 (accessed 29 November 2008). For a general discussion of the legal issues surrounding political asylum, see Nicole LaViolette, 'The Immutable Refugees: Sexual Orientation in *Ward* v. *Canada*', *University of Toronto Faculty of Law Review* 55, no. 1 (1997): 1; Suzanne

B. Goldberg, 'Give Me Liberty or Give Me Death: Political Asylum and the Global Persecution of Lesbians and Gay Men', *Cornell International Law Journal* 26, no. 3 (1993): 605.

25. Ghassan Kassisieh, *From Lives of Fear to Lives of Freedom: A Review of Australian Refugee Decisions on the Basis of Sexual Orientation* (Sydney: Gay & Lesbian Lobby, 2008), 32.

26. James Hathaway, *The Rights of Refugees under International Law* (Cambridge: Cambridge University Press, 2005), 91–3.

27. 1951 UN Convention Relating to the Status of Refugees, 28 July 1951, 189 UNTS 150, Can. TS 1969 No. 7 (entered into force: 22 April 1954) [Convention].

28. 1967 Protocol Relating to the Status of Refugees, 16 December 1967, 606 UNTS 267, Can. TS 1969 No. 6 (entered into force: 4 October 1967). The Protocol renders international protection for refugees universal, since the Convention covered only persons whose reason to flee was linked to an event that occurred in Europe prior to 1951.

29. Immigration and Refugee Protection Act, SC 2001, c. 27. The definition of 'Convention refugee' is as follows: 'A Convention refugee is a person who, by reason of a well-founded fear of persecution for reasons of race, religion, nationality, membership in a particular social group or political opinion, (a) is outside each of their countries of nationality and is unable or, by reason of that fear, unwilling to avail themself of the protection of each of those countries; or (b) not having a country of nationality, is outside the country of their former habitual residence and is unable or, by reason of that fear, unwilling to return to that country.'

30. *Ward* v. *Canada (Attorney General)* [1993] 2 SCR 689, reversing [1990] 2 FC 667, affirming (1988) 9 Imm. LR (2d) 48, 709. The agents of persecution can be authorities of the state as well as persons not attached to the government. According to *Ward*, it must be shown that the state is tolerating the persecution by non-state agents or is incapable of protecting the individual who is the target of the persecution. See *Ward*, 709, 713, 717, 720, 721, LaForest J.

31. Convention, Art. 33.

32. *Adjei* v. *Canada* (1989) 7 Imm. LR (2d) 169.

33. Ibid., 171, citing Immigration Appeal Board in its decision of 19 May 1988.

34. Ibid., 172. The court held that a claimant's fear of persecution would be well founded if there was a 'reasonable chance' that persecution would take place. This test requires that there need not be more than a 50% chance but there must be more than a minimal possibility: ibid., 173.

35. James Hathaway, *The Law of Refugee Status* (Toronto: Butterworths, 1991), 71. For a discussion of the subjective element of 'well-founded fear', see Michael Bossin and Laila Demirdache, 'A Canadian Perspective on the Subjective Component of the Bipartite Test for "Persecution": Time for Re-evaluation', *Refuge* 22, no. 1 (2004): 108.

36. Hathaway, *The Law of Refugee Status*, 89. It is important to note that, because an individual need only fear a future risk of persecution, evidence of individualised past persecution is not necessary, but it is certainly an important indicator of the treatment awaiting the claimant if he or she should return home: ibid., 87.

37. Ibid., 84. The Federal Court of Appeal has stated that a claimant's testimony will be presumed to be credible if the applicant swears to the truth of the allegations.

38. Nurjehan Mawaani, 'Evidentiary Matters at the Immigration and Refugee Board in an Age of Diversity', *Canadian Journal of Administrative Law & Practice* 8, no. 1 (1994): 42.

39. Immigration & Refugee Act, s. 170(i).

40. Ibid., s. 170(g).

41. Ibid., s. 162(2).

42. Ibid., s. 170(h).

43. *Re R. (U.W.)* [1991] CRDD No. 50 (QL). My analysis of IRB decisions regarding sexual orientation is based on a review of all cases reported in writing by the Convention Refugee Determination Division, now known as the Refugee Protection Division (RPD), and some cases reported by the media. The IRB has a statutory requirement to provide written reasons only when it renders negative decisions. Because of the heavy workload of IRB adjudicators, positive decisions are usually delivered orally and rarely put down in writing unless otherwise requested by a claimant's lawyer: see Gerald H. Stobo, 'The Canadian Refugee Determination System', *Texas International Law Journal* 29 (1994): 391. My examination thus relies on a larger number of negative decisions than positive ones.

44. Marina Jimenez, 'Gay Refugee Claimants Seeking Haven in Canada', *Globe and Mail*, 25 April 2004, http://www.theglobeandmail.com/servlet/story/RTGAM.20040423.wrefugee24/BNStory/Front/?query=%22Gay+refugee+claimants%22 (accessed 29 November 2008).

45. Sean Rehaag, 'Patrolling the Borders of Sexual Orientation: Bisexual Refugee Claims in Canada', *McGill Law Journal* 53 (2008): 70.
46. Ibid., 71: Rehaag determined that '[t]he grant rates in sexual-orientation cases in 2004 were 49% overall, 48% for female claimants, and 50% for male claimants' and that the average grant rate for the whole of refugee claims for the same period was 45%.
47. For an analysis of case law pertaining to the definition of 'particular social group' and sexual minorities, see LaViolette, 'The Immutable Refugees'. For specific cases that raised this issue, see *Re R. (U.W.)* [1991] CRDD No. 501 (QL); *Re N. (K.U.)* [1991] CRDD No. 1140 (QL); *Re N. (L.X.)* [1992] CRDD No. 47 (QL); *Re L. (M.D.)*, note 13 above; *Re X. (J.K.)* [1992] CRDD No. 348 (QL); *Re V. (O.Z.)*, note 11 above; *Re E. (Q. R.)* [1993] CRDD No. 331 (QL); *Re H. (Y.F.)* [1994] CRDD No. 185 (QL); *Re H.(Y.N.)* [1994] CRDD No. 13 (QL); *Re W.(U.K.)* [1995] CRDD No. 123 (QL); *Re F.I.N.* [1995] CRDD No 151 (QL); *Re N. (O.I.)* [1995] CRDD No. 112 (QL); *Re B. (W.B.)* [1995] CRDD No. 108 (QL); *Re C.X.S*, note 10 above; *Re U.Y.O.* [1996] CRDD No. 163 (QL); *Re J.K.D.* [1997] CRDD No. 307 (QL); *Re K.V.R.* [1997] CRDD No. 312 (QL); *Re B.Q.D.* [1997] CRDD No. 308 (QL).
48. *Ward* v. *Canada (Attorney General)*.
49. Even though *Ward* had a significant impact on sexual orientation claims, the facts in *Ward* did not revolve around a gay or lesbian claimant. Rather the case involved a member of the Irish National Liberation Army (INLA) who, after helping two hostages escape, was sentenced to death by the terrorist organisation. He fled to Canada, and sought refugee status based on his fear of persecution for membership in a particular social group, i.e. the INLA. In the course of deciding whether the INLA could be considered a 'particular social group', the Supreme Court of Canada set forth a definition of the concept that at the same time resolved the status of sexual minorities as a social group in Canadian refugee law.
50. *Pizarro* v. *Canada (Minister of Employment and Immigration)* [1994] FCJ No. 320 ¶ 5 (QL).
51. Sexual minority claimants have also founded their fear of persecution on political opinion: see *Re U.L.X.*. In addition, sexual minority claimants have founded their fear of persecution on membership in a particular social group based on gender: see *Re C.L.Q.* [1996] CRDD No. 145 (QL).
52. See *Re W. (U.K.)*; *Re I.O.D.* [1995] CRDD No. 167 (QL); *Re F.I.N.* [1995] CRDD No. 151 (QL); *Re N. (O.I.)*; *Re B. (W.B.)*; *Re C.X.S*; *Re C.D.H.* [1996] CRDD No. 210 (QL); *Re X.Q.P.* [1996] CRDD No. 222 (QL); *Re E.N.U.* [1997] CRDD No. 67 (QL); *Re G.P.E.* [1997] CRDD No. 215 (QL); *Re C.R.H.* [1997] CRDD No. 178 (QL); *Re G.W.M.* [1997] CRDD No. 238 (QL); *Re S.E.X.* [1997] CRDD No. 277 (QL); *Re K.V.R.*; *Re T.B.E.* [1997] CRDD No. 304 (QL); *Re J.M.E.* [1998] CRDD No. 19 (QL); *Re F.V.Y.* [1998] CRDD No. 20 (QL); *Re B.S.J.* [1998] CRDD No. 32 (QL); *Re T.Q.B.* [1998] CRDD No. 101 (QL); *Re C.Y.T.*; and *Re U.O.L.* [1998] CRDD No. 166 (QL).
53. It is important to underscore that a claimant does not actually have to be a member of the particular social group. According to *Ward*, it is sufficient that the agents of persecution believe the person to be a member of the particular social group. This principle was applied by the Federal Court to claims based on sexual orientation in *Dykon* v. *Canada (Minister of Employment and Immigration)* [1994] FCJ No. 1409 (QL). The Federal Court held that 'it is totally irrelevant … whether [the refugee claimant] was in fact a homosexual or not' (para. 3). It is the beliefs of the persecutors that are important, and whether the individuals responsible for the persecution perceive the claimant to be a homosexual.
54. The IRB has conducted professional development training with its members on several occasions since 1995 to respond in part to concerns about the use of human rights documentation evidence in claims based on sexual orientation and gender identity. The author developed and presented these professional training seminars to RPD staff in 1995, 1999, 2003, and 2004; see Nicole LaViolette, 'Sexual Orientation and the Refugee Determination Process: Questioning a Claimant about their Membership in the Particular Social Group', in *Asylum Based on Sexual Orientation: A Resource Guide*, ed. Sydney Levy (San Francisco: IGLHRC, 1996). This particular training document was updated in 2004; see Nicole LaViolette, 'Sexual Orientation and the Refugee Determination Process: Questioning a Claimant about their Membership in the Particular Social Group' (on file with author). The training is also mentioned in Maria Jiménez, 'Nicaraguan Wins Reprieve in Bid to Remain in Canada', *Globe and Mail*, 10 February 2007; Jen Lahey, 'Sweating Bullets: How Canada's Gay Refugees Get Stuck in Legal Limbo', *Capital Xtra*, 20 February 2008, 14.

55. See *Re H.F.P.*, ¶ 9; *Re V.P.F.* [1999] CRDD No. 191 ¶ 4 (QL); *Re Y.J.E.* [1999] CRDD No. 288 ¶ 6 (QL); *Re P.L.Z.* [2000] CRDD No. 97 ¶ 11 (QL); *Re J.Q.U.* [2001] CRDD No. 90 ¶ 3 (QL).
56. See *Re U.O.D.* [1999] CRDD No. 106 ¶ 10 (QL); *Valdes* v. *Canada (Minister of Citizenship and Immigration)* [2004] RPDD No. 140 ¶ 30 (QL); see also *Re H.S.O.* [2001] CRDD No. 19 ¶ 17–19 (QL) (where the RPD rejected a video that had been submitted by the claimant which showed the claimant having sex with another man, and stated that the 'videotape was shot purposely to be used as evidence in the refugee hearing and the story about the claimant and xxxxx was a concoction to support his allegation that he was persecuted as a homosexual').
57. See *Re H.F.P.*; *Re G.J.M.*, ¶ 16; *Re P.L.L.* [2005] RPDD No. 21 ¶ 28; see also *Re U.P.V.* [1999] CRDD No. 145 (QL) (where a claimant's failure to provide corroborating letters from gay organisations he stated he was involved in led the adjudicator to conclude that he was not gay).
58. See *Re W.X.S.* [2004] RPDD No. 15 (QL) (where a Ugandan claimant filed a medical report in which a Ugandan doctor concluded that the claimant had been having regular anal sex. The claimant testified that this caused him to be expelled from school. The RPD accepted this document as credible in relation to establishing his homosexuality).
59. Matt Mills, 'Nicaraguan Refugee Goes into Hiding', *Xtra!*, 16 August 2007, http://www.xtra.ca/public/viewstory.aspx?AFF_TYPE=3&STORY_ID=3497&PUB_TEMPLATE_ID=2 (accessed 29 November 2008); Kevin Ritichie, 'Queer Refugees Unfairly Rejected, Critics Say', *Xtra!*, 11 October 2007, http://www.xtra.ca/public/viewstory.aspx?AFF_TYPE=3&STORY_ID=3717&PUB_TEMPLATE_ID=1 (accessed 29 November 2008).
60. Tracy J. Davis, 'Opening Doors of Immigration: Sexual Orientation and Asylum in the United States', *Human Rights Brief* 6, no. 3 (1999): 19.
61. Ibid.
62. See *Re R. (U.W.)*; *Re N.(K.U.)* [1991] CRDD No. 1140 (QL); *Re N. (L.X.)*; *Re P.(E.U.)*; *Re X. (W.B.)* [1992] CRDD No. 549 (QL); *Re J.(F.H.)* [1993] CRDD No. 98 (QL); *Re Q. (B.C.)* [1993] CRDD No. 209 (QL); *Re T. (F.N.)* [1993] CRDD No. 326 (QL); *Re H. (Y.F.)*; *Re H. (Y.N.)*; *Re I.O.D.*; *Re D. (C.J.)* [1995] CRDD No. 86 (QL); *Re C.L.Q.*; and *Re O.R.C.* [1997] CRDD No. 66 (QL).
63. This section is based in part on a previous paper published by the author: Nicole LaViolette, 'Proving a Well-Founded Fear: The Evidentiary Burden in Refugee Claims Based on Sexual Orientation', in *Asylum Based on Sexual Orientation: A Resource Guide*, ed. Sydney Levy (San Francisco: IGLHRC, 1996). For an examination of evidentiary issues related to sexual orientation claims in both the Canadian and Australian refugee determination processes, see Catherine Dauvergne and Jenni Millbank, 'Burdened by Proof: How the Australian Refugee Review Tribunal Has Failed Lesbian and Gay Asylum Seekers', *Federal Law Review* 31(2003): 299.
64. James D. Wilets, 'International Human Rights Law and Sexual Orientation', *Hastings International and Comparative Law Review* 18, no. 1 (1994): 72. Amnesty International had been lobbied for 17 years before finally deciding to regard those imprisoned for their sexuality as prisoners of conscience.
65. For instance, it was only in 1994 that Human Rights Watch, a well-respected human rights organisation based in the United States, adopted a statement opposing human rights violations against gay men and lesbians; see Human Rights Watch, 'Two Recent HRW Actions', press release, 24 July 1995. The International Commission of Jurists incorporated sexual minority equality into its mandate in 1994; see John Fisher, 'A Revolution that's Going Global', *Xtra!*, 5 August 1994, 13. The first Canadian NGO report on human rights violations against gay men and lesbians was published in April 1996 by the Inter-Church Committee on Human Rights in Latin America (ICCHRLA): ICCHRLA, *Violence Unveiled: Repression against Lesbians and Gay Men in Latin America* (Toronto, 1996), http://www.choike.org/documentos/gays_violence.pdf (accessed 29 November 2008).
66. The resistance of the international NGO community was evident at the 1993 UN World Conference on Human Rights held in Vienna. A first draft of the report of the NGO forum to be presented to a Plenary Session of the World Conference made no mention of the sexual minority issues that were discussed in several workshops of the Forum. Only after extensive lobbying were gay men and lesbians mentioned in the Final Report: ILGA, *The International Lesbian and Gay Association at the United Nations World Conference on Human Rights* (Brussels: ILGA 1993).

67. UN Economic and Social Council, Commission on Human Rights, *The Legal and Social Problems of Sexual Minorities*, E/CN.4/Sub.2/1988/31, 1987.

68. *Gay Times*, 'UN Briefed on Lesbian and Gay Human Rights', October 1992.

69. Rex Wockner, 'A Critical Mass', *Advocate*, 17 October 1995, 20–1.

70. *Re R. (U.W.)*.

71. *Re P. (E.U.)*.

72. See *Re X. (W.B.)*; *Re Q. (B.C.)*; *Re T. (F.N.)*; and *Re H. (Y.F.)*.

73. Juan Pablo Ordoñez, *No Human Being Is Disposable* (San Francisco: IGLHRC, 1995), 65–6. Ordoñez had his life threatened for investigating abuses against sexual minorities and had to leave Colombia as a result.

74. Ibid., 9.

75. IGLHRC, *The International Tribunal on Human Rights Violations against Sexual Minorities* (New York, 1995), 8–9, http://www.iglhrc.org/files/iglhrc/reports/Tribunal.pdf (accessed 29 November 2008).

76. *Re H. (Y.F.)*.

77. Ibid.

78. *Re N. (L.X.)*.

79. Ibid.

80. Ibid.

81. *Re H. (Y.F.)*.

82. Ibid. The same evidence was presented in an American asylum case when Dr Luis Mott, the sociologist who had investigated the murders, testified about his findings. The gay man from Brazil was granted asylum by an immigration judge in that case, who found that 'based on the testimony and the documentation submitted … the respondent's fear of persecution … is objectively reasonable'; see Jin S. Park, 'Pink Asylum: Political Asylum Eligibility of Gay Men and Lesbians under U.S. Immigration Policy', *UCLA Law Review* 42 (1995): 1153.

83. *Re H. (Y.N.)*.

84. Ibid.

85. For instance, IRB cited information from the Quaker Council for European Affairs on conscientious objectors in a National Documentation Package on the Ukraine: IRB, *National Documentation Package – Ukraine*, 19 March 2008, http://www.irb-cisr.gc.ca/en/research/ndp/index_e.htm?id=614 (accessed 29 November 2008). Information produced by Reporters Without Borders was included in a National Documentation Package on China: IRB, *National Documentation Package – China*, 19 March 2008, http://www.irb-cisr.gc.ca/en/research/ndp/index_e.htm?id=598 (accessed 29 November 2008). In a similar package about El Salvador, the IRB cited a report from the International Confederation of Free Trade Unions: IRB, *National Documentation Package – El Salvador*, 19 March 2008, http://www.irb-cisr.gc.ca/en/research/ndp/index_e.htm?id=605 (accessed 29 November 2008).

86. Amnesty International, letter to ILGA Members, 'AI Members for Lesbian and Gay Concerns', 28 June 1994.

87. Amnesty International members attended ILGA's international conference held in New York in June 1994.

88. *Re H. (Y.F.)*.

89. Amnesty International USA, *Breaking the Silence* (New York: Amnesty International USA, 1994), 37.

90. Julie Dorf, 'International Human Rights: Advocating for Gays and Lesbians' (lecture, University of Ottawa, Ottawa, Canada, 15 March 1994).

91. El-Farouk Khaki, interview by Nicole LaViolette, Toronto, May 1995.

92. See *Re H. (Y.N.)*.

93. Canadian Council for Refugees, Working Group on Refugee Protection, 'Addressing Claims Based on Sexual Orientation', policy statement, 1995, 4.

94. Amnesty International USA, *Breaking the Silence*; Amnesty International, *Violations of the Human Rights of Homosexuals: Extracts from Amnesty International Action Materials* (London, 1994); idem, *Killings of Gay Men in Chiapas: The Impunity Continues* (London, 1994); idem, *Human Rights Are Women's Rights* (New York, 1995), 169–210; see also *Re N. (O.I.)*, n. 17 (which relied on a news story which that reported that Amnesty International feared that sexual minorities were being persecuted in Venezuela); *Re J.J.Y.* [1996] DSSR

No. 50 (QL) (where information from Amnesty International was cited in relation to a Venezuelan claimant).

95. Committee to Protect Journalists, *Double Jeopardy: Homophobic Attacks on the Press, 1990–1995* (New York: Committee to Protect Journalists, 1995).
96. ICCHRLA, *Violence Unveiled*.
97. In 1996, the Lawyers Committee for Human Rights criticised the United States Department of State's *Country Reports on Human Rights Practices for 1993* for failing to report the persecution and murder of gay men in Mexico and the failure or lack of appropriate police investigations: see *Re N.K.O.* [1996] CRDD No. 238 ¶ 13 (QL).
98. Human Rights Watch, Free Expression Project, *A Ruling by U.S. Anti-Pornography Activists is Used to Restrict Lesbian and Gay Publications in Canada* (New York, 1994); Human Rights Watch/Helsinki, letter to the Russian Federation about the harassment of a gay journalist, 18 July 1995; Human Rights Watch/Americas, letter to the Salvadoran government about death threats to AIDS and gay groups, 6 July 1995; Human Rights Watch, *Unsettled Business; Human Rights in Chile at the Start of the Frei Presidency* (New York, 1994), 32–3; Scott Long, *Public Scandals: Sexual Orientation and Criminal Law in Romania* (New York: Human Rights Watch and IGLHRC, 1998), http://www.hrw.org/reports97/romania/ (accessed 29 November 2008); *Re S.E.X.* (citing information gathered by Human Right Watch in support of a claim from a Romanian gay man).
99. See, *e.g.*, IGLHRC and Human Rights Watch, *More than a Name: State-Sponsored Homophobia and Its Consequences in Southern Africa* (New York: Human Rights Watch, 2003), http://www.hrw.org/reports/2003/safrica/safriglhrc0303.pdf (accessed 29 November 2008); see also Cynthia Rothschild and Scott Long, *Written out: How Sexuality Is Used to Attack Women's Organizing* (IGLHRC and Center for Women's Global Leadership, 2005), http://www.iglhrc.org/files/iglhrc/WrittenOut.pdf (accessed 29 November 2008); Long, *Public Scandals*.
100. *Re H.F.P.*, ¶ 14–16.
101. *Re G.J.M.*, ¶ 23.
102. Amnesty International, *Crimes of Hate, Conspiracy of Silence: Torture and Ill-Treatment Based on Sexual Identity* (London, 2001), 33, http://www.amnesty.org/en/library/asset/ACT40/016/2001/en/dom-ACT400162001en.pdf (accessed 29 November 2008).
103. *Re F.C.B.* [1999] CRDD No. 89 ¶ 19 (QL).
104. *Re L.(O.V.)* [1995] CRDD No. 4 (QL). The same report was cited in *Re U.Y.O.*; and *Re Z.P.O.* [1996] DSSR No 47 (QL).
105. *Re W. (U.K.)*, n. 7; see also *Re G.U.S.* [1996] CRDD No. 239 (QL) (where a statement of Julie Dorf, then Executive Director of the IGLHRC, was cited in support of another Ukrainian claimant).
106. *Re B. (W.B.)*; see also *Re C.D.H.*; and *Re B.Q.D.* (citing IGLHRC information in support of certain Chilean lesbian claimants).
107. *Re W.R.O.* [2000] CRDD No. 284 ¶ 10 (QL); but see *Neto v. Canada (Citizenship and Immigration)* 2007 FC 664, [2007] FCJ No. 893 (QL) (where the RPD accepted a report from ILGA provided by IRB as reliable, but rejected an ILGA report produced by the claimant because it did not come from a reliable and independent source).
108. *Re Q.N.W.* [1998] CRDD No. 38 (QL).
109. *Re F.O.K.* [1998] CRDD No. 228 ¶ 33 (QL).
110. Ibid., ¶ 32.
111. Stobo, 'The Canadian Refugee Determination System', 387.
112. The author reviewed responses of the Directorate entitled 'Information Requests', which represent answers to questions received from then Convention Refugee Determination Division Board adjudicators.
113. IRB, Research Directorate, Documentation, Information and Research Directorate, *Question and Answer Series – Iran: Chronology of Events June 1989 – July 1994*, August 1994, 3 and 18.
114. As a contractor with Human Rights Internet, the author researched and produced the bibliography and selection of articles that was published by the Documentation, Information and Research Branch of IRB in June 1996.
115. IRB, 'Mexico: Treatment of Sexual Minorities', issue paper, April 1999, http://www.irb-cisr.gc.ca/en/research/publications/index_e.htm?docid=108&cid=0&disclaimer=hide (accessed 29 November 2008).

116. IRB, Research Directorate, 'Poland: Situation of Gays and Lesbians', extended response to information request, 11 May 1999, http://www.irb-cisr.gc.ca/en/research/publications/index_e.htm?docid=32&cid=0 (accessed 29 November 2008).

117. IRB, Research Directorate, 'Russia: Situation of Gays and Lesbians', extended response to information request, 14 May 1999, http://www.irb-cisr.gc.ca/en/research/publications/index_e.htm?docid=34&cid=0 (accessed 29 November 2008).

118. See, e.g., IRB, Research Directorate, 'Jamaica: Treatment of Homosexuals by Society and Government Authorities; Availability of Support Services (2004–2006)', responses to information requests, 22 February 2007, http://www.irb-cisr.gc.ca/en/research/rir/?action=record.viewrec&gotorec=450935 (accessed 29 November 2008); IRB, Research Directorate, 'Mongolia: The Treatment of Homosexuals by Authorities and by Society in General; Recourse Available to Those Who Have Been Harassed Based on Their Sexual Orientation (2004–March 2007)', responses to information requests, 16 March 2007, http://www.cisr-irb. gc.ca/en/research/rir/index_e.htm?action=record.viewrec&gotorec=451031 (accessed 29 November 2008) IRB, Research Directorate, 'Saudi Arabia: Treatment of Homosexuals by Authorities and by Society in General; Recourse Available to Those Who Have Been Targeted because of Their Sexual Orientation (2004–2007)', responses to information requests, 19 March 2007, http://www.irb-cisr.gc.ca/en/research/rir/index_e.htm?action=record.viewrec&gotorec=451049 (accessed 29 November 2008).

119. *Re L.L.R.* [1999] CRDD No. 18 ¶ 31 (QL).

120. Ibid., ¶ 46.

121. Ibid., ¶ 49–56.

122. *Re U.F.S.*

123. The author developed and presented professional training seminars on sexual orientation claims to IRB staff in 1995, 1999, 2003, and 2004. For a discussion of professional development training at IRB: see François Crépeau and Delphine Nakache, 'Critical Spaces in the Canadian Refugee Determination System: 1989–2002', *Journal of Refugee Law* 20, no. 1 (2008), 50, 94–6.

124. In fact, the professional development workshop addressed another recommendation made by the Canadian Council for Refugees, which called on the Board to provide training for staff and RPD adjudicators on issues relating to documentation; see Canadian Council for Refugees, *Addressing Claims Based on Sexual Orientation*.

125. In their 2003 comparative study, Dauvergne and Millbank concluded that the Canadian tribunal developed better evidentiary practices in relation to sexual orientation claims than its counterpart in Australia: Dauvergne and Millbank, 'Burdened by Proof', 317–20. Similar findings are made in Kassisieh, *From Lives of Fear to Lives of Freedom*.

126. Hathaway, *Law of Refugee Status*, 84.

127. *Re H. (Y.N.)*.

128. See Hathaway, *Law of Refugee Status*, 84, citing *Thind* v. *Canada (Minister of Employment and Immigration)* [1983] FCJ No. 939 (FCA).

129. Dauvergne and Millbank, 'Burdened by Proof', 309.

130. ARC International, 'ARC Annual Report 2006', http://www.arc-international.net/report2006.html (accessed 29 November 2008). The Yogyakarta Principles can be found at http://www.yogyakartaprinciples.org/ (accessed 29 November 2008).

131. ARC International, 'About Us', http://www.arc-international.net/about.html (accessed 29 November 2008).

132. United Nations High Commissioner for Human Rights (UNHCHR), 'Discrimination on the Basis of Sexual Orientation', http://www2.ohchr.org/english/bodies/chr/special/sexualorientation.htm (accessed 29 November 2008).

133. UNHCHR, *Resolution on Extrajudicial, Summary or Arbitrary Executions*, CHR Res. 2004/37, 55th Mtg., UN Doc. E/CN.4/2004/127 (19 April 2004), ¶ 6.

134. ILGA, ILGA Files, 'Supportive governments: 60 countries have publicly supported sexual orientation at the CHR/HRC between 2003 and 2008', http://www.ilga.org/news_results.asp?FileCategory=61&ZoneID=7&FileID=583 (accessed 20 November 2008).

135. Louise Arbour, 'Presentation of the Office of the United Nations High Commissioner for Human Rights', presentation to the International Conference on LGBT (Lesbian, Gays, Bisexual and Transgender) Human Rights, Montreal, 26 July 2006), http://www.unhchr.ch/huricane/

huricane.nsf/view01/B91AE52651D33F0DC12571BE002F172C?opendocument (accessed 29 November 2008).

136. Kassisieh, *From Lives of Fear to Lives of Freedom*, 38 (internal citations omitted).
137. IRB, 'Mongolia'.
138. IRB, Research Directorate, 'Turkey: Military and Societal Treatment of Homosexuals Who Have Been Deemed Unfit to Serve in the Military and/or Who Have Been Discharged from the Military Due to Their Sexual Orientation (January 2002 – September 2004)', responses to information requests, 10 September 2004, http://www.cisr-irb.gc.ca/en/research/rir/index_e.htm?action=record.viewrec&gotorec=44449 (accessed 29 November 2008).
139. For instance, a search of Amnesty International's online library yields full-length country reports on only a handful of countries: Amnesty International, *Poland and Latvia: Lesbian, Gay, Bisexual and Transgender Rights in Poland and Latvia* (London, 2006), http://www.amnesty.org/en/library/info/EUR01/019/2006/en (accessed 29 November 2008); idem, *Ecuador: Pride and Prejudice: Time to Break the Vicious Circle of Impunity for Abuses against Lesbian, Gay, Bisexual and Transgendered People* (London, 2002), http://www.amnesty.org/en/library/info/AMR28/001/2002/en (accessed 29 November 2008); idem, *Egypt: Torture and Imprisonment for Actual or Perceived Sexual Orientation* (London, 2001), http://www.amnesty.org/en/library/info/MDE12/033/2001/en (accessed 29 November 2008). Human Rights Watch lists the following reports on their website: Human Rights Watch, *'We Need a Law for Liberation': Gender, Sexuality, and Human Rights in a Changing Turkey* (New York, 2008), http://hrw.org/reports/2008/turkey0508/ (accessed 29 November 2008); idem, *Hated to Death: Homophobia, Violence, and Jamaica's HIV/AIDS Epidemic* (New York, 2004), http://hrw.org/reports/2004/jamaica1104/ (accessed 29 November 2008); idem, *In a Time of Torture: The Assault on Justice in Egypt's Crackdown on Homosexual Conduct* (New York idem, 2004), http://hrw.org/reports/2004/egypt0304/ (accessed 29 November 2008) idem, *Uniform Discrimination: The 'Don't Ask, Don't Tell' Policy of the U.S. Military* (New York, 2003), http://hrw.org/reports/2003/usa0103/ (accessed 29 November 2008) IGLHRC and Human Rights Watch, *More than a Name*; idem, *Hatred in the Hallways: Violence and Discrimination against Lesbian, Gay, Bisexual, and Transgender Students in U.S. Schools* (New York, 2008), http://www.hrw.org/reports/pdfs/c/crd/usalbg01.pdf (accessed 29 November 2008).
140. Mexico is apparently the largest source of refugee claimants generally in Canada; see Samantha Sarra, 'New Hearing for Rejected Mexican', *Xtra!*, 16 April 2008, http://www.xtra.ca/public/viewstory.aspx?AFF_TYPE=3&STORY_ID=4648&PUB_TEMPLATE_ID=9 (accessed 29 November 2008).
141. Ordoñez, *No Human Being Is Disposable*; Masha Gessen, *The Rights of Lesbians and Gay Men in the Russian Federation* (San Francisco: IGLHRC, 1994); Rachel Rosenbloom, *Unspoken Rules: Sexual Orientation and Women's Human Rights* (San Francisco: IGLHRC, 1995); Long, *Public Scandals*; and Luiz Mott, *Epidemic of Hate: Violations of the Human Rights of Gay Men, Lesbians, and Transvestites in Brazil* (San Francisco: IGLHRC, 1997).
142. IGLHRC and Human Rights Watch, *More than a Name*.
143. For instance, on 8 July 2008, the description for IGLHRC's programme in Africa did not appear to have been updated since 2003 when it announced the publication of *More than A Name*.
144. Ottosson, *State-Sponsored Homophobia*.
145. *Garcia* v. *Canada (Minister of Citizenship and Immigration)* [2005] FCJ No. 1008 (QL).
146. Ibid. ¶ 17.
147. United Nations Economic and Social Council, Commission on Human Rights, *Report of the Special Representative of the Secretary-General on Human Rights Defenders*, UN ECOSOC, 57th Sess., E/CN.4/2001/94 (2001), 24, http://www.unhchr.ch/Huridocda/Huridoca.nsf/0/d6c1b351bf405ad3c1256a25005109bc/$FILE/G0110638.pdf (accessed 29 November 2008).
148. Arbour, 'LGBT Human Rights'.
149. Ottosson, *State-Sponsored Homophobia*.
150. Human Rights Watch, *'We Need a Law for Liberation'*, 5.
151. Ibid., 5.
152. Human Rights Watch, *Homophobia*, 11.
153. Ibid.

154. Michael Battista, letter to Jean-Guy Fleury, Chairperson, IRB, 4 December 2002 (on file with author); see also Joel Dupuis, 'Believe the Hype: Refuge Evaluated According to Tourist Info', *Xtra!*, 9 January 2003, http://archives.xtra.ca/Story.aspx?s=14751297 (accessed 29 November 2008).

155. Battista, letter to Jean-Guy Fleury.

156. Dauvergne and Millbank, 'Burdened by Proof', 317–20.

157. But see *Re V.P.F.*, para. 12 (where the 'dearth of country conditions' information available on sexual minorities in Mongolia did not prejudice the claimants' case).

158. The RPD added, 'It is reasonable to infer that if gays and lesbians were being persecuted then these reports would have said so because Amnesty reports makes a point of referring to violations of human rights.' IRB, *Reasons for Decision – File A99-01249*, 28 June 2000, 3–4 (on file with author).

159. *Canada (Minister of Citizenship and Immigration)* v. *Shwaba* 2007 FC 80, [2007] FCJ No. 119 (QL).

160. Ibid., ¶ 20.

161. Kassisieh, *From Lives of Fear to Lives of Freedom*, 38, citing RRT Reference *N04/49352* (unreported, O'Brien, 30 September 2004).

162. See Mirko Bagaric and Penny Dimopoulos, 'Discrimination as the Touchstone of Persecution in Refugee Law', *International Journal of the Sociology of Law* 32, no. 4 (2004): 303.

163. *Ward* v. *Canada (Attorney General)*, 734.

164. *Rajudeen* v. *Canada (Minister of Employment and Immigration)* [1984], 55 NR 129, 133–4 (FCA).

165. Ibid.: the Federal Court of Appeal defined persecution thus: '[t]o harass or afflict with repeated acts of cruelty or annoyance ... to afflict or punish because of particular opinions ... a particular course or period of systematic infliction of punishment'.

166. See *Chan* v. *Canada (Minister of Employment and Immigration)* (1993) 20 Imm. LR (2d) 181, 208, [1993] 3 FC 675, 156 NR 279 (FCA), affirmed on other grounds (1995) 128 DLR (4th) 213; see also *Thirunavukkarasu* v. *Canada (Minister of Employment and Immigration)* (1993) 109 DLR (4th) 682 (FCA); *Surujpal* v. *Canada (Minister of Employment and Immigration)* (1985) 60 NR 73 (FCA).

167. *Ranjha* v. *Canada (Minister of Citizenship and Immigration)* 2003 FC 637, [2003] FCJ No. 901 ¶ 42 (QL); *N.K.* v. *Canada (Solicitor General)* [1995] FCJ No. 889 ¶ 21 (QL).

168. United Nations High Commissioner for Refugees (UNHCR), *Handbook on Procedures and Criteria for Determining Refugee Status under the 1951 Convention and the 1967 Protocol Relating to the Status of Refugees*, UN Doc. HCR/IP/4/Eng/Rev.1 (1979), http://www.unhcr.org/publ/PUBL/3d58e13b4.pdf (accessed 29 November 2008).

169. Ibid., ¶54.

170. *Sagharichi* v. *Canada (Minister of Employment and Immigration)* [1993] FCJ No. 796 (FCA) ¶ 3.

171. *Kaish* v. *Canada (Minister of Citizenship and Immigration)* [1999] FCJ No. 1041 ¶ 9 (QL).

172. *Sagharichi* v. *Canada (Minister of Employment and Immigration)*, ¶ 3. It is true also that identification of persecution behind incidents of discrimination or harassment is not purely a question of fact but a mixed question of law and fact.

173. *Gutkovski* v. *Canada (Secretary of State)* [1995] FCJ No. 566 ¶ 28 (QL).

174. *Re D.C.J.* [1995] CRDD No. 86 (QL); *Re N.K.O.* [1996] CRDD No. 238 (QL); *Re U.Y.O.*; *Re C.L.Q.*; and *Re U.V.G.* [1997] CRDD No. 250 (QL).

175. Kevin Ritchie, 'Successful Refugee Claims Decrease: Burgeoning Queer Movements at Home May Work against Homos', *Xtra!*, 17 January 2007, http://www.xtra.ca/public/viewstory.aspx?AFF_TYPE=3&STORY_ID=2556&PUB_TEMPLATE_ID=2 (accessed 29 November 2008).

176. Ibid.

177. *Cuesta* v. *Canada (Minister of Citizenship and Immigration)* [2003] RPDD No. 603 ¶ 34.

178. *Re N.E.V.* [2004] RPDD No. 225 ¶ 7 (QL).

179. *Titus-Glover* v. *Canada (Minister of Citizenship and Immigration)* [2006] RPDD No. 79 ¶ 25 (QL).

180. *Re S.T.V.* [2006] RPDD No. 11 ¶ 16 (QL).

181. For a discussion of how this has been an issue in Australian cases, see Kassisieh, *From Lives of Fear to Lives of Freedom*, 37.

182. *A.J.M.* v. *Canada (Minister of Citizenship and Immigration)* [2005] FCJ No. 142 ¶ 9 (QL).
183. Kassisieh, *From Lives of Fear to Lives of Freedom*, 38.
184. Amnesty International, *Crimes of Hate*, 27.
185. Kassisieh, *From Lives of Fear to Lives of Freedom*, 37.
186. *Zakka* v. *Canada (Minister of Citizenship and Immigration)* 2005 FC 1434, [2005] FCJ No. 1759 ¶ 11 (QL).
187. *Birsan* v. *Canada (Minister of Citizenship and Immigration)* [1998] FCJ No. 1861 (QL).
188. Ibid., ¶ 4.
189. *Oviawe* v. *Canada (Minister of Citizenship and Immigration)* 2006 FC 1114, [2006] FCJ No. 1421 ¶ 14.
190. *Sagharichi* v. *Canada (Minister of Employment and Immigration)*, ¶ 3.
191. *Inigo Contreras* v. *Canada (Minister of Citizenship and Immigration)* 2006 FC 603, [2006] FCJ No. 763 ¶ 12.
192. *Re J.Q.U.*
193. *Re E.K.G.* [1999] CRDD No. 54 ¶ 13-14 (QL).
194. Ibid., ¶ 15.
195. Ibid., ¶ 12–15.
196. *Re N.W.P.* [1999] CRDD No. 3 ¶ 9 (QL).
197. Ibid.
198. Kassisieh, *From Lives of Fear to Lives of Freedom*, 34.
199. Ibid.
200. Sonia Katyal, 'Sexuality and Sovereignty: The Global Limits and Possibilities of *Lawrence*', *William & Mary Bill of Rights Journal* 14, no. 4 (2006): 1448.
201. *De Seram* v. *Canada (Minister of Citizenship and Immigration)* 2007 FC 1123, [2007] FCJ No. 1487 ¶ 25. The Federal Court of Canada concluded that RPD committed a reviewable error by not considering contrary evidence that the police harassed, assaulted, and extorted money from gay men. Ibid., ¶ 30.
202. *Abdul Hameed* v. *Canada (Minister of Citizenship and Immigration)* [2004] RPDD No. 256 (QL).
203. *Re J.F.E.* [2007] RPDD No. 6 ¶ 21 (QL).
204. *Peiris* v. *Canada (Minister of Citizenship and Immigration)* [2004] FCJ No. 1510 ¶ 10.
205. Ibid., ¶ 21.
206. Ibid.
207. *Canada (Minister of Citizenship and Immigration)* v. *Flores Carrillo* (2008) 69 Imm. L.R. (3d) 309 ¶ 17 and 20.
208. Ibid., ¶ 30.
209. *Ward, Ward* v. *Canada (Attorney General)*, 724–5.
210. Ibid.
211. *Canada (Minister of Employment and Immigration)* v. *Villafranca* (1992) 18 Imm. LR (2d) 130 (FCA); *Sampayo* v. *Canada (Minister of Citizenship and Immigration)* [2004] RPDD No. 324 (QL); *Valdes* v. *Canada (Minister of Citizenship and Immigration)*.
212. *K.N.* v. *Canada (Minister of Citizenship and Immigration)* [1996] FCJ No. 1376 ¶ 5 (QL).
213. See *Re O.V.D.* [2002] CRDD No. 364 (QL).
214. *Re B.X.Y.* [2003] RPDD No. 8 (QL). For a description of jurisprudential guides and the two decisions designated as such, see IRB, 'Jurisprudential Guides', http://www.irb-cisr.gc.ca/en/references/policy/juriguides/index_e.htm (accessed 29 November 2008).
215. Immigration & Refugee Act.
216. Shannon Minter, 'Lesbians and Asylum: Overcoming Barriers to Access', in *Asylum Based on Sexual Orientation: A Resource Guide*, ed. Sydney Levy (San Francisco: IGLHRC, 1996), IB/3, IB/5–6; see also *Re D.A.K.* [2000] CRDD No. 338 ¶ 23 (QL) (where the RPD noted that discrimination against lesbians in Mexico happened 'usually only within the realm of private life'). An Amnesty International report confirmed that '[t]he imposition of such penalties for same-sex relations must be viewed in the context of the repression of other forms of consensual sexual behaviour which are seen to transgress strict religious or political codes, such as sexual relations between men and women outside marriage. Where gender discrimination is enshrined in law, women accused of any sexual activity outside marriage are particularly at risk of such penalties': Amnesty International USA, *Human Rights and Sexual Orientation and*

Gender Identity (New York, 2004), http://www.amnestyusa.org/outfront/document.do?id=9
F25DB548B5696C680256E5C00688E96 (accessed 29 November 2008); Amnesty
International, *Crimes of Hate*, 19.

217. *Re U.J.Y.* [2003] RPDD No. 23 (QL); *Perez* v. *Canada (Minister of Citizenship and Immigration)* [2004] RPDD No. 78 (QL).

218. *Re F.I.N.* [1995] CRDD No. 151 (QL); *Re L.U.M.* [1996] CRDD No. 193 (QL); *Re O.P.K.* [1996] CRDD No. 88 (QL); *Re G.U.S.* [1996] CRDD No. 66 (QL); *Re O.R.C.*; *Re E.N.U.*; *Re U.V.G.* [1997] CRDD No. 250 (QL); *Re Q.N.W.*; *Re U.O.D.*; *Re V.P.F.*. It was ironic that, in certain cases, a marriage or relationship of convenience was the only possible way to escape persecution: see *Re L. (M.D.)*; *Re P. (E.U.)*; *Burgos-Rojas* v. *Canada (Minister of Citizenship and Immigration)* [1999] FCJ No. 88 (QL); *Re O.R.R.* [2000] CRDD No. 122 (QL); *Re C.R.N.* [2001] CRDD No. 526 (QL).

219. *Re L.U.M.*: 'Being unmarried and without children would always subject me to ridicule and detection as a homosexual, and therefore always at risk'); see also *Re C.Y.T.*; *Re U.F.S.*; *Re K.V.T.* [1999] CRDD No. 64 (QL).

220. *Re A.M.A.* [2000] CRDD No. 103 ¶ 4 (QL).

221. *Re O.R.C.*

222. For an extensive review of documentary evidence on state protection, see *Re S.C.E.* [2004] RPDD No. 8 (QL).

223. *Re U.E.T.* [2000] CRDD No. 66 (QL).

224. Ibid., ¶ 34–6.

225. Ibid., ¶ 34.

226. Ibid., ¶ 35.

227. *Re J.M.Y.* [2000] CRDD No. 506 (QL).

228. Ibid., ¶ 9.

229. *Re E.K.G.*

230. Ibid., ¶ 12.

231. Tamara Letkeman, 'Gay Man Killed after Refugee Claim Denied', *Xtra!*, 6 July 2007, http://www.xtra.ca/public/viewstory.aspx?AFF_TYPE=1&STORY_ID=3287&PUB_TEMPLATE_ID=2 (accessed 29 November 2008).

232. Ibid.

233. Kassisieh, *From Lives of Fear to Lives of Freedom*, 55.

234. Ibid., 57.

235. Amnesty International, *Love, Hate and the Law: Decriminalizing Homosexuality* (London: Amnesty International, 2008), 7, http://www.amnesty.org/en/library/asset/POL30/003/2008/en/d77ce647-4cd3-11dd-bca2-bb9d43f3e059/pol300032008eng.pdf (accessed 29 November 2008).

236. Kassisieh, *From Lives of Fear to Lives of Freedom*, 57.

237. Ibid., 37, citing RRT Reference *060931294* [2006] RRTA 229 (unreported, Jacovides, 21 December).

238. Amnesty International, *Love, Hate and the Law*, 8.

239. Kassisieh, *From Lives of Fear to Lives of Freedom*, 37.

240. Authors have expressed general concerns that '[m]any cases show little consideration for the documentary evidence provided by the counsel for the claimant, and often this evidence is not even mentioned in the reasoning for rejection of the claim': Cécile Rousseau, François Crépeau, Patricia Foxen, and France Houle, 'The Complexity of Determining Refugeehood: A Multidisciplinary Analysis of the Decision-Making Process of the Canadian Immigration and Refugee Board', *Journal of Refugee Studies* 15, no. 1 (2002): 43, 56.

241. *Re D.I.Z.* [2000] CRDD No. 211 (QL).

242. Ibid., ¶ 17–18.

243. Ibid., ¶ 19.

244. *Pitrowski* v. *Canada (Minister of Citizenship and Immigration)* [2004] RPDD No. 449 (QL).

245. The case referred to the following report: LAMBDA Warsaw Association, *Report on Discrimination on Grounds of Sexual Orientation in Poland* (Warsaw, 2001).

246. Twenty-two per cent of respondents reported experiencing beatings, rapes, and physical assaults, and 51% experienced harassment; see *Pitrowski* v. *Canada (Minister of Citizenship and Immigration)*, ¶ 94 and 98.

247. Seventy-seven per cent of those who experienced violence did not report it to the police for fear of reaction of law enforcement officers and related social implications and 93.5% of those who experienced harassment did not report it to the police. *Pitrowski v. Canada (Minister of Citizenship and Immigration)*, ¶ 95, 98.
248. Ibid., ¶ 104.
249. Ibid., ¶ 106.
250. *Re B.B.Y.*
251. *Re J.V.D.* [2003] RPDD No. 237 ¶ 26–7 (QL): 'In the circumstances, the panel is of the opinion that, despite some restrictions, it is possible for the claimant to live as a homosexual, as he apparently did during all of the last years he spent in Lebanon. The panel is of the opinion that using the *Immigration and Refugee Protection Act* is not the appropriate way to shield the claimant from the prejudices that the Lebanese government and Lebanese society allegedly still have against homosexuality.'
252. *Garcia v. Canada (Minister of Citizenship and Immigration)*, ¶ 29; *Re U.O.D.*, ¶ 14.
253. Human Rights Watch, *Hated to Death*, 2.
254. *Re V.Z.D.* [2001] CRDD No. 37 (QL).
255. Ibid., ¶ 26.
256. *Re U.O.D.*, ¶ 23.
257. *Re A.M.A.*, ¶ 10.
258. *Re J.O.U.* [2007] RPDD No. 18 ¶ 14 (QL).
259. Ibid., ¶ 13.
260. James C. Hathaway, 'The Michigan Guidelines on the Internal Protection Alternative', *Michigan Journal of International Law* 21, no. 1 (1999): 211.
261. *Rasaratnam v. Canada (Minister of Employment and Immigration)* [1992] 1 FC 706, [1991] FCJ No. 1256.
262. *Thirunavukkarasu v. Canada (Minister of Employment and Immigration)* [1994] 1 F.C. 589, [1993] FCJ No. 1172.
263. *Rasaratnam v. Canada (Minister of Employment and Immigration)*, ¶ 4 and 6.
264. IRB, Legal Services, *Interpretation of the Convention Refugee Definition in the Case Law*, 31 December 2005, para. 8.3, citing *Chauhdry v. Canada (Minister of Citizenship and Immigration)* [1998] FCJ No. 1169.
265. *Re Q.L.O.* [2001] CRDD No. 471.
266. Ibid.
267. Candace Joseph, 'Refugees: So Near and Yet So Far', *Xtra!*, 5 July 2007, http://www.xtra.ca/public/viewstory.aspx?AFF_TYPE=3&STORY_ID=3259&PUB_TEMPLATE_ID=2 (accessed 29 November 2008).
268. *Orozco Gonzalez v. Canada* [2004] RPDD No. 120 ¶ 16–17.
269. Ibid., ¶ 17.
270. *Re P.L.L.*, ¶ 48.
271. Human Rights Watch, '*We Need a Law of Liberation*'.
272. *Gutierrez v. Canada (Minister of Citizenship and Immigration)* [2005] RPDD No. 179 (QL).
273. IRB, 'Notice of Revocation of Persuasive Decisions', policy note, May 2008, http://www.irb-cisr.gc.ca/en/references/policy/polnotes/rev_ta417681_10800203_18833_e.htm (accessed 29 November 2008).
274. IRB, 'Persuasive Decisions', policy note, December 2005, http://www.irb-cisr.gc.ca/en/references/policy/polnotes/persuasive_e.htm (accessed 29 November 2008).
275. Ibid.
276. *Re H.K.T.* [2007] RPDD No. 28 ¶ 15 (QL).
277. Andrew Reding, *Sexual Orientation and Human Rights in the Americas* (New York: World Policy Institute, 2003), 55–62. The report was cited in *Gutierrez v. Canada (Minister of Citizenship and Immigration)*, 3, n. 5.
278. *Parrales v. Canada (Minister of Citizenship and Immigration)* [2005] RPDD No. 326 ¶ 43–4 (QL); *Re Z.C.J.* [2007] RPDD No. 46 ¶14 (QL); *Re F.Y.G.* [2007] RPDD No. 44 ¶ 18 (QL); *Martinez v. Canada (Minister of Citizenship and Immigration)* [2005] RPDD No. 68 ¶ 22 (QL).
279. Letkeman, 'Gay Man Killed after Refugee Claim Denied'.
280. *Re H.K.T.* [2007] RPDD No. 28, 15 (QL).
281. Ibid.

282.   *Re H.W.X.* [2007] RPDD No. 4 ¶ 26 (QL).
283.   IRB, 'Treatment of Homosexuals and Availability of State Protection', responses to requests for information, June 2006, http://www.cisr-irb.gc.ca/fr/recherche/rdi/index_f.htm?action= record.viewrec&gotorec=450264 (accessed 29 November 2008).
284.   IRB, 'Notice of Revocation of Persuasive Decisions'.

Same-sex marriage and the Irish Constitution

Aisling O'Sullivan

Irish Centre for Human Rights, National University of Ireland, Galway, Ireland

This paper examines the recent Irish High Court case of *Zappone and Gilligan* v. *Revenue Commissioners and Others*, a challenge to the constitutionality of the state's interpretation of the Irish Tax Code vis-à-vis the foreign marriage of a same-sex couple and their right to marry each other under Irish law. The right to marry and the nature of marriage are undefined in the Irish Constitution. Thus, a progressive interpretation may take into account contemporary knowledge of sexuality and sexual orientation and norms of equality and non-discrimination. This paper also discusses the 'living document' approach to constitutional interpretation and argues that the High Court misapplied the methodology of Supreme Court Justice Murray in *Sinnott* v. *Minister for Education*, a methodology which may offer the means to interpret the Irish Constitution as protecting the right to marry another person of the same sex.

Introduction

The case of *Zappone and Gilligan* v. *Revenue Commissioners and Others*[1] was the first detailed judicial discussion in Ireland on an individual's right, if any, to marry another person of the same sex under the Irish Constitution and laws together with one's right to private and family life and to marry under the European Convention on Human Rights. In analysing the High Court judgment, I will focus solely on the constitutional questions that it poses, as the appellate proceedings currently pending before the Supreme Court will rest on the constitutional questions of the right to marry and not on compatibility with the Convention. I will examine the judicial interpretive approach underpinning the High Court judgment, namely, the 'living document' approach, and argue that the approach adopted by the High Court did not comport with that of the Supreme Court Justice Murray in *Sinnott* v. *Minister for Education*[2] upon which the High Court approach was supposedly based. Indeed, I argue that the *Sinnott* approach offers hopes for an interpretation alternative to the High Court's finding that would recognise a constitutional right to marry another person of the same sex.

Bunreacht na hÉireann (Constitution of Ireland) 1937

The drafting of the Irish Constitution preceded the process of international human rights standard-setting within the United Nations and regional organisations, a fact which is much reflected in the language and substantive content of its fundamental rights provisions

(Articles 40–4). As Whyte argues,[3] the language of the Constitution demonstrates the fusion of Christian and liberal democratic ideology, with Christian democratic ideology being influenced 'to some extent' by the Catholic teachings and doctrines of the time.[4] While this fusion, or perhaps tension, subsumes the entire text of the Constitution, it is particularly glaring in the fundamental rights provisions. For example, it has been argued that Article 40, which guarantees the personal rights of the citizen, including equality and the right to life, derives from 'secular and rationalist theory'.[5] In contrast, Article 41, which protects the rights of the family, and Article 42, which guarantees the right to education, are both considered to have been influenced by papal encyclicals and contemporary Catholic social teachings.[6] The family, which the Constitution defines as 'a natural and fundamental unit group' and whose rights are 'inalienable', 'imprescriptible' and 'antecedent and superior to all positive law',[7] is a 'moral institution' founded upon 'marriage'.[8]

Chubb has applied Martin's theory of secularisation to early twentieth-century state-building in Ireland on the basis of a religious and nationalist identity,[9] wherein Martin argues that an 'indissoluble union' of Church and state occurs in circumstances where the Church constitutes the sole agent of nationalism against political and cultural domination by a foreign power.[10] Thus, nations with such a union remain 'areas of high practice and belief'.[11] Keogh explains that in the decade following the Irish war of independence and a bitter civil war in Ireland, there was 'a pressing need for common ground where citizens could gather irrespective of political affiliation, which found expression in the search for marks of national identity, which were identifiably different from those that have long characterised the British national ethos'.[12] In particular, religion and language became 'the two most obvious hallmarks of independent Ireland'.[13] More recently, however, Hogan criticises previous literature on the drafting of the Constitution for over-emphasising the influences of the Church and for failing to acknowledge the extent of improvements upon the 1922 Saorstát Éireann (Free State) Constitution and the role of drafters other than the incumbent Taoiseach (Prime Minister) Eamon de Valera, and further argues that as a result of the Northern Ireland conflict many commentators focused on aspects of the Irish Constitution considered to be confessional or to be offensive to the minority religious or political traditions.[14] Instead, the more remarkable facet of the Constitution, Hogan discerns, is the extent of its secular or liberal democratic values, its respect for individual rights, its separation of Church and state, and the extent to which it does *not* reflect the Catholic teachings of the 1930s.[15] Based on a comparative analysis, he contends that the Constitution in many respects is not dissimilar to other constitutions of its age. The original text of Article 44, respecting freedom of religion yet explicitly recognising the special position of the Roman Catholic Church, is often cited as a prime example of the Irish Constitution's overt Catholic influences and its uniqueness.[16] However, from 'a necessarily incomplete' survey of written or 'unwritten' constitutions from other European states in the pre- and post-Second World War periods,[17] Hogan concludes that a 'broad pattern' emerged: predominantly Protestant or Lutheran states would provide for an established church; predominantly Catholic states the 'special position' status of the Roman Catholic Church; and predominantly Orthodox states either an established or a specially positioned church.[18] Thus, judging by the contemporary European standards of 1937, Hogan argues that the 'special position' of the Roman Catholic Church in the original text of Article 44 was not of an exceptional character.[19]

Another provision often cited as embodying and representing the influences of Catholic social teachings is the express constitutional protection for the institution of marriage in Article 41. However, this was not an idea original to the drafters. Hogan refers to Article 119 of the 1919 Constitution of the Weimar Republic, which expressly conferred special constitutional protection on the institution of marriage.[20] In fact, the Irish and the Weimar Constitutions had other similarities,[21] demonstrating the influence of comparative constitutional traditions already prevalent at the time. Hogan argues that Articles 41 and 42 most probably 'reflect a diverse jumble of sources, ranging from papal encyclicals to the Weimar provisions to Article 16 of the [Anglo-Irish Treaty of 1921]'.[22] Expectation for a wholly secular document would be unrealistic given Ireland's pre-Constitution history, and the Constitution's language and content reflect a wider range of sources than has previously been considered.[23]

Interpretation of Bunreacht na hÉireann

How important is the source of inspiration for Articles 41 and 42? Hogan argues that even if the provisions were exclusively inspired by Catholic social teachings, 'the case law has long since broken loose of that particular inspirational source'.[24] This independence began with *McGee* v. *A.G.*,[25] where the Supreme Court ruled that a right to marital privacy protected a spouse from state interference with the use of contraceptives within marriage through the criminal law. However, the inspiration did also enable the natural law approach to constitutional interpretation to have particular vibrancy in early jurisprudence, most notably through application of the doctrine of unenumerated rights developed in *Ryan* v. *A.G.*[26] There the High Court held that Article 40(3)(2), which respected 'in particular' the right to life, person, good name and property, was a 'detailed statement' of the rights protected under the general guarantee of Article 40(3)(1), which 'must extend to rights not specified in Article 40' as derived from 'the Christian and democratic nature of the State'.[27] Thus, it fell upon individual judges to determine the existence of such unenumerated rights, which the courts have since undertaken as part of the common law tradition.[28]

As one of the factors for its continuing prevalence, the 'willingness' of some judges to invoke a natural legal order enabling the natural law approach to have a 'stubborn vibrancy' has been cited.[29] However, Hogan and Whyte argue that there has also been growing 'judicial unease' with determining the theoretical source for the rights protections.[30] For example, in *T.F.* v. *Ireland*,[31] the High Court refused to admit the expert testimony of theologians on natural legal theory regarding marriage or the essential features of Christian marriage,[32] holding that while the constitutional order may recognise a natural legal order the determining factor for the judge was the express or implied terms of the fundamental rights provisions, 'from whatever source they are derived'.[33] In *Re Article 26 and the Information (Termination of Pregnancies) Bill, 1995*,[34] the Supreme Court rejected the notion that natural law as the fundamental law of the state prevailed over the express determination of the people, who are 'paramount',[35] in exercising their power to amend the Constitution through a referendum.[36] However, the courts have failed to reach a consensus on the philosophy underpinning the rights protections, *North Western Health Board* v. *H.W.*[37] being a clear demonstration of the differing views. There the Supreme Court offered two philosophies underpinning Article 41: natural law in common with other philosophies[38] and the pre-Reformation common law tradition.[39] In this respect, Hogan advocates a focus solely on the 'inherent value of the right' to be protected rather than on the probable philosophical underpinnings.[40]

The natural law approach is one of five different interpretative approaches traditionally identified within the jurisprudence; the others are, namely, the literal, the broad, the harmonious and the historical.[41] As Hogan and Whyte emphasise, there is no consistency within the case law regarding any of the particular approaches, raising worry that 'individual judges are willing to rely on any such approach as will offer adventitious support for a conclusion' already reached.[42] These approaches, in particular the natural law approach, have been discussed elsewhere.[43]

The right to marry and the institution of marriage in Ireland

In 1951, the High Court adjudicated on a provision within the code of practice for members of An Garda Síochána (Irish Police) requiring police officers to inform the Garda Commissioner of their intention to marry. *Donovan* v. *Minister for Justice*[44] is noteworthy as the first judgment to find that a right to marry was implied in the Constitution. Subsequently, in *Ryan*, the High Court discerned that a right to marry derived from Article 41 of the Constitution, particularly the reference to 'the institution of marriage' in Article 41(3)(1), but that such a right was protected also as a personal right under Article 40(3)(1). The court reasoned that the terms 'constitution and authority' in Article 41 determined the scope of the rights of the family as a 'moral institution' founded upon marriage.[45] The ruling was then followed by the High Court in *Murray* v. *Ireland*[46] and subsequently upheld by the Supreme Court; the High Court in *Murray* supported the finding of Article 41 as a provision protecting the collective rights of the family whereas 'personal rights, which each individual member might enjoy by virtue of membership of the family', must be protected under Article 40(3).[47]

The courts have interpreted the nature of marriage in accordance with the common law tradition. The oft-cited definition of marriage originated from the English family court's decision in *Hyde* v. *Hyde and Woodmansee*,[48] where polygamy was at issue. The court concluded that 'marriage, as understood in Christendom, may ... be defined as the voluntary union for life of one man and one woman, to the exclusion of all others'.[49] In *Ussher* v. *Ussher*,[50] the Irish High Court of Justice described the common law and canon law of England and Ireland as identical in the pre-Reformation period and 'all were substantially governed, so far as marriage law is concerned, by the Canon law, as decreed and expounded from Rome'[51] but administered by the ecclesiastical court sometimes referred to as the 'Court Christian'.[52]

However, pre-1937 statute law and case law must be consistent with the Irish Constitution.[53] According to *Pigs Marketing Board* v. *Donnelly (Dublin)*[54] and *Educational Company* v. *Fitzpatrick*,[55] a statute enacted by Parliament of Saorstát Éireann (Irish Free State) or of the United Kingdom does not enjoy a presumption of constitutionality that attaches to post-1937 Acts of the Oireachtas (Houses of Parliament of Ireland). The courts apply a presumption of constitutionality to guarantee judicial deference to the Oireachtas and place the burden on the petitioner to prove otherwise. The only exception for a pre-1937 law is where the Oireachtas has effectively re-enacted the common law or statutory rule.[56] The common law definition of marriage has been applied by Irish courts and re-enacted by the Oireachtas through the Civil Registration Act 2004, which lists 'both parties are of the same sex' as an impediment to a valid marriage.[57] Express reference to the common law definition of marriage was made in *B.* v. *R.*,[58] where the High Court prescribed marriage, as previously and contemporaneously conceived, as 'the voluntary and permanent union of one man and one woman to the exclusion of all others for life'.[59] In *Murray*, the High Court described marriage as 'derived from a Christian notion of partnership', 'a partnership based on an irrevocable personal consent given by both spouses which establishes a unique and very special life-long relationship'.[60] Supreme Court Justice McCarthy in *N.* v. *K.*[61] went further to hold that marriage, as a 'civil contract', created 'reciprocating rights and duties between the parties' and constituted a 'status' relationship affecting the individual parties and the community as a whole.[62] *Murray* and

N. v. K. were subsequently approved by the Supreme Court in *T.F. v. Ireland*.[63] In *T. (D.) v. T. (C.)*,[64] Supreme Court Justice Murray held marriage to be 'a solemn contract of part-nership entered into between a man and a woman with a special status recognised by the Constitution'.[65]

In *Foy v. An t-Ard Chláraitheoir*,[66] the High Court discussed the issue of capacity. The petitioner, who suffered from gender dysphoria, challenged the refusal of the Registrar to amend her birth certificate to accord with her male-to-female gender reassignment[67] and sought a declaration of unconstitutionality vis-à-vis the Registration of Births and Deaths (Ireland) Act 1863 (as amended) for breaching her rights to equality, privacy and dignity as well as her right to marry under the Constitution.[68] While the court refused relief, it called upon the Oireachtas to urgently review the matter that had such impact on many indi-viduals 'in a most personal and profound way ... of deep concern to any caring society'.[69] It must be noted that the petitioner claimed that the state arbitrarily interfered with her right to marry a biological male and was not seeking to be or remain married to a biological female. Hence, the petitioner challenged not the common law definition of marriage as opposite-sex-based but the legal concept of gender as solely based on biological factors determined at birth. Importantly for the court, she was legally married to (albeit separated from) a biological female and had not sought divorce or annulment.[70] Thus, her existing marriage was more immediately relevant to her lack of capacity than her birth certificate.[71] Notwithstanding, the court reaffirmed the common law definition of marriage as opposite-sex-based[72] and held that the right to marry was not absolute and must be evaluated in the context of other constitutional rights, including the 'rights of society'.[73] It is clear that the potential dissolution of the petitioner's marriage weighed heavily in the court's decision.[74] Such 'unease', in the light of the fact that all of her other legal documents recognised her reassigned gender identity, struck a 'fair, reasonable and just balance' in the context of com-peting constitutional rights.[75] Thus, it would appear that the right to marry under Article 40(3) was evaluated *against* the rights of the family under Article 41. As for the 'rights of society', the court stressed the need to be 'conscious of society as a whole',[76] which appeared to be invoking concepts such as the 'common good' that the Preamble prescribes as an aim pursued by the state in order to ensure the dignity of the individual and to attain true social order. In its judgment, the court referred to the harmonious approach,[77] whereby a provision of the Constitution must be construed in such a way that it would not 'lead to conflict with other Articles and which conforms with the Constitution's general scheme'.[78] The courts, thus, must interpret provisions not in isolation but must harmonise a particular provision with the Constitution as a whole.[79] The doctrine has been described as 'no more than a presumption that the people who enacted the Constitution had a single scale of values and wished those values to permeate their charter evenly and without internal discor-dance'.[80] Thus, in *Foy* the court must harmoniously interpret the right to marry within the context of the fundamental rights provisions as a whole and the avowed aspirations of the Constitution. Again, it is clear that the controlling issue was the inability of the petitioner's marriage to remain legally valid if her reassigned gender identity were to be legally recognised on her birth certificate given that under the law as it stood marriage must be between two persons of opposite sexes. The High Court, then, appeared to find that the right to marry must not impinge upon the rights of the family or bring about the dissolution of a valid marriage other than by divorce or annulment.

As Eardly argues, however, by interpreting the Constitution on the basis of the common law and statute, the court in *Foy* effectively sidestepped the petition, that the definition of marriage under the common law and statute was itself unconstitutional.[81] Thus, the Constitution must 'reflect the common law and statute rather than the other way round'.[82]

As Supreme Court Justice Walsh has pointed out in his extra-judicial writings, the Constitution as the 'basic law of the State' 'controls the Statute and Common law' and, in cases of conflict, prevails.[83]

It is also of note that the court's judgment was delivered immediately before the European Court of Human Rights rendered its judgment in *Goodwin* v. *United Kingdom*,[84] where the Strasbourg court ruled that gender may be determined by criteria other than ones 'purely biological',[85] thus recognising the gender of post-operative transgender persons. After *Goodwin*, the European Convention on Human Rights Act 2003 was enacted, which incorporated the Convention into Irish law through an interpretative mode of incorporation at sub-constitutional level.[86] The courts must thenceforth interpret and apply any statutory provision or rule of law 'as far as possible' in a manner compatible with Ireland's obligations under the Convention[87] and, in cases where no other legal remedy is adequate, issue a declaration of incompatibility.[88] In 2007, Foy became the first person to be granted a declaration of incompatibility by the High Court.[89] There the court strongly reprimanded the state for its failure to legislate for gender recognition[90] given the intervening five-year period since its initial decision and *Goodwin*. The court noted the petitioner's ongoing divorce proceedings[91] but maintained that if the petitioner had been divorced it would have held the reasoning in *Goodwin* on the right to marry under Article 12 to be compelling and applicable in Ireland notwithstanding Articles 41 and 42 of the Constitution.[92] Consequently, while it has not been definitively stated,[93] it seems certain that the right to marry in Irish law extends to persons who have undergone post-gender reassignment and who seek to marry someone of the opposite sex.

In *Zappone and Gilligan* v. *Revenue Commissioners and Others*, the petitioners challenged the Revenue Commissioners' decision to preclude them from availing of tax benefits afforded exclusively to married couples under the Taxes Consolidation Act 1997.[94] The petitioners supported their claim as a married couple with their marriage certificate from British Columbia, Canada.[95] However, the commissioners refused their claim on the basis of the phrase 'husband and wife' in the taxes legislation as defined by the Oxford English dictionary, which referred to an opposite-sex marital relationship.[96] In their application before the High Court, the petitioners argued that by failing to recognise their marriage the state 'acted without lawful authority, subjected the plaintiffs to unjust and invidious discrimination and acted in breach of the constitutional rights of the plaintiffs' under Articles 40 and 41. Further and alternatively, the state's refusal to legally recognise their foreign marriage constituted discrimination on grounds of gender and/or sexual orientation in breach of Article 14 of the European Convention on Human Rights in conjunction with Article 8 (right to private and family life) and Article 12 (right to marry).

The petitioners argued that the right to marry was a gender-neutral 'right to marry the one you love' and the state arbitrarily interfered with their right to marry through unjustifiable legal restrictions on capacity such as gender or sexual orientation as opposed to justifiable restrictions such as degrees of relationship or marriageable age.[97] The petitioners argued that gender and sexual orientation constituted prima facie discriminatory grounds[98] and the burden shifted to the state to justify such restrictions on their right to marry each other.[99]

While the petitioners conceded that the framers of the Constitution considered the nature of marriage as opposite-sex-based, they nonetheless emphasised that the courts had never considered 'whether marriage could encompass same sex marriage'.[100] Importantly, the description of marriage as a 'very special life-long relationship' equally applied to marriage between two persons of the same sex.[101] Furthermore, while the common law exclusion of same-sex marriage was based on capacity, there was no equivalent provision in the Constitution.[102] Underpinning their case was that the Constitution should be interpreted as a 'living document'.[103] Thus, the definition of marriage was not constitutionally fixed or frozen but must be interpreted in accordance with 'prevailing ideas and concepts'. In this respect, they cited a changing consensus on marriage with reference to decisions from the United States and Canada.[104]

By contrast, the state argued that the established methods of interpreting the Constitution could not give rise to a right to marry for the petitioners.[105] Otherwise, the court would 'rewrite the plain wording of Article 41' as well as the recent social policy choice of the Oireachtas.[106] Instead of harmoniously construing Article 41 with the fundamental rights provisions as a whole, the provision was clearly intended to be for 'the family constituting a mother, father and children of a heterosexual marriage'.[107] For the court to rule otherwise would amount to an amendment to the Constitution without requisite referendum.[108] Furthermore, the state contended that no jurisprudential basis had been presented that would allow for such radical alteration of the nature of marriage. The 'living document' approach, advocated by the petitioners, did not allow 'the courts to depart from what the Constitution says or implies or was understood in 1937'.[109] While the courts may interpret the Constitution in light of prevailing ideas, this did not mean that 'the words of the Constitution can be divorced from their historical context'.[110] Although the High Court considered that the Constitution should be interpreted as a 'living document', it agreed with the state that there was a difference between discovering unenumerated rights in *McGee* and re-defining a right 'clearly understood ... to mean something which it has never done to date'.[111] Based on its analysis of Supreme Court Justice Murray's methodology in *Sinnott*,[112] the court ultimately found that marriage, as contemporaneously understood, was opposite-sex-based and refused relief.

The 'living document' approach to constitutional interpretation is one yet to be entrenched within the jurisprudence. It may be traced to Supreme Court Justice Walsh's dictum in *McGee* where he proposed the virtues of prudence, justice and charity as jurisprudential guides to 'discovering' the existence of unenumerated rights, holding that '[i]t is but natural that from time to time the prevailing ideas of these virtues may be conditioned by the passage of time; no interpretation of the Constitution is intended to be final for all time. It is given in the light of prevailing ideas and concepts.'[113] It ought to be noted that Justice Walsh himself interpreted the Constitution in *McGee* on the basis of the natural law approach,[114] reiterating that Articles 40–4 subordinated law to justice,[115] the highest virtue in ancient Greek and early Christian philosophy, reinforced by prudence and charity, two other virtues that were also highly esteemed in ancient Greece and Christianity.[116] These three virtues were expressly stated in the Preamble to the Constitution as part of the central aim 'to promote the common good ... so that the dignity and freedom of the individual may be assured [and] true social order attained'.[117] Thus, judges must 'as best they can from their training and their experience interpret these rights in accordance with *their* ideas of prudence, justice and charity'.[118]

However, can his analysis have a broader application than as a jurisprudential tool for discovering unenumerated rights? Support may be derived from Justice Walsh's use of the semi-colon. *Hart's Rules* state that a semi-colon 'separates two or more clauses which are of more or less equal importance and are linked as a pair or series'.[119] Thus, the conditioning of prevailing ideas of prudence, justice and charity by the passage of time and the lack of a fixed interpretation of the Constitution are independent clauses. They have a close relation to one another and possess equal importance. My argument is further supported by the final sentence in Justice Walsh's dictum. 'It' refers to the interpretation of the Constitution, which must be interpreted in accordance with 'prevailing ideas and concepts'. In addition, as Justice Walsh has stated extra-judicially, the courts should view the Constitution as a 'contemporary fundamental law that speaks in the present tense'.[120] Thus, 'as a document, [the Constitution] speaks from 1937, but as law it speaks from today',[121] and it should be interpreted not as 'having a static meaning determined 50 years ago but on the basis that it lays down broad governing principles that can cope with current problems'.[122] It is argued that Justice Walsh advocated contemporaneous interpretation of the Constitution on the basis of 'prevailing' ideas of prudence, justice and charity. However, the 'prevailing ideas and concepts' are to be determined by individual judges who may or may not be influenced by their own subjective ideas and concepts when interpreting the Constitution. Subsequently, the Supreme Court in *State (Healy)* v. *O'Donoghue*[123] invoked Justice Walsh's dictum and argued that the 'rights given by the Constitution' must be 'considered' or determined in accordance with prudence, justice and charity, concepts that may gradually change and develop according to prevailing ideas and concepts.[124] The court held that such an approach to constitutional interpretation inhered in the Preamble to the Constitution.[125]

More recently in *Sinnott*, Supreme Court Justices Murray, Geoghegan and Denham agreed with the thesis that the Constitution should be regarded as a living document and interpreted in accordance with 'contemporary circumstances', including prevailing ideas and mores.[126] Justice Murray, however, qualified that an interpretation 'in accordance with contemporary circumstances' cannot be 'divorced from its historical context';[127] 'by definition that which is contemporary is determined by reference to its historical context'.[128] Justice Murray endorsed Kelly's guidance for balancing competing claims between the historical and the 'present tense' approaches.[129] Kelly contended that the 'present tense' approach was appropriate to standards and values; personal rights, the common good, social justice, and equality 'can (indeed can only be) interpreted according to the lights of today as Judges perceive and share them'.[130] Yet the historical approach was appropriate 'where some law-based *system* is in issue, like jury trial, county councils, the census'.[131] This, however, did not mean that 'the shape of such systems is in every respect fixed in the permafrost of 1937. The courts ought to have some leeway for considering which dimensions of the system are secondary, and which are so material to traditional constitutional values that a willingness to see them diluted or substantially abolished without a referendum could not be imputed to the enacting electorate.'[132]

In *Sinnott*, the petitioner was a 22-year-old person with profound general learning disability and autism, who succeeded in his claim before the High Court that the state was under a duty to provide free primary education beyond the age of 18 and for so long as his educational needs required.[133] The Supreme Court by majority allowed a limited appeal by the state and ruled that the duty of the state was owed children not adults and the petitioner was entitled to free primary education up to the age of 18 as appropriate to his needs as an autistic child.[134] There, Justice Murray held that historically the meaning of 'primary education' was always understood to be education for children in the primary school cycle. While the ages at which the primary cycle was to begin and to end might be 'a variant of history, culture and policy in any given country', it was understood to be the primary school cycle in which children and not adults were taught.[135] However, the judge held that the 'nature and concept' of primary education may be determined in light of present-day circumstances (to paraphrase Kelly's guidance), as the concept of primary education is an 'abstract concept with connotations of standards and values'.[136] Historically, as at the time of the promulgation of the Constitution, persons with intellectual disability were not able to benefit from primary education as was traditionally available, for it would not have been considered to encompass the provision of basic education and training skills, such as toilet training and basic mobility, but rather the primary school cycle and curriculum.[137] Justice Murray maintained that 'with greater insight into the nature of people's handicaps, the evolution of teaching methods, new curricula as well as new tools of education, there is no doubt that the nature and content of primary education must be defined in contemporary circumstances',[138] and that where children 'are capable of benefiting from primary education (however its content is defined), the State is under an obligation to ensure that it is provided free to children'.[139] As for the duration of childhood, Justice Murray considered it a secondary matter and reasoned that limitations were for the government and the Oireachtas to determine although they were subject to judicial review by the courts in cases where their determination may have failed their constitutional obligations.[140] Justice Murray's emphasis on 'contemporary circumstances' modified Justice Walsh's dictum that the judge ought to interpret the Constitution in accordance with his or her prevailing ideas of prudence, justice and charity, and arguably lessened the room for judicial subjectivity by focusing on contemporary knowledge in medical, scientific and sociological research rather than on abstract philosophical concepts. Justice Murray then supported his reasoning through the harmonious approach, interpreting the duty of the state in the context of Article 42 as a whole and concluding that the provision was 'child-centred'.[141] The reference in Article 42(1) to the 'Family' as the natural educator of the 'child' set the tone, and subsequent paragraphs in Article 42 outlined the parameters for state interference with the rights and duties of parents in its role as 'guardian of the common good.[142]

In *Zappone and Gilligan*, then, the High Court held that on the basis of *Sinnott* the concept of marriage as at 1937 ought to be established, whereas capacity must be determined in accordance with the prevailing law.[143] Thus, the court acknowledged that the framers of the Constitution could not have contemplated a same-sex union within the concept of marriage in 1937, but the prevailing law, including the High Court decision in *Foy* and the Supreme Court decision in *T. v. T.*,[144] clearly did not support a concept of marriage as 'fossilised'.[145] The court also referred to the recent reform of marriage law through the Civil Registration Act 2004, which enjoyed the presumption of constitutionality and must constitute a clear indication of the prevailing 'ideas and concepts' of marriage.[146]

This, however, begs the question of whether, in dealing with capacity to exercise a right constituting a traditional constitutional value, recently enacted legislation or regulation can suffice. Clearly, deference should be had to the Oireachtas, which is under a constitutional duty to legislate in accordance with the Constitution, and such deference by the courts is mandated by the presumption of constitutionality that must be rebutted by a petitioner. In *Zappone and Gilligan*, success for the petitioners would have rendered the Civil Registration Act 2004 unconstitutional despite the fact that they did not directly challenge the particular statute; the subject of their challenge was the Taxes Consolidation Act 1997, which applied the same interpretation of marriage as the Civil Registration Act.

Furthermore, while legislation may indicate the contemporary majority view, the majority view itself, in the words of South African Constitutional Court Justice Albie Sachs, 'can often be harsh to minorities that exist outside the mainstream'.[147] Thus, the function of the Constitution is 'to step in and counteract rather than reinforce unfair discrimination against a minority'.[148] Vindicating rights under the Constitution protects groups who have been discriminated against by the ordinary law and who cannot 'count on popular support and strong representation in the legislature'.[149] The judge considered that the test under the South African Constitution was whether the measure 'promotes or retards the achievement of human dignity, equality and freedom'.[150] In a similar vein, the Irish Constitution embodies and enshrines the objective that measures taken by the state ensure the dignity of the individual so that true social order may be attained.[151]

As the High Court held in *Murray*, when dealing with limitations imposed by the state, it is to balance not the right of the state and the right of the individual but the power of the state and whether the exercise of its power is constitutionally permissible. Thus, the Constitution imposes 'very clear and specific correlative duties' upon the state to protect and vindicate the personal rights of the citizen but it also designates the state as the guardian of the common good, which as such is empowered to restrict a personal right in certain circumstances.[152] In *Zappone and Gilligan*, the High Court did not examine whether *the relevant case law and statute* undermined a personal right. In other words, can an indefinite bar to exercising the right to marry, rather than an age-related limitation, constitute a legitimate exercise of state power?

It is important to note that the approach to contemporaneous constitutional interpretation taken by the High Court in *Zappone and Gilligan* differed from Supreme Court Justice Murray's methodology in *Sinnott*, where capacity to partake in a law-based system (state primary education) was first discerned against historical and contemporary circumstances to derive a traditional constitutional value (right to education) and then assessed through a harmonious textual analysis of Article 42. To adopt the approach in relation to the question of marriage, it is clear that marriage as an institution is a law-based system derived from what is a core 'traditional constitutional value', namely, the right to marry. Therefore, the nature and content of marriage as a law-based system must be examined from a historical context and yet interpreted in accordance with 'contemporary circumstances'; thus, the institution of marriage must be interpreted in accordance with contemporary standards and values, including greater insights into sexuality and sexual orientation, relevant advances in technologies, and, above all, contemporary standards of equality and non-discrimination. Then, a harmonious textual analysis of Articles 40(3) and 41 must support such an examination with regard to capacity to marry.

While the institution of marriage in Ireland was conceived in accordance with the common law tradition as exclusive to opposite-sex couples and has been repeatedly and consistently upheld by the courts and recently re-enacted by the Oireachtas, it is noteworthy that certain jurisdictions where this common-law definition was applicable have now moved forward to recognise the equal worth and dignity of sexual minorities in all aspects of their lives. As the Canadian Supreme Court pointed out in its *Reference re Same-Sex Marriage*:[153]

> The reference to 'Christendom' is telling. *Hyde* spoke to a society of shared social values where marriage and religion were thought to be inseparable. This is no longer the case. Canada is a pluralistic society. Marriage, from the perspective of the state, is a civil institution. The 'frozen concepts' reasoning runs contrary to one of the most fundamental principles of Canadian constitutional interpretation: that our Constitution is a living tree which, by way of progressive interpretation, accommodates and addresses the realities of modern life.[154]

Recognition of pluralism and maintenance of religious neutrality have always been noted in Irish jurisprudence.[155] Thus, while bearing in mind the historical origins and context of marriage, the Irish Constitution ought to be interpreted in the light of 'contemporary circumstances', including the recognition that sexuality is 'a feature of the human condition'.[156] In Ireland, sexual orientation already constitutes a prohibited ground of discrimination in employment[157] and access to goods and services.[158]

Under the Constitution, all citizens are equal before the law.[159] In *In re Article 26 and the Employment Equality Bill 1996*,[160] the Supreme Court held that while presumptive forms of discrimination under the Constitution were not particularised, discrimination on grounds of 'sex, race, language, religious or political opinion' was clearly prohibited.[161] Where a piece of legislation discriminates in favour of a certain class of persons, it need not be justified if justification can be found within the Constitution.[162] However, such legislation objectively must not be arbitrary, unreasonable or unjust and as such incapable of justifying the discrimination.[163] In *In re Article 26 and the Employment Equality Bill 1996*, the Supreme Court approved the approach of the High Court in *Brennan* v. *Attorney General*[164] that a classification must be 'for a legitimate legislative purpose ... It must be relevant to that purpose, and ... each class must be treated fairly'.[165]

Thus, the exclusion of a same-sex couple from their capacity to marry each other is based solely on grounds of sexual orientation, and Irish marriage law favours persons who are sexually inclined towards others of the opposite sex. Is there a different physical or moral capacity or social function between same-sex and opposite-sex relationships? The state in *Zappone and Gilligan* argued that Article 41 expressly contemplated a distinction between the committed relationship of the petitioners and a marriage between two persons of opposite sexes.[166] The argument, however, circularly circumvented the central issue: the agreed component of marriage – a 'unique and special life-long relationship' to the exclusion of all others – is clearly applicable to both a committed opposite-sex relationship and a committed same-sex relationship equally. The committed life-long unions that result from both kinds of relationships serve an equal, and equally important, social function within the community: that of life-long partnership in love and support within a broader family unit.

Some words should be laid on the welfare of children reared by same-sex couples, which was a key issue for the High Court where there was disagreement among psychologists as to the adequacies, methodologies and conclusions of relevant empirical studies. In the absence of scientific consensus within the evidence, the court took a cautious stance calling for longitudinal studies before definite findings could be made. However, the absence of scientific consensus over the welfare of children cannot normatively deny a same-sex couple from marrying each other if doing so is *their* right. Furthermore, as de Londras has pointed out, a gay man or a lesbian may already apply as an unmarried individual to adopt a child and is subject to a rigorous assessment process as to his or her suitability as a parent, in the same manner as an unmarried heterosexual, with the best interests and welfare of the child being a paramount consideration.[167]

As stated above, the right to marry is implied in the reference to marriage in Article 41, but it is also protected as an unenumerated personal right under Article 40(3), which imposes upon the state the duty to guarantee in its laws and vindicate by its laws 'as far as practicable' the personal rights of the citizen. As a personal right, it is not absolute and its exercise may be restricted by the state within constitutionally permissible limits, namely, protection of other constitutional rights and maintenance of the 'common good'. There is, however, no textual exclusion in the Constitution precluding a same-sex couple from exercising a personal right to marry each other.

Furthermore, under Article 41, the family is a unit group founded upon marriage with its nature and content undefined. A duty, however, is imposed upon the state to guard with special care the institution of marriage. In its analysis in *Zappone and Gilligan*, using the harmonious approach, the High Court found that Article 41 as a whole clearly excluded a same-sex union and that the duty of the state to guard marriage and protect it from attack justified the exclusion based on the historical and prevailing definition of marriage and the lack of conclusive longitudinal studies of the long-term psychological and psychosexual developmental effect on the welfare of children of being reared by same-sex parents.[168]

However, I argue that the only potential exclusionary textual references (similar to references to the word 'child' in Article 42) are references to a 'woman's life within the home' and 'mothers' in Article 41(2), which connote a 'nuclear' family. Given that contemporaneously there are different kinds of committed relationships, textually a lesbian couple could be encompassed by such references. Article 41(2) is a highly controversial provision, which, within the lifetime of the Constitution, has largely been dormant and appears to be little more than a convenient tool for judges in times of need. The provision has been heavily criticised for its evident gender stereotyping, and the Constitutional Review Group has recommended that it be amended to embrace a gender-neutral recognition of carers in the home,[169] which unfortunately has been rejected by the All-Party Oireachtas Committee on the Constitution.[170] To justify the exclusion of all committed same-sex relationships from access to the institution of marriage requires a stronger basis than a textual difficulty. This textual difficulty contrasts with the significance of the terms 'child' and 'parents' in Article 42 as dissected in *Sinnott*.

Conclusion

This paper has shown that the High Court in *Zappone and Gilligan* misapplied the approach of Supreme Court Justice Murray in *Sinnott* when interpreting the Constitution contemporaneously. While *Sinnott* offers hopes for an individual to vindicate his or her right under the Constitution to marry another person regardless of gender or sexual orientation, it is likely that the Supreme Court in the appellate *Zappone and Gilligan* proceedings currently pending will uphold the High Court judgment out of deference to the Oireachtas given its recent re-enactment of the common law definition of marriage through the Civil Registration Act 2004.[171] Full recognition of the equal worth and dignity of sexual minorities in Ireland, thus, lies in the hands of the Oireachtas.[172]

Acknowledgements

I am deeply grateful to Phil C.W. Chan for his invaluable comments and improvements on my paper at every stage.

Notes

1. [2006] IEHC 404. For unreported High Court Judgements, see http://www.courts.ie/Judgements.nsf/Webpages/HomePage
2. [2001] 2 IR 545.
3. G. Whyte, 'Some Reflections on the Role of Religion in the Constitutional Order', in *Ireland's Evolving Constitution 1939–1997*, ed. P. Twomey and T. Murphy (Dublin: Hart, 1998), 51, 60–1.
4. J.M. Kelly, *Fundamental Rights in Irish Law* (Dublin: Allen Figgis, 1967), 57–8. See also M. Gallagher, 'The Constitution and the Judiciary', in *Politics in the Republic of Ireland*, ed. J. Coakley and M. Gallagher, 4th edn (Dublin: Routledge, 2005), 72.
5. D. Costello, 'The Natural Law and the Irish Constitution', *Studies* 45 (1956): 403, 414.
6. J.H. Whyte, *Church and State in Modern Ireland 1923–1970* (Dublin: Gill & Macmillian, 1980), 51–2. See also W.R. Duncan, 'Supporting the Institution of Marriage in Ireland', *Irish Jurist* 13 (1978): 215, 221.
7. Article 41(1)(1) states that '[t]he State recognises the Family as the natural primary and fundamental unit group of Society, and as a moral institution possessing inalienable and imprescriptible rights, antecedent and superior to all positive law'. See *The State (Nicolaou) v. An Bord Úchtála* [1966] IR 567.
8. Article 41(3)(1) states that '[t]he State pledges itself to guard with special care the institution of Marriage, on which the Family is founded, and to protect it against attack'.

9. B. Chubb, *The Politics of the Irish Constitution* (Dublin: Institute of Public Administration, 1991), 40.
10. D.A. Martin, *A General Theory of Secularisation* (Oxford: Blackwell, 1978), 107.
11. Ibid.
12. R. Fanning, 'Mr de Valera Drafts a Constitution', in *De Valera's Constitution and Ours*, ed. B. Farrell (Dublin: Gill & Macmillian, 1988), 33, 42.
13. Ibid.
14. G. Hogan, 'De Valera, the Constitution and the Historians', *Irish Jurist* 40 (2005): 293.
15. Ibid., 294.
16. D. Keogh, 'The Irish Constitutional Revolution: An Analysis of the Making of the Irish Constitution', in *The Constitution of Ireland: 1937–1987*, ed. F. Litton (Dublin: Institute of Public Administration, 1988), 4, 39.
17. Hogan, 'De Valera, the Constitution and the Historians', 301 (referring to the Act of Settlement 1701 [England], the 1814 Constitution of Norway, the 1921 Constitution of Poland, the 1948 Constitution of the Italian Republic, the 1978 Constitution of the Republic of Spain, and the 2001 Constitution of the Hellenic Republic of Greece).
18. Hogan, 'De Valera, the Constitution and the Historians', 301.
19. Ibid., 302.
20. Ibid., 303. Article 119 of the 1919 Constitution of the Weimar Republic, quoted ibid., stated that 'marriage, as the foundation of the family and the preservation and expansion of the nation, enjoys the special protection of the constitution'.
21. Hogan, 'De Valera, the Constitution and the Historians'.
22. Ibid., 306.
23. Ibid.
24. G. Hogan, 'The Constitution, Property Right and Proportionality', *Irish Jurist* 32 (1997): 373, 396.
25. [1974] IR 384.
26. [1965] IR 294.
27. Ibid., 312. Article 40(3)(1) states that '[t]he State shall guarantees in its laws to respect and, as far as practicable, by its laws to defend and vindicate the personal rights of the citizen'.
28. *Ryan*, ibid., 313.
29. G.W. Hogan and G.F. Whyte, *J.M. Kelly: The Irish Constitution*, 4th edn (Dublin: Tottel, 2006), 31.
30. Ibid., 1827.
31. [1995] 1 IR 321.
32. Ibid., 333.
33. Ibid.
34. [1995] 1 IR 1.
35. Ibid., 38.
36. Ibid.
37. [2001] 3 IR 662.
38. Ibid., 687.
39. Ibid., 757.
40. Hogan, 'De Valera, the Constitution and the Historians', 306. His position was supported by the Supreme Court in *North Western Health Board*.
41. Hogan and Whyte, *J.M. Kelly*, 3.
42. Ibid.
43. For more recent criticisms, see, e.g., O. Doyle, 'Legal Validity: Reflections on the Irish Constitution', *Dublin University Law Journal* 25 (1993): 56; G.F. Whyte, 'Natural Law and the Constitution', *Irish Law Times* 14 (NS) (1996): 8; M. de Blacam, 'Justice and Natural Law', *Irish Jurist* 32 (1997): 323; S. Mullally, 'Searching for Foundations in Irish Constitutional Law', *Irish Jurist* 33 (1998): 333; A. O'Sullivan and P.C.W. Chan, 'Judicial Review in Ireland and the Relationship between the Irish Constitution and Natural Law', *Nottingham Law Journal* 15, no. 2 (2006): 18.
44. (1951) 85 ILTR 134.
45. *Ryan*, 308. The Supreme Court approved the reasoning of the High Court.
46. [1985] ILRM 545.
47. Ibid., 547.

48. (1866) LR P & D 130.
49. Ibid., 133.
50. [1912] 2 IR 445.
51. Ibid., 458.
52. Ibid., 459.
53. Article 50(1) states that '[s]ubject to this Constitution and to the extent to which they are not inconsistent therewith, the laws in force in Saorstát Éireann immediately prior to the date of the coming into operation of this Constitution shall continue to be of full force and effect until the same or any of them shall have been repealed or amended by enactment of the Oireachtas'.
54. [1939] IR 413.
55. [1961] IR 345.
56. *ESB* v. *Gormley* [1985] ILRM 494.
57. Civil Registration Act 2004, No. 3/2004, Art. 2(2)(e). There was no debate on this paragraph in the Dáil (Chamber of Representatives); see Dáil debates 578, col. 276. The only disquiet raised in the Seanad (Senate) was from Senator David Norris; see Seanad debates 175, col. 652.
58. [1995] 1 ILRM 491.
59. Ibid., 495.
60. *Murray*, 536.
61. [1985] IR 733.
62. Ibid., 754.
63. [1995] 1 IR 321.
64. [2002] 3 IR 355.
65. Ibid., 405. However, the appellate judgment examined the terms of a divorce settlement awarded by the High Court and consequently neither the Chief Justice for the majority nor the dissenting judgments made declarations on the concept of marriage under Article 41.
66. [2002] IEHC 116.
67. Ibid., para. 62.
68. Ibid., para. 65.
69. Ibid., para. 177.
70. Ibid., para. 175.
71. Ibid.
72. Ibid.
73. Ibid., para. 131.
74. Ibid., para. 128.
75. Ibid.
76. Ibid., para. 126.
77. Ibid., para. 101.
78. *The State (Director of Public Prosecutions)* v. *Walsh* [1981] IR 412, 425.
79. Hogan and Whyte, *J.M. Kelly*, 8. See also *Dillane* v. *Ireland* [1980] IRLM 167.
80. Ibid.
81. J. Eardly, 'The Constitution and Marriage – The Scope of Protection', *Irish Law Times* 11 (2006): 167, 168.
82. Ibid.
83. B. Walsh, 'The Constitution: A View from the Bench', in *De Valera's Constitution and Ours*, ed. B. Farrell (Dublin: Gill & Macmillian, 1988), 188, 191.
84. (2002) 35 EHRR 447.
85. Ibid., para. 99.
86. A. Lowry, 'Practice and Procedure under the European Convention on Human Rights Act 2003', *Bar Review* (November 2003): 183, 185.
87. European Convention on Human Rights Act 2003, No. 20/2003, s. 2(1).
88. Ibid., s. 5(1).
89. *Foy* v. *An t-Ard Chláraitheoir and Others* [2007] IEHC 470. In light of *Goodwin* and the enactment of the European Convention on Human Rights Act 2003, the petitioner sought to raise new issues in her appeal before the Supreme Court, which instead re-directed her case to the High Court to re-determine the question of compatibility at first instance.
90. Ibid., paras 100–2.
91. Ibid., para. 104.

 92. Ibid.
 93. It was, however, mentioned in *Zappone and Gilligan*, 530, as a caveat to the traditional concept of marriage.
 94. Taxes Consolidation Act 1997, No. 39/1997, Pt. 15, ch. 1. Under sections 1017 and 1019, married persons may elect to be jointly assessed for taxation purposes.
 95. Under section 29(1) of the Family Law Act 1995, No. 26/1995, a foreign marriage may be recognised in Ireland where the applicants are domiciled in Ireland at the date of application or have ordinarily been resident in Ireland for a period of one year ending on that date.
 96. *Zappone and Gilligan*, 407.
 97. Ibid., 444.
 98. Ibid.
 99. Ibid., 445.
100. Ibid., 470.
101. Ibid., 471.
102. Ibid., 450.
103. Ibid., 477.
104. Ibid., 454–77.
105. Ibid., 479.
106. Ibid., 483.
107. Ibid., 484.
108. Ibid., 483.
109. Ibid., 501.
110. Ibid., 484.
111. Ibid., 530.
112. *Sinnott*.
113. *McGee*, 319.
114. Ibid., 310.
115. Ibid., 318.
116. Ibid., 319.
117. Bunreacht na hÉireann 1937, Preamble.
118. *McGee*, 319 (emphasis added).
119. R. Hart, *Hart's Rules for Compositors and Readers at the University Press*, 39th edn (Oxford: Oxford University Press, 1983).
120. Walsh, 'The Constitution', 195.
121. Ibid.
122. Ibid.
123. [1976] IR 325.
124. Ibid., 347.
125. Ibid.
126. *Sinnott*, 680. However, Justice Denham subscribed to the 'living document' approach in her dissenting judgment and did not explore the 'living document' approach in any detail: ibid., 652.
127. Ibid., 680.
128. Ibid.
129. J.M. Kelly, 'Law and Manifesto', in *The Constitution of Ireland: 1937–1987*, ed. F. Litton (Dublin: Institute of Public Administration, 1988), 208, 215.
130. Ibid.
131. Ibid.
132. Ibid.
133. *Sinnott*, 582.
134. Ibid; see esp. Murray J.'s opinion, 682; Hardiman J.'s, 690; Geoghegan J.'s, 720; and Fennelly J.'s, 726.
135. Ibid., 680.
136. Ibid., 681.
137. Ibid., 682.
138. Ibid.
139. Ibid.

140. Ibid. In a similar vein, Justice Geoghegan, ibid., 721–2, explicitly approved the High Court judgment in *O'Donoghue* v. *Minister for Health* [1993] IEHC 2.

141. *Sinnott*, ibid., 682.

142. Ibid., 683.

143. *Zappone and Gilligan*, 531.

144. [2003] 1 ILRM 321.

145. *Zappone and Gilligan*, 530.

146. Ibid.

147. *Minister of Home Affairs and Another* v. *Fourie and Another*, 2006 (3) BCLR 355, para. 94.

148. Ibid.

149. Ibid., para. 74.

150. Ibid.

151. Bunreacht na hÉireann 1937, Preamble.

152. *Murray*, 549.

153. [2004] 3 SCR 698.

154. Ibid., para. 22.

155. *McGee*, 317. See also *T. (D.)* v. *T. (C.)*.

156. *Zappone and Gilligan*, 416, per evidence of Henry Kennedy, Professor of Forensic Psychiatry, University of Dublin.

157. Employment Equality Act 1998, No. 21/1998, s. 6(2)(d).

158. Equal Status Act 2000, No. 8/2000, s. 3(2)(d).

159. Bunreacht na hÉireann 1937, Art. 40(1).

160. [1997] 2 IR 321.

161. Ibid., 347.

162. *O'B.* v. *S.* [1984] IR 316; *De Burca* v. *A.G.* [1976] IR 38.

163. *Dillane* v. *A.G.* [1980] IRLM 167.

164. [1983] ILRM 449.

165. Ibid., 480.

166. *Zappone and Gilligan*, 497.

167. F. de Londras, 'The Law that Dare Not Speak its Name?', *Irish Journal of Family Law* 2 (2006): 24.

168. *Zappone and Gilligan*, 533.

169. Constitutional Review Group, *Report of the Constitutional Review Group* (Dublin: Stationary Office, 1996), 311.

170. All-Party Oireachtas Committee on the Constitution, *Tenth Progress Report: The Family* (Dublin: Stationary Office, 2006), 106.

171. Equally, Justice Murray himself had previously referred to marriage as opposite-sex-based: *T. (D.)* v. *T. (C.)*, 405.

172. However, it is clear that section 2(2)(e) of the Civil Registration Act 2004 is unlikely to be amended in the near future. Parliamentary debate has focused on civil partnership legislation, and the government has stalled debate on the only Bills to date, the Civil Partnership Bill 2004 moved by Senator Norris in the Seanad and the Civil Unions Bill 2006 moved by the Labour Party in the Dáil. Nevertheless, in June 2008, the Department of Justice, Equality and Law Reform published its scheme for civil partnership legislation, which has not yet been submitted to the Oireachtas and if enacted would accord same-sex partners legal rights regarding wrongful death, pensions and immigration albeit not joint tax assessment; see Department of Justice, Equality and Law Reform, 'General Scheme of Civil Partnership Bill', http://www.justice.ie/en/JELR/Pages/General_Scheme_of_Civil_Partnership_Bill (accessed 31 December 2008).

INDEX

For Product Safety Concerns and Information please contact our EU
representative GPSR@taylorandfrancis.com
Taylor & Francis Verlag GmbH, Kaufingerstraße 24, 80331 München, Germany